"Though it concluded only fifty years ago, Vatican II played out in a different world and in ways that seem complicated and even mysterious to today's readers. This collection will long remain a valuable resource for unlocking the meaning of the council and its interpretation. Some of the best scholars in this field contributed to several issues of *Theological Studies* during the council's jubilee, and these selections comprise a truly fitting tribute to the council that created the contemporary Catholic Church and shaped relations among Christians and among all people of goodwill into the present century."

—John Borelli
Georgetown University

"Fifty years after the Second Vatican Council (1962–1965) some of the world's finest Catholic scholars explore the continuing significance of the council's teaching for our time, including its capacity to inform the mission of the church in a vastly different context. This collection is required reading for anyone interested in exploring the interpretation and reception of the council's insights today."

—Catherine E. Clifford
Saint Paul University, Ottawa, Ontario Canada

"Finally, there is no longer the need to search repeatedly through the issues of *Theological Studies* looking for recent articles on Vatican II. In celebration of the 50th anniversary of the council's closing, the journal's editor, David Schultenover, has gathered in one volume a masterful and contemporary compendium of the finest contributions by top scholars. The cohesion and complementarity of the collection is truly remarkable, allowing it to be read easily from cover to cover. In fifty years, it will still stand as one of the most valuable contributions of our time. This is a golden collection to mark a golden anniversary!"

—Michael Attridge
University of St. Michael's College, Toronto, Ontario Canada

"This book offers very challenging and diverse insights on the worldwide reception and hermeneutics of Vatican II and postconciliar Catholic thought."

—Dr. Jürgen Mettepenningen
Katholieke Universiteit, Leuven, Belgium
Author of *Nouvelle Théologie—New Theology: Inheritor of Modernism, Precursor of Vatican II*

"Already when reading many of these articles in *Theological Studies* I was hoping they would become available as a book. I am sure that this collection will become a landmark in the reception of Vatican II 50 years on, as was the case with the *Herder Theologischer Kommentar zum Zweiten Vatikanischen Konzil* 10 years ago. Even if the Council documents hesitated to use the term "reform," the famous 2005 speech by Pope Benedict on the hermeneutics of reform inspires many authors in this volume to take the implicit pleas of Vatican II for a reform of the Church more seriously. Very prophetic indeed, if one realizes that most contributions were written before the start of the current pontificate.

"Most of all, this book asks critical questions to the postconciliar magisterium in the name of the Council: Do they not overestimate their own authority? Are they really willing to listen to the *sensus fidelium* (as expressed, e.g., by American nuns)? What has happened to the primacy of the conscience as expressed in *Dignitatis Humanae*? Has the Catholic Church in Africa truly received the reflections of the Council on the mission of the laity? Whence the suspicious attitude of Rome toward attempts to develop a decentralized magisterium in Asia and Latin America? Has the Catholic Church somehow lost its prophetic enthusiasm in its relationship to the Jews since Vatican II? For specialists in Vatican II studies the most important advice comes at the end, in the postscript by Gilles Routhier: now the time has come to leave the detailed redaction history of particular paragraphs behind and to develop a synthetic approach on the Council."

—Peter De Mey
Katholieke Universiteit
Leuven, Belgium
Chair of the Vatican II Studies Group within the American Academy of Religion

50 Years On

Probing the Riches of Vatican II

Edited by David G. Schultenover, SJ

Introduction by Stephen Schloesser, SJ

A Michael Glazier Book

LITURGICAL PRESS
Collegeville, Minnesota

www.litpress.org

The cover image—of a segment of the all-male hierarchy—is intentionally meant to illustrate a focus of significant progress around the notions of council, synod, "The Vatican," and global and intercultural dialogue *ad intra* over the last fifty years while at the same time emphasizing that there is still much work to do on behalf of the people of God on many levels.

A Michael Glazier Book published by Liturgical Press

Cover design by Jodi Hendrickson. Photo courtesy of Catholic News Service.

1 2 3 4 5 6 7 8 9

Library of Congress Control Number: 2015931097

ISBN: 978-0-8146-8301-9 ISBN: 978-0-8146-8326-2 (ebook)

Contents

Preface

Let me here confess to a primary motive for publishing this collection of articles commemorating the 50th anniversary of the Second Vatican Council. As a youth I found church history boring. Everything seemed to happen by divine plan. So I took up something more interesting: I was working on a PhD in organic chemistry while the world's bishops met for the council in Rome. In 1966, however, when I was just one year from completing my degree, Vatican II happened for me personally—and expelled boredom. That was the year when the collected *Documents of Vatican II* (edited by Walter Abbott and Joseph Gallagher) appeared in English translation.

How can I convey the excitement I felt upon reading them? The documents fired my imagination for what this council could mean for Catholics as well as for all with whom a renovated Church might interact. This was a council like none other: a reform council addressed to Catholics and a pastoral council addressed to all persons of good will, believers and unbelievers alike. Its vision was breathtaking. That experience of reading in 1966 changed my life in the most literal way. It impelled me to end my quest for the scientific doctorate and turn instead to a quest for the once and future Church.

Fifty years later, the council's anniversary seems an appropriate moment to take stock: to return to those documents, reconsider them, and assess their reception and effect not only on the Catholic Church but also on all other churches, religions, and indeed the world itself. This collection of articles is an effort in that direction.

My intention from the moment I first considered running a series of articles in *Theological Studies* to commemorate the council's golden jubilee was to eventually gather them under one cover as a textbook for upper-level college students, graduate students, and educated laypersons in parishes, as well as for clergy, religious, and seminarians. My motive, apart from the one already mentioned, was twofold: (1) to provide a text that informs readers about the reception of the conciliar documents during the 50 years following the council; and (2) to inspire readers to return to the documents themselves to see where the articles published here came from. Older readers will remember the council, while nobody under 50 will have the slightest memory of it. But all will benefit by reading the assessments of Vatican II experts 50 years on, and by returning to the documents themselves over and over again.

Initially, I had a plan for the articles' order of appearance, but early on, the plan had to give way to reality. Circumstances beyond control prevented some manuscripts from arriving on my schedule. Now, however, having all the articles in hand, I was able to group them in what seems a reasonable sequence: general interpretations of the council; specific interpretations; the Church's mission; reception of the council worldwide; treatments of specific documents; and finally an afterword assessing the council, its reception, and promise. The tone is scholarly, as befits such a deeply theological, momentous event in living history, but the articles are also accessible to nonspecialists.

Without context, however, authorial intention of documents is indiscernible and the documents themselves unintelligible. Stephen Schloesser's introduction to this collection provides the necessary historical context. Readers will notice that Schloesser spends roughly 75 percent of his introduction on the long 19th century (from the Enlightenment to the beginning of World War I) and 25 percent on the period from WWI to the present.

His rationale, as I interpret it, is this: a number of events—including the Enlightenment, French Revolution, Napoleon, and post-1815 liberal nationalism—led the papal monarchy to construct a bitter opposition between Church and world. However, post–World War I circumstances—especially the Vatican concordats concluded with both Fascist Italy and Nazi Germany—led to horrifying unintended consequences. After the defeat of those regimes in World War II, the Cold War binary offered stark alternatives: a choice between American-led liberalism and Soviet-led communism. Both the popes and the council needed to realize that the world had changed profoundly and irrevocably: the papal monarchy had disappeared a century earlier; and "liberalism" was no longer its enemy. It was time to transcend the church–world opposition. The end result of that transcendence was enshrined in the opening paragraph of *Gaudium et spes*: "The joys and the hopes, the griefs and the anxieties of the people of this age . . . are the joys and hopes, the griefs and anxieties of the followers of Christ. . . . [This Church] community realizes that it is truly linked with humanity and its history by the deepest of bonds."

I wish to express my profound gratitude first to all the contributing authors, who generously gave their time, energy, and talent to produce such outstanding works for the benefit of the Church; to my astute editorial consultants, who advised me in this project; and to Stephen Schloesser, who interrupted his already overcommitted schedule to provide the introduction. Special thanks to Hans Christoffersen, publisher of Liturgical Press, who happened to be seated next to me on a long flight . . . ; to Colleen Stiller, his production manager, and Lauren Murphy, his managing editor, who had to pick up the pieces consequent on that conversation; and finally, to my own graduate assistant, Andrew Harmon, who applied his highly developed skills and sharp eye to all the texts as they reached his inbox. These and many others contributed to this collection in the hope that it will provide reliable guidance to the council's meaning and our ongoing appropriation of it.

Reproach vs. *Rapprochement*

Historical Preconditions of a Paradigm Shift in the Reform of Vatican II

STEPHEN SCHLOESSER, SJ

> *But we cannot pass over one important consideration in our analysis of the religious meaning of the council: it has been deeply committed to the study of the modern world. Never before perhaps, so much as on this occasion, has the Church felt the need to know, to draw near to, to understand, to penetrate, serve and evangelize the society in which she lives; and to get to grips with it, almost to run after it, in its rapid and continuous change. This attitude, a* response to the distances and divisions we have witnessed over recent centuries, in the last century and in our own especially, between the Church and secular society—*this attitude has been strongly and unceasingly at work in the council; so much so that some have been inclined to suspect that an easy-going and excessive responsiveness to the outside world, to passing events, cultural fashions, temporary needs, an alien way of thinking . . . may have swayed persons and acts of the ecumenical synod, at the expense of the fidelity which is due to tradition, and this to the detriment of the religious orientation of the council itself. We do not believe that this shortcoming should be imputed to it, to its real and deep intentions, to its authentic manifestations.*
>
> —*Pope Paul VI*
>
> *Address during the last general meeting of the Second Vatican Council (December 7, 1965)*[1]

1. Emphasis added. Except where noted, council documents, papal speeches and documents, and synod documents are taken from the Vatican website (www.vatican.va).

What is the religious meaning of Vatican Council II? How should it be interpreted? Does it represent continuity or discontinuity with Catholicism's past? Did anything happen—did anything change—at the council? Was the Church any different in its wake? And if so, what significance, if any, does this change have for the present moment—a half century later—and for the future? As a professor of mine liked to say, the most important question in theology is: "So what?"

As the essays collected in this volume abundantly demonstrate, theologians and historians have been debating the meaning of Vatican II for 50 years—asking "So what?" in multiple ways. And as Paul VI's words at the closing meeting demonstrate, the "religious meaning" of the council had been hotly contested even before it had been completed. Conservative critics had accused the event (in Paul's words) of being "an easy-going and excessive responsiveness to the outside world, to passing events, cultural fashions, temporary needs, an alien way of thinking." In wanting to keep up with the trends of a quickly changing world, it had minimized its "fidelity" to the "tradition." Discontinuity—rupture—had outweighed continuity. Even worse, the council was accused of having lost its "religious orientation," a specifically "religious" meaning. It had engaged psychology, sociology, economics, geopolitics, history, postwar existentialism, and atheism—but in doing so, its final meaning and purpose had not been religious.

Clearly, Paul VI interpreted Vatican II from a vastly different perspective. For him, the desire to "get to grips" with the modern world—"almost to run after it"—was itself the council's fundamental "religious meaning." The council's explicit, overt, and self-conscious overtures to "secular society" were not accidents of the moment, not whimsical enthusiasms for getting in groove with the 1960s. Rather, the council's *rapprochement* had been long in the making: a studied and deliberate response "to the distances and divisions we have witnessed over recent centuries, in the last century and in our own especially." Paul VI viewed the council from the long-duration perspective. Although the conciliar events happened to take place within the very brief 1962–1965 time span, they were in fact the culmination of unhealed wounds and fissures festering since at least the 1700s.

Reading the December 1965 closing address with a half-century's hindsight, one can see the picture inverted. Paul VI's critics seem to have been caught up in the moment's uncertainty, while he spoke with surety. He understood what had been at stake. A yawning chasm had separated church and world. The council had built a bridge. The bridge answered the question: "So what?"

In his essay on "The Hermeneutic of Reform," John O'Malley proposes that we too step back and attempt to synthesize the larger picture in order to interpret the council's religious meaning.[2] Considered superficially, the council appears to have spread itself very thin as it touched on a dizzying number of topics: liturgy; ecumenism; religious liberty; Judaism; atheism; media; nuclear war; environment and population; the nature, purpose, and structure of the Church; the place of laity within that structure; and so on. Such an expansive canvas defies the viewer to comprehend the whole in a single grasp.

And yet, without such synthesis, the parts spin off into splendid isolation; no overall meaning can be discerned within them; and the whole becomes even less than the sum of its parts. O'Malley specifies the challenge:

> The further, absolutely essential step of considering the documents as constituting a single corpus and thus of showing how each document is in some measure an expression of larger orientations and part of an integral and coherent whole. . . . Once the documents are thus examined, they are striking in that they express themselves in a style different from the legislative, judicial, and often punitive style employed by previous councils.

That seismic shift in style, argues O'Malley, is a "reform that is a system replacement or paradigm replacement, not merely an adjustment or correction of the status quo."

O'Malley's "paradigm shift" metaphor draws on Thomas Kuhn's now classic *Structure of Scientific Revolutions* (1962), a work published—not insignificantly—the same year the council opened.[3] In it, Kuhn argues that scientific "paradigms" are the basic assumptions in a scientific community's "ruling theory." Historically speaking, a paradigm shift is provoked when "normal science" has become inadequate to—can no longer accommodate—new factual data produced by experiment and experience. The fundamental ruling assumptions or paradigms of "normal science" have to change in order to account for incommensurable data. This change entails a "paradigm shift" or "revolutionary science."

Extending the metaphor: what was the fundamental ruling assumption—what was the underlying paradigm or "normal science"—that had governed the Church's interactions with the "modern world" since the 1700s? In a word: *opposition*. In reaction to a monolithic conception of

2. John W. O'Malley, SJ, "'The Hermeneutic of Reform': A Historical Analysis," in the present volume, 3–34.

3. Thomas S. Kuhn, *The Structure of Scientific Revolutions* (Chicago: University of Chicago, 1962).

Enlightenment thought and its offspring—incommensurable data—the Church constructed a self-image in which it stood intransigently over and against the "modern world." What was this opposition's corresponding style? In a word: *reproach*—rebuke, disapproval, blame.

Historical theologian Joseph Komonchak has situated this construction within an even more precisely delimited historical period. He argues that the construction of "modern *Roman* Catholicism" between 1815 and 1914 (i.e., over the "long nineteenth century") "took the form of a counter-society, legitimated by a counter-culture, as a response to and in opposition to the emerging liberal culture and society which advanced with such apparent inexorability throughout those years."[4] Distinguishing "between the Church in its theological definition and the social form in which it is embodied at different times and in different places," Komonchak identifies post-1815 Catholicism as a distinctly ultramontanist "*Roman* Catholicism" that had been "largely unknown in previous centuries": "A single interpretation of the challenge of modernity was everywhere considered to be applicable and normative by a Roman authority." These distinctions allow Komonchak to offer a causal explanation for a fact agreed upon by theologians and historians from left to right: the social form of "everyday Catholicism that had existed right up through the reign of Pius XII had collapsed." Although interpreters on the left "welcomed its disappearance" and those on the right "deplored its loss," both sides agreed: the modern Roman Catholic edifice constructed during the previous 150 years was gone.[5]

In the pages that follow, I offer a rapid chronicle of historical events contributing to the construction of this "modern Roman Catholicism." As O'Malley suggests, if interpretive concepts like a "paradigm of opposition" or a "style of reproach" are to be helpful and make sense, they need to be grounded in historical reality.[6] For readers familiar with modern Church history, this survey will serve as a refresher. For readers without such background, the sketch provides a starting point. In either case, the survey lays out the long-duration historical awareness with which Paul VI

4. Joseph A. Komonchak, "Modernity and the Construction of Roman Catholicism," *Cristianesimo nella storia* 18 (1997): 353–85, at 356.

5. Ibid., 357, 373 (emphasis original), 379, 355. Quoting Joseph Ratzinger eight years after the council (1973): "In an apparent clash between faith and world, it is not Christianity that is being defended against the world, but only a particular form of its relationship to the world that is being defended against another form" (357 n. 9).

6. O'Malley, "Hermeneutic of Reform," 7.

interpreted the council: "a response to the distances and divisions we have witnessed over recent centuries."

The historical landscape of those "distances and divisions" consisted of a mutually exclusive binary opposition: an emerging liberal paradigm descended from the Enlightenment on the one side, and a reactionary counterparadigm descended from the "enemies of the Enlightenment" on the other. The reactionary style was "reproach." By contrast, the conciliar style of *rapprochement* constituted a radical paradigm shift—the council's religious meaning.

Enlightenment (ca. 1689–1789)

The notion of a single entity called "The Enlightenment" has been challenged and come under heavy scrutiny by scholars in recent decades. New understandings of multiple "Enlightenments"—including "Catholic Enlightenment"—add important nuances to an epoch often reduced to a one-dimensional caricature of what was in fact a complex process.[7] Nevertheless, some general concepts generated by the period's thinkers define the era. The Church, by contrast, came to define itself over and against these key ideas. In spite of the overgeneralization, then, it is still useful to speak of an "Enlightenment" and the revolutionary concepts it generated. Two of these would prove to be especially problematic for Roman Catholicism: the "social contract" and "toleration."

Among the most important Enlightenment notions was the "social compact" or "contract."[8] The English version, drawing on the earlier thought of Thomas Hobbes, was formulated by John Locke in his *Second Treatise of Government* (1689). The French version was formulated by Jean-Jacques Rousseau in *Of The Social Contract, or Principles of Political Right* (1762). Although these versions differ in significant ways, both embraced an attitude toward the world that broke with millennia of tradition—a

7. Dale K. Van Kley, *The Religious Origins of the French Revolution: From Calvin to the Civil Constitution, 1560–1791* (New Haven, CT: Yale University, 1996); *Religion and Politics in Enlightenment Europe*, ed. James E. Bradley and Dale K. Van Kley (Notre Dame, IN: University of Notre Dame, 2001); *A Companion to the Catholic Enlightenment in Europe*, ed. Ulrich L. Lehner and Michael O'Neill (Boston: Brill, 2010).

8. For an accessible overview, see Margaret C. Jacob, *The Enlightenment: A Brief History with Documents* (Boston: Bedford/St. Martin's, 2001). For Anglo-American and French comparisons, see Susan Dunn, *Sister Revolutions: French Lightning, American Light* (New York: Faber & Faber, 1999).

radical paradigm shift. For them, a government's legitimacy comes from the "contract" made by the governed. Individuals are conceived as atoms who, for reasons of self-preservation, band together to form a collective body by mutual agreement (contract). Government's legitimacy is artificial, contingent, and comes from below.

Because this worldview is taken for granted today in all societies descended from the Enlightenment, it may be difficult to imagine what the alternative was. Briefly put, the traditional image of society was organic, not atomistic. An individual was born into a society and played his or her destined role in the social organism. Eyes, ears, arms, hands, legs, feet, hearts, heads—all played their parts in the social body that preceded their births and would endure after their deaths. In practical terms, this meant hierarchical divisions of society largely perpetuated by blood inheritance.

Medieval society in particular was imagined as divided into three "orders" or "estates." The First Estate was composed of those who "pray": clergy, monks, and nuns. The Second Estate derived from those who "fight," i.e., those descended from knights of former days. This was the nobility or aristocracy, families who owned great tracts of land and passed this property down via blood inheritance. The Third Estate—composed of the other 97 percent of people—was made up of those who "work": peasants on landed estates, artisans who worked in villages and urban areas, merchants, and so on. Over these estates reigned the divinely appointed and anointed monarchs. The legitimacy of such social and political bodies was considered to be rooted in both "nature" (blood inheritance) and "God."

The notion of legitimacy deriving from a social contract agreed upon by mutually consenting individuals demolished traditional notions of society. At the heart of the Enlightenment worldview was a society whose hierarchical ranks were based on individual "merit," not on privileges derived from land ownership and blood inheritance.

A second concept essential to the demolition of traditional society was "toleration" of those whose faith deviated from the official state religion. Enlightenment thought drew upon earlier precedents: the Peace of Augsburg (1555) was settled by allowing both Catholic and Lutheran states in the Holy Roman Empire, depending on the religion of the ruler (*Cuius regio, eius religio* = "Whose realm, his religion"); the Dutch and English had tolerated various forms of Protestantism not conforming to the state church (e.g., the Church of England); and Henri IV had ended France's Wars of Religion by issuing the Edict of Nantes (1598), tolerating Huguenots (Calvinists) in certain regions of the officially Catholic state. These precedents had been set a full century before the Enlightenment of the 1700s.

However, it was Locke (again) who systematically argued for religious toleration in "A Letter Concerning Toleration" (again in 1689). The most popular French version was Voltaire's "Treatise on Tolerance" (1763). Voltaire wrote his impassioned work in response to that year's excruciating torture and eventual execution of Jean Calas, a Huguenot merchant wrongfully convicted of murder. Voltaire developed a variation on Locke's thought just as Rousseau had adapted Locke's social contract. Although here again English and French thinkers differed, the differences were outweighed by commonalities. Both refuted centuries of practices in which deviations from state-sanctioned religions were not tolerated.

Indeed, in traditional European states (both Catholic and Protestant), religious nonconformists were disciplined and punished in ghastly ways, including torture, drawing and quartering, beheading, and burning at the stake. Nontoleration was based on at least two presuppositions: first, error has no rights; second, a unitary nation state must have only one head (the monarch), one language, one religion, and, more broadly, one people.

Within this overall landscape of nontoleration, Jews occupied an ambivalent position in prerevolutionary Europe. On the one hand, their presence was "tolerated" for the most part—excepting numerous occasions in which various states either expelled or executed them (e.g., Spain's Alhambra Decree [1492]). On the other hand, they were not actually citizens. They occupied an unsteady third place, not unlike "resident aliens" in the ancient Roman Empire. They were obviously not orthodox Christians, but they were also not subject to the punishments dealt out to nonconformist or heterodox Christians ("heretics").

Eighteenth-century popes vacillated on the "Jewish Question."[9] In 1769, Clement XIV relaxed some of the restrictions on Jews and reassigned control over Rome's Jewish ghetto from the Holy Office of the Inquisition to the city's cardinal vicar. However, just six years later, Clement's successor, Pius VI, reversed those measures and instituted draconian ones. He rescinded all of the Jews' previous privileges, set up ghettoes in all the towns of the Papal States, forbade Jews to "speak familiarly" to Christians, and reintroduced a 16th-century papal provision requiring Jews to wear a special badge of identification. Note that the measures took place in the very midst of the Enlightenment—just one year before the American

9. For fuller treatment of the "Jewish Question" with references, see Stephen Schloesser, "Against Forgetting: Memory, History, Vatican II," *Theological Studies* 67 (2006): 275–319, at 289–97.

Declaration of Independence (1776). Jewish emancipation was a logical corollary of "toleration."

The French Revolution (1789–1799)

The French Revolution's causes and meanings have been debated ever since the revolution itself.[10] Some historians have argued that it was a peasants' revolt; others a revolt of the newly arrived bourgeoisie. Some have argued that the Terror was an accidental byproduct of particular choices made by particular individuals; others have argued that it was a necessary outcome of the way "social contract" was articulated. Here again, differences in interpretation are outweighed by commonalities, i.e., concrete events with which Catholicism would struggle to reconcile itself. Two in particular are of significance: the abolition of feudalism (and monarchy in particular) and the dechristianization project. A corollary event should be noted: Jewish emancipation in late 1791.

In August 1789, the National Assembly put an end to the feudal system of "Three Estates" by mutual agreement—the two privileged estates (clergy and aristocrats) sacrificed their ancient privileges and inaugurated a new era. At the same time, the state confiscated church properties (the old "First Estate"), including especially the vast landowning monasteries and convents. These would soon be sold and the monies used to assist the nearly bankrupt government—monetary problems having been an initial catalyst for the revolution—just as Henry VIII's dissolution of the English monasteries had filled royal coffers two centuries earlier.

Although perhaps not intended, the practical effect of these two legislative acts was the demolition of Christianity as it had existed for at least twelve centuries. Without monasteries, abbeys, and convents, the world of monks and nuns—male and female "religious"—had come to an end. All that was left of the "Church" was the "diocesan" or "secular" clergy: that is, (male) bishops and priests. Even this remnant of the old religion would be radically changed just eleven months later. According to the "Civil Constitution of the Clergy" (July 1791), bishops and priests effectively became civil servants paid by the state. On the positive side, this meant that the gross inequalities that had divided the clergy into princes

10. For an overview, see Lynn Hunt, *The French Revolution and Human Rights: A Brief Documentary History* (Boston: Bedford/St Martin's, 1996); Jack Richard Censer and Lynn Hunt, *Liberty, Equality, Fraternity: Exploring the French Revolution* (University Park: Pennsylvania State University, 2001).

and paupers—bishops and privileged priests living in luxury paid for by great benefices, while lowly parish priests lived in dire poverty—was eliminated. On the negative side, however—at least for those (including the pope) who thought of religion and the "church" as being something separate from the state—this meant that the Church effectively became a state subsidiary, not unlike the post office. Clerics were required to swear (*jurer*) an oath of loyalty to the state alone, severing ties to any nonstate authority (e.g., the foreign pope). Catholicism in France became divided into "jurors" (those who swore the oath) and "nonjurors" (those who refused). Laity also split in their allegiances toward jurors and nonjurors.[11]

The larger story of the revolution is well known: as events wore on and national unity turned out to be more difficult to achieve than previously thought, the revolution was exported abroad in wars against (Catholic) Austria and (Lutheran) Prussia. Meanwhile, domestic massacres were perpetrated against former members of the privileged two estates (religious and aristocrats) accused of being counterrevolutionaries. Eventually the monarchy itself was abolished and both Louis XVI and Marie Antoinette were executed. As the Terror was carried out by Robespierre and the Committee of Public Safety, thousands more suspected counterrevolutionaries would meet their deaths at the guillotine. Drowning was another method of executing clergy and nuns: they were fastened to boats filled with holes that sank to river bottoms. (Drowning a priest and nun tied together by ropes was known as a "Republican Wedding.") Stiffened penalties proscribed death not only for nonjuring priests but also for sympathetic laity sheltering them. In November 1793, dechristianization seemed to have reached its symbolic peak when prostitutes were enthroned as "Goddesses of Reason" in cathedrals at Paris and Strasbourg. In June 1794, Robespierre, convinced that atheism could not provide necessary social cohesion, invented the "Cult of the Supreme Being." He was soon thereafter deposed and guillotined in the hot month of "Thermidor" (July 1794).

To what extent were the abolition of the monarchy, dechristianization, and the Terror contingent accidents or logical consequences? These questions have been debated during the two centuries since. Regardless of the causes, the fact remains: the Revolution—and, as a corollary, Enlightenment thought seen as having caused it—profoundly traumatized

11. For background, see Nicholas Atkin and Frank Tallett, eds., *Religion, Society, and Politics in France since 1789* (London: Hambledon, 1991); Joseph F. Byrnes, *Catholic and French Forever: Religious and National Identity in Modern France* (University Park: Pennsylvania State University, 2005).

Catholicism. In its aftermath, Catholic "enemies of the Enlightenment" would intransigently insist on monarchy being the sole legitimate form of government; on government's identification with a single state religion; on the erroneous character of social contract, tolerance, and rights; and, as a corollary, on Jewish citizenship in Christian states.[12]

Above all these particulars, counterrevolutionaries would deny the very possibility of human progress—indeed, deny any positive value to historical change itself, which had been a cornerstone of Enlightenment thought and value extending as far back as the *Encyclopédie*.[13] In 1795, one year after the Marquis de Condorcet mysteriously died in prison, his *Sketch for a Historical Picture of the Progress of the Human Spirit* had been published posthumously. Five years later, in 1800, a royalist countered:

> Not only does human reason not perfect itself with time, but this perfection is impossible. It would be necessary to discover new relationships among men, new duties, new moral truths—something that cannot take place in the wake of the Gospel. . . . Nothing beyond Christian morality has been discovered. It is evident that it is the *non plus ultra* of true philosophy, that it is beyond the capacity of human faculties to go further.[14]

Napoleon Bonaparte (1799–1815)

Napoleon is famous for reputedly having declared: "The French Revolution is over. I am the French Revolution."[15] What does this cryptic paradox mean? On the one hand, Napoleon is the figure who, by seizing control

12. Darrin M. McMahon, *Enemies of the Enlightenment: The French Counter-Enlightenment and the Making of Modernity* (New York: Oxford University, 2001); *Critics of the Enlightenment: Readings in the French Counter-Revolutionary Tradition*, ed. and trans. Christopher Olaf Blum (Wilmington: ISI, 2004).

13. Philipp Blom, *Enlightening the World: Encyclopédie, the Book That Changed the Course of History* (New York: Palgrave Macmillan, 2005).

14. Julien Louis Geoffroy; in Schloesser, "Against Forgetting: Memory, History, Vatican II," 307. For more on "temporalization," see ibid., 306–7; and Schloesser, "*Vivo ergo cogito*: Modernism as Temporalization and Its Discontents: A Propaedeutic to This Collection," in *The Reception of Pragmatism in France and the Rise of Roman Catholic Modernism, 1890–1914*, ed. David G. Schultenover, SJ (Washington, DC: Catholic University of America, 2009), 21–58.

15. For succinct overviews, see Rafe Blaufarb, *Napoleon, Symbol for an Age: A Brief History with Documents* (Boston: Bedford/St. Martin's, 2008); Blaufarb and Claudia Liebeskind, *Napoleonic Foot Soldiers and Civilians: A Brief History with Documents* (Boston: Bedford/St. Martin's, 2011).

of France in his *coup d'état* of November 1799 ("Brumaire"), put an end to the chaotic succession of unstable governments following the fall of Robespierre. Naming himself "Consul for Life," Napoleon was able to rule largely as an autocratic military dictator, thus ending the revolution. In 1800, he granted amnesty to French emigrés, "counterrevolutionary" aristocrats and clergy who had sought refuge abroad from the Terror, especially by fleeing to England. Returning exiles brought their riches and bloodlines back to France as well as devotion to the old Catholic religion.

On the other hand, Napoleon continued France's revolutionary wars abroad—they now became the "Napoleonic Wars"—and as he conquered Europe, he dethroned monarchs (including the pope), abolished the feudal system, and instituted his Napoleonic Code based on Enlightenment ideals. For example, he emancipated Jews in all the areas he conquered. In this way, paradoxically, he continued the French Revolution's exportation abroad even as he ruled at home with an autocrat's iron fist.

In 1801, Napoleon concluded a concordat with Pope Pius VII.[16] Napoleon's reasons were at least in part politically expedient and cynical. Not unlike Robespierre before him, Napoleon believed that a state needed religion—or at least religious structures, symbols, and rituals—for social cohesion. In concluding his concordat with the pope, Napoleon acted out of self-interest. Catholicism's symbols and rituals would strike a deep chord in much of the French populace. Religion could forge ties that bind.

However, the concordat is at least as significant for what it did *not* do. First, while it established "that the Catholic Apostolic and Roman religion is the religion of the great majority of French citizens," it did not restore Catholicism as a state religion.[17] Religious toleration was maintained, protecting Protestants, Jews, and nonbelievers. Second, the Church did not regain any of the vast tracts of land confiscated in the early days of 1789. In other words, Catholicism did not return in its ancient form—primarily marked by numerous monasteries, abbeys, and convents filled with religious men and women. Instead, the revolutionary form of Catholicism remained largely in place: the Church's institution—and, by extension, French "religion" itself—was composed almost exclusively of "secular" bishops and priests serving in diocesan structures. And with the elimination of religious orders, the face of the French Catholic Church became

16. "Concordat between the Holy See and the Republic of France, 15 July 1801," in *Readings in Church History*, ed. Colman J. Barry, 3 vols. (Westminster, MD: Newman, 1965), 3:13–15.

17. See Schloesser, "Against Forgetting," 298.

effectively male. Thus, the 1801 concordat was what historians call an "invention of tradition": although it has the outward appearance of "restoring" something ancient, it is in fact a modern invention.[18] In this case, it was the beginning of postrevolutionary "modern" Roman Catholicism: a private and voluntary choice not intrinsically connected to the state's social body; and a largely diocesan (male) institution stripped of the many monks and nuns with their vast landed abbeys, monasteries, and convents of old.

In his foreign wars of aggression as well, Napoleon irrevocably altered the future of Catholicism. First, the imposed Napoleonic Code abolished feudalism (including the privileged estates based on land ownership by religious and aristocrats), enforced meritocracy (instead of blood-inherited privilege), legalized divorce, established religious toleration, emancipated Jews, and eliminated ghettoes. In 1809, after exiling Pius VII, Napoleon emancipated Jews and abolished the ancient ghetto in occupied Rome.

Second, after he deposed monarchs and installed puppet rulers, Napoleon rearranged state boundaries and streamlined Europe's maps, often by simply eliminating old states. Most important for Catholicism, he erased ancient divisions of the Italian peninsula, including the Papal States, and invented a "Kingdom of Italy," a political entity without precedent in the Roman Republic, Roman Empire, or multiple Renaissance city-states. The pope effectively became the bishop of Rome without temporal jurisdiction. These actions foreshadowed Roman Catholicism's conflicts for the next hundred years.

Romantic Invented Traditions (1815–1846)

After Napoleon's final defeat at Waterloo, the Congress of Vienna (1815) set about the "Restoration" of Europe. The word is misleading: since there was no going back to the old world, the 1815 "restoration" was yet another invented tradition. For example, by dismantling the old Holy Roman Empire and inventing the "Confederation of the Rhine," Napoleon had given German-speaking peoples the vision of a possible future nation state called "Germany." German nationalism would be a driving force throughout the century. The same held true for the Italian peninsula: by destroying various smaller states and inventing a "Kingdom of Italy," Napoleon had engendered the vision of a possible future "Italy." As the

18. E. J. Hobsbawm and T. O. Ranger, eds., *The Invention of Tradition* (New York: Cambridge University, 1983). See also Stephen Schloesser, *Jazz Age Catholicism: Mystic Modernism in Postwar Paris, 1919–1933* (Toronto: University of Toronto, 2005), 27.

peninsula gradually unified (*risorgimento*) over the coming decades—*la forza del destino*!—the Papal States faced the ever-growing prospect of extinction.[19] The ultimate nationalist goal was a "future past": ancient Rome as the capital of a modern nation state.[20]

In response, intransigent papal opposition to this political "modernity" gradually acquired the force of doctrine—literally. At every level of existence, "modern civilization"—ideas and values stemming from the Enlightenment and French Revolution—was judged as intellectually and morally wrong. By contrast, the Church imagined itself as a besieged remnant and guardian of truth. It defended monarchy as opposed to social contract, and it denounced the various "liberties" identified with liberal democracy: free speech, the right to assembly, freedom of the press, the right to vote (suffrage), and religious liberty. If Jewish emancipation served as a marker of the "modern," Pius VII's reinstatement of the Roman ghetto immediately upon his "restoration" as Rome's monarch symbolized Catholicism's antimodernism.

The Romantic movement provided this antimodernist stance with assistance from unexpected quarters.[21] Even artists and intellectuals who may not have believed in religious doctrines nevertheless embraced neo-Gothic Catholicism as an antidote to urban industrialized society. They saw in their nostalgic re-creations of the Middle Ages a bygone world of organic unity, sharply contrasting with their own felt class and national divisions. One important moment in this movement was a large work written by François-René de Chateaubriand, an aristocrat who had fled the Terror and taken refuge in England. After Napoleon's 1800 amnesty for emigrés, Chateaubriand returned to France and published *The Genius of Christianity, or Beauties of the Christian Religion* (1802). This work might be thought of as the first example of "cultural Catholicism": a lavishly detailed account of Catholicism's symbols and rituals, appealing even to those who might not religiously assent to doctrines. Chateaubriand laid the cornerstone in Romantic Catholicism's edifice.

19. For an overview, see Derek Edward Dawson Beales and Eugenio F. Biagini, *The Risorgimento and the Unification of Italy*, 2nd ed. (Harlow: Longman, 2002).

20. Reinhart Koselleck, *Futures Past: On the Semantics of Historical Time* (Cambridge, MA: MIT, 1985).

21. For an overview, see Warren Breckman, *European Romanticism: A Brief History with Documents* (Boston: Bedford/St. Martin's, 2008). See also Schloesser, *Jazz Age Catholicism*, 27–35.

Another such work was Joseph de Maistre's *On the Pope* (1819), published four years after the Congress of Vienna's "restoration" of the papal monarchy. De Maistre, one of the extreme right's most articulate and influential "enemies of the Enlightenment," theorized the pope as an absolutist global ruler possessed of "infallibility." As the papacy's temporal power became increasingly threatened by nationalist advances, de Maistre's invented tradition of the global papal monarch served as a powerful neomedievalist unifying symbol. Paradoxically, it modernized medieval and Baroque ultramontanism precisely through its antimodernism.[22]

In 1832, Gregory XVI summarized this adversarial stance in his encyclical *Mirari vos* (August 15, 1832).[23] During the 1830s, "liberalism" became consolidated as the dominant transatlantic political and cultural paradigm.[24] Gregory, by contrast, conservative to the point of being reactionary, refused to allow gas street lighting and steam engine trains in the Papal States. *Mirari vos* articulated the fear of "indifferentism," seen as the inevitable consequence of religious "toleration." "This perverse opinion," wrote Gregory,

> is spread on all sides by the fraud of the wicked who claim that it is possible to obtain the eternal salvation of the soul by the profession of any kind of religion, as long as morality is maintained. Surely, in so clear a matter, you will drive this deadly error far from the people committed to your care. With the admonition of the apostle that "there is one God, one faith, one baptism" [Eph 4:5] may those fear who contrive the notion that the safe harbor of salvation is open to persons of any religion whatever.

From indifferentism flowed liberty of conscience, and this too was condemned:

> This shameful font of indifferentism gives rise to that absurd and erroneous proposition which claims that *liberty of conscience* must be maintained for everyone. . . . Thence comes transformation of minds,

22. Useful excerpts from both Chateaubriand and de Maistre may be found in Joseph Fitzer, *Romance and the Rock: Nineteenth-Century Catholics on Faith and Reason* (Minneapolis: Fortress, 1989).

23. For what follows, see Gregory XVI, *Mirari vos* (August 15, 1832), in *The Papal Encyclicals*, 5 vols., ed. Claudia Carlen (Raleigh, NC: Pierian, 1990), 1:235–41, emphasis original.

24. Edmund Fawcett, *Liberalism: The Life of an Idea* (Princeton, NJ: Princeton University, 2014).

> corruption of youths, contempt of sacred things and holy laws—in other words, a pestilence more deadly to the state than any other. Experience shows, even from earliest times, that cities renowned for wealth, dominion, and glory perished as a result of this single evil, namely, immoderate freedom of opinion, license of free speech, and desire for novelty.

From liberty of conscience and free speech flowed freedom of the press:

> Here We must include that harmful and never sufficiently denounced freedom to publish any writings whatever and disseminate them to the people, which some dare to demand and promote with so great a clamor. We are horrified to see what monstrous doctrines and prodigious errors are disseminated far and wide in countless books, pamphlets, and other writings which, though small in weight, are very great in malice. We are in tears at the abuse which proceeds from them over the face of the earth. . . . Is there any sane man who would say poison ought to be distributed, sold publicly, stored, and even drunk because some antidote is available and those who use it may be snatched from death again and again?

Finally, Gregory condemned liberal political theories—stemming from the Enlightenment notion of social contract—that questioned the legitimacy of divinely appointed monarchy:

> We have learned that certain teachings are being spread among the common people in writings which attack the trust and submission due to princes; the torches of treason are being lit everywhere. . . . May all recall, according to the admonition of the apostle that "there is no authority except from God; what authority there is has been appointed by God. Therefore he who resists authority resists the ordinances of God; and those who resist bring on themselves condemnation" [Rom 13:2]. Therefore both divine and human laws cry out against those who strive by treason and sedition to drive the people from confidence in their princes and force them from their government.

As a corollary, Gregory also condemned the separation of church and state, breaking "the mutual concord between temporal authority and the priesthood. It is certain that that concord which always was favorable and beneficial for the sacred and the civil order is feared by the shameless lovers of liberty."

Mirari vos, published just a little over the quarter mark of the 19th century, summarized the Church's opposition to the Enlightenment's descendants. Opposition to liberal nationalism—the force of destiny—had acquired the force of doctrine.

Dueling Civilizations: Supernaturalism vs. Materialism (1846–1860)

In 1846, Gregory died and was succeeded by Pius IX ("Pionono"). Pius was initially seen and embraced as a progressive liberalizing monarch. Immediately after his accession to the throne, he issued a pardon freeing all political prisoners and opened the Jewish ghetto in Rome. He would later build gas lighting, railroads, and telegraph lines in the Papal States. However, there was underlying continuity: Pius's first encyclical, *Qui pluribus* (November 9, 1846), published immediately after his accession, extended his predecessor's concerns.[25] Pius condemned those "enemies of divine revelation, [who] with reckless and sacrilegious effrontery want to import the doctrine of human progress into the Catholic religion." In particular, he singled out scripture scholars and publishers who capitalized on freedom of the press: "the crafty Bible Societies which renew the old skill of the heretics and ceaselessly force on people of all kinds, even the uneducated, gifts of the Bible. They issue these in large numbers and at great cost, in vernacular translations, which infringe the holy rules of the Church." And he condemned the indifferentism resulting from conflicting biblical interpretations: "Also perverse is the shocking theory that it makes no difference to which religion one belongs, a theory which is greatly at variance even with reason. By means of this theory, those crafty men remove all distinction between virtue and vice, truth and error, honorable and vile action." This "filthy medley of errors which creeps in from every side" was a legacy of Enlightenment thought, "the result of the unbridled license to think, speak and write."

History, however, was against Pius. Almost immediately after his accession to the throne, Europe was rocked by the revolutions of 1848, revolts by liberal bourgeoisie against autocratic monarchs and by industrial workers against those same bourgeois capitalists who owned and ran factories. Fearing for his life, Pius IX had to flee Rome as the brief but fiercely anticlerical "Roman Republic" was established by republicans (later excommunicated by the pope). After 1850, when Pius was once again "restored" to Rome, the fragile papal monarchy was propped up against nationalists by foreign French troops. Traumatized by the events of 1848–1849, Pius passed a number of reactionary measures including the reinstatement of Rome's Jewish ghetto.

25. For what follows, see Pius IX, *Qui pluribus* (November 9, 1846); in Carlen, *Papal Encyclicals*, 1:277–84.

During the following 1850s, Pius IX used various means to create an emotionally charged antimodernist counterculture and countersociety. First, immediately on his return after the revolution, the pope instructed the Jesuits to found a journal titled *La Civiltà Cattolica*—"Catholic Civilization" or, equivalently in Rome's view, "Christian Civilization." Perhaps realizing that condemnations of "liberty of the press" were futile, he founded his own journalistic arm. This concept of an antimodernist "Christian civilization" was a seedling soon to blossom in Pius's imaginary. It might also be noted that *La Civiltà Cattolica* adopted a significantly anti-Semitic stance, of a piece with the accompanying reinstatement of the Jewish ghetto.

This anti-Semitism would surface in the journal eight years later during the bizarre affair of Edgardo Mortara.[26] The Jewish six-year-old had allegedly been surreptitiously baptized—perhaps out of malicious intent—by a Christian servant girl who sprinkled water on the boy and recited the trinitarian formula. (Needless to say, the implicit sacramental theology, in which no one except the mischievous servant made an affirmation of faith, was of a piece with the supernaturalist era.) Police then forcibly removed Edgardo from his parents' home in Bologna (Papal States) on the grounds that Jewish parents could not raise a baptized Christian. After authorities transported the boy to Rome to be raised under papal care, journalists throughout Europe waged a war of words on behalf of the Mortaras. By contrast, *La Civiltà Cattolica* ("Christian Civilization") defended the papal position.

In 1854, Pius IX defined the doctrine of the "Immaculate Conception of the Mother of God," the belief that Mary had been conceived in her mother's womb without inheriting the stain of Original Sin. Four years later, in 1858, the Virgin Mary seemed to confirm this doctrine herself. She was said to have appeared multiple times to Bernadette Soubirous, a young peasant girl in the remote French village of Lourdes. After Bernadette's numerous requests for a name, the apparition replied, "I am the Immaculate Conception." This belief had been debated for many centuries, and perhaps the main reason it had not received more official recognition is that it had been opposed by Saint Thomas Aquinas (while advocated by Duns Scotus). In its acute mid-19th-century context, however, it had a specifically supernaturalist function: it was directed against "naturalism"

26. See David I. Kertzer, *The Kidnapping of Edgardo Mortara* (New York: Alfred Knopf, 1997); Schloesser, "Against Forgetting," 302; and Kertzer, *The Popes against the Jews: The Vatican's Role in the Rise of Modern Anti-Semitism* (New York: Knopf, 2001).

(and its corollary determinism), the belief that everything in the world has only material or "natural" causes—or, more to the point, no divinely intervening "supernatural" causes. Pius correctly read the *Zeitgeist*: one year after Lourdes, Charles Darwin published *On the Origin of Species* (1859), a thoroughly materialist account of evolution by means of natural selection via species extinction.

The year 1858 has been highlighted by recent scholarship. Hubert Wolf's *The Nuns of Sant'Ambrogio*, based on Inquisition archives only recently opened by Pope John Paul II, uncovers a long-suppressed scandal at the Roman convent of Sant'Ambrogio.[27] Wolf's lurid yet mesmerizing account features the fraudulent visionary Sister Maria Luisa Firrao, whose intrigues included embezzlement, sexual abuse, and murder. They were enabled by her Jesuit confessor, Josef Kleutgen (with whom she was sexually involved). Kleutgen was one of his era's most influential conservative proponents of neo-Scholastic philosophy; he would soon be intimately involved with preparing for Pius IX's forthcoming Vatican Council.[28] Apart from moral blindness induced by sexual desire, what might account for the extreme gullibility that led Kleutgen and others to be duped by the fraudulent visionary? Wolf suggests one causal factor: a fervent supernaturalism, ideologically antimodernist, predisposed minds to imagine they had found the visions they sought.

The year 1858 marks three pertinent events: the Lourdes apparitions, the kidnaping of Edgardo Mortara, and the Sant'Ambrogio affair. All three vividly exemplify Catholicism's militant supernaturalism in the age of Darwin.

Spatial Turn: A Tale of Two Kingdoms (1861–1870)

On March 17, 1861, Victor Emmanuel II proclaimed the Kingdom of Italy with himself as its first monarch and Turin (1861–1864) as its capital city. The very next day, Pius IX quickly countered with his allocution, *Jamdudum cernimus* (March 18, 1861).[29] A transatlantic comparison might assist American readers in finding their bearings. Exactly two weeks

27. Hubert Wolf, *The Nuns of Sant'Ambrogio: The True Story of a Convent in Scandal*, trans. Ruth Martin (New York: Alfred A. Knopf, 2015).

28. John Inglis, *Spheres of Philosophical Inquiry and the Historiography of Medieval Philosophy* (Boston: Brill, 1998), 62–167.

29. For what follows, see Pius IX, *Jamdudum cernimus* (March 18, 1861); in Pius IX, *Les actes pontificaux cités dans l'encyclique et le syllabus du 8 décembre 1864: Suivis de divers autres documents*, ed. J. Chantrel (Paris: Poussielgue, 1865), 372–87.

earlier, Abraham Lincoln had been inaugurated president (March 4, 1861). One month later, the Confederate attack on Fort Sumter began the Civil War (April 12, 1861). Almost exactly four years later to the date, Lincoln would be assassinated (April 15, 1865). The Italian *risorgimento* was one episode in the broader transatlantic age of democratic civil wars.[30]

In *Jamdudum cernimus*, Pius IX laid out a vision of two irreconcilable forms of "civilization": "Christian civilization" versus modern liberal civilization. The purpose of the latter, he suggested, was the world's dechristianization—a reference to the French Revolution. The implicit opposition was an extremely concrete historical one between two conflicting monarchies: the Kingdom of Italy versus the Papal States. However, the pope's rhetorical transmutation of this opposition into a quasi-apocalyptic "clash of civilizations" solidified the Church versus world binary in play since Napoleon's defeat nearly 50 years earlier.

In 1864, this initial seed fully blossomed in the Syllabus of Errors (December 8, 1864).[31] The Syllabus was a compendium of 80 condemned propositions. In other words, the proposition stated a belief held by moderns but condemned by the Church. For example, the following four propositions related to indifferentism and disestablishment were condemned:

> 18: Protestantism is nothing else than a different form of the same Christian religion, in which it is permitted to please God equally as in the true Catholic Church.
> 55: The Church should be separated from the state, and the state from the Church.
> 77: In this our age it is no longer expedient that the Catholic religion should be treated as the only religion of the state, all other worships whatsoever being excluded.
> 78: Hence it has been laudably provided by law in some Catholic countries, that men thither immigrating should be permitted the public exercise of their own several worships.

The propositions were wide-ranging and provided a summary of 19th-century ideologies. They included philosophical schools like pantheism, naturalism, and rationalism; religious stances like indifferentism, church-state separation, and Bible societies (both historical exegesis and

30. See Philip Mark Katz, *From Appomattox to Montmartre: Americans and the Paris Commune* (Cambridge, MA: Harvard University, 1998).

31. For what follows, see "Pope Pius IX: Syllabus of Errors, 8 December 1864," in Barry, *Readings*, 3:70–74; and Schloesser, "Against Forgetting," 299.

publications); socioeconomic and political movements like liberalism, socialism, and Communism; and the legitimacy of the pope's temporal power as monarch of the Papal States. The Syllabus concluded with a fiery all-inclusive condemnation: "The Roman Pontiff can and ought to reconcile and harmonize himself with progress, liberalism, and with modern civilization" (no. 80).

The Syllabus was actually an annex to the encyclical *Quanta cura* (December 8, 1864).[32] Pius opened his encyclical by reminding Catholics that he had "again and again admonished and exhorted" them to "flee from the contagion of so dire a pestilence," that is, "the monstrous portents of opinion which prevail especially in this age." In a single sentence quoted from his predecessor Gregory's *Mirari vos*, Pius IX linked freedom of conscience, religion, speech, and (implicitly) assembly as erroneous beliefs that

> liberty of conscience and worship is each man's personal right, . . . and that a right resides in the citizens to an absolute liberty, which should be restrained by no authority whether ecclesiastical or civil, whereby they may be able openly and publicly to manifest and declare any of their ideas whatever, either by word of mouth, by the press, or in any other way.

At the end of this year (1864), Pius IX began preparations for an ecumenical council, the first to be held in three centuries. In particular, he wanted the council to address these post-Enlightenment and postrevolutionary issues: rationalism, materialism, liberalism, scriptural inspiration and interpretation, and—most radically—papal infallibility, an ultramontanist idea given a uniquely Romantic spin in de Maistre's *On the Pope* (1819) 50 years earlier.

Meanwhile, the Papal States' days were numbered. In 1864, after the September Convention, French Emperor Napoleon III agreed to withdraw his troops from Rome. However, in 1867, just one year after French troops had left, Italian nationalists attempted another invasion of Rome. Napoleon III immediately sent troops back to defeat them and left a garrison to protect the papal monarchy. It was a fragile measure completely dependent on the French Second Empire's stability. That was soon threatened in August 1866 when the northern German states were unified under Prussian direction following the Austro-Prussian War (or "Unification War").

32. For what follows, see Pius IX, *Quanta cura* (December 8, 1864); in Carlen, *Papal Encyclicals*, 1:381–86.

In 1870, this potent brew of intellectual, cultural, religious, and political ingredients boiled over. Pius IX's ecumenical council, in the planning since 1864 and announced in 1868, opened on December 8, 1869, the feast of the Immaculate Conception. Its title was "The Vatican Council."[33] Two constitutions were discussed and approved: the Dogmatic Constitution on the Catholic Faith (*Dei Filius*) and the Dogmatic Constitution on the Church of Christ (*Pastor Aeternus*).[34]

Dei Filius set boundaries limiting rationalism—"the natural light of reason"—and underscored the necessity of "supernatural revelation" for knowing truth. At the same time, it also set limits to "fideism," an irrational and blind faith that bypassed any need for human reason at all. Stating that the Catholic Church, "with one consent, has also ever held and does hold that there is a twofold order of knowledge"—that is, both faith and reason—"distinct both in principle and also in object," the constitution drew this remarkable conclusion:

> But although faith is above reason, there can never be any real discrepancy between faith and reason, since the same God who reveals mysteries and infuses faith has bestowed the light of reason on the human mind; and God cannot deny himself, nor can truth ever contradict truth. The false appearance of such a contradiction is mainly due, either to the dogmas of faith not having been understood and expounded according to the mind of the Church, or to the inventions of opinion having been taken for the verdicts of reason. We define, therefore, that every assertion contrary to a truth of enlightened faith is utterly false.[35]

Especially read within the light of relentlessly negative papal reproaches during the past hundred years, this paragraph seems surprisingly optimistic.

33. Herbert Vaughan, *The Year of Preparation for the Vatican Council: Including the Original and English of the Encyclical and Syllabus and of the Papal Documents Connected with Its Convocation* (London: Burns, Oates, 1869).

34. For what follows, see "First Vatican Council—1869–1870," in *Decrees of the Ecumenical Councils*, ed. Norman P. Tanner, 2 vols. (Washington, DC: Georgetown University, 1990), 2:801–16.

35. *Dei Filius*, chap. 4 ("De fide et ratione"): in Tanner, *Decrees*, 2:808. See also Stephen Schloesser, "Jesuit Hybrids, Catholic Moderns, Futural Pasts," in *For the City and the World: Conversations in Catholic Studies and Social Thought*, Lane Center Lectures 2005–2010, ed. Julia Dowd (San Francisco: University of San Francisco, Association of Jesuit University Presses, 2010), 114–41, at 116; and Stephen Schloesser, "The Unbearable Lightness of Being: Re-Sourcing Catholic Intellectual Traditions," *Cross Currents* 58 (2008): 65–94, at 75.

The second constitution, *Pastor Aeternus*, had a rougher ride. Although the majority party favored infallibility, the minority party included some extremely strong and articulate opponents. Moreover, since a war between France and Prussia was imminent and hence time short, discussion was limited. Once the French withdrew their troops and left Rome unprotected, Italian nationalists were sure to seize the day and capture the city. Thus, as the infallibility discussion took place in July 1870, the heat was unbearable, many bishops took sick, and the city braced for battle.[36] An initial vote on July 13 garnered 451 votes for, 88 against, and 62 in favor but with an amendment. As the outcome became clear, 60 bishops left Rome so as not to cast an opposition vote.

The final tally, offering only a yes or no option, was taken on July 18: 433 voted yes while only 2—Sicilian Aloisio Riccio and American Edward Fitzgerald of Little Rock, Arkansas—voted no. The next day, July 19, France sent a declaration of war to the Prussian government. As French troops departed Rome for battle, Foreign Minister Otto von Bismarck received what he had been looking for all along: southern German states joined the northern Prussian war effort. Six decades after Napoleon dissolved the Holy Roman Empire and invented the Confederation of the Rhine (1806–1813), a united German nation state had finally been achieved.

In contrast to 19th-century critics who joked that the pope would soon be infallibly predicting the weather, *Pastor Aeternus*'s final wording significantly circumscribed the definition. First, the pope needed to be explicitly speaking *ex cathedra*, i.e., from his "chair"; second, he had to be defining a doctrine regarding faith or morals; and third, it needed "to be held by the universal Church." Most significantly, "infallibility" was not an attribute possessed by the pope; rather, it was "that infallibility with which the Divine Redeemer willed that his Church should be endowed." Thus, the pope's teaching *ex cathedra* was infallible insofar as he—as head—articulated teaching "held by the universal Church."

Thus the paradox: just as Pius IX achieved defined infallibility in faith and morals, he became the first pope in over 1,100 years not to reign as a temporal monarch. After Rome was captured on September 20, 1870, Pius declared himself a self-imposed "Prisoner of the Vatican."[37] One month later, on October 20, he indefinitely suspended the Vatican Council.

36. Johann Joseph Ignaz von Döllinger, *Letters from Rome on the Council* (New York: Pott & Amery, 1870), 685, 689, 712.

37. David I. Kertzer, *Prisoner of the Vatican: The Popes' Secret Plot to Capture Rome from the New Italian State* (Boston: Houghton Mifflin, 2004).

Today, perhaps, the very notion of a papal state monarchy seems unimaginably quaint or archaic—something seen only on *The Borgias*. By contrast, for pro-papal antinationalists of the 1800s, the evaporation of a political entity that had survived since the mid-700s seemed unthinkable. In either case, papal monarchy today is a nonissue. And yet, a somewhat disturbing deeper issue is at play.

The "spatial turn" in recent decades reminds historians and other humanities scholars of the importance of particular geographical places situated in time: place matters.[38] Taking spatiotemporal location seriously reframes 19th-century Roman Catholic teaching. The "ordinary magisterium"—a term first coined by Kleutgen—is often imagined as transcending space and time, indeed, transcending history itself.[39] However, seen through the lens of spatiality, the heated rhetoric of a clash of civilizations actually concerned a highly specific and extremely circumscribed territorial dispute: the Papal States versus the Kingdom of Italy. Although this civil war soon fell down the memory chute, the binary opposition between Roman Catholicism and "modernity" would shape the Church for nearly another century. Far from being apocalyptic, it was human, all too human.

Restoration: Christian Philosophy for a Christian Civilization (1879)[40]

In February 1878, Pius IX died and was succeeded by Leo XIII. Only 18 months later, Leo promulgated *Aeterni Patris* (August 4, 1879).[41] The quickness with which this encyclical appeared testifies to Leo's vision of causal connections: bad thought leads to bad politics. The document

38. See Barney Warf and Santa Arias, eds., *The Spatial Turn: Interdisciplinary Perspectives* (New York: Routledge, 2009); Phil Hubbard and Rob Kitchin, *Key Thinkers on Space and Place* (London: Sage, 2010); Robert T. Tally Jr., *Spatiality* (New York: Routledge, 2013).

39. Paul Collins, *Upon This Rock: The Popes and Their Changing Role* (New York: Crossroad, 2000), 244; citing John P. Boyle, "The Ordinary Magisterium," *Heythrop Journal* 20 (1979): 380–98, and 21 (1980): 14–29.

40. For "Christian philosophy," see Stephen Schloesser's review of *Reason Fulfilled by Revelation: The 1930s Christian Philosophy Debates in France*, ed. and trans. Gregory B. Sadler (Washington, DC: The Catholic University of America, 2011), in *H-France Review* 11, no. 233 (October 2011): no. 233, http://www.h-france.net/vol11reviews/vol11no233 Schloesser.pdf.

41. For fuller treatment with references, see Schloesser, *Jazz Age Catholicism*, 33–35.

established the philosophy of Saint Thomas Aquinas as Roman Catholicism's official intellectual system and mandated its teaching in all Catholic institutions, including seminaries and universities:

> Domestic and civil society even, which, as all see, is exposed to great danger from this plague of perverse opinions, would certainly enjoy a far more peaceful and secure existence if a more wholesome doctrine were taught in the universities and high schools—one more in conformity with the teaching of the Church, such as is contained in the works of Thomas Aquinas.

Nine years earlier, the Vatican Council's declaration on faith and reason had sounded a surprisingly optimistic note: "there can never be any real discrepancy between faith and reason." But these eight years had been tumultuous: the Papal States had vanished; Rome became Italy's capital; and the popes—first Pius and now Leo—adopted the official position of being "Prisoners of the Vatican." Moreover, the decade had been traumatized by Pius's final struggle: the *Kulturkampf* (Culture Struggle) with Bismarck's Germany (1871–1878).[42]

Not surprisingly, then, Leo's estimation of human reason was somewhat more tempered than the Council's. His map of the faith-and-reason landscape made the two parties seem less like overlapping territories and more like divided continents:

> We know that there are some who, in their overestimate of the human faculties, maintain that as soon as man's intellect becomes subject to divine authority it falls from its native dignity, and hampered by the yoke of this species of slavery, is much retarded and hindered in its progress toward the supreme truth and excellence. Such an idea is most false and deceptive. . . . For the human mind, being confined within certain limits, and those narrow enough, is exposed to many errors and is ignorant of many things; whereas the Christian faith, reposing on the authority of God, is the unfailing mistress of truth, whom whoso followeth he will be neither enmeshed in the snares of error nor tossed hither and thither on the waves of fluctuating opinion. Those, therefore, who to the study of philosophy unite obedience to the Christian faith, are philosophizing in the best possible way. . . . For surely that is a worthy and most useful exercise of reason when men give their minds to disproving those things which are repugnant to faith and proving the things which conform to faith.

42. Michael B. Gross, *The War against Catholicism: Liberalism and the Anti-Catholic Imagination in Nineteenth-Century Germany* (Ann Arbor: University of Michigan, 2004).

What was reason's most useful function? It provided rational arguments defending truths already revealed in Scripture and tradition.

The rhetoric of this Thomistic "restoration" exemplified the word's 1854 definition by Eugène-Emmanuel Viollet-le-Duc: "RESTORATION. Both the word and the thing are modern. To restore an edifice means neither to maintain it, nor to repair it, nor to rebuild it; it means to reestablish it in a finished state, which may in fact never have actually existed at any given time."[43] As with the invented traditions already noted (e.g., Napoleon's Concordat Catholicism, Chateaubriand's *Genius of Christianity*, de Maistre's *On the Pope*), neo-Thomism (or neo-Scholasticism) wore antique clothing seemingly steeped in misty prehistoric origins. And yet, neo-Thomism was a modern invention responding to contemporary problems. Whereas neo-Thomism was primarily concerned with the problem of knowledge ("epistemology"), the historical Aquinas would not have doubted that we know things outside our minds. Indeed, by means of analogy, he was extremely optimistic that we could know a great deal even about the ineffable God.

In actual practice, seminarians did not read much of Aquinas's original texts. Rather, they were trained with "manuals" of philosophy and theology—a practice dubbed "manualist theology." These manuals were largely compilations of textual fragments from numerous sources—Scripture, magisterial teachings, philosophers, and theologians (including Thomas himself)—assembled in order to proof-text various doctrines and dogmas.[44] The method was deductive, not inductive. It began with a proposition and proceeded to prove it with internal evidence; it did not begin with observation or research and then see where the empirical data led.

More to the point: neo-Scholasticism was fundamentally ahistorical. It paid no attention to the original historical (or even textual) contexts in which its cut-and-pasted excerpts had been written or to what acute problems they had been responding. The claim can be made even stronger: neo-Scholasticism was intentionally *anti*historical. The method was explicitly meant to ignore the historical research that would retrieve the actual *tradition(s)*—as opposed to invented tradition—that might erode or undermine the doctrines or dogmas taken at face value. Reaction against this profound opposition to history—change itself—would soon lead to the "Modernist Crisis."

43. Eugène-Emmanuel Viollet-le-Duc, *The Foundations of Architecture: Selections from the* Dictionnaire raisonné, trans. Kenneth D. Whitehead (New York: Braziller, 1990), 195.

44. For an example in English, see Ludwig Ott, *Fundamentals of Catholic Dogma*, trans. Patrick Lynch, ed. James Canon Bastible (St. Louis: B. Herder, 1964).

Before leaving *Aeterni Patris*, it seems worth recalling that neo-Scholasticism's preeminent champion had been the Jesuit Josef Kleutgen who considered the encyclical a vindication of his life's work. Exactly 20 years earlier, he had been entangled in the 1858 Sant'Ambrogio sex scandal. The "purity and pollution" rhetoric in *Aeterni Patris* is muted when compared to the earlier fulminations of Gregory XVI and Pius IX: "perverse opinion"; "shameful font"; "corruption of youths"; "deadly pestilence"; "monstrous doctrines" (all from *Mirari vos*); "perverse and shocking theory"; "crafty men"; "vile action"; "filthy medley of errors" (all from *Qui pluribus*); "the contagion of so dire a pestilence"; "monstrous portents" (from *Quanta cura*). And yet, albeit muted, purity and pollution anxieties also underlay *Aeterni Patris*'s proposal to counter a "plague of perverse opinions" with "a more wholesome doctrine." Whether read through the lens of cultural anthropology or psychoanalytic theory, the condemnatory rhetorical style of the 19th-century magisterium is shot through with fears of impurity, pollution, and contamination. As anthropologist Mary Douglas notes: "The final paradox of the search for purity is that it is an attempt to force experience into logical categories of non-contradiction. But experience is not amenable and those who make the attempt find themselves led into contradiction."[45]

Anti-Semitism's Wages: From *Ralliement* to Divorce (1892–1905)

In 1892, departing from the tradition of encyclicals published in Latin, Leo XIII promulgated *Au milieu des sollicitudes* (February 16, 1892) in French. In it, he came to grips with the fact that republicanism (popularly elected government) needed to be accommodated. In fact, it had been exactly a century (September 21, 1792) since the French had abolished the monarchy and proclaimed the First Republic.

In 1875, France's Third Republic, originally intended as a transitional government after the disastrous defeat in the Franco-Prussian War (1870) and the end of Napoleon III's Second Empire, had become a permanent one. In 1881–1882, as part of a broader republican anticlerical agenda, the Jules Ferry Laws established free and mandatory public (i.e., "laicist") education and suppressed Catholic schools and religious teaching orders (like the Jesuits). In 1882, reacting to the growing laicist offensive, the Assumptionist religious order founded the daily newspaper *La Croix* (*The Cross*). It would quickly come to be treated as gospel truth by many clergy. This new "culture struggle" in France, coming immediately on the heels of the *Kul-*

45. Mary Douglas, as quoted in Schloesser, *Jazz Age Catholicism*, 49.

turkampf in Germany, alarmed Leo. He realized that the Republic needed to be accommodated if the Church were not to be completely shut out of the public sphere (recently attempted in the Paris Commune of 1870–1871).

In 1888, four years prior to *Au milieu des sollicitudes*, Leo had begun forging a middle way in his encyclical *Libertas* (June 20, 1888). He first reaffirmed continuity with his predecessors: "Justice therefore forbids, and reason itself forbids, the State to be godless; or to adopt a line of action which would end in godlessness—namely, to treat the various religions (as they call them) alike, and to bestow upon them promiscuously equal rights and privileges." But Leo then began a shift in tone. A certain measure of "tolerance"—even of a "godless" Republic—was permissible in particular circumstances: "While not conceding any right to anything save what is true and honest, [the Church] does not forbid public authority to tolerate what is at variance with truth and justice, for the sake of avoiding some greater evil, or of obtaining or preserving some greater good."

In 1892, applying and expanding this same line, Leo used *Au milieu des sollicitudes* to appeal directly to France's Catholics and urge them to embrace a policy of *ralliement*—"rallying to the Republic." How did he justify this appeal? He did not accept the legitimacy of popular sovereignty or the social contract. To do so would have reversed the magisterial papal teachings pronounced with such vehemence over the preceding 60 years; effectively it would also have undermined the legitimacy of his own teachings as well as his status as "Prisoner of the Vatican."

Instead, Leo made a razor sharp distinction between "constituted political power" and the "legislation" it produced. The most legitimately established government can pass bad laws; and a thoroughly illegitimate government can pass good laws: "In so much does legislation differ from political power and its form, that under a system of government most excellent in form legislation could be detestable; while quite the opposite under a regime most imperfect in form, might be found excellent legislation." From this distinction, Leo went on to note that the quality of laws depends on the quality of the legislators, "of men invested with power."

> [They] in fact, govern the nation; therefore it follows that, practically, the quality of the laws depends more upon the quality of these men than upon the power. The laws will be good or bad accordingly as the minds of the legislators are imbued with good or bad principles, and as they allow themselves to be guided by political prudence or by passion.

Catholics, therefore, needed to "rally" to the Republic, engage the political process, run for office and become representatives, regardless of whether the Republic was a legitimate government. The goodness or badness of laws depended on the quality of legislators: the "constituted political power" (the Republic) was distinct from those individuals "invested with power" (the legislators).

Leo's encyclical did, in fact, affect the French political scene, especially when taken in tandem with his encyclical *Rerum novarum* (May 15, 1891), published the previous year, and generally regarded as the inauguration of modern Catholic social teaching. Count Albert de Mun, for example, was a practicing Roman Catholic elected legislator who worked on behalf of Leo's social reforms.[46] However, many other Catholics saw in Leo a betrayal of everything the Church had stood for during the long century of intransigence since the French Revolution. They rallied to neither the Republic nor the pope.

Enter anti-Semitism. In 1892, the same year as Leo's *ralliement* encyclical, Edouard Drumont, the most powerful anti-Semitic voice of the fin-de-siècle, founded his newspaper *La Libre Parole* (*Free Speech*).[47] (Drumont's *La France juive* [*Jewish France*, 1886], published six years earlier, would reach 200 editions by the turn of the century.) With the founding of *Libre Parole*, Drumont launched a crusade to purge Jewish "pollution" in the French army. "The Semitic invasion is like the breeding of microbes," he wrote. "Though there have been some hints of weakness, the army has joined the combat with a remarkable strength of resistance. . . . We want to encourage the army in this holy struggle." Drumont's journal, like his earlier book, was popular among Catholic clergy and laity.

Two years later, the Dreyfus Affair erupted. In 1894, a Jewish artillery officer named Captain Alfred Dreyfus was indicted for passing on classified documents. A highly placed military source leaked word of the indictment to Drumont, who in turn published the news on November 1, 1894. Prominently displayed beneath the xenophobic masthead motto, "France for the French," the *Libre Parole* headline read: "High Treason: Arrest of the Jewish Officer A. Dreyfus." A month later, Dreyfus was found guilty of high treason. Four months later, he was transferred to Devil's Island to serve out his life sentence of solitary confinement.

After much cajoling over the next two years, the popular naturalist novelist Émile Zola, laicist by conviction, was persuaded to take up a campaign in favor of Dreyfus. On January 13, 1898, Zola published his now famous

46. Benjamin F. Martin, *Count Albert de Mun, Paladin of the Third Republic* (Chapel Hill: University of North Carolina, 1978).

47. For fuller treatment of the Dreyfus Affair with references, see Schloesser, *Jazz Age Catholicism*, 50–54. For an overview, see also Michael Burns, *France and the Dreyfus Affair: A Documentary History* (Boston: Bedford/St. Martin's, 1999).

open letter "J'Accuse!" The government brought Zola to trial, convicted him, and gave him the maximum sentence for libel. Zola's loss was the left's gain. Jean Jaurès founded the newspaper *La Petite République* and reanimated the moribund socialists. In reaction, fanatical Assumptionists waged a bitter campaign in *La Croix* to strip all Jews of citizenship. *La Croix* had an influence disproportionate to its circulation numbers, thanks to the clergy's dissemination of its ideas. The Assumptionists also used another of their journals, *Le Pèlerin* (The Pilgrim), published at the Lourdes healing shrine, to peddle a particularly violent racial anti-Semitism.

In 1899, the left triumphed when the Republic's president pardoned Dreyfus. (His innocence would wait several more years to be proven.) In the 1902 elections, a political backlash against the right swept in a radical left coalition government. Between 1902 and 1905 a series of anticlerical laws was passed, culminating in the 1905 Act of Separation of Church and State. The state confiscated all Church properties, and members of religious orders were exiled. Perhaps it is just as well that Leo XIII had died two years earlier; he was spared seeing the utter collapse of his *ralliement* dreams. French Catholics had snatched defeat from the jaws of victory.

Pius X, who had only just succeeded Leo in 1903, excommunicated all Catholic deputies who had voted for the separation. This action accorded with his namesake's condemned proposition in the Syllabus (1864): "The Church should be separated from the state, and the state from the Church." Pius also forbade Catholics to participate in the new lay committees that would oversee parishes. What effect did this have on the Church in France? Statistics from the Limoges area provide one limited yet illuminating case study. Between 1899 and 1914, the number of unbaptized children rose from 2.5 to 33.9 percent; the number of civil marriages from 14 to 60 percent; and the number of civil burials quadrupled. For France as a whole, the annual number of ordinations fell from 1,518 in 1904 to 704 by 1914. One catastrophic long-term effect of the Dreyfus Affair: Catholics chose state over Church.

Non-Integralists: "Cafeteria Catholics"? (1898–1914)

In addition to the external crisis of church-state relations, the Church also underwent one internal to itself, known to history as the "Modernist Crisis."[48] In 1905, besides excommunicating the Catholic deputies who

48. For fuller treatment of the following (Modernist Crisis) with references, see Schloesser, *Jazz Age Catholicism*, 54–56; "*Vivo ergo cogito*," 46–47, 49–51; and "Jesuit Hybrids," 122–23.

had voted for separation, the Holy See also placed five of the Abbé Alfred Loisy's books on the Index of Forbidden Books. Twenty-five years earlier, Leo XIII's encyclical mandating the restoration of Thomism in Catholic schools had causally linked thought and politics: "Many of those who, with minds alienated from the faith, hate Catholic institutions, claim reason as their sole mistress and guide." The events of 1902–1905 seemed to verify Leo's vision.

What was "Roman Catholic Modernism"? Fundamentally, it was an attempt to come to terms with the 19th century's embrace of history. Scripture scholars, Church scholars, historical theologians—all were using historical methods to trace developments in the Bible, the Church, and doctrines back to their beginnings. The embrace of history—or, more pointedly, the affirmation of change over time—challenged the Church's denial of change, especially as embodied in neo-Thomism and manualist theology.

Two years after France's Act of Separation, the Inquisition issued the syllabus *Lamentabili sane* (July 3, 1907). Like the Syllabus of Pius X's namesake issued 50 years earlier, it condemned 65 propositions expressing "dangerous errors concerning the natural sciences, the interpretation of Holy Scripture, and the principal mysteries of the faith." Proposition 22 exemplified the antihistorical stance: "The dogmas the Church holds out as revealed are not truths which have fallen from heaven. They are an interpretation of religious facts which the human mind has acquired by laborious effort." In other words, revealed church dogmas actually *had* fallen from heaven, fully formed and independently of human thought.

Whether any individual person actually believed all that "Modernists" were said to believe, the outcome of this episode was the reclothing of an old binary in new language: "integralists" versus "Modernists." Integralists (*intégristes*) imagined a total "integration" of all facets of life into an indivisible organic unity, hierarchically ordered beneath the ultramontanist pope. A simplistic metaphor with popular appeal, the term "integralism" suggested a body that was integrally perfect and hence pure. If one held fast to the whole and did not question the parts, one could be guaranteed safety from polluted contaminants. Although the *intégristes* had never shown much enthusiasm for Leo XIII or his *ralliement*, they were now ardent zealots for the fiercely antimodernist Pius X. "We are integral Roman Catholics," they announced. "That is, we set above all and everyone not only the Church's traditional teaching in the order of absolute truths but also the pope's directions in the order of practical contingencies. For the Church and the pope are one." In today's parlance, integralists regarded non-integralists—i.e., Modernists—as "cafeteria Catholics."

In 1909, a secret international antimodernist network was set up. Its Latin title, the Sodalitium Pianum (S.P., i.e., "Sodality of St. Pius V"), was known in France by its code name Sapinière. Pius X both encouraged and subsidized the activities of this "secret police." In 1910, the Holy See required all priests having pastoral charge to sign the "Oath Against Modernism." This oath included affirming an antihistorical agenda: dogmas were immutable. The integralist reaction peaked during the years 1912–1913.

This was the state of affairs on the eve of the Great War in July 1914: an absolute binary drawn between two opposing camps—Catholicism versus modern civilization. Ninety-nine years had passed since Napoleon's 1815 defeat at Waterloo and the Congress of Vienna's "restoration." Numerous tumultuous events located in space-time had reinforced and calcified the opposition. However, even as those events faded from spatiality into history, the opposition seemingly transcended time, a quasi-apocalyptic clash of civilizations.

Fascism: Making Liberalism Look Good (1919–1939)

In January 1919, the Paris Peace Conference was convened at Versailles to settle the Great War of 1914–1918.[49] On a basic level, it needed to negotiate the usual items of peace settlements: new boundaries with exchanges of land, war reparations, demands for demilitarization. However, like its predecessor exactly one century earlier (Vienna 1815), Paris 1919 had an unusually large number of additional tasks. As great powers sat at the negotiating table, they redrew much of the world's map as they invented new states. This was even truer in 1919 than in 1815 because three empires had collapsed as a result of the Great War: the Austro-Hungarian, Russian, and Ottoman empires. As a result, new states were invented: Czechoslovakia, Yugoslavia, and Poland (resurrected). The League of Nations, founded in 1920 after Paris 1919, established the "mandate" system to govern the former Ottoman territories. Nation states eventually created out of British and French mandates include present-day Iraq, Syria, Lebanon, and Israel.

The guiding aura of Paris 1919, embodied in the person of President Woodrow Wilson, was the liberal principle of "self-determination" descended from the Enlightenment's social contract. Just as individuals have

49. Margaret MacMillan, *Paris 1919: Six Months That Changed the World* (New York: Random House, 2002).

the inalienable right to self-determination, so too did a "people" or "nation"—what we today might call an "ethnicity"—have a right to their own nation state. The state's legitimacy was founded on popular sovereignty. Although reality substantially departed from rhetoric, Wilsonian self-determination—seen as the logical outcome of Enlightenment values—was meant to endow the 1914–1918 slaughterhouse with lasting meaning. The Great War had been the war to end all wars. Incalculable sacrifice had not been in vain. Mourning could end in comfort.

However, challenging this apparently final triumphant chapter in the Enlightenment story simmered two competing worldviews. The first was Communism: a driving intellectual and social force throughout the long 19th century, it had achieved political embodiment in 1917 during the Russian revolutions of February and then October.[50] In 1922, the Soviet Union would be created under the leadership of Vladimir Lenin. In 1924, Lenin died and was succeeded by Joseph Stalin. Soviet Communism imagined itself as the French Revolution's true heir. A proletarian dictatorship would enforce genuine equality and fraternity, social as well as political. Stalin's purges, state confiscation of private property, and forced collectivization could all be interpreted as distant echoes of Robespierre's Terror.[51]

However, also in 1922, another (and more recent) competitor for true political modernity appeared on the streets—quite literally.[52] One year after the Fascist Party was created (November 1921), it hit the pavement in the audacious and utterly improbable March on Rome (October 1922). The scheme worked. On October 30, one day after being summoned to the palace of King Victor Emmanuel III, Benito Mussolini became prime minister of the Kingdom of Italy. Like Napoleon Bonaparte a century earlier, Mussolini understood the advantages of solidifying political cohesion with religious symbols and rituals. In 1926, negotiations began in an attempt to settle the "Roman Question" of the papacy, now a self-imposed "Prisoner of the Vatican" for over two generations.

50. For an overview, see Jeffrey Brooks and Georgiy Chernyavskiy, *Lenin and the Making of the Soviet State: A Brief History with Documents* (Boston: Bedford/St. Martin's, 2007).

51. For differing but classic interpretations, see E. J. Hobsbawm, *The Age of Extremes: A History of the World, 1914–1991* (New York: Pantheon, 1994); and François Furet, *The Passing of an Illusion: The Idea of Communism in the Twentieth Century*, trans. Deborah Furet (Chicago: University of Chicago, 1999).

52. For an overview, see Marla Stone, *The Fascist Revolution in Italy: A Brief History with Documents* (Boston: Bedford/St Martin's, 2013).

Three years later, in February 1929, the Lateran Treaty was signed by Mussolini and Cardinal Pietro Gasparri, the Holy See's secretary of state.[53] The treaty created the state of Vatican City with independent sovereignty. In exchange, the pope, as head of state, promised perpetual neutrality in international affairs. Unlike the concordat with Napoleon a century earlier, the treaty affirmed that "the Catholic, Apostolic and Roman Religion is the only religion of the [Italian] State"; and the Vatican also received a financial settlement in exchange for properties lost in 1870. The good news for the papacy: the "Roman Question" had been settled. The bad news: Vatican City owed its existence to a Fascist government.

In late October 1929, eight months after the Lateran Treaty, the New York stock market crashed. The financial collapse set into motion a series of events that would result in a decade-long Great Depression. More particularly, it laid the groundwork for the Nazi accession to power in Germany under the strong arm of Adolph Hitler.[54] Because of unique circumstances owed to war reparations mandated in Paris 1919 (and heavy American postwar investments in German banks), the 1929 crash had a disproportionate and catastrophic effect on Germans. Electoral numbers tell the story. In 1928, the Nazis had received just 800,000 votes and 12 seats in parliament. But in 1930, just two years later—following the crash—they received 6,400,000 votes and 107 parliamentary seats. Mass panic fueled movement toward National Socialism.

In 1931, only two years after Mussolini's creation of the Vatican state, Pius XI felt compelled to publish an encyclical (in Italian, not Latin) titled *Non abbiamo bisogno* (June 29, 1931). Rebuking Fascist attacks on Catholic Action lay associations,[55] Pius wrote:

> We have protested against the campaign of false and unjust accusations which preceded the disbanding of the Associations of the young people and of the University students affiliated to Catholic Action. . . . How many acts of brutality and of violence there have been, even to the striking of blows and the drawing of blood! How many insults in the press, how

53. "The Lateran Treaty and Concordat Between the Holy See and Italy, 11 February 1929," in Barry, *Readings*, 3:348–63.

54. For an overview, see Robert G. Moeller, *The Nazi State and German Society: A Brief History with Documents* (Boston: Bedford/St. Martin's, 2010).

55. On "Catholic Action," see Jeremy Bonner, Christopher D. Denny, and Mary Beth Fraser Connolly, eds., *Empowering the People of God: Catholic Action before and after Vatican II* (New York: Fordham University, 2014). See also Tallett and Atkin, eds., *Religion, Society, and Politics in France*.

> many injurious words and acts against things and persons not excluding Ourself, have preceded, accompanied and followed the carrying into effect of this lightning-like police-order. . . . The inventions, falsehoods and real calumnies diffused by the hostile press of the party, which is the only press which is free to say and to dare to say anything and is often ordered or almost ordered what it must say, were largely summarized in a message which was cautiously characterized as unofficial and yet was broadcast to the general public by the most powerful means of diffusion which exist at present.

Non abbiamo marks a significant moment. In Pius XI's explicit acknowledgment that freedom of the press might have provided a counterpoint to the totalitarian state's monopoly on information dissemination—now made not only in printed matter but also on wireless radio ("the most powerful means of diffusion")—the pope embraced a fundamental Enlightenment principle. Fascism made liberalism look good.

In 1933, two years after *Non abbiamo*, Hitler effectively became the dictator of a German "Reich" (empire) dominated by the Nazi party. On July 20, a "Concordat Between the Holy See and the German Reich" was concluded in order "to consolidate and enhance the existing friendly relations between the Catholic Church and the state in the whole territory of the German Reich in a stable and satisfactory manner for both parties."[56] The Vatican's side was negotiated by the secretary of state, Cardinal Eugenio Pacelli, the future Pius XII. The Vatican received guarantees it customarily sought in concordats, including the right to appoint bishops, the administration of confessional (nonpublic) schools, and the regulation of Catholic marriages.

However, two Church concessions in particular foreshadowed storm clouds. Article 31 provided for the protection of "Catholic organizations and associations whose activity is devoted *exclusively to religious, purely cultural and charitable purposes* and which are, as such, subordinated to Church authorities" (emphasis added). The article's paragraph 2 further specified that associations having "other tasks such as social or professional aims" would also be tolerated "provided they guarantee to develop their activities *outside political parties*" (emphasis added). Paragraph 3 stipulated that it would be up to the "Reich government and German episcopate to determine, by mutual agreement," which organizations and

56. "Concordat Between the Holy See and the German Reich, 20 July 1933"; in Barry, *Readings*, 3:363–70.

associations qualified for such protection—that is, which associations were *not political.*

Article 32 extended this prohibition from associations to individuals: "The Holy See will issue ordinances by which the clergy and the religious will be forbidden to be members of political parties or to be active on their behalf." If a divergence of opinion were to arise about what constituted the "political," the Holy See and the German Reich would "arrive at an amicable solution by mutual agreement" (art. 33). In the additional protocol accompanying and explaining these provisions, the "duty for the German clergy and members of religious orders" in Article 32—that is, abstention from "political" parties or activity—was underscored as not meaning "any restriction on their preaching and exposition of the dogmatic and moral teachings and principles of the Church, as it is their duty to do."

Just as the concordat with Napoleon radically altered the nature of Catholicism, so too did the concordat with the German Reich. After all, how does a "dogmatic" or "moral" teaching differ from the "political"? Antimiscegenation laws, stripping Jews of citizenship, mass incarcerations in concentration camps, involuntary sterilization, euthanasia of the mentally disabled—are these "moral" issues? Are they "political" issues? Are the two mutually exclusive?

For a century and a half, the Church had struggled against being excluded from political and economic activity in everyday public life. In the classic terms of Ernst Troeltsch, the Church had militantly insisted on being a "church," not a "sect"; a player in the world (albeit on the Church's own terms), not an isolationist.[57] And yet now, just four years after achieving the victory of a papal city state with territorial sovereignty, it had acquiesced in effectively granting the *polis* its independent sovereignty. The concordat embodied a modern notion that the "secular" (*saeculum* = "worldliness") is the space (critiqued by Talal Asad) "in which real human life gradually emancipates itself from the controlling power of 'religion' and thus achieves the latter's relocation."[58] By signing the Reich concordat, the

57. Ernst Troeltsch, *The Social Teaching of the Christian Churches*, trans. Olive Wyon, 2 vols. (New York: The Macmillan Company, 1931); originally *Soziallehren der christlichen Kirchen und Gruppen* (1912).

58. Talal Asad, *Formations of the Secular: Christianity, Islam, Modernity* (Stanford, CA: Stanford University, 2003), 191–92; see also Asad, *Genealogies of Religion* (Baltimore: The Johns Hopkins University, 1993); and Brent Nongbri, *Before Religion: A History of a Modern Concept* (New Haven: Yale University, 2013).

Church seemed to accept modern "religion": a private voluntary sphere restricted to "faith and morals."

The first challenge to this newly invented "religion" would come just two years later in the form of the Nuremberg Laws (1935). Enacted on September 15, the laws used scientific racism to distinguish between "German or kindred blood," "mixed blood," and racially unacceptable (Jewish) blood. This distinction was then used in two laws. First, "The Reich Citizenship Law" provided for the distinction between "Reich citizens" and "state subjects." German blood was established as a prerequisite for citizenship. Jews had now been effectively stripped of citizenship. Given the long tortuous history—of Christians refusing citizenship to Jews; the inextricable link between Jewish emancipation and the French Revolution (especially under Napoleon); and the papacy's endless vacillation over its own Jewish ghettoes—the turned tables were now bitterly ironic.

Second, "The Law for the Protection of German Blood and German Honor" prohibited marriages and sexual intercourse more generally between "Germans" and "Jews" (now stripped of citizenship). Just five years earlier, in his encyclical *Casti connubii* (December 31, 1930), Pius XI had condemned such antimiscegenation laws—responding at that time to such laws in force for centuries in the United States, which served as precedent and model for the Nazis: "Finally, that pernicious practice must be condemned which closely touches upon the natural right of man to enter matrimony but affects also in a real way the welfare of the offspring. . . . Public magistrates have no direct power over the bodies of their subjects." And yet the question arose: could antimiscegenation be challenged without violating the 1933 concordat? Was such legislation a question of "politics" or merely "morals"?

Two years later, on Passion Sunday 1937, Pius XI promulgated his encyclical (in German, not Latin) *Mit brennender sorge* (March 14, 1937). (Perhaps to avoid any accusations of favoritism, he also promulgated *Divini Redemptoris* [March 19, 1937], an encyclical on atheistic communism, five days later on the feast of St. Joseph.) *Mit brennender Sorge* was smuggled into Germany and read from the pulpits the following Palm Sunday (March 21). "We thank you, Venerable Brethren," wrote the pope, "who have persisted in their Christian duty and in the defense of God's rights in the teeth of an aggressive paganism." He attacked the identification of God with the universe, "by pantheistic confusion," as atheism: "Whoever follows that so-called pre-Christian Germanic conception of substituting a dark and impersonal destiny for the personal God, denies thereby the Wisdom and Providence of God. . . . Neither is he a believer in God." Implicitly defending the role of Judaism in salvation history, the pope underscored the value of Hebrew Scriptures: "Nothing but ignorance and pride could blind one to the treasures hoarded in the Old Testament." Finally, without naming names, the pope equated Nazism with idolatry:

> Whoever exalts race, or the people, or the State, or a particular form of State, or the depositories of power, or any other fundamental value of the human community—however necessary and honorable be their function in worldly things—whoever raises these notions above their standard value and divinizes them to an idolatrous level, distorts and perverts an order of the world planned and created by God.

The following year, on November 9 and 10, 1938, a coordinated wave of anti-Jewish pogroms swept across Germany. The night came to be called *Kristallnacht*, the Night of Broken Glass. During a visit to Rome, American Jesuit John LaFarge was asked by Pius XI to write an encyclical specifically on racism. LaFarge did write this "hidden encyclical" in 1938, but it was never promulgated.[59] Pius XI died on February 10, 1939, and was succeeded on March 2 by Pius XII. On September 1, Hitler invaded Poland. The "Great War" became the "First World War" as a Second World War began.

Cold War Binary: Liberalism vs. Communism (1945–1962)

It would not be until Pius XII's Christmas allocution of 1945 that, for the first time in history, a pope unequivocally embraced the value of democratic government.[60] With the Allied defeat of Germany and Italy, Fascism had been eliminated as a third major political alternative (excepting the outlier Spain). This left liberal democracy and Soviet Communism as the two main alternatives in the postwar era. Communism had emerged from the war as a moral hero, embraced as the party of antifascist resistance; and Soviet-style Communism offered an international coalition. Pius XII faced the reality of a third phase in the politics of modernity. The first, liberal democracy versus divinely appointed monarchy, had disappeared after the First World War. The second, liberal democracy versus Communism and Fascism, evaporated at the end of the Second World War. This third

59. Georges Passelecq and Bernard Suchecky, *The Hidden Encyclical of Pius XI*, trans. Steven Rendall (New York: Harcourt Brace, 1997).

60. Schloesser, "Against Forgetting," 300.

phase, that of the Cold War, once again divided the political world into an absolute binary: liberalism (West) versus Communism (East). Pius XII chose liberalism. "Within the confines of each particular nation as much as in the whole family of peoples," he declared, "state totalitarianism is incompatible with *a true and healthy democracy*" (emphasis added).

Pius correctly perceived that there was little time to grieve over the recent catastrophe. A new world order demanded an immediate pivot away from the Church's long-standing antiliberalism. "Christian Democracy" was invented as a hybrid political movement that would ultimately rescue Catholicism across most of post-1945 Western Europe.[61] In April 1948, elections were held in Italy's newly formed "First Republic."[62] Partly mobilized by fear after the Communist coup in Czechoslovakia only weeks earlier, Christian Democrats won a sizable majority. They would dominate Italian politics for a half century, opposed by the Italian Communist Party. On July 15, 1948, *L'Osservatore Romano* published a decree excommunicating those propagating Communism. Other condemnations soon followed, including membership in Communist parties (1949).[63]

During the next decade of the 1950s, the world would be fundamentally reshaped by three overarching realities: a Cold War dividing the world into a liberal democratic "West" and a Soviet communist "East"; the ever-present threat of nuclear annihilation of the planet during the USA-USSR arms race; and the decolonization of Africa and Asia.[64] Within the Catholic Church, the 1940s and 1950s were also marked by an exhausting effort that often seemed futile to come to terms with "the Jewish Question" after the Holocaust.

On October 9, 1958, Pope Pius XII died and was immediately succeeded by John XXIII. Only three months later, on January 25, 1959, the pope surprised the world with his announcement of a Second Vatican Council. Documents prepared for consideration in October 1962 reflected the neo-Scholastic style. "All dangers were carefully noted. The predominantly negative tone was already perceptible in the titles: 'Maintaining the

61. Stathis N. Kalyvas, *The Rise of Christian Democracy in Europe* (Ithaca, NY: Cornell University, 1996); Wolfram Kaiser, *Christian Democracy and the Origins of European Union* (New York: Cambridge University, 2007); see also Atkin and Tallett, eds., *Religion, Society, and Politics in France*.

62. Robert Ventresca, *From Fascism to Democracy: Culture and Politics in the Italian Election of 1948* (Toronto: University of Toronto, 2004).

63. "Decree of the Sacred Congregation of the Holy Office on Joining or Supporting Communist Parties, 1 July 1949," in Barry, *Readings*, 503–4.

64. For fuller treatment with references, see Schloesser, "Against Forgetting," 279–85.

purity,' 'Moral order,' 'Chastity,' and these were then followed by lists of condemnations."[65] However, within weeks those documents were rejected and ordered rewritten. The continuity versus discontinuity contest had begun.

As O'Malley notes, in the council's final documents, a rhetoric of "adapting" and "accommodating" displaced the traditional rhetoric of "correcting" and "remedying." The Church embraced history. Latin equivalents of "evolution" and "development" occur 42 times in the documents; equivalents of "progress" and "advance" occur 120 times.[66] In 1966, one year after the council's conclusion, Bernard Lonergan explicitly identified the Church's transition from a classicist worldview to historical mindedness: one in which meaning is "not fixed, static, immutable, but [rather] shifting, developing, going astray, capable of redemption." In 1800, the royalist Geoffroy had claimed that nothing new could "take place in the wake of the Gospel." Some 166 years later, Lonergan stood that claim on its head: "I think our Scripture scholars would agree that [classicism's] abstractness, and the omissions due to abstraction, have no foundation in the revealed word of God."[67]

History of the Present: Reproach vs. *Rapprochement* Redux

This introduction began with a set of questions. Did anything happen—did anything change—at the council? Was the Church any different in its wake? And if so, what significance, if any, does this change have for the present moment—a half century later—and for the future? The Synod on the Family, called by Pope Francis to meet in two sessions (October 2014 and October 2015), offers a case study.

On October 13, 2014, the Synod received the *Relatio post disceptationem* for debate.[68] The *Relatio* explicitly and self-consciously retrieved

65. Mario von Galli and Bernhard Moosbrugger; in *History of Vatican II*, 5 vols., ed. Giuseppe Alberigo; English version ed. Joseph A Komonchak; trans. Matthew J. O'Connell (Maryknoll, NY: Orbis, 1995–2006), 1:415.

66. O'Malley, "Hermeneutic of Reform," 26.

67. Schloesser, "Against Forgetting," 307–8.

68. See Stephen Schloesser, "'Dancing on the Edge of the Volcano': Biopolitics and What Happened after Vatican II," in *From Vatican II to Pope Francis: Charting a Catholic Future*, ed. Paul Crowley, SJ (Maryknoll, NY: Orbis, 2014), 3–26; and Schloesser, "Biopolitics and the Construction of Postconciliar Catholicism," in *A Realist's Church: Essays in Honor of Joseph Komonchak*, ed. Christopher Denny, Patrick Hayes, and Nicholas Rademacher (Maryknoll, NY: Orbis, forthcoming).

what O'Malley has identified as Vatican II's "epideictic style," a humanist genre of "praise."[69] After first referencing the genre's use in *Nostra aetate* (October 1965)—"appreciating the positive elements present in other religions and cultures, despite their limits and their insufficiencies"—the *Relatio* then applied the principle to present-day challenges. In cases of cohabitation, civil marriages, and divorced and remarried persons, the Church was said to appreciate "the positive values they contain rather than their limitations and shortcomings." The same style was then applied to homosexuality: "Without denying the moral problems associated with homosexual unions, there are instances where mutual assistance to the point of sacrifice is a valuable support in the life of these persons." This reasoning followed the path opened by Leo XIII in *Libertas* (1888).

In the end, these formulations were not approved by the majority. However, the *Relatio* remains posted on the Vatican website, translated into five languages, an integral and permanent element in the process of the synod's first session. As I write this in March 2015, no one can foretell what the synod's second session will bring seven months from now. One thing is certain: 50 years after the council, two styles—reproach versus *rapprochement*—continue to collide. The paradigm shift in the reform of Vatican II may not always (or even often) have informed magisterial documents during the half century following it (1965–2015). Yet it remains waiting in the wings, ever ready for the wise scribe—in words used by Paul VI when paying homage to Leo XIII—who "knows how to bring both new and old things out" of the Church's treasure-house.[70]

69. John W. O'Malley, SJ, "Vatican II: Did Anything Happen?," *Theological Studies* 67 (2006): 3–33; see also Schloesser, "Against Forgetting," 277–78.

70. Matthew 13:52; in Paul VI, *Ecclesiam suam* no. 67 (August 6, 1964).

Part 1

General Interpretations

1 "The Hermeneutic of Reform" A Historical Analysis

JOHN W. O'MALLEY, SJ

Few ideas have impacted the church more than reform, but in recent centuries it virtually disappeared from theological discourse. That changed on December 22, 2005, when Pope Benedict XVI, in his address to the Roman Curia, introduced "hermeneutic of reform" as the proper category for interpreting Vatican II. John O'Malley here traces the history of the idea of reform, describes its meaning in different contexts, and shows how the problem of change is at its very core. He then shows how Vatican II dealt with the problem and concludes with an analysis of Benedict's address.

In the West few ideas have enjoyed a longer, more complex, and, in many instances, more disruptive history than reform. Expressed through a number of terms, of which the most direct and obvious is the Latin *reformatio*, reform has traditionally been defined as *mutatio in melius*, change for the better. Etymologically speaking, *reformatio*, whose English equivalents are both *reform* and *reformation*, indicates a re-forming or a restructuring of something already in place. Thus, although change is at its core, reform presupposes continuity with what has gone before. It is not *creatio ex nihilo*.

This definition presupposes, as well, that reform entails a self-consciously undertaken effort within an institution to effect change. It is thus different from changes that come about because of decisions taken by others. For instance, few events more radically changed the Christian church than Constantine's recognition of it and his granting it a privileged status in his empire. Yet the changes his decisions effected, which church leaders welcomed as "for the better," are never described as reform.

The definition also implicitly differentiates reform from changes that come about in a gradual fashion without deliberate decision making to effect the final result. Over the course of time, institutions, for instance, have a tendency toward greater sophistication in procedures. The change is incremental, as when a business bit by bit adds more staff and eventually opens branch offices. Or, to take a concrete example from the sphere of ideas: *renaissance* was first employed in the 15th century to indicate a literary rebirth, then got applied to designate a shift in standards in painting, sculpture, and architecture, and finally was applied to a whole period of history. Rather than call such changes reform, we tend to call them developments, about which I will say more later.

Although the synonyms, quasi-synonyms, and euphemisms for reform have slightly different nuances, they express the same idea of change for the better. They too have played such important roles in cultural and political history that it is almost impossible to speak of the course of Western civilization without employing them. I refer to words such as *renewal*, *renovation*, *restoration*, *revival*, *rebirth*, and *renaissance*. To that list can be added, with less cogency, terms such as *correction*, *emendation*, and *improvement*.[1] Important though these terms are, *reform* remains the most basic and most frequently invoked in almost every sphere of human activity to indicate deliberate efforts undertaken within an institution to improve the status quo.

Important as the idea of reform has been in secular history, it has been even more important in the history of Christianity.[2] After all, it cuts to the very heart of the Christian message, which is a call to repentance, conversion, and reform of life. Without rebirth, according to John's Gospel, there is no entrance into the kingdom of heaven. Reform was therefore originally directed to the individual Christian. Repent! Change your ways! Nonetheless, *reform* early on began to be applied also to the church as an organized social body and was thus launched on its impressive ecclesiastical trajectory. Councils, both local and ecumenical, emerged by the third and fourth centuries as the most unquestioned institutions responsible for reform.

Despite its importance for Christian history, scholarship on reform has been notably sparse.[3] Only two major monographs have ever explicitly

1. The Latin for such terms, used often in church documents: *corrigere*, *emendare*, *meliorare*, *recreare*, *regenerare*, *renovare*, *reparare*, *restituere*, *revocare*.

2. German scholars have been particularly interested in its use in political and social discourse. See, e.g., Martin Greiffenhagen, ed., *Zur Theorie der Reform: Entwürfe und Strategien* (Heidelberg: Müller, 1978).

3. Among the relatively few studies are Gerald Strauss, "Ideas of *Reformatio* and *Renovatio* from the Middle Ages to the Reformation," in *Handbook of European*

dealt with it. Both were published in the 1950s, on the eve of Vatican II. They remain to this day the classic studies. Gerhart B. Ladner's *The Idea of Reform: Its Impact on Christian Thought and Action in the Age of the Fathers* appeared in 1959.[4] It dealt almost exclusively with the idea's impact on personal asceticism and monastic discipline in late antiquity. Especially significant in it is Ladner's insistence on the multivalent character of the term: its meaning in any given instance depends on concrete circumstances.

The Idea of Reform, a work of superb historical scholarship and still indispensable for the sphere it covers, has attracted little attention outside a circle of specialists. The same cannot be said of Yves Congar's *Vraie et fausse réforme dans l'église*, published nine years earlier, in 1950.[5] It has been described as "arguably Congar's most important and original contribution to Christian theology."[6]

Shortly after the publication of *Vraie et fausse réforme*, the Holy Office of the Inquisition forbade its reprinting and translation into other languages and informed Congar that in the future everything he intended to publish had first to be submitted to the master general of the Dominican

History 1400–1600: Late Middle Ages, Renaissance, and Reformation, ed. Thomas A. Brady Jr. et al., 2 vols. (Leiden: Brill, 1995), 2:1–30; Konrad Repken, "Reform als Leitgedanke kirchlicher Vergangenheit und Gegenwart," *Römische Quartalschrift für christliche Altertumskunde und Kirchengeschichte* 84 (1989): 5–39; Giuseppe Alberigo, "'Réforme' en tant que critère de l'histoire de l'église," *Revue d'histoire ecclésiastique* 76 (1981): 72–81; John W. O'Malley, SJ, "Developments, Reforms, and Two Great Reformations: Towards a Historical Assessment of Vatican II," *Theological Studies* 44 (1983): 373–406; Wayne J. Hankey, "Self and Cosmos in Becoming Deiform: Neoplatonic Paradigms for Reform by Self-knowledge from Augustine to Aquinas," in *Reforming the Church before Modernity: Patterns, Problems, and Approaches*, ed. Christopher M. Bellitto and Louis J. Hamilton (Burlington, VT: Ashgate, 2005), 39–60. For case studies, see, e.g., John W. O'Malley, *Giles of Viterbo on Church and Reform: A Study in Renaissance Thought* (Leiden: Brill, 1968); and Nelson H. Minnich, "Concepts of Reform Proposed at the Fifth Lateran Council," *Archivum historiae pontificiae* 7 (1969): 163–251. Hans Norbert Janowski takes a quite different approach in "Reform als theologisch-ethisches Problem," in *Zur Theorie der Reform*, 211–40.

4. (Cambridge, MA: Harvard University, 1959). Ladner also wrote a number of important articles on the subject. For a listing, see O'Malley, *Giles of Viterbo*, 1 n. 1.

5. (Paris: Cerf, 1950); 2nd ed., rev. and corr. (Paris: Cerf, 1968); ET, *True and False Reform in the Church*, trans. Paul Philibert (Collegeville, MN: Liturgical Press, 2011). For an analysis of Congar's approach to church reform that takes off from *Vraie et fausse réforme*, see Gabriel Flynn, "Yves Congar and Catholic Church Reform: A Renewal of Spirit," in *Yves Congar: Theologian of the Church*, ed. Gabriel Flynn (Louvain: Peeters, 2005), 99–133.

6. Gabriel Flynn, introduction to *Yves Congar*, 1–24, at 9.

order for censorship.[7] These strictures were just the beginning of Congar's difficulties with Roman authorities.[8]

What was the Holy Office's problem with *Vraie et fausse réforme*? The book, unlike Ladner's, was not a historical study in the conventional sense, but one of the early ventures by a Catholic into historical theology. This attempt to correlate doctrine and practice with historical contingencies could not but seem dangerous in certain circles and cause unease. Much of the burden of *Vraie et fausse réforme* consists in Congar's attempt to justify the method and thus anticipate potential critics.

Moreover, for reasons I will discuss below, the application to the church of the word *reform* had by the 20th century become anathema. Congar in his foreword in fact noted that "a veritable curse" seemed to hang over the word.[9] Only in that light can we understand, for instance, how Cardinal Angelo Roncalli, the future Pope John XXIII, could ask, when questioned about the book while he was nuncio in Paris, "Reform of the church—is such a thing possible?"[10]

Congar had in fact phrased his title cautiously: reform *in* the church, not reform *of* the church, but his caution did not save him. After Vatican II, however, Congar, now fully rehabilitated, felt free to undertake and publish a revised edition, which only last year appeared in English translation.[11] By 1969 when Congar published the revision, the idea that the church might be reformed no longer seemed unthinkable. Yet, misgivings about it persisted.

The council itself had to tread warily. In its 16 final documents it applied *reformatio* to the church only once, in the often-quoted line from the Decree on Ecumenism, *Unitatis redintegratio*: "In its pilgrimage on earth Christ summons the church to continual reformation [*perennem reformationem*], of which it is always in need, in so far as it is an institution of human beings here on earth" (no. 6).[12] In the early 1960s that was a bold

7. See Yves Congar, *Journal d'un théologien (1946–1956)*, ed. Étienne Fouilloux (Paris: Cerf, 2001), 181–222.

8. See ibid., esp. 232–76. See also Thomas O'Meara, "'Raid on the Dominicans': The Repression of 1954," *America* 170, no. 4 (February 5, 1994): 8–16; and, more broadly, Étienne Fouilloux, *Une église en quête de liberté: La pensée française entre modernisme et Vatican II* (Paris: Desclée de Brouwer, 1998).

9. Congar, *Vraie et fausse réforme* (1950), 13, "une véritable malédiction."

10. Philibert, "Translator's Introduction," in Congar, *True and False Reform*, xi. Congar explicitly stated that Roncalli read the book in 1952: *Mon journal du concile*, 2 vols., ed. Éric Mahieu (Paris: Cerf, 2002), 2:441–42 (October 19, 1965).

11. See n. 5 above.

12. Norman Tanner, ed., *Decrees of the Ecumenical Councils*, 2 vols. (Washington, DC: Georgetown University, 1990), 2:913; "Ecclesia in via peregrinans vocatur a Christo ad

statement and was recognized as such at the time. *Reform* was not truly applicable to the Catholic Church. Moreover, in some ears the document's expression *perennis reformatio* sounded more Protestant than Catholic, for it seemed to be a paraphrase of the principle *ecclesia semper reformanda* that originated in 17th-century German Pietism, and was given currency in the early 20th century by Karl Barth's circle.[13]

Nowhere else in the council's final 16 documents is *reformatio* applied to the church. The word occurs in eight other instances but in reference to aspects of secular society needing improvement.[14] For the church the council preferred euphemisms such as *renewal* or *renovation* (*renovatio*), a term that occurs 64 times, most often to indicate changes in church life or practice, that is, to indicate some aspect of reform of the church.

This queasiness about *reformatio* explains why, even a half century after the council, Catholics continue to show a decided preference for softer words in referring to Vatican II. It was a council of "renewal." It was a council of "updating" or even "modernizing." It was almost anything but a reform council. In late 2005, however, that situation suddenly changed. When, on December 22, Pope Benedict XVI proposed in his Christmas allocution to the Roman Curia that the proper lens for understanding Vatican II is a "hermeneutic of reform," the term got instantaneously and powerfully rehabilitated. The pope authoritatively readmitted *reform* into Catholic theological vocabulary.[15]

In his allocution Benedict did not rest content with introducing the term. He went on to explain what he understood it to entail. In so doing he implicitly reinforced the point made by Congar in 1950 that the term is "a little vague" (*un peu vague*) and the point made later by Ladner that it was multivalent.[16] What *reform* means in concrete circumstances is not self-evident. It is revealed only when tested against the historical phenomena it professes to describe.

Examination of the "idea of reform" in the different historical circumstances in which it came into play is precisely what I attempt to do in what follows. Because of space limitations my review will be sketchy but, I hope, sufficient for a profitable exploration of the implications and problems

hanc perennem reformationem qua ipsa, quo humanum terrenumque institutum, perpetuo indiget." Throughout I use Tanner's English translation, sometimes with slight modification.

13. See Repgen, "Reform als Leitgedanke," 21–22.

14. See Tanner, *Decrees*, 2:888, 911, 915, 1067, 1114, 1115, 1120, 1128.

15. See *Acta apostolicae sedis: Commentarium officiale* 98 (2006): 40–53, at 45–53 (henceforth, *AAS*, allocution).

16. Congar, *Vraie et fausse réforme* (1950), 13; and Ladner, *Idea of Reform*, 1–35.

entailed in "a hermeneutic of reform" applied to Vatican II. Only by being grounded in historical reality can such a hermeneutic be helpful and make sense. When we deal with real historical happenings, it becomes clear that an abstract idea like reform has meaning only in relation to them. If, on the contrary, reform is explained by further abstractions, it degenerates into a platitude or even a mask for an ideology.[17]

In the survey that follows, patterns of reform emerge. I divide them into three types, each of which has different manifestations. The first type concerns leadership, which can come either "from above" or "from below." The leaders from above are persons or institutions with authority to impose a reform, such as bishops, popes, and councils. Leaders from below may be charismatic individuals like Francis of Assisi or intellectuals like Erasmus, persons who lead movements that directly affect the religious life and mentality of the faithful, including clergy.

The second type concerns the extent of reform. The reform might look to repairing a system in place and remedying "abuses" in it. The Council of Trent, for instance, did not challenge the place of bishops in the church but aimed at making them more effective in their traditional pastoral duties. Another type of reform, however, aims at displacing or replacing a given system within the church, as when the Gregorian reformers of the eleventh century sought to reintroduce the free election of bishops by the local clergy to replace the system of episcopal nomination by lay magnates.

The final type of pattern of reform concerns content, which most often and most obviously has referred to either doctrine or practice. For the former, reform traditionally consisted in a strong reaffirmation of what presumably had always been the orthodox belief, but more recently it has had to take account of process or "development," that is, change. The latter, which has often been designated simply "church discipline," has been the more obvious object of reform and readier to admit change, but even it has been hedged with problems.

There is in this last type, however, a third manifestation that is not usually taken into account, but that is particularly pertinent for Vatican II. It concerns values and mind-set. As such it entails a rethinking of received patterns. It is expressed and issued in new patterns of discourse. When taken seriously, it imposes new patterns of behavior, new ways of "doing business," and perhaps a new configuration of doctrine. Although it may seem distinct from doctrine and practice, it affects both.

17. See, e.g., Alberigo, "'Réforme.'"

Conceptually clear though these types are, in concrete historical happenings they are never quite so distinct from one another. A reform initiated "from below," for instance, can have repercussions on church authority and result in a decision "from above" clearly influenced by what has been going on "below." Still, naming these types helps us discern patterns in the seemingly infinitely complex and intractable thing that is history.

The Gregorian Reform: The Crucial Turning Point

As Ladner showed, the idea of reform was alive and well in the patristic period but applied principally to the ongoing amendment of life required of the Christian. However, both the local and ecumenical councils of the era were in fact convoked to correct deviations from received church teaching and practice.[18] Councils meted out sentences of guilt and innocence and made regulations to uproot abuses that here and there had sprung up. Although a number of these councils dealt with doctrinal issues and controversies, they all without exception dealt in some measure with "discipline," or "correction," that is, with reform. They were all, thus, "reform councils."

The councils assumed that what they enacted as correctives consisted in reassertions, reinforcements, or even reformulations of earlier Christian teaching and practice. They further assumed that these problems were localized. Change for the worse might affect individual persons or churches but not the church as a whole. The councils remedied the problems by defining orthodox teaching, by expelling deviant individuals from the body of the church, by instituting penalties for disciplinary infractions, and by installing once again the traditional modus operandi.

In the eleventh century, however, the conviction arose in a group of devout churchmen that certain abuses were widespread, almost universal. These men became convinced that certain practices that they believed deviated from "the fathers"—by which they generally meant church legislation enacted between the fourth and sixth centuries—infected virtually the whole church. Only with them did the idea clearly emerge that the system in place might itself be subject to reform or even replacement and, indeed, require it.

The reformers, eventually led by Pope Gregory VII (1073–1085), tried to abolish long-standing procedures and practices in the name of a return

18. See, e.g., Claire Sotinel, "The Church in the Roman Empire: Changes without Reform and Reforms without Change," in *Reforming the Church*, 155–72.

to ancient canonical provisions. They were determined, more specifically, to accomplish principally two changes: first, as mentioned, to reinstate the free election of bishops by local clergy and thereby displace the almost universal practice of episcopal appointments being made by secular rulers; second, to reinstate clerical celibacy and thereby abolish widespread clerical marriage and concubinage.

The idea that the current system of received operating procedures needed radically to be reformed had its genesis in a revival of the study of canon law in Germany and Italy, made possible by more settled political conditions. This study of the canons was the first great renaissance of learning in the Middle Ages that would from that point forward have a continuous history.[19] In it was born the first glimmerings of a sense of anachronism, of significant discrepancies between past and present—in this instance, the discrepancy between the feudal culture of the Middle Ages and the Roman culture of Christian antiquity. Although the reformers could not possibly have formulated the problem in such terms, they clearly saw that present practice differed radically from the past as they discovered it in the canons.

What they had engaged in was a process that in mid-20th century Congar called *ressourcement*, a neologism coined earlier in the century by the poet Charles Péguy.[20] The term came to mean returning to past sources in systematic fashion to discover what there might be of use in the present. Although *ressourcement* could be employed simply to trace how an idea or an institution got to be the way it was, it was more regularly employed in discovering discrepancies between past and present. It thus implied the possibility of a repudiation of aspects of the present in favor of a better or more authentic past. *Ressourcement* was not, therefore, an antiquarian project but a practical one and, in practice, often a virtual synonym of *reform*.

The popes and their allies, who waged against recalcitrants a vigorous war not only of propaganda but sometimes of spear and sword, became the first great church reformers. The upheaval that accompanied and followed their efforts resulted in civil war in Germany, in the most horrible sacking of the city of Rome in its history, and in several generations of bitter contest between popes and antipopes and between popes and secular rulers.

19. See the classic study by Charles Homer Haskins, *The Renaissance of the Twelfth Century* (Cambridge, MA: Harvard University, 1927). See also Erwin Panofsky, "Renaissance and Renascences," *Kenyon Review* 6 (1944): 201–36.

20. See Congar, *Vraie et fausse réforme* (1950), 43; in the note on this page Congar cites the pertinent passages from Péguy.

The reformers eventually had to settle for compromises on their stated goals. There was no way, for instance, that secular rulers were going to relinquish all control over the appointment of such important vassals as the bishops. Such a change would have upset the very foundations upon which feudal society operated. The reformers had more success with celibacy, not so much in its enforcement as in its firm installation in canon law.

Nonetheless, the Gregorian Reform constitutes a landmark in the history of the idea of church reform. Replacement of a system normatively in place by another system is what distinguished the Gregorian Reform from preceding reforms. Earlier reforms attempted to plug leaks and repair glitches in the status quo. The Gregorians, on the contrary, repudiated the status quo in favor of a different status, one presumably better and more authentic than what was in place. Their aims and ideals constituted a new paradigm, to use the expression made famous by Thomas Kuhn. They tried to establish that paradigm to replace the regnant paradigm. This was something new in the history of the church. The fact that the reform provoked such profound political and military reactions substantiates its radical character for its age. To distinguish it from less momentous reforms I have called it "a great reformation."[21]

From the Gregorian Reform to the Council of Trent

The Gregorian reformers gave *reform* as applied to social institutions a strikingly new prominence. Their movement helped generate a mind-set intimating that an improvement of corporate behavior and a return to more ancient norms was at times urgent in the church and in other institutions of society. By the time of the Fourth Lateran Council (1215), the word *reformare* had begun to appear in ecclesiastical sources with ever-greater frequency. From then until the 17th century, *reform* became one of the most characteristic and frequently invoked words in discussion of Catholic church life.

In Lateran IV, moreover, there appeared for the first time in council documents an unmistakably clear assertion that a change in discipline (*statuta humana*) might be required by a change in "the times." The assertion is notable not only for its straightforward affirmation of the necessity of adjustment to new conditions and therefore its suggestion of discrimination between past and present, but also because it provided a criterion for deciding when such a change should be adopted: when required by

21. See O'Malley, "Developments, Reforms," 378–91.

necessity or clear advantage—*urgens necessitas vel evidens utilitas*.[22] The assertion was an anticipation of the *aggiornamento* of Vatican II.

At just the time of Lateran IV, an impetus to ideas of radical church reform entered the stage through the newly founded Franciscan order. Saint Francis saw himself as anything but a challenge to the ecclesiastical status quo. His literal interpretation of Gospel passages concerning poverty set the stage, however, for the emergence after his death of a party within the order that aggressively pursued that interpretation and began to apply it in a sharply negative way to the church at large, which they saw as operating far from the ideals of the New Testament. This party became known as the Spirituals or Spiritual Franciscans. The Spirituals' stridency and the threat they posed brought them, not surprisingly, into conflict with ecclesiastical authorities and eventually with the papacy itself, which culminated during the pontificate of John XXII (1316–1334). The pope condemned their ideas and program, especially the idea that Christ and the Apostles had no money either individually or collectively. But it was easier to condemn such ideas than to stamp them out.

The Spirituals gave impetus to ideas and aspirations that spread in different but recognizable forms among both theologians and the rank and file of the faithful. The English theologian John Wycliffe held a number of heretical ideas, among them those concerning the church's deviation from the poverty demanded by the New Testament. It was in the wake of the Great Western Schism (1378–1418), however, that reform of the church surged as an insistent, persistent, and absolutely urgent theme in upper echelons of both secular and ecclesiastical society.

The scandal of two, then three, men claiming to be the legitimate successor of Saint Peter and their refusal over the course of two generations to resolve the problem on their own fed the persuasion that radical measures were required. Emperor-elect Sigismund pressured Pope John XXIII, who seemed to be the claimant with the best credentials for legitimacy, to convoke the Council of Constance (1414–1418). The council deposed two claimants, "persuaded" the third to resign, and elected a new pope, Martin V, who soon won almost universal recognition as the true successor of Peter. It is from the line established at Constance with Martin V that all subsequent popes have descended.

The Great Western Schism had turned eyes to the papacy in a newly critical way and focused attention on grievances that were already of

22. Tanner, *Decrees*, 1:257, "50. De restricta prohibitione matrimonii."

long standing, most especially on papal taxes, fines, and other financial exactions that, since the long residence of the popes in Avignon in the 14th century, seemed to be expanding without limit or oversight. It is no wonder, then, that in its very first document the Council of Constance set for itself the task of implementing the "necessary reform" (*debitam reformationem*).[23]

Four months later, on March 26, 1415, Constance even more emphatically took the task in hand by making its own the all-inclusive expression "reform of the said church in head and members" (*pro reformatione dictae ecclesiae in capite et in membris*).[24] The council's formal adoption of the expression propelled it into the imagination of concerned persons across Europe. It evolved into a powerful mantra. Reform, understood by different persons in different ways and applied to different entities, exploded as the great preoccupation of the century between Constance and the outbreak of the Reformation.[25] In that preoccupation "reform of the head," that is, the papacy, achieved a special preeminence. The slogan ran: "Reform Rome, [and you will] reform the world."

Constance itself legislated a number of reforms, many of which concerned the management and responsible use of church revenues. Other reforms concerned the proper functioning of papal conclaves and the behavior of clerics. Just before it elected Martin V, it issued a decree informing the pope-to-be that he was bound to "reform the church in head and the Roman curia" (*reformare ecclesiam in capite et curia Romana*). It then provided a list of 18 areas where abuses occurred that he was to remedy. The first was in "the number, quality, and nationality of the lord cardinals." Many of the rest concerned the use and misuse of church funds and goods, the proliferation of church taxes and fines, simony in papal elections and other transactions, and the amount of the revenues enjoyed by the pope and cardinals.[26]

With the Council of Constance, then, reform of the church developed into an ongoing project that preoccupied the leaders, clerical and lay, of

23. Tanner, *Decrees*, 1:406.

24. Tanner, *Decrees*, 1:407. William Durant the Younger did not coin the expression "reform of the church in head and members," but he gave it currency when, at the Council of Vienne in 1311, he demanded such a reform. See Constantin Fasolt, *Council and Hierarchy: The Political Thought of William Durant the Younger* (New York: Cambridge University, 1991), 1, 115–76.

25. See, e.g., Erika Rummel, "Voices of Reform from Hus to Erasmus," in *Handbook of European History*, 2:61–91.

26. See Tanner, *Decrees*, 1:438–50, at 444.

late-medieval society. In Italy at about the same time, the idea that a return to ancient sources would effect a reform of society arose in a powerfully influential mode outside ecclesiastical circles. It was set in motion principally by the poet Petrarch (1309–1374), who called for return to classical Latin prose and poetry and to a revival of the moral ideals that literature embodied. The result would be, he believed, a rebirth of good literature and good morals after the "darkness" (*tenebrae*) of the intervening centuries up to his own.[27] The venture, crowned with great success by the 16th century, came to be known, aptly, as the Renaissance—literally, a *rebirth*.

Ad fontes! To the sources! The leaders of the movement, known as humanists, wanted of course to revive the study of classical authors such as Virgil and Cicero but also of the Bible and the Fathers of the Church. In Erasmus (1469–1536) the reforming impulses of the humanist movement related to Christian issues found their most thoughtful, eloquent, and widely respected exponent. He was not the superficial litterateur and theological dilettante that he is often depicted as being. Virtually everything he wrote was directed, in one form or another, toward promoting *pietas*, a more authentically human and Christian style of life. He believed that the model for that *pietas* and the nourishment for it was to be found, yes, in the "good pagans," but more pointedly and authentically in the Bible and the Fathers.[28]

On that basis he promoted reform in several interlocking spheres, of which two are particularly pertinent. The first was reform of practices of devotion. He was an acerbic (and sometimes amusing) critic of the crass superstition that in his day often accompanied such phenomena as relics, indulgences, and pilgrimages. In place of those practices he promoted what he regarded as more authentic alternatives that he found in the Bible and the earlier Christian tradition. Important among these alternatives was the liturgy. Although virtually every line we have from him is in Latin, he in fact favored the idea of vernacular liturgy, as a proper expression of Christian devotion and *pietas*.

Even more basic to his program was installing Scripture as the principal focus of Christian life. In 1516 Erasmus published the first critical edition of the Greek New Testament along with a new Latin translation. In the preface he expressed the wish that the Scriptures be translated into every

27. See, e.g., Panofsky, "Renaissance"; and Theodore Mommsen, "Petrarch's Conception of the Dark Ages," *Speculum* 17 (1943): 226–49.

28. See John W. O'Malley, "Introduction," *Spiritualia: Enchiridion, De Contemptu Mundi, De Vidua Christiana*, Collected Works of Erasmus 66, ed. John W. O'Malley (Toronto: University of Toronto, 1988), ix–li.

language and made easily available to everybody. In reading and contemplating that text, he asserted, one encountered "the speaking, healing, dying, rising Christ himself."[29] Thus would Christians learn to live and appropriate "the philosophy of Christ."

The second sphere needing reform was theological method, and he campaigned against Scholastic theology because it was in its very procedures inimical to *pietas*. He attacked the method as having devolved into the pursuit of irrelevant and even irreverent questions. Its practitioners engaged in endless disputes among themselves over trivial issues and the very style in which they wrote and preached snuffed out the life of the Spirit. In its stead he promoted the "ancient and more authentic" style of the Fathers of the Church. The Fathers did not get lost in theological trivialities but kept the focus on the central mysteries of the faith—Trinity, Incarnation, Redemption, and the power of grace. They wrote in a style accessible to all and in a style that touched the heart as well as the mind.

In these ways, as in others, Erasmus's program was an anticipation of aspects of *la nouvelle théologie* of the mid-20th century promoted by theologians such as Yves Congar, Henri de Lubac, and Jean Daniélou. It is, therefore, also an anticipation of the effect "the new theology" had on Vatican II that refashioned the council into a mode different from all its predecessors.[30] The *ad fontes* of Renaissance reformers such as Erasmus is, after all, simply the Latin form of the French *ressourcement*—return to the past to correct the present. It was not a reform of doctrine or of church discipline, and in that regard it differs from "church reform" in the conventional sense, yet it fulfills the classic definition of reform: *mutatio in melius*. Erasmus's reform was like the Gregorians' in one extremely important regard. Like theirs, his was not an adjustment or repair of a system in place but the replacement of one system with another. Although he was willing at points to grant that Scholastic theology had certain merits, he wanted a different method and ethos to prevail over it. The same was true for his reform of the practices of piety. In other words, he was not engaged in paradigm adjustment but in paradigm replacement.

29. Erasmus, "Paraclesis" [preface to his *Novum Instrumentum*], in *Christian Humanism and the Reformation: Desiderius Erasmus, Selected Writings*, ed. and trans. John C. Olin (New York: Harper & Row, 1965), 106.

30. See John W. O'Malley, "Erasmus and Vatican II: Interpreting the Council," in *Cristianesimo nella storia: Saggi in onore di Giuseppe Alberigo*, ed. Alberto Melloni et al. (Bologna: Il Mulino, 1996), 195–211; and O'Malley, "*Fides quaerens et non quaerens intellectum*: Reform and the Intellectuals in the Early Modern Period," in *Reforming the Church*, 69–84.

He was passionate about his cause because he saw its goal as engendering a deeper, more heartfelt appropriation of values that he considered most authentically Christian. For him, for instance, Christ was the Prince of Peace, which meant that the Christian worked for peace on earth and attempted to understand "the other" rather than wipe him off the face of the earth. The ideal Christian held, for instance, that the canon of saints was "wider than we might believe." Rather than trying to solve all problems with apodictic pronouncements from on high, the Christian engaged in dialogue and conversation and was ready to assume good will on the part of "the other." The central discipline in the humanist program was not dialectics, as in Scholasticism, but rhetoric. The former was the art of winning an argument, whereas the latter was the art of winning consensus.[31]

What Erasmus required of the Christian—and therefore of the church—was a new mind-set and the appropriation of values that would be expressed in new patterns of behavior. These "reforms" rode on the wave of a "new" mode of discourse that was, as he saw it, the truly "ancient and venerable" mode, the mode of the Bible and the Fathers.

The Reformation and Its Catholic Aftermath

By the first few decades of the 16th century, reform was the emotionally charged cry of the day. Its most explosive instantiation was, of course, the Protestant Reformation, an immensely complex movement that, for reasons of space, I must reduce to Luther. In him the close relationship between conversion and reform could not have been clearer. Luther's discovery of "the gospel"—justification by faith alone—was for him a dramatically reorienting insight, a eureka experience, a conversion that led him to a sharp and irreversible break with his past. "Here I felt that I was altogether born again and had entered paradise itself through open gates."[32] He soon became convinced that he saw things differently from his contemporaries, who lived in blindness and bondage.

31. For manifestations of a "rhetorical theology" in Italian humanists of the period, see Charles Trinkaus, *In Our Image and Likeness: Humanity and Divinity in Italian Renaissance Thought*, 2 vols. (Chicago: University of Chicago, 1970); and John W. O'Malley, *Praise and Blame in Renaissance Rome: Rhetoric, Doctrine, and Reform in the Sacred Orators of the Papal Court, c. 1450–1521* (Durham, NC: Duke University, 1979).

32. Martin Luther, "Preface to the Complete Edition of Luther's Latin Writings" (1545), in *Works*, ed. Jaroslav Pelikan and H. T. Lehmann, 55 vols. (St. Louis: Concordia, 1955–1986), 34:337.

Luther's great and frightening insight, therefore, was that in the church the most vital and essential function, the preaching of the Good News, had for long ages been suppressed by the papacy in favor of a save-yourself-by-your-own-efforts Pelagianism. If the humanists saw a "dark age" of literature between themselves and the good past, Luther saw an even more dreadfully dark age of the suppression of the gospel. He took up the challenge to set things right once again.

He published his "Ninety-Five Theses" in 1517. Three years later, in 1520, he published his "Appeal to the German Nobility," a call to lay magnates to intervene and take church reform into their own hands. While the "Appeal" contained radical principles, it consisted for the most part in a vigorously worded compilation of widely held late-medieval grievances about how the church functioned on a practical level. Prominent in it were the standard complaints about papal financial exactions and the extravagant lifestyle of the papal court. Decades later prelates at the Council of Trent railed against many of the same problems.

Luther's insight into justification soon led him to a drastic restructuring of ministry, piety, and church order, based on his fundamental principle of the exclusive prerogatives of Scripture in all things Christian. He rejected five of the seven traditional sacraments, utterly repudiated the papacy as having any role in church order, and rejected the idea of ecclesiastical hierarchy as Catholics understood it. The ultimate result was a new paradigm, derived, Luther believed, from the authentic message of the word of God through a process of *ressourcement*. Luther's reform consisted not in making adjustments, however drastic, to a system in place but rather in replacing that system with another.

Along with these radical changes he demanded yet another—a change in mode of discourse. In his famous debate with Erasmus on justification, Luther insisted that the only Christian mode of discourse was the prophetic mode of assertion. In that mode the supreme value is "the cause," which does not admit either Scholastic qualifications and distinctions or the humanist mode of middle ground. This was an issue-under-the-issues that contemporaries were incapable of naming but that colored everything Luther said.[33] As a response to the doctrinal and reform issues raised by Luther and, to a lesser extent, by other Protestant reformers, Pope Paul III was finally able in 1545 to convoke the Council of Trent.

33. See John W. O'Malley, *Four Cultures of the West* (Cambridge, MA: Harvard University, 2004), esp. 1–75.

The council met intermittently in three distinct periods over 18 years, finally concluding on December 4, 1563. As its very length suggests, it was an extremely difficult enterprise, threatened by war, plague, internal conflicts, and political machinations of the first order. It lurched from major crisis to major crisis.

After the council, controversy over how it was to be interpreted and implemented emerged almost immediately. It contributed to distortions of what the council legislated and intended that entered into Catholic historiography as what "Trent decided." Not until quite recently, especially with the work of Hubert Jedin, has the distinction between what actually happened at the council and what often erroneously got attributed to it become clear, at least to specialists.[34]

The council's internal difficulties stemmed in large measure from a conflict of priorities that surfaced even before the council opened. Although Pope Paul III convoked the council, Holy Roman Emperor Charles V had for 20 years been the indefatigable, most persistent, and often frustrated voice insisting on its necessity. These two men formed an uneasy partnership that finally allowed the council to happen, but they disagreed about the council's agenda.

Paul III envisaged the council as principally a response to the doctrinal issues raised by "the Lutherans," a generic term that for long included other reformers such as Zwingli, Karlstadt, and, eventually, Calvin. Like all popes of the era, Paul III feared allowing the council to deal with reform, lest it touch the sensitive and explosive issue of the practices of the papal court. Reform, surely, was needed, but it was to be handled directly by himself, not by the council.

The Holy Roman emperor had for centuries been recognized as the Protector of the Church, a role emperors took seriously. Charles V's agenda for the council, which he felt was his prerogative to promote, was almost diametrically opposed to the pope's. A practical man, he was convinced that the real problem was reform. Just as the unreformed condition of the church had, in his analysis, caused the Lutheran crisis, a reform of

34. See John W. O'Malley, *Trent: What Happened at the Council* (Cambridge, MA: Harvard University, 2013). The standard and indispensable history of the council is Hubert Jedin, *Geschichte des Konzils von Trient*, 4 vols. in 5 (Freiburg im/Br.: Herder, 1949–1975). Only the first two volumes have been translated into English: *A History of the Council of Trent*, 2 vols., trans. Ernest Graf (London: Thomas Nelson, 1957, 1961). See also Giuseppe Alberigo, "Du concile de Trente au tridentinisme," *Irenikon* 54 (1981): 192–210.

the church was the first, most urgent, and absolutely indispensable step in resolving it.

During the first months of the council, the prelates at Trent, under pressure from both sides, wrestled with this conflict of priorities. They eventually adopted the sensible solution of treating both issues, and to do so in parallel tracts. For every doctrinal decree, the council would simultaneously issue a decree on reform, *de reformatione*. Through thick and thin this binary agenda prevailed to the very end of the council. Although Trent showed a decided preference for *reformatio* as the designation for what it was about, it employed other traditional terms—such as *restituere*, *revocare*, and *innovare*—to express the same idea.

The council never explicitly stated the parameters of its reform, but it in practice understood it to focus primarily, almost exclusively, on reform of three *offices* in the church—the papacy, the episcopate, and the pastorate, that is, pastors of parishes. It was never able to address reform of the papacy except in the most tangential way. The council therefore did not undertake a comprehensive review of Catholicism. For instance, it said not a word about the most impressive undertaking of the era, the evangelization of the newly discovered lands.

As the council evolved, its reform decrees took shape as radically pastoral. Its aim was to persuade or, more often, force the incumbents in church offices to act as shepherds of their flocks by attending to the basic and traditional duties the offices entailed. The council wanted bishops and pastors of parishes to do their jobs, as those jobs were traditionally understood and spelled out in canon law. Trent thus engaged in a specifically focused *ressourcement*.

Trent's doctrinal decrees had perhaps an even more precise focus than did the reform decrees. They dealt essentially with two issues: first, justification (with original sin as a kind of essential prelude), and, second, the sacraments. For anyone familiar with medieval Scholastic theology, Trent's decrees on the sacraments hold few surprises. One of their features, however, is of extreme importance for the future of the idea of reform.

Luther postulated a complete rupture in the handing on of the gospel, with the result that the teaching of the "papal church" criminally departed from the message of Christ and the Apostles.[35] In reaction to Luther's (and then other Reformers') accusation, Catholic apologists rushed to insist

35. See John M. Headley, *Luther's View of History* (New Haven, CT: Yale University, 1963).

upon the church's unbroken continuity with the faith and practice of the apostolic era. Trent imparted further force to this insistence and again and again stated that its enactments faithfully reflected what had been determined "from the beginning."

No previous council had ever so often and so explicitly declared the continuity of its teachings with the authentic Christian past. When Trent affirmed, regarding the sacrament of penance, that the Catholic practice of secret confession to a priest had been observed since "the beginning," it was only making explicit a principle that underlay almost all its doctrinal pronouncements.

The council thus gave force and validation to a characteristically Catholic historiographical tradition just emerging at the time. That tradition was of course heir to the substantialism that for long had marked historical thinking, but Trent developed it and made it into a hermeneutical principle. In its insistence on continuity, Trent helped develop the tradition and fostered the Catholic mind-set of reluctance to admit change in the course of church history. By the early 17th century, Catholic reluctance to see or admit change had become deeply rooted and pervasive. It persisted in different degrees and different forms up to the present.

That historiographical tradition, of course, holds important implications for the idea of reform, which is about change. It was a major factor in the gradual development of Catholic aversion to the idea that the church could or should be reformed and an aversion even to the very word "reform." This was the aversion dramatized so well by Roncalli's question in the early 1950s, "Reform of the church—is such a thing possible?"

A not unrelated factor was Protestants' appropriation of "reform" and their claim to it as properly their own. Calvinist communities almost from their beginning referred to themselves as "reformed churches" (*églises réformées*), and Lutherans by the last quarter of the 16th century were following a similar path. Catholic rulers and reformers in Germany continued for some time to assert a claim on the word by calling the sometimes forcible restoration of Catholicism in areas gone Lutheran "the reform of religion" (*die Reformation der religion*). The Protestant purchase on reform and reformation, however, was destined ultimately to triumph. *Reformatio*, which had played such a vital role in Catholic life up to that point and had inspired the Council of Trent to try to resolve glaring abuses in church practice, suffered banishment as foreign to Catholicism and subversive of it. Catholics surrendered the word to Protestants.

Only in 1946 when Hubert Jedin, the great historian of the Council of Trent, mounted a persuasive argument for the legitimacy of Catholic "reform" as a category to describe aspects of the 15th and 16th centuries, did *reform* begin to sneak back, in a limited and highly qualified sense, into Catholic vocabulary.[36] Congar's *Vraie et fausse réforme* appeared four years later.

The Long 19th Century

The Enlightenment threw history's goal into the future and gave 19th-century historiography its orientation toward progress.[37] The golden age now loomed in the future. This radical reorientation of thinking, which was previously retrospective, occurred, of course, gradually and was due to a number of factors. Since the beginning of the scientific revolution, progress in science and technology seemed undeniable. The *philosophes* saw humankind as emerging from the darkness of religion to enter into an era illumined by the clear light of reason. Hegel saw history culminating in the German *Reich*, and "Whig" historians in England saw it as leading inevitably to the triumph of the British Empire and the Anglican Church. Most tellingly, Darwin argued for the evolution of the species.[38]

On a less grandiose scale, professional historians, with critical skills newly honed by the revival of historical studies especially under the inspiration of Leopold von Ranke and his like, began to earn new respect and attention. They grew ever more aware of the distance in mentality, mores, and fundamental cultural assumptions that separated present from past and almost universally saw the present as improvement on what had gone before.

Ten years before Darwin's *On the Origin of Species* appeared, John Henry Newman published his *Essay on the Development of Christian Doctrine*, in which he used different analogies to show how church teachings had evolved while remaining fundamentally true to their origins. The book, still the classic on the subject, is ironic in that the idea behind the book helped lead Newman into a church that on the official and unofficial levels denied that such an evolution took place.

36. See John W. O'Malley, *Trent and All That: Renaming Catholicism in the Early Modern Era* (Cambridge, MA: Harvard University, 2000), 16–45.

37. See chapter 2, "The Long Nineteenth Century," in John W. O'Malley, *What Happened at Vatican II* (Cambridge, MA: Harvard University, 2008), 53–92.

38. See, e.g., Frank E. Manuel, *The Prophets of Paris* (Cambridge, MA: Harvard University, 1962); and John Edward Sullivan, *Prophets of the West: An Introduction to the Philosophy of History* (New York: Holt, Rinehart, & Winston, 1970), esp. 21–87, 245–90.

Newman had as a young man immersed himself in the study of the patristic era, and in 1833 published *The Arians of the Fourth Century*. His research and wide reading alerted him to the difference between patristic positions on doctrinal matters and the 19th-century teaching of both Roman Catholicism and Liberal Protestantism. Instead of seeing the current discrepancy as by definition a sign of decline from the purity of the past, he interpreted aspects of it as healthy and inevitable growth, as a providential fulfillment of impulses present at the beginning. From the acorn comes the oak.

Newman was certainly not an admirer of the culture of his times. Nonetheless, his theory of development was in essence a ratification of what had evolved into the present. It affirmed the validity of the status quo as it had "developed." He thus, for a restricted area and almost despite himself, gave his approval to aspects of the times in which he lived. "Development" recognizes the reality of historical change, but it inhibits *reformatio*.

Catholic officialdom, especially the papacy, did not share the positive view of the historical process that prevailed in the 19th century. Especially since the French Revolution and its Europe-wide repercussions, it felt beleaguered and the victim of vicious and lawless forces. The Revolution's call for liberty, equality, and fraternity sounded like a call for anarchy. In Italy the *Risorgimento*, with its aim of making Rome the new capital of a united Italy, exacerbated the papacy's fears and resentments.

For Catholics, led by the papacy, the "modern world," with all its works and pomps, was not the result of an upward trajectory of progress but of a dangerous and precipitous decline in the other direction that originated in the Reformation and that with ever greater strength and force hurtled the church downward, propelled by the Enlightenment, the French Revolution, the *Risorgimento*, and the corrosive results of modern science and historical methods. Official response came with measures like "The Syllabus of Errors" of Pius IX, in 1864.

A few years later Pius convoked Vatican I. *Reformatio* appears in the council's decrees not a single time. What does appear is *irreformabiles*, used by the council to describe papal decisions *ex cathedra*. Vatican I was, for reasons that by now should be clear, intellectually and emotionally fortified against admitting the possibility of reform, a striking contrast with Trent, the council that immediately preceded it.

Despite the impact of the draconian measures against Modernism launched by Pius X in 1907, Catholic scholars began with ever-greater intensity to apply historical methods to sacred subjects. As they did so, they found it impossible not to acknowledge significant changes in teaching and practice over the course of the centuries. By and large their efforts turned into exercises in *ressourcement*, that is, into the hope of using what they discovered in the past to correct and improve the present.

With Pius XII's encyclicals *Divino afflante Spiritu* (1943) on modern biblical methods and *Mediator Dei* (1947) on the sacred liturgy, such *ressourcement* won qualified official approval. By the eve of Vatican II, therefore, *ressourcement*, though not named as such, was ready for use in the council. Reform, partially under the quasi-pseudonym of *ressourcement*, got silently reintroduced into Catholic life.

Historians of dogma faced a more daunting problem in the discrepancy between past and present. How were they to explain it while holding to the principle that the church's teaching was in fundamental and unbroken continuity with the teaching of the Apostles. Newman's theory of development provided the solution. Yes, church teaching changed, but in the process of change it was as true to itself as in its beginning—or even truer. By the eve of Vatican II development as a way to explain change had, in widely diverging degrees, won almost universal acceptance in Catholic circles. It was a reassuring theory.

In the wake of the two World Wars the "modern world" was not nearly as cocky as before about its attainments and its future and, so it seemed, not so inimical to Catholicism. Moreover, the Western democracies had, in defiance of earlier assessments of their military and moral impotence, rallied to defeat the seemingly unstoppable Nazi onslaughts. They professed liberty, equality, and fraternity, not as a club to beat down monarchies but as a necessity in political life to ensure justice and safeguard human rights. When in 1944, just as World War II drew to a close, Pope Pius XII in his Christmas message commended democracy as a political form especially compatible with human dignity, he took a significant step toward reconciliation of the church with "the modern world" and thus laid the groundwork for the more profound implications of the *aggiornamento* that Pope John XXIII set as a goal of Vatican II.

By the time Vatican II got under way in the fall of 1962, therefore, three terms were in circulation among Catholics to deal with the problem of change: *aggiornamento*, development, and *ressourcement*. Although they overlapped in meaning, they more directly pointed to three ways change might take place in the church. In the atmosphere of reluctance to admit change that still strongly prevailed among many of the prelates at the council, they operated as euphemisms or soft synonyms for it. *Reform*, though by no means a word uttered in respectable ecclesiastical company, had begun its struggle for rehabilitation.

Aggiornamento, Development, and *Ressourcement* at Vatican II

The Problem of Change

As in previous councils, the documents of Vatican II evince a strong sense of continuity with the past and a determination to remain true to it. They reassert the church's continuity in faith, spiritual gift, and evangelical tradition from the time of the Apostles to the present, a continuity that in part stretches back even to Israel and that will continue to the end of time. The council underscored the undeviating nature of the church's tradition and its identification with it by its repeated, almost obsessive affirmation of its continuity with previous councils, especially Trent and Vatican I.

Nonetheless, Vatican II showed an awareness of change that in its pervasiveness and implications was new for a council and, at least on an official level, new for Catholicism as such. Unless the council stuck its head in the sand, it really had no choice. The problems for the church that the historically conscious culture of the modern world generated were too many and too deep to be avoided.

The council betrayed its awareness of the issue in the opening sentence of the first document it approved, the Constitution on the Sacred Liturgy, *Sacrosanctum concilium*. That sentence is replete with change words, including "change" itself, *mutatio*:

> It is the intention of this holy council to *improve* the standard of daily Christian living among Catholics; to *adapt* those structures that are subject to *change* so as better to meet the needs of *our time*; . . . it will, therefore, and with quite special reason, see the taking of steps towards the *renewal* and *growth* of the liturgy as something that it can and should do.[39]

It is certainly possible to quibble about the English equivalents here used for the Latin originals, but the Latin words, no matter how translated, have to do with change—*augere*, *accommodare*, *mutationes*, *nostra aetas*, *instaurare*, and, not so clearly, *fovere*.

As Massimo Faggioli has shown, *Sacrosanctum concilium* was not only a landmark document on the liturgy. It was also, and perhaps more importantly, an ecclesiological statement that contained in germ the ori-

39. "Sacrosanctum concilium, cum sibi proponat vitam christianam inter fideles in dies *augere*; eas institutiones quae *mutationibus* obnoxiae sunt, ad *nostrae aetatis* necessitates melius *accommodare*; . . . suum esse arbitratur peculiari ratione etiam *instaurandam* atque *fovendam* liturgiam curare" (Tanner, *Decrees*, 2:820, emphases added).

entations that guided the council in its subsequent course.[40] Among those orientations was the recognition of change and the need to take account of it—under the three headings of *aggiornamento*, development, and *ressourcement*.[41]

"Adapting to meet the needs of our time," almost the first words of the council's first document, is the definition of *aggiornamento*. In his opening allocution to the council on October 11, 1962, Pope John XXIII provided the basis for the "updating" that became a leitmotif in the council, to the point that Vatican II became known as the council of *aggiornamento*. Several comments are in order.

First, important though *aggiornamento* is for understanding Vatican II, it is not the only or the most significant way the council wrestled with the question of "change for the better." Second, though the term was new, the idea that change might be needed in view of new circumstances had been operative earlier in the church and even in councils, as indicated when Lateran IV approved change when it seemed "necessary or opportune."

Third, although previous councils invoked the equivalent of *aggiornamento* for changes they undertook, they did so rarely and by way of exception. In Vatican II, however, *aggiornamento* explicitly and implicitly affects virtually every document the council issued. The pervasiveness of the idea betrays a new mind-set in which accommodation to circumstances assumes a much more dominant role in how the church is to go about its mission. What is peculiar to Vatican II is the scope given to updating and the admission of it as a broad principle rather than as a rare exception.

Finally, the "adaptations" and "accommodations" the council enjoins are not presented as remedies for abuses in the system, nor are penalties enjoined for noncompliance with them. In effect "adapting" and "accommodating" displace the traditional "correcting" and "remedying," expressions virtually absent in Vatican II. *Aggiornamento* thus redefines reform in a way peculiar to Vatican II. The adaptations and accommodations are not measures taken against evils that have crept into the church from the outside. They are, rather, a form of *rapprochement* between church and the existing order in the world. It should come as no surprise, therefore, that this feature of the council's appropriation of *aggiornamento* is of a piece with a larger pattern in Vatican II of which the Pastoral Constitution on

40. See Massimo Faggioli, "*Sacrosanctum concilium* and the Meaning of Vatican II," *Theological Studies* 71 (2010): 437–52.

41. For further elaboration on these terms and their implications, see O'Malley, *What Happened at Vatican II*, esp. 36–43, 298–302.

the Church in the Modern World, *Gaudium et spes*, is the most impressive monument.

John Courtney Murray famously commented that "development of doctrine" was *the* issue-under-the-issues at Vatican II. The idea explicitly appears at crucial moments in the council's documents, as in the Dogmatic Constitution on Revelation, *Dei verbum*, where we are told that apostolic tradition "makes progress in the church." There is a "growth in understanding," as the centuries advance and as the church moves further toward "the fullness of God's truth."[42] The idea also appears explicitly in the opening paragraphs of the Declaration on Religious Liberty, *Dignitatis humanae*: the council "intends to develop [*evolvere*]" the teaching of recent popes on the subject.[43]

Murray was correct in his assessment about the centrality of the issue of doctrinal development, but he could have gone further. Development burst the limits of "development of doctrine." It was a mind-set that pervaded the thinking of the council on a much wider scope than doctrine, a fact revealed by how often the council has recourse to words that expressed it. The Latin equivalents of "evolution" and "development" (*evolutio* and *evolvo*), for instance, occur 42 times in the conciliar documents. The Latin equivalents of "progress" and "advance" (*progredior*, *progressio*, and *progressus*) occur 120 times.

Not only are these among the most characteristic words employed by the council; they are virtually absent from the vocabulary of previous councils. True, although the council applies them to aspects of church teaching and practice, it also often, especially in *Gaudium et spes*, applies them to aspects of secular society. This distinction, however, only strengthens the point that "development," a new form of *mutatio in melius* in the church, is a ubiquitous feature of Vatican Council II.

In contrast to development, *ressourcement* in the sense of return to the past to correct the present does not have in the council documents an obvious Latin equivalent that occurs with any frequency. The obvious candidate would be *reformatio*, but, as mentioned, it is, except in one important instance, altogether absent. "Renewal" (*renovatio*) does much

42. "Haec quae est ab apostolis traditio sub assistentia Spiritus sancti in ecclesia proficit; crescit enim tam rerum quam verborum traditorum perceptio. . . . Ecclesia scilicet, volventibus saeculis, ad plenitudinem divinae veritatis iugiter tendit" (Tanner, *Decrees*, 2:974).

43. "Summorum pontificum doctrinam . . . evolvere intendit" (Tanner, *Decrees*, 2:1002).

better, but it is a softer word. It seems to imply warming up or refurbishing something that has lost its luster rather than retrieving something lost in order to repair or replace a piece outmoded or gone wrong. Euphemism though it is, it still points to the fundamental fact that Vatican II is unintelligible without taking *ressourcement* into account.

Despite the fact that *Sacrosanctum concilium* opens by invoking *aggiornamento*, *ressourcement* is the idea much more responsible for its provisions. Yes, the council wanted to adapt the liturgy to make it more meaningful in the religious life of contemporaries, but it did so by making use of a century of *ressourcement*, a century of scholars searching ancient and medieval sources to discover how and why things got to be the way they were.

When the council insisted that the fundamental principle of liturgical reform was the participation of the whole assembly in the sacred action, it did so on the basis of a principle derived from ancient liturgical practice, not as a sop to hyperactive moderns. Restoring the dignity of the first part of the Mass, the Liturgy of the Word, was similarly derived. And so forth. The application of such principles to the present, the *aggiornamento*, was a consequence, not the starting point.

Other examples of *ressourcement* abound. The Decree on Ecumenism, *Unitatis redintegratio*, begins with hope for the restoration of Christian unity that prevailed before the Great Eastern Schism and the Reformation. In the contested passages of *Dei verbum* over the Scripture/tradition relationship, the majority voices wanted to recapture modes of thinking about it that predated the 16th-century controversies and their theological aftermath.

In *Dignitatis humanae*, the council in effect retrieved and refashioned the age-old teachings on the free character of the act of faith and on the primacy of conscience in moral decision making as arguments to displace a tradition of church-state relations that had its remote origins with Constantine; got refashioned in the 16th century with the principle of *cuius regio, eius religio*; refashioned again in the arrangements the Holy See negotiated with governments after the defeat of Napoleon; then rationalized in theological textbooks in the thesis-hypothesis model; and, on the very eve of Vatican II, not only officially professed but also instantiated in the Vatican's concordats with Franco in Spain and with other governments. Despite the "*evolvere*" of the text of *Dignitatis humanae*, this was system replacement.

The lightening-rod issue at the council was episcopal collegiality. No other section of any other document was more contested or received more minute scrutiny than chapter 3 of *Lumen gentium*. Even after the council overwhelmingly approved that chapter, the issue did not die but returned at the last moment in the famous *Nota praevia* attached to the decree by "a higher authority." The fierce and unrelenting opposition to collegiality from a small but powerful minority at the council, which surely provided the impetus for the *Nota*, indicates that something important was at stake, something more than an updating or a development.[44]

Proponents of collegiality saw it as a recovery of the predominantly collegial character of the church that had gradually but effectively been sidelined almost to the point of banishment by the way papal primacy had been interpreted and functioned especially in recent centuries. Yet, though the church had never officially defined collegiality as part of its constitution, for centuries it had taken collegiality for granted as its normal mode of operation. Collegiality surfaced at Vatican II as a result of the engagement of historians and theologians in *ressourcement*. Although its proponents presented collegiality at the council as simply an enhancement of the current mode in which the Holy See functioned, its opponents saw it as something much more threatening, a real *re-forming*, a paradigm replacement.

I have up to this point stressed the differences evinced by these three modes of "change for the better" operative at Vatican II: *aggiornamento*, development, and *ressourcement*. I now need to stress that in practice they were often not so distinct from one another. A given measure might from one perspective seem like *aggiornamento* and from another like development. Life is never as simple as theory. Even so, these three categories derive from the council's reality as a historical happening. They capture differences that we smooth over at our peril.

In particular, development and *ressourcement* are far from being synonyms. Development indicates a process of growth and efflorescence that has resulted in the status quo. It suggests, even, that the process might well continue to give us more of the same. It is thus profoundly confirmatory of the status quo and, as a theory, a formidable defense against *ressourcement* interpreted as reform. Development delivers the message "all's well" or "more of the same," which is precisely what reform denies.

Ressourcement, though it certainly can result in findings confirmatory of the present, most characteristically looks to the sources to see how the status quo needs to be modified, corrected, or replaced. It challenges the status quo, and it has in the history of the church sometimes challenged it radically. It might, moreover, call a halt to certain developments, as happened at Vatican II with the strong movement to define more prerogatives of the Virgin Mary.

44. On the *Nota praevia*, see O'Malley, *What Happened at Vatican II*, 244–45.

Mariology was a booming industry before the council, fueled by the apparitions at Lourdes, La Salette, Fatima, and elsewhere, but from a doctrinal viewpoint fueled especially by the definition in 1854 of the Immaculate Conception and in 1950 by the definition of the Assumption. Many bishops and theologians promoted and expected a further definition at Vatican II, such as, perhaps, Mary as coredemptrix.

But as the result of the heated debate over whether the council would issue a separate document on her, development in the form of a further definition went no further. *Ressourcement* was much responsible for this halt. Scholars argued for the patristic tradition of Mary as the model member of the church and not as someone enthroned above it.

In assessing the impact *ressourcement* had upon the council, however, we must avoid the big, but altogether common, hermeneutical mistake of resting content with examining the documents individually, one by one, and failing to take the crucial further step of examining them as a single corpus. Commentaries on the documents of the council commonly analyze them as discreet units, without reckoning in any consistent fashion with how they relate to and build upon one another.

The most authoritative of the early studies on the council is the multi-authored, five-volume commentary edited by Herbert Vorgrimler and written by theologians who took part in the council, including the young Joseph Ratzinger.[45] The most recent publication of similar scope is another five-volume commentary edited by Peter Hünermann and Bernd Jochen Hilberath.[46]

Commentaries like these are basic and absolutely indispensable, but they pave the way for the further, absolutely essential step of considering the documents as constituting a single corpus and thus of showing how each document is in some measure an expression of larger orientations and part of an integral and coherent whole. Unlike the determinations of previous councils, those of Vatican II are not a grab bag of ordinances without intrinsic relationship to one another. They implicitly but deliberately cross-reference and play off one another—in the vocabulary they employ, in the great themes to which they recur, in the core values they inculcate, and in certain basic issues that cut across them.

Once the documents are thus examined, they are striking in that they express themselves in a style different from the legislative, judicial, and

45. ET, *Commentary on the Documents of Vatican II*, 5 vols. (New York: Herder & Herder, 1967–1969).

46. *Herder theologischer Kommentar zum zweiten Vatikanischen Konzil*, 5 vols. (Freiburg i/Br: Herder, 2004–2006).

often punitive style employed by previous councils. That style, a consistent and characteristic feature of the council, is the result of a deliberate, even if somewhat haphazard, attempt to recover what the Council Fathers believed was the style of "Scripture and the Fathers." It is, therefore, a *ressourcement*.

It is, moreover, a *ressourcement* or reform that is a system replacement or paradigm replacement, not merely an adjustment or correction of the status quo. The Roman Synod of 1960, the purported "dress rehearsal" for Vatican II, issued 773 canons. Canons, prescriptive ordinances that often carried penalties for failure to comply, were not the only, but certainly the most characteristic, literary form of councils from Nicaea (325) forward. Vatican II issued not a single canon.

Two system replacements result from this seemingly innocuous style shift. In the first place, Vatican II replaced with an altogether different system the legislative/judicial system of councils operative since at least the local synods of the third century but authoritatively codified with Nicaea. It thereby redefined what a council is and is supposed to do. In a gentle and unobtrusive way, Vatican II effected a major replacement of one system with another.

The style shift, in the second place, conveyed a values shift that was also a system shift or paradigm shift. It called for new attitudes on the part of the church and of all Catholics. The values it conveyed were anything but new in Christianity and to that extent were in continuity with tradition, but they were a break with the official mode in place up to that point. In its vocabulary the style promoted a change in mind-set and in the modus operandi of the church, as from commands to invitations, from laws to ideals, from threats to persuasion, from coercion to conscience, from fault finding to a search for common ground.[47] The profound and far-reaching implications of such a shift in how the church conducts itself, in how it "does business," and how it relates to real, live human beings should be obvious.

The Hermeneutic of Reform

When Pope Benedict XVI proposed a hermeneutic of reform for interpreting Vatican II, he stepped away from the sharp dichotomy of rupture/continuity that he had earlier insisted upon. Historians, surely, must welcome the new category. They know that the sharp dichotomy of rupture/

47. For an elaboration of the implications of this shift in style, see O'Malley, *What Happened at Vatican II*, 43–52, 305–11.

continuity is never verified in historical events, which are always a mix of the old and the new. An event as radical as the French Revolution did not destroy the deep bond that continued to define what it meant to be French.

Continuities in history are always deeper and more long-lasting than any rupture, no matter how drastic that rupture might be, which is true even of paradigm replacement. This simple truth obtains a fortiori for the church, whose reason for being is to pass on a message received long ago. However, to press continuity to the exclusion of any discontinuity is in effect to say that nothing happened. As applied to Vatican II, it reduces the council to a non-event.

In his allocution the pope explicitly recognizes that reform, a self-aware effort to effect change, partakes of both realities: "It is precisely in this blending, at different levels, of continuity and discontinuity that the nature of true reform consists."[48] Reform is, according to him, a process that within continuity produces something new.[49] The council, while faithful to the tradition, did not receive it as inert but as somehow dynamic.[50] These are important statements, and they seem to be a change in the position the pope held before his election.

Scholars immediately went to work analyzing the allocution. How did this "hermeneutic of reform" relate to the "hermeneutic of continuity" that it replaced in the template the pope as Cardinal Ratzinger had insisted upon, beginning with the famous *Ratzinger Report* published in 1985?[51] Not surprisingly, scholars have found strong affinities between the new and the old.

48. *AAS*, allocution 49: "È proprio in questo insieme di continuità e discontinuità a livelli diversi che consiste la natura della vera riforma" (my translation, as in every instance below).

49. Ibid.: "In questo processo di novità nella continuità."

50. Ibid. 47: "come in un Concilio dinamica e fedeltà debbano diventare una cosa sola."

51. *The Ratzinger Report: An Exclusive Interview on the State of the Church* (San Francisco: Ignatius, 1985). See, e.g., Joseph A. Komanchak, "Benedict XVI and the Interpretation of Vatican II," *Cristianesimo nella storia* 28 (2007): 323–37; Lieven Boeve, "'La vraie réception de Vatican II n'a pas encore commencé': Joseph Ratzinger, révelation, et autorité de Vatican II," in *L'autorité et les autorités: L'herméneutique théologique de Vatican II*, ed. Gilles Routhier and Guy Jobin (Paris: Cerf, 2010), 13–50; Karim Schelkens, "La réception de 'Dei Verbum' entre théologie et histoire," ibid., 51–68; Massimo Faggioli, *Vatican II: The Battle for Meaning* (New York: Paulist, 2012), esp. 50–53, 68–75, 106–13, 133–38; and Gilles Routhier, "The Hermeneutic of Reform as a Task for Theology," *Irish Theological Quarterly* 77 (2012): 219–43.

Present in the allocution, for instance, is the same rejection of a "hermeneutic of rupture" as an instrument of interpretation for Vatican II that the pope had long insisted upon. As in the *Ratzinger Report*, the pope asserts, "The church is, as much before as after the council, the same church."[52] As that assertion stands, he would find little disagreement except from members of the Society of Saint Pius X who reject the council as heretical and an illegitimate break with tradition. Gilles Routhier has argued, in fact, that here and elsewhere the pope's hermeneutical proposals must be understood against his desire to effect an accommodation with that group.[53]

In any case, the assertion of no-before-and-after in itself weights the argument against change. The pontiff's definition of "principles" as immune to contingency, even though applicable to contingent circumstances, weights it in the same way.[54] When Benedict goes on to warn that we should not be deceived by "apparent discontinuities," he seems to take away with one hand what he gives with the other.

But he provides examples to clarify his meaning in these regards. Decisions of the church regarding something as contingent as 19th-century Liberalism, for instance, must themselves be regarded as contingent and therefore subject to change to meet changing circumstances. The "recent crimes of the Nazi regime" made it necessary to "define in a new way the relationship between the church and the faith of Israel." Although Benedict does not adduce the word *aggiornamento*, these examples of reconciliation with something outside the church fit the term's standard definition.

Regarding the council's affirmation of religious liberty in *Dignitatis humanae*, Benedict says, "The Council, recognizing and making its own a principle of the modern state, once again recovered [in that regard] the most profound patrimony of the church."[55] He therefore sees the affirmation

52. *AAS*, allocution 51: "La Chiesa è, tanto prima quanto dope il Concilio, la stessa Chiesa, una, santa."

53. See Routhier, "Hermeneutic of Reform." On January 31, 2012, Father Jean-Michel Gleize of the Society of Saint Pius X published on the Internet "A Crucial Question." It was a reply to an article dealing with the magisterial authority of Vatican II that appeared in *L'Osservatore Romano*, December 2, 2011, by Msgr. Fernando Ocariz, one of four experts representing the Holy See in conversation with the Society. In "A Crucial Question," Father Gleize comments extensively on the allocution of December 22, 2005, and thereby lends indirect support to Routhier's position. See http://www.sspx.org/theological_commission/a_crucial_ question_gleize_1-31-2012.pdf.

54. See *AAS*, allocution 49–50.

55. Ibid. 50: "Il Concilio Vaticano II, riconoscendo e facendo suo con il Decreto sulla libertà religiosa un principio essenziale dello Stato moderno, ha ripreso novamente il patrimonio più profondo della Chiesa."

as, on the one hand, an instance of returning to the sources ("the patrimony")—hence, *ressourcement*—and, on the other hand, an adaptation to a contemporary contingency—hence, *aggiornamento*. His is a fair analysis of precisely what the council did in this instance, which is a telling example of how in a particular circumstance more than one model of change may be operative.

At the very beginning of the section of the allocution related to hermeneutics, Benedict equates reform with development. In fact, for him development seems to be the model that best encapsulates what "true reform" is all about: "[The proper lens for understanding the council] is the 'hermeneutic of reform,' of renewal within the continuity of the one subject, the church, which [continuity] the Lord has granted her. The church is a subject that grows in time and develops, remaining, however, always the same, the unique subject of the People of God in journey."[56] This statement provides the occasion for Benedict to insist that there is no disjunction between the church before and after the council.

His Holiness thus blurs the distinction among the three categories of *aggiornamento*, development, and reform (or *ressourcement*). He cannot be too much faulted for such blurring. It is still common among interpreters of the council and does not lack, as we have seen, a basis in historical reality itself. Nonetheless, the distinction among the three is crucial for a fruitful exploration of the implications of a "hermeneutic of reform" as applied to Vatican II. Especially crucial is the distinction between reform and development.

Of course, the allocution of December 22, 2005, was just that, an allocution. It was not, nor was it intended to be, a theological treatise. It was not intended, we must assume, to provide a fully elaborated "theology of the hermeneutics of reform." Such an elaboration is, rather, the task the allocution opened up for theologians.

In that regard it is important to stress the pope's clear recognition of the fact of change, expressed in terms we can break down into the three categories. The function even of development is, we must remember, to explain why and how things today are different from the way they were yesterday. To use the lens of reform as the primary hermeneutical instrument to interpret the council imbues Vatican II with a dynamic character. It puts change at the very center of the interpretative enterprise, and it

56. Ibid. 46: "C'è l''ermeneutica della riforma,' del rinnovamento nella continuità dell'unico soggetto-Chiesa, che il Signore ci ha donato; è un soggetto che cresce nel tempo e si sviluppa, rimanendo però sempre lo stesso, unico suggetto del Popolo di Dio in cammino."

throws a glaring spotlight on the crucially important, yet often forgotten, assertion in the Decree on Ecumenism that Christ summons the church to ongoing reformation.

Because the word *reform* is not, except for one instance, explicitly present in the documents, a "hermeneutic of reform" might seem like an unwarranted imposition upon them from outside. I have shown, however, how the problem of change "as improvement" is a basic orientation of the council that runs through its debates and enactments as an issue-under-the-issues. Reform is thus based on the documents but in its pervasiveness transcends them taken individually. The council, we might now say, was animated by a *spirit of reform*.

Finally, no matter what else is to be said about the allocution, the description of reform Pope Benedict provides would be difficult to improve upon: "It is precisely in this blending, at different levels, of continuity and discontinuity that the nature of true reform consists." This is a description in accord with *ressourcement* as its proponents at the council understood it, and it is, as far as it goes, in accord with how reform has been understood in the West in the past millennium.

Theologians and historians now have license to address the council with a category that formerly was virtually off limits. In so doing they can assess in each instance and "at different levels" the degree present, respectively, of continuity and discontinuity. They will thereby be able to judge and then to tell us just how wide and deep (or how narrow and superficial) the reform of Vatican II was. In what areas and to what extent, we will perhaps then know, was Vatican II engaged in paradigm replacement and/or where and to what extent in paradigm adjustment.

2 Toward a Comprehensive Interpretation of the Council and Its Documents

ORMOND RUSH

Contemporary proposals regarding an appropriate hermeneutic for interpreting Vatican II vary in their emphasis on three elements: the conciliar process, the conciliar documents, and the shifting contexts from which future generations interpret the council and its documents. Drawing on these insights, this article outlines six principles, which the author proposes as basic for ensuring a comprehensive interpretation of the council.

The 1985 Extraordinary Synod of Bishops, 20 years after the close of Vatican II, proposed several hermeneutical principles that remain valuable for guiding discussion 50 years after the council's opening.[1] Since

1. "The theological interpretation of the conciliar doctrine must show attention to all the documents, in themselves and in their close inter-relationship, in such a way that the integral meaning of the Council's affirmations—often very complex—might be understood and expressed. Special attention must be paid to the four major Constitutions of the Council, which contain the interpretative key for the other Decrees and Declarations. It is not licit to separate the pastoral character from the doctrinal vigor of the documents. In the same way, it is not legitimate to separate the spirit and the letter of the Council. Moreover, the Council must be understood in continuity with the great tradition of the Church, and at the same time we must receive light from the Council's own doctrine for today's Church and the men of our time. The Church is one and the same throughout all the councils" ("The Church, under the Word of God, Celebrates the Mysteries of Christ for the Salvation of the World," Final Report of the 1985 Extraordinary Synod (hereafter Final Report) I.5, http://www.saint-mike.org

this synod, reflection has continued as to the appropriate hermeneutics for interpreting the council and its texts. The literature provides rich reflection on the range of issues at stake. Leaving aside one-dimensional approaches that, for example, exaggerate exclusively either "continuity" or "discontinuity," or either "spirit" or "letter," the major contributors to the hermeneutical debate, among many others, include Joseph Ratzinger, and now as Benedict XVI, Walter Kasper, Karl Lehmann, Giuseppe Alberigo, Hermann Pottmeyer, Giuseppe Ruggieri, Joseph Komonchak, Peter Hünermann, Gilles Routhier, Alberto Melloni, John O'Malley, Christoph Theobald, and Massimo Faggioli.[2] Different emphases are placed by these commentators on the three elements of (1) the conciliar process, (2) the conciliar documents, and (3) the reception of the council and its documents. Some take a more historical perspective, others a more theological perspective.

The framework proposed here attempts to bring together many of these insights under six hermeneutical principles. Each principle is formulated in terms of a dialectic, where the two terms of the dialectic are to be seen as mutually interpretative and existing in creative tension.[3] There is a certain overlap in the issues at stake in the dialectics. This overlap gives the framework a coherence. Furthermore, the overlap highlights how one principle alone, or just one term within a dialectic, can give a narrow view of the issues, and requires the other term or the other dialectics for mutual correction, for the sake of a more comprehensive and credible interpretation of the council and its documents 50 years on. At the beginning of the following six sections on each principle, a thesis states the central affirmations of the principle.

The Council/The Documents

Principle One: The documents of Vatican II must be interpreted in the light of the historical event (the council) that produced them; and the historical event must be interpreted in the light of the official documents that it promulgated.[4]

/library/synod_bishops/final_report1985.html). This and all other URLs cited herein were accessed on May 5, 2012.

2. For an examination of the different approaches to interpreting Vatican II, including his own contribution to the debate, see Massimo Faggioli, *Vatican II: The Battle for Meaning* (New York: Paulist, 2012).

3. I am not using the term "dialectic" here in a Hegelian sense.

4. I use the term "event" here in a broad sense, referring simply to all the elements that made up "the council" from its being announced by Pope John XXIII on Janu-

When referring to "Vatican II," a distinction can be made between "the council" as a multidimensional historical process and "the documents" it promulgated. A related distinction, used by the 1985 Synod of Bishops, is that between the "spirit" and the "letter" of the council. However, with both dialectics, as with all that follow, care must be taken not to set up the distinction as a dichotomy, pitting one pole against the other. They are mutually interpretive and require the careful interrelating of not only a hermeneutics of the authors and a hermeneutics of the texts but also a hermeneutics of the receivers (the ones who are interpreting and applying the council and its documents from the later perspectives of forever-changing contexts).[5] Several hermeneutical points can be selected as significant if an interpretation of "the council" and its "16 documents" is to be comprehensive, and if it is to avoid setting the "spirit" and "letter" of the council in opposition.

First, the documents, in one sense, constitute a "fixed" criterion, a collection of documents that long outlives those who authored them. Without falling into a "Romantic hermeneutic" privileging "authorial intention,"[6] they could be legitimately termed expressions of "the mind of the council," in the sense that, after much hard work and vigorous debate, they were voted on and promulgated by the overwhelming majority of the bishops of the world.[7]

---

ary 25, 1959, to the closing Mass on December 8, 1965. This includes the motives and intentions of individual protagonists (as revealed in private diaries or minutes of conciliar commissions), informal meetings of bishops outside the formal meetings, bishops' speeches in the aula, written interventions by individual bishops or groups of bishops, the work of drafting commissions and their *relationes* ("reports") back to the council assembly, and the bishops' voting on conciliar procedures, drafts, and final documents. When referring to Vatican II as a historic occurrence with greater epochal significance in the broad sweep of church history, the more narrow sense of "event" will be specified in the text.

5. See Ormond Rush, *Still Interpreting Vatican II: Some Hermeneutical Principles* (New York: Paulist, 2004).

6. "Any interpretation referring to 'the mind of the Council' . . . is problematic. It falls into the fallacy of a Romantic hermeneutic by reducing meaning to authorial intention and neglecting the complex compositional process behind the Council's texts. The final texts are agreed-upon statements that have meaning independently of any authorial intention and by their nature provide an openness to diverse receptions" (Francis Schüssler Fiorenza, "Vatican II," in *The Routledge Companion to Modern Christian Thought*, ed. Chad Meister and James Beilby (New York: Routledge, forthcoming 2013).

7. The successive drafts of the documents, including the *relationes* given by the drafting commissions to accompany each of the revised texts, with explanations of the

Second, while the documents constitute a "fixed" criterion once set in writing, they are nevertheless "finished in their unfinishedness."[8] They "overflow" the context of their original production and reception; there is a surplus of meaning that future generations might legitimately discover in the texts, meanings, however, that might very well go beyond what the bishops explicitly intended. Once set in writing, the documents take on a life of their own; readers, posing new questions to the texts from new contexts, take them in directions both legitimate and possibly illegitimate; interpretations of particular texts that go beyond authorial intention may well be faithful (or unfaithful) to the overall vision of the council. Criteria are needed to discern the difference.

Third, among the 16 documents, the four constitutions function analogously like the four gospels within the New Testament. They provide "the interpretative key"[9] for the other 12 documents. Nevertheless, subtlety is needed when applying this hermeneutical key; there is a certain hierarchy or ordering within the constitutions, a hierarchy of importance not necessarily captured and determined by the wording of the titles, with words such as "dogmatic" and "pastoral." In this sense, the theological focus of *Dei verbum* (*DV*) can function as a lens for interpreting the more ecclesio-

---

changes over the prior text, can be found in the detailed *Synopses* being produced on each of the documents. For example, see Francisco Gil Hellín, ed., *Constitutio de sacra liturgia Sacrosanctum Concilium: Concilii Vaticani II synopsis in ordinem redigens schemata cum relationibus necnon patrum orationes atque animadversiones* (Vatican City: Libreria Editrice Vaticana, 2003); Francisco Gil Hellín, ed., *Constitutio dogmatica de divina revelatione, Dei verbum: Concilii Vaticani II synopsis . . .* (Vatican City: Libreria Editrice Vaticana, 1993); Francisco Gil Hellín, ed., *Constitutionis pastoralis de ecclesia in mundo huius temporis Gaudium et spes: Concilii Vaticani II synopsis . . .* (Vatican City: Libreria Editrice Vaticana, 2003). Detailed accounts of the drafting history for each document can be found in works such as Antonio Acerbi, *Due ecclesiologie: Ecclesiologia guiridica ed ecclesiologia di comunione nella "Lumen Gentium"* (Bologna: EDB, 1975); Riccardo Burigana, *La Bibbia nel concilio: La redazione della costituzione "Dei verbum" del Vaticano II* (Bologna: Il Mulino, 1998); Umberto Betti, *La dottrina del Concilio Vaticano II sulla trasmissione della rivelazione: Il capitolo II della costituzione dommatica Dei verbum* (Rome: Antonianum, 1985); Giovanni Turbanti, *Un concilio per il mondo moderno: La redazione della costituzione pastorale Gaudium et spes del Vaticano II* (Bologna: Il Mulino, 2000).

8. "In der Unfertigkeit fertig" (Leo Popper, as quoted in Hans Robert Jauss, "Horizon Structure and Dialogicity," in *Question and Answer: Forms of Dialogic Understanding* [Minneapolis: University of Minnesota, 1989], 197–231, at 212).

9. Final Report I.5.

logically focused constitutions, *Sacrosanctum concilium*, *Lumen gentium*, and *Gaudium et spes*.

Fourth, the development in the bishops' thinking regarding issues across the four sessions of conciliar debate must be taken into account in interpretation, especially when interrelating the four constitutions. Over time, the conciliar assembly "learned" to be a council. Along the way it received into its thinking and its documents its own earlier documents. The bishops developed in their thinking, such that their later documents show development over the earlier ones, and therefore are to be seen as qualifying the previous statements.[10]

Fifth, the conciliar documents themselves are complex texts. In places they contain passages deliberately expressed either in an open-ended way or with juxtapositions of traditional and innovative formulations through which the council was able to reach a "consensus," in a form of text to which the vast majority of bishops, despite their theological differences, could vote on affirmatively. The bishops did not set out to present systematic treatises; they intended that theologians after the council should bring such open-ended formulations and juxtapositions into a new synthesis.

Sixth, given the complexity of the texts' history and final composition, the interpreter should beware of speaking in simplistic terms of "authorial intention." The conflict of interpretations around Vatican II in the contemporary church often tends to center exclusively on how the bishops themselves interpreted what they were doing, what they set out to achieve, and the complex debates over the final form of the documents they promulgated. While the "spirit" of the assembly is highly relevant

10. As Alberigo notes: "The conciliar assembly itself offered a model of a dynamic hermeneutic that takes into account the progressive expansion of its decisions. It is, in fact, perfectly clear that only the acquisition of an ecclesiology of communion, first in the constitution *Sacrosanctum concilium* and then in the constitution *Lumen gentium*, made further developments possible. The decree *Unitatis redintegratio* [*UR*] and the declaration *Dignitatis humanae*, but also the decree *Ad gentes* and finally the constitution *Dei verbum* contain propositions that presuppose the development already acquired by the council. This hermeneutical criterion, even if it was not always followed consistently, nevertheless constitutes a point of reference that cannot be ignored in postconciliar interpretation" (Giuseppe Alberigo, "Transition to a New Age," in *History of Vatican II*, vol. 5, *The Council and the Transition: The Fourth Period and the End of the Council, September 1965–December 1965*, ed. Giuseppe Alberigo and Joseph A. Komonchak [Maryknoll, NY: Orbis, 2006], 573– 644, at 604). On the shifts in perspective among the Australian bishops at Vatican II, see Ormond Rush, "The Australian Bishops of Vatican II: Participation and Reception," in *Vatican II: The Reception and Implementation in the Australian Church*, ed. Neil Ormerod et al. (Melbourne: John Garrett, 2012), 4–19.

and captured in their voting, the historical significance of the council and the meaning of their texts are not to be restricted solely to what even they foresaw or intended. "History often tells what contemporaries did not know or consciously 'live.' "[11]

Seventh, "the council" is more than its final documents, and what the council communicates goes beyond the written word of those documents. The documents cannot capture the whole of what the council was and is.[12] In this sense, the spirit is more than the letter. For example, Joseph Ratzinger wrote after the third session regarding the change that was taking place in the bishops:

> This spiritual awakening, which the bishops accomplished in full view of the Church, or, rather accomplished *as* the Church, was the great and irrevocable event of the Council. It was more important in many respects than the texts it passed, for these texts could only voice a part of the new life which had been awakened in this encounter of the Church with its inner self.[13]

As one example of how the documents did not capture the council's fullness, John O'Malley notes how the reform of the Roman Curia is mentioned only once in the entire collection of documents.[14] However, the issue was a cause of much heated discussion.[15] As O'Malley notes: "It is not the documents, therefore, that reveal how hot the issue was but the narrative of the battles for control of the council itself."[16] Furthermore, as the council would itself teach with regard to the nature of divine revelation occurring not only in words but also in deeds, the council likewise taught and continues to teach not only in its words (its 16 documents)

11. Joseph A. Komonchak, "Vatican II as an 'Event,' " in *Vatican II: Did Anything Happen?*, ed. David G. Schultenover (New York: Continuum, 2007), 24–51, at 37.

12. An analogy with Scripture highlights the point. The revelatory event to which the scriptural writings witness surpasses the written witness.

13. Joseph Ratzinger, *Theological Highlights of Vatican II* (New York: Paulist, 2009), 194, emphasis original.

14. Decree on the Pastoral Office of Bishops in the Church, *Christus Dominus*, nos. 9–10.

15. Cardinal Frings, in a speech to the assembly on November 7, 1963, allegedly written by his *peritus* Joseph Ratzinger, stated: "This reform of the Curia is necessary. Let us put it into effect." Quoted in Xavier Rynne, *Vatican Council II* (Maryknoll, NY: Orbis, 2002), 222.

16. John W. O'Malley, *What Happened at Vatican II* (Cambridge, MA: Harvard University, 2008), 304.

but also in its deeds or actions. The council made some symbolic gestures through which it taught by example, beyond the words expressed in its documents. These symbolic moments and gestures include the admission of Protestant observers and seeking out their observations; inviting Catholic lay observers, first men, then extended to a few women, including the Australian lay woman Rosemary Goldie.[17] Also papal gestures, although not strictly conciliar acts, did create a public perception as to what the council was doing—for example, Paul VI's gift of a papal tiara for the poor; his visits to India, Israel, and the United Nations; and his ecumenical gift of a Vatican reliquary of St. Andrew to the Greek Orthodox Church. All these too are related to the historical event of Vatican II and were, and are still, significant in shaping the contemporary reception of what the council was intending to do and the kind of church it was attempting to fashion.

Eighth, the hermeneutical points above, on the significance of the council being beyond what even the participating bishops understood or even imagined, as well as the council being more than its documents, can be further explored through the historical category of "event" (in the narrow sense): the further in time we get from the council is not necessarily a disadvantage; a retrospective 50 years after an event in some ways enables a clearer judgment to be made regarding that event's historical significance.[18] On December 8, 1965, the council itself entered into history to be received through time. From the viewpoint of a 50-year timeline, new perspectives on the historical significance of the council emerge.

In addition to these hermeneutical points concerning specifically the principle of interrelating the council and its documents, a further five hermeneutical principles can be singled out.

Pastoral/Doctrinal

Principle Two: The council and its documents are to be interpreted in light of the council's primarily pastoral orientation; Vatican II's

17. Goldie was present for the third and fourth sessions, sitting right up front, "on the plush chairs of St Andrew's tribune, alongside the male auditors and the theologians" (Rosemary Goldie, *From a Roman Window: Five Decades; The World, the Church, and the Catholic Laity* [Blackburn, Vic.: HarperCollinsReligious, 1998], 71). For more on the contribution by women auditors at the council and Goldie's particular role, see Carmel Elizabeth McEnroy, *Guests in Their Own House: The Women of Vatican II* (New York: Crossroad, 1996).

18. See Komonchak, "Vatican II as an 'Event.'"

reformulation of doctrine aimed to teach in words and actions that foster a more meaningful spiritual appropriation of God's salvation and revelation by the people of God.

While remembering the qualifications noted above regarding the interpretation and significance of "authorial intention," the intention of the pope who called and first orientated the council is an important element in interpreting the council and its documents. Pope John XXIII, in his opening speech, *Gaudet Mater Ecclesia*, at the first session, expressed his desire that the council be primarily "pastoral," and that consideration of doctrine be expressed in a pastoral way. Furthermore, the pope called for "a magisterium which is predominantly pastoral in character" and of a pastoral leadership style in which "the medicine of mercy rather than that of severity" characterizes the church's way of governing and teaching.[19] The papal discourse had significant influence on the Council Fathers and is to be considered, according to Jared Wicks, as "the Council's first great text."[20] It became more than an opening address.

In many ways over its years of deliberation, the council enthusiastically adopted Pope John's pastoral focus, from the first session's debates on liturgy and revelation to the last session's debates on the church in the world. The first line of the first document promulgated, *Sacrosanctum concilium*, begins: "The sacred Council has set out to impart an ever-increasing vigor to the Christian lives of the faithful" (*SC* no. 1).[21] In a footnote reference after the title of the document promulgated on the last working day of the council, *Gaudium et spes* (*GS*), the Pastoral Constitution on the Church in the World of Today states a principle that should be applied to all the council's constitutions, decrees, and declarations: "The Constitution is called

19. Pope John XXIII, "Pope John's Opening Speech to the Council," in *The Documents of Vatican II*, ed. Walter M. Abbott (New York: America, 1966), 710–19, at 715–16.

20. Jared Wicks, *Doing Theology* (New York: Paulist, 2009), 22. On John XXIII's opening address as a continuing guiding norm during the council debates, Wicks writes: "In the early weeks of the Council's deliberations, Council members began citing Pope John's address in their comments in St. Peter's as expressing the Council's purpose, namely, as assembled not to condemn errors, but to promote pastoral renewal and the cause of Christian unity. The address also served as a norm in some members' evaluation of draft texts prepared before the Council, for example, in positive assessments of the text on liturgical reform and in critical judgments on the text *The Sources of Revelation*, on scripture and tradition" (ibid., 141).

21. Austin Flannery, OP, ed., *Vatican Council II: The Conciliar and Postconciliar Documents* (Collegeville, MN: Liturgical Press, 2014); hereafter Flannery translation.

'pastoral' because, while resting on doctrinal principles, it seeks to set forth the relation of the Church to the world and to the [people] of today. In Part I, therefore, the pastoral emphasis is not overlooked, nor is the doctrinal emphasis overlooked in Part II."[22] In other words, *Gaudium et spes* is both a pastoral and a doctrinal constitution. Similarly, *Lumen gentium* is both "dogmatic" and pastoral, as are *Dei verbum* and *Sacrosanctum concilium*.

Christoph Theobald sees this "principle of pastorality" as *the* hermeneutical key for interpreting Vatican II.[23] According to him, the pastorality called for by John XXIII can be summed up in the axiom, "there can be no proclamation of the gospel without taking account of its recipients."[24] As the council would later teach: the primary receiver of God's revelation and salvation is the whole people of God; facilitating their reception of the gospel is of utmost importance for the effectiveness of the church's mission. The council's doctrinal statements regarding the church's life should be interpreted as directed to this pastoral aim; likewise, the ecclesiological reforms it proposed have as their ultimate purpose God's saving of human beings—which implies deep spiritual appropriation by believers of God's offer of salvation if God's intention is to be realized. The church is a servant of that salvific goal. The opening article of *Dei verbum* states this conciliar intention: "[This synod] wants the whole world to hear the summons to salvation." The pastoral/doctrinal principle is at play, in some way, in all the other dialectics that follow.

Proclamation/Dialogue

Principle Three: The church's mission is to proclaim boldly and steadfastly God's loving offer of salvation to humanity in Jesus Christ through the Holy Spirit; proclamation of the Christian gospel will be ineffective without dialogic openness to the perspectives and contexts of the intended receivers of the proclamation, whether they be believers or nonbelievers.

Related to the council's desire for pastoral effectiveness within the church was its desire for dialogic openness to the world and those "outside"

22. Flannery translation.

23. On the council's reception of John XXIII's "principle of pastorality" and its centrality for a hermeneutics of the council and its documents, see Christoph Theobald, *La réception du concile Vatican II: I. Accéder à la source* (Paris: Cerf, 2009), 281–493.

24. Christoph Theobald, "The Theological Options of Vatican II: Seeking an 'Internal' Principle of Interpretation," in *Vatican II: A Forgotten Future?*, *Continuum* 1005/4, ed. Alberto Melloni and Christoph Theobald (London: SCM, 2005), 87–107, at 94.

the church. Once again John XXIII set the tone in his opening address, a tone adopted by the council and his successor, Pope Paul VI. The council deliberately avoids condemnation. The word *rapprochement*, while not used in the documents,[25] nevertheless captures what was clearly perceived at the time, by both its opponents and promoters in the assembly of bishops, as a clear shift in ecclesial policy, away from a church deliberately hostile to those around it to a church desiring engagement with those "others." The council's intention was to rebuild broken relationships that had impeded God's effectiveness in the world. Furthermore, the church should seek to know the perspective, language, and mind-set of the receivers of its message, in order that the "other" may see more clearly in the face of the Catholic Church "the genuine face of God."[26]

Accordingly, the council sought a new start in relations with those "outside" it: with Eastern churches of the Great Schism of 1054; with the churches of the Reformation; with the Jewish people; with adherents of other religions; with those of no religious belief. The council extended this dialogic openness to "modernity," to "the world," to "culture," to "history." This openness manifests a clear desire to end the entrenchment mentality characteristic of the previous centuries of Catholicism, especially during "the long nineteenth century" since the French Revolution and its aftermath.[27] However, what is also clear is that neither John XXIII nor the council nor Paul VI ever understood such *rapprochement* as a capitulation to the Zeitgeist of liberalism, relativism, or indifferentism. The ending of a hostile stance was for the sake of a more compelling and more effective proclamation of God's Good News for all humanity.

The council embedded this deliberate shift in the language it used throughout its documents: a shift in tone away from hostile words toward "friendship words," such as brothers/sisters, cooperation, collaboration, partnership, freedom, and dialogue.[28] The last word "dialogue" (translating

25. "*Rapprochement* . . . is not part of the corpus of Vatican II in a material way, but it belongs fully to the aims of Vatican II" (Massimo Faggioli, "*Sacrosanctum concilium* and the Meaning of Vatican II," *Theological Studies* 71 [2010]: 437–52, at 452). Faggioli notes the frequency of the term *rapprochement* in the writings of Dom Lambert Beauduin (1873–1960), a pioneer in the liturgical and ecumenical movements prior to the council. O'Malley refers to Cardinal Léon-Joseph Suenens as "a disciple of Lambert Beauduin" (O'Malley, *What Happened at Vatican II*, 117).

26. *GS* no. 19.

27. On "the long nineteenth century," see O'Malley, *What Happened at Vatican II*, 53–92.

28. Ibid., 306–7.

both *dialogus* and *colloquium*) became a key leitmotif for capturing this element of the council's vision.[29] For O'Malley, the council was concerned not only about the "what" of the church but also and ultimately about "how" the church should be; John XXIII's call for pastoral reform and its adoption by the conciliar assembly expressed their desire to change the very "style" of being church.[30] Hermann Pottmeyer interprets the council's vision for ecclesial reform as a call above all to create "a culture of dialogue" *within* the Catholic Church itself.[31] It is significant that in its treatment of the four concentric circles of dialogue, *Gaudium et spes* no. 92 begins with dialogue *within* the church, before going on to speak of dialogue with other Christians, with adherents of other religions, and with nonbelievers.[32]

A stark example of the shift in attitude—from monologue to dialogue—toward those "outside" the church is evident in the heading and content of *Gaudium et spes* no. 44: "What the Church Receives from the Modern World."

> Nowadays when things change so rapidly and thought patterns differ so widely, the Church needs to step up this exchange by calling upon the help of people who are living in the world, who are expert in its organizations and its forms of training, and who understand its mentality, in the case of believers and nonbelievers alike. With the help of the Holy Spirit, it is the task of the whole people of God, particularly of its pastors and theologians, to listen to and distinguish the many voices of our times and to interpret them in the light of the divine Word, in order that the revealed truth may be more deeply penetrated, better understood, and more suitably presented.[33]

29. See James McEvoy, "Church and World at the Second Vatican Council: The Significance of *Gaudium et Spes*," *Pacifica* 19 (2006): 37–57; James Gerard McEvoy, "Proclamation as Dialogue: Transition in the Church-World Relationship," *Theological Studies* 70 (2009): 875–903.

30. For one formulation of his interpretation, see O'Malley, *What Happened at Vatican II*, 305–7.

31. Hermann J. Pottmeyer, "Die Mitsprache der Gläubigen in Glaubenssachen: Eine alte Praxis und ihre Wiederentdeckung," *Internationale katholische Zeitschrift "Communio"* 25 (1996): 135–47, at 146–47.

32. The council reverses the order in which Paul VI had treated the same circles of dialogue in his encyclical on dialogue, *Ecclesiam suam*, published on August 6, 1964, just five weeks before the start of the council's third session on September 14. See *Ecclesiam suam*, nos. 96–117.

33. *GS* no. 44, Flannery translation, slightly altered.

This passage was inserted just a few days before the last working day of the council, December 7, 1965, almost as a final reminder by the council of what it saw as one of its most important principles.

Ressourcement/Aggiornamento

Principle Four: Vatican II sought renewal and reform of the church by re-receiving many of the past forms and practices of the tradition; application of these past forms and practices to the present, however, demands critical adaptation for new times and contexts if genuine renewal and reform are to take place.

With the two terms *ressourcement* ("return to the sources") and *aggiornamento* ("updating"), we come to the issues of "history" and "historical consciousness." Bruno Forte has called Vatican II "the Council of history."[34] It was the first council in the history of the church that explicitly worked out of a historical awareness.[35] The two leitmotifs in this dialectic capture two necessarily interrelated dimensions of that consciousness.

The notion of *aggiornamento* had long been central to the vision of historian Angelo Roncalli.[36] As Pope John XXIII, his explicit use of and allusions to the leitmotif, both before the council and during his opening address, are important factors to be considered in the continuing interpretation of Vatican II, because his leitmotif would enter into the imagination of the bishops in council and shape both their agenda and their expression

34. Bruno Forte, "Le prospettive della ricerca teologica," in *Il Concilio Vaticano II: Recezione e attualità alla luce del Giubileo*, ed. Rino Fisichella (Milan: San Paolo, 2000), 419–29, at 420.

35. "The main novelty of Vatican II was rather its consideration of history as related to the gospel and the Christian truth. Whereas for the most part in the past there had been an awareness that history as experienced by human beings was ultimately of no importance for the understanding of the gospel (I use the term 'awareness', although 'in reality' it was never such a thing), the major question of the Second Vatican Council was precisely this, even if the words used (pastoral nature, *aggiornamento*, signs of the time [*sic*]) were not immediately understood clearly by all" (Giuseppe Ruggieri, "Towards a Hermeneutic of Vatican II," *Concilium* 1 [1999]: 1–13, at 3). See also Giuseppe Alberigo, "Cristianesimo e storia nel Vaticano II," *Cristianesimo nella storia* 5 (1984): 577–92.

36. See Max Vodola, "John XXIII, Vatican II, and the Genesis of *Aggiornamento*: A Contextual Analysis of Angelo Roncalli's Works on San Carlo Borromeo in Relation to Late Twentieth Century Church Reform" (PhD diss., School of Philosophical, Historical, and International Studies, Monash University, Melbourne, 2010); Michael Bredeck, *Das Zweite Vatikanum als Konzil des Aggiornamento: Zur hermeneutischen Grundlegung einer theologischen Konzilsinterpretation* (Paderborn: Schöningh, 2007).

of thought. Pope John's successor Paul VI also embraced *aggiornamento*, considering it to be "the guiding criterion of the Ecumenical Council," and indeed adopting it as an expression of "the aim and object" of his own pontificate.[37] Although the council documents never explicitly use the Italian word *aggiornamento*, the opening paragraph of its very first promulgated text, *Sacrosanctum concilium*, states: "It is the intention of this holy council . . . to adapt [*accommodare*] those structures which are subject to change [*mutatio*]."[38] For both popes of the council, as for the conciliar assembly, this *aggiornamento* could be characterized as a fresh reception (through personal and institutional renewal and reform) of "the treasure of revelation, entrusted to the church"[39] from the beginning: God's self-communication in Jesus Christ through the Holy Spirit, as it was witnessed to in Scripture and tradition, and as it is experienced in history and made evident through certain contemporary signs of the times. Without *aggiornamento*, this treasure would not be meaningfully communicated to (and, in turn, appropriated by) new generations.

While its aim was an *aggiornamento* of the church's liturgy, the council's first promulgated document, *Sacrosanctum concilium*, is simultaneously a work grounded on *ressourcement* of the tradition. According to Massimo Faggioli:

> The advocates of the anti-Vatican II "new liturgical movement" are indeed right as they identify in *Sacrosanctum concilium* the main target since this constitution is the most radical instance of *ressourcement* and the most obviously antitraditionalist document of the council. The principle of *ressourcement* affected *Sacrosanctum concilium* like no other conciliar document; it is hard to find in the corpus of the documents passages more expressive of the very essence of the Church and driven by the idea of *ressourcement*.[40]

Similarly, in the early debates on the document that would become *Dei verbum*, *ressourcement* of long-forgotten scriptural and patristic personalist notions of revelation and dynamic notions of tradition became important, as the bishops reflected on the nature of the divine revelatory event within history and its meaningful and effective transmission by the

37. *Ecclesiam suam*, no. 50, http://www.vatican.va/holy_father/paul_vi/encyclicals/documents/hf_p-vi_enc_06081964_ecclesiam_en.html.

38. Norman P. Tanner, ed., *Decrees of the Ecumenical Councils*, 2 vols. (Washington, DC: Georgetown University, 1990), 2:820.

39. *DV* no. 26, Tanner translation.

40. Faggioli, "*Sacrosanctum concilium* and the Meaning of Vatican II," 451.

church throughout history. Likewise, toward the end of the council, when discussing the church *ad extra*, these earlier theological discussions on revelation and tradition were never far from the surface of debate as they discussed the constant need for *aggiornamento*:

> The Church learned early in its history to express the Christian message in the concepts and languages of different peoples and tried to clarify it in the light of the wisdom of their philosophers: it was an attempt to adapt the Gospel to the understanding of all and the requirements of the learned, insofar as this could be done. Indeed, this kind of adaptation and preaching of the revealed word *must ever be the law of all evangelization*. In this way it is possible to create in every country the possibility of expressing the message of Christ in suitable terms and to foster vital contact and exchange between the Church and different cultures.[41]

In reaching back to the rich heritage of the faith for resourcing its updating, the work of the so-called *ressourcement* theologians in the decades prior to the council was vital.[42] This biblical, patristic, liturgical, historical, ecumenical, and theological scholarship was directly mediated to the council members through the theological *periti* present, either as assistants to individual bishops and national groups of bishops or as theological advisors on various conciliar committees.[43]

41. *GS* no. 44, Flannery translation, emphasis added.

42. On the historical consciousness grounding the *ressourcement* scholarship by theologians of the so-called *nouvelle théologie*, see Gabriel Flynn and Paul D. Murray, eds., *Ressourcement: A Movement for Renewal in Twentieth-Century Catholic Theology* (Oxford: Oxford University, 2011); Hans Boersma, Nouvelle Théologie *and Sacramental Ontology: A Return to Mystery* (New York: Oxford University, 2009); Jürgen Mettepenningen, Nouvelle Théologie—*New Theology: Inheritor of Modernism, Precursor of Vatican II* (New York: T. & T. Clark International, 2010). Mettepenningen considers Vatican II's appropriation (and, effectively, approbation) of the work of these theologians as the fourth phase in his history of *la nouvelle théologie*.

43. On the effects of *ressourcement* theology within the final texts, see Gerald O'Collins, "*Ressourcement* and Vatican II," in *Ressourcement: A Movement for Renewal*, 372–91. For a detailed study of the role before and during the council of theologians from the *ressourcement* Dominican "school" of Le Saulchoir (Marie-Dominique Chenu, Yves Congar, and Henri-Marie Féret), see Michael Quisinsky, *Geschichtlicher Glaube in einer geschichtlichen Welt: Der Beitrag von M.-D. Chenu, Y. Congar, und H.-M. Féret zum II. Vaticanum* (Berlin: LIT, 2007). For assessments on the role of such theologians at Vatican II, see Alberigo, "Transition to a New Age," 602–4; Jared Wicks, "Theologians at Vatican Council II," in *Doing Theology* (New York: Paulist, 2009), 187–223.

With a new historical consciousness, and a retrieval of the notion that the ultimate "source" of the faith throughout history is God's continuing self-communication in Christ through the Spirit, a greater appreciation emerged in the council assembly that all expressions of that source's reception by the church are historically conditioned, including Scripture itself. The council would teach that it was therefore appropriate for historical-critical methods to be applied to Scripture's interpretation, albeit within the historical process of ongoing interpretation and application in the church's living tradition. Similarly, the historical nature of doctrine was appreciated to a deeper degree; the American *peritus* John Courtney Murray believed that "development of doctrine" was "*the* issue under the issues" at Vatican II.[44] Such "development" was an element of ongoing *aggiornamento*. A further consequence of this engagement with recent historical methods of scholarship, when applied to interpreting the whole sweep of church history, was a rediscovery by the Council Fathers of great diversity within the tradition, and especially the rediscovery of a richly diverse Catholicism before the Counter-Reformation (or "Tridentine") Catholicism that still shaped the Catholic Church so pervasively up to the eve of the council.

Within the various streams of the tradition being resourced, the patristic period was especially privileged, particularly the writings of Augustine. The growing appreciation of the tradition's rich diversity led at times to significant differences in preferred elements for retrieval. For example, while the early sessions of the council showed a united group wanting to reject the then-dominant "neo-Scholasticism" in favor of a more biblical and personalist theology from the patristic period, there were those who, all the same, did not want to reject the deep Catholic insights of recent historical *ressourcement* of a Thomas Aquinas before the Scholasticism of the centuries following him, a Scholasticism that dominated Catholic theology immediately before the council and shaped the initial schemas presented to the council. The differences between these conciliar groups would more and more mark the council's work and can be found woven throughout the later documents.[45] It can be broadly described as the Augustinian and Thomist threads within Catholicism. In the end, the council documents attempt to safeguard *both* the Augustinian and the Thomist

44. John Courtney Murray, "This Matter of Religious Freedom," *America* 112, no. 2 (January 9, 1965), 40–43, at 43.

45. See Joseph A. Komonchak, "Le valutazioni sulla *Gaudium et spes*: Chenu, Dossetti, Ratzinger," in *Volti di fine Concilio: Studi di storia e teologia sulla conclusione del Vaticano II*, ed. Joseph Doré and Alberto Melloni (Bologna: Il Mulino, 2000), 115–53.

approaches. Both Incarnation and Cross are highlighted: God's coming as a human being consecrates creation and human history as the *locus* where God is to be found ever new; however, within that creation and history, evil and sin continue to impede God's reigning in the world.

The citations in the main text and footnotes of the documents reveal the council's desire to ground its positions in the rich tradition of Christianity highlighted by this *ressourcement*, going back to its first scriptural witness. Certainly there is an obvious concern to appeal to earlier popes, especially Pius XII (who makes up half the references to previous papal teachings). Showing the relationship with the previous council, Vatican I, was also seen to be important, as indeed was Vatican II's relationship with Trent. However, even here the appeal to Trent's authority, which had so dominated the period of "Tridentine Catholicism," is recontextualized, as Joseph Komonchak notes: at Vatican II, "the tradition was no longer read in the light of Trent; Trent was read in the light of the tradition."[46] That tradition was "the great tradition" of the church, a "living tradition" going back to the earliest church.[47] However, these footnote references are only surface indicators of the council's *ressourcement*. What is invisible, except for its pervasive effects, are the decades of preconciliar scholarship in biblical, patristic, liturgical, historical, ecumenical, and theological studies, mediated to the council through its *periti*.

46. Joseph A. Komonchak, "The Council of Trent at the Second Vatican Council," in *From Trent to Vatican II: Historical and Theological Investigations*, ed. Raymond F. Bulman and Frederick J. Parrella (New York: Oxford University, 2006), 61–80, at 76.

47. The notion of "living tradition" can be highlighted as one example of the council's appropriation of *ressourcement* scholarship (as indeed it can be highlighted as an example of how ongoing *aggiornamento* goes to the heart of the church's mission). The notion pervades the whole of *DV* no. 8, though the actual phrase *traditio viva* is not explicitly used. However, phrases can be found such as "the enlivening [*vivifica*] presence of this tradition" and "the living voice of the Gospel (ringing out) in the church." It is later used explicitly in *DV* no. 12, in reference to "the living tradition [*traditio viva*] of the whole church." The phrase *traditio viva* is found too in *UR* no. 17. Regarding the drafting of *DV* no. 8, Ratzinger notes: "It is not difficult . . . to recognize the pen of Y. Congar" (Joseph Ratzinger, "Chapter II: The Transmission of Divine Revelation," in *Commentary on the Documents of Vatican II*, vol. 3, ed. Herbert Vorgrimler [New York: Herder, 1969], 181–98, at 184). Le Saulchoir Dominican Yves Congar played a significant role on the subcommission that formulated *DV* no. 8. The two parts of his work on tradition in French were published just before (1960) and during the council (1963). See Yves M.-J. Congar, *La tradition et les traditions: Essai historique* (Paris: A. Fayard, 1960–1963), translated as *Tradition and Traditions: An Historical and a Theological Essay*, trans. Michael Naseby and Thomas Rainborough (London: Burns & Oates, 1966).

With this principle of *ressourcement/aggiornamento*, Vatican II took on a historical consciousness and embraced a dynamic understanding of tradition: *ressourcement* is to *aggiornamento* as tradition is to reception. The history of tradition shows continuous adaptation; what is constant in that process is the need for reinterpretation for new times and contexts.

Continuity/Reform

Principle Five: The church is the one community of faith through time as a sacrament of God's offer of salvation; the form this sacrament takes in a particular time and place requires continual reform and must always be adapted to that context for the sake of the church's ongoing effectiveness.

In the previous section, I indicated how *ressourcement* scholarship revealed rich diversity in the tradition and brought about the conciliar shift away from understanding Catholic identity in terms of a monolithic Tridentine Catholicism. There, continuity had been understood as "uniformity through time"; continuity had meant the continuation of Tridentine Catholicism. In the early 20th century, any theological attempts to go beyond that vision were severely resisted, as happened during the Modernist controversy. Many of the bishops at Vatican II, who had been formed as seminarians between 1910 and 1940, would have had that anti-Modernist Catholicism deeply engrained in them. This section now extends discussion of the issues of *ressourcement* and *aggiornamento*, but brings explicitly to the fore the tension that results in the interplay between them: the necessary tension between constancy and change, sameness and novelty, in effecting an *aggiornamento* of the tradition. "Although [the Italian *aggiornamento* and the French *ressourcement*] express almost diametrically opposed impulses—the first looking forward, the second backward—they are both geared to change."[48]

It should not be surprising that during the council and then during its aftermath we find being played out an ecclesiastical version of *la querelle des anciens et des modernes*, a seemingly eternal quarrel over the old and the new, tradition and innovation, the past and the present.[49] From the very first day of the council in his opening speech, John XXIII raised this

48. John O'Malley, "Vatican II: Did Anything Happen?," in *Vatican II: Did Anything Happen?*, 52–91, at 63.

49. The phrase comes from a 17th-century literary debate in France. See Hans Robert Jauss, "Ursprung und Bedeutung der Fortschrittsidee in der 'Querelle des Anciens et des Modernes,' " in *Die Philosophie und die Frage nach dem Fortschritt*, ed. Helmut Kuhn and Franz Wiedmann (München: Pustet, 1964), 51–72; Jauss, "Antiqui/moderni

issue of continuity and adaptation. Of course, he said, the deposit of faith (divine revelation) is a nonnegotiable; what demands constant attention is the effective proclamation of this good news; the church, through this council (he urged), must look to anything in its life that is impeding this proclamation, by removing it or reforming it. The council did go on to embrace an agenda for renewal (*renovatio*) and reform (*reformatio*).[50]

Much recent discussion has narrowed debate over the correct interpretation of Vatican II to the issue of continuity versus discontinuity. Benedict XVI has used this dichotomy to structure initially his own deliberate foray into the debate, nevertheless attempting thereafter to rename what he considers the proper terms of that debate—continuity/reform.[51] Joseph Komonchak, in his analysis of Benedict's 2005 speech to the Roman Curia, identifies Lefebvrites as the real target of the pope's criticism of a radical "hermeneutics of discontinuity." According to Komonchak, the pope's proposed "hermeneutic of reform" is much more subtle than its detractors would claim:

> The "reform" that Benedict sees as the heart of the council's achievement is itself a matter of "novelty in continuity," of "fidelity and dynamism"; indeed, in what is something like a definition, the pope says that "true reform" consists precisely in a "combination of continuity and discontinuity at different levels." It oversimplifies his position to see it as counterposing continuity and discontinuity, as is often done. It is no less an oversimplification to reduce the question of interpreting Vatican II to the same choice

(Querelle des Anciens et des Modernes)," in *Historisches Wörterbuch der Philosophie*, 13 vols., ed. Joachim Ritter et al. (Basel: Schwabe, 1971–), 1:410–14.

50. The two nouns are used in a few places in the documents. *Lumen gentium* no. 8 speaks of *renovatio* (renewal): "The church . . . , clasping sinners to its bosom, at once holy and always in need of purification, follows constantly the path of penance and renewal." *Unitatis redintegratio*, in two articles, uses together both *renovatio* (renewal) and *reformatio* (reform or reformation): all Christian communions are required to undertake "the task of renewal and reform" (*UR* no. 4); "Every renewal of the church essentially consists in an increase of fidelity to the church's own calling. . . . In its pilgrimage on earth Christ summons the church to continual reformation [*perennem reformationem*], of which it is always in need, in so far as it is an institution of human beings here on earth" (*UR* no. 6, Tanner translation). On the occurrence of the two terms, see Philippe Delhaye, Michel Guéret, and Paul Tombeur, eds., *Concilium Vaticanum II: Concordance, index, listes de fréquence, tables comparatives*, Informatique et étude de textes 7 (Louvain: CETÉ DOC, 1974), 553.

51. For the December 22, 2005, "Address of His Holiness Benedict XVI to the Roman Curia," see Benedict XVI, "Interpreting Vatican II," *Origins* 35 (2006): 534–39.

> between continuity and discontinuity. Is there anyone who sees only continuity in the council, or anyone who sees only discontinuity? Pope Benedict's description of "true reform" invites an effort to discern where elements of continuity and elements of discontinuity may be found.[52]

What constitutes the precise elements of discontinuity introduced by Vatican II has been variously listed. For example, Peter Hünermann notes that the council desired four major breaks with the past: a break with 1500 years of Christendom, where church and state have common goals and work as one; a break with the 1000-year division between Eastern and Western Christianity; a break with the 500-year separation between Catholics and Protestants; a break with the 100 years of tense Catholic "lingering on the threshold of the modern."[53] Karl Rahner's thesis is well known: Vatican II marks an epochal change in the history of the church, from a Hellenistic model to a truly "catholic" world church.[54] I have already noted O'Malley's thesis regarding the deliberate and dramatic shift in the desired "style" of being church. Others could be noted.

What constitutes the elements of continuity that Vatican II perpetuated, albeit in a renewed way? Certain fundamental features are considered by Vatican II to be permanently enduring elements of the Catholic Church: evangelization; the Scriptures; the seven sacraments; service of neighbor, especially the poor; ordination and the threefold order of bishop, priest, and deacon; religious life; the papacy; conciliar government; authoritative teaching; prayer and the call to holiness; etc. Vatican II addressed all these, and in its intention to bring about their renewal, it certainly saw itself and its vision to be in continuity with these elements of Catholicism.

I would argue, however, that Vatican II's fundamental enduring element is more *theo*logical than *ecclesio*logical. One of the most significant teachings of the council is its retrieval of the nature of divine revelation as first and foremost God's loving, personal self-communication to humanity in Christ through the Spirit, and not simply a communication of divine truths. Ultimately, in any discussion of the council and continuity, the *continuum* it

52. Joseph A. Komonchak, "Benedict XVI and the Interpretation of Vatican II," in *The Crisis of Authority in Catholic Modernity*, ed. M. Lacey and F. Oakley (New York: Oxford University), 93–110, at 105.

53. See Peter Hünermann, "Kriterien für die Rezeption des II. Vatikanischen Konzils," *Theologische Quartalschrift* 191 (2011): 126–47.

54. Karl Rahner, "Basic Theological Interpretation of the Second Vatican Council," in *Concern for the Church*, Theological Investigations 20 (New York: Crossroad, 1981), 77–89.

primarily focused on, in the end, was not so much "the church" but more so "the treasure of revelation entrusted to the church":[55] God's continuous revelatory and salvific presence and activity in human history in Jesus Christ, through the Holy Spirit.[56] It is this that never changes. Ecclesiologically, "continuity" relates to the church's ongoing reception of that *continuum*. In that reception, the church is *semper ipse sed nunquam idem* (always itself but never the same)—always itself as receiver of God's revelation, yet constantly needing to reform itself so that it might be a more effective sacrament of that salvific revelation. Preservation of ecclesial continuity is maintained by always being effective in that mission. *Dei verbum*'s notion of "living tradition" captures the ecclesial "mirror" of the divine *continuum* in history. In that sense *Dei verbum* is as much about the church as *Lumen gentium* and *Gaudium et spes*; the living tradition is the church living the gospel in its daily life in whatever period in history.

Vision/Reception

Principle Six: The bishops of Vatican II proposed a vision for renewing and reforming the Catholic Church; that vision requires ongoing reception and implementation by the whole people of God for its realization.

Vatican II envisioned a renewed and reformed Catholic Church. In fashioning its vision, "the Council by no means claims encyclopedic completeness";[57] moreover, "the Council did not claim to be expressing the final word on the subjects it treated, only to be pointing out the direction in which further reflection should develop."[58] However, it did try to be comprehensive.[59]

55. *DV* no. 26.

56. *DV* no. 2.

57. Peter Hünermann, "The Ignored 'Text': On the Hermeneutics of the Second Vatican Council," in *Vatican II: A Forgotten Future?*, 118–36, at 126.

58. Joseph Doré, "Vatican II Today," in ibid., 137–47, at 142.

59. "No subject escaped their attention: from Revelation to listening to the signs of the times, from marriage to international peace, from education and the communications media to ecumenical and interfaith dialogue, from the nature and mission of the Church to the redefinition of its various functions, ministries, and states of life, the bishops managed to depict a renewed vision of Christianity on a planet embarking on globalization, even to put forward a programme of reform that exceeds anything we might have dared to imagine earlier. None of the twenty preceding councils showed so much daring and ambition: allowing a consensus to emerge among those more than two thousand prelates from all continents and obtain their agreement on the responses

In hermeneutically reconstructing what the council envisaged and what it outlined in its documents, it is helpful to keep in mind "the hermeneutical function of distanciation."[60] An author of a text (in the world behind the text) commits a vision to writing by producing a text that imagines "a world" (the world of the text). The text projects and proposes this world to an implied reader and ultimately to a reader in the "real" world, inviting the reader to imagine that proposed world in his or her own context (the world in front of the text). In the reader's application to the real world, vision can become a reality, no matter how distant in time the receiver is from the production of the text.

Similarly, the bishops of Vatican II committed their vision to writing in 16 texts. The increasing distance in time from the council does not leave us at a disadvantage; through the dynamic nature of writing, of texts, and of reading, we have access to the conciliar vision—through hermeneutical reception. The council documents project a world in front of the text, and that world is a proposed way of being church in the face of the rest of humanity and ultimately before God. This projected world is what could be called "the vision of Vatican II." The dominant features of how the council imagined the church need to be brought to synthesis; receivers in new contexts must, however, reimagine and apply that vision for their own time and place. The conciliar vision requires reception for its realization—contemporary receivers of those texts are invited to imagine that envisioned church now, five decades later, in a very different context from the one in which those texts were first produced, the 1960s. New questions may arise in the new contexts and be posed to the conciliar texts for answers—questions, however, that individual conciliar texts did not intend to answer, or questions that the bishops could not have even envisaged at that time. Nevertheless, receivers may indeed find answers to those new questions, from a comprehensive interpretation of the council and all its documents, as they imagine the whole conciliar vision realized in their new context.

The vision of the Second Vatican Council is hermeneutically reconstructed from a new context by taking the council and its documents as a whole, along all time frames and from all hermeneutical perspectives

to be made to virtually all the questions facing the Church at the dawn of a new age for humanity—such is the absolutely unheard-of legacy of these great twentieth-century assizes" (Theobald, "Theological Options of Vatican II," 87).

60. For what follows, see Paul Ricoeur, "The Hermeneutical Function of Distanciation," in *From Text to Action: Essays in Hermeneutics, II* (London: Continuum, 1991), 75–88.

(authors-texts-receivers). First, the *documents* themselves are to be read as a whole, both intratextually and intertextually; furthermore, they are to be interpreted intertextually within the whole textual tradition of the church, reaching right back to the Scriptures.[61] Second, *the council* too has to be read within a longer context—as a historical ecclesial "event" to be now situated, 50 years later, in the context of a 2000-year living tradition. Third, since Vatican II (the *council* and the *documents*) has now entered history, it must be interpreted within a comprehensive theological epistemology, interrelating Scripture and tradition (of which Vatican II is now an element). According to the council's own "principle of pastorality" (as formulated by Theobald, "there can be no proclamation of the gospel without taking account of its recipients"[62]), it is the intended recipients of the conciliar vision who are now part of the council's history, because it is they who will apply it (or resist applying it). Those potential recipients make up the whole people of God, who the council emphasizes is the primary recipient of divine revelation. Therefore, there is a wide circle of voices and authorities within the contemporary church who are to participate in that comprehensive reception and assessment by the whole people of God (the *sensus fidelium*, theologians, and the magisterium).[63]

Alois Grillmeier has highlighted three dimensions of conciliar reception following councils in the early church: kerygmatic, theological, and spiritual reception.[64] They are helpful categories for examining the reception of the most recent council. *Kerygmatic reception* refers to the official interpretation, promulgation, and implementation through church law by church leadership once the council ends. *Theological reception* refers to the work of academic theologians attempting to bring to synthesis the vision of the conciliar decisions and documents. *Spiritual reception* is the

61. On the need to read the conciliar texts intratextually and intertextually, see Rush, *Still Interpreting Vatican II*, 40–48.

62. Theobald, "Theological Options of Vatican II," 94.

63. A full consideration of the relationship between these voices in the church, including particularly that of the laity, is a matter beyond this present article. For one proposal of that interrelation, see Ormond Rush, *The Eyes of Faith: The Sense of the Faithful and the Church's Reception of Revelation* (Washington, DC: Catholic University of America, 2009).

64. See Alois Grillmeier, "The Reception of Chalcedon in the Roman Catholic Church," *Ecumenical Review* 22 (1970): 383–411; Grillmeier, *Christ in Christian Tradition*, vol. 2, *From the Council of Chalcedon (451) to Gregory the Great (590–604)*, pt. 1, *Reception and Contradiction: The Development of the Discussion about Chalcedon from 451 to the Beginning of the Reign of Justinian* (Atlanta: John Knox, 1987), 7–10.

conversion of heart and mind by all the baptized to a greater fidelity to the gospel, no matter what particular aspects of the Christian life and church life a council might be wishing to address. Since this was John XXIII's pastoral intention for Vatican II—a more intense and meaningful proclamation and appropriation of the gospel—spiritual reception, therefore, is the ultimate goal of Vatican II's reception; it is here that the pastoral intention of the council is realized. Renewing the church for the sake of a greater facilitation of that spiritual reception, however, was never intended by the council to be focused only on personal renewal of individuals; it saw institutional reform as also key to its pastoral vision.

In terms of a theological epistemology, and from the perspective of what *Lumen gentium* called the "prophetic office" of the church, Grillmeier's three dimensions of conciliar reception can be seen to correspond to the three teaching authorities of the *sensus fidelium* (spiritual reception), theology (theological reception), and the magisterium (official reception). The reception—or nonreception—of Vatican II's vision occurs at all three levels: official, theological, and spiritual. It is here also, through the interaction of the *sensus fidelium*, theology, and the magisterium, that a proper assessment takes place regarding how faithfully the Catholic Church ("the whole body of the faithful")[65] has de facto received and applied the vision of Vatican II in the five decades since its close. If spiritual reception is the pastoral goal of the council, and if it is through the *sensus fidelium* that such spiritual reception can be found to be best articulated, then attention to the *sensus fidelium* by theologians and the magisterium is vital for accessing the lived application of Vatican II's vision within new contexts, five decades later. However, the fundamental condition for such ecclesial listening has yet to be effectively implemented: provision of structures of participation for enabling genuine interaction between the *sensus fidelium*, theologians, and the magisterium.

Conclusion

According to Alberigo, "Even from the viewpoint of its doctrinal accomplishments Vatican II seems to have been chiefly a point of departure rather than a point of arrival."[66] Grillmeier has highlighted the importance of "theological reception" in the reception of any council. One particular

65. *LG* no. 12.
66. Alberigo, "Transition to a New Age," 604.

task for theologians in their "theological reception" of Vatican II is to bring the elements of the conciliar vision into some form of comprehensive synthesis, keeping in mind the above hermeneutical principles. Such a synthesis cannot be attempted here. However, I wish to conclude with one aspect that emerges from the above considerations and that such a synthesis would need to highlight: the increasing emphasis given by the council to the saving activity of the tripersonal God's presence and activity in the movements of human history, but with a new appreciation of "history."

Over the council's four sessions, as the bishops discussed a vast range of ecclesiological issues, and particularly toward the end of the council, as they drafted *Nostra aetate*, *Dignitatis humanae*, and *Gaudium et spes*, their attention would also return regularly to the document that in the very first days of the council had caused such controversy, *De fontibus revelationis*—one of the seven schemas presented to the Council Fathers before they arrived in 1962, and the second to be brought to the floor of the council early in the first session (November 14, 1962). This first schema on revelation was famously rejected; after failing to reach the required two-thirds majority to send the schema back for total redrafting, John XXIII intervened to that effect. Consideration of further versions of the document remained on the agenda for all four sessions.[67] It would finally be promulgated (as *Dei verbum*) three weeks before the close of the council (November 18, 1965). Like the layers of an archeological dig, there is a sense in which the stages in the history of *Dei verbum* over four sessions can be seen to trace the history of the council's development. It was a development through which the bishops' Christocentric vision became more and more pneumatologically balanced,[68] resulting in a trinitarian vision of God's activity in the economy of salvation that pervades the 16 documents taken as a whole. The council's desire to renew and reform the Catholic Church spiritually and institutionally was for the sake of making the church a more effective sacrament of *God's mission* in the world.

67. In the second session, the second draft was not actually debated on the floor of the council in any of the plenary meetings. However, many bishops were able to submit written interventions that eventually reshaped this second draft considerably. For a detailed history of the document's development, see Burigana, *La Bibbia nel concilio*. For a summary account, see Ronald D. Witherup, *Scripture: Dei Verbum* (New York: Paulist, 2006), 15–31.

68. See, e.g., Jacques Dupuis, "Western Christocentrism and Eastern Pneumatology," in *Jesus Christ and His Spirit: Theological Approaches* (Bangalore: Theological Publications in India, 1977), 21–31.

During the third session, the Doctrinal Commission stated that the document on revelation was "in a way the first of all the constitutions of this council, so that its Preface introduces them all to a certain extent."[69] *Dei verbum* therefore has a central place among the four constitutions, as highlighted in the fourth session by the Relator, Cardinal Ermenegildo Florit from Florence, when introducing the near-final version of *Dei verbum* to the council assembly on October 29, 1965; the constitution, he stated, "formed the very bond among all the questions dealt with by this Council. It sets us at the very heart of the mystery of the Church and at the epicentre of ecumenical considerations."[70]

However, it is also important to see the development of *Dei verbum* as taking place in parallel to all the other 15 documents that the council produced. An internal conversation was taking place, as it were, among all the documents as they developed—despite the fact that, even as a collection, they do not present consistent, systematic treatises on individual themes. Over these four sessions, the ecclesiological elements of the council's emerging vision came to be presented in terms of a broader vista, that of the whole economy of salvation revealing the activity of the tripersonal God's ways within human history, now understood with a much keener historical consciousness. In turn, over these four sessions, this new appreciation of how God works in the economy of salvation began to bring forth an emerging appreciation of how God works *within* the church *throughout history*. A comprehensive interpretation of the council, five decades on, in the light of the hermeneutical principles outlined in this essay, must therefore bring to the fore the significance of that developing

69. Vatican Council II, *Acta synodalia sacrosancti concilii oecumenici Vaticani II*, 5 vols. with multiple parts (Vatican City: Typis Polyglottis Vaticanis, 1970–1978), IV/1, 341, quoted in Theobald, "Theological Options of Vatican II," 91. On the centrality of *Dei verbum* in the conciliar vision and on the significance of this statement by the Doctrinal Commission, Jared Wicks writes: "Vatican II stated revelation's evangelical content in [*Dei verbum*'s] opening six paragraphs. One can argue that in the overall logic of the council documents, this passage stands first, since the gospel that it states is the word by which the church is assembled as *congregatio fidelium* and priestly people for worship. This is the gospel that all church ministries and apostolates serve and promote. The same gospel creates the horizon of understanding within which Catholic Christians view the world and its structures for the unfolding of the human vocation. Because of this, Vatican II's Doctrinal Commission once said that the constitution on revelation is in a certain way (*quodammodo*) the first of all the council's constitutions" (Jared Wicks, "Vatican II on Revelation—From behind the Scenes," *Theological Studies* 71 [2010]: 637–50, at 640–41).

70. *Acta synodalia* IV/5, 741, quoted in Theobald, "Theological Options," 91.

preoccupation with the ways of God in history and its articulation across the texts. Ongoing interpretation of the ecclesiological reforms of Vatican II should be informed by this rejuvenated theology of God's activity within history in the economy of salvation, to be discerned through carefully reading "the signs of the times" in the light of the gospel.[71] As Bruno Forte states, Vatican II was "the Council of history."[72]

71. *GS* no. 4; see *GS* no. 11.
72. Forte, "Le prospettive della ricerca teologica," 420.

3 Vatican II
The History and the Narratives

MASSIMO FAGGIOLI

The author discusses the relationship between historical studies and the hermeneutics of the Second Vatican Council. He seeks to develop a critical understanding of the two-sided debate about how to understand and assess the event of the council by showing how one side argues not on the basis of historical understanding of the council but on the basis of "narratives," which are constructs governed more by ideologies than by historical research and analysis.

Who controls the past controls the future; who controls the present controls the past.

—George Orwell[1]

From a historical point of view, Vatican II is a complex event, given its global dimension, duration, agenda, and long-term consequences for the church and our world.[2] But the council is complex also in terms of

1. The "Party slogan," in George Orwell's novel *Nineteen Eighty-Four* (Cutchogue, NY: Buccaneer, 1949), 1.3.

2. Vatican II is not merely the 16 final *documents*, and not merely the *experience* of the council between its announcement on January 25, 1959, and its conclusion in 1965; it is also an *event*, because the evaluation of its consequences has elevated it to the level of an epochal change in the history of Christianity. Vatican II, as an ongoing phenomenon in the church, has assumed the character of "event": see Joseph A. Komonchak, "Riflessioni storiografiche sul Vaticano II come evento," in *L'Evento e le decisioni: Studi sulle dinamiche del concilio Vaticano II*, ed. Maria Teresa Fattori and Alberto

"institutional memory": memory of an event that has changed the church. It is indeed clear that "institutional memory" is often not the contrary, but the companion or the other side, of "institutional amnesia"—the need for institutions to forget some aspects of their past in order to maintain integrity and cohesion. On the other hand, memory is not always helped by the process of "memorialization," that is, the culture of constructing festivities, rituals, monuments, and memorials supposed to help us not just remember but also shape our national and political identities around a given interpretation of major events of our recent history.[3]

But after Vatican II, the Catholic Church took unambiguous steps to help Catholics remember the council. Paul VI's decision to create the "Archive of Vatican II" immediately after the conclusion of the council and to make it available to scholars was an act of trust in the ability and the will of theologians and historians to build an "institutional memory."[4] The pope trusted Msgr. Vincenzo Carbone (former aide to the powerful secretary general of Vatican II, Bishop Pericle Felici) to collect and publish the proceedings of the plenary congregations celebrated in the Basilica of St. Peter, the different *schemas* in the redaction history of each final conciliar document, and the minutes of the conciliar and preconciliar commissions.

After the completion of the publication of the *Acta synodalia*,[5] the recent (2002) decision to move that archive within the Secret Vatican Archives in order to make it even more available to scholars signaled the institution's continuing trust in the community of scholars of Vatican II.[6] This fact is often taken for granted, but it is indeed remarkable, because

---

Melloni (Bologna: Il Mulino, 1997), 417–49; and Joseph A. Komonchak, "Vatican II as an Event," in *Vatican II: Did Anything Happen?*, ed. David G. Schultenover (New York: Continuum, 2007), 24–51.

3. For a very different kind of event, see Harold Marcuse, "Holocaust Memorials: The Emergence of a Genre," *American Historical Review* 115, no. 1 (2010): 53–89.

4. See Vincenzo Carbone, "L'archivio del Concilio Vaticano II," *Archiva Ecclesiae* 34–35 (1991): 57–68.

5. *Acta et documenta Concilio Oecumenico Vaticano II apparando: Series I—Antepraeparatoria* (Vatican City: Typis Polyglottis Vaticanis, 1960–1961); *Series II—Praeparatoria* (Vatican City: Typis Polyglottis Vaticanis, 1964–1994); *Acta Synodalia Sacrosancti Concilii Oecumenici Vaticani II* (Vatican City: Typis Polyglottis Vaticanis, 1970–1999).

6. See Sergio Pagano, "Riflessioni sulle fonti archivistiche del concilio Vaticano II: In margine ad una recente pubblicazione," *Cristianesimo nella storia* 24 (2002): 775–812. For the availability of the archive of Vatican II in the Secret Vatican Archives, see the index carefully edited by Piero Doria, http://www.archiviosegretovaticano.va/en/patrimonio/ (all URLs cited herein were accessed on July 21, 2012).

Vatican II is still changing the church, and a particular "institutional interpretation" of the council is still able to influence the council's effect on the church. Vatican II was not only a religious event but also an institutional event. The "political" implications of the historiography of that event are not quite like those of other religious events that are less monopolized by the organizational dominance of one center of power that announces the event, manages it, and after its ending determines the process of the event's evaluation and concretization of its resolutions.[7]

Usually the starting point for this discussion is Vatican II as an event of church history that has both a textual dimension and a culture surrounding it—that is, both a "letter" and a "spirit" that, along with their relationship, have been defined by the Extraordinary Synod of 1985.[8] Both of these elements must be part of every hermeneutical effort regarding the council, and the history of the council's interpretations 50 years on has been marked by this complex relationship between text and context of the council.

Far less explored so far has been the issue of the role of Vatican II as a historical event in the "memory building" effort in the church. In other words, it is now clear that for the church the issue arises of finding in Vatican II a "usable past" in a rapidly changing world and in an even more rapidly changing global Catholicism.[9] The imagery, symbols, and data that the public discourse in the church associates with Vatican II are very powerful markers of the council itself, especially for future generations of Catholics, who will not be able to connect directly with the generation of

7. See John O'Malley, *What Happened at Vatican II* (Cambridge, MA: Harvard University, 2008), 311.

8. See *The Final Report of the 1985 Extraordinary Synod* (Washington, DC: National Conference of Catholic Bishops, 1986); Avery Dulles, "The Reception of Vatican II at the Extraordinary Synod of 1985," in *The Reception of Vatican II*, ed. Giuseppe Alberigo, Jean-Pierre Jossua, and Joseph A. Komonchak (Washington, DC: Catholic University of America, 1987), 349–63; Jean-Marie Tillard, "Final Report of the Last Synod," in *Synod 1985: An Evaluation*, ed. Giuseppe Alberigo and James Provost (Edinburgh: T. & T. Clark, 1986), 64–77.

9. See William J. Bouwsma, *A Usable Past: Essays in European Cultural History* (Berkeley: University of California, 1990), esp. 421–30 ("The History Teacher as Mediator"). The title of Bouwsma's book is derived from Nietzsche's essay, "*Vom Nutzen und Nachteil der Historie für das Leben*" (1874) (translated as "On the Uses and Disadvantages of History for Life," in Friedrich Nietzsche, *Untimely Meditations*, ed. Daniel Breazeale, trans. R. J. Hollingdale [New York: Cambridge University, 1997], 57–124). About the consequences of the "usable past" for contemporary church history, see Joseph P. Chinnici, "An Historian's Creed and the Emergence of Postconciliar Culture Wars," *Catholic Historical Review* 94 (2008): 219– 44.

those who lived through the council: in the church there are two generations of Catholics who have no direct, personal memory of the council.

What today's church makes of Vatican II depends on what the transmitters of the council's memory are able and willing to communicate. In the process of reception, the perception of the council as such—the "whole thing"—is not less but in fact more important than the reception of a single document (e.g., the Constitution on the Church, *Lumen gentium*) or of a single passage in a document (e.g., "*subsistit in*" in *LG* no. 8).

What we have seen emerge in the last few decades is a new prominence for narratives about Vatican II and the shape of contemporary Catholicism that take no account of the historical research on the council produced during this same period. We are left with narratives innocent of historical studies and even inimical to them.

Narrative and Narratives of Vatican II

The concept of "narrative" is relatively new; it comes from linguistics and literary science. Between the 1960s and 1970s the works by Tzvetan Todorov and Émile Benveniste, among others, have stressed the distinction between "story" and "discourse" or "narrative," and between the "narrator" and the "recipient of the narration."

"Narratologie" was born as a development of structuralism, whose first principle is that "meaning-making is a rule-governed activity."[10] Narrative is a formal system, but it can also be an ideological instrument. It is a way to decode the rules of social communication, but it is also a way to read the text not in the context that produced it, but in the context of the consequences supposedly created by the text.

Lately the relevance of the narrative has gone beyond the academic study of narrative. In recent times the pervasiveness of the concept of "narrative" has changed the way major historical events are offered to the public:

> We are living in the age of the Narrative Turn, an era when narrative is widely celebrated and studied for its ubiquity and importance. Doctors, lawyers, psychologists, business men and women, politicians, and political pundits of all stripes are just a few of the groups who now regard narrative as the Queen of Discourses and an essential component of their work.

10. Robert Scholes, Robert Kellogg, and James Phelan, *The Nature of Narrative*, rev., exp. ed., ed. James Phelan (1966; New York: Oxford University, 2006), 287.

> These groups acknowledge narrative's power to capture certain truths and experiences in ways that other modes of explanation and analysis such as statistics, descriptions, summaries, and reasoning via conceptual abstractions cannot.[11]

Theology has adopted the narrative theory, and in these last few years "narratologie" has become, especially in the French-speaking world, an important way for theology to understand and transmit the revelation in Scripture.[12] But outside the field of theological narratology, the idea of a "narrative" has imposed itself also on understanding and explaining what happened at Vatican II and after it. One of the phenomena typical of these last few decades in the church has been not only the growing separation and mistrust between theologians and the magisterium, but also the gap between Catholic church historians on one side (and historians of the councils in particular) and theologians, magisterium, and "secular historians" on the other side.[13] But for the understanding of Vatican II, the problem is even more acute due to the separation between historians and "narrators."

Usually the macronarratives are identified as the "conservative" and the "liberal" interpretations of Vatican II: the first one embodying the skeptical view of the new openness of the council vis-à-vis modernity and the modern world, the second one advocating a more positive view of the council as a necessary step to unlock Catholic theology from the reaction against modernity that was typical of the 19th and early 20th centuries, and a third narrative that might be called "neoconservative" or "neoliberal." But behind these macronarratives are other subnarratives that have marked these years of reception of the council. Others have already tried

11. See ibid., 285.

12. See Jean-Noël Aletti, *L'Art de raconter Jésus Christ: L'Écriture narrative de l'Évangile de Luc* (Paris: Seuil, 1989); and Daniel Marguerat, ed., *La Bible en récits: L'Exégèse biblique à l'heure du lecteur* (Geneva: Labor et Fides, 2003).

13. About the relationship between church historians and Catholic theology in the decades before Vatican II and during the council see Daniele Menozzi and Marina Montacutelli, eds., *Storici e religione nel novecento italiano* (Brescia: Morcelliana, 2011); Giuseppe Alberigo, "Hubert Jedin storiografo (1900–1980)," *Cristianesimo nella storia* 22 (2001): 315–38, and "Concili," in *Dizionario del sapere storico-religioso del Novecento*, ed. Alberto Melloni (Bologna: Il Mulino, 2010), 540–56; Heribert Müller, "Konzilien des 15. Jahrhunderts und Zweites Vatikanisches Konzil: Historiker und Theologen als Wissenschaftler und Zeitgenossen," in *Historie und Leben: Der Historiker als Wissenschaftler und Zeitgenosse; Festschrift für Lothar Gall zum 70. Geburtstag*, ed. Dieter Hein, Klaus Hildebrand, and Andreas Schulz (Munich: Oldenbourg, 2006), 117–35.

to catalogue them, and I will just begin here the work of decoding the "public discourse" of and on the Catholicism of Vatican II that will be a task for the church's future historians.[14]

A first narrative trying to undermine the legitimacy of the council, which emerged during Vatican II itself and is becoming more and more influential in the church, is the traditionalist narrative of the Lefebvrites, the Society of St. Pius X founded in 1970 by Archbishop Marcel Lefebvre (1905–1991), who denounced Vatican II as heretical. This narrative sees Vatican II as a product of early 20th-century theological "Modernism" condemned by Pius X in 1907. This "Modernist" theology allegedly took over Catholic theology and rehabilitated the worst enemies of modern Catholicism: Protestantism, Liberalism, Communism, and Freemasonry, among others. The definition of Vatican II as the ultimate and final moment of early 20th-century Modernism has almost become, at the beginning of the 21st century, common language in the neotraditionalist movement within contemporary Catholicism.[15] The view of Vatican II as "the French revolution in the church"[16] was fundamental in shaping Lefebvre's historical perception of the council, especially for a French bishop such as Lefebvre, who espoused the idea of a chain of "modern errors": the 16th-century Reformation followed by the Enlightenment, the French Revolution, Liberalism and socialism, and culminating in 20th-century Communism. In the 1940s Lefebvre had expressed support for the "Catholic order" of the authoritarian French Vichy régime (which collaborated with Nazi Germany); in the 1970s he commended authoritarian governments and military dictatorships in Spain, Portugal, Chile, and Argentina; and in

14. Peter Steinfels described a few years ago these tendencies active in American Catholicism: Vatican II as a tragic mistake (ultraconservative narrative); Vatican II misinterpreted and distorted (conservative); Vatican II as the needed change and reconciliation with the world (liberal); Vatican II as a false revolution (ultraliberal). See Peter Steinfels, *A People Adrift: The Crisis of the Roman Catholic Church in America* (New York: Simon & Schuster, 2003), 32–39.

15. For an example of such a mind-set, see Dominique Bourmaud, *Cent ans de modernisme: Généalogie du concile Vatican II* (Etampes: Clovis, 2003); ET, *One Hundred Years of Modernism: A History of Modernism, Aristotle to the Second Vatican Council*, trans. Brian Sudlow and Anne Marie Temple (Kansas City, MO: Angelus, 2006).

16. Marcel Lefebvre, *An Open Letter to Confused Catholics* (Herefordshire, UK: Fowler Wright Books for the Society of St. Pius X, 1986), 105; French edition: *Lettre ouverte aux catholiques perplexes* (Paris: Albin Michel, 1985). Lefebvre referred to Vatican II also as "the peace of Yalta of the Church with its worst enemies" (Marcel Lefebvre, *J'Accuse le Concile* [Martigny: Saint-Gabriel, 1976], 8).

the 1980s he supported the French far-right party "Front National" and added Vatican II as the final link in his chain of "modern errors." In his *Open Letter to Confused Catholics* (1986), Lefebvre described this chain of events: "The parallel I have drawn between the crisis in the church and the French Revolution is not simply a metaphorical one. The influence of the *philosophes* of the eighteenth century, and of the upheaval that they produced in the world, has continued down to our times. Those who injected that poison admit it themselves."[17]

Lefebvre's assessment of the state of the church after Vatican II was inextricably connected with his firm attachment to a very narrow idea of pontifical magisterium that developed after the French Revolution and to the Ultramontanist mind-set typical of 19th-century Catholicism. He identified the idea of church teaching with the contents and forms of 19th-century papal magisterium, culminating in Pius X's encyclical *Pascendi Dominici Gregis* (1907), which had condemned Modernism and brought about the most dramatic purge of theologians in the modern history of the Catholic Church. For Lefebvre, Vatican II represented the decisive point in the development of Catholicism in the modern world, a path that went from "Christian democracy" to "Christian socialism" and concluded with "Christian atheism" in which "dialogue" had become the most dangerous element: "The adulterous union of the Church and the Revolution is cemented by 'dialogue.' Truth and error are incompatible; to dialogue with error is to put God and the devil on the same footing."[18] According to Lefebvre, Vatican II had become the work of the devil against the church: "There is no more any Magisterium, no dogma, nor hierarchy; not Holy Scripture even, in the sense of an inspired and historically certain text. Christians are inspired directly by the Holy Spirit. The Church then collapses."[19]

In today's public discourse of Catholicism, this ultratraditionalist narrative is all but dead. Recent publications by self-appointed apologists very close to some Vatican circles are typical of the spirit of *revanche* against Vatican II. They also propagate a view of Vatican II in its texts as clearly discontinuous from the tradition. Such publications have gone far beyond the usual boundaries of the debate over "texts vs. the spirit of Vatican II." Among such apologists is Roberto de Mattei, a renowned proponent of ultratraditionalist Catholicism and a biographer of the Brazilian revanchist

17. Lefebvre, *An Open Letter to Confused Catholics*, 105; French ed.: *Lettre ouverte*, 8.

18. Lefebvre, *Open Letter*, 117.

19. Ibid., 118.

Plinio Corrêa de Oliveira. De Mattei sees in Vatican II the triumph of Modernism and the result of the infiltration of Communism and free masonry in Catholic theology at work at Vatican II. His hermeneutical effort provides interesting results in terms of archival discoveries from the ultratraditionalist Lefebvrians, but it is most interesting (and disconcerting) in its attempt to present itself as the historiographical translation of the call of Pope Benedict XVI for a renewed interpretation of Vatican II. In de Mattei's work, the rejection is not only of the "spirit" of Vatican II, but also of the very texts of the council, thus retrieving the conspiracy-driven Lefebvrian interpretation of Vatican II and proving essentially useless for developing a hermeneutical approach to Vatican II.[20]

A second narrative that has become more vigorous in the last few years sees in Vatican II a council whose major accomplishments were fatally weakened from the very beginning by excessive compromises between the reformers and the conservative forces in the Roman Curia and the church's leadership. This narrative maintains that Vatican II was despoiled of its major results even before it ended. What happened after the council is only the logical consequence of what had happened already at the council. The most important promoter of this narrative is Hans Küng, whose disappointment with Vatican II began already during the council, when he refused the invitation to become involved as a *peritus* in the work of a conciliar commission. He recently disparaged the council's achievements over against "what Vatican II should have said" but did not due to an alleged disconnect between the wishes of the Council Fathers and the texts of the approved documents:

> There is absolutely no decree that completely satisfies me and certainly even most of the bishops. Much of what the Council Fathers had wanted was not included in the decrees. And much of what was accepted in the decrees the Council Fathers did not want. What is lacking almost everywhere in the doctrinal decrees is a solid exegetical and historical foundation—I have often lamented as a fundamental defect the almost total absence of historical-critical exegesis in the council. Often very difficult issues such as Scripture/tradition or primacy/collegiality have been plastered over by diplomatic compromise.[21]

20. See Roberto de Mattei, *Il Concilio Vaticano II: Una storia mai raccontata* (Torino: Lindau, 2010); translations into other languages are forthcoming.

21. "Es gibt überhaupt kein Dekret, das mich und doch wohl auch die meisten Bischöfe ganz befriedigte. Vieles, was die Konzilsväter wollten, ist nicht in die Dekrete aufgenommen worden. Und vieles, was aufgenommen wurde, wollten die Konzils-

A few years after Vatican II (and the publication of his book on papal infallibility),[22] Küng had already expressed his views about the "betrayal" of Vatican II by Pope Paul VI:

> The bishops present there—advised and prompted by theologians—spoke a lot at that time about the breathing of the Holy Spirit; but under another Pope [Paul VI] they returned to their old surroundings and the papal curia tried to correct the mistakes of the new Pope's predecessor and to consolidate afresh its tottering rule over the Roman Empire.[23]

In the 1980s Küng's criticism of Vatican II as a betrayal continued. On the Extraordinary Synod of 1985 he commented: "Has the Second Vatican Council been forgotten, superceded, betrayed? . . . The ecclesiastical bureaucracy is fostering a restoration movement such as has taken hold of other churches, religions, and nations."[24] More recently, he substantially rejected the historians of Vatican II, accusing them not only of failing to take into account his own contribution to the formation of the council agenda (his books *Konzil und Wiedervereinigung* [1959] and *Strukturen der Kirche* [1962]), but also of being complicit with the Vatican and the papacy and thus unable to perceive the real Vatican II.[25]

A third narrative, that of the neoconservatives and neoliberals, emerged in the 1980s, but only recently, after the death of John Paul II and the election of Benedict XVI, has it entered into the discourse of Catholics on Vatican II. This narrative of Vatican II merges elements of the two master narratives—the ultratraditionalist and the ultraliberal. The

---

väter nicht. Fast überall felht mir gerade in den Lehrdekreten—die fast totale Abwesenheit der historisch-kritischen Exegese im Konzil habe ich oft als grundlegenden Mangel beklagt—ein solides exegetisches und historisches Fundament. Öfters sind gerade schwierigste Punkten wie Schrift/Tradition oder Primat/Kollegialität durch diplomatische Kompromisse überkleistert worden" (my translation from Hans Küng, *Erkämpfte Freiheit: Erinnerungen* [Munich: Piper, 2002], 577); for Küng's assessment of the council, see 230–580.

22. See Hans Küng, *Unfehlbar? Eine Anfrage* (Zürich, Einsiedeln, Köln: Benziger, 1970); ET, *Infallible? An Inquiry*, trans. Edward Quinn (Garden City, NY: Doubleday, 1983).

23. Hans Küng, *On Being a Christian*, trans. Edward Quinn (New York: Doubleday, 1976), 36.

24. Hans Küng, "On the State of the Catholic Church—or Why a Book Like This Is Necessary," in *The Church in Anguish: Has the Vatican Betrayed Vatican II?*, ed. Hans Küng and Leonard Swindler (New York: Harper & Row, 1987), 1.

25. Küng, *Erkämpfte Freiheit*, 501, 541.

ultratraditionalist elements come from a very narrow view of the tradition that allows neoconservatives to propagate an interpretation of Catholicism according to the theological and cultural markers of the "long nineteenth century,"[26] and, accordingly, of Vatican II as some kind of pacifist-Communist takeover of Catholicism. The ultraliberal elements come from a Jacobin-Leninist conception (typical of the neoconservative mind-set) of the role of theologians and intellectuals in the church: an *avant garde* that is entitled to move the state of the debate in the church according to a specific and idiosyncratic agenda, championing the rule of an elite over a Catholic population that will never be able to understand their intellectual masters.

The neoconservative narrative of Vatican II is embodied in the writings of Michael Novak, Richard John Neuhaus, and George Weigel, who take their philosophical inspiration from Irving Kristol, particularly his engagement with the philosopher Leo Strauss.[27] This narrative surfaced in the 1980s, coincident with the emergence of a "new breed" of neo-Catholics in the United States. For at least two decades it did not manage to infiltrate the leadership of the Catholic Church, thanks to the personal-biographical contribution of John Paul II to the church's interpretation of Vatican II, especially on the issues *ad extra* (ecumenism, interreligious dialogue, and global justice). But during John Paul's pontificate, a staunch defense of the council in the name of the personal experience of the pontiff as a Council Father did not exclude a sometimes casual labeling of phenomena, movements, and theological insights as the direct "fruit of Vatican II," thus endorsing a kind of Vatican II nominalism coming from the pope. On the other side, the doctrinal policy of Cardinal Joseph Ratzinger never disavowed a clearly conservative reading of Vatican II in the name of literalism: an interpretation of the literal texts of Vatican II aimed at countering the liberal interpretation allegedly based on the "pure spirit" of the council.

For many years the Vatican's doctrinal position on the council was characterized by two partially conflicting visions: John Paul II's fundamentally positive view of the council and Ratzinger's decidedly pessimistic reading of the post–Vatican II period. This "dialogue" of interpretations—at

26. See John O'Malley, *What Happened at Vatican II* (Cambridge, MA: Harvard University, 2008), 53–92.

27. On the intellectual roots of neoconservatives, see Irving Kristol, *The Neoconservative Persuasion: Selected Essays, 1942–2009* (New York: Basic, 2011), especially "Taking Religious Conservatives Seriously" [1994], 292–95), where Kristol defined "the three pillars of modern conservatism" as "religion, nationalism, and economic growth." For the personal experience with Vatican II of one of the leaders of neoconservative discourse in America, see William F. Buckley Jr., *Nearer, My God: An Autobiography of Faith* (New York: Doubleday, 1997), chap. 6, "Disruptions and Achievements of Vatican II."

the beginning under some control of the pope—gradually ceded place to Ratzinger's views. The conclave of 2005 put an end to the dialogue between the two most important interpreters of Vatican II in the first 50 years of its reception and opened a new phase in which the church could no longer count on Ratzinger's interpretation being offset by John Paul's.

In 2005, Ratzinger's accession to the papacy as Benedict XVI helped implant the neoconservative narrative in the vocabulary of the governing elites of Western Catholicism (European and North American especially). This transatlantic migration of the neoconservative narrative (opposite the direction of the migrations of Catholics in North America) has multiple consequences, most of which are still invisible and so far underappreciated. But the starting point of this approach to the issue of the presence of Catholicism in the modern world finds in the attack against Vatican II one of its favorite markers. This new breed of "public theologians" (in some cases, recent converts to Catholicism as their home of choice suited to their social and political conservatism) made the case for the fundamental need to promote the neoconservative interpretation of the First Vatican Council by fashioning a narrative against what Neuhaus called "the councils called Vatican II." In his *The Catholic Moment* (1987), Neuhaus took off from *The Ratzinger Report* (1985) to attack the interpretation of Vatican II coming from "the party of discontinuity." The need to attack these "councils in conflict" comes largely, for Neuhaus, from the fact that

> the cultural, intellectual, and political leadership of the country [the United States] is interested in American Catholicism because it has a stake in American Catholicism. The Catholic wars are surrounded by, and indeed are part of, the larger cultural warfare within American society. Those who view with anxiety the resurgence of fundamentalist and evangelical religion in the public arena view with undisguised alarm the possibility that that resurgence may converge with similar directions in American Catholicism. For such people "Vatican II," however vaguely understood, has become a totem, the last remaining and institutionally most formidable redoubt of a liberalism under conservative assault. . . . In all the changing definitions of sides and alignments, the contest over the interpretation of Vatican II constitutes a critical battlefront in our society's continuing cultural wars.[28]

Weigel inaugurated the political anti–Paul VI narrative of Vatican II, finding the positive content only in the council's teaching on religious freedom

28. Richard John Neuhaus, *The Catholic Moment: The Paradox of the Church in the Postmodern World* (San Francisco: Harper & Row, 1987), 61.

and portraying John Paul II's offensive against liberation theology as the much-needed correction against the social teaching of Paul VI and against the narrative connection between the pastoral constitution *Gaudium et spes* and the encyclical *Populorum progressio* (1967).[29] This effort needed to be accompanied by the push against "revisionist" Catholic historiography.[30] In the name of an *aggiornamento* carried by *ressourcement*, Weigel advocated a new "Americanist" reading of Vatican II that was able to push back the social and intellectual agenda of theologians and bishops in the United States in the two decades between 1965 and 1985.[31]

A similar identification of Vatican II with the neoconservative gospel of economic freedom is to be found in Michael Novak, once an enthusiast of Vatican II and a student of Bernard Lonergan at the Pontifical Gregorian University in Rome in the late 1950s.[32] The assessment of Vatican II by this former enthusiast of it could not be starker: "The very meaning of Catholicism as a coherent people with a coherent vision has been threatened. What the barbarian invasions, centuries of primitive village life, medieval plagues and diseases, wars, revolutions, heresies and schisms had failed to do, the Second Vatican Council succeeded in doing."[33]

The Narratives and the History of Vatican II

These narratives about Vatican II were all created in the first 20 years after the council, but also prior to the publication of the most significant contributions of theologians and historians to the scholarship on Vatican II. While the ultratraditionalist narrative kept going as if nothing had hap-

29. For Weigel's comparison between the "glumness" of Paul VI and John Paul II and their interpretations of the social message of Vatican II, see George Weigel, *Catholicism and the Renewal of American Democracy* (New York: Paulist, 1989), 27–44.

30. See George Weigel, *Freedom and Its Discontents: Catholicism Confronts Modernity* (Washington, DC: Ethics and Public Policy Center, 1991), esp. 43, 57, 87, 134–49.

31. See also George Weigel, *The Courage to Be Catholic: Crisis, Reform, and the Future of the Church* (New York: Basic, 2002), esp. 44–47, 220.

32. For a comparison with Novak's early positions, see his *The Open Church: Vatican II, Act II* (New York: Macmillan, 1964), a journalistic account of the events of the second session of the council. Of particular interest is the apologetic "Introduction to the Transaction Edition" (New Brunswick, NJ: Transaction, 2002), where Novak impugns "the spirit of Vatican II," but also—quite inconsequently— says that "for the history of Vatican II, there is no more thorough and scholarly source than *History of Vatican II*, whose general editor is Giuseppe Alberigo, and whose American editor is Joseph Komonchak" (xxxvii).

33. Michael Novak, *Confessions of a Catholic* (San Francisco: Harper & Row, 1983), 8.

pened between 1965 and the beginning of the 21st century (and ultratraditionalists now present themselves—misleadingly—as the "silent majority" of Catholics), both the ultraliberal and neoconservative narratives were fueled by the pivotal moment of the Extraordinary Synod of 1985 and the debate surrounding the synod and its conclusions on one side and the changing role of Catholics in increasingly secularized societies in Europe and North America on the other.

But the synod of 1985 was also the chronological starting point for the major scholarly work on Vatican II, *History of Vatican II*, edited by Giuseppe Alberigo.[34] It is remarkable to see how little these narratives have been touched and modified by the new information made available by Alberigo's international team of historians and theologians.[35] In the mid-1980s, the project for a *History of Vatican II* began at the Institute of Bologna as an attempt of "historicization" (not memorialization) of Vatican II. Leading the project was the consideration that the epochal change taking place in contemporary Catholicism was "the cause and purpose of Vatican II"; the council was "an experience of communion in search of action in the human story that not only affects a few privileged members, but involves the church as such."[36]

The first step of the project concerned the types of sources for the history of Vatican II. The need to resort to historical sources along with the official ones became clear, in order to develop a reconstruction that was as complete and comprehensive as possible. Vatican II was a complex event, as evidenced not only by the monumental official documentation published by the Holy See (*Acta et documenta* and *Acta synodalia*), but also by the unofficial documentation, political and diplomatic sources, and private records of bishops and theologians (projects, draft plans, diaries, correspondence). Such sources were used for publishing the acts of the Council of Trent, the 13-volume *Concilium Tridentinum*: "acta, epistulae, diarii"

34. Giuseppe Alberigo, ed., *Storia del concilio Vaticano II*, 5 vols. (Bologna: Il Mulino 1995–2001); ET, *History of Vatican II*, ed. Joseph Komonchak (Maryknoll, NY: Orbis, 1996–2006); also translated into French, German, Spanish, Portuguese, and Russian.

35. About Giuseppe Alberigo (1926–2007), see *Giuseppe Alberigo (1927–2007): La figura e l'opera storiografica*, a special issue of *Cristianesimo nella storia* 29, no. 3 (September 2008); and Giuseppe Ruggieri, "Lo storico Giuseppe Alberigo (1926–2007)," in *Storici e religione nel novecento italiano*, ed. Daniele Menozzi and Marina Montacutelli (Brescia: Morcelliana, 2011), 33–52.

36. Giuseppe Alberigo, "Il Vaticano II nella storia della chiesa," *Cristianesimo nella storia* 6 (1985): 441–44, at 443 (all translations are mine, unless otherwise indicated).

(proceedings, letters, diaries).[37] In the early stages of this research, the historians on Alberigo's team uncovered, researched, and made available more than 100 unofficial archives, after having inquired about the existence of papers kept by more than 700 persons and institutions connected with the council.[38] The intention of Alberigo and his team was to assume the Vatican II project as a multiyear research effort with no underlying apologetic or polemical purposes. They aimed to write a critically rigorous history of the council, based on archival sources and treating it as a historical event. This work aimed to document a multidimensional history of the council, which would require an interdenominational and intercontinental collaboration to achieve a perception of the "internal" aspects of Vatican II in their relationship with the "external" factors: "It is time to produce a historicization of Vatican II, not to relegate it to a distant past, but to facilitate the overcoming of the apologetical phase of its reception."[39] Alberigo's training under Hubert Jedin in Bonn in the early 1950s and his hands-on experience with the production and reception of Jedin's 4-volume *History of the Council of Trent* superbly qualified Alberigo to attempt a history of Vatican II just three decades after its completion.[40]

Alberigo had developed a reflection on the "hermeneutical criteria for the history of Vatican II" that would inform his work as a conciliar historian under the aspects of scholar, teacher, and Christian:

(1) *The council-event as a canon of interpretation*: Vatican II is much more than the sum of its decisions, since the nature of the assembly and the council have an important role for understanding and for the reception of the council itself. Vatican II is an "event" also because the council was a celebration in the liturgical sense, and trying to understand it without taking into account the nature of the gathering completely misses the point.

(2) *The intention of John XXIII*: Pope John XXIII was planning to convene a council that could set the church again in a position to speak

37. See *Concilium Tridentinum: Diariorum, actorum, epistularum, tractatuum*, 18 tomes in 13 vols., ed. Görres–Gesellschaft (Freiburg im Breisgau: Societas Gorresiana, 1901–2001).

38. See Massimo Faggioli and Giovanni Turbanti, *Il concilio inedito: Fonti del Vaticano II* (Bologna: Il Mulino, 2001).

39. See Giuseppe Alberigo, "Per la storicizzazione del Vaticano II," in *Per la storicizzazione del Vaticano II*, ed. Giuseppe Alberigo and Alberto Melloni, special issue of *Cristianesimo nella storia* 13 (1992): 473–74, at 473.

40. See Hubert Jedin, *Geschichte des Konzils von Trient*, 4 vols. (Freiburg: Herder, 1949–1975).

to modern men and women. He wanted to do this not by sacrificing the essentials of his message and his tradition, but by revising older forms to proclaim more effectively the gospel to the modern world.

(3) *The "pastoral" nature of the council*: The role of Vatican II was not to assuage guilt or to proclaim new dogmas, but at its center was pastoral teaching. The council did also teach, but its pastoral nature made *salus animarum* (the salvation of the souls)—and not the conservation of the old ways—the ultimate goal of theology.

(4) Aggiornamento *as the key goal of the council*: "update" is the effort to know, renew, and reform the cultural, theological, and spiritual patrimony of the church the more effectively to advance the gospel in our time.

(5) *The importance of compromise for interpreting the documents of Vatican II*: No decision of the council is a unique source to produce a "mind," school, or doctrine. The effort of the Council Fathers and conciliar committees to compromise in order to achieve as much consensus as possible (at least a moral consensus) on the texts under discussion greatly influenced the formulation of the final documents.[41]

The 5-volume *History of Vatican II* (and the many other volumes of a series published as its corollary) changed much of what the church knows about specific and very important issues regarding, for example, the "continuity/discontinuity" issue of Vatican II with respect to the tradition, especially thanks to the following new discoveries (among others):[42]

(1) The history of the preparation of the council (1960–1962) and the debate on the rejection of the preparatory schemas drafted by the Roman Curia;[43]

41. Giuseppe Alberigo, "Critères herméneutiques pour une histoire de Vatican II," in *À la veille du Concile Vatican II: Vota et réactions en Europe et dans le Catholicisme oriental* (Leuven: Peeters, 1992), 12–23; now republished in Italian in Giuseppe Alberigo, *Transizione epocale: Studi sul concilio Vaticano II* (Bologna: Il Mulino, 2009), 29–45.

42. See also Giuseppe Alberigo, "L'Histoire du Concile Vatican II: Problèmes et perspectives," in *Vatican II sous le regard des historiens*, ed. Christoph Theobald (Paris: Médiasèvres, 2006), 25–48.

43. See especially Antonino Indelicato, *Difendere la dottrina o annunciare l'Evangelo: Il dibattito nella Commissione centrale preparatoria del Vaticano II* (Genova: Marietti, 1992); Joseph A. Komonchak, "The Struggle for the Council during the Preparation of Vatican II (1960–1962)," in *History of Vatican II*, ed. Giuseppe Alberigo and Joseph A. Komonchak, vol. 1, *Announcing and Preparing Vatican Council II: Toward a New Era in Catholicism* (Maryknoll, NY: Orbis, 1995), 167–356.

(2) the history of the individual documents of Vatican II (constitutions, decrees, declarations) from their first drafts to the final versions, through the work in the conciliar commission and the debates on the floor of the aula of St. Peter;[44]

(3) the fundamental contribution provided by the commissions to the documents of the intersession periods (January to August 1963; January to August 1964; January to August 1965) that until the 1990s had been underestimated, if not neglected, by the scholarship on Vatican II;[45]

(4) the influence of non-Roman and nontheological factors in the decision-making process regarding major documents of Vatican II.[46]

Church History and the Church of Vatican II

Understanding the importance of the councils in Catholic theology requires much more than historical studies: *traditio* is not just *historia*. But if the *traditio* of the teachings of a council in the church goes beyond the passing down of the historical memory of the council as an event, this *traditio* is surely not detached from the kind of historical studies dedicated to the councils and cultivated by the church that celebrated them. In the last 30 years the historiography on Vatican II has offered the global church a valuable patrimony of studies necessary to know and understand what happened at Vatican II. But the narratives—especially the above-mentioned three master narratives: the ultratraditionalist, the ultraliberal, and the neoconservative—have not changed a bit. Their "spin" on the council has been untouched by what we now know about Vatican II— things we

44. See Massimo Faggioli, "Concilio Vaticano II: Bollettino bibliografico (2000–2002)," *Cristianesimo nella storia* 24 (2003): 335–60; "Concilio Vaticano II: Bollettino bibliografico (2002–2005)," *Cristianesimo nella storia* 26 (2005): 743–67; Faggioli, "Council Vatican II: Bibliographical Overview 2005–2007," *Cristianesimo nella storia* 29 (2008): 567–610; "Council Vatican II: Bibliographical Overview 2007–2010," *Cristianesimo nella storia* 32 (2011): 755–91.

45. See Jan Grootaers, "The Drama Continues between the Acts: The 'Second Preparation' and Its Opponents," in *History of Vatican II*, 2:359–514; Evangelista Vilanova, "The Intersession," in *History of Vatican II*, 3:347–490; Riccardo Burigana and Giovanni Turbanti, "The Intersession: Preparing the Conclusion of the Council," in *History of Vatican II*, 4:453–615.

46. See especially Alberto Melloni, *L'Altra Roma: Politica e S. Sede durante il Concilio Vaticano II, 1959–1965* (Bologna: Il Mulino, 2000); Stephen Schloesser, "Against Forgetting: Memory, History, Vatican II," *Theological Studies* 67 (2006): 275–319.

did not know before and when those narratives were developed. On the contrary, these narratives have only become louder in the last few years because of the struggle to control the recent past of the church beginning already in the years following the First Vatican Council. It is worth recalling what Francis Oakley wrote recently about his attempt to access the "repressed memory" of conciliarism—the theological foundations of the councils of the 14th to 15th centuries that saved the church from a papacy gone astray with the Great Western Schism—against the "papalist narrative" dominant until the 1950s:

> But in so doing I am acutely conscious of the fact that I will be arguing in the teeth of the high papalist constitutive narrative successfully installed, in the wake of Vatican I, not only in Catholic historiography but also in our general histories at large. Only in the past forty to fifty years at most has the revisionist process begun finally to gain traction and to succeed in calling into question that established narrative.[47]

All that has become evident in today's theological debate, as well as in the public posture of the Holy See toward the topic of Vatican II from the end of John Paul II's pontificate and the beginning of Benedict XVI's. Already in 1997 members of the entourage of the Roman Curia, feeling more secure in the decline of John Paul II's pontificate, began expressing more vocally their prior criticism of the volumes of *History of Vatican II* edited by Giuseppe Alberigo, because *History of Vatican II* challenged the favored narrative.[48]

This initially quiet reaction against the international, multiauthored, and respected historiographical work on Vatican II (polemically labeled "the

47. Francis Oakley, "The Conciliar Heritage and the Politics of Oblivion," in *The Church, the Councils, and Reform: The Legacy of the Fifteenth Century*, ed. Gerald Christianson, Thomas M. Izbicki, and Christopher M. Bellitto (Washington, DC: Catholic University of America, 2008), 82–97, at 85.

48. See Agostino Marchetto's review of *History of Vatican II*, vol. 2, in *Osservatore Romano*, November 13, 1997, and in *Apollinaris* 70 (1997): 331–51 (republished in Agostino Marchetto, *Il Concilio Ecumenico Vaticano II: Contrappunto per la sua storia* [Vatican City: Libreria Editrice Vaticana, 2005], 102–19). All the other historians and theologians had reviewed *History of Vatican II* favorably: from the same "Roman milieu," see, e.g., Giacomo Martina, in *La Civiltà Cattolica* 147, pt. 2 (1996): 153–60, and in *Archivum historiae pontificiae* 35 (1997): 356–59. On the reception of *History of Vatican II*, see Alberto Melloni, "Il Vaticano II e la sua storia: Introduzione alla nuova edizione, 2012–2014," in *Storia del Concilio Vaticano II*, ed. Giuseppe Alberigo, 2nd ed., vol. 1 (Bologna: Il Mulino, 2012), ix–lvi.

Bologna School") became gradually more visible over time and especially after 2005, but it never acquired a real scholarly standing as an alternative to the international research on Vatican II. The absence of Roman Curia theologians from the debate has been replaced by the political interpretation of Vatican II by curial officials—high-ranking members and cardinals included. Only a few historians and theologians active at the Vatican in Rome have taken part in serious debate.

A growing radicalization of positions around the council is perceivable during the pontificate of Benedict XVI: both the anti-Vatican II sentiment typical of traditionalism, closer and closer to the Lefebvrian narrative about the council as a total "rupture,"[49] and the ultraliberals' disappointment with Vatican II as a failed promise[50] have become typical of these times. The indirect, silent, and benevolent approval by some cardinals and bishops of the Lefebvrites' narrative on Vatican II has been undoubtedly a side effect (much wished by some in Rome and in Catholic traditionalist quarters) of the reconciliation talks with the Society of St. Pius X, especially since 2009.[51] Quite recently, Catholic ultratraditionalist intellectuals, ideologically much closer to the Lefebvrites than to the Roman "official" interpretation of Vatican II as an event of "continuity and reform," have been given honors and venues by prelates of the Roman Curia.[52]

The rise of the narratives in today's church has intellectually weakened the awareness of Vatican II as a historical event. Even worse, "politically," that is, from the church government standpoint, the rise of the narratives is weakening the idea of Vatican II as a "reform council":[53] for the ultratraditionalist narrative, Vatican II was a council of complete and illegitimate rupture from the past; for the ultraliberal narrative it was a totally failed promise; for the neoconservative narrative it was merely the ushering in of an agenda of economic freedom. This crisis of the consensus around

49. See *Penser Vatican II quarante ans après*: Actes du VIe congrès théologique de "Sì Sì No No" (Versailles: Courrier de Rome, 2004); and Dominic Bourmaud, *Cent ans de modernisme: Généalogie du concile Vatican II* (Étampes: Clovis, 2003).

50. Typical of this sentiment are some passages of Hans Küng's memoirs, *My Struggle for Freedom* (Grand Rapids, MI: Eerdmans, 2003).

51. See Peter Hünermann, ed., *Exkommunikation oder Kommunikation? Der Weg der Kirche nach dem II. Vatikanum und die Pius-Brüder* (Freiburg: Herder, 2009).

52. See Giovanni Miccoli, *La chiesa dell'anticoncilio: I tradizionalisti alla riconquista di Roma* (Rome: Laterza, 2011), 234–334.

53. O'Malley, *What Happened at Vatican II*, 300.

Vatican II is a crisis for the authority of the council that has spilled over into the credibility of the church as such.[54]

What is happening to the role of Vatican II in today's church and to the appreciation of the council as a decisive moment to engage the challenges facing Catholicism today has many roots; here it is possible to offer only a few hypotheses.

One possible cause is the backlog of post–Vatican II reforms that have been piling up between the pontificates of Paul VI and John Paul II: for example, the stop-and-go about the reform of the Roman Curia and the role of the papacy in the church (especially after John Paul II's encyclical *Ut unum sint*, 1995) in the direction of a decentralization in an increasingly globalized Catholicism. So many expectations regarding the power of Vatican II to reform the church have been disappointed, such that it has become easy for the ones who never believed in Vatican II as a real reform council to blame it for what happened *after* Vatican II.

A second probable reason is that the end of the first "global pontificate," John Paul II's, has given way to a surge in the new Westernization of the Catholic Church. This development and the crisis of the theory of secularization have left Catholicism with no defense against the outbreak of a theologically worded "culture war": the so-called "revanche de Dieu" has taken the form of a "revanche contre Vatican II" in Western Catholicism, especially among the younger generations of seminarians and priests.

Third, one difference between the force of the narratives on Vatican II and the previous councils is that Vatican II and contemporary theological discourse in Catholicism operate in a completely new environment: we live in a "mass society" and a "mass culture" that make historical scholarship more exposed to ideological manipulation. This also meets an idea of the church that was recast by Vatican II in a more embracing and participative fashion. In this new self-understanding of the church, the power of the old elites (Catholic bishops, theologians, and historians included) is weaker than before. This makes the history of Vatican II a more debated project, not a shared enterprise as it was for previous councils.

Finally, the crisis of the historical awareness of Catholics about Vatican II is a symptom of the crisis of church history as an academic discipline cultivated in pontifical universities, theological seminaries, departments of

54. See Andreas Battlogg, "Ist das Zweite Vatikanum Verhandlungsmasse?," *Stimmen der Zeit* 227 (2009): 649–50; Wolfgang Beinert, "Nur pastoral oder dogmatisch verpflichtend? Zur Verbindlichkeit des Zweiten Vatikanischen Konzils," *Stimmen der Zeit* 228 (2010): 3–15.

Catholic theology and religious studies, and also in history departments of non-Catholic academic institutions of higher education and research. The debate between Alberigo and Jedin about the status of church history as a "theological discipline" has now, at the beginning of the 21st century, very few descendants still dealing professionally with church history.[55] The crisis of church history in Catholic culture, compared to the golden age of church historians between Vatican I and Vatican II, means the escalating risk of leaving recent church history, and especially Vatican II, in the hands of "theological pundits" (journalists in the best of cases; bloggers in the worst) whose agenda is far more influenced by nontheological factors. The fact that church history has its own specificity but is part of global history is now rejected by many—as if it were intellectually possible to go back to the apologetics of *historia ecclesiastica*—on the grounds of a neo-Augustinian ecclesiology that sees the church not *in the modern world*, but opposed to it. In these last 50 years after Vatican II, there have not been conflicting *histories* but conflicting *narratives* at work on the interpretation of the council.[56] All the experts know that there is no trustworthy alternative, at least so far, to the history of Vatican II written in the last 20 years and represented by Alberigo, Komonchak, and O'Malley. In this cultural and theological environment, church historians have been accused of "discontinuism," of being uninterested in the tradition, that is, in Catholicism's past. But it is clear now, at 50 years from the opening of Vatican II, that those not interested in recovering the past—as well as tradition in its entirety—are actually the ideologues of the "narratives" on Vatican II, and certainly not church historians.[57]

55. See Hubert Jedin, *Chiesa della fede: Chiesa della storia* (Brescia: Morcelliana, 1972), especially "Storia della chiesa come storia della salvezza" and "La storia della chiesa è teologia e storia," 35–40 and 51–65. Contra Jedin's view of church history as a theological discipline, see Giuseppe Alberigo, "Conoscenza storica e teologia," *Römische Quartalschrift* 80 (1985): 207–22; and "Méthodologie de l'histoire de l'Église en Europe," *Revue d'histoire ecclésiastique* 81 (1986): 401–20.

56. About the development of the debate, see Massimo Faggioli, *Vatican II: The Battle for Meaning* (New York: Paulist, 2012).

57. "Some modern intellectuals believe, like many social historians, that, as Alan Megill put it, we are now 'under the reign of discontinuity': that, in short, to be 'modern' means, among other things, to recognize the irrelevance of the past. This sense of a break with the past, particularly on the part of alienated intellectuals, is not, however, to be confused with discontinuity itself; indeed, as a repetition of similar attitudes, for example among Renaissance humanists, it reflects, in a radical form, one possible attitude to the past perhaps unique to Western culture" (Bouwsma, *A Usable Past*, 6).

Church history as a "public utility"—an intellectual discipline providing a "public service" to the world of knowledge—is far from being without problems, but it certainly does not have more problems than the apparently more neutral "religious history." The intention of serving the church by discovering and publishing what happened at Vatican II was and is part of the intention of church historians researching Vatican II.[58] In this moment of passage between the *memory* of Vatican II and a dangerously sterilized *memorialization* of it,[59] church historians try, with their own scientific method, to remind the church "how much purposeful forgetting—repression or amnesia—is required to make a case for continuity."[60] The main difference between the history and the narratives of Vatican II is that the former keeps track also of the forgotten things.

58. See Hervé Legrand, "Relecture et é valuation de l'*Histoire du Concile Vatican II* d'un point de vue ecclésiologique," in *Vatican II sous le regard des historiens*, 49–82; John W. O'Malley, "Vatican II: Did Anything Happen?," in *Vatican II: Did Anything Happen?*, 52–91, esp. 52–59.

59. See Enrico Galavotti, "Le beatificazioni di Benedetto XVI e il mausoleo del Vaticano II," *Il margine* 30, no. 2 (2010): 22–33.

60. Schloesser, "Against Forgetting," 277.

4 Does Vatican II Represent Continuity or Discontinuity?

GERALD O'COLLINS, SJ

*The article examines changes in teaching and practice endorsed by Vatican II. What "combination of continuity and discontinuity" (Pope Benedict XVI) shaped those reforms? Several conciliar documents set out principles guiding the changes by retrieving neglected traditions (*ressourcement*) and bringing the church's life up to date (*aggiornamento*). The article suggests going beyond such schemes as "changing forms and permanent principles" or changes in "nonessentials but not in essentials" and instead recognizing that the council embraced reform with a view to renewing the church's apostolic identity.*

On the occasion of the 50th anniversary of Vatican II (1962–1965), publications, conferences, and other events probe and celebrate its achievements. What has the council represented in the history of Christianity and how should it be evaluated? The council obviously brought far-reaching changes in the life of the Catholic Church and in its relationship with "the others." Has this change involved discontinuity with past teaching and practice? Or are the changes compatible with claims about Vatican II's being in (total?) continuity with what went before? An address by Pope Benedict XVI to the Roman Curia on December 22, 2005, reinvigorated the debate about this issue.[1]

1. *Acta apostolicae sedis* (*AAS*) 98 (2006): 40–53; ET, "Interpreting Vatican II: Address to the Roman Curia," *Origins* 35 (2006): 534–39. Apropos of this address, see Massimo Faggioli, *Vatican II: The Battle for Meaning* (Mahwah, NJ: Paulist, 2012), 109–12; Joseph A. Komonchak, "Novelty in Continuity: Pope Benedict's Interpretation of Vatican II," *America* 200, no. 3 (February 2, 2009): 10–14, 16. An expanded

In that address the pope contrasted two contrary hermeneutics: "a hermeneutic of discontinuity and rupture" over against "a hermeneutic of reform, of renewal in the continuity of the subject-church that the Lord has given us. She is the subject that increases in time and develops yet always remains the same." The pope, however, went on to bring together "discontinuity," "reform," and "continuity" but not "rupture" when he said, "It is precisely [in a] combination of continuity and discontinuity at different levels that the very nature of reform consists."[2]

How might we understand and interpret "continuity" and "discontinuity," as well as the closely related language of "reform," "renewal," "review," "revise," and "rupture"? What reasons have we to recognize continuity and discontinuity? We should pay adequate attention to *both* continuity *and* discontinuity,[3] unlike many contributors to *Vatican II: Renewal within Tradition* who failed to face up to the elements of discontinuity found in the council's 16 documents.[4] Renewal and innovation are unthinkable without some measure of discontinuity, at least discontinuity with the recent and not-so-recent past. We need to examine in detail those texts if we are going to construct a well-founded position on the continuity and/or discontinuity that they embody. No position here will be convincing unless it recognizes the amount of change Vatican II ushered in. To introduce the discussion, I turn first to what the council itself had

---

version of this article ("Benedict XVI and the Interpretation of Vatican II") is found in *The Crisis of Authority in Catholic Modernity*, ed. Michael J. Lacey and Francis Oakley (New York: Oxford University, 2011), 93–110; the section of the pope's address that concerns interpreting Vatican II is reprinted in ibid., 357–62. See also John W. O'Malley, "Vatican II: Did Anything Happen?," *Theological Studies* 67 (2006): 3–33; O'Malley, *What Happened at Vatican II* (Cambridge, MA: Harvard University, 2008); Neil Ormerod, "Vatican II—Continuity or Discontinuity? Toward an Ontology of Meaning," *Theological Studies* 67 (2010): 609–36.

2. Benedict XVI, "Interpreting Vatican II," 536, 538. As Komonchak remarks, "A hermeneutics of reform, it turns out, acknowledges some important discontinuities" ("Novelty in Continuity," 13). In fact, if there were no discontinuity, there could be no reform. Moreover, unless discontinuity amounts to *total* discontinuity, there could be no real rupture or complete break. For a rich, historical reflection on the language of reform(ation), its partial equivalents, and its use by the pope in his December 2005 address, see John W. O'Malley, "'The Hermeneutic of Reform': A Historical Analysis," *Theological Studies* 73 (2012): 517–46.

3. See Ormond Rush, *Still Interpreting Vatican II: Some Hermeneutical Principles* (Mahwah, NJ: Paulist), 79–80.

4. Matthew L. Lamb and Matthew Levering, eds., *Vatican II: Renewal within Tradition* (New York: Oxford University, 2008); see Komonchak, "Benedict XVI and the Interpretation of Vatican II," 110 n. 22; and Komonchak, "Rewriting History," *Commonweal* 31, no. 2 (January 30, 2009): 22–24.

to say about continuity and discontinuity in the changes it mandated, and examine, in particular, 3 of its 16 documents.

What the Council Said about Changes

The Constitution on the Sacred Liturgy

The first document to be approved and promulgated by Vatican II was *Sacrosanctum concilium* (*SC*), the Constitution on the Sacred Liturgy (December 4, 1963). It is in the liturgical changes prescribed by the council and introduced later that the question of continuity/discontinuity would become most visible. How did Vatican II understand and express what it was doing in changing the liturgy and revising the rites?

In commenting on the constitution, Josef Jungmann wrote of its aiming at the "renewal of liturgical life," the "revival" and "reform" of the liturgy, and, in particular, the "reform of the Mass."[5] Yet, while closely related and often overlapping, "renewal," "revival," and "reform" are not strictly synonyms, if indeed any completely synonymous terms ever truly exist. Let us look at the terms the council used to describe its teaching on the liturgy and the changes ushered in by that teaching.[6]

In one place the constitution speaks of "reviewing/revising [*recognoscantur*]" the rites and "giving them new vigor [*novo vigore donentur*]" (no. 4). In another article, it prescribes that the "prayer of the faithful" should "be restored [*restituatur*]" (no. 53). But the favored term was *instaurare*, which means "to renew" or "to restore."

Thus the very first article speaks of the council's commitment "to renew and foster the Liturgy [*instaurandam atque fovendam Liturgiam*]."[7] In

5. Josef Jungmann, "Constitution on the Sacred Liturgy," trans. Lalit Adolphus, in *Commentary on the Documents of Vatican II*, 5 vols., ed. Herbert Vorgrimler (New York: Herder & Herder, 1967–1969), 1:1–88, at 2, 6, 8, 31.

6. *SC*, as Massimo Faggioli has argued, proved to be a "pillar" of the council's eucharistic ecclesiology (*Ecclesia de Eucharistia*), which has rediscovered "the centrality of Scripture" and, one can add, the central image of the church as the (worshiping) people of God (see *SC* no. 33). Faggioli also recognizes how the liturgical constitution prepared the way for the *rapprochement* manifestoes of Vatican II (*Unitatis redintegratio*, *Nostra aetate*, and *Gaudium et spes*) and initiated the council's *ressourcement* procedure (see below). In short, he champions "a hermeneutics of the council based on *Sacrosanctum concilium*" (Massimo Faggioli, "*Sacrosanctum concilium* and the Meaning of Vatican II," *Theological Studies* 1 [2010]: 437–52, at 450–52).

7. Walter M. Abbott and Joseph Gallagher, eds., *The Documents of Vatican II* (New York: America, 1965), translate the passage as providing for "the renewal and fostering of the liturgy" (137). In *Vatican II: The Conciliar and Post Conciliar Documents*, rev. ed., ed. Austin Flannery (Northport, NY: Costello, 1988), 1, this becomes undertaking "the

reverse order the two verbs recur in article 3, where the constitution indicates that it will introduce principles and norms concerned "with the fostering and renewing of the Liturgy [*de fovenda atque instauranda Liturgia*]." Chapter 1 puts the same verbs into its title: "On general principles for the renewal and fostering of the sacred Liturgy [*De principiis generalibus ad sacram Liturgiam instaurandam atque fovendam*]." Later, in no. 21 of chapter 1, *SC* uses the noun *instauratio* when indicating its "desire to undertake with great care the general renewal of the Liturgy itself [*ipsius Liturgiae generalem instaurationem sedulo curare cupit*]." Similar words provide the heading for section three: "On the renewal of the sacred Liturgy [*De sacrae Liturgiae instauratione*]." But two translations, those edited by Walter Abbott (with Joseph Gallagher) and Austin Flannery, both render the chapter heading as "The Reform of the Sacred Liturgy."[8] The translation edited by Norman Tanner rightly makes the heading "The Renewal of the Liturgy," but then presses on at once to render "*Liturgiae generalem instaurationem*" as "a general reform of the liturgy" (2:825). The constitution prefers, however, to present its task in the language of *instaurare* and *instauratio* and not in that of *reformare* and *reformatio*.

Unitatis redintegratio (*UR*), the Decree on Ecumenism, promulgated a year after the Constitution on the Liturgy, famously introduced the terminology of "reformation" when calling not only for a "renewal (*renovatio*)" of the church but also for her "constant reformation [*perennem reformationem*]" (no. 6). The lexical meaning of "*reformare*" is (a) "to transform" or "change radically for the better" and (b), simply and less dramatically, "to restore." Inevitably, however, in *UR*, a decree dealing in part with churches and ecclesial communities that came into existence in the 16th century, to speak of "reformation" inevitably conjures up nuances of "improving by removing faults and errors."

---

reform and promotion of the liturgy." But the original text does not read "*reformandam atque promovendam liturgiam*." In Norman Tanner, ed., *Decrees of the Ecumenical Councils*, 2 vols. (Washington, DC: Georgetown University, 1990), the phrase is rendered as "the renewal and growth of the liturgy" (2:820), and then "*de fovenda atque instauranda Liturgia*" (no. 3) is translated as "the renewal and progress of the liturgy" (820). But *fovere* means "foster" or "nourish"; the result will or can be "growth" and "progress." Somewhat dissatisfied with the Abbott, Flannery, and Tanner translations, I use my own translations throughout this article.

8. Flannery (p. 9) follows Abbott (p. 146) in rendering *Liturgiae generalem instaurationem* as "a general restoration of the liturgy," and, when *instauratione* recurs later in no. 21, again both render it as "restoration." Where *SC* puts "Liturgy" in the upper case, Abbott, Flannery, and Tanner persistently reduce it to lower case.

Putting matters within the focus of this article, however, one can ask: where the decision is taken through the liturgical constitution to give up some things, remove certain faults and even errors, and change matters radically for the better, are we not facing a situation of "reformation"? Without using the explicit language of "reformation" or "reform," *SC* gave up certain things (e.g., the obligatory use of the Latin language in the Roman rite [no. 36]), prescribed the removal of such faulty things as "useless repetitions" in the liturgy (no. 34; see no. 50), and wanted to change liturgical matters radically for the better by, for instance, introducing the Scriptures more abundantly and with a better representation from all "the treasures of the Bible" (no. 51). In fact, by allowing the liturgy to be celebrated in the vernacular, by stressing "the table of God's word" along with the importance of the homily (no. 52), and by granting to the laity—although restricted to certain circumstances—communion "under both kinds" (no. 55), Vatican II conceded the demands of Martin Luther and other 16th-century Protestant reformers, albeit in the 20th century. In short, while *SC* did not use explicitly the language of "reform" or "reformation," what it enacted can and should be described in those terms.[9]

In pressing for the renewal (or reform) of the liturgy, *SC* prescribed a revision "according to the mind of healthy tradition (*ad mentem sanae traditionis*)," which might give the rites new vigor "for the sake of today's circumstances and needs" (no. 4). The twin principles recurred in a later article that spoke of both "retaining healthy tradition" and "opening the way to legitimate progress" (no. 23). This was to set up two procedures: retrieving healthy tradition inherited from the past and discerning what present conditions call for. Thus the two procedures, retrieval (*ressourcement*) and updating to meet pastoral needs in the new contexts of the modern world (the *aggiornamento* that Pope John XXIII called for when convoking the council), featured right in the introduction to the first document promulgated by Vatican II. Some people continue to present *ressourcement* and *aggiornamento* as if they were opposed principles and procedures. But this is a mistake: remembering and recovering forgotten or neglected teaching and practice from the Scriptures and the great tradition serve the church's adaptation in the present and progress into the future. The postconciliar liturgical changes offer spectacular examples of the two procedures working in tandem: for instance, the Second

9. Hence recent calling into question of some of the changes mandated by *SC* have been widely called "the reform of the reform"; see Faggioli, *Vatican II: The Battle for Meaning*, 102–5.

Eucharistic Prayer retrieved from the *Apostolic Tradition* of Hippolytus (d. ca. 236);[10] the restoration of the ancient Rite of Christian Initiation of Adults (no. 64); and the reintroduction of the "prayer of the faithful," based on 1 Timothy 2:1-2 and now restored after the gospel reading and homily (no. 53). The process of retrieval concerns a major resource for renewal, whereas the task of *aggiornamento* may include retrieval but always involves discerning what should be changed and what should be introduced as being pastorally desirable. Thus *ressourcement* and *aggiornamento*, far from being in competition, are different but complementary principles and procedures, with the former often, but not always, making a major contribution to the latter.[11]

These two principles could be translated in terms of inherited *tradition* and contemporary *experience*. The constitution prescribes taking into account "the general laws of the structure and intention" of the liturgy (which obviously derive from Christian tradition), and doing so in the light of "the experience coming from more recent liturgical renewal" (no. 23). The spirit of *ressourcement* encourages retrieving healthy traditions that have fallen into abeyance,[12] while the spirit of *aggiornamento* encourages discerning the contemporary experience of liturgy and other areas of Christian life and practice.

When introducing norms for the renewal (or reform) of the liturgy and, in particular, what *aggiornamento* entailed, *SC* distinguished in the liturgy between (a) "a part that cannot be changed, inasmuch as it is divinely instituted [*parte immutabili, utpote divinitus instituta*]," and (b) "parts that are subject to change [*partibus mutationi obnoxiis*]." Apropos of (b), the constitution added at once that these parts can and indeed ought to be changed, "if by chance there have crept into them things that might respond less well to the inner nature of the liturgy or that might have become less suitable [than they once were]." After dealing with elements that might be inappropriate or unsuitable, the document pressed ahead to express what it positively expected from the renewal of the rites. They should, in their revised form, "express more clearly [*clarius exprimant*] the holy things that

10. See "The Apostolic Tradition," in *The Oxford Dictionary of the Christian Church*, ed. Frank Leslie Cross, 3rd ed., ed. Elizabeth Anne Livingstone (New York: Oxford University, 2005), 92.

11. See Gabriel Flynn and Paul Murray, eds., Ressourcement*: A Movement for Renewal in Twentieth-Century Catholic Theology* (New York: Oxford University, 2012).

12. Thus *SC* prescribed that valuable elements in the rites, which had been lost over the centuries, "should be restored (*restituantur*)."

they signify," so that "the Christian people" can "understand [these things] easily and share in them through a community celebration that is full, active and proper" (no. 21). In this way *SC* set out the principles governing the changes in the liturgy that a discerning *aggiornamento* calls for.[13]

The document came back to these principles when treating the sacraments (other than the Eucharist) and the sacramentals (chap. 3). It noted how "in the course of time, there have crept into the rites of the sacraments and sacramentals certain things by which their nature and purpose have become less clear [*minus eluceant*] in our days." Hence "there is much more need to adapt certain things in them [the rites] to the needs of our age" (no. 62). With the aim of purging what is unsuitable and fails to communicate clearly and of adapting to the needs of our times (*aggiornamento*), the constitution then enjoined that the rites of baptism, confirmation, penance, the "anointing of the sick" (a new name to replace "Extreme Unction"), ordination, marriage, and various sacramentals (e.g., the rites for burial) should be "reviewed/revised [*recognoscantur*]" (nos. 66–82). Over and over again the reason given for such changes was to let significant elements at the heart of the rites "become clearer [*magis pateant*]" (no. 67), to indicate them "more openly and more suitably [*apertius et congruentius*]" (no. 69), to express them "more clearly [*clarius*]" (no. 72), and to "signify more clearly [*clarius*] the grace of the sacrament" (no. 77). The desire for the rites to exercise more successfully their pedagogical function motivated and fashioned the far-reaching changes being prescribed.

Finally, two further principles were consciously operative to shape the changes the constitution envisaged. First, there were to be "no innovations unless a true and certain advantage of the church requires it [*innovationes ne fiant nisi vera et certa utilitas Ecclesiae id exigat*]." In other words, changes were not to be admitted unless obvious needs demanded them; and still less did *SC* tolerate change for its own sake. Second, and more importantly for the scope of what I am examining, "new forms should in some way *grow organically* from the already existing forms [*novae*

13. In "Theologischer Kommentar zur Konstitution über die heilige Liturgie, *Sacrosanctum Concilium*," *Herders theologischer Kommentar zum Zweiten Vatikanischen Konzil*, 5 vols., ed. Peter Hünermann and Bernd Jochen Hilberath (Freiburg im Breisgau: Herder, 2004–2005), Reiner Kaczynski sums up the prescriptions of no. 21: "the outer form of the liturgical celebration must allow its inner content to be experienced, in order that the community can in the easiest way possible grasp [this content] and celebrate the divine service with a fuller, more active, and more community [-oriented] participation" (1:87; translation mine).

formae ex formis iam exstantibus organice *quodammodo* crescant]" (no. 23, emphasis added).[14]

The first principle expressed the good sense enshrined in the proverbial wisdom of the question, "If it works, why fix it?" The second moves us toward John Henry Newman's first "note of a genuine development, preservation of type," which is "readily suggested by the analogy of physical growth." Newman explains this analogy of organic development as follows:

> The parts and proportions of the developed form, however altered, correspond to those which belong to its rudiments. The adult animal has the same make as it had on its birth; young birds do not grow into fishes, nor does the child degenerate into the brute, wild or domestic, of which he is by inheritance lord.

To clinch his case, Newman quotes Vincent of Lerins, who adopted the same analogy to illustrate the development of doctrine: "Let the soul's religion imitate the law of the body, which, as years go on, develops indeed and opens out its due proportions, and yet remains identically what it was. Small are the baby's limbs, a youth's are larger, yet they are the same."[15] Thus organic growth illustrates classically how, along with many obvious changes in size, in the capacity to do things, and in other regards, animals, birds, and human beings remain the same, identical beings. While passing through radical alterations, a certain correspondence persists between their rudimentary shape and their mature form. An unbroken succession or organic continuity links together the different stages of their lives and maintains their uninterrupted identity. Along with innumerable "alterations," which we might call "secondary discontinuities," at no point do they suffer a radical discontinuity, a deep break or "rupture" that would sever the connection with their past and cause them to go out of existence.

To sum up, *SC* never explicitly raises the question of continuity versus discontinuity. Nevertheless, on the one hand, the comprehensive and far-

14. When commenting on no. 23, Kaczynski has nothing to say about the "organic" analogy of development; he contents himself with remarking that "liturgical renewal stands in the field of tension between the preservation of healthy tradition and courageous, justified progress" ("Theologischer Kommentar," 89; translation mine).

15. John Henry Newman, *An Essay on the Development of Christian Doctrine* (New York: Doubleday, 1960), 177; Newman cites Vincent of Lerin's *Commonitorium*, 9. After proposing "preservation of type" as his first "note of a genuine development," Newman suggests a second, which also enjoys obvious relevance to the issue of appropriate liturgical change: "the continuity of principles" (*Essay*, 183–89) or what he calls "the continuous identity of principles" (ibid., 309–36, at 312).

reaching changes it mandates cannot be reconciled with any thesis of total continuity. On the other hand, it obviously rules out any suggestion of total discontinuity, in particular by insisting that "the divinely instituted part of the liturgy cannot be changed."[16] After mediating between tradition (*ressourcement*) and experience (from which discerning eyes can conclude to suitable and even necessary changes), the constitution aims at giving the rites new vigor and enhancing their pedagogical function. Throughout, *SC* embodies a deep pastoral desire to renew the church by renewing her liturgy. Like a growing organism, the liturgy can preserve an unbroken continuity with the past, but it will be a continuity amenable to widespread external adaptations and inner changes.

The Decree on the Up-to-Date Renewal of Religious Life

In the immediate aftermath of the Second Vatican Council, Friedrich Wulf wrote prophetically about one major area of renewal: "the Council's Decree on the Appropriate Renewal of Religious Life, despite its shortness and shortcomings, is a turning point in the history of religious orders" and "will, indeed, initiate that turning, the full sweep of which cannot yet be seen."[17] Whatever we conclude if we work our way through the stories of various religious institutes over the past 50 years, Wulf was correct in observing that the decree, *Perfectae caritatis* (*PC*), introduced into those institutes "a new theological and spiritual mentality."[18] In fashioning and promoting such a mentality, this document clearly endorsed two principles for change: *ressourcement* and *aggiornamento*. It emphasized that "an updated renewal of religious life comprises *both* a continual return to the sources of the whole Christian life and to the original inspiration of the institutes *and* their adaptation to the changed conditions of the times." Starting from the "supreme rule," "the following of Christ proposed in the Gospel," the decree spelled out norms for this renewal, which should be "promoted under the impulse of the Holy Spirit and the guidance of the Church" (no. 2, emphasis added).

The role of *ressourcement* comes into view constantly. Apropos of the prayer life for religious men and women, the decree recommends that

16. *SC* does not specify what comes under such a "divinely instituted" part, but presumably it would include, for instance, the trinitarian formula of baptism (Mt 28:19).

17. Friedrich Wulf, "Decree on the Appropriate Renewal of the Religious Life," trans. Ronald Walls, in *Commentary on the Documents of Vatican II*, 2:301–70, at 370.

18. Ibid., 330. See also Joachim Schmiedl's characterization of *PC* as one component in the larger paradigm shift to be found in Vatican II, in *Das Konzil und die Orden: Krise und Erneuerung des Gottgeweihten Lebens* (Vallendar-Schönstatt: Patis, 1999), 472.

they should "draw from the fitting sources of Christian spirituality." This means drawing not only from the Eucharist but also from daily contact with "the Sacred Scripture, so that by reading and meditating on the divine scriptures they might learn the surpassing knowledge of Jesus Christ (Phil 3:8)" (no. 6). The return to the sources also involves "faithfully recognizing and observing the spirit and particular aims of the founders, as well as the healthy traditions; all of these constitute the patrimony of each institute" (no. 2).

While stressing the indispensable role of "spiritual renewal" (ibid.), the decree called on religious to take into account "the conditions of the times," "the needs of the Church" (ibid.), "the present-day physical and psychological condition of the members," "the requirements of the culture" (no. 3), and so forth. All this amounted to acknowledging the place of *aggiornamento* in changing the legislation and customs that guide the life of religious institutes. *PC* spoke of "right updating/adaptation [*recta accomodatio*]" and of "the norms of an updated/adapted renewal [*normas accomodatae renovationis*]" (no. 4).

"Up-to-date renewal [*accommodata renovatio*]" entered, of course, into the very title of the decree. Abbott renders the two Latin words as "the Appropriate Renewal," whereas Tanner moves further away from the Latin and has "the Sensitive Renewal." Flannery's "the Up-to-date Renewal" opens up memories of John XXIII's call for *aggiornamento* and fills out what kind of "updating/adapting [*accommodatio*]" was intended. The words from the title, "up-to-date renewal [*accommodata renovatio*]," were to recur once in no. 2 and twice in no. 4.

PC initiated wide-ranging changes in religious life. Whatever one's verdict on those changes in postconciliar history, Vatican II fashioned its decree in the light of two principles, *ressourcement* and *aggiornamento*, which amounted to retrieving life-giving traditions and acting on a prayerful discernment of present experience. As with *SC*, these two principles brought about continuity-in-discontinuity, or what Newman might call "preservation of type" in a situation of far-reaching development.

Declaration on Religious Freedom

A third Vatican II document not only introduced change but also explicitly reflected, albeit more briefly, on the dramatic change it was mandating. According to Basil Mitchell, with *Dignitatis humanae* (*DH*), the Declaration on Religious Liberty, promulgated on December 7, 1965, the Catholic Church "finally abandoned the traditional doctrine that 'error has no rights' and embraced a more liberal theory based upon the rights of the person, and the individual's duty to follow his conscience."[19] *DH* went through six drafts before being finally approved on the last working day of the council, with 2,308 votes in favor and 70 votes against. An article that appeared in the Turin-based newspaper, *La Stampa*, spoke not of the church "abandoning" a traditional doctrine and "embracing" a "more liberal theory" but of development of doctrine: "The schema which deals with religious freedom constitutes by itself a genuine development of doctrine, perhaps the greatest and most characteristic progress achieved by the Council."[20]

In teaching the right of individuals to religious liberty—that is to say, their freedom in civil society to worship God according to their conscience—the council "intended to develop [*evolvere*] the teaching of more recent popes about the inviolable rights of the human person and about the juridical regulation of society" (no. 1). The declaration ended by calling this religious freedom "the greatest of the duties and rights of human beings" (no. 15). When, however, we recall how the Syllabus of Errors, published by Pope Pius IX in 1864, excluded public religious freedom, how could the council allege that its declaration represented a development in official teaching? In a footnote that accompanied no. 2, the document cited prior teaching by John XXIII, Pius XII, Pius XI, and Leo XIII. But, pointedly, it did not attempt to enlist any support from Pius IX. The "more recent popes" stopped at Leo XIII (pope 1878–1903). *DH*, when set over against the Syllabus of Errors, looks more like a reversal rather than a development of doctrine.[21]

In the Syllabus of Errors, Pius IX had condemned the proposition that "everyone is free to embrace and profess the religion which by the light of reason one judges to be true."[22] Set this over against the statement from

19. Basil Mitchell, "The Christian Conscience," in *The Oxford Illustrated History of Christianity*, ed. John McManners (New York: Oxford University, 1990), 602–27, at 602–3.

20. Quoted by Pietro Pavan, "Declaration on Religious Freedom," trans. Hilda Graef, in *Commentary on Vatican II* (1969): 4:49–86, at 62. For a thorough treatment of the writing of *DH*, see Silvia Scatena, *La fatica della libertà: L'Elaborazione della dichiarazione "Dignitatis humanae" sulla libertà umana del Vaticano II* (Bologna: Il Mulino, 2003).

21. See Francis A. Sullivan, "Catholic Tradition and Traditions," in *Crisis of Authority in Catholic Modernity*, 113–33, at 126–27. Joseph Ratzinger called *DH*, along with *Nostra aetate* (*NA*) and *Gaudium et spes* (*GS*), "a revision of the *Syllabus* of Pius IX, a kind of counter syllabus" (*Principles of Catholic Theology: Building Stones for a Fundamental Theology*, trans. Mary Frances McCarthy [San Francisco: Ignatius, 1987], 381).

22. *Enchiridion symbolorum, definitionum et declarationum*, 17th ed., ed. Heinrich Denzinger and Peter Hünermann (hereafter DzH) (Freiburg im Breisgau: Herder 1991), 2915; *The Christian Faith in the Doctrinal Documents of the Catholic Church*, 7th ed., ed. Josef Neuner and Jacques Dupuis (hereafter ND) (New York: Alba House, 2001), ND 1013/15.

DH that "the human person has the right to religious freedom" (no. 1). The Syllabus rejected the notion of the Catholic Church's surrendering or losing its position where it enjoyed a monopoly as state church, and so condemned the proposition: "In our age it is no longer advisable that the Catholic religion be the only state religion, excluding all the other cults."[23] For *DH*, "the other cults" were not to be excluded in countries where the Catholic Church or any other religious group was constitutionally recognized: "If in view of the particular circumstances of peoples, special recognition is assigned in the constitution to one religious community, the right of all citizens and religious communities to freedom in religious matters must at the same time be recognized and respected" (no. 6).

Earlier in its introduction, *DH* showed its readiness to hear the voices of our times (*Gaudium et spes* [*GS*] no. 44) and, in particular, the widespread "desires [*appetitiones*]" for "the free exercise of religion in society." The council "declared" these desires to be "in conformity with truth and justice" (*DH* no. 1). Later the text observed not only that "people of today want to be able to profess their religion in public and in private," but also that "religious liberty is already declared a civil right in many constitutions and solemnly recognized in international documents" (no. 15).[24] When *DH* disclosed its intention of catching up with the true and just concerns of contemporary humanity, the spirit of *aggiornamento* came into view.

But then at once, in the spirit of *ressourcement*, the council announced that it would "examine the sacred tradition and doctrine of the church, from which it produces new things always consistent (*congruentia*) with the old" (ibid.).[25] Obviously *DH* produced something strikingly "new," by insisting that governments should safeguard religious freedom. But what could be "the old things" that were consistent with this new teaching on

23. DzH 2977; ND 1103/77. In the spirit of "error has no rights," the Syllabus also condemned the proposition: "it is praiseworthy that in some Catholic regions the law has allowed people immigrating there to exercise publicly their own cult" (DzH 2978; ND 1013/78).

24. There is an obvious reference to no. 18 of the 1948 Universal Declaration of Human Rights: "Everyone has the right to freedom of thought, conscience and religion; this right includes freedom to change his religion or belief, and freedom, either alone or in community with others and in public or private, to manifest his religion or belief in teaching, practice, worship and observance."

25. Talking of *nova et vetera* inevitably conjures up the implied signature of the author of Matthew's Gospel, when he speaks about a "scribe trained for the kingdom of heaven bringing out of his treasure what is new and what is old" (Mt 13:52). But the evangelist does not (explicitly) claim that the "new" will be consistent with the "old."

religious freedom? They were certainly not "old things" authorized by the Syllabus of Errors, but rather things known "through the revealed word of God and reason" (no. 2). A later article reversed this order and, following the order in which *DH* treated matters, clarified the role of "reason": (a) "The demands [of human dignity] have become more fully known to human reason through the experience of centuries." (b) Furthermore, "this doctrine of [religious] freedom has roots in divine revelation" (no. 9).

When nos. 2–8 expressed what "centuries" of experience had made known, the declaration appealed to philosophical anthropology and insights into a constitutional order of society, based on justice (no. 3) and "human dignity." That phrase formed the title of the document and recurred in articles 2, 3, and 9. It was from the dignity of the human person created in the divine image that John XXIII in his 1963 encyclical, *Pacem in terris*, had drawn his extensive treatment of natural rights, which concerned such matters as life, education, and religious freedom.[26] This encyclical, cited four times in the footnotes to nos. 2–8, provided a major witness supporting the case for civil authority protecting the inviolable rights of citizens—in particular, religious freedom and equality of all before the law. The *ressourcement* at work in establishing "the general principle of religious freedom" (nos. 2–8) retrieved past teaching but only as far back as Leo XIII.

The process of retrieval showed up much more clearly in what came next, in the theological appeal to the revelation mediated through Christ and his apostles (nos. 9–15). Christ always respected human freedom, and specifically religious freedom, which meant that one's faith could not be coerced. His disciples followed him by maintaining that the human response to God must be free, as well as by asserting their own right to proclaim the Good News (nos. 9–11).[27] As part of this theological defense of religious freedom, *DH* cited the teaching of four Fathers of the Church (from Lactantius to Gregory the Great), as well as that of two medieval popes (Clement III and Innocent III). Here the document might also have referenced Pope Nicholas I. In a letter sent to the ruler of Bulgaria, he rejected any violent means for forcing people to accept the Christian faith, which had just been officially accepted in the country.[28]

26. DzH 3956–72; ND 2026–42.

27. Commenting on this example of *ressourcement*, Benedict XVI judged that the Declaration on Religious Freedom had "recovered the deepest patrimony of the church" by being "in full harmony with the teaching of Jesus himself" ("Interpreting Vatican II," 538).

28. DzH 647–48.

Retrieving the past also involved acknowledging that, while the church maintained the teaching that "no one should be coerced into believing," it had at times behaved in ways "not in keeping with the spirit of the Gospel and even opposed to it" (no. 12). Notoriously in 1252, Pope Innocent IV, in *Ad extirpanda*, authorized the use of torture to force suspected heretics to "confess," retract their errors, and reveal the names of "other heretics."[29] Catholic Christianity countenanced torture during the 13th-century anti-Albigensian crusade and later—all in the cause of maintaining religious unity which underpinned social and political stability. Through the 16th century and beyond, faith commitments were woven into the fabric of life: bishops, rulers, and their officials felt themselves answerable to God for supporting what they believed to be the true religion. Those who spread "heresy" brought eternal ruin on any who accepted their false views, and hence were deemed worse than thieves and murderers.[30] As *DH* acknowledged, it took "the course of time" for "the leaven of the Gospel" to contribute to the conviction that "in religious matters" the human person should be free from any "coercion" (no. 12). This section of *DH*, when retrieving the past, acknowledged past practice that must be judged incompatible with the Christian gospel. The principle of *ressourcement* can operate negatively as well as positively.

By retrieving the teaching and practice of Jesus, *DH* showed how Scripture can correct distorted and false traditions, in particular the long-standing conviction that "errors have no rights." Where *Dei Verbum* (*DV*), the Dogmatic Constitution on Divine Revelation, did not offer guidance about the role of the Scriptures in evaluating and criticizing particular traditions, we find such guidance embodied in *DH* and other Vatican II documents. They illustrated effectively how particular traditions can be corrected and even eliminated by the retrieval of the Scriptures.

Thus far I have examined three documents of Vatican II, which, respectively, mandated changes in the liturgy, updated religious life, and reversed 19th-century papal teaching in order to support religious freedom in civil society. I have shown how, when introducing these changes and so creating some discontinuity with the past, the council consciously invoked two complementary principles: that of *ressourcement* (retrieval of past tradition) and *aggiornamento* (an updating in the light of experience and

29. "Innocent IV, Pope," in *Oxford Dictionary of the Christian Church*, 840.

30. For a cross-confessional study of (mainly) 16th-century Protestant, Anabaptist, and Catholic martyrs, see Brad S. Gregory, *Salvation at Stake: Christian Martyrdom in Early Modern Europe* (Cambridge, MA: Harvard University, 1999).

contemporary society). I turn now to two further documents that brought far-reaching changes but with less self-conscious attention to the underlying principles involved when they embraced innovation.

Some Changes Introduced by Two Further Documents

The Dogmatic Constitution on the Church

Albert Outler called *Lumen gentium* (*LG*), the Dogmatic Constitution on the Church, promulgated on November 21, 1964, "the first full-orbed conciliar exposition of the doctrine of the Church in Christian history."[31] As a perceptive observer of the working of Vatican II, he also judged that "the Council intended the Constitution to be the major resource in the renovation and reform of the Catholic Church."[32] Through what changes did this "renovation and reform" express itself in *LG*? Let me single out four changes that concerned sharing in Christ's triple "office" as priest, prophet, and king; the collegiate authority of bishops; a positive vision of non-Catholic Christian churches and communities; and the religious situation of Jews, Muslims, and followers of other faiths.

(1) First, earlier work by John Henry Newman, Joseph Lécuyer, Yves Congar, Gérard Philips, and others on Christ's triple office as priest/prophet/king or shepherd had prepared the way for the constitution to incorporate this major theme in its new vision of the church.[33] Vatican II wished Catholics at large to relearn the long-neglected or even forgotten truth that each of the baptized shares in the dignity and responsibility of Christ's triple office. They are all priests, prophets/teachers, and kings/shepherds; some of them are ordained to ministry as deacons, priests, and bishops.[34]

LG names Christ as "Teacher, Shepherd, and Priest" (no. 21) or, using one equivalent title to express his threefold office, calls him "Teacher, King, and Priest" (no. 13). Distinguishing "the common priesthood of the faith-

31. Albert C. Outler, "A Response," in *Documents of Vatican II*, 102–10, at 102.

32. Ibid., 106. On *LG* see Peter Hünermann, "*Lumen Gentium*," in *Herders theologischer Kommentar*, 2:269–563; Gérard Philips, "History of the Constitution [*LG*]," trans. Kevin Smyth, in *Commentary on the Documents of Vatican II*, 1:105–37; Philips, *L'Église et son mystère au IIe Concile de Vaticane: Histoire, texte, et commentaire de la Constitution "Lumen Gentium,"* 2 vols. (Paris: Desclée, 1967).

33. For the ways Newman and others had already developed the triple office, see Gerald O'Collins and Michael Keenan Jones, *Jesus Our Priest: A Christian Approach to the Priesthood of Christ* (New York: Oxford University, 2010), 206–34.

34. Ibid., 273– 91.

ful" from "the ministerial or hierarchical priesthood," the constitution adds that "each in its own proper way shares in the one priesthood of Christ," which is a "*royal* priesthood" (no. 10, emphasis added). *LG* completes the threefold scheme when it moves on to say that "the holy people of God shares also in Christ's prophetic office" (no. 12).

Given its scope as a document on the church, *LG* does not set itself to explore and define the triple office of Christ himself. It is concerned rather to illustrate in detail how others participate in his priestly, prophetic, and kingly offices. Nevertheless, before doing that, it sets out the living presence and continuous activity of "the Lord Jesus Christ": in "the person of the bishops, to whom the priests render assistance," this "supreme High Priest is present in the midst of the faithful. Though seated at the right hand of God the Father, he is not absent." But, through the service of the bishops, he "preaches the Word of God to all peoples, administers ceaselessly" the "sacraments of faith," and "directs and guides the people of the New Testament on their journey toward eternal beatitude" (no. 21). This fresh vision of Christ as the ever-active prophet, priest, and shepherd/king shapes what the constitution wishes to say about the bishops as "teachers of doctrine, ministers of sacred worship, and holders of office in government" (no. 20).[35]

LG invests further in unpacking the prophetic, priestly, and kingly roles of *bishops* first as preachers, teachers, and "heralds of the faith" (no. 25); second as "stewards of the grace" of the fullness of priesthood (no. 26); and third as "*vicars* and legates of Christ," who "govern the particular churches assigned to them" (no. 27, emphasis added).[36] The text then applies the threefold office to *priests*: "they are consecrated in order to preach the Gospel and shepherd the faithful, as well as to celebrate divine worship" (no. 28). Where the bishops are pictured in their prophetic, priestly, and kingly roles, at least here the order is varied for priests: they "preach," "shepherd," and "celebrate divine worship."

Finally, chapter 4 of *Lumen gentium* elaborates the threefold office of the laity as priests, prophets, and kings (in that order). First of all, "Christ

35. In *Unitatis redintegratio* (UR), the Decree on Ecumenism, Vatican II pictures the triple office of the bishops and its hoped-for outcome: "Through their faithful *preaching* of the Gospel, administrating the *sacraments*, and *governing in love*, Jesus Christ wishes his people to increase, under the action of the Holy Spirit, and he perfects his people's communion in unity: in the confession of one faith, in the common celebration of divine worship, and in the fraternal harmony of God's family" (no. 2, emphasis added).

36. Here *LG* corrected the long-standing habit of limiting the title "vicar of Christ" to the bishop of Rome (see no. 19 on the pope as the vicar of Christ).

Jesus, the supreme and eternal Priest," "intimately joins" all the baptized to "his life and mission," and gives them "a share in his priestly office" to offer spiritual worship in the Holy Spirit "for the glory of the Father and the salvation of the world" (no. 34). Second, Christ, "the great prophet who proclaimed the kingdom of the Father," now "fulfills this prophetic office not only by the hierarchy who teach in his name . . . but also by the laity." He "establishes them as witnesses" and "powerful heralds of the faith" (no. 35). Third, "the Lord also desires that his kingdom be spread by the lay faithful" through their kingly office, which is described at even more length than their priestly and prophetic offices (no. 36).

In its fourth and final session, the council promulgated six decrees, three of which concern us here: *Christus Dominus* (*CD*), the Decree on the Pastoral Office of Bishops in the Church; *Apostolicam actuositatem* (*AA*), the Decree on the Apostolate of Lay People; and *Presbyterorum ordinis* (*PO*), the Decree on the Ministry and Life of Priests. These three decrees developed *LG* by spelling out in detail what sharing in the threefold office of Christ entailed in the lives of bishops, laypersons, and priests, respectively. Never before in the history of Roman Catholicism had a general council published documents dedicated to the life and ministry of bishops, laypersons, and priests. Never before had a council attended to the royal priesthood and prophetic office conferred on all the baptized. Even if the Council of Trent in its decrees on the Mass and the sacrament of order taught something about the ordained priesthood,[37] *Presbyterorum ordinis*, along with what we gleaned above from *Lumen gentium*, went beyond the limited view of priesthood offered by Trent. Most importantly, Vatican II insisted that preaching the word is an essential and, indeed, primary obligation of ministerial priests.

(2) A second change that *Lumen gentium* introduced and that caught the imagination of many commentators was its teaching about all the Catholic bishops around the world forming with the bishop of Rome a college (nos. 22–23), like "the one apostolic college constituted by St. Peter and the rest of the apostles" (no. 22).[38] What grounds membership in this college for local bishops is their episcopal ordination and "communion with the head and members of this college" (no. 22).

Expressing the organic unity between the pope and bishops and their joint responsibility for the universal church, this new doctrine of collegiality

37. DzH 1743, 1763–78; ND 1548, 1706–21.

38. See also the "explanatory note [*nota praevia*]" added by the council's doctrinal commission to clarify the nature of collegiality.

did not subordinate the pope to the bishops (even when they all meet in a general council) or make the episcopal college merely a gathering of equals (as happens in such bodies as national colleges of surgeons). Attention to the college of bishops filled out the one-sided picture left by the First Vatican Council with its definitions of papal primacy and infallibility. Episcopal collegiality complements rather than challenges the primacy of the pope.

LG reasserted the collegial authority of the bishops, who, in communion with the pope and united among themselves, share responsibility for the "shepherding" of the whole church. While primarily exercised by all the bishops meeting in an ecumenical council, collegiality also applies, analogously, to national bishops' conferences[39] and to other groups and situations: for instance, to the coresponsibility of laypersons, priests, and religious who constitute parishes.[40] How well or badly has collegiality functioned in the primary case of the worldwide episcopate and in particular through three organs: the synods of bishops in Rome, the national episcopal conferences, and such international bodies as CELAM (the Consejo Episcopal Latinoamericano), and FABC (the Federation of Asian Bishops' Conferences)? Neither the synods nor the bishops' conferences show collegiality to be already functioning fully.[41]

(3) A third, strikingly new development initiated by *LG* concerns relations with the other Christians. Apropos of the identity of the Roman

39. As no. 23 states, "the episcopal conferences can today make a manifold and fruitful contribution to the concrete application of the collegial disposition."

40. In a 1968 article that was a swinging attack on the wide scope of collegiality, Archbishop Marcel-François Lefebvre recognized what was involved, even if he dismissed collegiality as a modern introduction rather than acknowledging it as retrieving what we find in, e.g., the Acts of the Apostles (esp. chaps. 1–15): "The democratization of the magisterium has been naturally followed by the democratization of government. Modern ideas on this point have been translated into the Church by the famous slogan of 'collegiality.' It is supposed to be necessary to 'collegialize' the government: that of the pope or that of the bishops with a presbyteral college, that of the parish priest with a pastoral college of lay persons, all of it flanked by commissions, councils, assemblies etc., before authorities can think of giving orders and directives. The battle of collegiality, supported by the whole Communist, Protestant, and progressive press, will remain famous [he meant "infamous"] in the annals of the Council" ("Un peu de lumière sur la crise actuelle de l'Église" ["A Little Light on the Present Crisis in the Church"]), http://lacriseintegriste.typepad.fr/weblog/1968/03/article-de-mgr-lefebvre-dans-rivarol.html, translation mine.

41. On the counter-collegial current, see Faggioli, *Vatican II: The Battle for Meaning*, 10, 13–15, 24, 87; and Gerald O'Collins, *Living Vatican II: The 21st Council for the 21st Century* (New York: Paulist, 2006), 35–38, 154–56.

Catholic Church as "the holy Church" founded by Christ (no. 5), the constitution famously left behind the 1943 encyclical of Pius XII, *Mystici Corporis*, by saying that the holy church "continues to exist [fully] [*subsistit*]" in the Roman Catholic Church but is not simply identical with it. To be sure, the meaning of *subsistit in* remains controversial, with the Congregation for the Doctrine of the Faith offering over the years varying translations, as Francis Sullivan has pointed out.[42] But the conclusion that the church of God is not *tout court* identical with the Roman Catholic Church does not simply depend on the translation of *subsistit in*; it emerges clearly from several passages in Vatican II documents.

Recognizing how "many elements of sanctification and grace" are found outside the "visible" Roman Catholic Church (no. 8), *LG* went on to specify some of these elements present among other Christian churches and communities: "believing the Sacred Scripture" to be "the norm of faith and life"; faith in the Trinity; and the reception of baptism and "other sacraments in their own churches and ecclesial communities" (no. 15).[43] Here the council acknowledged as "churches" various bodies of Christians not (or not yet) in union with the Roman Catholic Church. Even more emphatically, in *UR*, which was promulgated on the same day as *LG* (November 21, 1964) and extended and applied to practice the teaching of the constitution, Vatican II broke new ground by recognizing how the principle "the Eucharist makes the church" operates also for the Eastern churches not in communion with the bishop of Rome: "through the celebration of the Eucharist of the Lord in each of these churches, the church of God is built up and grows" (no. 15).[44] In other words, while the church of God

42. For a guide to the meaning of *subsistit in* in this context and in some of the controversy surrounding its meaning, see the following by Francis A. Sullivan, SJ, "A Response to Karl Becker, SJ, on the Meaning of *Subsistit in*," *Theological* Studies 67 (2006): 395–409; "The Meaning of *Subsistit in* as Explained by the Congregation for the Doctrine of the Faith," *Theological Studies* 69 (2008): 116–24; and "Further Thoughts on the Meaning of *Subsistit in*," *Theological Studies* 71 (2010): 133–47. Alexandra von Teuffenbach, using the council diaries of Sebastian Tromp, has argued for a narrow version of *subsistit in* (as simply *is*) in *Die Bedeutung des* "Subsistit in"*(LG 8): Zum Selbstverständnis der katholischen Kirche* (Munich: Herbert Utz, 2002).

43. Apropos of no. 15, the official *relatio* explained that the "elements of sanctification and grace" belong primarily not to individuals but to the heritage and life of the ecclesial communities, which were now turning to each other through dialogue and in quest of visible unity: *Acta synodalia Sacrosancti Concilii Oecumenici Vaticani II*, vol. 3, part 1 (Vatican City: Vatican, 1973), 204.

44. On this principle, see the encyclical by John Paul II, *Ecclesia de Eucharistia*, AAS 95 (2003): 433–75.

continues to exist fully in the Roman Catholic Church, it also continues to exist in other churches or ecclesial communities, especially in the Eastern churches, which enjoy almost all the elements of Christian sanctification and truth. Here Vatican II innovated by officially recognizing that, beyond the visible Roman Catholic Church, the church of God also lives and grows among those whom the Council of Florence and the Council of Trent had labeled "heretics" and "schismatics"—language never used by *LG* or any other Vatican II document.

A sea change had taken place. The Catholic Church was a latecomer to the ecumenical movement in which many members of other churches were far ahead. There had been some Catholic trailblazers like Abbé Paul Couturier (1881–1953).[45] Through his vast correspondence and tracts on prayer for Christian unity, Couturier enjoyed contacts with Christians around the world and encouraged innumerable people to pray for "the unity Christ wills, by the means he wills." Nevertheless, praying with other Christians remained forbidden by the Catholic Church. The 1928 encyclical of Pius XI, *Mortalium animos*, forbade Catholics even to take part in conferences with non-Roman Christians; such participation, he believed, would imply that the Catholic Church was but one of the denominations. When the World Council of Churches began, Catholic observers were not allowed to attend the first assemblies (Amsterdam in 1948 and Evanston in 1954).

Vatican II expressed and approved an "important change to a positive vision of non-Catholic Christian communities,"[46] a change deeply desired by John XXIII and his great collaborator, Cardinal Augustin Bea. *UR* strongly endorsed theological dialogue with "the separated brethren" (no. 9), and opened the way for the establishment of numerous ecumenical commissions at an international, national, and diocesan level. It recommended that Catholics join in prayer with other Christians, not least at ecumenical gatherings and especially at services for Christian unity (no. 8).

(4) With its positive statements first about (a) Jews and then about (b) Muslims, *LG* (no. 16) signaled a fourth change, which closely paralleled the official "about face" on relations with other Christians. (a) For the first time in the story of Catholic Christianity, an ecumenical council had something positive to say about Jews. Citing Romans 11:28-29, *LG* declared that the chosen people remain "most dear" to God, who never "repents" of his

45. "Couturier, Paul Irénée," in *Oxford Dictionary of the Christian Church*, 428.

46. Johannes Feiner, "Commentary on the Decree [*Unitatis redintegratio*]," trans. R. A. Wilson, in *Commentary on the Documents of Vatican II*, 2:57–164, at 61.

"gifts and calling." Commenting on *Nostra aetate* (*NA*), the Declaration on the Relation of the Church to Non-Christian Religions, promulgated on October 28, 1965, John Oesterreicher wrote: "It is the first time that the Church has publicly made her own the Pauline view of the mystery of Israel" and "given glory to God for his enduring faithfulness toward this chosen people, the Jews."[47] *NA* would have more to say about Paul's view of the mystery of Israel. Nevertheless, it was a year earlier, when promulgating *LG* in November 1964, that for "the first time the Church publicly made her own the Pauline view."

(b) Apropos of Muslims, Georges Anawati correctly observed that "up to the beginning of the twentieth century, the constant attitude of the Church toward Islam was one of condemnation." But he ignored the official change embodied a year earlier in *LG* (November 1964), when he went on at once to attribute to *NA* (October 1965) "a change in the Church's attitude to Islam."[48] Eleven months before (in *LG*)—and for the first time since the Arab prophet Muhammad (d. 632) founded Islam—an ecumenical council of the Catholic Church offered some positive teaching on Islam.[49] This teaching highlighted common ground: the divine "plan of salvation also embraces those who acknowledge the Creator, in the first place among whom are the Muslims. They profess to hold the faith of Abraham, and together with us they adore the one, merciful God, who will judge human beings on the last day" (no. 16).[50] While describing Muslims as those "who profess to hold the faith of Abraham" rather than simply state that Muslims hold the faith of Abraham, the council agreed that they "acknowledge the Creator," "adore with us the one, merciful God," and also share with Christians an expectation of a general judgment "on the last day." A year later in *NA*, Vatican II would fill out its positive view of Islam and Judaism.

47. John M. Oesterreicher, "Declaration on the Relation of the Church to Non-Christian Religions," trans. Simon Young, Erika Young, and Hilda Graef, in *Commentary on the Documents of Vatican II*, 3:1–136, at 1.

48. George C. Anawati, "Excursus on Islam," trans. Simon and Erika Young, *Commentary on the Documents of Vatican II*, 3:151–54, at 151.

49. Meeting soon after the failure of the fifth and final (major) crusade, the Second Council of Lyons (1274) described "the Saracens" as "blasphemous," "faithless," and "the impious enemies of the Christian name" (*Decrees of the Ecumenical Councils*, 1:309).

50. In no. 107 of his first encyclical, *Ecclesiam suam* (August 6, 1964), Paul VI had anticipated by a few months the positive teaching on Islam found in *LG*. He wrote of Muslims, "whom we do well to admire on account of those things that are true and commendable [*vera et probanda*] in their worship" (AAS 56 [1964]: 609–59, at 654).

After the Muslims, the same article in *LG* turns to other believers in God: "Nor is this God distant from others who in shadows and images seek the unknown God, since to all he gives life and breath and all things (cf. Acts 17:23-28) and since the Savior wills all human beings to be saved (cf. 1 Tim 2:4)." Because God is both the Creator who gives life to all human beings and the Savior who wishes all to be saved, the council holds that the divine presence also enfolds all God-seekers, even if it is "in shadows and images" that they seek "the unknown God." Hence "those who through no fault [of their own] do not know Christ's Gospel and his Church and who, nevertheless, seek God with a sincere heart and, under the influence of grace, try in their actions to fulfill his will made known through the dictate of their conscience—those too may obtain eternal salvation."

When this article in *LG* considers believers in God other than Jews and Muslims, it prioritizes the divine initiative. It is God who comes close to all (as Creator) by giving them life and (as Savior) by willing them to be saved. It is through "the influence of grace" that these "others" can try to follow their conscience and do God's will. But when they "seek the unknown God" and "seek God with a sincere heart," can they do this only because God draws them? When they seek God, is this only because God has first found them? While not clearly stated, an affirmative answer seems presupposed when no. 16 speaks earlier of "all human beings without exception" being "called by God's grace to salvation."

While speaking of their salvation, *LG* remains silent about the other, inseparable dimension of the divine self-communication: revelation. This particular passage of *LG* has nothing to say, at least explicitly, about divine revelation and its correlative in human faith. Nevertheless, we should ask, While the voice of conscience dictates what the "God-seekers" should do, how has the will of God been "made known" to them at the heart of their conscience? Does the "making known" imply some measure of revelation? Although they can be described as seeking "the unknown God" and doing so "in shadows and images," this language suggests that something has been disclosed to them. Shadows are not equivalent to total darkness, and images imply some resemblance to truth and reality.

Retrieving teaching from Acts and 1 Timothy, these reflections in *LG* on the religious situation of those who are neither Jews nor Muslims broke new ground in the history of ecumenical councils. Osterreicher, writing about a later conciliar document (*NA*), forgot that *LG* had already acknowledged "the universal presence of grace and its activity in the many religions of mankind." It was in this constitution (and not in *NA*) that a general council had "for the first time in history" "honored the truth and holiness in other religions as the work of the one living God."[51] Unquestionably, *NA* would have more to say, but it was a year earlier that *LG* had spoken up positively on the other religions.

Thus far we have recalled four pieces of new teaching found in *LG*: all Christians share in Christ's "triple office" as priest, prophet, and king; the bishops enjoy universal, "collegiate" authority; a positive vision of non-Catholic Christian communities committed the Catholic Church firmly to the ecumenical movement; and the council recognized the work of God in other living faiths and in all who seek God. All four changes were intended to impact (a) life within the Catholic Church (through the teaching on the triple office and on episcopal collegiality) and (b) her relationship with "others" through a transformed vision of non-Catholic Christians and followers of other faiths. Furthermore, these changes, as well as embodying something new, also drew on ancient testimony—notably the Holy Scriptures (e.g., biblical teaching on the triple office). Thus the very changes themselves express a radical continuity with the past.

Beyond question, one could press on to list further changes of doctrine and practice incorporated in *LG*: the many biblical images that express the mystery of the church (no. 6); the universal call to holiness of all the baptized (nos. 39–42), which retrieves teaching from St. Paul and other ancient sources; the restoration of the permanent diaconate[52] in the Latin rite; and much else besides. But let me turn to the remarkable changes found in *NA*.[53]

51. Osterreicher, "Declaration on the Relationship," 1.

52. If Vatican II had met today, it might well have proposed the restoration of the diaconate for women. See Phyllis Zagano, "Remembering Tradition: Women's Monastic Rituals and the Diaconate," *Theological Studies* 72 (2011): 787–811; and the International Theological Commission, *From the Diakonia of Christ to the Diakonia of the Apostles* (London: Catholic Truth Society, 2003); the English title is a tendentious translation of the original French, "Le Diakonat: Évolution et perspectives," *La documentation catholique* 2.2284 (January 19, 2003): 58–107.

53. On the production of *NA*, see Giovanni Miccoli, "Two Sensitive Issues: Religious Freedom and the Jews," in *History of Vatican II*, 4:135–93; Riccardo Burigana and Giovanni Turbanti, "The Intersession: Preparing the Conclusion of the Council," ibid., 5:546–59; Mauro Velati, "Completing the Conciliar Agenda," ibid., 185–273, at 211–31. On the theological impact of the declaration, see Michael Fitzgerald, "*Nostra Aetate*, A Key to Interreligious Dialogue," *Gregorianum* 87 (2006): 700–713; Daniel A. Madigan, "*Nostra Aetate* and the Questions It Chose to Leave Open," ibid., 781–96; Gerald O'Collins, "Implementing *Nostra Aetate*," ibid., 714–26; Jacques Scheuer, "The Dialogue with the Traditions of India and the Far East," ibid., 797–809; Roman A. Siebenrock, "Theologischer Kommentar zur Erklärung über die Haltung der Kirche zu den nichtchristlichen Religionen *Nostra Aetate*," in *Herders theologischer Kommentar*, 3:591–693.

The Declaration on the Relation of the Church to Non-Christian Religions

While *LG* no. 16 had already broken new ground in the history of the 21 ecumenical councils of Catholic Christianity by its positive remarks about Judaism and Islam, *NA* took matters further by reflecting on other religions (in particular, on Hinduism and Buddhism) and by considering the human condition and "the riddles of the human condition" to which different religions provide an answer (no. 1). The opening words of the declaration (on human beings drawing closer together) loomed large as the first time any ecumenical council had ever reflected on the state of global humanity.[54] Popes had done so, notably John XXIII in *Pacem in terris* (1963), but never before was that kind of pronouncement to be found in any ecumenical council. *NA* named three basic reasons for acknowledging what all nations have in common, to the point of making them "one community": their origin in God, the divine providence that extends to all, and their common, heavenly destiny.

After having shown that the unity among all human beings has its foundation in what God has done, is doing, and will do, *NA* turns next to the common self-questioning that also—but this time, on the side of humanity—bonds everyone (no. 1). The declaration's eloquent exposé of the deep questions that haunt human beings has no precedent in the teaching of earlier councils. The same is true when the document reflects explicitly and positively on some aspects of Hinduism and Buddhism, two religious ways of life that existed centuries before the coming of Christ himself. In the history of Catholic Christianity no previous ecumenical council had ever reflected on these ancient Asian religions.

Before moving to Islam and Judaism, *NA* observes that "the Catholic Church rejects nothing of those things which are true and holy in these [other] religions." Rather, "it is with sincere respect that she considers those ways of acting and living, those precepts and doctrines, which, although they differ in many [respects] from what she herself holds and proposes, nevertheless, often reflect a ray of that Truth, which illuminates all human beings" (no.2). By recognizing what is "true and holy" in other religions, the declaration follows the lead of *LG* in using a Johannine, double-sided terminology that distinguishes but does not separate the two dimensions of the divine self-communication, revelation and salvation. What, or rather

54. *LG* had already adverted, albeit very briefly, to "the conditions of this time" and the way "all human beings are more closely joined today by various social, technical, and cultural bonds" (no. 1; see also the closing words of no. 28).

who, has given rise to "those things which are true and holy" in the other religions? *NA* responds by pointing to the person of Christ.

Without condemning various "ways of acting and living," as well as various "precepts and doctrines" to be found in other religions but simply noting that they may "differ" in many respects from what the Catholic Church teaches, the declaration then acknowledges something extraordinarily positive: the beliefs and practices of other religions "often reflect a ray of that Truth that illuminates all human beings" (John 1:9). Since what is "true" among the others reflects "the Truth" that is the Word of God, presumably what is "holy" among them also comes from the Word who is the life of human kind (John 1:4). If Christ is "the truth" for everyone, he is also "the life" for them. This paragraph does not expressly state that Christ is both universal Revealer and universal Savior, but what it says amounts to that. How can he "illuminate" all human beings, without conveying to them (through a personal divine self-disclosure) something of God's self-revelation and hence also the offer of salvation? All of this teaching, which retrieves and applies what we find in John's Gospel, boldly develops doctrine and, in fact, reverses the ugly way the Council of Florence in its decree for the Copts had indiscriminately relegated "pagans" (as well as "Jews, heretics, and schismatics") to eternal damnation.[55]

After its fuller treatment of Islam (no. 3) and Judaism (no. 4), *NA* recalls a theme from the Book of Genesis that fills out what has already been said about all people having a common origin in God (no. 5). Right from the very first, all human beings have been "created in the image and likeness of God" (Gen 1:26, 27). Seeing all men and women as not only created by God but also created in the divine image will prove an effective mind-set; it dramatically puts back on display how we should interpret and understand "the religious others," whoever they may be. The declaration draws a practical conclusion from the doctrine of all people being created in the divine image: there is no basis for any "discrimination" that offends or curtails "human dignity and the rights that flow from it" (no. 5). "Human dignity" would become a major theme of the Declaration on Religious Liberty, promulgated a few weeks later on December 7, 1965. *GS*, promulgated on the same day, would insist at greater length on "the extraordinary dignity of the human person" and the basic rights that flow from that dignity" (no. 26; see also no. 29). The use that *NA* (briefly) and *GS* (more fully) made of Genesis 1:26, 27 enjoys no precedent in any earlier

55. DzH 1351; ND 810.

councils. Here once again Vatican II innovated, this time by applying a basic biblical theme about the creation of humanity.

Understanding and Interpreting Changes

Thus far this article has set itself to illustrate how Vatican II introduced sweeping changes in liturgical practice and religious life, reversed set positions about religious freedom and relations with other Christians, and, for the first time in the story of 21 general councils, offered positive teaching on Judaism, Islam, Hinduism, Buddhism, and other religions. *LG*, as we saw, besides breaking new ground with its positive vision of other Christian communities and other living faiths, also innovated by teaching that all the baptized share in the triple office of Christ, and that the bishops enjoy universal, "collegiate" authority.

Much more could be added about the extent and nature of change in doctrine and practice brought about by Vatican II. For example, it retrieved the central importance of Sacred Scripture for liturgy, theology, and the whole life of the church (*SC* nos. 24, 51–52; *DV* nos. 21–26), and encouraged a theology of the local church (e.g., *Ad gentes*, the Decree on the Missionary Activity of the Church, nos. 19–23). It rejected the institution of slavery and the use of torture (*GS* no. 27), both of which the Catholic Church had for centuries found acceptable.[56] A dramatic language shift involved not only dropping standard talk about "pagans," "heretics," and "schismatics," but also introducing such positive terms as "collegiality," "dialogue," and "dignity." *Ressourcement* also meant retrieving biblical language that had long been neglected. In giving the Decree on the Ministry and Life of Priests the name of *Presbyterorum ordinis* (of the order of presbyters), Vatican II retrieved from early Christianity a typical term for church leaders.[57] We could amass further examples inspired by *aggiornamento* and *ressourcement*—not least the extent to which the retrieval

56. On the church's long-standing approval or at least tolerance of slavery, see John T. Noonan Jr., *A Church That Can and Cannot Change: The Development of Catholic Moral Teaching* (Notre Dame, IN: University of Notre Dame, 2005), 110–23; Sullivan, "Catholic Tradition and Traditions," 118–25. The 1948 Universal Declaration of Human Rights (articles 4 and 5) outlawed slavery and torture.

57. See Friedrich Wulf, "Decree on the Ministry and Life of Priests: Commentary on the Decree," trans. Ronald Walls, in *Commentary on the Documents of Vatican II*, 4:210–14; and Gerard Kelly, "Ordination in the Presbyteral Order," *Australasian Catholic Record* 73 (1996): 259–72.

of biblical themes such as creation in the divine image impacted deeply *NA* and *GS*.[58] But what should we make of all these changes brought by Vatican II? Let me respond by citing Neil Ormerod and Benedict XVI and then adding some suggestions of my own.

(1) Ormerod rightly warns that if we locate the changes within any "larger theory" of social and cultural crisis and change, we face something "extremely complex."[59] He himself speaks of "authentic" and "inauthentic" developments. Old ways of promoting the church's mission have become dysfunctional and need, after discernment, to be discarded and replaced. Ormerod also applies the language of Bernard Lonergan and speaks of the church being called to an intellectual, moral, and religious conversion.[60]

(2) In his 2005 address to the Roman Curia, Pope Benedict uses the scheme of permanent principles and changing forms to interpret the changes brought by Vatican II. In the "innovation in continuity," "only the principles" express "the permanent aspect." While he allows that "the practical forms depend on the historical situation and are therefore subject to change," he maintains "the continuity of principles."[61] This proposal opens up memories of Newman's "continuity of principles," his second "note" for distinguishing between "the genuine development of an idea" and its "corruption." While "doctrines grow and are enlarged," principles are "permanent."[62]

Along with the scheme of permanent principles and changing forms, the pope also introduces a term, "identity," when remarking: "in apparent discontinuity it [the church] has actually preserved and deepened her inmost nature and true identity."[63] That brief remark opens the way to my closing observations. But before examining "identity," I want to explore briefly the possibility of distinguishing between essentials and nonessentials.

(3) The widespread innovations sanctioned by Vatican II inevitably meant widespread discontinuities with the past—sometimes with the more

58. Significantly in opposing Vatican II and its implementation, Archbishop Lefebvre appealed to his own vision of "the church" and "tradition," but avoided the challenge of the Scriptures. Thus in an interview that appeared in *Newsweek* for December 19, 1977, he spoke 13 times of "the church" but never referred to the New Testament or Jesus Christ.

59. Ormerod, "Vatican II—Continuity or Discontinuity?," 611, 612.

60. Ibid., 613, 633.

61. Benedict XVI, "Interpreting Vatican II," 538.

62. Newman, *Essay*, 183–89, at 183; see also 309–36.

63. Benedict XVI, "Interpreting Vatican II," 538.

recent past but sometimes (e.g., in the case of the toleration of torture and slavery) with a past that reached back to the early centuries of Christendom. One might comment that in all these changes no essential or substantial belief (e.g., faith in the Trinity) or practice (e.g., baptism) was dropped, and so substantial continuity remained intact. Following *SC* no. 21, one might then distinguish between the permanence of essentials and change in what is nonessential. Nothing essential has been lost or removed, and nothing essentially or substantially new has been added. Thus a scheme of "essential" and "nonessential" (or "substantial/substantive" and "accidental") could be pressed into service.

Yet Pope Benedict's term "identity" may offer a richer theme to pursue and could lead us to ask, Is the pre–Vatican II and post–Vatican II church one and the same corporate subject? Has there been a loss of identity? Or has the church retained her authentic identity, so that all the faithful can continue to participate in a church structured by the same values and goals and living by the same essential beliefs and practices? There can be only one reply. The indwelling Holy Spirit maintains the church's true, deep, and lasting trinitarian identity as the body of Christ and the people of God.

Far from threatening the enduring continuity of the church, change makes possible that continuous identity of this corporate subject profoundly shaped by the tripersonal God. As with any living organism, for the church not to change would be to die. Or, making this point positively and with Newman's words, one can say, "In a higher world it is otherwise, but here below to live is to change and to be perfect is to have changed often."[64]

Finally, we need to enlarge our vision of the identity between the pre–Vatican II and post–Vatican II church. The continuous identity at stake is nothing less than *apostolic* identity. Newman admitted "the abstract possibility of extreme changes" that would bring a loss of "identity" and a kind of "counterfeit Christianity." But he argued for a "real continuity" that made Christianity of later centuries "in its substance the very religion which Christ and his apostles taught in the first, whatever may be the modifications for good or for evil which lapse of years, or the vicissitudes of human affairs, have impressed upon it."[65]

What Newman calls "real continuity" is nothing less than the continuity of apostolic identity. Far from threatening that "real continuity," Vatican II

64. Newman, *Essay*, 63.
65. Ibid., 33.

renewed the church's apostolic identity or its "real continuity," through the guidance of the Holy Spirit, with what the crucified and risen Christ and the original witnesses did in founding and propagating the church. With a reverential nod toward Newman, some have understood "development" to be *the* issue underlying both the events that constituted the council and the texts that it produced. Yet one goes closer to the heart of the matter by naming as *the* conciliar challenge that of maintaining and renewing the church's apostolic identity.[66]

66. On the apostolic character and identity of the church, see Lutheran–Roman Catholic Commission on Unity, *The Apostolicity of the Church: Study Document of the Lutheran–Roman Catholic Commission on Unity* (Minneapolis: Lutheran University, 2006). The author wishes to thank Jared Wicks, Ormond Rush, and two anonymous referees for generous help in providing valuable suggestions and corrections.

Part 2

Specific Interpretations

5 Developments in Teaching Authority since Vatican II

FRANCIS A. SULLIVAN, SJ

The author describes and comments on developments that have taken place since Vatican II with regard to teaching authority. Among subjects exercising such authority he treats episcopal conferences and the Congregation for the Doctrine of the Faith. Among objects of definitive teaching he treats truths that are not revealed but necessarily connected with revealed truth. As a way of exercising teaching authority, he discusses papal declarations that a doctrine has been taught infallibly by the ordinary universal magisterium.

During the year 2012 a half century will have passed since the opening of the Second Vatican Council. No doubt this "golden anniversary" will stimulate much serious reflection on the effects that this remarkable event has had on not only the Catholic Church but also the world with which the council encouraged the church to dialogue. One can expect articles to be written, and perhaps a book will be published with the title "What Has Happened since Vatican II?"

Having spent a good part of those 50 years teaching future priests (and some future bishops) about the magisterium, it seems useful for me to share these reflections on the developments that have taken place with regard to teaching authority in the Catholic Church since Vatican II. I will divide the matter into three parts: (1) the subjects (the authoritative teachers); (2) the object (what they teach about); and (3) the exercise (how they teach).

The Subjects of Teaching Authority

Between the years 1852 and 1884 all the Catholic bishops in the United States met together three times in plenary councils to enact laws that would adapt the church to life in this new nation. They have not gathered again in a plenary council since 1884. However, the archbishops began to hold annual meetings in 1890, and in 1919 the National Catholic Welfare Council was founded in which all the bishops would have a voice. At the insistence of the Holy See, the term "council" was changed to "conference." The preference of the bishops of the United States to meet in unofficial conferences rather than in canonically regulated plenary councils was shared by the bishops of many other nations, especially after the promulgation of the Code of Canon Law in 1917. The result of this development was that when the bishops of the whole world gathered in 1962 for the Second Vatican Council and were presented at once with a slate of candidates from which they were expected to choose the members of the conciliar commissions, the bishops insisted on drawing up new lists of candidates, whom they would choose in meetings of their conferences. Thus the reality of episcopal conferences was present from the very beginning of Vatican II.

Episcopal Conferences

The role that episcopal conferences would have in the life of the church was mentioned in three of the conciliar documents. In its Constitution on the Sacred Liturgy, Vatican II recognized the part that "groupings of bishops" with "territorial ecclesiastical authority" would play in the local adaptation of the liturgy.[1] In the Dogmatic Constitution on the Church, after speaking of organic groupings of churches, the council declared: "This variety of local churches, in harmony among themselves, demonstrates with greater clarity the catholicity of the undivided church. In a similar way episcopal conferences can today make a manifold and fruitful contribution to the concrete application of the spirit of collegiality."[2] In the Decree on the Pastoral Office of Bishops in the Church, an episcopal conference is described as "a kind of assembly (*coetus*) in which the bishops of some nation or region discharge their pastoral office in collaboration."[3] Since the pastoral office conferred on bishops at their ordination obviously includes the office of teaching the faith, it is not surprising that after Vatican II, episcopal conferences saw that it was within their competence to issue pastoral letters in which they were exercising their teaching office. Thus,

1. *Sacrosanctum concilium* nos. 22, 36, 39.

2. *Lumen gentium* no. 23. Throughout the article I quote the English translation of the conciliar documents from *Decrees of the Ecumenical Councils*, 2 vols., ed. Norman P. Tanner, SJ (Washington, DC: Georgetown University, 1990).

3. *Christus Dominus* no. 38.

our National Conference of Catholic Bishops (NCCB)[4] produced a number of doctrinal pastoral letters during the 15 years between Human Life in Our Day (1968) and The Challenge of Peace (1983).

During the preparation of the pastoral letter on peace, controversy erupted over the teaching role of episcopal conferences. With a view to promoting a broad consensus on issues concerning war and peace, the Holy See summoned representatives of the NCCB along with those of the episcopal conferences of six European nations to an "informal consultation" at the Vatican. The chairman of the consultation, Cardinal Joseph Ratzinger, prefect of the Congregation for the Doctrine of the Faith (CDF), proposed five points for discussion. The first began with the statement: "A bishops' conference as such does not have a *mandatum docendi*. This belongs only to the individual bishops or to the college of bishops with the pope."[5] In view of the controversy that arose on this question, the Extraordinary Synod of 1985 summoned by Pope John Paul II proposed that a study should be made concerning the theological status and the teaching authority of episcopal conferences. In January 1988, the prefect of the Congregation for Bishops, Cardinal Bernardin Gantin, sent the bishops a document entitled: "Theological and Juridical Status of Episcopal Conferences," along with a letter in which he described the document as a "working paper" (*instrumentum laboris*), and requested corrections and emendations from bishops and episcopal conferences before the end of 1988. This document echoed Ratzinger's view, saying, "The episcopal conferences do not, as such, properly speaking possess the *munus magisterii*."[6]

This "working paper" received severe criticism from many episcopal conferences, more than one of which suggested that an entirely new draft be prepared. In 1998 Pope John Paul II settled the question by issuing *motu proprio* his Apostolic Letter *Apostolos suos*.[7] In section 4 of this document, entitled "Complementary Norms Regarding the Conferences of Bishops," in Article 1, the pope prescribed the conditions under which

4. On July 1, 2001, the NCCB combined with the US Catholic Conference to become the US Conference of Catholic Bishops (USCCB).

5. "Rome Consultation on Peace and Disarmament: A Vatican Synthesis," *Origins* 12 (1983): 691–95, at 692.

6. "Draft Statement on Episcopal Conferences," *Origins* 17 (1988): 731–37, at 735. The term *munus magisterii* can be translated as "office of teaching authority."

7. The Vatican's English translation, with the title, "The Theological and Juridical Nature of Episcopal Conferences," was published in *Origins* 28 (1998): 152–58.

episcopal conferences can issue authoritative doctrinal statements in the name of the conference itself:

> Article 1. In order that the doctrinal declarations of the conference of bishops referred to in No. 22 of the present letter may constitute authentic magisterium and be published in the name of the conference itself, they must be unanimously approved by the bishops who are members, or receive the *recognitio* of the Apostolic See if approved in plenary assembly by at least two-thirds of the bishops belonging to the conference and having a deliberative vote.[8]

To my knowledge there is no historical precedent for the requirement that a conciliar decree must have been unanimously approved for it to be published in the name of a council. Councils have always sought, with the help of the Holy Spirit, to achieve consensus, which may be described as moral unanimity, but they have not required actual unanimity. One can reasonably expect that the difficulty of achieving unanimous approval would have the result that conferences would avoid controversial topics for doctrinal statements, and choose only those topics on which they were confident that their statement would receive the Holy See's *recognitio*. The topics on which the USCCB has produced doctrinal statements since those conditions were imposed strike me as being of that kind.[9]

One might speculate as to the reason that led John Paul II to introduce those conditions for the exercise of teaching authority by episcopal conferences. I suggest that his reason may have been the coherence between those conditions and Ratzinger's opinion referred to above, that episcopal conferences do not have a mandate to teach, since this belongs only to individual bishops, the pope, and the college of bishops with him. Meeting the conditions laid down by the pope would supply the authority that an episcopal conference would lack if it had no mandate to teach. A statement that was approved unanimously by the members of the conference would have the collective authority given it by all the individual bishops. And *recognitio* by Rome would give it the authority that a statement approved by only two-thirds of the bishops would not have. I find a con-

8. *Apostolos suos*, *Origins*, 157. The "doctrinal declarations of episcopal conferences" to which *Apostolos suos* no. 22 referred are "those to which the faithful are obliged to adhere with a sense of religious respect to the authentic magisterium of their own bishops." "Religious respect" is the Vatican translation here of *obsequium religiosum*.

9. The titles of these statements are listed on the USCCB's website, http://usccb.org/. (This and all other URLs cited herein were accessed on June 12, 2012.)

firmation of this interpretation of the effect of *recognitio* by the Holy See in the comparison that John Paul II made between the *recognitio* given to a doctrinal statement and the mandate of the Holy See that an episcopal conference needs in order to issue legislative decrees. Referring to the *recognitio* required for the publication by an episcopal conference of a doctrinal statement not approved unanimously, he said: "The intervention of the Apostolic See is analogous to that required by law in order for the episcopal conference to issue general decrees."[10]

I conclude that John Paul II's conditions for the publication of authoritative doctrinal statements by an episcopal conference are consistent with Ratzinger's opinion that teaching authority is properly held at only two levels: the universal level (the pope and by the whole college of bishops with him) and the local level (the individual bishops). In other words, episcopal conferences as such do not have teaching authority. This conclusion would imply that there is a basic theological difference between episcopal conferences and the regional councils of the early church that, by their exercise of teaching authority, played an important role in the faithful handing on and development of Christian doctrine. I do not see on what grounds one can judge that there is a basic theological difference between those regional councils and episcopal conferences.

The USCCB's Committee on Doctrine

In *Apostolos suos*, articles 2 and 3 of the "Complementary Norms," John Paul II prescribed the limits of the powers that an episcopal conference can grant its commissions, such as its committee on doctrine:[11]

> Article 2. No body of the episcopal conference outside of the plenary assembly has the power to carry out acts of authentic magisterium. The episcopal conference cannot grant such power to its commissions or other bodies set up by it.
>
> Article 3. For statements of a different kind, different from those mentioned in Article 2, the doctrinal commission of the conference of bishops must be authorized explicitly by the permanent council of the conference.

In view of a recent controversy, it would seem opportune to apply these norms to the question of the teaching authority of a statement issued on

10. *Apostolos suos*, *Origins*, 157.
11. Ibid.

March 24, 2011, by the USCCB's Committee on Doctrine entitled "Statement on *Quest for the Living God: Mapping Frontiers in the Theology of God*, by Sister Elizabeth A. Johnson."[12] One might begin by asking whether this statement of the Committee on Doctrine qualifies as an act of "authentic magisterium." Article 2 of the papal norms makes it clear that it does not, since the Committee on Doctrine does not have the power to carry out such an act, nor can the Conference grant it that power. It follows that the faithful of the United States are not obliged to respond to its statement with *obsequium religiosum*. According to Article 3 of the papal norms, the statement on Johnson's book would then be "of a different kind . . . from those mentioned in Article 2," for which the commission "must be authorized explicitly by the permanent council of the conference." That such authorization was given has been affirmed by the president of the USCCB, Archbishop Timothy M. Dolan, in his letter of July 7, 2011, addressed to Professor John E. Thiel, president of the Catholic Theological Society of America (CTSA).[13] Here Dolan wrote:

> I should also point out, that according to USCCB rules, any proposed statement by a committee must be approved by a vote of the Administrative Committee. As President of the Episcopal Conference I serve as chairman of that committee. At its March meeting, the Administrative Committee discussed both the content of and the procedure leading up to the statement of the Committee on Doctrine. In view of the pastoral concerns presented by the Committee on Doctrine, and following their proposal, the Administrative Committee unanimously authorized the immediate publication of the statement.

It is noteworthy that Dolan explicitly mentioned the discussion by the USCCB Administrative Committee of both the content and the procedure leading up to the statement, and their approval of its immediate publication. The controversial element of the procedure used in making this statement was its publication before any opportunity had been given to Johnson to respond to the severe criticisms it expressed concerning her book. This procedure was particularly deplored by the board of directors of the CTSA, in view of the fact that in 1989 the NCCB had approved the document *Doctrinal Responsibilities*, which provided that when misunder-

12. *Origins* 40 (2011): 704–11.

13. This letter was posted on the CTSA website: http://www.ctsa-online.org/pdf_doc_files/Letter%20of%20Archbishop%20Dolan%20to%20CTSA%20President,%20July%207,%202011.pdf.

standings arise between bishops and theologians about the teaching of the gospel and the ways of expressing it, "informal conversation ought to be the first step towards resolution."[14] Cardinal Donald Wuerl, archbishop of Washington and chairman of the Committee on Doctrine of the USCCB, replied to the criticism of the fact that his committee had not followed the procedure proposed in *Doctrinal Responsibilities* for the solution of conflicts between bishops and theologians. In his document entitled "Bishops as Teachers: A Resource for Bishops,"[15] he wrote:

> *Doctrinal Responsibilities* was intended to promote cooperation in resolving misunderstandings between individual diocesan bishops and theologians. *Doctrinal Responsibilities* did not address the special responsibilities of the Committee on Doctrine of our national episcopal conference. In addition the document is presented for consideration as one way of proceeding but not as obligatory.[16]

One may grant that the Committee on Doctrine is not obliged to follow the procedure for formal doctrinal dialogue proposed in *Doctrinal Responsibilities.* But it is surely obliged to follow a procedure that respects the rights of theologians, among which the same document names "the right . . . to a good reputation, . . . and, if needed, the defense of that right by appropriate administrative or judicial processes within the Church," and "in cases of dispute . . . the right to expect access to a fair process."[17] In his defense of the procedure followed by the Committee on Doctrine in Johnson's case, Wuerl mentioned the fact that his committee had been entrusted with a mandate by the CDF. This suggests that one could usefully compare the procedure followed by his committee with the procedure that John Paul II prescribed for the CDF to follow in its examination of books and other writings touching on faith and morals. In his apostolic constitution *Pastor bonus* John Paul decreed:

> [The Congregation] examines carefully writings and opinions that seem to be contrary or dangerous to true faith, and, if it is established that they are opposed to the teaching of the Church, reproves them in due

14. NCCB, *Doctrinal Responsibilities: Approaches to Promoting Cooperation and Resolving Misunderstandings between Bishops and Theologians* (Washington, DC: NCCB, 1989), 4. The CTSA statement was published in *Origins* 41 (2011): 18–19.

15. Published in *Origins* 41 (2011): 19–23.

16. Ibid., 23.

17. NCCB, *Doctrinal Responsibilities*, 8.

> time, having given authors full opportunity to explain their minds, and having forewarned the Ordinary concerned; it brings suitable remedies to bear, if this be opportune.[18]

As one would expect, when the CDF published the new Regulations for Doctrinal Examination in 1997, the rules for "ordinary procedure" gave the authors whose works were examined full opportunity to respond, first in writing and then orally, to the objections communicated to them, before the publication of any critical judgment on their work.[19] The Regulations also laid down the following rules for examination in cases of urgency:

> Article 23. An urgent examination is employed when the writing is clearly and certainly erroneous and, at the same time, its dissemination could cause or already has caused grave harm to the faithful. . . .
>
> Article 26. If the ordinary session judges that the above-mentioned propositions are in fact erroneous and dangerous, after the approval of the Holy Father they are transmitted to the author, through his ordinary, with the request that they be corrected within two canonical months.
>
> Article 27. If the ordinary, having heard the author, believes it is necessary to ask him for a written explanation, this text must be forwarded to the congregation together with the opinion of the ordinary. Such an explanation is then presented to the ordinary session for the appropriate decisions.[20]

In his defense of the decision of his committee to publish its critical judgment on Johnson's book *Quest for the Living God*, without having communicated its objections to her or given her an opportunity to respond, Wuerl said that she could have initiated a dialogue with a bishop by requesting an *imprimatur* for her book, a step that he noted is recommended by canon 827.2, even when it is not required. He went on to say: "Once a theological work is published, however, it is ipso facto open to response. It is like the tennis ball that has been hit in a tennis match. It is already in play. If it is called out of bounds, it is not an adequate defense to say that the referee did not enter into dialogue with the player beforehand."[21]

18. *Pastor bonus*, art. 51, http://www.vatican.va/holy_father/john_paul_ii/apost_constitutions/documents/hf_jp-ii_apc_19880628_pastor-bonus_en.html.

19. Regulations for Doctrinal Examination, sec. III, Ordinary Procedure for Examination, *Origins* 27 (1997): 222.

20. Ibid., sec. IV, Examination in Cases of Urgency.

21. Cardinal Wuerl, "Bishops as Teachers: A Resource for Bishops," *Origins* 41 (2011): 19–23, at 22.

Does this mean that Wuerl recommends that bishops enter into dialogue with authors about theological opinions they express in their books only if the authors have initiated such a dialogue by requesting the imprimatur? One would hope that the Administrative Committee of the USCCB would not approve this as the policy of its Committee on Doctrine, and that it would rather adopt as its own policy that it will not authorize the publication of a critical judgment on a theologian's work unless the objections of the Committee on Doctrine had been communicated to the author with ample opportunity to respond to them. This policy would enable authors to clarify the meaning of what they had written, and thus prevent the damage that the bishops' teaching authority would suffer if it could subsequently be shown that the severe judgment published by the Committee on Doctrine was based, at least in part, on a misunderstanding of what the author had written.

Congregation for the Doctrine of the Faith

Founded by Pope Paul III as the Sacred Congregation of the Universal Inquisition, renamed the Sacred Congregation of the Holy Office by Pope Pius X, it received its present name, the Congregation for the Doctrine of the Faith, from Pope Paul VI in 1965, when he added to its original function of protecting the faith from error, the positive task of promoting sound doctrine.[22] This twofold task is now expressed in the regulations given to the CDF by John Paul II in 1988.[23] Since the time of Paul VI, but especially during the pontificate of John Paul II, the CDF has been fulfilling its new positive task by issuing authoritative teaching documents on a variety of topics. It described its own magisterial function in its "Instruction on the Ecclesial Vocation of the Theologian" (*Donum veritatis*) where it said:

> The Roman Pontiff fulfills his universal mission with the help of the various bodies of the Roman Curia and in particular with that of the Congregation for the Doctrine of the Faith in matters of doctrine and morals. Consequently, the documents issued by this Congregation expressly approved by the Pope participate in the ordinary magisterium of the successor of Peter.[24]

For this reason, every document issued by the CDF must have received papal approval, and the fact of such approval is affirmed at the conclusion

22. Apostolic Letter *Integrae servandae*, *Acta apostolicae sedis (AAS)* 57 (1965): 953.

23. Apostolic Constitution *Pastor Bonus*, arts. 48–51, *AAS* 80 (1988): 873.

24. *Donum veritatis* no. 18, http://www.vatican.va/roman_curia/congregations/cfaith/documents/rc_con_cfaith_doc_19900524_theologian-vocation_en.html.

of the document. In his statement of approval, the pope may single out particular articles in the document, and declare that he is approving those articles *in forma specifica*. Articles that are thus specifically approved have the authority of statements made by the pope himself, while the rest of the document has teaching authority that is delegated by him.

As an example of ordinary papal approval it seems useful to cite the formula used at the conclusion of *Donum veritatis* referred to above:

> *This Instruction was adopted at a Plenary Meeting of the Congregation for the Doctrine of the Faith and was approved at an audience granted to the undersigned Cardinal Prefect by the Supreme Pontiff, Pope John Paul II, who ordered its publication.*[25]

My reason for citing the statement of papal approval at the conclusion of *Donum veritatis* is that no such statement is found at the conclusion of a document entitled "Commentary on Profession of Faith's Concluding Paragraphs," which was signed by the prefect of the CDF, Cardinal Joseph Ratzinger, and by its secretary, Archbishop Tarcisio Bertone, and was published along with the apostolic letter of Pope John Paul II, *Ad tuendam fidem*.[26] A new Profession of Faith, consisting of the Nicene-Constantinopolitan Creed followed by three paragraphs drawn up by the CDF, had been published in *L'Osservatore Romano* on February 25, 1989.[27] In the following year, in *Donum veritatis* no. 23, the CDF briefly explained the meaning of those paragraphs. One can well understand the assumption that a more extended commentary on them, signed by the cardinal prefect and the secretary of the CDF, would have the teaching authority of a document issued by the CDF. This assumption seemed to be confirmed by what Ratzinger and Bertone said in the cover letter they sent to all the bishops along with the "Commentary."[28] After speaking of the objections and questionable interpretations that had been published by theologians, especially with reference to the Profession of Faith's second paragraph, they wrote: "For these reasons, this congregation has judged it opportune to publish this doctrinal commentary on the concluding formula of the Profession of Faith, which is intended in the first place for bishops, the teachers of the faith."[29] However, the absence of a

25. Ibid., no. 42, emphasis original.

26. *Origins* 28 (1998): 114–16, with the "Commentary," 116–19.

27. Subsequently published in *AAS* 81 (1989): 104–6.

28. "Letter Regarding Commentary on the Profession of Faith," *Origins* 28 (1998): 163–64.

29. Ibid., 164.

concluding statement, affirming that the "Commentary" was published by the CDF with papal approval, still raised doubts about its doctrinal authority.

In the following year, Ratzinger responded to questions that had been raised about the "Commentary" by attaching a note to an article entitled *Stellungnahme*, which he published in *Stimmen der Zeit*. This note's importance justifies giving it here in full:

> This text was composed by the entire congregation and was presented to the meeting of the cardinals in its several drafts, and was finally approved by them; it also received the approval of the Holy Father. But it was agreed that this text should not be presented as having its own teaching authority, but solely as a help for understanding, and therefore should not be published in the form of an independent document of the congregation. On the other hand, in order to show that it was not a private writing of the prefect and secretary of the congregation, but rather an authorized aid to the understanding of the text, the way it was published was deliberately chosen. One conclusion that is correctly drawn is that the examples [we gave] have no greater doctrinal weight from their mention in the commentary than they already had.[30]

While this strikes me as a puzzling explanation of the way the "Commentary" was published, it clearly means that it does not have the doctrinal weight of a document of the CDF and therefore does not oblige Catholics to give *obsequium religiosum* to its doctrinal statements. The reference to "examples" has to do with the judgments its authors expressed as to the paragraph of the Profession of Faith to which various particular doctrines belong. Thus, it is significant that they described the doctrine that the church has no authority to ordain women to the priesthood as belonging to the second paragraph. This means that in their judgment that doctrine has not been taught as a revealed truth, but as one that is definitively taught and calls for a firm assent of the mind. I suggest that this judgment may account for the fact that the "Commentary" was published along with *Ad tuendam fidem*, which added to the Code of Canon Law a penalty for the obstinate rejection of a doctrine of that kind (c. 1371.1).

An interesting question one might raise about the "Commentary" is whether its teaching authority has been enhanced by the fact that the prefect and secretary of the CDF who signed it are now the supreme pontiff and his secretary of state.

30. *Stimmen der Zeit* 217 (1999): 169–71, at 171 (my translation).

The Secondary Object of Infallibility

The object of teaching authority, which has undergone significant development since Vatican II, is what theologians have called "the secondary object of infallibility," that is, truths that are not revealed but are intimately connected with revealed truth. There has been development on three issues: (1) the nature of the connection with revealed truth that qualifies something as a secondary object of infallible teaching; (2) the "theological note" of the proposition that the magisterium can speak infallibly about such nonrevealed truths; and (3) the assent that must be given to such truths when the magisterium proposes them in a definitive way.

The Nature of the Connection with Revealed Truth

At Vatican I, Bishop Vincent Gasser, the official spokesman for the *Deputatio de Fide*, explained the propositions that could be defined not as "dogmas of faith," but as "truths to be held," as those that are "required for the defense and explanation of the deposit of faith, since without these the deposit of faith could not be guarded and explained."[31]

Vatican II described the limits of the object of infallible magisterium by saying that it "extends just as far as the deposit of divine revelation that must be guarded as sacred and faithfully expounded."[32] This last phrase was explained by the Doctrinal Commission as referring to those things that "are required in order that the same deposit may be religiously safeguarded and faithfully expounded."[33]

In its declaration *Mysterium ecclesiae* of June 24, 1973, the CDF made its own the explanation that had been given at the two Vatican Councils, of the connection with revealed truth that is required for a nonrevealed truth to be taught infallibly. It declared: "According to Catholic doctrine, the infallibility of the Church's Magisterium extends not only to the deposit of faith but also to those matters without which that deposit cannot be rightly preserved and expounded."[34]

However, in *Donum veritatis* the CDF did not explain such truths as being necessary for the preservation or exposition of revealed truth, but

31. Mansi, *Sacrorum conciliorum nova collectio*, 52:1226.

32. *Lumen gentium* no. 25.

33. *Acta synodalia Sacrosancti Concilii Oecumenici Vaticani Secundi*, vol. 3, pt. 8, p. 89 (my translation).

34. *Mysterium ecclesiae* no. 3, http://www.vatican.va/roman_curia/congregations/cfaith/documents/rc_con_cfaith_doc_19730705_mysterium-ecclesiae_en.html.

as being "intimately connected with them in such a way that the definitive character of such affirmations derives in the final analysis from revelation itself."[35] In another place in the same document, the CDF described such truths as "strictly and intimately connected with revelation."[36] This description raised the question whether it was no longer the official position that for such connected truths to be taught infallibly they must be "matters without which the deposit of faith cannot be rightly preserved and expounded."

An authoritative answer to this question was given by John Paul II in his apostolic letter *Ad tuendam fidem*. Here he introduced into the Code of Canon Law a paragraph (c. 750.2) affirming the obligation of the faithful firmly to embrace and hold each and every proposition that is stated definitively by the magisterium and is "required for the sacred preservation and faithful explanation of the deposit of faith."[37] In the introductory section of his letter, the pope explained that such propositions are intimately linked to revealed truths "either for historical reasons or through logical connection."[38] But it clearly is not enough that there be a historical or logical connection with revealed truth. The new paragraph in the Code makes it clear that the propositions that the second paragraph of the Profession of Faith says must be firmly embraced and held are those required for the preservation and explanation of revealed truth.

"Theological Note" of the Proposition That the Magisterium Can Teach Infallibly about Its Secondary Object

At Vatican I, when Bishop Gasser spoke of the possibility that the pope could define a proposition that was not revealed but was required for the defense and explanation of revealed truth, he explained that it was not the council's intention to define papal infallibility in regard to such a matter as a dogma of faith, but to leave that infallibility in its actual state as "theologically certain."[39]

At Vatican II, an early draft of the paragraph treating the infallible ordinary magisterium of the whole body of bishops spoke of the object of such teaching as "revealed faith." To satisfy an objection, the text was amended to allow for the possibility of infallible teaching on matter connected with

35. *Donum veritatis* no. 16.
36. Ibid., no. 23.
37. *Ad tuendam fidem* no. 4A, *Origins* 28 (1998): 115.
38. Ibid., no. 3.
39. Mansi, *Sacrorum conciliorum nova collectio*, 52:1226–27.

revelation. The change of the text involved substituting "matters concerning faith and morals" for "revealed faith." The reason the Doctrinal Commission gave for this change was "lest the infallibility of the episcopal body seem to be restricted to that only which is proposed to be believed as divinely revealed."[40] Thus, Vatican II followed Vatican I in allowing for the possibility of infallible teaching regarding the secondary object, but can hardly be said to have expressly affirmed this as conciliar doctrine.

However, as we have seen above, in its declaration *Mysterium ecclesiae*, the CDF wrote: "According to Catholic doctrine, the infallibility of the Church's Magisterium extends not only to the deposit of faith but also to those matters without which that deposit cannot be rightly preserved and expounded."[41] The theological note "Catholic doctrine" usually refers to authoritative but nondefinitive teaching of the magisterium. The CDF did not explain its reason for classifying the infallibility of the magisterium with regard to its secondary object as "Catholic doctrine."

An even stronger affirmation of the official status of the doctrine that the magisterium can speak definitively about its secondary object was made when the CDF drew up the new formula for the profession of faith. In the second paragraph after the Creed, the person making the profession says: "I also firmly accept and hold each and everything definitively proposed by the Church regarding teaching on faith and morals."[42] The CDF, in *Donum veritatis* no. 23, explained that this paragraph of the Profession of Faith refers to definitive teaching about matters that are not revealed, but are "strictly and intimately" connected with revelation. To require firm adherence to such teaching in the Profession of Faith is obviously a strong assertion of the church's ability to speak definitively about matters that are not in themselves revealed.

John Paul II affirmed this ability even more strongly in *Ad tuendam fidem* no. 4A. Here he introduced the obligation to adhere to such teaching into the Code of Canon Law, and declared that anyone who rejects those propositions that are to be held definitively is opposed to the doctrine of the Catholic Church.[43] He further decreed that anyone who pertinaciously rejects such a proposition and who does not make a retractation after

40. *Acta synodalia* vol. 3, pt. 1, p. 251.

41. *Mysterium ecclesiae* no. 3.

42. CDF, Profession of Faith, http://www.vatican.va/roman_curia/congregations/cfaith/documents/rc_con_cfaith_doc_1998_professio-fidei_en.html.

43. C. 750.2.

being admonished by the apostolic see or the ordinary is to be punished with a just penalty.[44]

It is to be noted that in both the Profession of Faith and *Ad tuendam fidem*, in reference to matter that is only connected with revelation, the magisterium is described as proposing doctrine "definitively"; the term "infallibly" is not used in these texts. Some theologians have drawn the conclusion that here we have a new category of teaching that is definitive but not infallible. However, in their "Commentary," Ratzinger and Bertone clearly express their understanding that when the magisterium definitively teaches a doctrine that belongs to the second paragraph of the Profession of Faith, it also speaks infallibly. They explain that such doctrines can be either solemnly defined or taught infallibly by the ordinary universal magisterium. They conclude: "Every believer, therefore, is required to give *firm and definitive assent* to these truths, based on faith in the Holy Spirit's assistance to the Church's magisterium and on the Catholic doctrine of the infallibility of the magisterium in these matters."[45]

The development that has taken place with regard to the infallibility of the magisterium when it speaks definitively about truths not revealed but required for the defense or explanation of revealed truth can be summed up by observing that what was considered only "theologically certain" at Vatican I is now described as "Catholic doctrine." This development is implied in the second paragraph of the Profession of Faith and is enforced by canon law.

The Nature of the Response to Be Given to Propositions of the "Secondary Object" When They Are Taught Definitively

The *Catechism of the Catholic Church*, in its original edition of 1994, in paragraph no. 88, under the heading, "The Dogmas of the Faith," states:

> The Church's Magisterium exercises the authority it holds from Christ to the fullest extent when it defines dogmas, that is, when it proposes truths contained in divine Revelation or having a necessary connection with them, in a form obliging the Christian people to an irrevocable adherence of faith.[46]

Here the *Catechism* espoused the opinion that by defining a doctrine that is not revealed but has a necessary connection with revealed truth, the

44. C. 1371.1.
45. "Commentary," no. 6, emphasis original.
46. *Catechism of the Catholic Church* (St. Paul, MN: Wanderer, 1994): no. 88.

magisterium makes that unrevealed truth into a dogma that requires the irrevocable adherence of faith. This opinion has been held by a few theologians, but it was never before proposed as the doctrine of the Catholic Church. Previous official statements had said that such doctrines, when proposed definitively, were to be "firmly accepted and held," but did not speak of an "irrevocable adherence of faith."

Three years later, the definitive Latin edition of the *Catechism* was published with a corrected version of no. 88, which in the second English edition reads:

> The Church's magisterium exercises the authority it holds from Christ to the fullest extent when it defines dogmas, that is, when it proposes, in a form obliging the Christian people to an irrevocable adherence of faith, truths contained in divine revelation, or also when it proposes, in a definitive way, truths having a necessary connection with these.

Here there is a clear distinction between truths contained in divine revelation and truths having a necessary connection with them. Only of the former is it now said that they can be proposed as dogmas obliging the Christian people to an irrevocable adherence of faith. Of the latter it is now said only that the church's magisterium exercises its authority to the fullest extent also when it proposes such truths in a definitive way. It says nothing about the response due them when they are so taught. One can presume that the proper response is that expressed by the words "firmly accept and hold" used in the second paragraph of the Profession of Faith.

In the "Commentary" signed by Ratzinger and Bertone, the distinction between dogmas of faith and definitively proposed "connected truths" is expressed by the two terms: "doctrines *de fide credenda*" and "doctrines *de fide tenenda*."[47] While I think the distinction between doctrines "to be believed" and doctrines "to be held" is clear enough, it strikes me as misleading to say that truths that are not revealed are "to be held *de fide*," since the term *de fide* normally refers to faith in revealed truth. At Vatican I an earlier draft of the definition of papal infallibility said that the pope is infallible when he defines "what is to be held as of faith" (*tamquam de fide tenendum*).[48] Archbishop Henry Edward Manning and some other bishops objected to this formula on the grounds that the term *de fide tenendum*

47. "Commentary," no. 8.

48. Mansi, *Sacrorum conciliorum nova collectio*, 52:7.

would limit the object of papal infallibility to revealed truth.[49] I think that to describe the definitively proposed "connected" truths as *de fide tenenda* is a way of expressing the required response that can only cause further confusion about a matter that has already caused a good deal of confusion.

The Exercise of Teaching Authority

A significant development has taken place since Vatican II with regard to the exercise of teaching authority in the form of official declarations that certain doctrines have been taught infallibly by the ordinary universal magisterium. Vatican I's Dogmatic Constitution on the Catholic Faith declared: "By divine and catholic faith all those things are to be believed which are contained in the word of God as found in scripture and tradition, and which are proposed by the church as matters to be believed as divinely revealed, whether by her solemn judgment or in her ordinary and universal magisterium."[50] Vatican I did not explicitly attribute infallibility to what is taught by the ordinary universal magisterium, but Vatican II did so, spelling out the conditions under which it enjoys the charism of infallibility, namely, that the Catholic bishops dispersed throughout the world but maintaining the bond of communion among themselves and with the successor of Peter are agreed in teaching a doctrine concerning faith and morals as to be held definitively.[51] While Catholic theologians had been accustomed to speaking of certain doctrines as taught by the ordinary universal magisterium, the first official document that specifically named particular doctrines as having been so taught was the 1995 encyclical *Evangelium vitae* of John Paul II. Here he declared that the grave immorality of the direct and voluntary killing of an innocent human being,[52] of direct abortion,[53] and of euthanasia[54] is "taught by the ordinary and universal magisterium." It is noteworthy that he did not say that those doctrines had been taught infallibly, even though in each case the footnote referred to *Lumen gentium* no. 25, which includes the statement cited

49. See Umbento Betti, *La constituzione dommatica "Pastor Aeternus" del Concilio Vaticano I* (Rome: Pontifical University "Antonianum," 1961): 390, 401.

50. Denzinger-Schönmetzer, *Enchiridion symbolorum*, 34th ed., no. 3011 (my translation).

51. *Lumen gentium* no. 25.

52. *Evangelium vitae* no. 57.

53. Ibid., no. 62.

54. Ibid., no. 65.

above about the infallible teaching of the whole body of bishops when they are in agreement that a particular doctrine is to be held definitively.

Later in the same year 1995, the CDF issued its "Reply to the *dubium* concerning the teaching contained in the apostolic letter *Ordinatio sacerdotalis*."[55] Here, referring to the teaching that the church has no authority to confer priestly ordination on women, which in that letter John Paul II had said must be held definitively, the CDF declared: "This teaching requires definitive assent, since, founded on the written word of God and from the beginning constantly preserved and applied in the tradition of the church, it has been set forth infallibly by the ordinary and universal magisterium."[56] Here we have the first official statement explicitly identifying a particular doctrine as having been taught infallibly by the ordinary universal magisterium. In the "Reply to the *dubium*" this doctrine was twice described as *pertinens ad depositum fidei,* which seemed to mean that it was proposed as a divinely revealed truth. However, it was later made clear that the word *pertinens* in the "Reply to the *dubium*" meant "related to" rather than "belonging to," since, as I have noted, Ratzinger and Bertone, in their "Commentary," placed the doctrine excluding women from the priesthood among truths that were not taught as revealed, but as necessarily connected with revelation.

In that same "Commentary" they named other doctrines as having been taught infallibly, including the doctrines of the grave immorality of the direct and voluntary killing of an innocent human being, and of euthanasia.[57] In those two instances, their footnotes refer to the passages of *Evangelium vitae* in which the pope declared that those doctrines had been taught by the ordinary universal magisterium.[58] They clearly take the pope's statements to mean that those doctrines had been taught infallibly. They offer the following explanation of the significance of a papal declaration that a doctrine has been taught by the ordinary universal magisterium:

> The magisterium of the church . . . teaches a doctrine to be *believed as divinely revealed* (first paragraph) or to be *held definitively* (second paragraph) with an act which is either *defining* or *nondefining*. . . . In the case of a *nondefining* act, a truth is taught *infallibly* by the ordinary

55. *Origins* 25 (1995): 402–3.

56. Ibid., 403.

57. "Commentary," no. 11.

58. On the killing of an innocent person, their footnote refers to *Evangelium vitae* no. 57; on euthanasia, it refers to no. 65.

> and universal magisterium of the bishops dispersed throughout the world who are in communion with the successor of Peter. *Such a doctrine can be confirmed or reaffirmed by the Roman pontiff, even without recourse to a solemn definition,* by declaring explicitly that it belongs to the teaching of the ordinary and universal magisterium as a truth that is divinely revealed (first paragraph) or as a truth of Catholic doctrine (second paragraph). Consequently, when there has not been a judgment on a doctrine in the solemn form of a definition, but this doctrine, belonging to the inheritance of the *depositum fidei,* is taught by the ordinary and universal magisterium, which necessarily includes the pope, such a doctrine is to be understood as having been set forth infallibly. The declaration of *confirmation* or *reaffirmation* by the Roman pontiff in this case is not a new dogmatic definition, but a formal attestation of a truth already possessed and infallibly transmitted by the church.[59]

The problem that Catholic theologians have always had with the doctrine of the infallible teaching of the ordinary universal magisterium is with the verification of the fact that the bishops along with the pope have been and are in agreement in teaching a particular doctrine as definitively to be held. Three criteria for such verification have been invoked in the past. The first is the positive response given by the bishops to the pope when he asked them what they believed and were teaching about a doctrine on which the pope planned to issue a statement. Pius IX, when he defined the Immaculate Conception, and Pius XII, when he defined the Assumption, each named the common affirmative response he had received from the bishops among the grounds on which he based his definition. John Paul II likewise invoked the "unanimous agreement of the bishops, albeit dispersed throughout the world," in response to his consultation of them about abortion, when he declared that the grave immorality of abortion "is taught by the ordinary and universal magisterium."[60] A second criterion was proposed by Pius IX, who invoked the universal and constant consensus of Catholic theologians that a doctrine called for the response of faith, as proof that it was being taught by the ordinary and universal magisterium as revealed truth.[61] A third is found in the Code of Canon Law, where Canon 750 says that when a doctrine is taught as divinely

59. "Commentary," no. 9, emphasis original.

60. *Evangelium vitae* no. 62.

61. Pius IX, *Tuas libenter* (December 21, 1863), Denzinger-Schönmetzer, *Enchiridion*, 2879.

revealed by the ordinary and universal magisterium, this is manifested by the common adherence of Christ's faithful.

The recent development in this matter is that a new criterion has been proposed which is easier to verify than the last two: this is an exercise of ordinary papal magisterium, or a statement by the CDF, declaring that a particular doctrine has been taught infallibly by the ordinary universal magisterium. In neither case would the declaration as such be infallible. It would seem to be understood that when such a declaration has been made, there would be no need of further verification of the fact that the bishops were in agreement in teaching that doctrine as definitively to be held. With regard to such a doctrine as the grave immorality of the direct and voluntary killing of an innocent person, the question would hardly arise whether the Catholic bishops agreed in teaching that doctrine as definitively to be held. But this was not the case when, in the "Response to the *dubium*," the CDF declared that the doctrine that the church has no authority to ordain women to the priesthood was taught infallibly by the ordinary universal magisterium. It was evident that Catholic bishops had not been ordaining women to the priesthood, and that in this regard they had been following a tradition that went back to the apostolic age. But it was not so evident that the bishops had been in agreement in teaching that the faithful must hold definitively that the church has no authority to ordain women to the priesthood. In the "Commentary" by Ratzinger and Bertone a footnote suggests how they might have responded to someone who asked for the evidence that prior to the publication of *Ordinatio sacerdotalis*, the bishops had been agreed in teaching that doctrine. This footnote reads:

> It should be noted that the infallible teaching of the ordinary and universal magisterium is not only set forth with an explicit declaration of a doctrine to be believed or held definitively, but is also expressed by a doctrine implicitly contained in a practice of the church's faith, derived from revelation or, in any case, necessary for eternal salvation and attested by the uninterrupted tradition.[62]

It seems to me that this response would be based on the assumption that if the bishops were asked why they ordained only men to the priesthood, they would have given a reason that would explain and justify that tradition, and that the reason they gave would be the doctrine implicitly

62. "Commentary," note.

contained in their practice. But this assumption raises two questions. In the years before the publication of *Ordinatio sacerdotalis* is it likely that the reason that all the bishops would have given for not ordaining women to the priesthood was that Christ had not given the church the authority to do so? And even if this doctrine had been implicit in their practice, would that satisfy the condition laid down by Vatican II for the infallible teaching of the ordinary universal magisterium? It strikes me that the idea that a doctrine that was *implied* in a traditional *practice* could for that reason be understood as having been infallibly *taught* by the ordinary universal magisterium needs further discussion.

Another question that needs serious theological examination is whether a papal declaration that a particular doctrine has been taught by the ordinary universal magisterium definitively settles the question whether the conditions laid down by Vatican II for the infallible teaching of the ordinary universal magisterium have been fulfilled in this case. It is well known that after Vatican I defined the dogma of papal infallibility, more than one attempt was made to extend the pope's infallibility to his ordinary magisterium.[63] One can hardly be surprised that the question has been raised whether this recent development would not introduce another way of attributing infallibility to the ordinary magisterium of the pope if, as it seems, it would mean that, without solemnly defining a doctrine, he could render it irreformable by declaring that it has been taught infallibly by the ordinary universal magisterium.[64]

Conclusion

In looking back over the developments in teaching authority that have taken place since Vatican II, I have been struck by the fact that each of them has been the result of an intervention of the Holy See, either by the pope himself or by the CDF acting by his authority.

John Paul II in 1998 decreed that for a doctrinal statement of an episcopal conference to have teaching authority it must either be approved by all the members of the conference or obtain the *recognitio* of the Holy See if it was approved by two-thirds. The difficulty of obtaining a unanimous vote for a doctrinal statement would be likely to have the effect of limiting

63. The most serious of these was by Alfred Vacant, in his work *Le magistère de l'Église et ses organes* (Paris: Delhomme et Briquet, 1887).

64. See, for instance, Bernard Sesboüé, SJ, *Le magistère à l'épreuve: Autorité, vérité, et liberté dans l'Église* (Paris: Desclée de Brouwer, 2001), 275.

the choice of topics to those on which the leadership could be confident that the conference could produce statements that would receive the Holy See's *recognitio*.

Two initiatives by John Paul II, the promulgation of a new formula for the Profession of Faith and the introduction of a new paragraph into the Code of Canon Law, have had the effect of giving the status of definitive doctrine to an opinion that, at Vatican I, was judged to be only theologically certain, namely, that the magisterium can teach infallibly about doctrines that are not revealed, but that are required for the defense or explanation of some revealed truth. As a result of these initiatives, Catholics who are obliged to make the Profession of Faith must declare that they firmly accept and hold such doctrines when they are definitively taught, and a canonical penalty can now be imposed on one who obstinately rejects such a doctrine.

Finally, a new way of exercising teaching authority by the Holy See was first seen in the encyclical *Evangelium vitae*, where John Paul II declared that three moral doctrines had been taught by the ordinary universal magisterium, in each instance referring to *Lumen gentium* no. 25, where the council named the conditions for its infallibility. The CDF soon followed this precedent by declaring that the doctrine that the church has no authority to ordain women to the priesthood had been infallibly taught in this way. I believe further discussion is needed of the grounds on which those making such declarations base their assurance that the conditions laid down by Vatican II for the infallibility of the ordinary universal magisterium have been fulfilled.

6 The Trinitarian Depths of Vatican II

ANNE HUNT

Central to Vatican II's deliberations on the church was a fundamental rediscovery: the church's origin in the mystery of the Trinity. How this rediscovery permeates and shapes the council's ecclesial vision is what this article addresses. Four leitmotifs exemplify the expanded horizon for the council's understanding of the church that this rediscovery afforded: church as mystery, as communio, as mission to the world, and as community of dialogue.

At the heart of the Second Vatican Council lay its deliberations on the church itself[1] and, at their core, its most fundamental rediscovery of all: the church's origin in the mystery of the Trinity. The rediscovery of her trinitarian origins opened up new avenues and vistas, an expanded horizon and a new mind-set for the council's understanding of the church, both *ad intra* in regard to her life and mission and *ad extra* in regard to her dialogical outreach to others. As Giuseppe Alberigo commented toward the end of his magisterial history of the council, "It does not seem an exaggeration to claim that the action of the Spirit and the dynamism of the Trinity were a constant running through the Council itself and the

1. Karl Rahner writes: "The Council . . . was a Council of the Church about the Church, a Council in which all the themes discussed were ecclesiological ones; which concentrated upon ecclesiology as no previous Council had ever done" ("The New Image of the Church," *Theological Investigations*, vol. 10, trans. David Bourke [London: Darton, Longman, & Todd, 1973], 10–24, at 4).

body of its decrees."[2] I here propose to demonstrate how this rediscovery permeates and profoundly shapes the council's leitmotifs, major themes, and overarching ecclesial vision.

Trinitarian references in the Vatican II corpus occur at highly significant points: *Sacrosanctum concilium*, the Constitution on the Sacred Liturgy (hereafter *SC*), describes the church's nature and mission as deriving from the will of the triune God who wishes all to be saved (no. 5).[3] God's salvific will is realized through the missions of the Son and Holy Spirit and celebrated in the church's Eucharistic liturgy (no. 5). The "whole of liturgical life" (no. 6) revolves around the work of salvation and thus manifests "the sort of entity the true church really is" (no. 2). Here in *SC* is not only the council's chronological starting point but also its theological starting point, adumbrating the key conciliar themes and priorities, as they would subsequently emerge.[4] Here indeed lies Vatican II's ecclesiological core. It is a distinctly paschal-eucharistic ecclesiology, and it is deeply trinitarian.[5] *Dei verbum*, the Dogmatic Constitution on Divine Revelation (hereafter *DV*), is likewise of remarkable significance for the council and its ecclesiology. As Pope Benedict XVI has noted, it "gave an intense impulse to the appreciation of the Word of God from which has derived a profound renewal of the life of the ecclesial community."[6] Moreover, the return to the Word of God prompted a renewed appreciation of the missions of the Son and Spirit in the world and of the life of the Trinity *ad intra* from which the missions emanated. The explicit reference to Father, Son, and Spirit in the opening paragraphs of the constitution signals the deeply trini-

2. Giuseppe Alberigo, "Transition to a New Age," in *History of Vatican II*, 5 vols., ed. Giuseppe Alberigo and Joseph A. Komonchak (Maryknoll, NY: Orbis, 2000), 5:573–644, at 632.

3. All English translations of Vatican II texts are taken from *Decrees of the Ecumenical Councils*, ed. Norman P. Tanner (Washington, DC: Georgetown University, 1990).

4. *SC*'s first sentence is programmatic: "It is the intention of this holy council to improve the standard of daily christian living among Catholics; to adapt those structures which are subject to change so as better to meet the needs of our time; to encourage whatever can contribute to the union of all who believe in Christ; and to strengthen whatever serves to call all people into the embrace of the church" (no. 1).

5. See Massimo Faggioli, "*Sacrosanctum Concilium* and the Meaning of Vatican II," *Theological Studies* 71 (2010): 437–52.

6. Benedict XVI, "On 'Dei Verbum' and Reading Scripture," *Zenit*, November 6, 2005, ref. ZE05110601, http://www.zenit.org/article-14473?l=english (all URLs cited herein were accessed on November 11, 2012). See Karim Schelkens, *Catholic Theology of Revelation on the Eve of Vatican II: A Redaction History of the Schema* De fontibus revelationis *(1960–1962)* (Boston: Brill, 2010).

tarian orientation of the entire document (no. 2). Revelation is described in terms of a personal trinitarian self-communication (nos. 2, 4). It leads humankind to the Father, through Christ and in the Spirit, and to a sharing in the divine nature (no. 2). Our eschatological end is the trinitarian communion (no. 2). The Son's mission took place so that humankind would know of God's inmost being (no. 4). Only after the trinitarian grounding of revelation does the document proceed to a discussion of Scripture and tradition (no. 7). While the christological dimension of *DV* is strong, a clear pneumatological emphasis is also evident (nos. 5, 7–11).

Lumen gentium, the Dogmatic Constitution on the Church (hereafter *LG*), describes the church first in terms of its inner reality as mystery, not as structure or institution or even society.[7] The mystery of the church is, then, grounded in the mystery of the Trinity (nos. 2–4). Here, a strong trinitarian seal is firmly placed on the whole document. The church is "a people made one by the unity of the Father and the Son and the holy Spirit" (no. 4). The trinitarian missions are the source of her life and mission, just as union with the triune God and the unity of the whole human race are her goal (no. 1). *LG* recognizes the founding of the church at Pentecost as manifestly a work of the Trinity (no. 5). The church *itself*, and not merely its missionary dynamism or catholicity, originates in the trinitarian life of God. The church's nature, mission, and identity manifest a trinitarian form: the church is *Ecclesia de Trinitate*, people of God, Body of Christ, and Temple of the Holy Spirit (no. 17). The universal call to holiness in the church is expressed in explicitly trinitarian terms (nos. 39, 47). The eschatological nature of the pilgrim church is also expressed in trinitarian terms (no. 48). The vocation of the church is unity with one another in mutual charity and in praise of the Trinity (no. 51). The trinitarian resonances of the constitution sound through to the end with the prayer that all people "be happily gathered together in peace and harmony into one people of

7. This theological rhetoric—symbolic and metaphorical as distinct from juridical and legislative—signals the clear change in the style and tenor of the council's ecclesiological discourse, a change registered not only in *LG* but also in the other conciliar documents. There is also immediate evidence of the council's shifting from the neo-Scholastic theological style and the apologetic concerns of the preconciliar period. Joseph Ratzinger has noted the "one-sided" view of the nature of the church that focuses on the juridical and hierarchical that persisted up to the council. See Joseph Ratzinger, *Theological Highlights of Vatican II*, 2nd ed., intro. Thomas P. Rausch, SJ (New York: Paulist, 2009): 73–74. See also Joseph A. Komonchak, "Theology and Culture at Mid-Century: The Example of Henri de Lubac," *Theological Studies* 51 (1990): 579–602; Avery Dulles, "A Half Century of Ecclesiology," *Theological Studies* 50 (1989): 419–42.

God to the glory of the most holy and undivided Trinity" (no. 69). *LG* also describes the vital pneumatic dimension of the church (nos. 2, 4, 7, 13).[8]

Gaudium et spes, the Pastoral Constitution on the Church in the Modern World (hereafter *GS*), in its famous opening words explains in explicitly trinitarian terms that all that is genuinely human is of concern for the followers of Christ (no. 1). On the topic of human community and interpersonal relationships, *GS* also assumes an expressly trinitarian frame of reference (no. 24). It is precisely the church's trinitarian origins that inspire dialogue and engagement with today's world (no. 40). As in the case of *LG*, what at first appears as a Christocentrism in fact opens out into a differentiated trinitarian vision. The strong pneumatological statements in *GS* also unfold in a comprehensively trinitarian manner. The trinitarian resonances throughout *GS*, as in *LG*, rise to an explicitly trinitarian conclusion with a distinctly trinitarian comprehension of the faith, hope, and love that unite the human community in God even now (no. 93).

Ad gentes, the Decree on the Mission Activity of the Church (hereafter *AG*), provides what is arguably the trinitarian highlight of the Vatican II documents.[9] *AG* describes the nature of the church as fundamentally missionary, with the foundation for its missionary activity lying in its participation in the trinitarian missions: "The pilgrim Church is of its very nature missionary, since it draws its origin from the mission of the Son and the mission of the holy Spirit, in accordance with the plan of God the Father" (no. 2). Mission is thus not merely just one aspect of the church's nature, but is essentially constitutive of it, springing from the church's grounding in the trinitarian mystery of God. Furthermore the church's missionary activity pertains not only to missionaries but also to all the faithful by virtue of their participation through baptism in the very life of the Trinity, in which all the faithful share (no. 6).

When read in conjunction with *LG* and *AG*, *Unitatis redintegratio*, the Decree on Ecumenism (hereafter *UR*), offers further insight into the deep

8. The documents of Vatican II frequently refer to the Holy Spirit—92 times in *LG* alone. For the rich Pneumatology of Vatican II, see Yves Congar, "The Pneumatology of Vatican II," in *I Believe in the Holy Spirit*, trans. David Smith (New York: Crossroad, 1983), 167–74; see also Sally M. Vance-Trembath, "The Pneumatology of Vatican II with Particular Reference to *Lumen gentium* and *Gaudium et spes*" (PhD diss., University of Notre Dame, 2003).

9. For a detailed account of the history of *Ad gentes*, see Stephen Bevans and Jeffrey Gros, *Evangelization and Religious Freedom:* Ad gentes *and* Dignitatis humanae (New York: Paulist, 2009), 3–38. See also James B. Anderson, *A Vatican II Pneumatology of the Paschal Mystery: The Historical-Doctrinal Genesis of* Ad Gentes *1, 2–5* (Rome: Gregorian University, 1988).

trinitarian roots of the council's ecclesial vision. *UR* ascribes the impetus for Christian unity to the Holy Spirit (no. 1). The principles of ecumenism are articulated in trinitarian terms (no. 2). The mystery of the unity of all the followers of Christ finds its exemplar, as well as its source, in the mystery of the unity of the Trinity (no. 2). *UR* exhorts Christians to holiness—union with the persons of the Trinity—as a way to advance Christian unity: "For the closer their union with the Father, the Word and the Spirit, the more deeply and easily will they be able to grow in mutual brotherly love" (no. 7).

The council's rediscovery of the church's origins in the mystery of the Trinity, reflected in these references to the mystery, exercised a profound influence on the council's understanding of the church, its nature, life, and mission. It is the key that opens the door to an understanding of the whole. Indeed, one might well make the same comments on the teachings of Vatican II that then-Cardinal Joseph Ratzinger made in a foreword to Henri de Lubac's book, *Catholicism*:

> [De Lubac] makes visible to us in a new way the fundamental intuition of Christian Faith so that from this inner core all the particular elements appear in a new light. He shows how the idea of community and universality, rooted in the trinitarian concept of God, permeates and shapes all the individual elements of Faith's content. The idea of the Catholic, the all-embracing, the inner unity of I and Thou and We does not constitute one chapter of theology among others. It is the key that opens the door to a proper understanding of the whole.[10]

The Trinitarian Roots of the Council's Leitmotifs

The influence of Vatican II's heightened consciousness of the relationship between the Trinity and the church is evident particularly in the council's more dynamic conception of church, in her origins, mission, and eschatological goal. I suggest that it is also evident in the language, style, and tone of the council's documents. As some scholars have noted, the Vatican II documents, in contrast to those of prior councils, are persuasive rather than dogmatic in tone, pastoral rather than juridical in genre, dialogical rather than didactic in style, and inclusive and open rather than defensive and hostile in their vision of the church in relation to the world.[11]

10. Joseph Ratzinger, foreword to Henri de Lubac, *Catholicism: Christ and the Common Destiny of Man* (San Francisco: Ignatius, 1988), 11–12, at 12. Ratzinger goes on: "For me, the encounter with this book became an essential milestone on my theological journey."

11. See John W. O'Malley, *What Happened at Vatican II* (Cambridge, MA: Belknap of Harvard University, 2008), 305–11; and O'Malley, "Trent and Vatican II: Two Styles

This most fundamental *ressourcement* afforded a change of horizon and mind-set and thus a fresh consideration of the church's life and mission. The ecclesiology that emerged as a consequence contrasts in significant ways with the dominant ecclesiology of preconciliar papal and conciliar statements.[12] I now turn to consider four leitmotifs, each of immense import in the council's ecclesial vision, and each traceable to the rediscovery in the church's trinitarian origins.

Church as Mystery

LG begins its programmatic first chapter under the heading "The Mystery of the Church (*De ecclesiae mysterio*)." There is arguably no more significant development in Vatican II than its understanding of the nature and mission of the church as mystery. As Pope Paul VI expressed it, the church is "imbued with the hidden presence of God";[13] it is not simply the bearer or proclaimer of the mystery, but mystery itself. This leitmotif was decisive not only for its theological significance in *LG* but also for the corpus of conciliar teachings and the key themes they addressed.

In sharp contrast to previously prevailing notions of the church as perfect society or mystical body of Christ, the vision of the church as mystery, deriving from the trinitarian mystery itself, situated the council's ecclesiology in a specifically theological context, as distinct from a juridical or institutional one.[14] Envisioning the church as mystery also highlighted the pilgrim nature of the church as a community of *viatores*, not perfect but continually journeying, on the way to an essentially eschatological fulfilment. Ever in anticipation of this fulfilment, the church is not an end in itself, but rather the sign, sacrament, and instrument of God's will for the salvation of all.

---

of Church," in *From Trent to Vatican II: Historical and Theological Investigations*, ed. Raymond F. Bulman and Frederick J. Parrella, foreword Jill Raitt (New York: Oxford University, 2006), 301–20; Ghislain Lafont, *Imagining the Catholic Church: Structured Communion in the Spirit* (Collegeville, MN: Liturgical Press, 2000), 69–78; and Ormond Rush, *Still Interpreting Vatican II: Some Hermeneutical Principles* (New York: Paulist, 2004).

12. For example, Pius XII's encyclical *Mystici corporis* (1943) and Vatican I's *Dei Filius* (1870) and *Pastor aeternus* (1870).

13. Pope Paul VI, allocution opening the second session of the Second Vatican Council, September 19, 1963, http://www.vatican.va/holy_father/paul_vi/speeches/1963/documents/hf_p-vi_spe_19630929_concilio-vaticano-ii_lt.html.

14. "Mystery" also afforded the recognition of the church as *una realitas complexa* (*LG* no. 8), allowing the council to hold in tension both the social and transcendent dimensions of the church's reality, and avoiding an overemphasis on either the mystical or the institutional aspects of her existence.

Given an understanding of mystery as primordial and intrinsic to the church's very being, she is then recognized as ever in process, on her pilgrim way, developing and maturing, always incomplete and short of her goal, and never fully possessing or understanding her own nature and mission.[15] As ever imperfect and *in via*, she is called to continual renewal and reform, not merely institutionally and structurally but also spiritually and interiorly. Indeed she is ever called to conversion. A renewed appreciation of the church as mystery, grounded in the mystery of the Trinity, thus prompts recognition of the need for continuing renewal.

This appreciation also prompts a sense of ecclesial humility in the realization that the church is not immune to criticism or reproach. *UR*, for example, speaks of the church as summoned by Christ "to continual reformation, of which it is always in need" (no. 6),[16] and that, if there have been deficiencies in moral conduct, church discipline, or the formulation of church teaching, "these should be set right in the proper way at the opportune moment" (no. 6). *UR* also speaks of a kind of fraternal rivalry among separated Christians by means of which *all* will be stirred to "a deeper awareness and a clearer manifestation of the unfathomable riches of Christ" (no. 11).

A dynamic notion of church and of the development of doctrine emerges—in contrast to institutional rigidity and static doctrinal approaches.[17] Similarly, the way is opened for assimilation of the faith in new cultures and contexts. As Pope John XXIII had explained in his

15. *LG* also employs the metaphor of a seed sprouting, unfolding, growing, developing, maturing, and dying into something else (no. 5). Similarly the pilgrim church is on the way, developing, maturing, and imperfect. See nos. 8 and 43 for the council's reflections on the church's imperfections.

16. This text is notable particularly in that it is the only time the council uses the word *reformatio* in relation to the church.

17. Ratzinger commented: "In the era of liberalism that preceded the First World War, the Catholic Church was looked upon as a fossilized organization, stubbornly opposed to all modern achievements. Theology had so concentrated on the question of the primacy as to make the Church appear to be essentially a centralized organization that one defended staunchly but which somehow one related to from the outside. Once again it became clear that the Church was more than this. . . . It became clear that the Church has experienced organic growth over the centuries, and continues to grow even today" (Ratzinger, "The Ecclesiology of Vatican II," Conference of Cardinal Ratzinger at the Opening of the Pastoral Congress of the Diocese of Aversa, Italy, September 15, 2001, Ratzinger Archives, http://www.ewtn.com/library/curia/cdfeccv2.htm). John Courtney Murray, *peritus* at the council, argued that development of doctrine was "the issue underlying all the issues at the Council" (Murray, "This Matter of Religious Freedom," *America* 112, no. 2 [January 9, 1965]: 40–43; http://woodstock.georgetown.edu/library/Murray/0_murraybib.html).

address at the opening of the council, "For the deposit of faith, the truths contained in our venerable doctrine, are one thing; the fashion in which they are expressed, but with the same meaning and the same judgement, is another thing."[18]

This stance of humility and openness also moved the council from *ad intra* considerations of church life to *ad extra* considerations of her relation to the world. The church emerged as more positively attuned to the world, open to learning from it, and freshly attentive to the voices of the times. As *GS* explains:

> It is for God's people as a whole, with the help of the holy Spirit, and especially for pastors and theologians, to listen to the various voices of our day, discerning them and interpreting them, and to evaluate them in the light of the divine word, so that revealed truth can be increasingly appropriated, better understood and more suitably expressed. (no. 44)

A renewed sense of revelation as God's loving tripersonal self-disclosure released the council from static neo-Scholastic notions of revelation as objective formulae and merely abstract propositional information. Together with the council's fresh comprehension of the church as mystery grounded in the mystery of the Trinity, it afforded an appreciation of revelation as most fundamentally personal and dialogical. The council was thus freed for personal and dialogical engagement, for *communio* and mission.

Church as Communio

As has often been lamented, for much of the church's history in the West a certain Christomonism had seemed to overshadow the role of the Holy Spirit, so much so that Yves Congar was moved to comment that until recently the Holy Spirit was rightly described as "the 'unknown' or 'half-known' one."[19] The council's heightened awareness of the pneumatic dimension of the church prompted an appreciation of the Holy Spirit as the life-principle or soul of the church (*LG* no. 7), and of the people of God as a communion of persons, who are created, animated, and sustained in union by the Spirit of Christ. This fresh insight into the role of the Spirit

18. The pope added: "This way of speaking will require a great deal of work and, it may be, much patience: types of presentation must be introduced which are more in accord with a teaching authority which is primarily pastoral in character" (*Acta apostolicae sedis* 54 [1962]: 785–96, at 791; ET, http://jakomonchak.files.wordpress.com/2012/10/john-xxiii-opening-speech.pdf).

19. Yves Congar, *I Believe in the Holy Spirit*, 3 vols., trans. David Smith (New York: Crossroad, 1997), 3:5.

served to correct limited Christomonistic understandings of church. It also reinforced the council's sense of the church's distinctly trinitarian origins. The result, as noted above, was a focus on the church's inner life and its people *qua* mystery, as distinct from an unbalanced emphasis on the juridical, legislative, and institutional aspects of church life.

The council's new emphasis on both the pneumatological and christological dimensions of the church was also accompanied by a heightened sense of *all* the faithful sharing in the one Spirit of unity. This realization inevitably called into question notions of a rigidly hierarchical and highly centralized ecclesial structure and inspired a shift toward an understanding of church in terms of *communio*, based on the analogy with the mystery of the Trinity. Indeed, according to Ladislas Orsy: "*Communio* was the central theme of the Council. . . . The Council Fathers made a profession of faith in the church of Christ as the *communio* of believers. . . . The Council lifted up the church to a new vision, or into a new field of vision."[20]

The notion of church as *communio* emerged under three aspects: (1) the church herself as mystery of trinitarian *communio* (*LG* no. 4; *UR* no. 2); (2) the church as sign and sacrament of *communio* (*LG* no. 9); and (3) the church's origin and end as the trinitarian *communio* (*LG* nos. 2–4).[21] A heightened comprehension of the Trinity as both the original mystery of unity in diversity and exemplar for the church prompted a fresh openness to unity in diversity and a new impetus for a *communio* model of church. A *communio* ecclesiology thus emerged, albeit in a variety of forms, as the principal ecclesiology of Vatican II.

The *communio* model of church yielded rich ecclesiological fruits, although not without attendant challenges.[22] While *communio* is not

20. Orsy adds that the council, however, "left little guidance for its implementation" (*Receiving the Council: Theological and Canonical Insights and Debates* [Collegeville, MN: Liturgical Press, 2009], xiii). In "The Ecclesiology of Vatican II," Ratzinger comments: "First of all one must admit that the word 'communio' did not occupy a central place in the Council. All the same if properly understood it can serve as a synthesis of the essential elements of the Council's ecclesiology" (http://www.ewtn.com/library/curia/cdfeccv2.htm).

21. For elaboration on these three aspects, see Maximilian Heinrich Heim, *Joseph Ratzinger: Life in the Church and Living Theology; Fundamentals of Ecclesiology with Reference to* Lumen Gentium, trans. Michael J. Miller (San Francisco: Ignatius, 2004), 62–73.

22. See Avery Dulles, "A Half Century of Ecclesiology," *Theological Studies* 50 (1989): 419–42; Leonardo Boff, *Trinity and Society*, trans. Paul Burns (Maryknoll, NY: Orbis, 1988); Dennis Doyle, *Communion Ecclesiology: Vision and Versions* (Maryknoll, NY: Orbis, 2000); Jean-Marie Roger Tillard, *Church of Churches: The Ecclesiology of Communion*, trans. R. C. De Peaux (Collegeville, MN: Liturgical Press, 1992).

primarily concerned with institutional structures, the momentum for such a model and for the relationship between unity and plurality in the church fashioned accordingly served to challenge a more Rome-centered, institutional, juridical model. One of those ecclesiological fruits was a renewed emphasis on the importance of the local church in relation to the universal church, understood as a *communio ecclesiarum*, and a sense of unity as issuing from below rather than from above. The *communio* model also afforded a fresh appreciation of the plurality of human cultures (*GS* nos. 44, 53, 58) and of inculturation in the work of evangelization, although it inevitably also raised the challenge of legitimate diversity in relation to the concern for unity.

Very importantly, the *communio* model prompted a renewed appreciation of the collegiality of the episcopacy in the exercise of its shared responsibility for the teaching and authority of the universal church (*LG* no. 22). While affirming Vatican I's teaching on the primacy of the papacy, Vatican II envisioned the pope and the bishops as together forming a college in which the bishops share with the pope, as bishop of Rome, the leadership of the universal church. Just as the universal church is comprised of a *communio* of local churches, the college of bishops is comprised of the *communio* of bishops. Both communions find their exemplar in the Trinity.

The rediscovery of the people of God as one reality, a mutuality of hierarchy and laity, in which all are called to holiness, was another of the profound insights of Vatican II. This recognition of the fundamental equality and dignity of all the faithful gave impetus to a more mature theology of the laity. The council envisaged the vital role of the laity in the church, wherein they are no longer regarded as mere subjects but as participants; as no longer passive recipients of the directions of the hierarchy, nor even merely collaborators with the hierarchy, but as active members of the people of God, with all the baptized sharing in the priestly, prophetic, and kingly offices of Christ. As *Apostolicam actuositatem*, the Decree on the Apostolate of the Laity (hereafter *AA*) explained, "Laypeople, sharing in the priestly, prophetic and kingly offices of Christ, play their part in the mission of the whole people of God in the church and in the world" (no. 2). Moreover the layperson is not merely a noncleric or nonreligious. Rather, each member of the church, through new birth at baptism, is gifted by the Holy Spirit and has a legitimate role to play in the church's mission and its quest for the fullness of grace and truth. "Through receiving these gifts of grace, however unspectacular, everyone of the faithful has the right and duty to exercise them in the church and in the world for the good of humanity and for the building up of the Church" (no. 3). The Holy Spirit "leads the church into all truth (Jn 16:23), and he makes it one in fellowship and ministry, instructing and directing it through a diversity of gifts both hierarchical and charismatic, and he adorns it with his fruits (see Eph 4:11–12; 1 Cor 12:4; Gal 5:22)" (*LG* no. 4). The council described the relationship between clergy and laity as one of mutual respect and esteem.[23] Thus, in contrast to a strongly hierarchical, monarchical model of church with the laity firmly and passively situated at the bottom of a pyramidal structure, a much-expanded vision of the laity emerged.[24]

Moreover, given the presence of the Holy Spirit in the whole baptized people of God, the laity together with the hierarchy is imbued with a sense of the faith (*sensus fidei*, *LG* no. 35). While Vatican II affirms the teaching of Vatican I that the solemn "definitions [of the Roman pontiff] are rightly said to be irreformable of themselves, and not from the consent of the church, for they are delivered with the assistance of the holy Spirit which was promised to him in blessed Peter" (*LG* no. 25), it also unambiguously affirmed the dignity of *all* the faithful, and that the sense of the faithful (*sensus fidelium*) pertains to hierarchy *and* laity. Reception too, like mission, is a coresponsibility.[25] Indeed, the council also recognized that the laity are not only entitled but are also sometimes duty-bound to express their opinions on matters that concern the good of the church (*LG* no. 37).

Church as Mission to the World

In recognizing that the church is missionary by her very nature, and that her mission derives from the Trinity itself, *AG* no. 2 marked a momentous breakthrough in the church's self-understanding in terms of mission. The council recognized that not only are the dynamic quality of her missionary activity and her outreach in catholicity sustained and inspired by the missions of the triune God, who wishes all to be saved, but also her very nature and mission *qua* church derive from the Trinity. As *LG* nos. 2–4 also explain, it is from this trinitarian source that the church receives the mission to proclaim and spread among all peoples the kingdom of Christ and of God. This insight was crucially important in the council's mindset, direction, and dynamism, and it derives directly from the council's rediscovery of the church's trinitarian origins.

23. *AA* no. 23.

24. *Monarchia*/monarchy does not appear in any of the final Vatican II documents.

25. See Cardinal Léon Joseph Suenens, *Coresponsibility in the Church*, trans. Francis Martin (New York: Herder & Herder, 1968), 29.

Being missionary by her very nature, organizational, structural, and legislative questions take second place in service to mission. Moreover, the mission of the church cannot be limited to that of the hierarchy alone, for the laity, by virtue of their baptism, are endowed with the gifts of the Holy Spirit and share in the abiding charismatic character of the church and in the priestly, prophetic, and kingly functions (*triplex munus*) of Christ (*LG* nos. 34–36), and so participate in the church's mission. Theirs is an active participation that belongs to *all*, hierarchy and laity alike, whatever their distinct gifts, vocations, and responsibilities.

A distinctly new ecumenical openness also arises from the sense of the "church as mission," giving an enduring impetus to a renewed quest for unity with other Christians, and inspiring the church's positive recognition of other religions and indeed of all people who seek God with a sincere heart (*LG* nos. 16, 22). As Congar noted, when *UR* speaks of a fraternal emulation, a kind of fraternal rivalry, "to incite all to a deeper understanding and a clearer manifestation of the unfathomable riches of Christ" (*UR* no. 11), the council expresses deep respect for the theological and spiritual life of the reformed churches.[26] Stressing what unites rather than what divides separated Christians, *LG* no. 15 states: "They lovingly believe in God the almighty Father and in Christ, the Son of God and saviour. They are marked by baptism, by which they are joined to Christ; and indeed there are other sacraments that they recognise and accept in their own churches or ecclesiastical communities." Hence the council, in another striking development, makes frequent mention of dialogue in regard to other Christian communities.[27]

Few developments were more radical than that expressed in *Nostra aetate*, the Declaration on the Church's Relation to Non-Christian Religions (hereafter *NA*), namely, that the church "rejects nothing of those things which are true and holy in these religions," and that "those ways of acting and living and those precepts and teachings which, though often at variance with what it holds and expounds, frequently reflect a ray of that truth which enlightens everyone" (no. 2). While *NA* makes no references to the Trinity as such—it refers to the Father and to the Son but not to the Holy Spirit[28]—the council's unprecedented openness to dialogue and collaboration with other religions is necessarily situated in terms of its reflection on the nature and mission of the church, particularly as

26. Yves Congar, *My Journal of the Council*, trans. Mary John Ronayne and Mary Cecily Boulding, ET ed. Denis Minns (Collegeville, MN: Liturgical Press, 2012), lv.

27. *UR* nos. 4, 9, 11, 14, 18, 19, 21, 22, 23.

28. *NA* nos. 2, 4, 5.

articulated in *LG*. This openness to other religious paths is clearly adumbrated in the council's awareness of the church's trinitarian origins and of her sharing in the missions of the Son and Spirit: God is Father of all (*NA* no. 5), "since he gives to all life and breath and everything (see Acts 17:25-28), and the Saviour wills all to be saved" (*LG* no. 16). The triune God's will for the salvation of *all* provides the theological foundation for the church's universal evangelizing mission, and thus for her dialogue and engagement with the whole world, including other Christian churches and other religions. For as *LG* reiterates, "All human beings are called to the new people of God" (no. 13).

Church as Community of Dialogue

The council also recognized that the church's mission is undertaken not in a dogmatic or didactic fashion, but in dialogue and engagement with the world in its joys and hopes, sorrows and anxieties (*GS* no. 1). Dialogue—accompanied by such notions as colloquium, conversation, cooperation, and collaboration—is another of the council's leitmotifs.[29] The principle of dialogue as fundamental to the mission of the church also flows directly from its refreshed trinitarian consciousness and is rightly regarded as another of the most important insights of Vatican II. The principle derives from a dialogical understanding of communal life of the Trinity itself as exemplar par excellence. As Ormond Rush explains: "If the church is called to be the icon of the Trinity, and dialogue is at the heart of trinitarian *communio*, . . . then dialogue must be at the heart of, and indeed constitute, ecclesial *communio*—vertical, horizontal, and temporal."[30] The principle of dialogue also derives from the mystery of salvation whereby the triune God, through Christ and in the Holy Spirit, entered into dialogue with humanity, a dialogue that the church undertakes by continuing Christ's mission. To recognize that the church is missionary by her very nature, with her mission deriving from the Trinity, is also to recognize that she is dialogical by nature, both *ad intra* and *ad extra*.

The council's awareness of the church's multidimensional relation to the mystery of the Trinity—as origin, form, exemplar, and goal—thus also allowed for a fresh framing of the question of its relationship to the world. *LG* acknowledged that the church is not untouched by the world or remote from its history, but rather is immersed in an evolving reality and is part

29. "Dialogue" occurs 24 times in the Vatican II corpus, frequently in connection with other Christians and the contemporary world.

30. Ormond Rush, *The Eyes of Faith: The Sense of the Faithful and the Church's Reception of Revelation* (Washington, DC: Catholic University of America, 2009), 49.

of the movement toward the eschaton when God will be all in all (nos. 5, 9, 48). *GS* similarly brought a new approach to the mutuality of the world-church relationship when it begins, not with the timeless abstract truths of faith, but with the human person and the human condition in the world.[31] The universal call to holiness, another vital element in the council's vision, is an invitation to communion with the triune God and with the whole human family. The council thus recognized the world as a genuine dialogue partner and the church–world relationship as one that involved both mutual benefits and mutual obligations (*GS* nos. 40–45).

The council thus also signalled a shift from conflict with the world to *rapprochement* with it, from defensively denouncing the world to appreciating and engaging it in dialogue.[32] As *GS* explains, "The wish for such conversations, undertaken solely out of love for the truth and with all due prudence, excludes nobody, as far as we are concerned, neither those who cultivate the value of the human spirit while not yet acknowledging their source, nor those who are hostile to the church and persecute it in various ways" (no. 92). In this respect, the council also defended with unprecedented conviction the role of conscience and religious freedom,[33] and expressed an appreciation even of the church's critics and persecutors: "Indeed the church affirms that it has derived, and can derive, much benefit from the opposition of its opponents and persecutors" (*GS* no. 44).

Conclusion: The Council's Trinitarian Depths

Vatican II was an occasion of effervescent, dynamic self-awareness, inspired by its most fundamental *ressourcement*: the rediscovery of the transcendent mystery of the triune God as the mystery at the heart of the church's existence and the ultimate source of its life. The result of this trinitarian *ressourcement* was a renewed insight into the church's relation to the Trinity as her origin, exemplar, source of her mission, and eschatological goal. Indeed, the Council Fathers' recognition of the church as *Ecclesia de Trinitate* led them to a fresh framing of the questions of her identity, mission, and relation to the world.

31. See James McEvoy, "Church and World at the Second Vatican Council: The Significance of *Gaudium et Spes*," *Pacifica* 19 (2006): 37–57.

32. See, e.g., James Gerard McEvoy, "Proclamation as Dialogue: Transition in the Church–World Relationship," *Theological Studies* 70 (2009): 875–903.

33. See *Dignitatis humanae*, the Declaration on Religious Freedom (hereafter *DH*).

John XXIII had prayed for a new Pentecost, and indeed, according to the accounts of many who were there, it was so. Alberigo observed:

> From its first announcement and throughout its entire course, the Council was motivated by reliance on the Holy Spirit. It is worth noting that with increasing frequency John XXIII emphasized "the need of a continuous outpouring of the Holy Spirit as if on a new Pentecost that will renew the face of the earth." The image of a new Pentecost was regularly associated with the Council which "will be truly a new Pentecost that will cause the interior riches of the Church to blossom."[34]

Gregory Baum, *peritus* at the council, writes:

> I have experienced that pentecostal events are possible in the church. The sociologist Emile Durkheim speaks of "times of effervescence" in the life of societies that allow them to renew themselves. Pentecostal events happen; they cannot be manipulated; institutions may initiate them, but they cannot foretell whether the Spirit will summon forth effervescence.[35]

Finally, Ratzinger commented on his experience:

> The Council is a Pentecost—that was a thought that corresponded to our own experiences at that time; not only because Pope John had formulated

34. Alberigo, "Transition to a New Age," 632. He adds: "The call for a revival of pneumatology is inherent in the Council's conception of the Church. This conception, which moved beyond the Christo-monistic limitations typical of *Mystici corporis*, was based precisely on a rediscovery of the role of the Spirit."

35. In *Voices from the Council*, ed. Michael R. Prendergast and M. D. Ridge (Portland, OR: Pastoral, 2004), 143, Bishop Frank Markus Fernando remarked that the presence of the Holy Spirit was palpable at the council ("Interview," in *Voices from the Council*, 19). John A. Coleman reports: "In the Caporale interviews, and in other memoirs or accounts of the Council, it is very clear that a large number of those who participated in the Council—as *periti* or bishops— felt such strong surges of solidarity and alternative possibility. They saw the Council as an historical event. Cardinal Suenens, in his interview with Caporale, captures this: 'surely, we all have changed considerably between the first and second sessions, very much so. The action of the Holy Spirit was evident. One could almost touch it everywhere' " (*The Belgian Contribution to the Second Vatican Council*, ed. D. Donnelly et al. [Leuven: Peeters, 2008], 17). See Thomas Hughson, "Interpreting Vatican II: 'A New Pentecost,' " *Theological Studies* 69 (2008): 3–37; and Cardinal Léon Joseph Suenens, *A New Pentecost?*, trans. Francis Martin (London: Darton, Longman, & Todd, 1975). For Durkheim's notion of collective effervescence, see Émile Durkheim, *The Elementary Forms of Religious Life*, trans. Joseph Ward Swain (London: Allen & Unwin, 1954), 214–23.

> it as a wish, as a prayer, but because it reflected what we experienced on our arrival in the city of the Council: meetings with bishops of all countries, all tongues, far beyond what Luke . . . could have imagined and, thus, a lived experience of real Catholicity with its Pentecostal hope.[36]

As a consequence of its trinitarian *ressourcement*, the council experienced an effervescent bubbling up of a new freedom and creativity in the task of *aggiornamento*. It began to imagine the church anew— in her nature, identity, and mission, and in her relationship to the world. Admittedly, the council offered no fully articulated blueprint for renewal, but it pointed to the sources of a new vitality and vision and gave new impetus for renewal in the church, both *ad intra* and *ad extra*. The result was a fresh openness and sense of mutuality in regard to the world, a receptivity to the other, and a readiness for dialogue, engagement, and commitment.

While I do not presume to reduce the council's ecclesiology to the four leitmotifs identified here, the ones I have examined—mystery, *communio*, mission, and dialogue—figure very strongly and decisively in the council's ecclesiology. I have demonstrated that each derives from and expresses the council's trinitarian consciousness. They are, moreover, mutually related and inextricably interconnected in their own kind of perichoretic unity. In this way, the council's rediscovery of the church's origins in the mystery of the Trinity suffuses the conciliar texts and the great ecclesiological themes they address. While the council's trinitarian assumptions were often subtle, this most fundamental *ressourcement* of the council provides an indispensable frame of reference for the deep, internal, intertextual coherence of the conciliar corpus and is a vital key to a proper understanding of the whole.[37]

36. Joseph Ratzinger, *Principles of Catholic Theology: Building Stones for a Fundamental Theology*, trans. Mary Frances McCarthy (San Francisco: Ignatius, 1987), 367.

37. On the intertextual character and coherence of the Vatican II documents, see O'Malley, *What Happened at Vatican II*, 309–12. Most recently, O'Malley comments, "Unlike the determinations of previous councils, those of Vatican II . . . implicitly but deliberately cross-reference and play off one another—in the vocabulary they employ, in the great themes to which they recur, in the core values they inculcate, and in certain basic issues that cut across them" ("'The Hermeneutic of Reform': A Historical Analysis," *Theological Studies* 73 [2012]: 517–46, at 541). In his own way, Congar also attests to the coherence of the conciliar texts: "a very serious attempt at integration was made at Vatican II. There was, for instance, no Scripture without Tradition and no Tradition without Scripture. There was no sacrament without the Word. There was no Christology without pneumatology and no pneumatology without Christology. There was no hierarchy without the people and no people without the hierarchy. There was no episcopate without the Pope and no Pope without the episcopate. There was no local Church that was not missionary and no mission that was not ecclesial. There was

In conclusion, my analysis compels me to endorse Alberigo's judgment that the council expressed its ecclesial vision within a distinctly *trinitarian horizon*:

> There is no denying that the preconciliar work in the area of pneumatology and the trinitarian dimension was fragmentary and inadequate. During the work of the Council no proposal was even made for a treatment of these subjects, and yet they really, and increasingly, formed the horizon against which the Council developed its subjects, inasmuch [as] and to the extent that the great majority of fathers felt an urgent need to escape from an overly static doctrinal approach incapable of being assimilated by new cultures. It does not seem an exaggeration to claim that the action of the Spirit and the dynamism of the Trinity were a constant running through the Council itself and the body of its decrees. Perhaps as a result also of the witness given by the observers, especially in view of the dynamic action of the Spirit, the Council was not deaf but showed an impulse, weak as it may have been, to reintegrate the trinitarian and pneumatological dimensions in Catholic thought and devotion.[38]

The tasks of *aggiornamento* and of *ressourcement* for the sake of the gospel are as urgent for us now as they were then for the Council Fathers. So too the challenge to hold in ever creative tension and balance the juridical and communal, administrative and charismatic, local and universal, papacy and episcopacy, hierarchy and people, clergy and laity, unity and diversity, tradition and renewal, continuity and discontinuity. John Henry Newman observed that "there has seldom been a council without great confusion after it."[39] Clearly, reflection on the message of Vatican II will be confused and its reception seriously impeded if its profound and pervasive trinitarian consciousness is lost. Should it be so, all that would be left is a few—and basically disconnected—doctrinal formulations and ecclesiastic arrangements, along with the risk of withdrawal into legalism and juridicism to the detriment of the Spirit-led, charismatic, and profoundly trinitarian character of the church.

But the mystery of the Trinity is a mystery of life ever surging forth inexhaustibly, drawing all to itself, calling the church into life, and ever

---

no Church which was not mindful of the whole Church and which did not provide universality within itself and so on" (quoted in *Vatican II by Those Who Were There*, ed. Alberic Stacpoole [London: Geoffrey Chapman, 1986], 343–44).

38. Alberigo, "Transition to a New Age," 632.

39. John Henry Newman, letter to W. J. O'Neill Daunt, August 7, 1870, in *The Letters and Diaries of John Henry Newman*, vol. 25, *The Vatican Council (January 1870 to December 1871)*, ed. Charles Stephen Dessain and Thomas Gornall, SJ, electronic ed. (Charlottesville, VA: InteLex Corp., 1995), 174–75, at 175.

active in its renewal. As we look back and move forward—not without the anxieties, preoccupations, and challenges of our own day—it is well to be mindful that it is not so much a matter of finding the Trinity in the documents of Vatican II as of finding the whole event of Vatican II, its history, its spirit, and the texts it produced, within the infinities of love, light, and life that are the grace of the Trinity, now and always, for the church and for each of her members.

7 Ecclesial Conversion after Vatican II

Renewing "the Face of the Church" to Reflect "the Genuine Face of God"

ORMOND RUSH

The Second Vatican Council was an event of conversion for the participating bishops, and the council's documents propose a vision for the conversion of the Catholic ecclesial imagination. The author argues that this ecclesial conversion entails a refashioning of the Catholic Church's understanding of the divine-human relationship in history. This relationship includes the divine-ecclesial relationship and, consequently, relationships within the Church. The article concludes by examining two particular dimensions of the council's call for ongoing ecclesial conversion that remain unfulfilled.

Conversion for the individual Christian is a constant calling, embedded in the tug of faith itself. God is always drawing the believer to deeper and deeper intimacy with God, away from a self-absorbed life to a life directed toward God, and to a way of living that embraces self-giving love: "Love God with all your heart"; "Love your neighbor as yourself." So too with ecclesial conversion. God continually calls the church, as a people, to greater fidelity to God in its covenant commitment as a community of faith, to a more authentic worship, to a spirit of reconciliation within and outside the community, and to a deeper commitment to generosity, justice, and compassion.

Like other councils before it, the Second Vatican Council set out to reform the Catholic Church. As Pope John Paul II later saw it, in *Ut unum sint*: "In the teaching of the Second Vatican Council there is a clear connection between renewal, conversion and reform."[1] Moreover, he says: "The council calls for personal conversion as well as for communal conversion."[2] Joseph Ratzinger called the council a "spiritual awakening" for the Church.[3] According to Ladislas Örsy, it was "an event of conversion."[4] This conversion event and the call to ecclesial conversion, which its documents encapsulate, continue to challenge us.

In this essay, I propose that Vatican II, in turning anew to God, marks a conversion of the Catholic ecclesial imagination. Specifically, I argue that this entails a refashioning of the Church's understanding of the divine-human relationship in history.[5] This includes the divine-ecclesial relationship and, consequently, relationships within the Church. I then comment on just two particular dimensions of the council's call for ongoing ecclesial conversion that remain unfulfilled.

Levels of Ecclesial Conversion

The actual Latin noun *conversio* appears only 12 times in the Vatican II documents; the verb *convertere*, 26 times.[6] Many references relate either to new Christian converts or, for those already converted, to a closer adherence to Christian life. For example, *Lumen gentium* speaks of "continual conversion" (*conversione continua*) in the lives of lay people.[7] *Unitatis redintegratio*, in the context of "continual reformation," states: "There

1. John Paul II, *Ut unum sint* no. 16, translation from *Ut unum sint* (Vatican City: Libreria Editrice Vaticana, 1995). All quotations from Vatican II documents are taken from Austin Flannery, ed., *Vatican Council II: The Basic Sixteen Documents: Constitutions, Decrees, Declarations; A Completely Revised Translation in Inclusive Language* (Northport, NY: Costello, 1996).

2. Ibid. no. 15.

3. Joseph Ratzinger, *Theological Highlights of Vatican II* (New York: Paulist, 2009), 194.

4. Ladislas Örsy, "Law for Life: Canon Law after the Council," in *Receiving the Council: Theological and Canonical Insights and Debates* (Collegeville, MN: Liturgical Press, 2009), 74–90, at 79.

5. Regarding the orthography of "church" in this article, wherever the word refers specifically to the Roman Catholic Church, I have made it upper case—to avoid giving the impression that what pertains to the Catholic Church also pertains to the whole church, even though in some cases it surely could.

6. See Philippe Delhaye, Michel Guéret, and Paul Tombeur, eds., *Concilium Vaticanum II: Concordance, index, listes de fréquence, tables comparatives* (Louvain: Publications du CETÉDOC, 1974), 148.

7. *LG* no. 35.

can be no ecumenism worthy of the name without interior conversion [*interiore conversion*]."[8]

However, a philological analysis of the technical words for "conversion" found throughout the documents does not give us the full picture. We need also to examine the word usage of other overlapping, related themes concerning the Church "turning to God." A cluster of Latin nouns and their verb forms capture the themes most closely related to ecclesial conversion: renewal, purification, reform, restoration, change, updating, adaptation, development.[9] Of these, "renewal" and "renew" (*renovatio* and *renovare*) are the most often used.[10]

The postconciliar literature tends to focus on the pair of terms "renewal" and "reform."[11] Views among the interpreters of Vatican II differ. Some propose that the council makes a clear distinction between their meanings—"renewal" relates only to personal and collective spiritual transformation, and "reform" only to institutional and structural change. Christoph Theobald, for example, proposes that the two terms "renewal" and "reform" in the final documents capture two juxtaposed perspectives, one in *Lumen gentium* and the other in *Unitatis redintegratio*, both promulgated on the same day.[12] Others, including Joseph Ratzinger, propose that, according to the council, only personal conversion is needed; reform of the Church as a collective will automatically follow, including institutional change.[13]

8. *UR* no. 7.

9. The Latin forms are *renovatio*, *purificatio*, *reformatio*, *instauratio*, *mutatio*, *accommodatio*, *aptatio*, *evolutio*. The verb forms are *renovare*, *purificare*, *reformare*, *instaurare*, *mutare*, *accommodare*, *aptare*, and *evolvere*. In a few cases, only the noun or the verb form is found.

10. For a discussion of all instances of these words, see Peter De Mey, "Church Renewal and Reform in the Documents of Vatican II: History, Theology, Terminology," *Jurist* 71 (2011): 360–400. See also John O'Malley, "'The Hermeneutic of Reform': A Historical Analysis," *Theological Studies* 73 (2012): 517–46, at 536–42.

11. With regard to the related terms "renewal" and "reform," Peter De Mey writes: "A more profound study on renewal and reform in the documents of Vatican II would also need to pay attention to the relation between the council's explicit references to renewal and reform and its entire ecclesiology" (De Mey, "Church Renewal and Reform," 400).

12. For Theobald's interpretation, see his "The Theological Options of Vatican II: Seeking an 'Internal' Principle of Interpretation," in *Vatican II: A Forgotten Future?*, ed. Alberto Melloni and Christoph Theobald (London: SCM, 2005), 87–107.

13. On this position in the thought of Joseph Ratzinger, see Maximilian Heinrich Heim, *Joseph Ratzinger: Life in the Church and Living Theology: Fundamentals of Ecclesiology with Reference to* Lumen Gentium (San Francisco: Ignatius, 2007), 194–97, 425–29.

I find Peter De Mey's conclusion in his study of these terms in the council debates and final documents convincing. He proposes that, although these two terms are not exactly synonymous and each term has its own nuances, the council was using these two overlapping terms in reference to individual and collective spiritual transformation, as well as to structural change on the institutional level.[14]

Vatican II called for conversion on all levels of ecclesial life: personal, collective, institutional, and structural. Setting up any sharp dichotomy between any of these levels—for example, between the spiritual renewal of individuals in the Church, and organizational, structural reform of the institutional Church—is a false dichotomy. Ecclesial conversion involves all levels. The great historian of ecclesial reform, Gerhart Ladner, emphasized that writers in the early centuries mainly conceived of reform as "personal transformation."[15] Yet recent commentators have rejected Ladner's sharp distinction between the categories of "reform" and "conversion."[16] Certainly, as Avery Dulles notes, "In the ancient Church, the idea of reform was operative almost from the beginnings, but the early [patristic] reformers

14. De Mey concludes his careful examination of the philological usage in all the relevant final documents, as well as the oral and written interventions of the bishops during their drafting: "My historical research has . . . shown that the majority of the fathers intervening in the debate on *De oecumenismo* did not in the first instance make a contrast between renewal and reform but rather asked that the plea for internal church renewal be complemented with the issue of the (external) renewal of the church. . . . When the bishops proposed to improve the paragraph on church renewal, they found inspiration in the *aggiornamento* program of Pope John XXIII; but they also regularly referred to Paul VI. In my opinion one should not separate *Unitatis Redintegratio* and *Lumen Gentium* too much. The reflections on ecumenism in the former presuppose what the latter had to say on the relation of communion which the Catholic Church maintains with non-Catholics" (De Mey, "Church Renewal and Reform," 386). Regarding the original pastoral vision of John XXIII, which was deliberately endorsed by bishops in their council speeches and became the agenda of the council body itself, Yves Congar notes: "John XXIII more than once described the aim of the Second Vatican Council as, optimally, both a renewal of the pastoral structures of the Church (the emphasis was often put, at first, on the revision of canon law), and a renewal—an increase—of faith and Christian life" (Yves Congar, "Renewal of the Spirit and Reform of the Institution," in *Readings in Church Authority: Gifts and Challenges for Contemporary Catholicism*, ed. Gerard Mannion et al. [Burlington, VT: Ashgate, 2003], 512–17, at 515).

15. See Gerhart B. Ladner, *The Idea of Reform: Its Impact on Christian Thought and Action in the Age of the Fathers*, rev. ed. (New York: Harper & Row, 1967).

16. See the introduction and essays in Christopher M. Bellitto and David Zachariah Flanagin, eds., *Reassessing Reform: A Historical Investigation into Church Renewal* (Washington, DC: Catholic University of America, 2012).

were concerned with the reformation of persons in the Church rather than with the reformation of the Church itself." However, Dulles continues: "Only in the middle ages did it become apparent that in some cases moral and spiritual reform could not be achieved without doctrinal and structural reform."[17] Yves Congar's work highlights examples in church history that demonstrate the ideal; he calls them "reforms which were both spiritual and structural."[18] This is certainly the vision of Vatican II.[19]

The biblical category of conversion is helpful in these discussions, since it captures many nuances regarding renewal and reform in its individual, collective, and institutional dimensions, and referring to both spiritual and structural change. The approach of the interdenominational/ecumenical Groupe des Dombes has influenced the debate, as Catherine Clifford's work shows.[20] For the Groupe, *metanoia* is "a New Testament term currently translated by 'conversion' or 'repentance.' We use it to indicate a change affecting not just interior dispositions and personal behaviour, but also the manner in which ecclesial institutions function, and even, if necessary, their structure."[21]

To summarize: The continual divine call to ecclesial conversion demands spiritual renewal at both the individual and collective levels; institutional ecclesial conversion demands both spiritual and structural reform.

17. Avery Dulles, "The Church Always in Need of Reform: *Ecclesia Semper Reformanda*," in *The Church Inside and Out: Baptist-Catholic Regional Conference . . .* (Washington, DC: United States Catholic Conference, 1974), 37–50, at 37.

18. Congar, "Renewal of the Spirit and Reform of the Institution," 514. Congar adds here: "It is true that purely spiritual attitudes also have an impact on social structures. . . . It is necessary; yet it is not sufficient. There is in fact a density proper to impersonal and collective structures which has to be reached: otherwise the most generous reformist intentions would exhaust themselves in a never-ending effort that the opposing structures, keeping their place, would condemn to remain only half-effective."

19. Dulles uses the word "reform" for both the individual and the institutional levels, speaking of "personal reform" and "institutional reform," and intends by the latter phrase no distinction between "institutional" and "structural" reform. Avery Dulles, "True and False Reform," *First Things* 135 (2003): 14–19.

20. E.g., Catherine E. Clifford, *The Groupe des Dombes: A Dialogue of Conversion* (New York: Peter Lang, 2005).

21. Groupe des Dombes, "The Episcopal Ministry: Reflections and Proposals Concerning the Ministry of Vigilance and Unity in the Particular Church," in *For the Communion of the Churches: The Contribution of the Groupe des Dombes*, ed. Catherine E. Clifford (Grand Rapids, MI: Eerdmans, 2010), 37–58, at 38 n. 2 (no.7). Quoted in Groupe des Dombes, *For the Conversion of the Churches* (Geneva: WCC, 1993), 25 (article 36).

The Conciliar Vision and the Conversion of the Catholic Imagination

Presupposing the work of writers on reform and its history, particularly Congar,[22] Ladner,[23] and O'Malley,[24] Dulles has provided a historical survey of the notion of *ecclesia semper reformanda*. His framework is helpful for examining ecclesial conversion during and after Vatican II. With his characteristic sharpness, Dulles analyzes reform under three captions: "types," "areas," and "arguments."[25] Throughout the church's history, he notes five types of reform: purification, adaptation, accretion, development, and creative transformation. These, he says, have been applied to four major areas of church life: morality, discipline, governing structures, and doctrine. In addition, he sees two major arguments for reform: sinfulness and historicity.

Dulles notes that the Catholic Church since the Protestant Reformation has strongly resisted calls for reform in two of those four areas in particular: governing structures and doctrine.[26] I will treat doctrinal reform later. Regarding calls for reform of the Church's governing structures, one need only read O'Malley's recent history of the Council of Trent to see that calls for reform of the Roman Curia are not new, and that popes and the Curia have long resisted them.[27]

The election of Pope Francis gives hope that he will address the preconclave desire of so many cardinals for reform in the governance of the Church, and in particular of the Roman Curia. His decision to create a globally representative group of mainly noncurial cardinals to assist him in structural reform seems to be a deliberate move toward a more collegial

22. Yves Congar, *True and False Reform in the Church*, rev. ed. (Collegeville, MN: Liturgical Press, 2011). See the critique of Congar in Joseph Famerée, "True or False Reform: What Are the Criteria? The Reflections of Y. Congar," *Jurist* 71 (2011): 7–19. See also Dulles, "True and False Reform."

23. Ladner, *Idea of Reform*. For review and critique of Ladner's contribution to reform studies, see the contributions in Bellitto and Flanagin, eds., *Reassessing Reform*.

24. John W. O'Malley, SJ, "Reform, Historical Consciousness, and Vatican II's *Aggiornamento*," *Theological Studies* 32 (1971): 573–601. This was later published as John W. O'Malley, SJ, "Reform, Historical Consciousness, and Vatican II's *Aggiornamento*," in *Tradition and Transition: Historical Perspectives on Vatican II* (Wilmington, DE: Michael Glazier, 1989), 44–81.

25. For the following, see Dulles, "Church Always in Need of Reform."

26. Ibid. 37.

27. John W. O'Malley, *Trent: What Happened at the Council* (Cambridge, MA: Belknap of Harvard University, 2013).

governance of the Church. Time will tell. Many have written—and I need not expand—on the unfulfilled dimensions of what Vatican II was calling for: genuine episcopal collegiality; the participation of lay women and men in the three offices of Christ as prophet, priest, and king (the teaching, sanctifying, and governing dimensions of church life); respect for the integrity of the lived faith and liturgical rituals of local churches within their own culture and circumstance; the need for dialogue not only with those outside the Church but also within—if indeed the Church is to be a credible witness in its dialogue with others (in other words: regarding dialogue, begin by putting our own house in order). Full conversion to the vision of Vatican II regarding all these matters of governance not only requires attitudinal, cultural change but also structural reform, including new "structures of participation," as John Paul II called them.[28]

What is missing from the types of reform in the past (as Dulles lists them) is reform relating to *the way* the Church fulfills its mission in the world—what O'Malley calls "style."[29] The council shows a particular concern for the kind of face the Church presents to the world. Vatican II wants to stop the scowl and give a smile—and even shed a tear. In attempting to balance the centripetal and centrifugal forces of *communio* and *missio*, the council gives equal attention to the Church's life *ad intra* and its mission *ad extra*. Likewise, with Pope Francis, it seems that *ad intra* reform of governance will certainly not be his only focus. He has already spoken often of a more missionary church, and one that is less "self-referential."[30] Coming from Argentina, he sees the Church differently. I myself come from a land down-under (as a popular Australian song puts it), where tourist shops sell maps of the world with the world turned upside down—the southern hemisphere up top and Europe in a bottom corner. Not only is this the emerging demographic reality of the Church, but also, I suspect, this is Pope Francis's mental map of the Church—turned upside down, with the poor of the global south a prominent concern. He has stated to a gathering of journalists: "Oh, how I would like a poor Church, and for

28. On the relationship between "a spirituality of communion" and "structures of participation," see John Paul II, *Novo millennio ineunte: Apostolic Letter of John Paul II* (Strathfield, Australia: St Pauls, 2001), nos. 43–45.

29. For a recent formulation of this thesis, see O'Malley, *What Happened at Vatican II*.

30. Reported in a summation of preconclave meetings of cardinals, from March 4–11, 2013. See James Martin, SJ, "Pope Francis' Plan for the Church?"—online blog for March 27, 2013, http://americamagazine.org/content/all-things/pope-francis-plan-church. (All URLs cited herein were accessed on August 27, 2013.)

the poor."[31] With this dimension of his *ad extra* focus, Pope Francis may well be deliberately echoing the spiritual conversion evident at Vatican II, which Pope Paul VI referred to in his address to the council on its last working day, December 7, 1965, when he said: "The old story of the Good Samaritan has been the model of the spirituality of the council. A feeling of boundless sympathy has permeated the whole of it. The attention of our council has been absorbed by the discovery of human needs."[32] This conciliar impulse has echoes of some elements of what Letty Russell would later call for when she says that "justice" should be "the fifth mark of the church," along with unity, holiness, catholicity, and apostolicity.[33]

Although we are only early into Francis's pontificate, there are signs of hope regarding reform in the issues mentioned above. Therefore, I would like to focus now on what Dulles lists as the two major arguments for reform: sinfulness and historicity—to see them at work at Vatican II and to assess reception of the council's vision of reform 50 years on.[34]

The first argument for reform is prompted by sinfulness, a central theme of the biblical vision regarding conversion with its call for ongoing personal and communal faithfulness to the demands of the covenant, the demands of

31. During an audience for journalists, Saturday, March 16, soon after his election. See Joshua J. McElwee, "Pope Francis: 'I would love a church that is poor,' " NCR Online (March 16, 2013), http://ncronline.org/blogs/pope-francis-i-would-love-church-poor.

32. Final Address by Pope Paul VI, Last Working Day of the Council, December 7, 1965 (Floyd Anderson, ed., *Council Daybook: Vatican II, Session 4* [Washington, DC: National Catholic Welfare Conference, 1966], 360, translation corrected: The Latin text reads: "Vetus illa de bono Samaritano narratio exemplum fuit atque norma, ad quam Concilii nostri spiritualis ratio directa est. Etenim, immensus quidam erga homines amor Concilium penitus pervasit. Perspectae et iterum consideratae hominum necessitates, quae eo molestiores fiunt, quo magis huius terrae filius crescit, totum nostrae huius Synodi studium detinuerunt").

33. See Letty M. Russell, *Church in the Round: Feminist Interpretation of the Church* (Louisville: Westminster John Knox, 1993), 135. If anything captures the hopes that might just be fulfilled in Pope Francis, it is John O'Malley's summary of Vatican II's shift in ecclesial self-understanding and the face it wishes the Church to project to the world. He states: "At stake were almost two different visions of Catholicism: from commands to invitations, from laws to ideals, from definition to mystery, from threats to persuasion, from coercion to conscience, from monologue to dialogue, from ruling to serving, from withdrawn to integrated, from vertical to horizontal, from exclusion to inclusion, from hostility to friendship, from rivalry to partnership, from suspicion to trust, from static to ongoing, from passive acceptance to active engagement, from fault-finding to appreciation, from prescriptive to principled, from behavior modification to inner appropriation" (O'Malley, *What Happened at Vatican II*, 307).

34. See Dulles, "Church Always in Need of Reform," 47–48.

the gospel. Here the type of ecclesial reform demanded, in Dulles's schema, is "purification," a term used by Vatican II.[35] Central to its pastoral aim of ecclesial renewal and reform is, as expressed in chapter 5 of *Lumen gentium* (nos. 39–42), the council's "universal call to holiness," a call to greater fidelity to Jesus Christ in the Holy Spirit—a call from which we theologians, of course, are not excluded. This call to holiness has a collective dimension, as the Decree on Ecumenism states: "Every renewal of the Church essentially consists in an increase of fidelity to her own calling."[36]

In our own time, sinfulness at all levels of our Catholic ecclesial life has become scandalously public—from child sexual abuse by clergy, to ecclesial corruption and inner power struggles, to what Pope Francis has already on several occasions decried as "careerism" and "clericalism" in the Church.[37] Certain kinds of collective culture can only enfeeble the Church. What is clear is that this sinfulness *in* the Church goes beyond just a matter of *individual* sin. In the 50 years since the council, diverse theologies have highlighted the social dimension of sin and the need in the Church for *collective* ecclesial conversion. This includes conversion from the sins of patriarchy, clericalism, sexism, racism, and collusion with economic, political, and social exclusion and oppression, all of which can become ideologically embedded in ecclesial collective and institutional culture and structures.[38] Whatever its form, such structural sin is, in the words of Oscar Romero, "the crystallization of individual egoisms in permanent structures which maintain this sin and exert its power over the great majorities."[39] All are forms of individual and structural sin that deface the Church.

35. *LG* no. 8; 15.

36. *UR* no. 6.

37. On June 6, 2013, when addressing the members of the Pontifical Ecclesiastical Academy in Rome, which trains priests for the diplomatic corps and the Secretariat of State of the Holy See, Pope Francis stated: "Careerism is leprosy! Leprosy! Please, no careerism!"; http://en.radiovaticana.va/news/2013/06/06/pope_francis_to_future_diplomats:_no_to_careerism/en1-698966.

38. On the social, structural dimension of sin, see Patrick Kerans, *Sinful Social Structures* (New York: Paulist, 1974). Specifically on conversion, see Peter J. Henriot, "Social Sin and Conversion: A Theology of the Church's Social Involvement," in *Conversion: Perspectives on Personal and Social Transformation*, ed. Walter E. Conn (New York: Alba House, 1978), 315–26. For a summary of the issues, see Roger Haight, "Sin and Grace," in *Systematic Theology: Roman Catholic Perspectives*, ed. Francis Schüssler Fiorenza and John P. Galvin, 2nd and rev. ed. (Minneapolis: Fortress, 2011), 375–430, at 398–402.

39. Oscar Romero's Second Pastoral Letter (1977), quoted in José Ignacio González Faus, "Sin," in *Mysterium Liberationis: Fundamental Concepts of Liberation Theology*, ed. Ignacio Ellacuría and Jon Sobrino (Maryknoll, NY: Orbis, 1993), 532–42, at 537.

This metaphor of "the face" is used on several occasions throughout the council documents. *Lumen gentium* in its very first paragraph boldly proclaims: "the light of Christ . . . is resplendent on the face of the church [*super faciem ecclesiae*]." That this is not quite the case in the church's history the document acknowledges in no. 8: "The church . . . clasping sinners to its bosom, at once holy and always in need of purification [*sancta simul et semper purificanda*], follows constantly the path of penance and renewal [*poenitentiam et renovationem*]." Further on, no. 15 states, "Mother church . . . exhorts her children to purification and renewal [*purificationem et renovationem*] so that the sign of Christ may shine more brightly over the face [*super faciem*] of the church." And in its last document, when reflecting on why people do not believe or no longer believe, the council, in *Gaudium et spes* no. 19, laments that Christian believers (*credentes*) themselves are often the very ones to blame for such nonbelief—because they fail to reveal "the genuine face of God [*revelare . . . Dei genuinum vultum*]."

The acknowledgment that the face of the church is not always resplendent with the light of Christ constitutes a fundamental concern in the overall reform agenda of Vatican II: that the face of the church would faithfully mirror *the genuine face of the God whom she proclaims*. Some have written on the implications of ecclesial sinfulness for ecclesial repentance, raising the issue of whether sinfulness *in* the church means that we must indeed speak, as Karl Rahner does, of "a sinful church."[40] Bradford

40. Karl Rahner, in an article tellingly titled "The Sinful Church in the Decrees of Vatican II," has proposed that a distinction be made between objective and subjective holiness of the church, and that within the latter category the church is de facto a sinful church. See Karl Rahner, "The Sinful Church in the Decrees of Vatican II," in *Theological Investigations*, vol. 6 (New York: Seabury, 1976), 270–94. Regarding the statement in *LG* no. 8, that the church is "at one and the same time holy and always in need of purification [*sancta simul et semper purificanda*]," Peter Hünermann interprets this phrase as stating that the church is here "identified as equally holy and sinful [*als eine zugleich heilige und sündhafte bezeichnet*]" (Hünermann, "Theologischer Kommentar zur dogmatischen Konstitution über die Kirche," in *Herders theologischer Kommentar zum Zweiten Vatikanischen Konzil*, 5 vols., ed. Peter Hünermann and Bernd Jochen Hilberath [Freiburg: Herder, 2004], 2:265–582, at 369). Likewise, Michael Becht sees in *GS* no. 43 the possibility of a similar interpretation open to seeing the church itself as sinful. See Michael Becht, "*Ecclesia semper purificanda*: Die Sündigkeit der Kirche als Thema des II. Vatikanischen Konzils," *Catholica* 49 (1995): 218–37; 239–60, at 254. Yves Congar too refers to the need for reform of the whole church as a collective body, not just the sinful members of the church. See his discussion on this point in De Mey, "Church Renewal and Reform," 388.

Hinze has highlighted the importance of public acts of ecclesial repentance, so tellingly expressed in Pope John Paul II's public *mea culpas*.[41] Ongoing ecclesial conversion demands processes of ecclesial repentance.

Alongside liberationist critiques of patriarchy and oppressive structures, of increasing importance for this theological reflection are background theories from ancillary disciplines that study group cultures and dynamics.[42] One such discipline is the dialogue partner of business studies. While serving on the Board of the Faculty of Business at Australian Catholic University, I came to learn something of that discipline's language and terms, particularly recent research into the pathology of business companies. For example, the area of what is termed "organizational change" examines how to bring about transformation in dysfunctional company cultures.[43] If culture is simply "the way we do things around here," then ecclesial conversion means cultural change, from the local parish level with its suborganizations through to the culture of episcopal and papal leadership and of the Roman Curia. O'Malley's well-known thesis proposes that the fundamental aim of Vatican II's reform was to change the style, the how, of being a Catholic Church. In other words, Vatican II set out to reform the culture of the Catholic Church.

The second argument for reform is historicity, the condition of the church in time and place. That ongoing reform is always necessary throughout history, Dulles notes, arises from the very nature of the divine-human encounter: "The revelation of God cannot be received except in fragile human vessels, limited by the particularities of time and place."[44] His formulation has echoes of the medieval Scholastic axiom: *quidquid recipitur ad modum recipientis recipitur* (whatever is received is received in the mode

41. Hinze has developed Rahner's proposal and its implications for ecclesial repentance: see "Ecclesial Repentance and the Demands of Dialogue," *Theological Studies* 61 (2000): 207–38. On John Paul II's petitions for forgiveness, see Luigi Accattoli, *When a Pope Asks Forgiveness: The Mea Culpa's of John Paul II*, trans. Jordan Aumann (Boston: Pauline, 1998). See also the International Theological Commission, *Memory and Reconciliation: The Church and the Faults of the Past* (Strathfield, NSW: St Pauls, 2000).

42. For a cultural anthropological perspective, see, e.g., Gerald A. Arbuckle, *Violence, Society, and the Church: A Cultural Approach* (Collegeville, MN: Liturgical Press, 2004).

43. See, e.g., Kim S. Cameron and Robert E. Quinn, *Diagnosing and Changing Organizational Culture: Based on the Competing Values Framework*, 3rd ed. (San Francisco: Jossey-Bass, 2011); Dianne Waddell, Thomas G. Cummings, and Christopher G. Worley, *Organisational Change: Development and Transformation*, 4th ed. (South Melbourne, Vic.: Cengage Learning, 2011).

44. Dulles, "The Church Always in Need of Reform," 48.

of the receiver).[45] The bishops at Vatican II begin to understand this ancient reception principle in a new way: beyond its being a merely pedagogical principle, it is also a *theological* principle regarding revelation and faith, faith and history. Dulles's description of the argument from historicity has parallels with what Christoph Theobald sees as *the* hermeneutical key for interpreting Vatican II, what he terms "the principle of pastorality,"[46] a pastorality called for by John XXIII in his opening conciliar address. Theobald summarizes this principle of pastorality with the axiom, "There can be no proclamation of the gospel without taking account of its recipients."[47] For the teaching office, as I will touch on later, taking account of the recipients of the gospel means taking seriously the *sensus fidelium*,[48] "the intimate sense of spiritual realities which [believers] experience."[49] The council's emphasis on inculturation and vernacular liturgies are just two other examples of this principle of reception coming to the fore at the council.

With this focus on reception we are now at the heart of the conversion of the Church's Catholic imagination begun at Vatican II. Types of reform attempted in the past, and also evident at the council, have been accretion, adaptation, and development. At Vatican II, however, we see also the beginnings of a new sense of historicity and the opening up to a new understanding of the relationship between faith and history. This is evident throughout the council and in its documents in a number of ways.

First, as Giuseppe Alberigo has shown, a whole new vocabulary of "history words" appears regularly throughout the documents and for the first time in any council; he lists 38 of them.[50] Second, according to O'Malley, "historical consciousness" for the first time in the Church's history becomes explicit in the thinking of the bishops;[51] Joseph Ratzinger wrote of the "historical thinking" informing their decisions.[52] This his-

45. See, e.g., Thomas Aquinas, *Summa theologiae* 1, q. 75, a. 5; 3, q. 5.

46. On the council's reception of John XXIII's "principle of pastorality" and its centrality for a hermeneutics of the council and its documents, see Christoph Theobald, *La réception du concile Vatican II: I. Accéder à la source* (Paris: Cerf, 2009), 281–493.

47. Theobald, "Theological Options of Vatican II," 94.

48. *LG* no. 12. The passage refers to the *supernaturalis sensus fidei totius populi*. This is generally referred to in the literature as *sensus fidelium*.

49. *DV* no. 8.

50. See Giuseppe Alberigo, "Cristianesimo e storia nel Vaticano II," *Cristianesimo nella storia* 5 (1984): 577–92, at 577 n. 1.

51. O'Malley, "Tradition and Transition."

52. Joseph Ratzinger, in commenting on the "bitterness" injected into the conciliar assembly by the late and nonconciliar addition of the *Nota explicativa praevia* to

torical consciousness begins to shape the bishops' imagination through the work of *ressourcement* theologians, who, as *periti*, are highlighting richly diverse forms and practices of Catholicism beyond the monolithic Tridentine Catholicism of the previous centuries.[53] They come to see that things have been different in the past, and could be now. Third, this historical consciousness underlies a basic intuition of the leitmotif *aggiornamento*, an intuition that, according to O'Malley, is "new in the history of the idea of reform and reformation."[54] Fourth, this new historical approach is evident in the shifts away from static to dynamic understandings of God, human being, and the nature of divine revelation and human faith, understood now primarily as an ongoing personal encounter in history. These perceptions then come to underpin leitmotifs such as "living tradition" and "the signs of the times."

Taken together, these four features of the conciliar vision alone show how Vatican II, in its approach to faith and history, constitutes an opening up to a model of reform beyond what is captured either individually or collectively by the three key terms "*ressourcement*," "development," and "*aggiornamento*."[55] Something new is happening here; the whole is greater than the sum of the parts. Yves Congar, writing in 1972, hints at such a different and indeed new model of reform that is present at Vatican II, albeit in an inchoate way:

Lumen gentium, remarks on the "historical thinking" being attacked in this addition: "The conservatism of this view is based on its aloofness from history, and so it basically suffers from a lack of tradition—i.e., of openness to the totality of Christian history. It is important that we see this because it gives us an insight into the inner pattern of the opposing alignments of thought in the Council, often mistakenly described as an opposition between progressives and conservatives. It would be more correct to speak of a contrast between historical thinking and formally juridical thinking. The 'progressives' (at least the large majority of them) were in fact concerned precisely with 'tradition,' with a new awareness of both the breadth and depth of what had been handed down in Christian tradition. This was where they found the norms for renewal which permitted them to be fearless and broad in their outlook. It was an outlook which came from the intrinsic catholicity of the Church" (Ratzinger, *Theological Highlights of Vatican II*, 171–72).

53. On the *ressourcement* theologians at Vatican II, see, e.g., Gerald O'Collins, "*Ressourcement* and Vatican II," in *Ressourcement: A Movement for Renewal in Twentieth-Century Catholic Theology*, ed. Gabriel Flynn and Paul D. Murray (New York: Oxford University, 2011), 372–91.

54. O'Malley, "Developments, Reforms, and Two Great Reformations," 108.

55. For this triad in O'Malley's work, see his *What Happened at Vatican II*, 299–302; and "'The Hermeneutic of Reform,'" 536–42.

> Our epoch of rapid change and cultural transformation (philosophical ferments and sociological conditions different from those which the Church has accustomed itself to until now) calls for a revision of "traditional" forms which goes beyond the level of adaptation or *aggiornamento*, and which would be instead a new creation. *It is no longer sufficient to maintain, by adapting it, what has already been; it is necessary to reconstruct it.*[56]

Likewise, Dulles, writing in 1974, notes the implications of the new type of reform beginning to emerge at Vatican II, a type he calls "creative transformation": "In dialogue with the contemporary world, the Church can make innovations that do not simply grow out of its own previous tradition."[57]

Such a shift constitutes nothing less than a conversion of the Catholic imagination regarding God and humanity, faith and history. One could well call it a hermeneutical turn in the history of the Catholic Church's self-understanding regarding its life, doctrine, and worship. As the Church moves into ever-new historical contexts, new questions arise and are addressed to the tradition, questions that the Church has never asked before—because it was inconceivable, given the worldviews at the time, even to have thought of them. The authoritative past here needs the present receiver to find answers. Vatican II marks a significant recalibration of the Catholic imagination concerning a truth always held but now newly perceived: the present too, not just the past, is revelatory and authoritative.[58] As the Holy Spirit leads the Church in history through conversion to the fullness of truth, God is challenging the Church to discern the new things that God is doing in Christ through the Spirit—by scrutinizing the signs of the times in the light of the gospel.

56. Congar, "Renewal of the Spirit and Reform of the Institution," 516, emphasis added.

57. Dulles, "The Church Always in Need of Reform," 42–43. The full passage states: "I would hold that, although the Church cannot accept what is simply alien, it can discern the presence of Christ in the signs of the times. In dialogue with the contemporary world, the Church can make innovations that do not simply grow out of its own previous tradition. Reform by development and assimilation may have seemed an adequate model when the Church was the controlling influence in Western culture. But today [1974] a proper respect for the autonomy of human culture demands a less possessive and a more dialogic relationship. The Church must creatively respond to the initiatives of others."

58. See Ormond Rush, *The Eyes of Faith: The Sense of the Faithful and the Church's Reception of Revelation* (Washington, DC: The Catholic University of America Press, 2009), 241–91.

In that quest for the fullness of truth, the answers to such new questions proposed by other Christian churches and ecclesial communities may well also be the Spirit's promptings for the Catholic Church to embrace. As our esteemed colleague Margaret O'Gara would have put it: In an "ecumenical gift exchange," the other may just have a gift from the Holy Spirit not to my liking! Something of a conversion in one's perspective may be what the Spirit is demanding.[59] This ecumenical openness was central to the council's vision for ecclesial conversion.

Over the decades since the council ended, "historical consciousness" has had its own history and turned critically toward itself. It has become more reflexive, more aware of distortions in the tradition, and more acutely aware of the distorting lenses through which present-day receivers of the council can view the past—and the present.[60] So many examples could be given of diverse contextual theologies that have developed over the last 50 years, and that are faithful to the emerging model of reform embedded in the conciliar vision when taken as a whole. In the light of this more critical historical consciousness, ongoing ecclesial conversion to the vision of Vatican II also includes attention to possible distorting elements in the conciliar vision itself, so that any retrieval in the present does not perpetuate any distortions of the past. For example, to state the obvious, Vatican II was an all-male affair, except for the women on some subcommissions and the women auditors in the third and fourth sessions.[61] New questions have arisen in the last 50 years and are posed to the conciliar texts for answers—questions, however, that the individual texts did not intend to answer, or questions that the bishops could not even have envisaged at that time. Receivers may nevertheless find answers to those new questions

59. See Margaret O'Gara (d. August 16, 2012), *The Ecumenical Gift Exchange* (Collegeville, MN: Liturgical Press, 1998). On Catholic learning from other churches, see Ormond Rush, "Receptive Ecumenism and the *Sensus Fidelium*: Expanding the Categories for Catholic Ecclesial Discerning," in *Receptive Ecumenism and Ecclesial Learning: Learning to Be Church Together; Joint 2nd International Receptive Ecumenism Conference*, ed. Paul D. Murray (New York: Oxford University, forthcoming).

60. On this, the literature is vast. For example, on the importance of Foucault for theology, see Vincent J. Miller, "History or Geography? Gadamer, Foucault, and Theologies of Tradition," in *Theology and the New Histories*, ed. Gary Macy (Maryknoll, NY: Orbis, 1999), 56–85. For more on Foucault and history, see Alun Munslow, *Deconstructing History*, 2nd ed. (New York: Routledge, 2006), 129–48.

61. See Adriana Valerio, *Madri del Concilio: Ventitré donne al Vaticano II* (Rome: Carocci, 2012); Carmel Elizabeth McEnroy, *Guests in Their Own House: The Women of Vatican II* (New York: Crossroad, 1996).

from a comprehensive interpretation of the council and all its documents, as they imagine the whole conciliar vision realized in their new context.[62]

Ecclesial Conversion, the Holy Spirit, and the *Sensus Fidelium*

The council's vision has some of the structural elements of conversion as presented throughout the Old and New Testaments.[63] For example, God is the one who brings about conversion; it is an event of divine grace. In the New Testament, the Holy Spirit is the agent of conversion. Also, in the Bible, God demands conversion not only away from sinful deeds but also from spiritual blindness and hardness of heart. Furthermore, as biblical scholar Ronald Witherup notes, "conversion [in the Bible] takes place in the context of relationship,"[64] and, he says, such relational conversion has interrelated vertical and horizontal dimensions—conversion to God always has implications for human relationships. We find these structural elements in the council's call for conversion.

Vatican II's most profound *ressourcement* was above all its turning to God, a turning of its mind and heart to the God of revelation.[65] In the

62. On principles for reconstructing the vision of the council, see Ormond Rush, "Toward a Comprehensive Interpretation of the Council and Its Documents," *Theological Studies* 73 (2012): 547–69.

63. On the theme of conversion in the Bible, see, e.g., Frederick J. Gaiser, "A Biblical Theology of Conversion," in *Handbook of Religious Conversion*, ed. H. Newton Malony and Samuel Southard (Birmingham, AL: Religious Education, 1992), 93–107; Beverly Roberts Gaventa, "Conversion," in *The Anchor Bible Dictionary*, 6 vols., ed. David Noel Freedman (New York: Doubleday, 1992), 1:1131–33; A. Hulsbosch, *The Bible on Conversion*, trans. F. Vander Heijden (De Pere, WI: St. Norbert Abbey, 1966); S. Kim, "Repentance/Conversion," in *Dictionary of Biblical Theology*, ed. Xavier Léon-Dufour, 2nd ed. (New York: Seabury, 1973), 486–91; Francis J. Moloney, "Conversion, I (In the Bible)," in *New Catholic Encyclopedia*, 15 vols., 2nd ed. (New York: Gale, 2003), 4:231–34; Marc-François Lacan, "Conversion and Grace in the Old Testament," in *Conversion: Perspectives on Personal and Social Transformation*, ed. Walter E. Conn (New York: Alba House, 1978), 75–96; Marc-François Lacan, "Conversion and Kingdom in the Synoptic Gospels," in ibid., 97–118; Ronald D. Witherup, *Conversion in the New Testament* (Collegeville, MN: Liturgical Press, 1994); Beverly Roberts Gaventa, *From Darkness to Light: Aspects of Conversion in the New Testament* (Philadelphia: Fortress, 1986); Roy A. Harrisville, *The Concept of Newness in the New Testament* (Minneapolis: Augsburg, 1960).

64. Witherup, *Conversion in the New Testament*, 17.

65. On this, see Bishop Michael Putney, "Vatican II: A New Relationship with God" (unpublished paper, presented for the eConference, "Vatican II: An Event of Grace" on Wednesday, October 10, 2012, sponsored by the Australian Catholic Bishops Conference and the Broken Bay Institute).

council's turning to God, there emerged over the four years a new perspective on how God works in history, and how, through the guidance of the Holy Spirit, the Church must respond to God working in history. From that new understanding of its own relationship to God, it perceived a new style of relationship within the Church, and of relating to those outside it, even though the bishops deliberately eschewed the "us" and "them" language of previous eras.

The council's call for a more outward-looking Church becomes increasingly clear as the council proceeds; we could say, to take up the words of Pope Francis, the council did not want its vision to be "self-referential." Primarily, it is more about God than about us. The Church is a sign or instrument of something greater than itself. Nevertheless, the directions *ad intra* and *ad extra* and the aspects of *communio* and *missio* are necessarily interrelated. How we are in our inner life will determine the face we present to the world and ultimately our credibility in mission.

Vatican II's call to conversion is multidimensional. I would like to select just two dimensions of the council's call to ecclesial conversion that deal with the Church's inner life, dimensions that determine the face the Church presents to outsiders. They relate to the vertical and the horizontal aspects of relational conversion. Both impinge directly on the last of the areas of reform listed by Dulles: doctrinal reform. Fifty years on, conversion in these two dimensions is far from profound.

The first dimension relates to vertical conversion: ecclesial conversion is fundamentally the Church relating to God in a new way. With its trinitarian theology of revelation and the focus on *communio* in God, the council calls on the Church to mirror the trinitarian life, to reflect "the genuine face of God" to the world as the universal sacrament of salvation. In *Lumen gentium* no. 17, the Church is named, at once, "the People of God," "the Body of Christ," and "the Temple of the Holy Spirit." However, from the personal, to the collective, to the institutional, canonical, and structural levels, the Church de facto still lacks this trinitarian balance in its life; we are still far from conversion to a genuinely trinitarian Church. A major issue is that the Holy Spirit, the Breath of God, is given little institutional breathing room. Ecclesial conversion cannot take place if the very divine agent of conversion is not given opportunities to convert the Church.

The council's teachings on the Holy Spirit—such as the Spirit's gift of diverse charisms, or the *sensus fidei* given by the Spirit to all the baptized, or the Spirit's working discernibly in history through attention to the signs of the times—still have yet to impact deeply on the spiritual and institutional life of the whole Church. Concerning the governing office in the Church, the 1983 Code of Canon Law lacks any mention of the Holy Spirit and structures for discernment of the Spirit, an ecclesial process so critical to the New Testament ecclesiological vision, especially in the Pauline and the Johannine literature.[66] Concerning the teaching office in the Church, there are no concrete "structures of participation" for explicitly acknowledging the authority of the *sensus fidelium*, that gift of the Holy Spirit—as *Lumen gentium* emphatically teaches—that ensures the Church's infallibility in believing.[67] This downplaying of the Spirit has long been a problem; the Council of Constantinople, for example, condemned those "Spirit-fighters," the Pneumatomachians, who denied the divinity of the Holy Spirit.[68] If we are not recognizing and acknowledging the Spirit at work *within*, we will have no gift for discernment of the Spirit also at work *outside* the Church.

Second, this relational vertical conversion to the triune God, especially concerning the role of the Holy Spirit, demands relational conversion on the horizontal level, *ad intra* and *ad extra*. Not wanting to be too "self-referential" here, I have space now only to focus on aspects of the Church as a *communio*, which nevertheless do have implications for the Church's mission *ad extra* and the necessary *perichoresis* between communion and mission.

66. Concerning canon law, Walter Kasper notes: "The degree to which a full reception of the council is still lacking in this respect is shown even by the new *Codex juris canonici*, which—contrary to *Lumen gentium* no. 14—in describing the full *communio* with the church, manages to get by without mentioning the Holy Spirit at all, confining itself to institutional criteria. This shows with sufficient clarity that we are only at the beginning of a reception of the council" (Walter Kasper, "The Church as Communion: Reflections on the Guiding Ecclesiological Idea of the Second Vatican Council," in *Theology and Church* [New York: Crossroad, 1989], 148–65, at 153). On the lack of recognition of the Holy Spirit in the Code of Canon Law, James Coriden writes: "The exclusion of the Holy Spirit and charisms from the code was not due to ignorance or casual neglect; it seems to have been a conscious choice. It is difficult to detect the real reasons for this deliberate exclusion. It may have been motivated by a fear of a mysterious charismatic element that might be difficult to verify or control, and that might prove disruptive or dangerous. Or the revisers of the code may have been reluctant to acknowledge any source of authority in the Church other than the exclusively Christocentric and hierarchic sources recognized for centuries. They may have been unwilling to recognize the Spirit who dwells within each one of the Christian faithful and gives them gifts for the building of the Church" (James A. Coriden, "The Holy Spirit and Church Governance," *Jurist* 66 [2006]: 339–73, at 372).

67. *LG* no. 12.

68. See Norman P. Tanner, *Decrees of the Ecumenical Councils*, 2 vols. (Washington, DC: Georgetown University, 1990), 2:31.

The primary way in which Vatican II envisaged vertical and horizontal ecclesial relationships *ad intra* was in terms of *communio*: *communio* in God, *communio* in the Church. The council documents use those three expressions, which capture key aspects of the Church's visible and invisible mystery: *communio hierarchica* (hierarchical communion, expressed in the council's teaching on collegiality);[69] *communio ecclesiarum* (communion of local churches, "in which and out of which" the one church of Christ exists);[70] and the often-forgotten third, *communio fidelium* (the communion of the faithful throughout the world-church, all the individual baptized believers).[71] If the invisible mystery of the church is to be realized, all three modes of *communio* must be given structural expression.

However, despite Vatican II's deliberate desire to balance out a juridical image of the Church with ones that highlight the Church as mystery, a juridical emphasis still lingers, with priority de facto given to a church seen primarily as a hierarchical communion. "Relational conversion" on the horizontal level, and a proper balancing of its three modes of *communio*, 50 years after Vatican II, are still in need of spiritual and structural realization. A genuine *affectus collegialis* ("collegial spirit")[72] between pope and bishops needs to be complemented by a genuine respect for the integrity of local churches and their lived faith within a diversity of cultures, and a respect for the *communio fidelium* and the Spirit speaking through the *sensus fidelium*. This becomes highly significant for any discussion of Dulles's last area of reform, doctrine. Horizontal relational conversion presupposes a "culture of dialogue,"[73] and doctrinal reform must be the result of dialogue within the Church between the three voices of the *sensus fidelium*, theologians, and the magisterium.

If one takes *Dei verbum* as one's lens, with its focus on the fundamental Christian realities of divine revelation and its reception in faith down through history, the Church is first and foremost a community *of faith*. It is a *communio fidelium*, a communion of those baptized faithful who have responded to God's revelatory offer of salvation in Christ through the

69. *LG* no. 21.

70. *LG* no. 23.

71. *UR* no. 2; *LG* no. 13; *AA* no. 18. On these three terms in the council, see Kasper, "Church as Communion."

72. *LG* no. 23.

73. Hermann J. Pottmeyer, "Die Mitsprache der Gläubigen in Glaubenssachen: Eine alte Praxis und ihre Wiederentdeckung," *Internationale katholische Zeitschrift "Communio"* 25 (1996): 135–47, at 146–47.

Spirit. Faith is the Spirit's gift for receiving revelation and—accompanying the gift of faith—the Spirit gives a sense for the faith, a *sensus fidei*. All the baptized individually and the Church as a whole receive this gift for interpreting and applying the gospel. Here is the powerhouse for incarnating the faith in diverse localities, cultures, times, and circumstances. It is here, on the ground, that personal and communal conversion begins.

If, as *Dei verbum* no. 8 teaches, God "continues to converse" with the Church through the Holy Spirit,[74] and if the *sensus fidelium* is a significant voice box for the Spirit, then genuine ecclesial conversion demands more than lip service to the role of the Holy Spirit in the Church, and to the Spirit's instrument for all things related to the faithful interpretation and application of the gospel in daily life, the *sensus fidelium*.

To conclude briefly. In his work on the development of doctrine, John Henry Newman highlighted a particular class of development, which he called "historical development." Such development, he said, is

> the gradual formation of opinion concerning persons, facts, and events. Judgments, which were at one time confined to a few, at length spread through a community, and attain general reception by the accumulation and concurrence of testimony. Thus some authoritative accounts die away; others gain a footing, and are ultimately received as truths.[75]

Vatican II was just such an event of accelerated and concentrated "historical development" over four years. Using a more critical hermeneutical model than the organic one of "development," Vatican II was certainly an event of ecclesial conversion to a new worldview, a new way of seeing, a new ecclesial self-understanding, a conversion of the Catholic imagination regarding faith and history.

74. "Thus God, who spoke in the past, continues to converse [*sine intermissione . . . colloquitur*] with the spouse of his beloved Son [i.e., the church]. And the Holy Spirit, through whom the living voice of the Gospel rings out in the church—and through it in the world—leads believers to the full truth and makes the word of Christ dwell in them in all richness" (*DV* no. 8).

75. John Henry Newman, *An Essay on the Development of Christian Doctrine*, 6th ed. (Notre Dame, IN: University of Notre Dame, 1989), 46–47.

8 Sin, Intimacy, and the Genuine Face of the Church

A Response to Ormond Rush

NATALIA IMPERATORI-LEE

Almost 50 years ago, the Second Vatican Council acknowledged that the face of the Church is not always resplendent with the light of Christ. This constitutes a fundamental concern in the council's overall pastoral and reform agenda. Ormond Rush reminds us that the goal of the council was at least in part that the face of the Church would faithfully mirror the genuine face of the God that the Church presents. My goal here is to consider the notion of the face of the Church, along with how the Church might more authentically reflect God's face in genuine encounter by facing reality, and particularly by facing the poor.

Our faces are the most visible and most naked part of our bodies. They are a primary way in which we interact with the world and with one other in relationship. The face is intimate, even as it remains constantly exposed. It is rarely fully covered, and even the practice of veiling points to the powerful intimacy of the face.[1] Though we may embellish our faces with

1. I do not wish to oversimplify the veiling of women as a religious practice, but rather to indicate that the impulse to cover the face has been rooted in the very power or intimacy of the face, and in the desire to confine this power or intimacy whether within the institution of heterosexual marriage or some other social, often patriarchal, construct. However, the practice of veiling, particularly in Muslim communities, is not viewed monolithically even in feminist circles. One example of feminist theological insight on the wearing of the hijab can be found in Bahar Davary, "Miss Elsa and the Veil: Honor, Shame, and Identity Negotiations," *Journal of Feminist Studies in Religion*

makeup or with paltry attempts at "putting on a good face," or vow "*al mal tiempo, buena cara*," as was frequently said in my family, the face is a locus of disclosure. Our faces reveal our emotions, our moods, our age, our confusion or understanding, our empathy or hardness of heart. Much of our humanity resides there, in our faces. This confers power on the face-to-face encounter—the meaningfulness of eye contact with a child, or a lover, or an enemy, or, as in the thought of Immanuel Levinas, the face-to-face encounter with the Other that brings us into subjectivity.[2] For Levinas, the face [of the Other] "denudes, undresses and disarms the subject,"[3] and the face-to-face encounter with the Other exacts a demand on the subject to enter into relationship with that other, an uneasy relationship where the subject must "care for the other in non-totalizing ways,"[4] including through "gestures of justice, generosity, and sacrifice."[5] Ultimately, the ethical demand of the face-to-face encounter with the Other is a kenotic one, inviting the subject to divest itself of prestige and power in favor of a posture of seeking justice.

If the Church were somehow to embody this ethical demand—to genuinely have a face-to-face encounter or to "get its house in order in terms of dialogue," to use Rush's image—how would it do so? If there were to be this perichoresis of hierarchical magisterium, theological insight, and *sensus fidelium*, what would it look like? My hope, and the council's, is that there would be a genuine face-to-face encounter, within the Church, of these three realities. But in effect we leave that encounter to chance—or, more realistically, we have relegated it to an eschatological hope. While it is true, as Orlando Espín reminds us, that the *sensus fidelium* is an intuition,

---

25, no. 2 (2009): 47–66. On veiling, women, and the face, see Fatima Mernissi, *The Veil and the Male Elite: A Feminist Interpretation of Women's Right in Islam*, trans. Mary Jo Lakeland (New York: Addison Wesley, 1991).

2. The notion of the face is thematic in Levinas's phenomenology and ethics. See, e.g., his *Difficult Freedom: Essays on Judaism*, trans. Seán Hand (London: Athlone, 1990); "Philosophy and Transcendence," in *Alterity and Transcendence*, trans. Michael B. Smith (New York: Columbia University, 1999); "Meaning and Sense," in *Basic Philosophical Writings*, ed. Adriaan T. Peperzak, Simon Critchley, and Robert Bernasconi (Indianapolis: Indiana University, 1996); *Otherwise than Being*, trans. Alphonso Lingis (Pittsburgh: Duquesne University, 1998). A secondary source, to which I am greatly indebted here, is Michele Saracino's *On Being Human: A Conversation with Lonergan and Levinas* (Milwaukee: Marquette University, 1993).

3. Saracino, *On Being Human*, 97.

4. Ibid., 96.

5. Ibid.

and that intuitions require interpretation,[6] the *sensus fidelium* further requires avenues for expression, and authentic dialogue also requires structures that do not presently exist.

My question is not merely what mechanisms exist through which the *sensus fidelium* is expressed, but more importantly, do mechanisms for the reception of the *sensus fidelium* exist at all? I tend to think not. If there were mechanisms for listening, perhaps the Church would look different. Perhaps theology would less often be viewed with suspicion by the hierarchy. Perhaps women's experience beyond motherhood would be taken into account in discussions of baptismal dignity and full humanity. Where are the venues for a face-to-face encounter between the hierarchy and the laity, where the laity speak and the power structure listens kenotically? Moreover, who is listening to the *sensus fidelium* on sexism? racism? heterosexism?

We all know the Church's failings when it comes to this justice-seeking posture, that the Church has turned away from the Others in its midst, or worse, dismissed or erased the Other in totalizing, colonializing ways. The Church is indeed sinful, and, as Rush asserts, its sinfulness goes beyond the sins of individuals. The patriarchy, racism, colonialism, homophobia remain embedded in the Church's structure and thought-patterns; our history is replete with such "isms." They seem inescapable for us. This is a reality we must face.

In addition to facing the fact of the sin in, of, and by the Church, I would invite us as church to face the demographic reality. This includes the pull of the Majority World that, though somewhat reflected in the Argentine/Italian pope, has yet to be reflected in the Church's hierarchy and the power structure, and even in the theological academy. It also must include the racial and ethnic reality of the soon-to-be Latino/a majority of American Catholics and how this reality stands in contrast (sometimes silently or invisibly) to the way the story of American Catholicism is told, originating

6. "The main problem with the study of the *sensus fidelium* . . . is its being a sense, an intuition. This sense is never discovered in some kind of pure state" (Orlando Espín, *The Faith of the People: Theological Reflections on Popular Catholicism* [Maryknoll, NY: Orbis, 1997], 66). US Latino/a theologians have pioneered the study of popular religious practices as sources of theological reflection. In addition to Espín's work, see Roberto Goizueta, "The Symbolic Realism of US Latino/a Popular Catholicism," *Theological Studies* 65 (2004): 255–74; Mark Francis, "Popular Piety and Liturgical Reform in a Hispanic Context," in *Dialogue Rejoined: Theology and Ministry in the United States Hispanic Reality*, ed. Ana Maria Pineda and Robert Schreiter (Collegeville, MN: Liturgical Press, 1995), 162–77; and most recently Timothy Matovina, *Latino Catholicism: Transformation in America's Largest Church* (Princeton, NJ: Princeton University, 2012).

from the Northeast and expanding West and South.[7] The sins of commission and omission, and of invisibility-making, are rampant. And we must face this failure with honesty, compassion, repentance, and forgiveness. Many believed that the election of a Latin American pope would remedy the problem of the Eurocentric hierarchy and the Eurocentric vision that pervades the Church. This young pontificate has shown promise. However, the fact of the sin is not erased by the face of the pope—although this pontificate might begin to indicate ways we can face the sins of the Church.

The image that has been most present in my mind as I thought about the relationship between the face of the Church and God's face is that of Pope Francis on Holy Thursday, with his face quite literally at the feet of a young Muslim woman. The posture and the positioning, the intimacy of that image and its radical nature, signify for me what the council meant when it talked about reflecting the genuine face of God to the world, about the Church as a sacrament or as leaven in the world.

The notion of "facing" as a posture or positioning—a preferential option—is the final aspect of "God's face" that I want to emphasize. In exegeting the story of the widow's mite, Gustavo Gutiérrez highlights the importance of perspective—Jesus' perspective, his point of view in the parable.[8] Jesus sees the woman offering her disproportionately large gift because he chooses to sit outside the Temple's door to the treasury. His decision to place himself precisely there allows Jesus to witness things that others might miss. This is the crucial notion of the word *face*: that the central mission of the Church, the way it is a reflection of God's own face, is that it is obligated to face the poor, the rejected, the excluded, the ones who cannot take life tomorrow for granted. Though no one has ever seen God, we know the posture of God toward the destitute, toward the Other. God loves the stranger, the widow, the orphan, and all the poor. To conclude, I offer these words from a homily of Augustine on 1 John:

7. According to the Instituto Fé y Vida Research and Resource Center, in 2012 approximately 41% of US Catholics were Hispanic. The majority of millennial Catholics and younger Catholics are also Hispanic. For a full picture of their studies see http://www.feyvida.org/research/. Research from The Pew Research Center supports the notion of a coming Hispanic majority in the US Catholic Church: see http://www.pewforum.org/2013/02/13/the-global-catholic-population/#know. (All URLs cited herein were accessed August 28, 2013.)

8. Olle Kristenson, *Pastor in the Shadow of Violence: Gustavo Gutiérrez as a Public Pastoral Theologian in Peru in the 1980s and 1990s* (Uppsala: Uppsala Universitet, 2009), 3.

> But let no one imagine God for himself in keeping with the concupiscence of his eyes. For he makes a huge shape for himself; or he stretches out some immeasurable vastness through space, as though spreading across open places—as much as he can— the light that he sees with these eyes; or he makes for himself some old man of, as it were, venerable aspect. Do not think of these. This is what you should think of if you want to see God: *God is love*. What sort of countenance does love have? What sort of shape does it have? What sort of feet does it have? What sort of hands does it have?[9]

The notion of ecclesial conversion must contain these three aspects—venues for face-to-face encounter, kenotic repentance for and continual uneasy relationship with ecclesial sinfulness, and a genuine justice-seeking posture and positioning. Though we cannot know how God looks, we can and should work to have the sort of face that love has (no more scowls!), and sorrowfully work to wipe away the tears from our broken Church and the broken world in which it journeys.

9. Augustine, *Homilies on the First Epistle of John*, The Works of St. Augustine: A Translation for the 21st Century III/14, intro., trans., notes by Boniface Ramsey, ed. Daniel Doyle and Thomas Martin (Hyde Park, NY: New City, 2008), 111.

Part 3

Church Mission

9 Revisiting Mission at Vatican II
Theology and Practice for Today's Missionary Church

STEPHEN B. BEVANS, SVD

The author argues that a closer and fresh reading of the Vatican II documents with an eye to the theme of mission might suggest that it is closer to the heart of the council's original intention than a cursory and dated reading might indicate. Indeed the church's mission is more urgent today than ever, given the shift of Christianity's center of gravity to the Global South, massive migration to the Global North, and widespread secularism. Revisiting the council's documents can offer substantial help for developing a theology and practice for today's missionary church.

At first glance, it might seem that the theme of the church's mission, particularly as developed in the Decree on the Mission Activity of the Church *Ad gentes* (*AG*), was not seen as a major issue at the Second Vatican council, nor as a major factor in its subsequent hermeneutic. As Italian missiologist Gianni Colzani reflects, "The usual reading of Vatican II does not consider it [*AG*] as one of the criteria that has influenced its [the council's] course; the biblical, liturgical, patristic, and ecumenical movements are the ones cited as influential at the council while the missionary movement is set rather to the side."[1] An indication of this might be the fact that, in the judgment of the 1985 Extraordinary Synod of Bishops, called precisely

1. Gianni Colzani, *Missiologia contemporanea: Il cammino evangelico delle chiese: 1945–2007* (Milan: San Paolo, 2010), 75 (translation mine).

to assess the council after 20 years, "the ecclesiology of communion is the central and fundamental idea of the council's documents."[2] The Final Report of the synod did indeed speak of the importance of the church's mission in the world, and even quotes *AG* no. 2's lapidary phrase regarding the church's essential missionary nature. Nevertheless, mission seems not to have been regarded as fundamental for the council's interpretation. Although John O'Malley, in his monumental work on what happened at Vatican II, certainly speaks about the evangelical spirit of the council, he devotes only about three pages to the development of the mission document itself. Unfortunately, he points out, the debate on the council floor on mission was held in three-and-a-half sessions, a "meager allotment of time given that about one-third of the bishops came from mission territories and were facing unprecedented difficulties in the new political, economic, and cultural situations in most of their countries."[3] Colzani's observations are justified as well by the fact that in their important recent work, Richard Gaillardetz and Catherine Clifford do not cite any passage from *AG* as one of the "keys" to the council.[4] They do, to be sure, include a chapter on the church's mission in the world, and they do mention *AG* no. 2 in that chapter, but mission is understood more along the lines of living out the rich tradition of the church's social teaching.[5] Perhaps along with the Constitution on the Sacred Liturgy, *Sacrosanctum concilium* (*SC*), the mission decree and the theme of mission might be classified as the "impoverished cousin of the council's hermeneutic."[6]

Nevertheless, a closer reading of the council and the council documents reveals that mission was very much at its heart. One might even say that in

2. The Church, in the Word of God, Celebrates the Mysteries of Christ for the Salvation of the World, The Final Report of the 1985 Extraordinary Synod, http://www.saint-mike.org/library/synod_bishops/final_report1985.html, II.b.C.1. This and all other URLs cited herein were accessed on February 8, 2013.

3. John W. O'Malley, *What Happened at Vatican II* (Cambridge, MA: Belknap of Harvard University, 2008), 269.

4. Richard R. Gaillardetz and Catherine E. Clifford, *Keys to the Council: Unlocking the Teaching of Vatican II* (Collegeville, MN: Liturgical Press, 2012).

5. Ibid., 87–94.

6. See Massimo Faggioli, *True Reform: Liturgy and Ecclesiology in* Sacrosanctum Concilium (Collegeville, MN: Liturgical Press, 2012), 15, citing Patrick Prétot, "La Constitution sur la liturgie: Une herméneutique de la tradition liturgique," in *Vatican II et la théologie: Perspectives pour le XXIe siècle*, ed. Philippe Bordeyne and Laurent Villemin (Paris: Cerf, 2006), 17–34.

its deepest intuitions, Vatican II was a "missionary council."[7] My contention here is that the theme of mission at the council in general, and in the council's document on mission in particular, needs to be revisited. This is especially true in our time of the shift in the center of gravity of Christianity to the Global South, the vast migrations of peoples, particularly toward what were formerly "mission sending countries" of the Global North,[8] and growing secularism and unbelief in the Global South as well. This latter reality prompted Pope John Paul II to speak of a "New Evangelization," and Benedict XVI to create the Pontifical Council for the New Evangelization and convoke the 2012 Synod of Bishops to deliberate on that topic,[9] but this article will suggest that "New Evangelization" or a "renewed evangelization" might be apt terms for *any* efforts of evangelization in what has become today a missionary church. Perhaps it is time to reaffirm the council's missionary intentions and methods, particularly in the face of this new world situation in which we find ourselves today.

Revisiting Mission at the Council

Colzani is correct in his judgment that other movements were the "drivers" of the council's major themes of the church as community and communion, episcopal collegiality, liturgical reform, and a renewed understanding of baptism and lay identity. Underneath, however, there ran a strong missionary current evident in some of the very first aims of the council articulated by Pope John XXIII and expressed in many documents and in several ways. Another Italian missiologist, Serena Noceti,

7. Johannes Schütte, "Ce que la mission attendait du Concile," in *Vatican II: L'Activité missionaire de l'église*, ed. Johannes Schütte (Paris: Cerf, 1967), 107–20, at 120.

8. There is no satisfactory way to make the distinction I am making here. Nations of the Global North in fact include Australia and New Zealand, even though they are geographically in the Southern Hemisphere. Some scholars prefer the term "Majority World" to speak of the Global South, but do not use the terminology of "Minority World." Some speak of the "Two-Thirds World" and the "One-Third World." In any case these terms are certainly better than the older terms "developed" and "developing nations," and perhaps better than "First" and "Third World," though the latter terms are still in use.

9. See Robert J. Schreiter, "The New Evangelization," in *Word Remembered, Word Proclaimed: Selected Papers from Symposia Celebrating the SVD Centennial in North America*, ed. Stephen Bevans, SVD, and Roger Schroeder, SVD (Nettetal, Germany: Steyler, 1997), 44–56; and Benedict XVI's *Moto Proprio*, *Ubicumque et semper*, establishing the Pontifical Council, http://www.vatican.va/ holy_father/benedict_xvi/apost_letters/documents/hf_ben-xvi_apl_20100921_ubicumque-et-semper_en.html.

speaks of mission as a defining factor in the reception and interpretation of the council's documents. Through the lens of mission, these texts can be understood in a new way.[10]

The Four Constitutions

As Giuseppe Alberigo points out, John XXIII's understanding of the goals of the council evolved between his first announcement on January 25, 1959, and his famous opening speech on October 11, 1962. As this understanding developed over the three years of preparation for the council, Alberigo says, it became clear that the pope "wanted a council that would mark a transition between two eras, that is, that would bring the Church out of the post-tridentine period and . . . into a new phase of witness and proclamation." In this way "the Church would then be able to present the gospel message to the world and explain it to human beings with the same power and immediacy that marked the first Pentecost."[11] The four goals outlined in the first paragraph of *SC*, comments Josef Jungmann, summarize the program that the pope had outlined in various speeches and documents during the preparatory period:[12] growth in the Christian life, becoming responsive to the present time, seeking the unity of Christians, and strengthening "those aspects of the Church which can help summon all of humanity into its embrace" (*SC* no. 1).[13]

Massimo Faggioli argues that the council understood that the liturgy could be "a powerful tool for the Church's missionary identity and activities."[14] *SC*'s acceptance of the vernacular (no. 36.2) and the sensitivity of the liturgy document to local cultures and customs (no. 37) won the support of many missionary bishops. In addition, the famous statement that "the liturgy is the summit toward which the activity of the Church

10. Serena Noceti, "Pensare il post-concilio: Tra recenzione ed ermeneutica," *Ad gentes: Teologia et antropologia della missione* 16, no. 1 (2012): 11–24, at 20.

11. Giuseppe Alberigo, "The Announcement of the Council: From the Security of the Fortress to the Lure of the Quest," in *History of Vatican II*, vol. 1, *Announcing and Preparing Vatican Council II: Toward a New Era in Catholicism*, ed. Giuseppe Alberigo and Joseph A. Komonchak (Maryknoll, NY: Orbis), 1–54, at 42.

12. Josef Andreas Jungmann, *Constitution on the Sacred Liturgy*, vol. 1 of *Commentary on the Documents of Vatican II*, 5 vols., ed. Herbert Vorgrimler (New York: Herder & Herder, 1967), 8.

13. Quotations from Vatican II are from Walter M. Abbot, ed., *The Documents of Vatican II* (New York: Herder & Herder, 1966). I have altered some citations for inclusive language.

14. Faggioli, *True Reform*, 38.

is directed; at the same time it is the fountain from which all her power flows" is a missionary statement. The liturgy, particularly the Eucharist, I submit, is a missionary act, to which we come to be nourished for more selfless and more effective apostolic service.

The Dogmatic Constitution on the Church, *Lumen gentium* (*LG*), opens with a missionary vision. By proclaiming the gospel to the ends of the earth, Christ's light will be shed on all peoples. The church is, as it were, a *sacrament*—not only a *sign* but also an *instrument* of the unity of God and humanity and women and men with each other (see *LG* no. 1). In *LG* no. 5 the council cautiously but certainly distinguishes between the church and the reign of God, intimating that the church receives its *raison d'être* from its missionary witness, service, and proclamation of that reign. Unfortunately, remarks Gaillardetz, this phrase was a late addition, and so did not influence the overall document as much as it might have.[15] It would be the postconciliar documents *Evangelii nuntiandi* (*EN*), *Redemptoris missio* (*RM*), and the 1991 statement Dialogue and Proclamation (DP) that would develop this important distinction further—though always insisting on the close connection between the church and God's reign.[16] *LG* nos. 13–17 lay out how various people belong to, are linked with, or related to the church, stating that while non-Christians and those not yet with faith can, with God's grace, find salvation, such salvation is difficult to achieve without the full means of grace that the church, in its missionary activity, offers. The end of *LG* no. 16 and the whole of *LG* no. 17 sketch out the motives, content, and method of mission. *LG* no. 17 insists both that mission should treat cultures with respect and that "the obligation of spreading the faith is imposed on every disciple of Christ, according to his or her ability."

The Constitution on Divine Revelation, *Dei Verbum* (*DV*), like *LG*, opens with a missionary vision. Like Trent and Vatican I, the preface states, the document intends to present the church's authentic teaching on revelation and tradition, "so that by hearing the message of salvation the whole world may believe; by believing, it may hope; and by hoping, it may love" (*DV* no. 1). The second paragraph, which presents a more personal rather than propositional understanding of revelation, also describes the *missio Dei*: God speaks to women and men as friends, lives among them, and invites and takes them into communion with Godself.[17] This revelation,

15. Richard R. Gaillardetz, *The Church in the Making:* Lumen Gentium, Christus Dominus, Orientalium Ecclesiarum (New York: Paulist, 2006), 22.

16. These developments are found in *EN* no. 8, *RM* nos. 12–20, and DP nos. 34, 35, 58.

17. See Ronald D. Witherup, *Scripture:* Dei Verbum (New York: Paulist, 2006), 34.

then, is entrusted to the apostles, who are commissioned "to preach to all women and men that gospel which is the source of all saving truth and moral teaching" (*DV* no. 7). Australian theologian Ormond Rush notes how the development of *DV* over the four sessions of the council also traces the history of the council's theological development. As the council progressed, he writes, the original more christological focus became more balanced with a pneumatological dimension "that pervades the 16 documents taken as a whole. The council's desire to renew and reform the Catholic Church spiritually and institutionally was for the sake of making the church a more effective sacrament of *God's mission* in the world."[18]

Cardinal Suenens's famous speech calling for the council to treat the church both in its *ad intra* and *ad extra* dimensions bore fruit in the development and promulgation of the Pastoral Constitution on the Church in the Modern World, *Gaudium et spes* (*GS*).[19] Behind this document is the conviction that the church finds its identity and purpose by being fully immersed in the service of and dialogue with the world—a marked contrast with attitudes held only a century earlier. So powerful and often quoted are the opening words of the constitution, proclaiming that the joys, hopes, griefs, and anxieties of every human being are also those of Christians, that the next missionary lines are often neglected: "United in Christ, they [Christians] are led by the Holy Spirit in their journey to the kingdom of their Father and they have welcomed the news of salvation which is meant for every human being" (*GS* no. 1). The whole document is a mission document *par excellence*, but several passages are particularly significant. Part 1 of chapter 4, for example, deals with the role of the church in the world as one of mutuality. Not only is the church in mission to and among individuals (*GS* no. 41), within society (no. 42), and in terms of human development (no. 43), but the document also goes on to say that the church is helped in its mission by the world's various cultures and by women and men "versed in different institutions and specialties" (no. 44), no doubt in terms of scientific expertise, political savvy, scholarly wisdom, and artistic creativity. Here and in part 2 of chapter 2, the role of culture in the church's life and evangelizing mission takes on real prominence. Preaching the gospel in tune with particular cultures and contemporary movements "ought to remain the law of all evangelization" (no. 44).

18. Ormond Rush, "Toward a Comprehensive Interpretation of the Council and Its Documents," *Theological Studies* 73 (2012): 547–69, at 568, emphasis original.

19. See Gaillardetz, *Church in the Making*, 14.

The Decrees and Declarations

Chapter 1 of the Decree on the Instruments of Social Communication, *Inter mirifica* (*IM*), anchors the church's interest in the means of social communication in Christ's commission "to bring salvation to every person," and so is "bound to proclaim the gospel" (*IM* no. 3). The Decree on Ecumenism, *Unitatis redintegratio* (*UR*), begins with the ecumenical movement's motives that seeking the unity of the church is not only against the will of Christ, but it also "inflicts damage on the most holy cause of proclaiming the good news to every creature" (*UR* no. 1). The council's Decree on Bishops' Pastoral Office in the Church, *Christus Dominus* (*CD*), opens with the statement that the Holy Spirit has been poured upon the church so that it might glorify God and "save humanity" (*CD* no. 1). It also understands an aspect of episcopal collegiality as bishops' duty "to be especially concerned about those parts of the world where the Word of God has not yet been proclaimed" (*CD* no. 6). In its Decree on the Apostolate of the Laity, *Apostolicam actuositatem* (*AA*), the council declares that the lay apostolate is founded in the church's mission, in which the laity participate directly (*AA* nos. 3–4). "For this the Church was founded: that by spreading the kingdom of Christ everywhere for the glory of God the Father, it might bring all peoples to share in Christ's saving redemption; and that through them the whole world might in actual fact be brought into relationship with Him" (no. 2).

Mission concerns figure prominently as well in the two declarations that, though brief, have had a huge impact in the postconciliar church: the Declaration on Non-Christian Religions, *Nostra aetate* (*NA*), and the Declaration on Religious Freedom, *Dignitatis humanae* (*DH*). In the former document, the "deeper study" that the church gives to other religious ways is part of its mission, namely, the "task of fostering unity and love among women and men, and even among nations" (*NA* no. 1). And although the religions of humankind "reflect a ray of that Truth which enlightens all humanity," there is still the necessity of always proclaiming Christ, "in whom humanity finds the fullness of religious life and in whom God has reconciled all things to Godself" (*NA* no. 2). Respect and dialogue does not take away the importance of the missionary task. Indeed, it points to the attitudes by which such work is to be carried out. *DH* no. 1 asserts forthrightly the need to "make disciples of all nations" (Mt 28:19), but nevertheless insists that "truth cannot impose itself except by virtue of its own truth, as it makes its entrance into the mind at once quietly and with power." It is because of every person's "right to religious freedom" (no. 2) that the council has abrogated the traditional doctrine that "error has no rights," but that right is also the basis for the council's insistence that "religious bodies also have the right not to be hindered in their public teaching and witness to their faith, whether by the spoken or by the written word" (no. 4). It is this dual aspect of religious freedom—expressing the right of the church to evangelize and guiding it in its basic method—that prompted eminent churchman Thomas Stransky to encourage Paulist Press to publish its recent commentaries on *AG* and *DH* in the same volume.[20]

Beyond the Documents

Revisiting mission in the texts of Vatican II makes it evident that mission is a significant perspective in the council's overall hermeneutic, and a theme that might well shape postconciliar thinking and practice. Perhaps more important, however, than the *fact* that mission is a constant theme in the council documents is what they presented regarding the *way* mission should be engaged, employing the symbols and attitudes of cultures and broader contexts, respecting the freedom of women and men to respond to the gospel and recognizing the truth in other religious ways and the goodness of women and men as they search for meaning in their lives. In other words mission is to be done in a way that appreciates culture, takes into account the way the gospel is proclaimed and more deeply reflected upon, and this in ways that recognize the prior presence of God's Spirit among the world's peoples. Mission is to reflect Pope Paul VI's powerful conviction in his 1964 encyclical, *Ecclesiam suam*, that, while other methods of evangelization are certainly possible, "the sort of relationship for the Church to establish with the world should be more in the nature of a dialogue" (no. 78).[21]

O'Malley's keen insight about the distinctive *style* of the council documents is also relevant to the hermeneutical importance of mission both for the interpretation of Vatican II and for mission's relevance today. This distinctive style is perhaps signaled already in John XXIII's opening speech, in which he spoke of how the church today prefers, rather than condemnation, "the medicine of mercy."[22] O'Malley notes that instead of a vocabulary of pessimism, juridicism, and dismissal of peoples and institutions beyond the church, the documents are filled with words like "brothers/sisters, friendship, cooperation, collaboration, partnership, freedom, dia-

20. Stephen B. Bevans and Jeffrey Gros, *Evangelization and Religious Freedom:* Ad Gentes *and* Dignitatis Humanae (New York: Paulist, 2009), ix.

21. Paul VI, *Ecclesiam suam*, http://www.vatican.va/holy_father/paul_vi/encyclicals/documents/hf_p-vi_enc_06081964_ecclesiam_en.html.

22. "Pope John's Opening Speech to the Council," 710–19, at 716.

logue, pilgrim, servant ('king'), development, evolution, charism, dignity, holiness, conscience, collegiality, people of God, priesthood of believers."[23] The implications of such language for mission are far-reaching. It is to be carried out in full confidence in the life-giving and liberating power of Jesus the Christ and the saving significance of membership in the church; at the same time it is to be lived out in vulnerability, respect, and gentleness. Witness and proclamation of the gospel should be done—to use two contemporary phrases rooted in the council's style—in "bold humility" and "prophetic dialogue."[24]

In his seventh principle for understanding the council, Rush points beyond the written texts to the full meaning of the "event" that was Vatican II. Like *DV*, which speaks of revelation in terms of both words and deeds, Rush indicates several conciliar and papal actions during the council that reveal its underlying missionary and evangelical intent. The council's invitation to Protestant observers certainly connected with its ecumenical aims, which, as I indicated above, had a missionary dimension to them. The invitation to lay observers—first men and then also women—was a concrete manifestation of the council's dialogical attitude. Rush also mentions Paul VI's donation of his tiara for the poor, and his visits to India, the Holy Land, and the United Nations, and the donation to the Greek Orthodox Church of a reliquary of the Apostle Andrew are all connected to the council's meaning. These "were, and are still, significant in shaping the contemporary reception of what the council was intending to do and the kind of church it was attempting to fashion."[25]

Revisiting Ad Gentes

The centerpiece of the council's explicit reflections on mission was its Decree on the Church's Missionary Activity, *Ad gentes*. Drafted toward the end of the council, and approved only after a tortuous development,[26] it was able to incorporate many of the key ideas in other documents. *AG* is grounded in the missionary, trinitarian ecclesiology that was more subtly developed in *LG* (*AG* no. 2) and had emerged as the council progressed. Indeed, it seems no accident that the titles of both documents speak of

23. O'Malley, *What Happened at Vatican II*, 306.

24. See David J. Bosch, *Transforming Mission: Paradigm Shifts in Theology of Mission* (Maryknoll, NY: Orbis, 1991), 489; Stephen B. Bevans and Roger P. Schroeder, *Prophetic Dialogue: Reflections on Christian Mission Today* (Maryknoll, NY: Orbis, 2011).

25. Rush, "Interpretation of Vatican II," 552.

26. See Bevans and Gros, *Evangelization and Religious Freedom*, 9–29.

Gentes/Gentium. *AG* takes for granted the theology of the local church in the church constitution (chap. 3), and expresses a practical episcopal collegiality in regard to the fact that it is the episcopal college, in union with the pope, that has the primary responsibility "to proclaim the gospel throughout the world" (*AG* no. 29; see also no. 5). *AG* contains a robust theology of the laity that reflects both *LG* chapter 4 and *AA*. It has the positive regard toward non-Christian religions present in *LG* no. 16 and *NA*. It contains several important and even lyrical passages on the importance of context in general and cultures in particular, reflecting *SC* no. 37 and *GS* part 2, chapter 2. Finally, it possesses the same sensitivity of style highlighted by O'Malley as so significant for engaging in ministry and mission worthy of the God who sends. *AG* is definitely worth revisiting.

Trinitarian Ecclesiology

The first four paragraphs of *LG* root the church in the missions of the Trinity, concluding with Cyprian of Carthage's dictum that the church is "a people made one with the unity of the Father, the Son, and the Holy Spirit" (*LG* no. 4). *AG*'s ecclesiology of mission is no less trinitarian, but perhaps more dynamic. In what missiologist William Burrows calls the document's "most memorable line," the one that "the decree's promoters wanted etched in the minds both of the council fathers and the church at large,"[27] *AG* defines the church and its radical missionary nature: "The pilgrim church is missionary by its very nature. For it is from the mission of the Son and the mission of the Holy Spirit that it takes its origin, in accordance with the decree of God the Father" (*AG* no. 2). This passage leaves no doubt that mission is not simply one among many of the things that the church does or an activity that is optional. Rather, mission is constitutive of the church itself, existing, as missiologist Wilbert Shenk expresses it, *prior* to the church.[28] As the saying goes, the church does not have a mission; the mission has a church. We could say in the light of this statement in *AG* that trinitarian faith is about engagement in mission—if one professes belief in the Trinity, one is caught up in the Trinity's saving work.

Connected with the trinitarian perspective of mission—but little commented on—is a rather fresh and powerful theology of the Holy Spirit, one that grounds the openness to cultures and religions that mark *AG*'s and the council's approach to mission. Acknowledging that the Spirit was sent by

27. William R. Burrows, "Decree on the Church's Missionary Activity: *Ad Gentes Divinitus*," in *Vatican II and Its Documents: An American Reappraisal*, ed. Timothy E. O'Connell (Wilmington: Michael Glazier, 1986), 180–96, at 180.

28. Wilbert R. Shenk, *Changing Frontiers of Mission* (Maryknoll, NY: Orbis, 1999), 7.

Christ from the Father at Pentecost, the text notes that "doubtless, the Holy Spirit was already at work in the world before Christ was glorified" (*AG* no. 4). This is because, as a note citing Leo the Great explains, Pentecost "was not so much the beginning of a gift as it was the completion of one already bountifully possessed: because the patriarchs, the prophets, the priests, and all the holy men who preceded them were already quickened by the life of the same Spirit, . . . although they did not possess his gifts to the same degree."[29] This presence of the Spirit already in Israel's history might well be extended, as theologians like Elizabeth Johnson and Denis Edwards acknowledge, to an active presence of the Spirit since the first instant of creation, pervading all things and people always and everywhere with God's grace and gentle prompting toward the good.[30] It points to the truth that, in the famous phrase of Anglican missiologist Max Warren, God was present long before the missionaries' arrival.[31]

Attention to Context and Culture

It may well be that the aspect of *AG* that deserves revisiting the most is the attention paid throughout the text to the importance, the usefulness, and even the holiness of contexts and cultures in which missionaries work. This attention to culture appears in *AG* no. 9, toward the end of the long chapter (the longest of the document) on the theological foundation of mission. It states that "truth and grace are to be found among the nations, as a secret presence of God," and that the work of Christian mission is in large part the task of freeing and perfecting that truth and grace, so that nothing is really lost in an encounter with the gospel. *AG* no. 11 repeats this idea in some of the most eloquent words of the decree. "Truth and grace" are now spoken of in terms of Justin Martyr's "seeds of the word," and missionaries are encouraged to immerse themselves in the continuing and changing history of people, be in critical contact with science and technology, and know the people among whom they live. "Thus they themselves can learn by sincere and patient dialogue what treasures a bountiful God has distributed among the nations of the earth."

In the context of a discussion of seminary training in a local church, students are to be taught ways of connecting "with the particular way of

29. The reference is to Leo the Great, Sermon 76, Migne, PL 54.405–6.

30. Elizabeth A. Johnson, *She Who Is: The Mystery of God in Feminist Theological Discourse* (New York: Crossroad, 1992), 124–49; Denis Edwards, *Breath of Life: A Theology of the Creator Spirit* (Maryknoll, NY: Orbis, 2004), 171–79.

31. M. A. C. Warren, introduction to John V. Taylor, *The Primal Vision: Christian Presence amid African Religion* (Philadelphia: Fortress, 1963), 5–12, at 10.

thinking and acting characteristic of their own people" and enabled to be in critical conversation with their culture (*AG* no. 16). In both philosophical and theological studies, students should be helped to discern "the points of contact between the traditions and religion of their homeland and the Christian religion" (*AG* no. 16). In other words, theological education should be geared to training in effective evangelization. In their ministry, bishops and clergy alike should live in contact with the universal church, but in a way that, while preserving communion with the whole, the wider traditions of the church should be embedded in their own cultures, "thereby increasing the life of the Mystical Body by a certain mutual exchange of energies" (*AG* no. 19).

AG no. 22 speaks straightforwardly about the need to adapt theology to local contexts and cultures (today we would say "inculturate" or engage in "contextual theology"). "From the customs and traditions of their people, from their wisdom and their learning, from their arts and sciences, these Churches borrow all those things which can contribute to the glory of their Creator, the revelation of the Savior's grace, or the proper arrangement of Christian life." As faith seeks understanding in this way, the document says, a whole new interpretation of the biblical witness and the witness of the early theologians and the church's theological tradition will be developed. If this process is done well, misunderstandings of the faith and interpretations that ignore the wider tradition will be avoided.

Proclamation in Dialogue

Like the language and attitude of the council in general, *AG* is shot through with passages that call for mission to be lived out in solidarity and dialogue. The trinitarian rooting of mission suggests that mission is done not so much to save women and men from wickedness and depravity—although they are caught often in the "devil's domain" and the "manifold malice of vice" (*AG* no. 9)—but in the overflowing love and life of a "bountiful God" (*AG* no. 11). *AG* no. 9 proclaims that "missionary activity is nothing else and nothing less than a manifestation or epiphany of God's will, and the fulfillment of that will in the world and in world history." Proclamation and witness to the gospel offer to women and men in today's world new, astounding knowledge that can reshape, recolor, and transform their lives.[32] Salvation, in other words, is not so much a negative

32. For an important reflection on this, see Clemens Sedmak, "Mission as Transformation: Commemorating the Second Vatican Council," The Thirteenth Louis J. Luzbetak, SVD, Lecture on Mission and Culture, in *New Theology Review* 25, no. 2 (March 2013): 35–55.

reality—being snatched from eternal punishment, from the hands, as it were, of an "angry God." Rather, salvation is here conceived as the entry into a new way of being human, into a community that can offer fullness of life through relationship and celebration, into a way of life that finds the greatest fulfillment in service and sharing of the gospel with others.

Witness begins with solidarity. Christians in mission must identify themselves with those among whom they live. They need to know and appreciate the culture; they need to understand the national and religious traditions where they live, because in that way they will lay bare "the seeds of the Word which lie hidden in them" (*AG* no. 11). They treat the local people equally, "without distinction of race, social condition, or religion, and they should identify with the poor and suffering and "take part in the strivings of those peoples who are waging war on famine, ignorance, and disease and thereby struggling to better their way of life and to secure peace in the world" (*AG* no. 13).

The gospel cannot be proclaimed indiscriminately, but "wherever God opens a door of speech," it should be announced "with confidence and constancy." In no uncertain words, the decree "strictly forbids" any kind of cheap proselytism (*AG* no. 13). It is perhaps said obliquely, but *AG* recognizes that there are places where the gospel cannot be openly preached, and where only a gradual, careful approach is appropriate (*AG* no. 6). In any case, missionaries need to be adequately trained—in the local language, in local customs and culture, but especially in respect for these (*AG* no. 26). The most famous speech at the 1910 Edinburgh World Missionary Conference was given by Indian churchman V. S. Azariah; it concluded with the words, "Give us FRIENDS!"[33] It is this attitude that is expressed over and over again in *AG*. To witness and preach effectively, cultivating relationships is fundamental.

Mission, *Ad Gentes*, and Today's Missionary Church

Exactly *where* mission is to be carried out is ambiguous in the texts and in the "event" of the council.[34] This is the case both in regard to mission in general and in particular to the council's document that addresses mission. When the council speaks of mission, does it mean the basic task of the

33. See Brian Stanley, *The World Missionary Conference, Edinburgh 1910* (Grand Rapids, MI: Eerdmans, 2009), 124.

34. On the meaning of "event" in this context, see Joseph A. Komonchak, "Vatican II as 'Event,' " in *Vatican II: Did Anything Happen?* ed. David G. Schultenover (New York: Continuum, 2007), 24–51.

church wherever it finds itself? Or does it mean the work of "Christian" "sending churches" moving beyond borders and cultures—i.e., the "mission"? On the one hand we read that "the pilgrim Church is missionary by its very nature" (*AG* no. 2), that "the whole Church is missionary, and the work of evangelization is a basic duty of the People of God" (*AG* no. 35), that the church is a sacrament, a sign and instrument of unity in the world (*LG* no. 1), and—albeit in a more tentative way—that the church takes its existence from its mission to witness to and proclaim the reign of God (*LG* no. 5). On the other hand, the council distinguishes between missionary work as such and "pastoral activity exercised among the faithful (*AG* no. 6). *LG* no. 16 speaks of the need for the church painstakingly to promote "missionary work," and the whole tenor of *AG*, especially after chapter 1, seems finally to refer to "foreign missions." The decree still seems to have in its imagination the white "First World" missionary working in exotic lands and cultures. On the one hand mission can be read as *constitutive* of the church; on the other it can be read as a very important, even indispensable, activity, but one of very many activities carried out by women and men with a specific "missionary" vocation.

In today's world, however, a half century later, this ambiguity may no longer obtain. Today there is no Christian center. Every church exists in a "missionary situation." Today there is only a missionary church, as the church expands rapidly, and yet often without adequate personnel resources, in lands formerly considered "missionary"; as members of those "missionary churches" migrate into lands where there exist what were formerly considered "sending churches"; as missionaries come from the "missionary churches" to care for those who have migrated there, or to evangelize their former evangelizers; as the church in the West finds itself in numerical decline, and recognizes a need to witness to and preach the gospel in new ways and with new urgency in pluralist and secularist societies. It is this missionary church that can revisit the doctrine of mission in the Vatican II documents with profit.

Revisiting missiology at Vatican II in the light of today's universal missionary situation will point to the fact that there is no longer dichotomy between every church's missionary nature and its task of preaching the gospel in a way that requires dialogue, knowledge of and empathy for the concrete contexts in which women and men live, and skills of intercultural communication. The church is indeed "missionary by its very nature," requiring missionary practice for its very existence. Without mission the church will cease to exist as church—both literally and theologically. Mission today is lived out among people of varying cultures and the world's many religions, and/or among people who do not believe or who have ceased to believe. Mission in every situation might well profit from the experience of traditional "cross-cultural" missionaries, for that is the situation in which every church today exists.[35] What was originally meant at Vatican II for certain kinds of ministers in certain kinds of churches now has relevance for all ministers and all churches. What was seen as basically irrelevant for some churches, and so was pushed to the side, is now amazingly relevant for all.

A Missionary Theology

In theology, this recognition of today's missionary church calls for radical rethinking of theological methods and content in the light of its missionary task. Theology has to serve an evangelical purpose. It has to reflect on the faith with real attention to the particular customs and traditions, wisdom and learning, scientific knowledge, and artistic achievement, as *AG* no. 22 and *GS* no. 44 encourage missionaries and ministers to do. Ilia Delio, reflecting on doing theology in the context of contemporary physics and evolutionary thinking, insists that as a result of such thinking all of theology needs to be rethought.[36] The same goes for theology in the political, social, cultural, and artistic contexts in which the church witnesses to and preaches the gospel. Contextual theology in today's missionary church is not optional. It is more than ever a "theological imperative."[37] In addition, because of the multicultural and intercultural nature of today's world, theology needs to be done, on the one hand, in a dialogue with individual contextual theologies, that is, in "global perspective."[38] On the other hand, in our highly interreligious world, theology has to be done, as Peter Phan has put it, "intereligiously," with a comparative method.[39] Of course, every effort of theologizing cannot include all these dimensions,

35. See Severino Dianich, "Evangelizzare: Dal Vaticano II alla problematica contemporanea," *Ad gentes* 16, no. 1 (2012): 77–87, at 82.

36. Ilia Delio, *The Emergent Christ: Exploring the Meaning of Catholic in an Evolutionary Universe* (Maryknoll, NY: Orbis, 2011), 32, u.a.

37. Stephen B. Bevans, *Models of Contextual Theology* (Maryknoll, NY: Orbis, 2002), 3–15.

38. Stephen Bevans, "A Theology for the Ephesian Moment," *Anvil* 27, no. 2 (November 2011), http://anviljournal.org/174. The "Theology in Global Perspective" series, published by Orbis Books and edited by Peter Phan, is one attempt, with varied success, to think theologically in this way.

39. Peter C. Phan, *Being Religious Interreligiously: Asian Perspectives on Interfaith Dialogue* (Maryknoll, NY: Orbis, 2004); Francis X. Clooney, *Theology after Vedanta: An Experiment in Comparative Theology* (Albany: State University of New York, 1993); Paul F. Knitter, *Without Buddha I Could Not Be a Christian* (Oxford: Oneworld, 2009).

but the context should dictate which methods and perspectives ought to be included.

Ecclesiology in particular needs to be conceived as a consistent *missionary* ecclesiology in order to give a theological foundation to today's missionary church. Some efforts have been made in this regard by members of the largely Protestant "Gospel and Our Culture Network," and Gaillardetz has offered an important volume from a Catholic perspective.[40] Work still needs to be done, however, in connecting ecclesiology even more closely with mission. Such an ecclesiology—working out the church's essential missionary nature according to *AG* no. 2—could, in a first move, begin with the trinitarian missions. Starting, however, with the Holy Spirit "already at work in the world before Christ was glorified" (*AG* no. 4) and present from the first nanosecond of creation, the missionary God sent the Son to take on flesh in Jesus of Nazareth. At his baptism, Jesus was anointed with this Spirit for mission and so preached, served, and witnessed to the reign of God, calling all who would listen to communion with "that fountain of love" (*AG* no. 2) that is overwhelming, ineffable Holy Mystery. Such witness and preaching led, sadly yet inexorably, to the cross, but his way of life was vindicated in his being raised from the dead, and the Spirit by which he was anointed is now lavished upon his disciples and their disciples after them. God's mission, active from the first instant of creation, shared by Jesus the Christ, is now the mission of Jesus' disciples. Sharing his mission is indeed constitutive of the church, which, like the Trinity, is a communion-in-*mission* (a more dynamic understanding of the quotation from Cyprian in *LG* no. 4).

In a second move, reflection could focus on the *communion* aspect of the church, still recognizing its essential missionary nature. This might be done, first, by focusing on the three major images cited at the end of chapter 2 of *LG* (no. 17), and giving them a distinct missionary interpretation. The church is the pilgrim people of God (*LG* nos. 48–51; *AG* no. 2), receiving its identity in its service of the reign of God and striving to live as its sacrament. The church is the Body of Christ, embodying and

40. See, e.g., Darrell L. Guder, ed., *Missional Church: A Vision for the Sending of the Church in North America* (Grand Rapids, MI: Eerdmans, 1998); Craig van Gelder, *The Essence of the Church: A Community Created by the Spirit* (Grand Rapids, MI: Baker, 2000); Darrell L. Guder, *The Continuing Conversion of the Church* (Grand Rapids, MI: Eerdmans, 2000); Richard R. Gaillardetz, *Ecclesiology for a Global Church: A People Called and Sent* (Maryknoll, NY: Orbis, 2008)—this volume appears in Phan's "Theology in Global Perspective" series.

continuing Jesus' mission of preaching, serving, and witnessing to God's reign. And the church is the temple of the Holy Spirit, called into being by that Spirit, challenged by the Spirit to cross new boundaries and to respond to new contexts, and, like a temple, being the place where God's mystery is palpably present within the world. A second section reflecting on the church's nature as a missionary communion might focus on the four traditional marks of the church, recognizing that each one is threefold in the light of mission: the church *is* apostolic, one, catholic, and holy; it is called to *become* more fully what it is; and it is called to *make* all peoples servants of the gospel (apostolic), all peoples one, all peoples clear in their cultural distinctiveness and yet connected in communion, and all peoples conscious of their beloved, holy status in the eyes of God.

Finally a missionary ecclesiology in service of today's missionary church would reflect on its structure as a communion-of-*ministers*-in-mission. This section takes as a starting point the fundamental equality and basic call to ministry and mission of all believers (*LG* nos. 10–12, 32; *AG* nos. 28, 35). Then it would develop a theology of the laity as rooted in the church's mission (*LG* no. 33; *AA* no. 3; *AG* no. 21), and a theology of ordained ministry as having its chief duty the ordering of the entire church— depending on one's level of responsibility, whether presbyteral, episcopal, or papal—in its faith, its worship, and its ministry. It would be in the context of church leadership for mission that a reflection could be made regarding the autonomy and universal responsibility of the local church at the regional, diocesan, parochial, or small-community level. *AG*'s fresh approach to the local church in its third chapter (especially no. 19) would be an important source for this. Through their vows and in community life, religious serve the church by being radical signs of the church's commitment to the reign of God and unencumbered workers at the church's edges, challenging the church to new and creative forms of missionary engagement.

The "Age of Migration,"[41] in which we live, challenges theology to reflect on mission and migration and develop a theology of migration. Some work in this area has been done, but much work remains.[42] Already

41. See Stephen Castles and Mark J. Miller, *The Age of Migration: International Population Movements in the Modern World*, 4th ed. (New York: Guilford, 2009).

42. See in particular Gaetano Parolin, *Chiesa postconciliare e migrazioni: Quale teologia per la missione con i migranti* (Rome: Gregorian University, 2010); Daniel G. Groody and Gioacchino Campese, eds., *A Promised Land, A Perilous Journey: Theological Perspectives on Migration* (Notre Dame, IN: University of Notre Dame, 2008);

important connections have been made between migration as a way to understand better the pilgrim nature of the church and Christian life, and new and intriguing images of God such as pilgrim, refugee, migrant, and guest. Recognizing the dialogical nature of mission as prescribed in *AG*, mission is not so much directed *at* migrants as carried out *among* them. And realizing that every Christian has a ministerial and missionary call, an essential part of the church's missionary work among migrants is their empowerment as missionary subjects.

Other issues that might be taken up in a missionary theology are reflections on the meaning of salvation, a theological anthropology adequate to particular cultural contexts and in relationship to a more cosmic, less anthropocentric vision, the uniqueness of Christ in a pluralistic world of religions, the criteria by which a particular ethical or doctrinal expression might be judged adequate and orthodox, and the increasing importance of reconciliation and peacemaking. A missionary theology of the Trinity will be crucial for a solid ecclesiological and missiological foundation. A missionary theology will serve missionary practice.

Missionary Practice

Revisiting Vatican II on mission urges the church to engage in what might be called "prophetic dialogue."[43] Such a stance anchors all mission in deep listening, respectful attitudes toward the world (business, art, science, culture, current trends) in which the church witnesses reverence for the heritage of people's religions, readiness to learn from people's experiential wisdom, and sensitivity to those who do not or cannot believe. At the same time, however, as a result of such a dialogical posture, Christians humbly, yet clearly and confidently, witness to and proclaim the gospel—telling the marvelous story that "God is like Jesus,"[44] offering his perspectives on life and life's problems, embodying a future of human and cosmic harmony, demonstrating an alternative yet attractive way to

---

Gioacchino Campese, "The Irruption of Migrants: Theology of Migration in the 21st Century," *Theological Studies* 73 (2012): 3–32; Stephen Bevans, "Migration and Mission: Pastoral Challenges, Theological Insights," in *Theology and Migration in World Christianity*, ed. Peter C. Phan and Elaine Padilla (New York: Palgrave MacMillan, 2014).

43. Bevans and Schroeder, *Prophetic Dialogue*. The entire issue of *Missiology: An International Review* 41, no. 1 (January 2013) is on prophetic dialogue, including Roger P. Schroeder's presidential address at the June 2012 annual meeting of the American Society of Missiology.

44. Juan Luis Segundo, *Christ in the Spiritual Exercises of St. Ignatius* (Maryknoll, NY: Orbis, 1987), 22–26, quoted in Roger Haight, *Jesus, Symbol of God* (Maryknoll, NY: Orbis, 1999), 116.

live, denouncing any and all evil and injustice, and working toward a just society both within and outside the church. Any kind of missionary practice, therefore, should always be tempered with what John XXIII called the "medicine of mercy."[45]

In his recent book on the council's teaching in regard to the motive of missionary work, Ralph Martin argues that—particularly in terms of contemporary Western society but applying this to *ad gentes* evangelization as well—"while there were many sound reasons to emphasize the positive in the Church's relations with the modern world, it has also become clear that an adjustment in her pastoral strategy is needed."[46] For Martin, this new strategy—which is actually a return to a previous strategy—emphasizes the sinfulness and corruption of women and men who do not believe in the gospel, very many of whom will most likely not be saved. Martin believes that such a strategy reaffirms the urgency of mission and will provide a more effective motive for mission than mere obedience to Christ's command and the enhancement of human and religious life. It is this strategy that he urges for the New Evangelization.

Much of what Martin argues is well taken. There has been, perhaps, a reading of Vatican II on mission that has glossed over human sinfulness, minimized the danger of the possibility of losing salvation, minimized the help of Christian faith, Christian community, and Christian sacraments in achieving salvation, and offered what Martin calls (referring to Karl Rahner, Richard McBrien, and Francis Sullivan) a "salvation optimism" that quickly slides down a slippery slope to a facile universalism.[47]

Nevertheless, Martin's caution does not seem to warrant a reversal of Vatican II's basic dialogical stance toward the world and basic pastoral strategy.[48] Perhaps rather than reversing such a strategy, a revisiting of Vatican II's missionary practice should be a renewal of efforts to concretize at every turn a practice of prophetic witness and proclamation that is rooted not in severe condemnations but in the medicine of mercy.[49] Thus revisiting Vatican II on mission will bring about a true New Evangelization

45. John XXIII, "Opening Speech," 716.

46. Martin, *Will Many Be Saved?*, 195. Martin's extension of the context is seen, for example, on p. 208.

47. Ibid., 54–55.

48. Gilles Routhier points out that official Vatican documents do not at all understand the New Evangelization as an adjustment of Vatican II's basic perspectives. See Routhier, *Un concilio per il XXI secolo: Il Vaticano II cinquant'anni dopo* (Milan: Vita et Pensiero, 2012), 39.

49. See the review of Martin's work by Stephen B. Bevans and Roger P. Schroeder in *International Bulletin of Missionary Research* 37, no. 2 (April 2013).

in the Majority World, in an "Age of Migration," and in a world of the unchurched and secular unbelief.

We have already seen how Faggioli connects the council's liturgical renewal to mission, as indeed the council itself did.[50] Any kind of renewal of evangelization efforts in today's world surely must pay heed to the evangelizing power of liturgy and the challenge to cultural relevance proposed by *SC* no. 37. Ideally, a New Evangelization will make further efforts at liturgical inculturation not only in the countries of the Global North but also among migrant groups, contemporary Western congregations, youth, young adults, and other particular groups. Sadly, however, with the abandonment of the conciliar principle of decisions being made at a more local level, the liturgical movement has reached something of an impasse. Nevertheless liturgy as it is celebrated today presents all sorts of opportunities for more worthy celebrations, cultural adaptations within the parameters allowed, more beautiful and relevant music, more graceful presiding, prayers that reflect international and local concerns, greater lay participation, particularly by women, and better prepared, better informed, evangelically focused homilies. People are either attracted to or repelled by liturgy. It is a missionary act.

GS no. 44 speaks about how "accommodated preaching" (we might say "inculturated" or "contextual" preaching) "ought to remain the law of all evangelization." This need not be confined to liturgical preaching or the homily. In a renewed practice of evangelization, *any* church communication needs to be attuned to the "signs of the times," the local culture, or broad cultural movements like contemporary movements in the United States toward social equality. It is not always a question of *agreeing* with what is going on—i.e., agreeing with current cultural values or social movements. However, a church that preaches the gospel needs to have a deep respect for the opinions of people of apparent good will, and needs to teach its own, perhaps countercultural, position in ways that are clear and well argued, based on scientific and philosophical truth, and presented clearly and nonjudgmentally. Truth, *DH* says, "cannot impose itself except by virtue of its own truth, as it makes its entrance into the mind at once quietly and with power" (no. 1). Mission eschews all "unworthy techniques" of preaching the gospel (see *AG* no. 13); real prophecy, however strong, is not violent.

And a missionary church should know when to keep silent. The council's dialogical approach to mission is beautifully summed up in the intervention of the 2012 Synod on the New Evangelization of (now Cardinal) Luis

50. See Faggioli, *True Reform*, 37–38.

Antonio Tagle, archbishop of Manila. He called for an evangelization in humility, respect, and silence, saying in respect to the third: "The Church must discover the power of silence. Confronted with the sorrows, doubts and uncertainties of people, she cannot pretend to give easy solutions. In Jesus, silence becomes the way of attentive listening, compassion and prayer. It is the way to truth."[51] Perhaps the church in its official teachings and official pronouncements should indeed keep silent more than it does. A sense of humility and listening—essential to dialogue— might proclaim the gospel more clearly. This might in itself be a prophetic stance. As *AG* no. 6 wisely counsels, "The appropriate actions and tools must be brought to bear on any given circumstance or situation." Perhaps, as the subtitle to Maryknoller John Sivalon's recent book suggests, the missionary church today might profit from "the gift of uncertainty."[52]

The council, and especially *AG* no. 15, calls for the formation of Christian communities that are examples of the power of the gospel to transform lives. The evangelizing influence of such communities can hardly be exaggerated, because "people will always believe their eyes first."[53] Communities in which Christians are seen to support one another, share deeply with one another, celebrate joyfully, challenge one another, console one another are truly what the great 20th-century missiologist Lesslie Newbigin called "a hermeneutic of the gospel."[54] The formation of this kind of community should be a real priority for the church's leadership, particularly at the parish and small-community level. In his intervention at the 2012 Synod, Archbishop Socrates Villegas of Lingayen-Dagupan, the Philippines, suggested that the New Evangelization calls for new saints— and that *we* must be those saints.[55] It is in the witness of true holiness, which is ultimately authentic, vibrant humanity found in individuals and pulsating in a community, that women and men will be attracted to ask the questions that can lead them to faith in Christ.

51. Thirteenth Synod of Bishops, October 7–28, 2012, on the New Evangelization, http://www.vatican.va/news_services/press/sinodo/documents/bollettino_25_xiii-ordinaria-2012/xx_plurilingue/b07_xx.html (unofficial translation).

52. John C. Sivalon, *God's Mission and Postmodern Culture: The Gift of Uncertainty* (Maryknoll, NY: Orbis, 2012).

53. World Conference on Mission and Evangelization (San Antonio, Texas, 1989), "Mission in Christ's Way: Your Will Be Done" no. 22, in *New Directions in Mission and Evangelization*, vol. 1, *Basic Statements 1974–1991*, ed. James A. Scherer and Stephen B. Bevans (Maryknoll, NY: Orbis, 1992), 73–81, at 78.

54. Lesslie Newbigin, *The Gospel in a Pluralist Society* (Grand Rapids, MI: Eerdmans, 1989), 222–33.

55. Thirteenth Synod of Bishops.

Something that has perhaps been lost in the years since the council has been the close tie between mission and ecumenism. Along with "missionary activity among the nations," *AG* no. 6 mentions both pastoral work and "undertakings aimed at restoring unity among Christians" as "most closely connected with the missionary zeal of the Church." As *UR* has said, the continuing divisions among Christians constitute a real scandal to people among whom Christians witness to and proclaim the gospel today. Doctrinal differences are real and in many cases fundamental. There still remain, however, many ways in which Christians can work together, especially in the areas of theological education, action for social and ecological justice, and reconciliation work. Praying together, as the council recommends, is also a witness to a more profound unity than appears on the surface. There needs to be a new ecumenism for the renewed evangelization that revisiting Vatican II requires.

Often one of the most prophetic actions Christians can take is to continue the practice of dialogue, especially in the face of the many religious tensions—in Nigeria, for example, or India, France, or the post-9/11 United States. As Hans Küng has constantly insisted, there can be no real peace without peace among the world's religions, and this peace is the hoped-for fruit of interreligious dialogue.[56] Whether it is the dialogue of life, of common action, of theological exchange, or of spiritual experience,[57] dialogue is a sine qua non of mission today. Often this will not be easy; often, as has been the case in several places in the world, the price of dialogue is martyrdom.[58] But openness and vulnerability are key aspects of mission that we discover when we visit Vatican II on mission, and key as well to a renewed vision of evangelization in the light of the council. Clemens Sedmak suggests that the church set up "intellectual base communities" in which "ethical issues (such as abortion, euthanasia, same-sex marriage) can be discussed in a climate of friendship. There is as yet little real encounter between Church members and representatives of positions

56. See, for example, Hans Küng, *Christianity: Essence, History, and Future* (New York: Continuum, 1995), 783.

57. See Pontifical Council for Interreligious Dialogue and Congregation for the Evangelization of Peoples, Dialogue and Proclamation no. 42, http://www.vatican.va/roman_curia/pontifical_councils/interelg/documents/rc_pc_interelg_doc_19051991_dialogue-and-proclamatio_en.html.

58. Perhaps the most famous recent example of this is the martyrdom of the Trappist monks in Tibhirine, Algeria, powerfully portrayed in the film *Of Gods and Men*. See John Kiser, *The Monks of Tibhirine: Faith, Love, and Terror in Algeria* (New York: St. Martin's Griffin, 2003). See also Jean-Jacques Pérennès, *A Life Poured Out: Pierre Claverie of Algeria* (Maryknoll, NY: Orbis, 2007).

that cannot be reconciled with the Church."[59] In a similar way, Proposition 55 of the 2012 Synod of Bishops suggests that various churches and institutions open a kind of "Courtyard of the Gentiles" "where believers and non-believers can dialogue about fundamental themes."[60] A missionary church in dialogue could not only be a teaching church; it could be a learning church as well.

Over and over again the council reminds us in so many words that the joys, the hopes, the griefs, and the anxieties of humanity—"especially those who are poor or in any way afflicted" (*GS* no. 1; see also *AG* no. 12) are the same as those of Christians. If this was not clear enough, the 1971 Synod of Bishops made a direct link between preaching the gospel and working for justice.[61] Although ecological concerns hardly appear in the Vatican II documents, today work for justice needs to be extended to the entire cosmos in ecological commitment, moving beyond the rather strong anthropocentrism of the council (e.g., *GS* nos. 9, 33). More than ever today, the church needs to work for justice and transparency within its own boundaries. How the church's leadership has treated women in some cases, how it has gone about its task of preserving the faith from error, and how it has treated victims of sexual abuse have greatly hindered Christian credibility in the world today. On the other hand, the brave acknowledgments of guilt that the church has made at Vatican II in terms of its partial blame for the lack of Christian unity (*UR* no. 3) or, perhaps obliquely, anti-Semitism (*UR* no. 5), and the humble apologies made during the Jubilee Year of the millennium have been powerful proclamations of how the gospel claims Christian life. A new, renewed evangelization can in no way be reduced to witnessing to and working for justice, but it surely is the condition of the possibility for the believability of a church that preaches and lives the gospel with the new ardor, new methods, and new expression that the New Evangelization calls for.

Conclusion: Mission at the Center

Revisiting mission at Vatican II, in its rather pervasive presence in the council's documents and in the decree dedicated to it specifically, can be a fruitful task, particularly in this time of seismic shifts in the world's

59. Sedmak, "Mission as Transfiguration," 55.

60. "Final List of Propositions of the Synod of Bishops," Proposition no. 55, http://www.zenit.org/article-35831?l=english.

61. World Synod of Bishops 1971, *Justice in the World* no. 6, http://jpicformation.wikispaces.com/file/view/Catholic+Bishops+on+Justice+in+the+world+1971.pdf.

Christian population. Such a shift calls the church in every part of the world to realize its essential missionary nature in a way not completely clear at the council itself. Nevertheless, the council gives us in its missionary emphases and missionary document—to borrow the words of John Paul II—a "sure compass by which to take our bearings"[62] in this extraordinary time of World Christianity, great migrations, and seemingly inevitable secularism and unbelief. That compass points in the direction of the church's duty to witness to and preach the gospel not only because of Christ's command, but especially because Christians are caught up in that overflowing fountain of the triune God's love and mercy toward the world. At the same time, that compass calls the missionary church to preach and witness in a way that—in the words of Paul VI at the end of the council—feels the need "to know, to approach, to understand, to penetrate, to serve . . . the surrounding society, and to comprehend it, almost to pursue it in its rapid and continuous change."[63] Fifty years after the council, this is a reliable compass indeed.

62. John Paul II, apostolic letter *Novo millennio ineunte* (January 6, 2001) no. 57, http://www.vatican.va/holy_father/john_paul_ii/apost_letters/documents/hf_jp-ii_apl_20010106_novo-millennio-ineunte_en.html.

63. Paul VI, Discorso di chiusura del concilio ecumenico Vaticano II, http://www.unavox.it/doc25_PVI_chiusura.htm (my translation).

10 "I Am Joseph, Your Brother"
A Jewish Perspective on Christian-Jewish Relations since *Nostra Aetate* No. 4

EDWARD KESSLER

The article reviews the impact of Nostra aetate *on Christian-Jewish relations and offers a Jewish perspective, including consideration of the Jewishness of Jesus as well as proposing a covenantal theology that grapples with supersessionism. It also explores the implications of the Holy See's assertion in 1974 that "Christians must strive to learn by what essential traits the Jews define themselves in the light of their own religious experience" and suggests that the church did not know then, nor yet knows, the challenges this raises.*

As Mary Boys has shown in her fine contribution to this volume, it is not too bold to suggest that *Nostra aetate* (*NA*), published October 28, 1965, toward the end of the Second Vatican Council, helped transform Jewish-Christian relations. According to Edward Flannery, it "terminated in a stroke a millennial teaching of contempt for Jews and Judaism and unequivocally asserted the Church's debt to its Jewish heritage."[1] The *aggiornamento* ("a bringing up to date") marked the beginnings of a fresh

1. Edward Flannery, "Seminaries, Classrooms, Pulpits, Streets: Where We Have to Go," in *Unanswered Questions: Theological Views of Jewish-Catholic Relations*, ed. Roger Brooks (Notre Dame, IN: University of Notre Dame), 128–29.

approach when the Roman Catholic Church "came in from out of the cold" and joined the Protestant churches in reflecting positively on the "mystery of Israel." Looking back 50 years later, it is noticeable that the document was forceful in deploring antisemitism, although it omitted any mention of the Holocaust or the Christian contribution to antisemitism (nor did it mention the existence of the state of Israel). Most of all, *NA* ushered in a new era, fresh attitudes, a new language of discourse never previously heard in the Catholic Church concerning Jews, which can be seen in phrases such as "God holds the Jews most dear" and "mutual understanding and respect." However, the document's possibilities were one thing, its success another, and the latter was dependent upon "things still to be worked out."[2]

Since then the Holy See has issued four major documents on Jews and Judaism:

- 1974, Guidelines and Suggestions for Implementing the Conciliar Declaration *Nostra aetate*
- 1985, Notes on the Correct Way to Present the Jews and Judaism in Preaching and Catechesis
- 1998, We Remember: A Reflection on the Shoah[3]

These three documents were produced by the Pontifical Commission for Religious Relations with the Jews. It is somewhat surprising that, as far as I am aware, no further documents are expected in the near future.

More encouragingly, however, is that in 2001 the Pontifical Biblical Commission produced the fourth major statement, The Jewish People and Their Sacred Scriptures in the Christian Bible.[4] This is significant because it implies that consideration of the Christian-Jewish encounter extends

2. Austin Flannery, OP, *Vatican Council II: The Conciliar and Post Conciliar Documents* (Dublin: Dominican, 1981), 741.

3. For a review of these three statements, see my "Jewish-Christian Relations in the Global Society: What the Institutional Documents Have and Have Not Been Telling Us," in *Jews and Christians in Conversation: Crossing Cultures and Generations*, ed. Edward Kessler, John Pawlikowski, and Judy Banki (Cambridge, UK: Orchard Academic, 2002), 53–73.

4. Pontifical Biblical Commission, The Jewish People and Their Sacred Scriptures in the Christian Bible (2001), II.A.7.22, par. 4. This and all Vatican documents cited herein can be found on the Vatican website by searching their titles on the Internet. All URLs cited herein were accessed on January 19, 2013.

beyond the Commission for Religious Relations with the Jews. It is the concern of the Roman Catholic Church as a whole.

Consequently Christians, so long instigators of negative attitudes toward Jews, began to rediscover a respect and admiration for Judaism, and the once-close relationship, which had become a distant memory, has been to a large extent restored. For Jews, the traditional view that Christianity was simply an enemy has been replaced by a realization that collaboration with Christians is possible.

Over the course of the last half-century, the Roman Catholic Church has become aware of the need to learn about developments in postbiblical Judaism, as demonstrated by the 1974 Guidelines, which asserted that "Christians must strive to learn by what essential traits the Jews define themselves in the light of their own religious experience"[5] and the 1985 Notes, which called on preachers and catechists to "'assess it [the patrimony common to Judaism and the church] carefully in itself and with due awareness of the faith and religious life of the Jewish people *as they are professed and practiced still today*.'"[6]

Two themes emerge: first, the history of Judaism did not end with the destruction of the Second Temple but developed an ongoing innovative and living religious tradition, and second, Christians need to understand Judaism as a living faith. I do not think the church knew in 1974, nor yet knows, the challenges these two themes present. This ignorance is neatly illustrated by Yossi Klein Halevi's portrait of an encounter with a Sister of the Beatitudes in Israel. The danger of the reassertion of the "old theology," the sister informed Klein Halevi, is illustrated when Christians simply say, "'Thank you, Jewish people, for giving us the Bible. Thank

5. Commission for Religious Relations with the Jews, Guidelines and Suggestions for Implementing the Conciliar Declaration "Nostra Aetate" (no. 4) (1974). See also similar Protestant statements such as the World Lutheran Federation's assertion that "Christians also need to learn of the rich and varied history of Judaism since New Testament times, and of the Jewish people as a diverse, living community of faith today. Such an encounter with living and faithful Judaism can be profoundly enriching for Christian self-understanding" (Church Council of the Evangelical Lutheran Church in America, Declaration of ELCA to Jewish Community [1994], http://www.elca.org/Who-We-Are/Our-Three-Expressions/Churchwide-Organization/ Office-of-the-Presiding-Bishop/Ecumenical-and-Inter-Religious-Relations/Inter-Religious-Relations/Christian-Jewish-Relations/Declaration-of-ELCA-to-Jewish-Community.aspx).

6. Notes on the correct way to present Jews and Judaism in preaching and catechesis in the Roman Catholic Church I.3, quoting a speech of John Paul II, emphasis original.

you for being the people of Jesus.' But that's archaeology. Am I ready to encounter Judaism as it is or just for nostalgia?"[7]

For their part, many Jews initially responded with distrust to the changes in Christian teaching; others engaged in the study of Christianity and in dialogue with Christians for defensive reasons, that is, in order to tackle prejudice and antisemitism. There were, of course, individual Jewish figures who called for a positive encounter, such as Martin Buber, who reminded Jews that Jesus was a fellow Jew, their "great brother," but this approach was highly unusual.[8]

However, in recent years there have been stirrings of a new and more widespread interest in Christianity among Jews, illustrated by the publication in 2000 of *Dabru Emet* ("Speak Truth"), a Jewish statement on Christians and Christianity.[9] A broad range of signatories, from both Orthodox and Progressive Judaism, ensured that *Dabru Emet* became the first detailed, widely supported, cross-denominational statement. Until its publication, the changes in Christian attitudes toward Jews and Judaism had been lacking a Jewish response. No longer. The eight-paragraph statement, similar in length to *NA*, demonstrates awareness among Jews of a common purpose with Christianity:

- Jews and Christians worship the same God.
- Jews and Christians seek authority from the same book (the Bible).
- Christians can respect the claim of the Jewish people upon the Land of Israel.
- Jews and Christians accept the moral principles of Torah.
- Nazism was not a Christian phenomenon.
- The humanly irreconcilable difference between Jews and Christians will not be settled until God redeems the entire world as promised in Scripture.

7. Yossi Klein Halevi, *At the Entrance to the Garden of Eden: A Jew's Search for Hope with Christians and Muslims in the Holy Land* (New York: Harper Collins, 2002), 203.

8. Buber writes: "From my youth onwards I have found in Jesus my great brother. That Christianity has regarded and does regard him as God and Saviour has always appeared to me a fact of the highest importance which, for his sake and for my own, I must endeavour to understand. . . . I am more than ever certain that a great place belongs to [Jesus] in Israel's history of faith" (Martin Buber, *Two Types of Faith*, trans. Norman P. Goldhawk [London: Routledge & Paul, 1951], 12–13).

9. Tikva Frymer-Kensky et al. of the National Jewish Scholars Project, *Dabru Emet*: A Jewish Statement on Christians and Christianity (July 15, 2001), http://www.jcrelations.net/Dabru_EmetA_Jewish_Statement_on_Christians_and_Christianity.2395.0.html.

- A new relationship between Jews and Christians will not weaken Jewish practice.
- Jews and Christians must work together for justice and peace.

Changes in Jewish attitudes were reinforced by the impact of the papal visit to Israel in the same year, which made an indelible mark on the Jewish psyche.

Of course, there continue to be divisions among and between Christians and Jews over, for example, attitudes toward the state of Israel and its relationship with the Palestinians as well as with its other Arab neighbors and assessment of the actions of the Catholic Church and Christians in general during the Second World War. Evidence of increasing antisemitism today, particularly in Europe and the Middle East, has also led to a corresponding increase in Jewish sensitivity to criticism, particularly Christian criticism.

Nevertheless, my view is that in the mainstream of both Judaism and Christianity, many of the principal divisive issues have been either eliminated or taken to the furthest point at which agreement is possible. The efforts of Catholics and Protestants toward respect for Judaism project attitudes that would have been unthinkable in 1965.

The Study of Relations and the Practice of Dialogue

As a subject of study, Jewish-Christian relations can rightly be said to be a child of the 20th century. From pioneering writers such as James Parkes to the establishment of organizations such as the London Society of Jews and Christians and the National Conference of Christians and Jews (both in 1927), the subject has been a point of discussion.[10] It is true that the previous centuries saw many contributions to the issue, but for the most part the intentions were other than honorable. It might even be said that an early writer such as Justin Martyr, who wrote a fictional dialogue between a Jew and a Christian, was presenting the relationship between Jews and Christians and, given the differences in scholarly attitudes between then and now, was thus engaging in the same activity. There is some truth in this, but Justin Martyr's purposes, and those of many like him, were confessional.[11] It is the aim and the tools that separate a scholarly from an apologetic approach.

10. James W. Parkes, *Conflict of the Church and Synagogue* (New York: Hermon, 1934).

11. See, e.g., Timothy J. Horner, *Listening to Trypho: Justin Martyr's Dialogue Reconsidered* (Leuven: Peeters, 2001).

The scholarly approach should analyze, using the interpretative tools and data of its time, in order to attempt to present a dispassionate and balanced understanding of a subject. This is not to say that students or scholars should not then use the evidence to make moral judgments or to speak out for causes they believe in—there are many well-known cases of leading scholars taking political or moral stances. Rather, the first task is to understand and evaluate the evidence, and from there to make a judgment.

We should therefore distinguish Jewish-Christian *relations* from Jewish-Christian *dialogue*. "Relations" covers the whole history and significance of the contact of Jews and Christians, including the positive contacts and influence upon each other. It might also include the external influences upon each or the question as to how each will fare in the modern world. "Dialogue" is a subset of relations, the most popular subset to be sure, and is predicated on the need for reconciliation between the two faiths, and is generally founded upon theological issues.

The word "dialogue" (and the nature of dialogue activity) is itself ill defined. A casual conversation between Jews and Christians that may add up to no more than a loose restatement of entrenched theological positions is sometimes claimed to be dialogue. Equally, any communication between persons of two differing religious points of view (e.g., by phone, Facebook, or email) may be on occasion described loosely as dialogue. However, dialogue is not simply synonymous with "communication." For dialogue to take place, there must be a genuine hearing of the Other.

In reality, dialogue consists of a direct meeting of two people and involves a reciprocal exposing of the full religious consciousness of the one with the Other. Dialogue speaks to the Other with a full respect for what the Other is and has to say. This is never less than personal but can develop in such a way as to be extended to a group and even to communities. However, it begins with the individual, not with the community.

Such a quest is never easy, because it is not merely about the Other, nor about where the Other differs from us. The thoughts and experience of dialogue are expressed in the writings of the Jewish philosopher Franz Rosenzweig, whose emphasis is not on "the subject matter that connects the speaker with the listener but the I confronting the Thou. The word is not only an expression of reality but also a means by which to express it."[12] This means that dialogue depends on the presence of another person.

12. Franz Rosenzweig, *The Star of Redemption*, trans. William Hallo (1971; Notre Dame, IN: University of Notre Dame, 1985), 423. See Jeremy F. Worthen, *The Internal Foe: Judaism and Anti-Judaism in the Shaping of Christian Theology* (Newcastle: Cambridge Scholars, 2009).

Rosenzweig asserted that truth could exist in two forms, in Judaism and in Christianity, which he expounded in *The Star of Redemption* (1921). It is not difficult to see how Rosenzweig became one of the main sources out of which Buber developed his "I and Thou" formula.

Buber, one of the most influential Jewish theologians of the 20th century, is known for his exposition of the I-Thou relationship, which maintains that a personal relationship with God is truly personal only when there is not only awe and respect on the human side, but also when we are not overcome and overwhelmed in our relationship with God. This comportment has implications for human-human dialogue too; it means that two people must meet as two valid centers of interest. Thus, one should approach the Other with respect and restraint so that the validity of the other center is in no sense belittled.[13]

Dialogue therefore involves a respect that takes the Other as seriously as one demands to be taken oneself. Rosenzweig's famous response to "No-one can reach the Father except through me" (John 14:6) is pertinent here. He acknowledges that millions of Christians have been led to God through Jesus Christ. But he continues: "It is different if one does not have to come to the Father because he or she is with him already. And that is the case with the people of Israel (not the individual Jew)."[14]

In these few sentences Rosenzweig introduces us to the crucial question of the Jewish-Christian relationship today: can Christians view Judaism as a valid religion on its own terms (and vice versa)?

Questions to be considered from the Jewish perspective include: What was the purpose behind the creation of Christianity and that two billion Christians read the *Tanakh*? Does Jesus the Jew have implications for Jews? It is well known that Jews are very proud of the Albert Einsteins, the Heinrich Heines, and the Sigmund Freuds; yet, Israel's most famous Jew is generally ignored. Now, in a freer climate as far as Jewish-Christian relations are concerned, is it not time that there was a greater Jewish interest in the Jew Jesus?

For Christians, does John 14:6 deny the legitimacy of Judaism? Directly related to this question is the need for reflection on the survival of the Jewish people and of the vitality of Judaism over 2000 years. Does it indicate a continuation of God's election of the Jewish people? The question of the validity of Judaism challenges some of the proclamations of Christian triumphalism.

13. Martin Buber, *I and Thou*, 2nd ed., postscript by Buber, trans. Ronald Gregor Smith (New York: Scribner, 1958).

14. Franz Rosenzweig, *Der Mensch und sein Werk: Gesammelte Schriften*, vol. 1, *Briefe und Tagbücher: 1900–1918* (The Hague: Nijhoff, 1976), 132–33 (my translation).

The last 50 years have seen a demonstrable shift from a pre-*NA* monologue about Jews to an instructive (and sometimes difficult) dialogue with Jews. A monologue generally fails to understand the reality of the Other, while a dialogue requires a respect for the Other as it understands itself. The challenge of making the transition from monologue to dialogue remains immense, as demonstrated by the controversy following the 2002 publication of Reflections on Covenant and Mission by the National Council of Synagogues and the US Conference of Catholic Bishops' Committee for Ecumenical and Interreligious Affairs.

Christianity, Antisemitism, and the Holocaust

While deploring antisemitism, *NA* avoided the topic of the Holocaust, possibly because few leaders of the Christian churches did much to help Jews. Eugenio Pacelli, Pope Pius XII from 1939 to 1958, was (and remains) a controversial figure, with some claiming that he knew much and did nothing of importance to help Jews, whereas others retort that he did what he could and encouraged others to do more.[15] In my view, the impression of Vatican policy of the 1930s and 1940s—indeed, of the two popes of that time, Pius XI and Pius XII—is hardly a positive one. Yet, it is essential for Jews and Catholics to remember that in Nazi-occupied countries, the churches themselves were often targeted, and were thus preoccupied with protecting their own flocks rather than with the fate of Jews.

However, individual Catholic (and some other Christian) leaders did extend their support to Jews. One of the most honorable examples was Angelo Giuseppe Roncalli who, as papal Nuncio for Turkey and Greece, made available baptismal certificates to thousands of Hungarian Jews in a bid to persuade Germans to leave them unmolested. He later became Pope John XXIII and initiated Vatican II.[16]

One of the most dramatic transformations arising from Vatican II is the shift from what was, for the most part, an inherent need to condemn Judaism to a need to condemn Christian anti-Judaism. This led not to

15. See, e.g., Pierre Blet, *Pius XII and the Second World War: According to the Archives of the Vatican*, trans. Lawrence J. Johnson (New York: Paulist, 1999); John Cornwell, *Hitler's Pope: The Secret History of Pius XII* (New York: Viking, 1999); Carol Rittner and John K. Roth, ed. and intro., *Pius XII and the Holocaust* (New York: Continuum, 2002); Jose M. Sánchez, *Pius XII and the Holocaust: Understanding the Controversy* (Washington, DC: Catholic University of America, 2002).

16. See Peter Hebblethwaite, *Pope John XXIII: Shepherd of the Modern World* (New York: Doubleday, 1985).

a separation from all things Jewish but, in fact, to a closer relationship with "the elder brother." As German theologian Johannes Metz observed, "Christian theology after Auschwitz must stress anew the Jewish dimension of Christian beliefs and must overcome the forced blocking-out of the Jewish heritage within Christianity."[17]

This blocking-out included the issue of Christian antisemitism. However, in 1987 in the wake of the controversy over the pope's reception of Austrian President Kurt Waldheim, who had been an active Nazi, the Vatican promised to reflect on the Holocaust; its document We Remember: Reflections on the Shoah was published in 1998. It stresses the evils of antisemitism, concluding: "We wish to turn awareness of past sins into a firm resolve to build a new future in which there will be no more anti-Judaism among Christians or anti-Christian sentiment among Jews but rather a shared mutual respect."[18] It is primarily a sincere call for the renunciation of antisemitism, reaching not only Catholics in Western Europe and North America, where relations have progressed, but also those in regions such as Africa, Asia, and Latin America where many have never encountered a Jew.

But its treatment of the Holocaust had some disappointing aspects for those who had hoped for a formal apology, on the lines of that issued by the French bishops who stated: "It is important to admit the primary role played by the consistently repeated anti-Jewish stereotypes wrongly perpetuated by the Christians in the historical process that led to the Holocaust."[19] We Remember speaks both of those Christians who helped Jews and of those who failed to do so, but it also implies a balanced picture. It fails to give a plain statement on the role of Christian teachings and stereotypes in motivating the Nazis and their antisemitic supporters and sympathizers.

In recent years Pope Benedict XVI's statements on the Shoah have caused different concerns, because they seem to depict Nazism simply as a pagan phenomenon, in which the church was not complicit. This ignores the reality that without the long history of Christian anti-Judaism and Christian violence against Jews, Nazi ideology could not have taken hold, nor could it have been carried out.

17. Johannes-Baptist Metz, "Facing the Jews: Christian Theology after Auschwitz," in *The Holocaust as Interruption*, Concilium 175, ed. Elisabeth Schüssler-Fiorenza and David Tracy (Edinburgh: T. & T. Clark, 1984), 26–33, at 27.

18. We Remember: Reflections on the Shoah, V, par. 3.

19. Roman Catholic Bishops of France, Declaration of Repentance (September 30, 1997), http://www.jcrelations.net/Declaration_of_Repentance_seeking_forgiveness_for_the_failings_of_the_Church_dur.2407.0.html?L=9&page=1.

There remains a special European and a special Christian angle to dealing with the Shoah. It happened in the midst of a supposedly liberal, democratic, and well-developed civilization. The vast majority of Europeans looked on while their Jewish neighbors were being taken away and murdered. As far as Christianity is concerned—and most Europeans were of course, at least nominally, Christians—the problem is even more serious: some 1,900 years after the life of Jesus the Jew, his people were murdered by baptized pagans who, by their action and inaction, denied their baptism, while most other Christians, from the highest to the lowest, looked aside.

In my view, the Holocaust remains as much a threat to Christian self-understanding today as it did at the end of World War II. This is perhaps one reason why John Paul II, whose pontificate witnessed more progress between Catholics and Jews than any other pope's, was the first pope to visit a concentration camp (Auschwitz) and to pray there (1979), the first to visit Yad Vashem in his pilgrimage to Israel (2000), and the first to place words of apology for antisemitism in the church in cracks of the Western Wall, when he called on Catholics (and all Christians) to do *teshuva* (repentance) for misdeeds against Jews:

> God of our fathers, you chose Abraham and his descendants to bring your Name to the Nations: we are deeply saddened by the behaviour of those who in the course of history have caused these children of yours to suffer, and asking your forgiveness we wish to commit ourselves to genuine brotherhood with the people of the Covenant.[20]

Understandably, in the last 50 years the Christian contribution to fostering antisemitism has been a central concern of Jewish-Christian relations. Although this had already been noted by Parkes before the Holocaust, the events of World War II brought into sharp focus the extent to which anti-Jewish teaching had taken root in Christian Europe. It was necessary to undertake a proper appraisal of antisemitism, anti-Judaism, and the significance of the Shoah, and this required an *unlearning* of attitudes and beliefs that had been learned before.[21] In the words of Catholic social

20. See Cardinal Edward Idris Cassidy's discussion of this prayer and visit to the Holy Land in his address at the annual meeting of the Interreligious Coordinating Council in Israel, March 13, 2001, at http://www.bc.edu/content/dam/files/research_sites/cjl/texts/cjrelations/resources/articles/cassidy.htm.

21. For example, the Leuenberg Church Fellowship (2001) states, "The churches failed because of indifference and fear, pride and weakness; but they also failed, above all, as a consequence of wrong interpretations of texts from the Bible and the terrible

ethicist John Pawlikowski, "the Holocaust has made it immoral for Christians to maintain any Christology that is excessively triumphalistic or that finds the significance of the Christ Event in the displacement of the Jewish people from an ongoing covenantal relationship with God."[22]

The need to reflect on the Shoah is self-evident, but there are dangers if reflection is not conducted in perspective. A case in point is Jewish philosopher Emil Fackenheim's proclamation that the Shoah resulted in a new commandment, the 614th, which stressed that it was incumbent upon Jews to survive as Jews. According to Fackenheim one remained a Jew so as not to provide Hitler a posthumous victory.[23] However, as a result, Jewish identity became Shoah-centered as did Jewish-Christian relations. The danger is that by focusing solely on the Shoah, Jews and Christians will gain a distorted view of themselves and of each other. To take a hypothetical example, a young Jew who knows nothing of Judaism and experience apart from the events of the Shoah will inevitably construct a negative Jewish identity, associated with suffering and victimhood. A young Christian will come away with an exclusive picture of the Jew as victim without an awareness of the positive aspects of Jewish culture.

While reaction to the Shoah is an important driving force, positive relations cannot be built solely on responses to antisemitism and Christian feelings of guilt. If recent Christian soul-searching in the aftermath of the destruction of European Jewry leads to a new approach and a repudiation of the *Adversus Iudaeos* tradition, so much the better. However, the

---

theological errors to which they led. Sometimes in Christianity there has been an idea that the rejection and devaluation of Judaism, even to the extent of overt antisemitism, could be considered an important aspect of how Christians understand themselves" (Church and Israel: A Contribution from the Reformation Churches in Europe to the Relationship between Christians and Jews, I.1.1, http://www.jcrelations.net/Church_and_Israel_A_Contribution_from_the_Reformation_Churches_in_Europe_to_the.2392.0.html?L=6.2011&page=2).

22. John T. Pawlikowski "Christology after the Holocaust," *Encounter* 59 (1998): 345–68, at 346.

23. "Fackenheim, himself a survivor, seeks to interpret the significance of the Shoah, where evil went beyond all explanation. God and Israel are still in relationship, and the Jewish people are precluded from despair or abdication of responsibility. Fackenheim's thesis of a 614th commandment gained wide recognition among Jews and Christians, and he called on Christians to support Israel as a guarantor for the future survival of the Jewish people and for Jews and Christians to work together for *tikkun olam* (mending of the world)" (Emil Fackenheim, 1969, "Transcendence in Contemporary Culture: Philosophical Reflections and a Jewish Theology," in *Transcendence*, ed. Herbert W. Richardson and Donald R. Cutler [Boston: Beacon, 1969], 150).

future relationship cannot be built on the foundations of guilt. The sense of guilt is transient and does not pass to the next generation; moreover, it is unstable, inherently prone to sudden and drastic reversal. Thus, the relevant statement in *Dabru Emet*:

> Nazism was not a Christian phenomenon. Without the long history of Christian anti-Judaism and Christian violence against Jews, Nazi ideology could not have taken hold nor could it have been carried out. . . . But Nazism itself was not an inevitable outcome of Christianity. . . . We encourage the continuation of recent efforts in Christian theology to repudiate unequivocally contempt of Judaism and the Jewish people. We applaud those Christians who reject this teaching of contempt, and we do not blame them for the sins committed by their ancestors.[24]

I would suggest that, as far as the Christian contribution to antisemitism is concerned, the Roman Catholic Church (and the Protestant churches) instead of being part of the problem have now become part of the solution, and it is therefore timely to move on to more positive bases for relations.

The Jewish Origins of Christianity

One consequence of *NA* was a reawakening among Catholics to the Jewish origins of Christianity. Catholics were reminded that Jesus was a faithful Jew and "that from the Jewish people sprang the apostles," the foundation stones and pillars of the Church who "draw sustenance from the root of that good olive tree onto which have been grafted the wild olive branches of the Gentiles" (no. 4).[25]

Pope John Paul II, followed by Pope Benedict XVI, spelled out what this statement means: God's covenant with the Jewish people had never been broken and retains eternal validity; God does not renege on his promises. If the Jews were not rejected, then Judaism is not a fossilized faith, as had been taught previously, but a living, authentic religion.

24. *Dabru Emet*.

25. Documents earlier than *NA* emphasized the Jewishness of Jesus, such as the 1947 Seelisburg document that commended Christians to "2. Remember that Jesus was born of a Jewish mother of the seed of David and the people of Israel, and that His everlasting love and forgiveness embraces His own people and the whole world. 3. Remember that the first disciples, the apostles and the first martyrs were Jews" (International Council of Christians and Jews, The Ten Points of Seelisberg [1947], http://www.bc.edu/dam/files/research_sites/cjl/texts/cjrelations/resources/documents/interreligious/Seelisberg.htm).

Thus, Christians reawoke to the Jewish origins of Christianity: that Jesus was born, lived, and died a Jew; that the first Christians were Jews; indeed, is it too bold to suggest that the New Testament is primarily a collection of Jewish writings?

Jesus and his family would have been observant of Torah, paid tithes, kept the Sabbath, circumcised their males, attended synagogue, observed purity laws in relation to childbirth and menstruation, kept the dietary code, etc. While the Gospels record disputes about Jesus' interpretation of a few of these laws, the notion of a Christian Jesus, who did not live by Torah or only by its ethical values, does not fit historical reality. Jesus was a Jew, not an alien intruder in first-century Palestine; a reformer of Jewish beliefs, not an indiscriminate faultfinder of them.

Although Jesus lived his life not as a Christian but as a Jew, within a few decades of his death, his Jewish followers espoused a rather different kind of religion from that followed by most Jews. Judaism, like Islam after it, is strongly rooted in religious law; Christianity ceased to be so. Judaism, also like Islam, has a strong belief in the unity of God; Christianity came to place such great store in Jesus and, centuries later, in the doctrine of the Trinity that it has seemed to many other monotheists to be, in essence, a refined form of polytheism. Gradually, the Christian religion came to look less like an authentic, even if eccentric, form of Judaism, and more like a completely different religion.

Nevertheless, the rediscovery of the Jewishness of Jesus among Christians has had an impact on Jews, although, of course, for Jews his significance is in his life rather than his death. Some have begun to view the New Testament in a more positive light, although there is, of course, no reason intrinsic to their faith why they should take much interest in it, since it is not their sacred Scripture. Indeed, there is every reason why they should ignore it, since it has been used to justify antisemitic actions by Christians. Yet an increasing number of Jewish scholars have turned their attention to studying Jesus. The pioneers lived in the first half of the 20th century,[26] but since *NA* Jewish academic interest has increased and significant studies have been penned by Pinchas Lapide, Géza Vermès, David Flusser, and Amy-Jill Levine.

Lapide argued that the resurrection actually happened, though he is unconvinced by the "strange paraphrases" of many modern Christian theologians about the resurrection. He believes these paraphrases to be

26. E.g., Abraham Geiger, Joseph Klausner, Claude Montefiore, and Martin Buber.

"all too abstract and scholarly to explain the fact that the solid hillbillies from Galilee who, for the very real reason of the crucifixion of their master, were saddened to death, [but] were changed within a short period of time into a jubilant community of believers."[27] Only resurrection could have accomplished that.

Building on the thought of Rosenzweig, Lapide suggested that Christianity is the "judaising" of the pagans. He refers approvingly to Catholic theologian Clemens Thoma, who argued that through the resurrection of Jesus, an access to faith in the one, until then unknown, God of Israel was opened to the Gentiles.[28] In other words, Jesus is the way for the Gentiles, but Jews, who already know God, do not need Jesus. This conviction has not gained wide acceptance among either Jews or Christians, though it is an intriguing one.

Vermès depicted Jesus as a Galilean Hasid, a holy man. In his examination of Jesus' titles he concluded that none link him with the Messiah, that no titular use of "Son of Man" is attested in Jewish literature, and that "prophet," "lord," or even, figuratively, "son of God" could be easily applied to holy men in the Judaism of Jesus' day. For Vermès, Jesus was a charismatic teacher, healer, and prophet:

> Whereas none of the claims and aspirations of Jesus can be said definitely to associate him with the role of the Messiah, . . . everything combines . . . to place him in the venerable company of the Devout, the ancient Hasidim. . . . [This] means that any new enquiry may accept as its point of departure the safe assumption that Jesus did not belong among the Pharisees, Essenes, Zealots or Gnostics, but among the holy miracle-workers of Galilee.[29]

Jesus died, said Vermès, because he was perceived as a potential threat to the authorities, and the real Jesus, Jesus the Jew, challenges Christianity as well as Judaism. The significance of Vermès's work can be illustrated by the fact that the title of his book published in 1973, *Jesus the Jew*, seemed revolutionary. Now it is almost taken for granted in New Testament scholarship.[30]

27. Pinchas Lapide, *The Resurrection of Jesus: A Jewish Perspective*, trans. Wilhelm C. Linss (London: SPCK, 1984), 125.

28. Clemens Thoma, *A Christian Theology of Judaism*, trans. and ed. Helga Croner (New York: Paulist, 1980).

29. Géza Vermès, *Jesus the Jew: A Historian's Reading of the Gospels* (London: Collins, 1973), 223.

30. A synthesis of Vermès's writings on Jesus can be found in his *The Changing Faces of Jesus* (London: Allen Lane, 2000).

David Flusser, Israeli scholar of first-century Judaism, accepts Jesus as a charismatic figure with an extraordinary sense of mission. He invites his readers to listen to Jesus himself and wonders out loud whether the responses that Jesus gave in connection with human conflict may be the best that anyone has proposed. Flusser commends Jesus for remaining aloof from the zealotism that would eventually destroy the Temple and Jerusalem.[31]

Amy-Jill Levine's thesis is that Jesus was a good Jew who taught Jews in a Jewish land. She is particularly concerned with anti-Jewish New Testament interpretations that occur when, in the attempt to depict Jesus as unique, the Jewish people and/or leaders of his time are depicted as monolithic, obsessively rule-following, unconcerned with the poor and outcast, and particularly oppressive to women. She encourages Jews to appreciate Jesus in continuity with other leaders and prophets of Israel. She describes how Jesus dressed, ate, taught, and prayed like a Jew, argued like a Jew with other Jews, and amassed Jewish followers.[32]

The Bible

Reflection on the New Testament brings us to the question of the relationship between the Old and New Testaments, a question as old as Christianity itself. In the second century CE Marcion had argued, albeit unsuccessfully, that Christianity should reject the Jewish Scriptures (as well as most of the Gospels). In response, the church has since then insisted simultaneously on the continuity and the discontinuity of the relationship between the Old and New Testaments. *Continuity* centered on the claim that the God of the Old Testament was the same as the God of Christ. *Discontinuity* derived from the belief that the Old Testament pointed to a future saving event—to Christ. While Marcion's teaching became regarded as heresy, residual Marcionism survived in a selective, comparative reading of Scripture, a tendency still in existence today in some Christian writings that depict the Old Testament as presenting a wrathful God of law in contradistinction to the New Testament portrait of a loving God of grace.

According to 2 Timothy 3:16, "all Scripture is inspired by God and profitable for teaching." Inevitably the Hebrew Bible, to which Jesus and

31. David Flusser, *Jesus* (1969; Jerusalem: Magnes, 2001).

32. See Amy-Jill Levine, *The Misunderstood Jew: The Church and the Scandal of the Jewish Jesus* (San Francisco: HarperSanFrancisco, 2006). The book she coedited with Marc Zvi Brettler, *The Jewish Annotated New Testament* (New York: Oxford University, 2012), is another important work consisting of the Christian holy book edited entirely by Jews.

his earliest followers appealed as a divine sanction for their message, was viewed not only as divinely inspired but also as the continuing normative authority for the faith and life of the people of God—a view consistent with the contemporary Jewish environment. The New Testament's use of the Old Testament and the claims made about Jesus demonstrate a deep reluctance to posit any breach between Christianity and Israel.[33]

Since the first Christians were Jews, and since Christianity is rooted in early Judaism, it is to be expected that the New Testament would exhibit many aspects of traditional Jewish interpretation. Both as an authority for the authors and as a hermeneutical key for readers, the Old Testament is indispensable for understanding the earliest New Testament interpretations about Jesus. However, unlike classical rabbinic interpretation, which seeks to discover some hidden element in the biblical text itself, the New Testament, with its eschatological orientation, generally applies the biblical text to some aspect of Jesus' life. This is because, for the rabbis, the biblical text is primary; for New Testament writers, however, Jesus is primary, and it is he whom the Old Testament serves to illuminate.

The early church distinguished between those elements of the Old Testament that continued to carry force after the coming of Christ and those that were no more than a shadow: one approach emphasizes a break with Scripture involving a new covenant with God (Lk 22:20; Heb 8:8–13), depicting Judaism as old and superseded; a second describes Jesus as a fulfillment of what was prophesied in the Bible, which remains in a typological relationship to it (1 Cor 10:1–11; Mt 5:17).

Neither *NA* nor the 1974 Guidelines commented on issues associated with typology. *NA*, for example, simply stated: "Since the spiritual patrimony common to Christians and Jews is thus so great, this Sacred Synod wants to foster and recommend that mutual understanding and respect which is the fruit above all of biblical and theological studies as well as of fraternal dialogues" (no. 4).

The 1985 Notes, however, highlighted that the church still had matters to resolve, warning that "we should be careful to avoid any transition from the Old to the New Testament which might seem merely a rupture" (40.4), and that "typological reading only manifests the unfathomable riches of the Old Testament, its inexhaustible content and the mystery of which it is

33. This is exemplified by Matthew's gospel, which uses explicit fulfillment citations throughout the birth narrative (with variations on the formula, "this took place in order to fulfill what had been spoken through the prophet") and the prominent place given to quotations from the Pentateuch, Isaiah, and Psalms.

full, and should not lead us to forget that it retains its own value as Revelation that the New Testament often does no more than [recapitulate]" (2.7). The 2001 document, The Jewish People and their Sacred Scriptures in the Christian Bible, also acknowledges that links between the Old with the New were abused, and that Scripture could be "severed" from their context. As a result "interpretation . . . became arbitrary" (no. 3), and it "would be wrong to consider the prophecies of the Old Testament as some kind of photographic anticipation of future events" (no. 21), particularly messianic prophecies. One way to overcome an unhealthy dependence upon typological interpretation, it suggested, is by familiarity with the rabbinic literature and Jewish biblical interpretation:

> Christians can and ought to admit that the Jewish reading of the Bible is a possible one, in continuity with the Jewish Sacred Scriptures from the Second Temple Period, a reading analogous to the Christian reading which developed in parallel fashion. Both readings are bound up with the vision of their respective faiths, of which the readings are the result and expression. Consequently, both are irreducible. On the practical level of exegesis, Christians can, nonetheless, learn much from Jewish exegesis practised for more than two thousand years, and, in fact, they have learned much in the course of history. For their part, it is to be hoped that Jews themselves can derive profit from Christian exegetical research. (no. 22)

These words are both bold and significant because they call on Catholics to take into consideration rabbinic and contemporary Jewish interpretations of Scripture. Catholics are also told that the Old Testament contains a divine revelation unrelated to the coming of Christ. This was not only valid at the time of its writing, it is also still valid for contemporary Judaism. By stating that Jewish interpretation of Scripture is possible, the Pontifical Biblical Commission is applying John Paul II and Benedict XVI's oft-repeated comment about the "covenant remaining with the Jews" to the interpretation of the Jewish Scriptures. If the covenant remains with the Jewish people, their interpretation of Scripture, alongside that of Christians, must at the very least remain "possible." The document's radical call for the use of Jewish commentaries responds to the emerging theme identified above, calling for Christians to learn about Judaism as it developed.

There is, however, another question posed by then-Cardinal Ratzinger in his preface to the Pontifical Biblical Commission's document The Jewish People and the Sacred Scriptures in the Christian Bible (2001): "Has not the New Testament itself contributed to creating a hostility towards the Jewish people that provided a support for the ideology of those who wished to destroy Israel?"

In 1965, *NA* no. 4 stated that nothing was to be taught or preached that was "out of harmony with the truth of the Gospel," but it was too soon to consider why texts in Matthew and John tended to excuse the disciples, but accuse more and more Jews by excluding more and more Romans. Indeed, why have the Christian Scriptures been used to justify persecution of Jews? Why have the consequences of the New Testament polemic toward Jews proved so destructive?

One of the problems in answering this question is the fact that Jesus was a Jew who taught his fellow Jews, some of whom followed his teaching and some others who did not. Most of his contemporaries, of course, had never heard of Jesus. After his death, his Jewish followers, encouraged by their experience of the resurrection, argued for the validity of his teaching and their own, against their fellow Jews who had not been persuaded. To complicate the position further, Jesus' Jewish followers argued among themselves about the conditions under which Gentiles might be admitted to this new Jewish movement. In addition, some of the Jewish communities within the Jesus movement—with or without Gentile members—found themselves further at odds with other Jews over issues such as Torah observance and claims about Jesus.

The New Testament bears witness to all this, and many of its texts illustrate the debates and arguments that were taking place. These disputes were serious, vigorous, and often bitter. Nevertheless, what must not be forgotten—but which over time has been almost completely neglected—is the fact that the arguments were between Jews, about a Jew, or about Jewish issues (even when they concerned Gentile converts). The problem of polemic is magnified greatly when we read the passages as if they were "Christian" arguments against "Jews." To read them this way is to misread them and this misreading contributed to the Christian teaching of contempt.

Since the ministry of Jesus can be understood only in the context of first-century Palestinian Judaism, it is essential to emphasize that the concerns of Jesus and his followers are Jewish concerns; that despite the disagreements, much of the polemic reflects the situation in which the Gospels were written when Jews and Jewish followers of Jesus had come to view each other in terms of hostility and disagreement.

The criticism of the Pharisees is especially pronounced because it was rabbinic Judaism, based on Pharisaic Judaism, that survived the destruction of the Temple and the dispersion from the Land of Israel. This is the background to the bitter intra-Jewish feud portrayed by the Gospels. The conflict is over interpretation and over who should lead in light of the destruction of the Temple.

The final text of the Gospels was edited long after the events described, and the authors were sometimes concerned with denigrating those Jews who did not follow Jesus. At the same time they were equally concerned with vindicating the Romans, whose goodwill they were seeking. This was courageously admitted by the Vatican's 1985 Notes, which stated forthrightly:

> It cannot be ruled out that some references hostile or less than favorable to the Jews have their historical context in conflicts between the nascent Church and the Jewish community.

Certain controversies reflect Christian-Jewish relations long after the time of Jesus.

> To establish this is of capital importance if we wish to bring out the meaning of certain Gospel texts for the Christians of today (IV.1.A).

Israel and Palestine

Although there have not been any pertinent statements from the Pontifical Commission for Religious Relations with the Jews, Israel stands out as a prominent issue in Christian-Jewish relations. Zionism and the establishment of the state of Israel are central in today's Jewish-Christian encounter, demonstrating numerous tensions and conversations often brimming with emotion and passion. Motions tabled at synods or in rabbinical assemblies are controversial, as speakers tend to be advocates of one side or another. Why is it so rare to find Christian organizations, let alone Jewish, that are both pro-Palestinian and pro-Israeli? Blinkered views prevail.

While for Jews it is more obvious: the centrality of the land of the Bible, as well as the survival of over one-third of world Jewry, is at stake. Christians, for their part, not only disagree as to the place of Israel in Christian theology, but feel particular concern for Christians who live in the Holy Land as well as for Palestinians in general. There are, of course, also many Christians and Jews who are deeply concerned about the Other, making this a picture complicated to understand.

Israel is controversial because it cannot be viewed simply as a geographical and political entity whose emergence is like the establishment of any new state. Political, social, cultural, and religious concerns all affect its place in the Jewish-Christian relationship. Indeed, the complexity and sensitivity surrounding Israel meant that when Paul VI briefly visited in

1964, he did not use the word "Israel" during any of his public addresses, did not visit any Israeli monuments, and declined to meet with Israel's chief rabbi—largely because of differences over Israel's political statehood and a desire that the visit be seen as a purely religious act, avoiding any kind of political considerations.[34] Even today, it is not easy to choose the appropriate words in discussions. Are we to use the term "Holy Land," perhaps with a qualifier such as "Christian," or, alternatively, "the Promised Land"? Or must we seek ostensibly more neutral terms such as "Israel" and "Palestine"?

As I have noted earlier, there have been great changes in Christian teaching on Judaism and especially a tackling of the traditional teaching of contempt. Nevertheless, attitudes toward the land and state of Israel continue to be difficult, making a Christian reorientation to Israel problematic. Simply put, it has been easier for Christians to condemn antisemitism as a misunderstanding of Christian teaching than to come to terms with the reestablishment of the Jewish state.[35]

Thus, although Christians acknowledge that Jews feel a spiritual attachment to the Land of Israel, they have found it harder to accommodate the consequences of the Jewish desire for and creation of a Jewish state. The Notes declare that "the existence of the State of Israel and its political options should be envisaged not in a perspective which is in itself religious, but in their reference to the common principles of international law" (VI.1).

The attitude of Roman Catholicism toward Zionism changed greatly in the course of the 20th century. In 1904, Pope Pius X famously gave an audience to Theodor Herzl, who asked for support in his endeavor to bring Jews back to the Land of Israel. The pope told him unequivocally that because "the Jews have not recognised our Lord, therefore we cannot recognise the Jewish people."[36]

34. The visit also took place before the publication of *NA*, making the visit a very sensitive topic. In its desire to avoid controversy, it was deliberately brief.

35. Alice Eckardt points out the contrast between Christian willingness to tackle antisemitism and reflect on the Shoah with Christian reticence on the subject of Zionism and the state of Israel. Christians are more likely to think about the Shoah than the state of Israel, she suggests, because the former accords with the traditional stereotype of Jews as a suffering and persecuted minority. Israel, however, challenges this assumption and transforms the victim into a victor. See Eckardt, "The Place of the Jewish State in Christian-Jewish Relations," *European Judaism* 25, no. 1 (Spring 1992): 3–14, esp. 3.

36. Theodore Herzl, *The Diaries of Theodor Herzl*, ed. Marvin Lowenthal (New York: Dial, 1956), 429–30.

Since then, however, attitudes have changed significantly. Although *NA* did not explicitly mention Israel, it began the process that eventually led to the Vatican's recognition of the state in 1994. A more general awareness among Roman Catholics of the significance of Israel became noticeable during John Paul II's papacy. In his 1984 Good Friday apostolic letter he wrote: "The Jewish people who live in the State of Israel, and who preserve in that land such precious testimonies to their history and their faith, we must ask for the desired security and the due tranquillity that is the prerogative of every nation and condition of life and of progress for every society."[37]

Ten years later the state of Israel and the Holy See exchanged ambassadors and reached another significant landmark with the pontiff's pilgrimage to Israel in 2000 and the iconic image of his visit to the Western Wall. His visit and Benedict XVI's in 2009 helped mark the final repudiation of a "theology of perpetual wandering" for the Jewish community on the part of Christianity, which argued against the very possibility of a restored, sovereign Jewish state as part of the punishment Jews incurred for rejecting Jesus and supposedly putting him to death.[38]

In the first decade of the 21st century, relations between the Holy See and the state of Israel have become strained, epitomized by the lack of agreement over juridical and tax issues. Occasional bilateral talks have failed to produce agreement over "the fundamental accord" that has been sought since 1993. The majority of the Holy See's religious communities own properties that were purchased in the 19th century, when they were often deserted; today, they are generally surrounded by modern neighborhoods. By virtue of a privilege granted by the Ottoman Empire, and then upheld throughout the British Mandate, these communities were exempted from taxes. Today, there is disagreement about whether these communities should continue to benefit from this exemption or pay taxes in Israel.

In 2007, the papal nuncio, Archbishop Antonio Franco, threatened not to attend the annual Holocaust Memorial day event at Yad Vashem, Israel's main Holocaust museum, unless the museum agreed to remove or rewrite a caption of Pope Pius XII that he found offensive. Although he changed his mind after the controversy became public, Franco's action was a sign of a

37. John Paul II, *Spiritual Pilgrimage: Texts on Jews and Judaism, 1979–95*, ed. Eugene J. Fisher and Leon Klenicki (New York: Crossroad, 1995), 34.

38. See John T. Pawlikowski, "The Vatican-Israeli Accords: Their Implications for Catholic Faith and Teaching," in *A Challenge Long Delayed: The Diplomatic Exchange between the Holy See and the State of Israel*, ed. Eugene J. Fisher and Leon Klenicki (New York: Anti-Defamation League, 1996), 10–19.

chill in the relationship. Benedict XVI's 2007 *motu proprio*, *Summorum pontificum*, on the expanded use of the 1962 Latin Missal (containing phraseology offensive to Jews), also raised concerns in Israel, and the controversy over Holocaust-denier Bishop Richard Williamson, in 2009, resulted in the Israeli chief rabbis temporarily breaking off formal ties with the Vatican.

Further tensions were raised in the pursuit of boycott, divestment, and sanctions against Israel among some churches, primarily Protestant but with support from Roman Catholics. When churches adopt initiatives directed against Israel, a country whose policies they sometimes liken to the former apartheid regime in South Africa, many see these as attempts to delegitimize Israel's very existence. They recall the long-standing Arab boycott that was designed to undermine Israel's economy and existence, and that still prevails to no small extent. The fact that the churches rarely act similarly regarding human rights abuses and state violence in many other places in the world adds to the strain.

In Israel itself, there have been signs of a positive shift in Israeli Jewish attitudes to Christianity. To see the pope at Yad Vashem demonstrating solidarity, weeping at the suffering of the Jewish people; to learn that he had helped save Jews during the Holocaust and that subsequently, as a priest, he had returned Jewish children adopted by Christians to their Jewish families; and to see the head of the Catholic Church placing a prayer of atonement for the sins of Christians against Jews between the stones of the Western Wall—all these scenes had a profound effect on many Israelis.

A survey of attitudes in 2009 showed that 75% of Israeli Jews do not see Christians as missionaries and are not bothered by encountering a Christian wearing a cross. Furthermore, 41% stated that Christianity is the religion closest to Judaism, with 32% according Islam second place.[39]

In 1999, The Center for the Study of Christianity was founded at the Hebrew University in Jerusalem, and the work of interreligious institutes such as the Hartman Institute and the Elijah School have also been influential. Even some in the religious Settler Movement have been motivated to engage with Christians as potential mediators in the struggle between the spiritual children of Isaac and those of Ishmael. One example is Shlomo Riskin's Center for Jewish-Christian Understanding and Cooperation in Efrat, which is primarily aimed at Evangelical Christians.

Nevertheless, the situation of Christians in the Holy Land is awkward and a five-year synod that started in 1995 involving the Catholic churches

39. The survey was carried out by the Jerusalem Institute for Israel Studies and the Jerusalem Center for Jewish-Christian Relations.

of the Holy Land, comprising not only the Roman Catholic Church but also the Oriental churches, makes clear that the local church does not have the same starting point as its European counterparts, for it sees itself as free of antisemitic practice, policy, and the responsibility for the fate of European Jewry. David Neuhaus, a Jesuit living in Jerusalem, explains further:

> Christians live as a minority face to face with a Jewish majority (those in Israel), under Israeli military occupation (those in the West Bank) or confronting a regional economic and military power (those in Jordan and Gaza). This is an absolutely unique historical situation. Nowhere else in the world do Christians experience directly the sovereignty and power of a Jewish polity, and never in history have Christians experienced Jewish sovereignty and power (these only having been reestablished in 1948 with the creation of the State of Israel). This unique situation must inform dialogue that takes place in this land between local Christians and Jews, predominantly in Israel. For many of the Holy Land faithful, unfortunately, the Jew is often first and foremost a policeman, a soldier or a settler.[40]

Thus, a key factor to reckon with is Christian status as a minority in the Middle East. Not only are Christians a minority within the state of Israel—approximately 2% of the Israeli population are Christian—they are also a minority within the Arab minority. Purely on the psychological level, their church representatives feel under pressure. Although integrated in Palestine, Christian Palestinians are clearly concerned at the prospect of the gradual Islamization of the nascent state and of a time when Hamas and other Islamist parties might take over completely. Yet, the Christian Arab and the Muslim Arab, whatever their religious differences might be, live in one society, speak one language, and share one culture. Dialogue with Muslims is sometimes a priority for Christians and in some dioceses it is only the dialogue with Muslims that is real—in Jordan and Gaza, for example, where there are no Jews.

In addition, there have been occasional violent attacks on Christians and Christian properties by ultra-Orthodox Jews. In the 1970s the attacks were linked to the extremist right-wing party of Meir Kahane, "Kach," which was banned by the government for its overt racism. In 2004, a controversy erupted when some yeshiva students spat at Nourhan Manougian, the Armenian Archbishop of Jerusalem, to protest idol worship. Antagonism

40. David Neuhaus, SJ, and Jamel Khader, "A Holy Land Context for *Nostra Aetate*," *Studies in Christian-Jewish Relations* 1, no. 1 (2005–2006), http://ejournals.bc.edu/ojs/index.php/scjr/article/view/1360.

toward Christians by some ultra-Orthodox Jews and West Bank Settlers has grown, especially since 2010.

Elsewhere in the Middle East the significant reduction in the Christian population (especially from Iraq, but also witness the concerns of Copts today in Egypt) add to feelings of insecurity. Nablus, a city that once had a sizeable Christian population, now has almost none, and in Bethlehem Christians are under pressure. Evangelical Christian Arabs have encountered special problems, against which they are to some extent shielded in Israel.

Divisions between Christians sometimes spill over into acts of violence. For example, fights between Catholic and Greek Orthodox priests in Easter 2005 and Greeks and Armenians in Easter 2008 at the Church of the Holy Sepulcher, illustrate an intra-Christian conflict that has marked the history of Christianity in the region since its earliest days. The intervention of the state may formally be decried, but the reluctance of Christian representatives to dialogue among themselves on the difficulties means that Israeli intervention is also quietly welcomed.

There remains one overarching factor to remember: the danger for Christians and Jews of focusing solely on Israel by, for example, arguing that what was once an interpretation about the nature of the biblical word and promise is now, in the situation of Israel, concretized in a contemporary event. The challenge to Jewish-Christian relations as a result of an emphasis on fulfillment of biblical prophecy can be seen in the writings of some Evangelical Christians as well as fundamentalist Jews. What happened 100 years ago to the Jews outside Israel is considered historically remote compared to biblical events, which are viewed as almost contemporary. The present becomes transfused with biblical language and geography, which leads to the danger of giving metaphysical meaning to geographical places. The fundamentalist may interpret the ownership of the Land of Israel in terms of a divine gift. This creates a great danger of bestowing divine importance on the state of Israel, and the vocation of the Jew becomes a dedication to the existence and the restoration of the cosmic state. Thus, the return to the Land is a fulfillment of the divine promise and reflects a return to the original fullness. However, the biblical promises did not define the same borders, and by choosing the widest ones, the fundamentalist abuses the idea of the promise, which is related to the Land.

Replacement Theology

Few biblical concepts are as troubling to theologians as the Christian claim to be the successor covenant people elected by God to replace Israel because of the latter's faithlessness. Known as "substitution theory" or "replacement theology," this is the teaching that, since the time of Jesus, Jews have been replaced by Christians in God's favor, and that all God's promises to the Jewish people have been inherited by the Christians.

Cardinal Walter Kasper, president of the Pontifical Commission for Religious Relations with the Jews from 2000–2011, has suggested that the term "unabrogated covenant," taken from Paul, should become the starting point for a renewed theology of Judaism. It is not by chance that *NA* bases its reflections on Paul's Letter to the Romans, not on the Letter to the Hebrews. Romans reminds Christians that the Jewish people remain part of the people of God. Paul's attempt to explain the "mystery of Israel" is based on the impossibility for him that the Jewish people as a whole could first have been elected by God and then later displaced. For Paul, God would not simply elect and then reject. As *NA* states:

> Nevertheless, God holds the Jews most dear for the sake of their Fathers; He does not repent of the gifts He makes or of the calls He issues [Rom 11:28–29 referenced here]—such is the witness of the Apostle. In company with the Prophets and the same Apostle, the Church awaits that day, known to God alone, on which all peoples will address the Lord in a single voice and "serve him shoulder to shoulder" (Zeph. 3:9).

The church's election derives from that of Israel, but this does not imply that God's covenant with Israel is broken. Rather, it remains unbroken—irrevocably (Rom 11:29). For Paul, the mystery of Israel is that her rejection and her stumbling do not mean that she ceases to be accepted by God. Rather, Israel allows the Gentiles to participate in the peoplehood of Israel.

Indeed, so strongly does Paul make this point that he offers a severe warning that Gentile Christians should not be haughty or boastful toward unbelieving Jews, much less cultivate evil intent and engage in persecution. His words remained a warning almost totally forgotten by Christians over the centuries, for Jews have been remembered as "enemies," not as "beloved," of God (Rom 11:28), and Christians took to heart Paul's criticisms, forgetting his love for Jews (Rom 9:1-5).

Of course, one could argue that if Jews have not kept faith with God, then God has a perfect right to cast them off. It is interesting that Christians who argue this way have not often drawn the same deduction about Christian faithfulness, which has not been a notable characteristic of the last two millennia. Actually, God seems to have had a remarkable ability to keep faith with both Christians and Jews, when they have not kept faith with God, a point of which Paul is profoundly aware in Romans 9–11.

He goes out of his way to deny claims that God has rejected the chosen people, and asserts that their stumbling does not lead to their fall.

It seems to me that today the Jewish-Christian encounter needs to turn a negative term ("unabrogated [or unrevoked] covenant") into a positive formulation. If God is faithful to the covenant with Israel, then what? This question remains open. To assert that the "old covenant" has not been revoked carries little import, if there is no theological reason for the existence of Judaism after the coming of Jesus Christ.

For their part, Jews might begin with reflecting on the covenant with Noah,[41] the laws of which are an attempt to formulate moral standards without a concomitant demand for conversion to Judaism. As such, they acknowledge the right of peoples to their own formulation of faith provided only that a minimum standard is met.[42] The rejection of idolatry, rather than any doctrinal definition of God, is the foundation of Noahide laws and may provide a basis on which to affirm the theological and existential validity of Christianity.

There are other Jewish resources such as the concept of "Righteous Gentiles," referring to Rabbi Joshua ben Hananya, who propounded the view, later generally accepted, that "the righteous of all nations have a share in the world to come."[43] Jews might also turn to the rabbinic principles of *tiqqun 'olam* ("establishing the world aright"), *darkhe shalom* ("the ways of peace"), and *qiddush Hashem* ("sanctifying God's name," that is, behaving in such a manner as to bring credit to God). Each can be brought to govern the Jewish relationship to Christianity and seeks to create the "theological space" for Christians while remaining faithful to Torah, similar perhaps to Paul's reflection in Romans 9–11, which also seeks to create "theological space" for Jews while remaining faithful to Christ.

From a Christian perspective, it is generally acknowledged that supersessionism needs to be challenged to repudiate the belief that Christ's coming entails the abrogation or obsolescence of God's covenant with Israel. Alternatives to supersessionism concur in affirming the ongoing validity

41. Tosefta *Avoda Zara* 9.4: "The children of Noah (that is, people other than Israel) were given seven commandments: Laws (i.e. to establish courts of justice), (the prohibitions of) Idolatry, Blasphemy, Sexual Immorality, Bloodshed, Theft, and the Limb from a Living Animal."

42. See Rabbi Johanan of Tiberias (third century CE): "Whoever denies idolatry is called a Jew" (BT *Megilla* 13a).

43. Tosefta, *Sanhedrin* 13: Judaism does not have an equivalent to Cyprian of Carthage's "*extra ecclesiam non est salus*" (256 CE: Epistola 73.21, s. Cypriani ad Jubaianum, *De haereticis baptizandis*, *Patrologia Latina*, vol. 3, cols. 1123A– B).

of God's covenant with the Jewish people, but beyond that alternatives vary widely among themselves. Some emphasize the relative independence of Christianity and Judaism as different, but equally valid, appropriations of a common religious inheritance rooted in biblical Israel ("two covenant" approaches). Others interpret the church and the Jewish people as interdependent players in a common history of salvation ("one covenant" approaches).[44] Clearly, the rejection of replacement theology entails some affirmation of the continuing validity of God's covenant with the Jewish people. But Christians differ on the implications for other central Christian doctrines such as the Trinity, the person and work of Jesus Christ, and the universality of the church's mission.

In their search for a replacement of replacement theology, Christian theologians may do well to reflect on a speech by John Paul II in 1997:

> This people has been called and led by God, creator of heaven and earth. Their existence is not a mere natural or cultural happening. . . . It is a supernatural one. This people continues in spite of everything to be the people of the covenant, and, despite human infidelity, the Lord is faithful to his covenant.[45]

Giant strides may have been made, but we are talking of a dynamic and relentless process. We will never be able to sit back and say, "The work is done. The agenda is completed." So, despite great advances, Jewish-Christian relations still face major challenges as well as opportunities. Rising to meet these challenges requires a concerted and collaborative effort: it is a joint covenantal endeavor.

44. See Philip Cunningham et al., eds., *Christ Jesus and the Jewish People Today: New Explorations of Theological Interrelationships* (Grand Rapids, MI: Eerdmans, 2011). I would like to thank Professor Cunningham for his comments on a draft of this article.

45. The quotation is from *Documentation Catholique* 94 (1997): 1003.

11 What *Nostra Aetate* Inaugurated

A Conversion to the "Providential Mystery of Otherness"

MARY C. BOYS, SNJM

The Second Vatican Council's declaration Nostra aetate (NA) *is regarded as a "watershed" document. NA no. 4, on relations with the Jewish people, is frequently cited as evidence of a turning point in the Catholic Church's attitudes toward the religious Other. Yet the full significance of NA no. 4 becomes manifest only when it is situated in the complex history of the church's understanding of Judaism, including the contentious debates at the council and current theological disputes.*

Vatican II's *Nostra aetate*, the Declaration on the Relation of the Church to Non-Christian Religions, might best be understood as a conversion to the "providential mystery of otherness" for the life of the church, and as a call to extend and deepen that conversion.[1] For the first time in history, an ecumenical council spoke positively of other religions to which people look for an "answer to the unsolved riddles of human existence." While the Catholic tradition differs in many particularities, these religions "nevertheless often reflect a ray of that truth which enlightens all men [and

1. Michael Barnes, SJ, *Theology and the Dialogue of Religions*, Cambridge Studies in Christian Doctrine (New York: Cambridge University, 2002), 239. For an argument that Vatican II represents a development of doctrine with regard to the salvation of the religious Other, see Francis A. Sullivan, SJ, "Vatican II on the Salvation of the Adherents of Other Religions," in *After Vatican II: Trajectories and Hermeneutics*, ed. James L. Heft (Grand Rapids, MI: Eerdmans, 2011), 68–95.

women].” Thus, the council encouraged “discussion and collaboration with followers of other religions.”[2]

At the vantage point of nearly 50 years, *NA*’s brevity and relative blandness may obscure not only its groundbreaking character but also the complex history that preceded its drafting. This is particularly true of *NA* no. 4, the point of departure of my article—which must be interpreted against the backdrop of centuries of church teachings that distorted Judaism, disparaged Jews, and contributed to the rise of antisemitism. Only when *NA*’s revolutionary character is revealed will relations between Catholics and Jews today be situated in their proper context.

Thus, to understand contemporary issues and tensions in the Jewish-Catholic relationship, it is first necessary to trace the evolution of theological thought about Judaism prior to Vatican II, and then to sketch the contentious debates over its five drafts that resulted in the most radical change in the ordinary magisterium of the church that emerged from the council.[3] Further, it is necessary to review the biblical and theological developments in the wake of the council that provide the context for the most salient issues confronting Catholic-Jewish relations today.

Judaism and the Evolution of Catholic Theology I: Traditional Tropes

Few people anticipated the immense impact of the 15 Latin sentences of *NA* no. 4 that began the process of reconciliation between the Catholic Church and the Jewish people—certainly not the bishops of Belgium, France, Germany, the Netherlands, Poland, and the United Kingdom: they made no mention of relations with Jews in the more than 800 pages of recommendations they submitted to the Vatican as part of the preparatory process after Pope John XXIII’s announcement of the council in 1959.[4] Nor is any mention of relations with Jews found among the 250 pages of recommendations the US bishops submitted.[5] The Vatican officials who

2. *NA* nos. 1 and 2, in *Vatican Council II: The Conciliar and Post Conciliar Documents*, rev. ed., ed. Austin Flannery (Collegeville, MN: Liturgical Press, 1984).

3. See Gregory Baum, “The Social Context of American Catholic Theology,” in *Proceedings of the Catholic Theological Society of America* 41 (1986): 83–100, esp. 87.

4. See John Connelly, *From Enemy to Brother: The Revolution in Catholic Teaching on the Jews, 1933–1965* (Cambridge, MA: Harvard University, 2012), 182.

5. See Joseph A. Komonchak, “U.S. Bishops’ Suggestions for Vatican II,” http://jakomonchak.files.wordpress.com/2012/01/us-bishops-suggestions-for-vatican-ii.pdf;

earlier in the 20th century had looked with suspicion, if not overt hostility, at the advocates for rethinking the church's stance on Judaism would not have envisioned an ecumenical council addressing this topic. Nor would the vast majority of Catholics, who were generally oblivious to the church's long and bitter history vis-à-vis the Jewish people. Like most Christians in the late 1950s and early 1960s, Catholics typically saw their church as having superseded Judaism.

Still other Catholics opposed consideration of the church's relationship with the Jewish people. Many Eastern bishops, particularly in Arab and Muslim lands, feared that their minority status could be further endangered. The scurrilous antisemitic texts distributed by anonymous or pseudonymous parties at all four sessions of the council testified to an undercurrent of opposition that persisted throughout the deliberations. The arguments of these texts, however, "were so vile, their allusions so repulsive, their origin apparently so uncertain and even suspect" that this hate literature exercised little or no influence on the conciliar participants.[6]

If few envisioned the need for the council to address relations with Jews, others had been rethinking traditional understandings of Judaism and advocating for a new stance on the part of the church. Prominent among these advocates was the association *Amici Israel*, founded in 1926. Inspired by a convert to Judaism, Sophie Franziska van Leer, it promoted reconciliation between Jews and Catholics by seeking to deepen understanding of Judaism and eliminating negative references to Jews in preaching and liturgy. In its early years, the association encouraged prayer for the conversion of Jews. Eventually, however, *Amici Israel* turned away from seeking conversions, a turning that became a pattern among many promoters of a renewed relationship with the Jewish people.

The efforts of *Amici Israel* to promote reconciliation exemplify divergent views of Judaism at high levels in the Vatican. In early January 1928, the association appealed to Pope Pius XI to reform the Good Friday prayer for the Jews, calling for removal of the terms *perfidis* and *perfidiam*, and recommending that the practice of not genuflecting during the prayer for the Jews on Good Friday, first specified in the 1570 Roman Missal, be

Komonchak, "What They Said before the Council: How the U.S. Bishops Envisioned Vatican II," *Commonweal* 117 (1990): 714–17.

6. Cited in John M. Oesterreicher, "Declaration on the Relationship of the Church to Non-Christian Religions," in *Commentary on the Documents of Vatican II*, 5 vols., ed. Herbert Vorgrimler (New York: Herder & Herder, 1969), 3:31–136, at 122.

abolished.[7] The *Amici Israel* offered a sample prayer as an alternative to the traditional one. The pope forwarded their request to the Congregation of Rites.[8] This office in turn sent it to a liturgical expert, Benedictine Abbot Alfred Ildefons Schuster, who indicated his approval of the arguments of *Amici Israel* as "fully justified by the classical tradition of the Roman liturgy."[9]

Yet, reform of a prayer involving matters of faith also required the approval of the Holy Office (now called the Congregation for the Doctrine of the Faith [CDF]). Here the recommendation met opposition. Its expert, papal court theologian and Dominican priest Marco Sales, citing texts such as Acts 7:51 ("You stiff-necked people") and Matthew 27:25 ("His blood be upon us and our children"), concluded that the Bible bore witness to Jewish faithlessness. Only the Jews, Sales said, had a "pact with God and a covenant with him, and only the Jews constantly violated this pact, and only they would continue constantly to violate it. It should come as no surprise, then, that they are called perfidious, and that we use the expression *perfidia Judaica* to distinguish them from the pagans."[10] Nothing should be changed, he mandated.

The secretary of the Holy Office, Cardinal Rafael Merry del Val, a zealous anti-Modernist, concurred with Sales.[11] Moreover, in identifying a list of "erroneous or offensive-sounding statements" that had appeared from advocates for reform of the Good Friday liturgy, an expert commissioned by Merry del Val asked "how it was possible that the Jews, who had made

7. The Roman Missal of 1570 was the prescribed text for celebrations of the Eucharist. See *The Roman Missal in Latin and English, Arranged for the Use of the Laity to Which Is Added a Collection of Usual Public Prayers* (Tournay, Belgium: Society of St. John the Evangelist and Desclée, 1911), 490–91. In 1960 John XXIII had the word *perfidis* removed.

8. See Hubert Wolf, *Pope and Devil: The Vatican's Archives and the Third Reich*, trans. Kenneth Kronenberg (Cambridge, MA: Belknap of Harvard University, 2010), 81–125.

9. Cited in ibid., 96.

10. Cited in ibid., 99.

11. The 1864 *Syllabus errorum* of Pope Pius IX listed 80 propositions that the church held to be false. Among them was the notion that "everyone is free to embrace and profess the religion which by the light of reason one judges to be true" (no. 15). Also held to be erroneous was that "we should at least have good hopes for the eternal salvation of all those who are in no way in the true Church of Christ" (no. 17). Similar in message and tone were the 1907 encyclical of Pope Pius X, *Pascendi dominici gregis*, and the decree of the Holy Office that same year, *Lamentabile sane exitu*; the latter listed 65 errors of those alleged to be Modernists. Among the propositions condemned was that "Christian Doctrine was originally Judaic" (no. 60).

common cause with those who nailed Jesus to the cross, thereby killing the son of God, could even have belonged to the Kingdom of the Eternal Father in the first place."[12] As had Sales, Merry del Val found ample evidence in the biblical texts. The Good Friday prayers, he maintained, were about "stiff-necked Jewish people burdened with the curse that they as a people with their principles undertook the responsibility for having spilled the blood of the holiest of the holy."[13] The Good Friday liturgy, according to Merry del Val, had been "inspired and sanctified" over the centuries, and it aptly expressed the "abhorrence for the rebellion and treachery of the chosen, disloyal, and deicidal people."[14] He warned against the possibility that *Amici Israel* could fall into the "trap devised by the self-same Jews who everywhere insinuate themselves into modern society and attempt by all means to dispel the memory of their history, and to exploit the good faith of Christians."[15] Merry del Val's antagonism reflects the way traditional anti-Jewish tropes intertwined with antisemitism.[16]

On March 25, 1928, Pope Pius XI settled the argument in favor of the opponents of the reform of the Good Friday prayer with the following statement:

> The Catholic Church has always been accustomed to pray for the Jewish people, the recipients of divine promises up to the coming of Jesus Christ, in spite of this people's blindness. More than that, it has done so on account of that very blindness. Ruled by the same charity, the Apostolic See has protected this people against unjust vexations, and just as it reproves all hatred between peoples, so it condemns hatred against the people formerly chosen by God, the hatred that today customarily goes by the name of anti-Semitism.[17]

12. Cited in Wolf, *Pope and Devil,* 103.
13. Cited in ibid., 106.
14. Cited in ibid., 105.
15. Cited in ibid., 107.
16. See Mary C. Boys, "Beyond 'Removing' Anti-Judaism: The Theological and Educational Task of Reframing Christian Identity," in *Removing the Anti-Judaism from the New Testament*, ed. Howard Clark Kee and Irvin J. Borowsky (Philadelphia: American Interfaith Institute, 1998), 88–102.
17. Cited in Wolf, *Pope and Devil*, 82. The author of the petition from *Amici Israel*, Abbot Benedict Gariador, and the liturgical experts who had recommended that the petition be granted were summoned before the Holy Office and admonished. Abbot Schuster demonstrated his "abject submission" and recanted his recommendation; see ibid., 114.

The papal statement also praised *Amici Israel*'s desire for the conversion of Jews (although the association's founders had in fact rethought the desirability of fostering such conversions). Nevertheless, Pius XI censured the association for "a manner of acting and thinking that is contrary to the sense and spirit of the Church, to the thought of the Holy Fathers and the liturgy."[18] Because of the association's "erroneous initiatives," it was suppressed. Only after Vatican II would the Good Friday prayer be reworded—and then, in 2008, revised by Pope Benedict XVI for the Tridentine Rite.[19]

Ironically, the *Monitum* that suppressed *Amici Israel* also expressed the official magisterium's first formal condemnation of antisemitism. The decree, although condemning hatred of Jews, nonetheless retained the idea of a sinful Jewish people whose rejection of Jesus led to their suffering.[20] It also suggested that God had rejected the Jews, "the people formerly chosen by God." Nevertheless, it manifested an awareness of the dangers of racial antisemitism—a peril about which the official magisterium would be largely silent until Vatican II.

The representation of Judaism expressed in the response to *Amici Israel*—Jews as perfidious, treacherous, disloyal, deicidal, and blind—typified

18. *Acta Apostolicae Sedis* 20 (1928): 103–4. See also Jean Levie, SJ, "Décret de suppression de l'Association des 'Amis d'Israel,' " *Nouvelle revue théologique* (1928): 532–37; and Lieven Sarans, "The Attitude of the Belgian Roman Catholic Clergy toward the Jews Prior to Occupation," in *Belgium and the Holocaust: Jews, Belgians, Germans*, ed. Dan Mikhman (Jerusalem: Yad Vashem, 1998), 117–58.

19. In the *motu proprio Summorum Pontificium* of July 7, 2007, Pope Benedict XVI gave greater latitude for the celebration of the Tridentine Rite. On February 6, 2008, the pope released his version of the prayer for this rite only: *Oremus et pro Iudaeis: Ut Deus et Dominus noster illuminet corda eorum, ut agnoscant Iesum Christum salvatorem omnium hominum. (Oremus. Flectamus genua. Levate.) Omnipotens sempiterne Deus, qui vis ut omnes homines salvi fiant et ad agnitionem veritatis veniant, concede propitius, ut plenitudine gentium in Ecclesiam Tuam intrante omnis Israel salvus fiat. Per Christum Dominum nostrum. Amen.* The prayer is headed: "*Pro Conversione Iudaeorum.*" One translation reads: "Let us pray also for the Jews. That our Lord and God may enlighten their hearts, that they may acknowledge Jesus Christ as the savior of all men [and women]. Almighty, ever living God, who wills that all men [and women] would be saved and come to the knowledge of the truth, graciously grant that all Israel may be saved when the fullness of the nations enter into Your Church. Through Christ Our Lord. Amen." For an eschatological interpretation of Benedict XVI's prayer, see Cardinal Walter Kasper, "Striving for Mutual Respect in Modes of Prayer," *L'Osservatore Romano*, weekly edition (April 16, 2008): 8–9. See also Rita Ferrone, "Anti-Jewish Elements in the Extraordinary Form," *Worship* 84 (2010): 498–513.

20. Anna Łysiak, "Rabbinic Judaism in the Writings of Polish Catholic Theologians," in *Antisemitism, Christian Ambivalence and the Holocaust*, ed. Kevin P. Spicer (Bloomington: Indiana University, 2007), 26–49, at 29.

long-standing church teaching.[21] From the *Adversus Judaeos* literature of the early centuries through the late medieval accusations of blood libel and ritual crucifixion, Christians portrayed Jews as the quintessential Other. Early in the 20th century, German theologians spoke of a "permissible antisemitism" that "combats, by moral and legal means, a truly harmful influence of the Jewish segment of the population in the areas of economy, politics, theater, cinema, the press, science, and art [liberal-libertine tendencies]."[22]

Jesuits Gustav Gundlach, Gustav Desbuquois, and John LaFarge developed this distinction at greater length in a draft encyclical for Pius XI in 1938. Although never published, perhaps because of the pope's failing health, the logic of the draft provides a glimpse of the kind of thinking at the highest levels of the church in the late 1930s.[23] On the one hand, the authors criticized the "struggle for racial purity [that] ends by being uniquely the struggle against the Jews"; as a consequence, millions of people were denied their rights as citizens and "many thousands of helpless persons" were left without resources. "Wandering from frontier to frontier, they [Jews] are a burden to humanity and to themselves."[24] Nevertheless, while "unjust and pitiless," awareness of the plight of Jews underscored the "authentic basis of the social separation of the Jews from the rest of humanity. This basis is directly religious in character." Thus, the authors concluded: "The so-called Jewish question is not one of race, or nation, or territorial nationality, or citizenship in the state. It is a question of religion and, since the coming of Christ, a question of Christianity."[25] From the Jewish people, the only people in history to have a call from God, came Jesus Christ, the fulfillment of Israel's prophecies and types. Yet:

21. See Mary C. Boys, *Redeeming Our Sacred Story: The Death of Jesus and Relations between Jews and Christians* (New York: Paulist, 2013).

22. Gustav Gundlach, SJ, "Antisemitismus," in *Lexikon für Theologie und Kirche*, 10 vols., 2nd rev. ed. (Freiberg: Herder, 1930–1938), 1:504; cited by Georges Passelecq and Bernard Suchecky, *The Hidden Encyclical of Pius XI*, trans. Steven Rendall (New York: Harcourt, Brace, 1977), 47–48. The concept of dual antisemitism had appeared in earlier sources. See Olaf Blaschke, *Offenders or Victims? German Jews and the Causes of Modern Catholic Antisemitism* (Lincoln: University of Nebraska, 2009), 32–33.

23. Pius XI died February 10, 1939; his successor, Pope Pius XII, typically avoided the more confrontational policies of his predecessor. As it became more apparent that Europe would go to war, Pius XII took a more neutral stance in the hopes of mediating the conflict. See Michael Marrus, "The Vatican on Racism and Antisemitism, 1938–39," *Holocaust and Genocide Studies* 4 (1997): 378–95, esp. 385–87.

24. Citations from *Humani generis unitas* nos. 131–32, in *Hidden Encyclical* 246–47 (all further references to this draft encyclical are taken from this source).

25. *Humani generis unitas* no. 133.

> The Savior, whom God had sent to His chosen people after they had prayed and longed for Him for thousands of years, was rejected by that people, violently repudiated, and condemned as a criminal by the highest tribunals of the Jewish nation, in collusion with the pagan authorities who held the Jewish people bondage. Ultimately, the Savior was put to death.[26]

Although the redemption gained by the suffering and death of Jesus was for all humanity, the consequences for Jews were dire:

> Blinded by a vision of material domination and gain, the Israelites lost what they themselves had sought. . . . This unhappy people, destroyers of their own nation, whose misguided leaders had called down upon their own heads a Divine malediction, doomed, as it were to perpetually wander over the face of the earth, were nonetheless never allowed to perish, but have been preserved through the ages into our own time.[27]

Yet, Jewish rejection of Jesus allowed the Gentiles to enjoy the fruit of the promises rejected by the Jews. Israel may have incurred God's wrath, but thereby it "hastened the evangelization and . . . conversion of the Gentiles." Thanks to God's mercy, Israel may eventually share in redemption, but this possibility exists in the realm of the supernatural. In the realities of historical time, however, "we find a historic enmity of the Jewish people to Christianity, creating a perpetual tension between Jew and Gentile which the passage of time has never diminished, even though from time to time its manifestations have been mitigated."[28]

Judaism and the Evolution of Catholic Theology II: New Directions

Despite such negative judgments of Judaism, efforts to advance reconciliation continued on various fronts. The evolving theological arguments of Johannes Oesterreicher (1904–1993) and Karl Thieme (1902–1963)

26. Ibid., no. 135.

27. Ibid., no. 136.

28. Ibid., nos. 140–41. Marrus concludes: "The 'lost encyclical' turns out not to have been a tragically spurned instrument that might have restrained Nazism, but part of a wider cultural distaste for Jews, despite its rejection of Fascist antisemitism" ("The Vatican on Racism and Antisemitism," 392). Connelly also argues that the encyclical's suppression is fortunate: "Had it been issued, the pope would have reinforced traditional anti-Judaism, and in the pervasive racism of that day, that meant bolstering antisemitism. One could not shun Jews 'religiously' without marginalizing actual Jewish human beings" (*From Enemy to Brother*, 98).

proved particularly significant. Also influential were the work of the Freiburg Circle and its journal the *Freiburger Rundbrief*, the Dutch Catholic Council, and the 1947 meeting of the International Emergency Conference on Antisemitism.[29] Moreover, the decision of the Sisters of Sion in the late 1950s to rethink their original mission of converting Jews gave further indication of changing perspectives.[30] Cooperation between Jewish organizations and Catholic groups also advanced new possibilities. The meeting in June 1960 of the 83-year-old French Jewish historian Jules Isaac with the 79-year-old John XXIII may have been the direct cause of the church's relationship with Judaism being placed on the agenda of Vatican II. Isaac presented his research on what Christians had taught about Judaism over the centuries: a "teaching of contempt."[31] Deeply moved, Pope John XXIII summoned Cardinal Augustin Bea to lead the process of rethinking traditional teaching. Fortunately, Bea could call upon the advocates for a transformed relationship with Jews to help establish the foundational arguments of *NA* no. 4.

Connelly identifies Thieme and Oesterreicher as preeminent among a group of "border crossers," men and women who were not only converts to Catholicism but also polyglots who moved fluidly across European borders

29. Gertrud Luckner, whose courageous work on behalf of German Jews resulted in her imprisonment in the concentration camp at Ravensbrück, founded the *Freiburger Rundbrief* in 1948 as a way of countering antisemitism and keeping alive the memory of the Holocaust. She recruited Karl Thieme as theological adviser to the journal. Miriam Rookmaaker van Leer founded The Dutch Catholic Council for Israel in 1951, and Antonius Ramselaar served as its theological adviser; he later served on the drafting committee for *NA*. The 1947 International Emergency Conference on Antisemitism met in Seelisberg, Switzerland, from July 30 to August 5, and is regarded as one of the events in which Christians, both Protestant and Catholic, confronted the Christian roots of antisemitism. See Christian M. Rutishauser, "The 1947 Seelisberg Conference: The Foundation of Jewish-Christian Dialogue," *Studies in Jewish-Christian Relations* 2.2 (2007): 34–53; and Victoria Barnett, "Seelisberg: An Appreciation," *Studies in Jewish-Christian Relations* 2, no. 2 (2007): 54–57.

30. See Charlotte Klein, "From Conversion to Dialogue—The Sisters of Sion and the Jews: A Paradigm of Catholic-Jewish Relations?" *Journal of Ecumenical Studies* 18 (1981): 388–400; and Mary C. Boys, "The Sisters of Sion: From a Conversionist Stance to a Dialogical Way of Life," *Journal of Ecumenical Studies* 31 (1994): 27–48. The Fathers and Brothers of Sion, technically the Congregation of Religious of Our Lady of Sion, also engaged in countering antisemitism and published a journal, *Cahiers Sioniens*.

31. Jules Isaac, *Enseignement du mépris vérité historique et mythes théologiques* (Paris: Fasquelle, 1962); ET, *Teaching of Contempt*, trans. Helen Weaver (New York: Holt, Rinehart, & Winston, 1964).

and were thus able to transcend the limitations of a single culture.[32] Thieme was a German who became a Catholic in part as protest against the acquiescence of his Lutheran colleagues to the Aryan Paragraph.[33] Oesterreicher, who became one of the drafters of *NA* no. 4, was brought up in a Jewish home in Moravia and had been active in a Zionist youth group. A religious experience led him to seek baptism and then the priesthood; he was ordained in 1927. Although in the early years of his priesthood he founded an organization, *Pauluswerk*, to missionize Jews, he was among the first to condemn the racist attitudes many Catholics held toward Jews. Countering claims by prominent Catholics that Nazi racial laws were in accord with God's will and that even baptism could not cure the moral defects of Jews because of their "bad genetic material," he spoke out passionately against racism, founding a journal, *Erfüllung*. In 1937 Oesterreicher published a 40-page memorandum by Thieme and Waldemar Gurian that criticized antisemitism.[34]

A number of Catholic intellectuals, including Jacques Maritain and Dietrich von Hildebrand, supported the memorandum, but none of the European bishops would sign it. Despite the lack of support from the hierarchy, Oesterreicher and Thieme persevered. They sought, unsuccessfully, to meet with Pope Pius XI in December 1938 in hopes of encouraging him to speak out against antisemitism in his Christmas address. When that tactic failed, Oesterreicher began broadcasting Sunday sermons into the Reich, calling Hitler an anti-Christ and the Nazis enemies of the cross. In

32. Connelly, *From Enemy to Brother*. See Peter E. Gordon's review of this book: "The Border Crossers," *New Republic* 243, no. 9 (June 7, 2012): 26–30, http://www.tnr.com/print/article/books-and-arts/magazine/103331/catholic-jewish-anti-semitism-pope-vatican-nazis.

33. The 1933 Civil Service Law of the Third Reich stipulated that only Aryans could serve as civil employees. Because pastors were included in the structure of the civil service, this "Aryan Paragraph" became church law. Pastors were thus required to prove their racial purity, that is, that neither their parents nor grandparents were Jewish. Protest against this law became one of the founding rationales of the Confessing Church, although even within its ranks, there was dispute about whether Jews who had converted to Christianity could continue to function as pastors. See Victoria Barnett, *For the Soul of the People: Protestant Protest against Hitler* (New York: Oxford University, 1992), 128–29.

34. In addition to *Erfüllung*, three other Catholic journals in Vienna in the late 1930s were critical of Nazism: Irene Harand's *Gerechtigkeit* (Justice), Dietrich von Hilldebrand's *Der Christliche Ständestaat* (The Christian Corporatist State), and Ernst Karl Winter's *Wiener politische Blättern* (Viennese Political News).

1940, writing from Paris, Oesterreicher published *Racisme, antisémitisme, antichristianisme: Documents et critique*.[35]

Yet, even as both Oesterreicher and Thieme condemned racism among Catholics, at this juncture they remained convinced of the necessity of Jewish conversion. They believed that Jews would continue to suffer until they recognized Jesus Christ as their messiah; once Jews turned toward Jesus, their mass conversion would inaugurate the messianic age. Both men, however, had experiences that led them to rethink this position and move to a radically different judgment. Oesterreicher, whose mother had been murdered in Auschwitz and whose father had died in Theresienstadt, became increasingly opposed to theological formulations that spoke of Jews as, for example, "enemies of the Christian name," a wording Thieme used in his 1945 book, *Kirche und Synagoge*. Thieme initially resisted such criticism, but by the late 1940s he underwent, by his own admission, a "conversion."

The postwar years afforded Thieme opportunity to engage Jews in conversation; Martin Buber was his most important interlocutor. Significantly, Thieme began to hear what his conversionary language sounded like to Jewish ears, and to realize how problematic a Christian mission to Jews was after Auschwitz. He questioned the ethics of his earlier eschatological perspective: Did not the command to love neighbors imply loving them as Jews? In addition, the founding of the State of Israel in 1948 upended the Augustinian notion that Jews were forever consigned to wander the earth as a punishment for the death of Jesus.

In a public letter in August 1950, he announced his "conviction that a Jewish person, not only as an individual person, but also in a certain sense precisely as '*Jew*' can be pleasing to God."[36] Thieme continued: "Precisely for the Jews according to the entirety of divine revelation certain promises continue to be in force so that one can assume that even in distance from Christ the Jewish people enjoys special guidance and special grace."[37] Therefore, he reasoned, "I am certain that if God's grace permits 'Israel according to the flesh' to continue to exist to the end of time, and then makes them recipients of very great compassion, then their character as chosen people has not been abolished, but only suspended in some of its effects."[38]

35. John Oesterreicher, *Racisme, antisémitisme, antichristianisme: Documents et critique*, preface Jacques Maritain, translated from the German (New York: Maison française, 1943).

36. Cited in Connelly, *From Enemy to Brother*, 204–5.

37. Ibid., 205.

38. Ibid.

Thieme, as Connelly notes, was the first major Catholic thinker to grasp Paul's claim in Romans that Jews remained God's "beloved" people (Rom 11:28).[39] The transformation in his thinking represents, with the exception of Anglican James Parkes, the "most sudden and radical shift in a Christian theologian's view of the Jews in modern history."[40]

Thieme continued his theological journey as the adviser to the *Freiburger Rundbrief* and in extensive correspondence with various church officials.[41] He challenged the deicide charge and collaborated in issuing theses for Catholic teaching about Judaism. Speaking at the Second Assembly of the World Council of Churches in Evanston, Illinois, 1954, Thieme repeatedly spoke of Jews as "elder brothers." Laying out what he saw as common ground and differences between Christians and Jews, he spoke of God's revelation to the patriarchs and in the Sinai covenant as leading to eternal life; "God's mercy to His people was unbreakable," and by God's love they were bound "indissolubly" to Christians.[42] While Christians believed in Jesus Christ and in the authority of the church, Thieme acknowledged an indebtedness "to our brothers" for not concealing existing differences; he expressed desire that they might discuss "with us in brotherly cooperation, wherever this can tactfully be done until the day comes when there will be 'one flock, one Shepherd' (John 10:16), when 'all people will serve God in united worship' (Zeph 3:9)."[43]

Oesterreicher initially took such umbrage at Thieme's use of "older brothers" in reference to Jews that in 1960 he ended his correspondence

39. Ibid., 187.

40. Ibid., 205. Parkes was a prolific author; see especially his *Conflict of the Church and the Synagogue: A Study in the Origins of Antisemitism* (London: Soncino, 1934); *Antisemitism* (London: Valentine, Mitchell, 1963); and *Emergence of the Jewish Problem, 1878–1939* (Westport, CT: Greenwood, 1970). See also, Robert Everett, *Christianity without Antisemitism: James Parkes and the Jewish-Christian Encounter* (Oxford: Pergamon, 1993).

41. The Freiburg Circle's advocacy of dialogue with Jews and demands for restitution for survivors aroused suspicion from members of the hierarchy, particularly Cardinal Joseph Frings, who regarded their efforts as manifesting religious indifferentism. The Vatican investigated the members of the Freiburg Circle, but Cardinal Bea acted as their protector. See Michael Phayer, *The Catholic Church and the Holocaust, 1930–1965* (Bloomington: Indiana University, 2000), 186–202.

42. Karl Thieme, "The Hope of the World: God's Redemption in Union with His Anointed," in *Christ, the Church, and Grace in the Economy of Christian Hope: Roman Catholic Views on the Evanston Theme* (Boulogne-sur-Seine: Istina, 1954), 30–32, published as an offprint of the journal *Istina* 2 (1954).

43. Ibid.

with him.[44] Nevertheless, Oesterreicher also reversed himself, albeit without explaining his rationale. By the early 1960s he no longer referred to a "mission" to Jews, but rather of a "ministry of reconciliation." By 1970 he spoke of Christianity and Judaism as "two ways of righteousness that have complementary functions."[45] Having emigrated to New York in 1940 and founded the Institute for Judeo-Christian Studies at Seton Hall University in 1953, Oesterreicher (now John rather than Johannes) was increasingly in conversation with Jews, including his close friends Rabbi Jacob Petuchowski and Dr. Joseph Lichten, pioneers of Jewish-Catholic dialogue.

Catholics like Thieme and Oesterreicher who were interested in relations with Jews in the 1950s were, as Michael Phayer writes, like "sixteenth-century scientists who suspected the sun did not revolve around the earth but could not explain heliocentrism."[46] Yet they and others with whom they collaborated had begun articulating the basic elements of an ecclesiastical heliocentrism, that is, the theological groundwork for *NA* no. 4.

A Perilous Journey at the Council: A Declaration Debated

After his meeting with Jules Isaac, John XXIII entrusted the formulation of a new understanding of the church's relationship with Jews to Cardinal Augustin Bea. Bea, then 79, served as president of the newly established Secretariat for the Promotion of Christian Unity and thus supervised the drafting of a statement. Bea appointed Oesterreicher, Gregory Baum, AA (also a convert from Judaism), and Leo Rudloff, OSB, to a subcommission.[47] Over the course of three meetings in 1961, they developed six principal elements of a draft. Among them was the claim that Jews were beloved of God; although separated from Christ, Jews were not accursed, and the church condemns wrongs done to them.[48] Yet political complications meant that the draft they presented to the Central Coordinating

44. Gregory Baum also registered his disagreement with Thieme's formulation. See Connelly, *From Enemy to Brother*, 227.

45. Cited in ibid., 236.

46. Phayer, *Catholic Church and the Holocaust*, 186.

47. Bea also solicited the assistance of the American Jewish Committee. In response, the AJC submitted three memoranda to the council regarding Jews in Catholic teaching, anti-Jewish elements in Catholic liturgy, and ways of improving relations with Jews. See Gary Spruch, *Wide Horizons: Abraham Joshua Heschel, the AJC, and the Spirit of Vatican II* (New York: American Jewish Committee, 2008).

48. Later in 1961 Bea appointed George Tavard to the subcommission. In 1964 the drafting committee expanded to include Barnabas Ahearn, CP, Pierre Benoit, OP, Bruno Hussar, OP, Nicholas Persich, CM, Thomas Stransky, CSP, and Antonius Ramselaar.

Commission never made it to the council floor. Thus, Cardinal Bea wrote to Pope John XXIII in December 1962, seeking his intervention in reinstating the schema on the Jews as a manifestation of a "purification of spirit and conscience" necessitated by the "appalling crimes of National Socialism against six million Jews."[49]

The conciliar draft of a statement on Jews, *De Iudaeis*, had a difficult time finding a home. In November 1963, a draft decree reappeared as chapter 4 of the schema on ecumenism, *De oecumenismo*, but the draft itself was not formally discussed in the second session of the council.[50] Yet, in the discussion of other chapters of *De oecumenismo*, widely varying views were expressed about the appropriateness of a statement on Jews. Bishops of the Middle East reiterated their reluctance to have the question on the conciliar agenda. Others, especially bishops in Asia, insisted that any statement on Jews should be part of the wider framework of other world religions. Still others argued for a text on the Jews that would stand as an independent document.

Controversy broke out over the Roman Curia's hand in formulating a third draft. In this iteration, not only had the condemnation of deicide disappeared but also language was inserted that insinuated the conversion of Jews:

> It is also worth remembering that the union of the Jewish people with the Church is part of Christian hope. Therefore, following the teaching of the Apostle (cf. Romans 2:5), the Church waits with unshaken faith and deep longing for the entry of that people into the fullness of the people of God established by Christ.[51]

Rabbi Abraham Joshua Heschel, who had developed a close relationship with Bea, was especially distraught with this draft of *NA*. In a mimeographed memorandum of September 3, 1964, he addressed all the Council Fathers; it included the following dramatic declaration:

> A message that regards the Jews as a candidate for conversion and proclaims that the destiny of Judaism is to disappear will be abhorred by the Jews all over the world and is bound to foster reciprocal distrust as

49. Connelly, *From Enemy to Brother*, 249.

50. At this juncture, chapter 5 of the schema *De oecumenismo* was on religious freedom. By spring 1964, *De Iudaeis* was placed as an appendix to the schema on ecumenism.

51. Cited in Connelly, *From Enemy to Brother*, 253.

> well as bitterness and resentment. . . . I am ready to go to Auschwitz any time, if faced with the alternative of conversion or death.[52]

Oesterreicher, too, was deeply disturbed. In May 1964 he sought intervention from Cardinal Franz König of Vienna and the support of Cardinal Richard Cushing of Boston. When the conciliar participants returned to Rome in September 1964, they joined in the "Great Debate" of September 28–29 in which Bea introduced a new draft for discussion. Responding to Oesterreicher's prompting, Cushing addressed the council, proposing three amendments: (1) that the statement be more positive, illustrating what Jews and Christians share in common; (2) that Jews should not be regarded as culpable for the death of Jesus; and (3) that Christians have too often remained indifferent to the fate of Jews.[53]

At the conclusion of the Great Debate, Archbishop John Heenan of Westminster announced that the text implying Jews should ultimately join the church would be replaced with the following formulation, suggested by Oesterreicher: "In company with the Prophets and the same Apostle, the Church awaits the day, known to God alone, when all people will call

52. Text in *Merton and Judaism: Holiness in Words*, ed. Beatrice Bruteau (Louisville: Fons Vitae, 2003), 223–24. Heschel also sent a copy of his memorandum to Thomas Merton, whom he had met at Gethsemane Abbey in July 1964. Merton responded to Heschel: "It is simply incredible. I don't know what to say about it." He then wrote in his journal: "Abraham Heschel sent a memo on the new Jewish chapter. It is incredibly bad. All the sense has been taken out of it, all the light, and it has become a stuffy and pointless piece of formalism, with the incredibly stupid addition that the Church is looking forward with hope to the union of the Jews with herself. As a humble theological and eschatological desire, yes, maybe; but that was not what was meant. It is this lack of spiritual and eschatological sense, this unawareness of the real need for profound change that makes such statements pitiable. Total lack of prophetic insight and even of elementary compunction. It is precisely in prophetic and therefore deeply humiliated and humanly impoverished thirst for light that Christians and Jews can begin to find a kind of unity in seeking God's will together. For Rome simply to declare itself, as she now is, the mouthpiece of God and perfect interpreter of His will for Jews (with the implication that He in no way speaks to them directly) is simply monstrous!" (quoted in *Merton and Judaism*, 225). For an assessment of Heschel's role as a consultant to the American Jewish Committee during the council, and of his tense meeting with Pope Paul VI, see Edward K. Kaplan, *Spiritual Radical: Abraham Joshua Heschel in America, 1940–1972* (New Haven, CT: Yale University, 2007), 238–76.

53. Text in A. James Rudin, *Cushing, Spellman, O'Connor: The Surprising Story of How Three American Cardinals Transformed Catholic-Jewish Relations* (Grand Rapids, MI: Eerdmans, 2012), 108–9.

on the Lord with a single voice and 'serve him with one accord.' "[54] This was precisely the language Thieme had used in the theses he had drafted for the Evanston meeting in 1954.

During the third session of the council in November 1964, the tract *De Iudaeis* was placed in a new context: as the core of *Declaratio De Ecclesiae habitudine ad religiones non-Christianas*. This had required adding advisers competent to draft wording on Hinduism, Islam, and Buddhism. The drafters also endeavored to find language expressive of Judaism as both a people and a religion. In the end, they chose "stock of Abraham" (*stirps Abrahae*); in German, this was *Stamm Abrahams* ("tribe of Abraham"), the phrase used by Thieme in his Evanston theses.[55] They also made clear that the promises made to the "stock of Abraham" remained in force by using the present tense: "theirs is the sonship and the glory and the covenant and the law and the worship and the promises." Moreover, their wording echoed that of *Lumen gentium* (*LG*), the Dogmatic Constitution on the Church no. 16, which had been approved that same month:

> Finally, those who have not yet received the gospel are related to the People of God in various ways. There is, first, that people to which the covenants and promises were made, and from whom Christ was born according to the flesh (cf. Rom. 9:4–5): in view of the divine choice, they are a people most dear for the sake of the fathers, for the gifts of God are without repentance (cf. Rom. 11:28–29).

On October 28, 1965, the council took up the final version. It maintained the eschatological perspective of the November 1964 draft: "Together with the prophets and the same apostle [Paul], the Church awaits the day, known to God alone, when all peoples will call on God with one voice and 'serve him shoulder to shoulder.' "[56] Yet in other respects, the text had been weak-

54. The various drafts of *NA* are available in Latin and English in *Merton and Judaism*; citation, 352. The Sisters of Sion wrote to Archbishop Heenan in 1964 to record their disappointment with the draft calling for Jewish conversion; see Emma Green, "Sisters of Sion: The Nuns Who Opened Their Doors for Europe's Jews," *Atlantic*, http://www.theatlantic.com/international/archive/2012/10/sisters-of-sion-the-nuns-who-opened-their-doors-for-europes-jews/263525.

55. Connelly, *From Enemy to Brother*, 259–60.

56. Here the text cites Zephaniah 3:9: "At that time I will change the speech of the peoples to a pure speech, that all of them may call on the name of the Lord and serve him with one accord" (NRSV). The November 1964 draft cited Wisdom 3:9, but this seems a mistaken reference; see Isa 66:23; Ps 65:4; Rom 11:11-32.

ened. The term *deicide* had been removed. Whereas the November 1964 draft stated that the "Jewish People is never to be represented as a reprobate race or accursed or guilty of deicide," the final version read: "It is true that the Church is the new people of God, yet the Jews should not be spoken of as rejected or accursed, as if this followed from holy Scripture." Similarly, in previous versions antisemitism was "deplored and condemned," but in the final text it was "deplored."[57] The pastoral concern, more evident in the first draft, had lost its vigor by the time of the final text. Nevertheless, the final declaration "created a space both in breadth and depth within the Roman Catholic Church for genuine inter-religious dialogue."[58]

And yet:

> In October 1965, many bishops raised their hand in ethical assent while unthinkingly keeping to their anti-Judaic views. Even Cardinal Bea . . . wrote that Jerusalem had once been destroyed because of the "guilt" of its inhabitants, "since they directly witnessed the preaching, the miracles, the solemn entrance of Jesus." . . . During Lent 1965 Pope Paul preached on the crucifixion: "It is a grave and sad page. It describes in fact the clash between Jesus and the Jewish people. That people predestined to receive the Messiah, who awaited him for thousands of years and [were] completely absorbed in the hope . . . at the right moment when Christ came, spoke, and presented himself, not only did not recognize him, but fought him, slandered him, and injured him; and in the end they killed him."[59]

It is hardly surprising that the formulations of *NA* did not immediately change the thinking even of those who voted in its favor. The traditional tropes of the teaching of contempt were firmly entrenched, and most of the bishops knew very little about Judaism other than through the lens of Catholic views.

It has now been nearly 50 years since the promulgation of *NA*. Yet, in the phrase of Cardinal Walter Kasper, "We stand only at the beginning of a new beginning."[60]

57. References to the November 1964 draft are from *Merton and Judaism*, 353.

58. Mathijs Lamberigts and Leo Declerck, "Vatican II on the Jews: A Historical Survey," in *Never Revoked:* Nostra Aetate *as Ongoing Challenge for Jewish-Christian Dialogue*, ed. Marianne Moyaert and Didier Pollefeyt (Leuven: Peeters, 2010), 13–56, at 55.

59. Connelly, *From Enemy to Brother*, 268–69.

60. Cardinal Walter Kasper, foreword to Philip A. Cunningham et al., *Christ Jesus and the Jewish People Today: New Explorations of Theological Interrelationships* (Grand Rapids, MI: Eerdmans, 2011), x–xviii, at xiv.

Postconciliar Developments

Rabbi Arthur Gilbert, writing shortly after the council, observed that many of its texts, including *NA*, encompassed a "bipolarity of tendencies."[61] For example, *NA* no. 4, citing Paul, speaks of the Jews as remaining "very dear to God" yet asserts that the "Church is the new people of God." Does the claim that the church is the "new" people of God imply that the church has replaced the Jews as God's people, even if they remain "very dear to God"?[62] A similar bipolarity is even more pronounced in the postconciliar period. For example, the Vatican's *Dialogue and Proclamation* speaks of interreligious dialogue as "truly part of the dialogue of salvation initiated by God" (no. 80); dialogue "implies reciprocity and aims at banishing fear and aggressiveness" (no. 83). *Dominus Iesus*, by contrast, asserts: "If it is true that the followers of other religions can receive divine grace, it is also certain that *objectively speaking* they are in a gravely deficient situation in comparison with those who, in the Church, have the fullness of the means of salvation" (no. 22).[63]

While not resolving all the tensions, Vatican commissions and numerous episcopal conferences have promulgated significant documents that expand

61. Arthur Gilbert, *The Vatican Council and the Jews* (Cleveland: World, 1968), 215. In his judgment, such a bipolarity could not be maintained: "As the Church moves inevitably toward a fuller ecumenicity, a more profound dialogue with non-Christians, and a more active involvement in the world, laggards will fall in the breach or change their direction" (215).

62. See Carol Ann Martinelli, "'People of God' in Selected Vatican II and post–Vatican II Documents" (PhD diss., University of St. Michael's College, 2002).

63. CDF, Declaration "Dominus Iesus," http://www.vatican.va/roman_curia/congregations/cfaith/documents/rc_con_cfaith_doc_20000806_dominus-iesus_en.html, emphasis original. Vatican II spoke of elements in the religious tradition of non-Christians that encompass "elements which are true and good" (*LG* no.16). *Ad gentes*, the Decree on the Church's Missionary Activity, exhorts missionaries to take cognizance of the "traditions of asceticism and contemplation" that are "sown by God" (no. 18); they will find "elements of truth and grace" manifesting a "secret presence of God" (no. 9), "seeds of the Word" (nos. 11 and 15). On May 19, 1991, the Pontifical Council for Interreligious Dialogue issued *Dialogue and Proclamation*; on August 6, 2000, the CDF issued *Dominus Iesus*. *Dialogue and Proclamation* has its own "bipolarity of tendencies"; see *Redemption and Dialogue: Reading* Redemptoris Missio *and Dialogue and Proclamation*, ed. William Burrows (Maryknoll, NY: Orbis, 1993); and Mark Plaiss, "Dialogue and Proclamation a Decade Later: A Retreat?" *Journal of Ecumenical Studies* 38 (2001): 191–95. See Stephen J. Pope and Charles C. Hefling, eds., *Sic et Non: Encountering* Dominus Iesus (Maryknoll, NY: Orbis, 2002); and Terrence Tilley, "Christian Orthodoxy and Religious Pluralism," *Modern Theology* 22 (2006): 51–63; he and Gavin D'Costa exchanged views in *Modern Theology* 23 (2007): 435–68.

and refine *NA*. These include three instructions from the Commission on Religious Relations with the Jews (CRRJ), established in October 1974: *Guidelines* (1974); *Notes* (1985); and *We Remember* (1988).[64] In the United States various committees and secretariats of the US Conference of Catholic Bishops issued teaching documents on how to preach or dramatize potentially anti-Jewish texts (*God's Mercy Endures Forever* and *Criteria for the Evaluation of Dramatizations of the Passion*, both in 1988).[65]

Complementing this documentary trajectory has been the establishment of numerous institutions and organizations committed to enhancing relations between Catholics and Jews. Many Catholic universities now have positions in Jewish studies. Further, some 20 Catholic institutions of higher education in the United States and Canada house a Jewish-Christian center of learning or holocaust study center.[66] These centers provide, in addition to public programs, opportunities for scholarly exchange, and contribute to the burgeoning scholarly literature on relations between Christians and Jews, including the online, peer-reviewed journal, *Studies in Christian-Jewish Relations*, published under the auspices of Boston College's Center for Christian-Jewish Learning. Moreover, religious textbooks have been revised to make *NA*'s teachings widely accessible.[67]

64. The full titles: *Guidelines and Suggestions for Implementing the Conciliar Declaration "Nostra Aetate" (n. 4)*; *Notes on the Correct Way to Present the Jews and Judaism in Preaching and Catechesis in the Roman Catholic Church*; *We Remember: A Reflection on the Shoah*. These documents are all available on the Vatican website and easily found by inserting the titles into an Internet search engine.

65. See, e.g., http://www.ccjr.us/dialogika-resources/documents-and-statements/roman-catholic. A recent anthology collects Protestant, Roman Catholic, ecumenical, and joint Christian-Jewish statements and provides commentary; see Franklin Sherman, ed., *Bridges: Documents of the Christian-Jewish Dialogue*, vol. 1, *The Road to Reconciliation, 1945–1985* (New York: Paulist, 2011); vol. 2 is forthcoming.

66. See the website of the Council of Centers on Jewish-Christian Relations, http://www.ccjr.us.

67. See John T. Pawlikowski, *Catechetics and Prejudice: How Catholic Teaching Materials View Jews, Protestants, and Racial Minorities* (New York: Paulist, 1973), which summarizes the findings of Rose Thering's 1961 doctoral dissertation; Claire Hutchet Bishop, *How Catholics Look at Jews: Inquiries into Italian, Spanish, and French Teaching Materials* (New York: Paulist, 1974); Eugene J. Fisher, *Faith without Prejudice: Rebuilding Christian Atttiudes toward Judaism* (New York: Paulist, 1977); Peter Fiedler, "Categories for a Correct Presentation of Jews and Judaism in Current Roman Catholic Religious Teaching," *Journal of Ecumenical Studies* 21 (1984): 470 –88; and Philip A. Cunningham, *Education for Shalom: Religion Textbooks and the Enhancement of the Catholic and Jewish Relationship* (Philadelphia: American Interfaith Institute, 1995).

What, then, are the "bipolarities" regarding the interpretation of *NA* and the ecclesial documents intended to facilitate its implementation? Debate around the following four questions highlights key tensions and exposes significant differences between the USCCB and theologians of the Catholic-Jewish relationship: (1) Is God still covenanted with the people Israel, and with what implications? (2) Does the language of promise-fulfillment imply that the promises to Israel are fulfilled only in Christ? (3) What is the mission of the Catholic Church with regard to the Jewish people? (4) What role should the largely "tormented history" vis-à-vis Jews play in a Catholic theology of relationship with Jews?[68] The first three questions are closely intertwined, as will be evident in the brief analyses that follow. Moreover, the extent to which one is affected by the church's historical relationship with Jews in part shapes one's response to the other three questions.

Covenant

The issue of covenant is multifaceted. In some theological quarters, whether or not Jews remain in a covenantal relationship since the coming of Christ is disputed. Further, differing biblical texts and hermeneutical principles are employed in the course of substantiating theological judgments. Review of the conciliar and postconciliar documents illustrates these differences.

Although *NA* does not directly address the question of Jewish covenantal status, its claim that the Jews remain "most dear to God" may be read as an implicit affirmation that God's covenant remains in effect. The 1974 *Guidelines* recommends that efforts be made to "acquire a better understanding of whatever in the Old Testament retains its own perpetual value (cf. *Dei Verbum*, 14–15), since that has not been canceled by the later interpretation of the New Testament." Presumably, that "perpetual value" exists for Jews as well as for Catholics. *Guidelines* also speaks of the "continuity of our faith with that of the earlier Covenant. . . . We believe that those promises were fulfilled with the first coming of Christ. But it is nonetheless true that we still await their perfect fulfillment in his glorious return at the end of time" (part II). Thus, *Guidelines* suggests that fulfillment be regarded eschatologically.

68. The third section of *We Remember: A Reflection on the Shoah* begins: "The history of relations between Jews and Christians is a tormented one" (http://www.ccjr.us/dialogika-resources/documents-and-statements/roman-catholic/vatican-curia/278-we-remember).

Pope John Paul II added significant commentary on the phrase "perpetual value of the Old Testament" in his assertion in 1980 that Jews are the "people of God of the Old Covenant, never revoked by God." In that same speech, he referred to Judaism as "a living heritage, which must be understood and *preserved in its depth and richness* by us Catholic Christians" (emphasis added).[69] Over the years, the pope's wording has assumed greater importance, as is evident by its inclusion in the 1985 *Notes*. In addition, the iconic moments associated with his papacy—embracing Rabbi Elio Toaff in the Rome Synagogue, inserting a prayer for forgiveness into the Western Wall, and meeting with Holocaust survivors at Yad Vashem—signal a high regard for Judaism as irrevocably covenanted with God.

Although the 1985 *Notes* does not speak explicitly about covenant, it does claim (sec. VI) that "the permanence of Israel is . . . a historic fact and a sign to be interpreted within God's design. . . . It remains a chosen people, 'the pure olive on which were grafted the branches of the wild olive which are the gentiles' (John Paul II, 6 March 1982, alluding to *Rom* 11:17–24)."

Seeking to build on these notions, a group of theologians and persons involved in Catholic ecumenical and interreligious work composed a brief study document in 2002, "Reflections on Covenant and Mission."[70] The authors took issue with what they viewed as a narrow construal of evangelization: inviting persons with whom one is engaged in interreligious dialogue to faith in Christ, and thus to baptism and the church. Rather, they argued, inviting the other to baptism is but one aspect of evangelization—and not appropriate in interreligious dialogue. Catholics engaged in such dialogue are involved in "a mutually enriching sharing of gifts devoid of

69. The text of the pope's 1980 address in Mainz, Germany, is published in *Spiritual Pilgrimage*, ed. Eugene J. Fisher and Leon Klenicki (New York: Crossroad, 1995), 13–15, at 15. See also *Notes* I.3.

70. This statement grew out of consultations among delegates of the USCCB's Committee on Ecumenical and Interreligious Affairs and of the National Council of Synagogues. "Reflections on Covenant and Mission" has two sections, one authored by the Jewish working group, the other authored by a Catholic group. The latter included staff persons from the Committee on Ecumenical and Interreligious Affairs and other USCCB offices, members of the Advisory Committee for the Secretariat, and Cardinal William Keeler. In the interests of full disclosure, I was a member of that working group. It is inaccurate, however, to assign authorship simply to John Pawlikowski, Philip Cunningham, and me (see John Connelly, "The Catholic Church and Mission to the Jews," in *After Vatican II: Trajectories and Hermeneutics*, 96–133, at 117. See also John Borelli, "Troubled Waters," *America* 202, no. 5 [February 22, 2010]: 20–23).

any intention whatsoever to invite the dialogue partner to baptism." This witness to their faith is indeed a dimension of evangelization because it is a "way of engaging in the Church's mission."[71]

Citing Cardinal Walter Kasper, then president of the CRRJ, "Covenant and Mission" continued: "God's grace, which is the grace of Jesus Christ according to our faith, is available to all. Therefore, the Church believes that Judaism, i.e., the faithful response of the Jewish people to God's irrevocable covenant, is salvific for them, because God is faithful to his promises."[72] It thus follows that "Jews already dwell in a saving covenant with God." Even if Jewish witness to God's reign did not originate with the church's experience of "Christ crucified and raised," it should not be "curtailed" by seeking to convert Jews to Christianity. "The distinctive Jewish witness must be sustained if Catholics and Jews are truly to be, as Pope John Paul II has envisioned, 'a blessing to one another.' "[73]

This document elicited a sharp critique from the late Jesuit theologian and cardinal Avery Dulles, who became the most prominent critic of the notion that Jews remained covenanted with God. Dulles believed the council had left open the question of whether the Old Covenant remained valid. Taking issue with *NA*'s use of Romans 9–11 as its scriptural grounding, Dulles countered that the Letter to the Hebrews should instead be regarded as "the most formal statement on the status of the Sinai covenant under Christianity." Hebrews, he argued, "points out that in view of the new covenant promised by God through the prophet Jeremiah, the first covenant is 'obsolete' and 'ready to vanish away' (Heb. 8:13). The priesthood and the law have changed (Heb 7:12). Christ, we are told, 'abolishes the first [covenant] in order to establish the second (Heb 10:9)."[74]

71. Text available at http://www.bc.edu/dam/files/research_sites/cjl/texts/cjrelations /resources/documents/interreligious/ncs_usccb120802.htm.

72. Ibid.

73. Ibid. See also Eugene B. Korn and John T. Pawlikowski, eds., *Two Faiths, One Covenant? Jewish and Christian Identity in the Presence of the Other* (Lanham, MD: Rowman & Littlefield, 2005); and Peter A. Pettit, "Covenants Old and New," in *Covenantal Conversations: Christians in Dialogue with Jews and Judaism*, ed. Darrell Jodock (Minneapolis: Fortress, 2008), 26–41.

74. Avery Dulles, "Covenant and Mission," *America* 187, no. 12 (October 21, 2002): 8–11, http://www.americamagazine.org/content/article.cfm?article_id=2550&comments=1#readcomments. Philip A. Cunningham deals at length with what he terms the "minimalist reading" of Dulles's interpretation of *NA*; see "Official Ecclesial Documents to Implement Vatican II on Relations with Jews: Study Them, Become Immersed in Them, and Put Them into Practice," *Studies in Christian-Jewish Relations* 4 (2009):

Dulles was not alone in his critique, as is evident in my next section on promise and fulfillment.

Promise and Fulfillment

Questions about the status of the covenant are related to how one understands fulfillment. Although *Notes* says that promise and fulfillment "throw light on each other" (sec. I), the document moves only in the direction of a one-way road: how the Old Testament prepares for the New. Its emphasis lies on the unity of biblical revelation and of the divine plan, particularly through typology as the traditional method through which the church has held the Testaments together. The Exodus, for example, should be interpreted as an "experience of salvation and liberation that is not complete in itself, but . . . has the capacity to be developed further." Indeed, "salvation and liberation are already accomplished in Christ and gradually realized by the sacraments in the Church. This makes way for the fulfillment of God's design" (sec. II).

Notes, however, does hint at problems with the conventional presentation of promise-fulfillment, asserting: "Typology, however, makes many people uneasy and is perhaps the sign of a problem unresolved." Strangely, it provides no explicit indication of what might stir this unease, although it does distinguish between Christian and Jewish readings of the Old Testament (sec. II) and reiterates that the Old Testament retains its own revelatory value (sec. II). Overall, however, *Notes* works along the traditional lines of salvation history in which the promises to the people Israel are fulfilled in Christ and the church.[75] Even as it speaks of Jews as remaining a chosen people, and of Judaism's "continuous spiritual fecundity," the document undercuts its own claims: God has chosen the Jews "to prepare for the coming of Christ"; they have "preserved everything that was progressively revealed and given in the course of that preparation, notwithstanding their difficultly in recognizing in Him their Messiah" (sec. I). By continuing to define Jews according to a hermeneutic of promise and fulfillment, *Notes* ties "Judaism to a procrustean bed of theological

1–36, http://ejournals.bc.edu/ojs/index.php/scjr/issue/view/130. Biblical scholars see Hebrews through a lens quite different from Dulles's; see especially Jesper Svartvik, "Reading the Epistle to the Hebrews without Presupposing Supersessionism," in *Christ Jesus and the Jewish People Today*, 77–91.

75. See Bradford E. Hinze, "The End of Salvation History," *Horizons* 18 (1991): 227–45; and Mary C. Boys, *Biblical Interpretation in Religious Education: A Study of the Kerygmatic Era* (Birmingham, AL: Religious Education, 1980).

suppositions. By implication Judaism is presented as a failed religion. Judaism fails to save its adherents, fails to understand its Scriptures, fails to accept its Messiah."[76] Ironically, *Notes* ignores an important principle expressed in the earlier *Guidelines*: Christians must "strive to acquire a better knowledge of the basic components of the religious tradition of Judaism; *they must strive to learn by what essential traits Jews define themselves in the light of their own religious experience*" (Preamble, emphasis added).[77] Even this important principle reveals a problem, since Jews do not define themselves solely in terms of religion. This difference between Jewish and Christian self-definition compounds the complex nexus of issues concerning the Land and State of Israel.[78]

Progress in transcending the linear understanding of fulfillment and in manifesting a sensitivity to Jewish self-definition is apparent in the PBC's 2001 monograph, *The Jewish People and Their Sacred Scriptures in the Christian Bible*.[79] The PBC argues that fulfillment is an "extremely complex" notion that can be distorted when one overemphasizes either continuity or discontinuity. Christianity recognizes Christ as the fulfillment of the Scriptures and of Israel's hopes, but it does not "understand this fulfillment as a literal one," because "Jesus is not confined to playing an already fixed role— that of Messiah—but he confers, on the notions of Messiah and salvation, a fullness which could not have been imagined in advance" (II.A.5).

Reading the Old Testament as Christians, the PBC instructs, involves "retrospective re-readings" (II.A.6). One finds there neither direct reference to Christ nor to Christian realities. Rather, the Christian reading is a *theological interpretation* that must be complemented by historical-critical exegesis:

76. Judith Banki and Alan L. Mittelman, "Why the 'Notes' Were Disappointing—Jews and Catholics: Taking Stock," *Commonweal* 112, no. 15 (September 6, 1985): 463–68, at 467.

77. *Notes* speaks of the "urgency and importance of precise, objective and rigorously accurate teaching on Judaism for our faithful" (I.8), and confesses that "there is evident in particular a painful ignorance of the history and traditions of Judaism, of which only negative aspects and often caricature seem to form part of the stock ideas of many Christians" (Conclusion).

78. See Ruth Langer, "Theologies of the Land and State of Israel," *Studies in Jewish-Christian Relations* 3 (2008): 1–17, http://escholarship.bc.edu/scjr/vol3. Israel may well be the most difficult issue in current relations between and among Jews and Christians—a topic deserving of its own essay.

79. At http://www.ccjr.us/dialogika-resources/documents-and-statements/roman-catholic/vatican-curia/282-pbc2001#5.%20The%20Unity%20of%20God%27s%20Plan%20and%20the%20Idea%20of%20Fulfilment.

> Although the Christian reader is aware that the internal dynamism of the Old Testament finds its goal in Jesus, this is a retrospective perception whose point of departure is not in the text as such, but in the events of the New Testament proclaimed by the apostolic preaching. It cannot be said, therefore, that Jews do not see what has been proclaimed in the text, but that the Christian, in the light of Christ and in the Spirit, discovers in the text a surplus of meaning that was hidden there (II.A.6).

The PBC draws an important conclusion from its argument about fulfillment as involving a "retrospective re-reading":

> Christians can and ought to admit that the Jewish reading of the Bible is a possible one, in continuity with the Jewish Sacred Scriptures from the Second Temple period, a reading analogous to the Christian reading which developed in parallel fashion. Each of these two readings is part of the vision of each respective faith of which it is a product and an expression. Consequently, they cannot be reduced one into the other (II.A.7).

Yet, recent editorial decisions at the USCCB fail to incorporate even the insights of *Guidelines* and *Notes*, let alone those of the PBC document. An example may be seen in a change made to *The United States Catholic Catechism for Adults*. Published in 2006, it initially included the following statement about the relations of the Jewish people to Catholicism: The call of Abraham "began the history of God's revealing his divine plan of salvation to a chosen people with whom he made *enduring* covenants. Thus the covenant that God made with the Jewish people through Moses *remains eternally valid for them*."[80] In 2008, however, the US bishops voted to replace the claim about the covenant's eternal validity with a citation from Paul: "To the Jewish people, whom God first chose to hear his word, 'belong the sonship, the glory, the covenants, the giving of the law, the worship and the promises; to them belong the patriarchs, and of their race, according to the flesh, is the Christ' (Rom 9:4–5; cf. CCC [*Catechism of the Catholic Church*], no. 839)."[81]

This seemingly minor edit becomes more problematic in view of the rationale provided by two spokesmen. According to the then-general secretary of the USCCB, Msgr. David Malloy:

> Catholics understand that all previous covenants that God made with the Jewish people have been fulfilled in Jesus Christ through the new

80. *The United States Catholic Catechism for Adults* (Washington, DC: USCCB, 2006), 131, emphasis added.

81. At http://old.usccb.org/mr/mediatalk/backgrounder_recognitio.shtml.

> covenant established through his sacrificial death on the cross. The prior version of the text might be understood to imply that one of the former covenants imparts salvation without the mediation of Christ, whom Christians believe to be the universal savior of all people.[82]

Similarly, the then-executive director of the Secretariat for Ecumenical and Interreligious Affairs of the USCCB, Rev. James Massa, a former doctoral student of Avery Dulles, said the change was intended to remove ambiguity. Massa stated that while church teaching affirms that Jews are "in a real relationship with God based on a covenant that has never been revoked," nevertheless, "all covenants with Israel find fulfillment in Christ, who is savior of all."[83]

The refusal to teach that God's covenant with Jews is "eternally valid" constitutes a "cloud on the horizon of Jewish-Catholic relations," according to Jesuit New Testament scholar John Donahue. The editorial change, he says, obscures the eschatological context of Romans and presages "disturbing developments that may make future dialogue less fruitful":

> In removing the original wording of the *Catholic Catechism for Adults*, are the ambiguity and stimulus to reflection evoked by the phrase "covenant never revoked" qualified or are they nullified? Unless cited elsewhere, Pope John Paul II's strong statement will never be read in the revised catechism. . . . The toning down of the strong statements of John Paul II on "the covenant never revoked" " may herald a return to a discredited supersessionism, one that ultimately disregards the past and continuing action of God among the Jewish people.[84]

82. Citation from the Catholic News Service story, "Bishops Vote to Change U.S. Catechism on Jewish Covenant with God" (August 12, 2008), http://www.usccb.org/stories/bishops_vote_catec.shtml. In March 2012, Malloy was appointed the bishop of the Diocese of Rockford, Illinois.

83. Ibid. Gavin D'Costa, in arguing for the theological legitimacy of a mission to the Jews, asserts that in principle fulfillment avoids both abrogation of Judaism and supersessionism; it "thus provides the argumentative link for why mission pertains to the Jews, who are still especially favored by God and to whom revelation has been granted in the Old Testament." It is not clear, however, how this is the case. See his "What Does the Catholic Church Teach about Mission to the Jewish People?" *Theological Studies* 73 (2012): 590–613, at 604. Because this issue of *TS* includes two essays that challenge D'Costa's arguments, I have chosen not to focus on his essay. See Edward Kessler, "A Jewish Response to Gavin D'Costa," ibid., 614–28; and John T. Pawlikowski, "A Catholic Response to Gavin D'Costa," ibid., 629–40.

84. John R. Donahue, "Trouble Ahead? The Future of Jewish-Catholic Relations," *Commonweal* 136, no. 5 (March 13, 2009): 19–23.

Indeed, ambiguity seems to be a problem for the USCCB, as may be seen in the June 2009 "A Note on Ambiguities Contained in *Reflections on Covenant and Mission*." In their critique of the study document, the Committee on Doctrine and the Committee on Ecumenical and Interreligious Affairs asserts that it is "incomplete and potentially misleading . . . to refer to the enduring quality of the covenant without adding that for Catholics Jesus Christ as the incarnate Son of God fulfills both in history and in the end of time the special relationship God established with Israel" (no. 5).[85] They continue, quoting Vatican II's *Dei verbum* no. 15: "'The principal purpose to which the plan of the old covenant was directed was to prepare for the coming of Christ, the redeemer of all and of the messianic kingdom, to announce this coming by prophecy, and to indicate its meaning through various types'" (no. 5).

In their aspiration to be unambiguous, the bishops here are either unacquainted with or reject the PBC's argument that fulfillment is "extremely complex." Further, the insistence in "Note on Ambiguities" that Christ fulfills the Scriptures stands in tension with the PBC's interpretation that such a claim should be seen as an element of a Christian retrospective rereading, not a literal claim. Rather than wrestle with how to communicate a more nuanced and complex understanding that has developed among biblical scholars and scholars of the Catholic-Jewish relationship, they simply reiterate and insist on a timeworn formulation.[86] A similar tension is evident in the question of mission.

Mission

In their June 2009 "Note on Ambiguities," the bishops criticized the claim that interreligious dialogue should be understood as a "mutually enriching sharing of gifts devoid of any intention whatsoever to invite the dialogue

85. USCCB, "A Note on Ambiguities Contained in *Reflections on Covenant and Mission*," http://old.usccb.org/doctrine/covenant09.pdf. See the news release issued by the USCCB's Office of Communication shortly after the 2002 release of "Reflections on Covenant and Mission," in which Cardinal Keeler is quoted as saying that the document "presents the state of thought among the participants of a dialogue that has been going on for a number of years between the U.S. Catholic Church and the Jewish community in this country" (http://www.ccjr.us/dialogika-resources/documents-and-statements/interreligious/bceia-ncs/1092-ncs-bceianews2002aug16).

86. See Ralph W. Klein, "Promise and Fulfillment," in *Contesting Texts: Jews and Christians in Conversations about the Bible*, ed. Melody D. Knowles et al. (Minneapolis: Fortress, 2007), 47–66.

partner to baptism."[87] While the bishops agreed that Catholics participating in interreligious dialogue would not normally explicitly invite their dialogue partners to be baptized and join the church, yet "the Christian dialogue partner is always giving witness to the following of Christ, *to which all are implicitly invited*."[88] This formulation raised immediate concern in American Jewish circles; within two months, five major Jewish agencies collaborated in sending a letter of concern. So too did others experienced in Catholic-Jewish dialogue.[89] In response, five members of the USCCB said that some Catholics and Jews had "misinterpreted" their "Note on Ambiguities." Nevertheless, they indicated they would excise that sentence so as to "address the concerns you and others have raised about the relationship between dialogue and witness." Thus, in the October 2009 revised "Note on Ambiguities," the bishops appended a "Statement of Principles for Catholic-Jewish Dialogue," including the assertion that this dialogue "has never been and will never be used by the Catholic Church as a means of proselytism—nor is it intended as a disguised invitation to baptism."[90]

The bishops also repeated the claim that Jesus Christ "fulfills in himself all of God's promises and covenants with the people of Israel."[91]

The bishops, "acting in harmony with the Pope," also reserve authoritative representation of Catholic belief to themselves. The work of theologians makes "an invaluable contribution to interreligious dialogue," but the bishops "have a responsibility to our Jewish partners to distinguish for them when a statement refers to Church teaching and when it is a theological opinion of scholars."[92] Since, however, the bishops have ignored the more nuanced understandings evident in postconciliar documents, their division between church teaching and the (mere) theological opinion of scholars is problematic.

87. USCCB, "Reflections on Covenant and Mission," August 12, 2002.

88. Ibid., emphasis added.

89. The leadership team of the Sisters of Sion, the Council of Centers for Christian-Jewish Relations, and the International Council of Christians and Jews were among those expressing disagreement with the suggestion that interreligious dialogue includes an implicit invitation to the following of Christ.

90. This is the third of six principles issued in October 2009, "Statement of Principles for Catholic-Jewish Dialogue," http://www.ccjr.us/dialogika-resources/documents-and-statements/roman-catholic/us-conference-of-catholic-bishops/584-usccbdialogue09oct2. The statement was issued by Cardinals Francis George and William Keeler, Archbishop Wilton Gregory, and Bishops William Lori and William Murphy.

91. Ibid. This is taken from the second of the six principles.

92. Ibid. This is based on the fourth of the six principles.

One wonders what the bishops would say to Johann Baptist Metz: "Ask yourselves if the theology you are learning is such that it could remain unchanged before and after Auschwitz. If this be the case, be on your guard."[93]

Facing History

In their monograph, *The Jewish People and Their Sacred Scriptures*, the PBC acknowledges the imperative of post-Shoah theology: "The horror in the wake of the extermination of the Jews (the *Shoah*) during the Second World War has led all the Churches to rethink their relationship with Judaism and, as a result, to reconsider their interpretation of the Jewish Bible, the Old Testament."[94] Unlike the authors of the 1985 *Notes* who declared that catechesis should "help in understanding the *meaning for Jews* of the extermination during the years 1939–1945, and its consequences" (sec. VI, emphasis added), the PBC acknowledges that the Shoah necessitates Christian rethinking of its relationship with Judaism. Yet here too the bipolar tendencies are evident.

Three years before the promulgation of PBC's monograph, the CRRJ released its own reflection on the Shoah, *We Remember*.[95] The horrors of this genocide, the CRRJ said, cannot be measured by ordinary criteria of historical research but must become the subject of moral and religious reflection. Unfortunately, the document distorts the historical record and obfuscates the extent of the church's complicity both in the Shoah itself and in the long centuries of the "teaching of contempt," as a considerable literature attests.[96] Despite the document's significant shortcomings, it nevertheless expresses, at times quite eloquently, a deep sorrow "for the

93. Johann Baptist Metz, *Emergent Church*, trans. Peter Mann (New York: Crossroad, 1981), 29.

94. *The Jewish People and Their Sacred Scriptures in the Christian Bible* II.A.7. While *NA* makes no specific reference to the Holocaust, the preamble to the *Guidelines* situates *NA* in "circumstances deeply affected by the memory of the persecution and massacre of Jews which took place in Europe."

95. See Secretariat for Ecumenical and Interreligious Relations, National Conference of Catholic Bishops, *Catholics Remember the Holocaust* (Washington, DC: USCC, 1998) 47–55. This edition complements the statement of the Holy See by including statements of other episcopal conferences, including the more forthright 1977 "Declaration of Repentance" by the bishops of France.

96. See John T. Pawlikowski, "The Vatican and the Holocaust: Putting 'We Remember' in Context," *Dimensions* 12, no. 2 (1998): 11–16; Michael Phayer, "Pope Pius XII, the Holocaust and the Cold War," *Holocaust and Genocide Studies* 12, no. 2 (1998): 233–56; Randolph L. Braham, "Remembering and Forgetting: The Vatican, the German Hierarchy, and the Holocaust," *Holocaust and Genocide Studies* 13, no. 2 (1999):

failures of her sons and daughters in every age" and a summons to repentance (*teshuvah*): "The Church approaches with deep respect and great compassion the experience of extermination, the *Shoah*, suffered by the Jewish people during World War II. It is not a matter of mere words, but indeed of binding commitment."[97]

But what is the nature of the church's repentance?[98] What might it mean to take responsibility, morally and religiously, for our "tormented history" with the Jewish people? Let me suggest three dimensions of the church's *teshuvah*: facing this history, engaging in a rigorous theological examination of what the church is teaching about Judaism in the course of teaching about the Christian life, and incorporating the scholarship that has emerged from Christian-Jewish dialogue.

To face our history means being affected by the wounds Christianity has inflicted on the Jewish people throughout the centuries. This requires a willingness to be attentive to disturbing truths about one's own tradition—a vulnerability that refuses defensiveness in the face of disquieting truths. For this we need the virtue of humility, as Elizabeth Groppe writes. Drawing on Augustine's *Confessions*, she suggests that human pride (*superbia*) is a fundamental misdirection of human desire. Augustine believed that the antidote to pride was God's love as mediated by the humility of the crucified Christ; Christ is the *medicus humilis*, the doctor of humility. Yet while walking the streets of Jerusalem in 2007 in the company of Jewish and Muslim scholars, Groppe muses about what the Bishop of Hippo would say of a "history in which *crucesignati* (crusaders, those signed by the cross) murder Jews in an archbishop's palace [in Mainz in 1096] and kill Muslim women and children seeking sanctuary in a mosque [Jerusalem's al-Aqsa mosque in 1099]." Such atrocities mean that the cross that served for Augustine as such a meaningful symbol of humility has today become a symbol associated with Christian violence. In response, she suggests, we follow Augustine in practicing theology in the mode of confession. Further, we need to scrutinize Christian teaching and worship

---

222–51; and Kevin Madigan, "A Survey of Jewish Reaction to the Vatican Statement on the Holocaust," *Cross Currents* 50 (2000): 488–505.

97. NCCB, *Catholics Remember the Holocaust*, 72. In a March 2000 service of repentance in St. Peter's Basilica, Pope John Paul II and various Vatican officials offered prayers that explicitly named sins committed by members of the church. These sins included causing Jewish suffering, violation of the rights of ethnic groups and peoples, failure to acknowledge women's equality, and intolerance.

98. See Bradford E. Hinze, "Ecclesial Repentance and the Demands of Dialogue," *Theological Studies* 61 (2000): 207–38.

to discern whether they "contain elements that may legitimate or even sacralize humiliation and violence."[99]

Precisely because Christian identity is linked to Judaism, shallow or uninformed depictions of Judaism distort Christian self-understanding. Particularly after the Shoah, Christians are obliged to replace the "teaching of contempt" with educational materials that accurately represent Judaism. Again, a recent publication from the USCCB fails to engage postconciliar texts that present a more adequate understanding of Judaism. The section on Judaism in the 2008 *Doctrinal Elements of a Curriculum Framework for the Development of Catechetical Materials for Young People of High School Age* provides a striking case in point. Intended to provide guidance for the doctrinal content in Catholic secondary education, this 53-page manual, written in the form of sentence outlines, includes a section on the relationship of the Catholic Church to the Jewish people. While it notes that the church has a special link with the Jewish people, many propositions lack critical nuance. For example, the manual claims that the "Jewish people are the original Chosen People of God; Christians are the new People of God."[100] The sentence implies that Christians have replaced Jews as God's people. Granted, *NA* makes a similar assertion, but given the rich scholarship in the postconciliar years, simply to retain its formulation is highly problematic, if not irresponsible.[101] Similarly, the document states that the "New Covenant with Jesus Christ is the fulfillment of the promises of the first Covenant between God and the Jewish people." After these claims, the document limns two fundamental differences between Judaism and Catholicism: (1) Jews "do not acknowledge Jesus as a Divine Person, the Son of God, or the promised Messiah, nor do they accept the revealed truth of the Triune God, which is what is unique to Christian Revelation"; (2) Jews have "no sacramental economy; they continue to rely on the ritual prescriptions of the first Covenant reinterpreted for post-Temple Judaism."[102]

Passed over in silence is any sense of the "continuous spiritual fecundity" spoken of in the *Notes*. A simplistic promise-fulfillment schema is promulgated without any sense of the concept of "retrospective rereading,"

99. Elizabeth Groppe, "After Augustine: Humility and the Search for God in Historical Memory," in *Learned Ignorance: Intellectual Humility among Jews, Christians, and Muslims* (New York: Oxford University, 2011), 191–209, at 200, 202.

100. *Doctrinal Elements* 51, http://old.usccb.org/education/framework.pdf. This assertion cites the *Catechism of the Catholic Church* (1994): no. 840.

101. See Elizabeth T. Groppe, "Revisiting Vatican II's Theology of the People of God after Forty Years of Catholic-Jewish Dialogue," *Theological Studies* 72 (2011): 586–619.

102. *Doctrinal Elements*, 52.

as the PCB instructed. The writers leave no theological space for the Jewish people today. Drawing only on the *Catechism of the Catholic Church*, they make no reference whatsoever to *NA*, to the 1974 *Guidelines*, to the 1985 *Notes*, or to the formulations of the PBC's *The Jewish People and their Sacred Scriptures* (2001). To assert that Jews lack a "sacramental economy" reveals a sort of Catholic narcissism in which the "other" is viewed only in accord with one's own framework. Similarly, the caricature of Jewish worship as a reliance on ritual prescriptions of the Old Testament reveals an astonishing ignorance of Jewish liturgy.[103]

Doctrinal Elements does admit that anti-Judaism or antisemitism "was evident among Catholics for many centuries," but it provides neither a definition of the terms nor any sense of what befell Jews because of the "teaching of contempt." Immediately following that admission, the document states that the Catholic Church condemns "all unjust discrimination," including antisemitism, but makes no reference to the church's anti-Jewish teachings and complicity in antisemitism. Further: "In the twentieth century, the Catholic Church dropped from its liturgy any inference that the Jewish people as a whole were responsible for the Death of Christ *because the truth is that the sins of all humanity were the cause of his Death*" (emphasis added). This is specious; *NA* no. 4 was not composed because the conciliar participants wanted to revive a classic teaching about the death of Jesus, but because the deicide charge had proven tragic for Jews.

Finally, *Doctrinal Elements* includes a number of points about dialogue with Jews, listing four aims: mutual respect, common witness on issues of peace and justice, mutual understanding of the one God, and conversion ("bring all to Jesus Christ and to his Church").[104] Thus, the USCCB has endorsed conversion as one of the goals of dialogue. So much for the eschatological vision of *NA* no. 4 that the church "awaits the day, known to God alone, when all peoples will call on God with one voice and serve him shoulder to shoulder (Zeph 3:9)."

The dependence on the *Catechism of the Catholic Church* rather than on the postconciliar documents that develop and refine *NA* is particularly problematic, because a supersessionist perspective pervades the *Catechism*. For example, it calls the OT divinely inspired and says its books retain

103. See the excellent six-volume series, "Two Liturgical Traditions," including vol. 4, *Life Cycles in Jewish and Christian Worship*, ed. Paul F. Bradshaw and Lawrence A. Hoffman (Notre Dame, IN: University of Notre Dame, 1995).

104. This last aim cites Romans 11:12, 15, 25; and the *Catechism of the Catholic Church* nos. 674, 1043.

a permanent value, "for the Old Covenant has never been revoked" (no. 121). Yet many other passages suggest that Judaism is obsolete. A simplistic salvation history schema is evident in the claim that God "makes everything converge on Christ: all the ritual and sacrifices, figures and symbols of the 'First Covenant' " (no. 522). Further, "all the Old Covenant prefigurations find their fulfillment in Christ Jesus" (no. 1223). Some passages seem to suggest that Israel's infidelity has led to the end of the Old Covenant: "But the prophets accuse Israel of breaking the covenant and behaving like a prostitute. They announce a new and eternal covenant. 'Christ instituted this New Covenant' " (no. 762). Even Passover and Shabbat, so central to Jewish identity, are presented as fulfilled in Jesus: "By celebrating the Last Supper with his apostles in the course of the Passover meal, Jesus gave the Jewish Passover its definitive meaning" (no. 1340). "The Sabbath, which represents the completion of the first creation, has been replaced by Sunday, which recalls the new creation inaugurated by the Resurrection of Christ" (no. 2190).

Overall, the *Catechism* manifests a reluctance to draw on the biblical scholarship that situates the ministry of Jesus in the context of Second Temple Judaism. Thus its authors draw sharp contrasts between Jesus and his contemporaries (no. 576), ignore the complexities of the "partings of the ways," and recycle the stereotypical portrayal of the "extreme religious zeal" of the Pharisees (no. 579).[105] In contrast, however, the documentary expansion and refinement of *NA* appears largely absent from the *Catechism*. Changes to the *Adult Catholic Catechism* reveal a narrow interpretation of ways in which Jesus Christ "fulfills" God's covenantal relation with Jews. It contradicts one of the most formative principles to emerge from the post-Vatican period, namely, Christians should learn how Jews define themselves.

According to the "Statement of Principles for Catholic-Jewish Dialogue" cited above, a catechism is a "compendium of the articles of faith, and

105. Ironically, the US bishops produced a brief monograph in 1988 that provides a more complex and nuanced portrait of the Pharisees; see *God's Mercy Endures Forever: Guidelines on the Presentation of Jews and Judaism in Catholic Preaching* (Washington, DC: USCC, 1988), nos. 17–20. Among the many studies on the Pharisees, see E. P. Sanders, *Judaism: Practice and Belief, 63 B.C.E.–66 C.E* (London: SCM, 1992); Anthony J. Saldarini, "Pharisees," in *Anchor Bible Dictionary*, vol. 5, ed. David Noel Freedman (New York: Doubleday, 1992), 289–303; Joseph Sievers, "Who Were the Pharisees?," in *Hillel and Jesus: Comparative Studies of Two Major Religious Leaders*, ed. James H. Charlesworth and Loren L. Johns (Minneapolis: Fortress, 1997), 138–53; John Meier, *A Marginal Jew*, vol. 3, *Companions and Competitors* (New York: Doubleday, 2001), 289–388; J. Patrick Mullen, *Dining with Pharisees* (Collegeville. MN: Liturgical Press, 2004).

therefore contains only settled teaching." Yet, what the bishops regard as "settled teaching" many scholars of the Catholic-Jewish relationship may view as "premature finality."[106] The "bipolarities of tendencies" that have characterized the reception of *NA* now seem resurgent.

Wherein lies the divide? It seems to lie first of all in the experience of dialogue, which provides an understanding and appreciation of the depths of Judaism that cannot readily be grasped at the level of abstract theologizing. This is evident in the substantive conversations with Jewish figures that led Karl Thieme and John Oesterreicher to turn away from their earlier desire to convert Jews. In the postconciliar era, these dialogical exchanges have given rise to close friendships and allowed Catholic participants to see Judaism through the eyes of learned and passionately committed Jews.[107] It seems inconceivable that those intensely involved in Catholic-Jewish relations could ever speak, as does D'Costa, of Jews as in a state of "inculpable ignorance."[108]

Second, the divide involves the realms of biblical and historical scholarship not as familiar to those writing episcopal statements and crafting catechetical documents. Recent developments in biblical studies offer a far more complex view of Second Temple Judaism and the Jewish Jesus than many recent church documents mirror. The "new perspective on Paul" portrays him as faithful to Judaism, committed to thinking theologically about the relationship of non-Jews to the God of Israel and about the relationship of Jewish and non-Jewish followers of Jesus.[109] Connelly's his-

106. Michael Barnes, a Jesuit scholar of the religions of India, aware that Christianity, particularly Catholicism, runs the risk of seeking a "premature finality," suggests that the experience of Christians learning how to relate to the religious other mirrors Christ facing death. In the language of Christian spirituality, interreligious encounter is an experience of the paschal mystery, a dying of self in order to live a transformed life (Barnes, *Theology and the Dialogue of Religions*, 59).

107. See James Fredericks, "Interreligious Friendship: A New Theological Virtue," *Journal of Ecumenical Studies* 35 (1998): 159–74.

108. D'Costa, "What Does the Catholic Church Teach about Mission to the Jewish People?," 600–601.

109. In brief, the origin of the "new perspectives on Paul" originated with the work of Krister Stendahl in the 1960s, and has been developed in various ways by E. P. Sanders and James D. G. Dunn, among others. See Krister Stendahl, *Paul among Jews and Gentiles, and Other Essays* (Philadelphia: Fortress, 1976); E. P. Sanders, *Paul and Palestinian Judaism: A Comparison of Patterns of Religion* (Philadelphia: Fortress, 1977); James D. G. Dunn, *The New Perspective on Paul*, rev. ed. (Tübingen: Mohr Siebeck, 2005). For a superb overview, see Magnus Zetterholm, *Approaches to Paul* (Minneapolis: Fortress, 2009).

torical research documents the evolution in thought by which the ultimate draft of *NA* no. 4 drew upon the eschatological vision of the prophet Zephaniah ("The Church awaits that day, known to God alone, on which all peoples will address the Lord in a single voice and 'serve him shoulder to shoulder' [Zeph 3:9])" in order to express the mystery of God's covenantal relations with both Jews and Christians. This decision of the drafters was immensely significant. Indeed, Connelly concludes: "A glance into the history of *Nostra Aetate* suggests that the controversies of recent years in Catholic-Jewish relations has been counterproductive and probably unnecessary. The essential thing that has been forgotten is that Catholic teaching does not obligate Christians to imagine Jews as Christians."[110]

A glimpse into Zephaniah's vision of the end time could be seen at the 2005 conference in Rome celebrating the 40th anniversary of *NA*. Hosted by the Pontifical Gregorian University, the participants included Buddhist scholars from Sri Lanka, Japan, and Turkey; Hindu scholars from India and the United States; Muslim scholars from Egypt, Lebanon, Malaysia, and Scotland; and Jewish and Christian (including Orthodox and Protestant) scholars from Europe, Israel, and North America. The presence of scholars, women as well as men, from diverse religious traditions engaging one another with respect, seriousness, and sensitivity was a true moment of interreligious hospitality. As the program read:

> With the promulgation of *Nostra Aetate* in 1965, the Catholic Church's highest teaching authority initiated a new and unaccustomed discourse in which the religious Other is greeted with respect and esteem, and is seen as a partner in dialogue and action. This positive inclusion of the Other in our official discourse has brought about a dramatic change in the Church's sense of itself, and it is this transformation of identities in dialogue on which we wish to focus in this conference. We reflect on the distance we have come together, and we celebrate it. At the same time we look to the future and map the more difficult paths we have yet to take if the dialogue of believers is not to remain simply an official policy practised by a few, but to become a key element of contemporary culture.[111]

110. Connelly, "Catholic Church and Mission to the Jews," 125. See also Mary C. Boys, "Does the Catholic Church Have a Mission 'with' or 'to' the Jews?," *Studies in Christian-Jewish Relations* 3 (2008): 1–19.

111. This introductory note, included in the conference program, was authored by Islamic scholar Daniel Madigan, SJ, then-director of the Gregorian's Institute for the Study of Religions and Cultures and now a professor at Georgetown University.

There we were, shoulder to shoulder. It was, of course, not yet "that day, known to God alone." Nevertheless, the participants bore witness that a conversion to the "providential mystery of otherness" had brought new life to the church in a way previously unimaginable.

Part 4

Reception of Vatican II

12 "After All, Africa Is Largely a Nonliterate Continent"

The Reception of Vatican II in Africa

AGBONKHIANMEGHE E. OROBATOR, SJ

The article examines critical factors that determined the impact, reception, and implementation of Vatican II in Africa. Drawing on historical accounts, the author identifies and analyzes personalities, contexts, and issues that conditioned and shaped Africa's participation in the council. Looking back 50 years, he argues that while the continent's participation was negligible, shaped by a combination of events and attitudes that either facilitated or hampered reception, concrete examples abound of how the council generated impetus for growth, renewal, and reform in inculturation, interreligious dialogue, theological reflection, and ecclesial collaboration in Africa.

Of Africa's role in the Second Vatican Council, Patrick Kalilombe, recently deceased theologian and bishop of Lilongwe, Malawi, wrote:

> The presence of Africa at Vatican II was marginal and by proxy. . . . Although technically and juridically the Church was no longer 'missionary,' it is hardly possible to imagine that the African Church counted very much as an influence on the Council. Apart from regular interventions from the principal spokesman, Cardinal L. Rugambwa, only sporadic voices were heard from Africa.
>
> It is obvious from an examination of the sixteen documents that the Council was largely a forum for the concerns of the Churches of Europe and America in the 1960s. . . .

> Africa's problems and preoccupations, therefore, came only indirectly: they did not determine the central perspective from which the Council's deliberations were moving. . . . Moreover, real acquaintance with the documents must not be exaggerated, even though efforts were made to publish them and diffuse their message widely in the African continent. . . . After all, Africa is largely a non-literate continent.[1]

The Context

To describe and assess the reception, impact, and implementation of the Second Vatican Council in Africa requires understanding the social and political context of the continent during the period of announcement, convocation, deliberation, and conclusion of the council (1959–1965). Viewed from the perspective of contemporary events in Africa, the council did not happen in a vacuum. "For the Catholic Church in Africa the vast internal revolution set in motion by Pope John more or less coincided with the political and cultural revolution of Independence."[2] Vatican II occurred at a momentous time in the history of Africa when nationalist tumult and agitation slowly and intensely rose to a combustible crescendo. During the conciliar years, that movement would culminate in precipitated transfer of political power from bewildered and beleaguered colonialists to exuberant and inexperienced African leaders.

Thus the religious excitement occasioned by the sudden announcement and convocation of the council coincided with the secular excitement over Africa's political emancipation. Symbolically, Pope John XXIII's radical objective of *aggiornamento* bore notable resemblance to aspirations for political independence in several African countries in the 1960s. In church as in secular society the promise of change and a future of hope struck a deep and optimistic resonance in the hearts and minds of Africans. This parallel movement offers a first clue to the impact of Vatican II in Africa:

> Probably in no other continent did the Vatican Council coincide quite so neatly and sympathetically with a major process of secular change as in Africa. . . . The conciliar themes of localization and pluralism, of the recognition of the positive values of different cultures and even

1. Patrick A. Kalilombe, "The Effect of the Council on World Catholicism: Africa," in *Modern Catholicism: Vatican II and After*, ed. Adrian Hastings (London: SPCK, 1991) 310–18, at 310–11.

2. Adrian Hastings, *A History of African Christianity, 1950–1975* (New York: Cambridge University, 1979), 167–68.

> other religious traditions, the new use of the vernacular in the liturgy, the ecumenical rapprochement, all this conformed with the general early 1960s' stress on African political and cultural values, on decolonization, on the social necessity of cooperation and unity across the division of tribe, race and religion.[3]

Yet this correlation of the promise and hope of Vatican II for the church and the wave of sociopolitical change in Africa needs to be critically examined before being adopted as the basis for analyzing and assessing Africa's reception of the council.

For setting this positive evaluation in context, two points are noteworthy. First, we may not overlook the fact that nationalism/independence and the conciliar event represented distinct interests and divergent preoccupations in Africa. Whereas the former interest was orchestrated by mission-bred and mission-educated Africans who hardly distinguished colonial adventure from missionary agenda, the latter interest was led by missionary ecclesiastics and clergy suspicious of the pulsating waves of political emancipation and self-determination. In the aftermath of independence, tension surfaced promptly between the missionary church and nascent political regimes around issues of schools, political system of one-party rule, and an elitist cast of ideologues eager to appropriate the spoils of independence.[4] Second, Adrian Hastings, to whom is credited these positive impressions of Vatican II in relation to Africa, wrote at a time much closer to the council and, as I will point out in this essay, from the perspective of arguably the most vigorous promoter and advocate of the directives of Vatican II. Much has transpired on the continent since then. Looking back 50 years, the temptation is strong to conclude that just as the promise and hope of political independence failed to deliver progress and development, so too did the *aggiornamento* of Vatican II become tepid in Africa.

This article examines some of the factors that have conditioned and shaped Africa's reception of Vatican II. It premises this exploration on the thesis that due to a complex interplay of personalities, attitudes, events, and contexts, what was heralded as a radical renewal and change in direction, or an *aggiornamento*, for the church has progressed along a checkered path on the African continent.

3. Adrian Hastings, "The Council Came to Africa," in *Vatican II: By Those Who Were There*, ed. Alberic Stacpoole (London: Geoffrey Chapman, 1986), 315–23, at 315–16.

4. Hastings, *History of African Christianity*, 151–52.

I begin by analyzing three primary factors that were determinant of Africa's role during the sessions of Vatican II. These factors fall under the broad categories of demography, ecclesiology, and theology. Following this analysis, I provide a concise account of the reception and principal achievement of Vatican II for the church in Africa—using appropriate examples—and indicate paths to the future inspired by the spirit of the council.

It is important to concede the spatial limitation of this analysis, focusing as it does primarily on eastern Africa—an option influenced largely by the relative scarcity of materials covering the entire continent of Africa. Besides, considering the characteristic diversity of the continent, any account of Vatican II's reception, impact, and implementation would be of necessity partial and offer only a basic overview.

Factors Influencing Africa's Participation at Vatican II

Counting Bodies and Weighing Voices

If we proceed from the assumption of the adage that *synodus episcoparum est*, we could perhaps form a preliminary impression of Vatican II and its impact on *ecclesia in Africa*. In the first place, African bishops constituted a small percentage of the overall composition of the council. The presence of Africa in terms of representation by so-called native bishops and ecclesial leaders was numerically insignificant. Besides the question of meager representation, an additional focal point of analysis is the influence that this minority had on the proceedings and outcomes of the council. It would not be an exaggeration to contend that none of the African bishops present at Vatican II had a major voice or played a decisive role, a factor routinely attributed to their unpreparedness in regard to the complex themes, documents, and conciliar process.[5] Those who had a major voice were expatriates either as Council Fathers or as *periti*.[6]

5. Albert de Jong, *The Challenge of Vatican II in East Africa: The Contribution of Dutch Missionaries to the Implementation of Vatican II in Tanzania, Kenya, Uganda, and Malawi, 1965–1975* (Nairobi: Paulines, 2004), 28; Hastings, *History of African Christianity*, 168.

6. It is important to note that African voices at the council raised issues of pertinence to the continent that unfortunately were not reflected in any of the final documents. An example of this was the matter of tribalism and "the feminist cause" reputedly championed at the council by Archbishop Malula of Kinshasa, DRC (formerly Leopoldville, Zaire). See Dennis Hurley, OMI, *Vatican II: Keeping the Dream Alive* (Pietermaritzburg, South Africa: Cluster, 2005), 105–6. On the whole, however, it would seem that the in-

Historical accounts of Africa's presence and participation at Vatican II identify some of the leading figures that flew the banner of the continent. Expectedly almost all of them were expatriates. One of the leading bishops at Vatican II from Africa was the charismatic and energetic Bishop Joseph Blomjous of Mwanza, Tanzania. Alongside was Bishop Vincent McCauley of Fort Portal, Uganda, variously characterized by Richard Gribble as a "driving force," "catalyst," and "spokesman" of the bishops from East Africa.[7] The insignificant participation of African-born bishops at the council seems confirmed by Dutch church historian Albert de Jong's claim that Dutch bishops ghostwrote the interventions of African bishops.[8] This claim, however, should not be generalized. Archbishop Denis Hurley's account of events at the council proffers some qualification of De Jong's assertion. While Hurley—himself a leading figure from Africa at the council—received help from some prominent European *periti*, his intervention reflected his authorship and his untiring appeal for a council that is pastoral in its approach to the issues of the day.[9] Yet, contrary to Hastings's contention that the participation and contribution of Africa was "not insignificant,"[10] the view held by Philippe Denis—and shared by Patrick Kalilombe noted above—is representative of the consensus among scholars regarding the influence of African bishops at Vatican II:

> Most observers agree, however, that the African bishops failed significantly to influence the work of the Council itself. The African representation—260 of a total 2,358 at the first session in 1962—had relatively little weight in the final outcome of the Council. The themes discussed were perceived as "too European" not only by the 61 African-born

tervention of African bishops was limited to pithy comments and reactions to particular issues. See, e.g., ibid., 108, 109, 129, 138. By far the most active in terms of number of oral interventions and written submissions at the council were Archbishop Dennis Hurley (Durban, South Africa) and the first African cardinal, Laurean Rugambwa (Bukoba, Tanzania). See Philippe Denis, "The Historical Significance of Hurley's Contribution to Vatican II," in Hurley, *Vatican II*, 207–8. That the voices of African bishops at Vatican II had limited impact or influence is further confirmed by the fact that no African bishop appears in John W. O'Malley's list of "Council Participants Frequently Mentioned" (*What Happened at Vatican II* [Cambridge, MA: Harvard University, 2008], 321–28).

7. Richard Gribble, *The Implementation of Vatican II in Eastern Africa: The Contribution of Bishop Vincent McCauley, CSC* (Lewiston, NY: Edwin Mellen, 2009), 70, 74.

8. De Jong, *Challenge of Vatican II in East Africa*, 30.

9. Hurley, *Vatican II* 30, 162–78.

10. Hastings, *History of African Christianity*, 173.

> bishops present at the opening of the Council, but also by the missionary bishops.[11]

Notwithstanding the numerical insignificance and theological unpreparedness of African Council Fathers, the accounts also concur in stressing that the modus operandi of African bishops was well organized and highly efficient during the conciliar sessions.[12] A minor but highly symbolic fact was the presence of a lay auditor from Togo, Eusebe Adjakpley.[13]

A Church in the Making

The second factor is ecclesiological. In the early 1960s, the church in Africa could hardly be qualified as "African." As the preceding point demonstrates, in terms of leadership and direction, the church in Africa prior to and during Vatican II represented a native outpost of a Eurocentric ecclesial organization. Understandably, therefore, the concerns of the universal church as outlined and debated at the council barely intersected with the pressing issues that the "young" churches in places like Africa had to contend with. Thus, as the conciliar drama unfolded in the aula, and European and North American ecclesiastical grandees fought running battles across doctrinal and ideological lines, African bishops watched with bemusement and fascination variously as spectators, cheerleaders, and voting bloc.[14]

African Theology en Route

The third and final point concerns the status of theology in Africa as local production. In the 1960s, African theology was still in its formative years. At the time of Vatican II the popular debate centered on the desirability, feasibility, and possibility of African theology as a viable discipline. Consequently, at this watershed event, Africa lacked the theological expertise and institutional capacity to engage the pertinent issues on Vatican II's

11. Denis, "Historical Significance of Hurley's Contribution," 197–98.

12. A firsthand account by Hurley corroborates the claim of organizational superiority of African bishops at the council: "The African Bishops had not wasted any time in getting themselves organised. South Africa had taken the lead in regard to the English-speaking African bishops and secured the use of a very convenient hall in a street off the Via della Conciliazione. . . . The African bishops got together in two groups, the Anglophone (i.e. English-speaking) and the Francophone (the French-speaking)" (Hurley, *Vatican II*, 23–24; see also O'Malley, *What Happened at Vatican II*, 122).

13. Hurley, *Vatican II*, 139.

14. O'Malley, *What Happened at Vatican II*, 291–95.

agenda. A telling illustration of this lacuna appears in the composition of the African delegation. Alongside the majority of expatriate bishops the corps of *periti* was exclusively European and North American.[15] Unlike "the bishops of the Western European bloc," the council's African contingent did not have "the advantage of this magnificent pool of theologians and also of Scripture scholars, historians, liturgical experts and prominent promoters of lay apostolates, social concern and catechetics."[16] Regrettable as this observation might seem at first sight, closer examination suggests that it contains a positive element in regard to the topic under consideration. It can be plausibly argued that to a large extent the impetus to develop an African theology came from Vatican II: "Vatican II brought to Africa a theology and a catechesis whose central themes showed how the power of Jesus Christ supplanted the power of local gods. This theology became concrete in the church's sacramental system where signs and words expressed initiation, maturity, healing, forgiving, and nourishment."[17]

The factors outlined above provide some evidence of the unpreparedness of the church in Africa for Vatican II. The cadre of ecclesial leadership and, much less, the body of the church in Africa were not prepared for the council.

Reception and Implementation

Richard McBrien defines reception as the "process by which the body of the faithful, or a significant portion thereof, accepts and abides by an official teaching or disciplinary decree of the hierarchical Church."[18] Reception, however, is not a straightforward process; in church history, councils have encountered objection, resistance, and rejection. Historian of church councils Norman Tanner notes that "other major councils, such as Nicea I or Chalcedon, had laboured receptions precisely because of the importance and challenging nature of their teaching. So too with Vatican II."[19]

As mentioned above, the event of Vatican II paralleled significant historic political events in Africa in the 1960s. The intersection of events

15. Hastings, "The Council Came to Africa," 316.

16. Hurley, *Vatican II*, 71–72.

17. Bede Jagoe, "Vatican II Comes to Africa," *Worship* 79 (2005): 544–54, at 548.

18. Richard P. McBrien, *The Church: The Evolution of Catholicism* (New York: HarperOne, 2008), 322.

19. Norman Tanner, "How Novel Was Vatican II?" *Asian Horizons* 6 (2012): 401–10, at 408.

held out fresh promise for church and society in Africa. "The fresh new breeze of *aggiornamento* and the new energy of the political and cultural revolutions in Eastern Africa made Vatican II quite acceptable to the African Church."[20] This assertion calls for a twofold qualification. First, it presupposes a homogeneous and established reality called the "*African* Church." At the time of the council, such a reality did not exist; at best, it was still in the making. Second, acceptability would have been limited to the hierarchy largely comprised of expatriate missionary bishops and clergy, and not to any recognizable, informed, and active community of African Christians. The general assessment is that in "the rather untheological world of the Catholic Church in Africa," Vatican II had very little impact on the ground, beyond academic circles and hierarchical concerns.[21] Yet De Jong's contention that Vatican II "formed the starting point for the self-reliance, the inculturation and the renewal of the African Church"[22] is largely correct, if interpreted in a strict sense, that is, as a task that was yet to be fully accomplished rather than as a finished product.

The reception and implementation of Vatican II in Africa can be assessed in the context of a broad set of factors that either facilitated or impeded this process. These factors are not exhaustive. The following represents and illustrates some of the most important considerations.

The Challenge of Literacy

Vatican II produced a corpus of constitutions, decrees, and declarations of varying themes, degrees of authority, lengths, and styles for dissemination, study, and implementation in the church. "Indeed the texts of Vatican II, in words, amount to twice that of all the first seven councils taken together."[23] For a continent steeped in orality and unremarkable for its literacy levels, this factor constituted a formidable challenge. The texts of Vatican II delivered in high ecclesiastical Latin would have been incomprehensible to the vast majority of African Christians and clergy in the postconciliar years. "The average lay person with no understanding of English had no possibility whatever of reading and studying the Vatican II documents [in Latin]."[24]

20. Gribble, *Implementation of Vatican II in Eastern Africa*, 77.
21. Hastings, "Council Came to Africa," 317.
22. De Jong, *The Challenge of Vatican II in East Africa*, 30.
23. Tanner, "How Novel Was Vatican II?," 404.
24. De Jong, *Challenge of Vatican II in East Africa*, 34.

The linguistic challenge was equally true for bishops and priests, as Hastings points out: "The bishops returned to their dioceses with a heap of Latin documents to redirect a clergy far less informed about what had been going on than their counterparts in Europe but also, for the most part, far more willing to be redirected. The laity, of course, were still more uninformed."[25] The clergy (and laity) were as unprepared for the implementation of Vatican II as the latter's documents were inaccessible and incomprehensible. This situation, however, was mitigated by approximations of translation in English and Swahili.[26]

To extend this argument on literacy, from a historical perspective, the reception of Vatican II and the realization (or lack thereof) of its promise in Africa was the result of an absence of a sustained initiative to inform the people of God "on the mind of the Church, as expressed in Vatican II."[27] There is, however, evidence that some bishops created platforms in their dioceses to speak informally about their experiences at Vatican II to a mixed audience of clergy, religious, and lay people.[28] While this practice would have been common in the postconciliar years, it gradually declined as the excitement of renewal and reform ebbed, and as interest in the study of Vatican II's documents receded to the exclusive domain of seminary formation.

Semper Idem*: Resistance of Bishops and Priests*

A recurring theme in the assessment of the reception and implementation of Vatican II in Africa concerns the attitude of bishops and priests. De Jong lambasts African bishops and clergy for deliberately mounting resistance to orientation sessions and the implementation of Vatican II. The reasons he adduces for their formidable resistance stems from various factors. Steeped as they were in a legalistic, clericalist, and ultramontane theological upbringing, they showed little sympathy for indigenous religion and culture as useful sources of the inculturation of liturgy and catechetical reform. Nor were they enamored of the prospect of diminishment

25. Hastings, "The Council Came to Africa," 316.

26. Bishop Vincent McCauley of Fort Portal, Uganda, for example, published and distributed English texts of the documents of Vatican II. Yet, when it comes to accessibility and familiarization with the documents of Vatican II, it would seem that they were "probably the least read and studied books in the presbyteries" (De Jong, *Challenge of Vatican II in East Africa*, 33).

27. Alex B. Chima, "Africanising the Liturgy: Where Are We Twenty Years after Vatican II?," AFER 25 (1983): 280–91, at 291.

28. Hurley, *Vatican II*, 32.

of clerical authority, social status, and living standard that a postconciliar ecclesiology seemed to indicate with the recognition of the important roles of the laity in the church. The reactions of African bishops and clergy to Vatican II seemed an exercise in surreptitious self-preservation and safeguarding of ecclesiastical and clerical privileges.[29] This is De Jong's account; while it is too biased to form the basis of a general statement on the attitude and positions of African ecclesiastics and clergy vis-à-vis Vatican II, it merits further critical consideration as will become clear further on.

Notwithstanding the challenges posed by the illiteracy of ill-informed laity and the opposition of conservative and ill-prepared bishops and priests, evidence exists of credible attempts at propagating and implementing the directives and orientations of Vatican II in Africa. By way of illustration, three such attempts are noteworthy: Adrian Hastings's writings, *African Ecclesial Review* (AFER), and the Pastoral Institute of the Association of Member Episcopal Conferences of East Africa (AMECEA) in Gaba, Uganda.

Adrian Hastings

Available resources on the reception and implementation of Vatican II in Africa, particularly in East Africa, give considerable credit to the initiative, effort, and ingenuity of British Roman Catholic priest, theologian, and historian Adrian Hastings. "Hastings personally stoked the fires of Vatican II enthusiasm through his publication of a fortnightly bulletin."[30] In response to the initiative of the AMECEA bishops to launch a program of postconciliar reeducation and reorientation for Kenya, Malawi, Tanzania, Uganda, and Zambia, Hastings produced critically acclaimed study guides and commentaries on the documents of the council pared down to the level of comprehension of missionary priests and religious, indigenous clergy, and lay people. Over a period of two years, this fortnightly bulletin, "Post Vatican II: A Guide to the Documents of the Second Vatican Council," became the staple of conferences, seminars, workshops, meetings, and discussion groups on Vatican II of priests and religious, and, in some cases, of catechists and lay people in several parts of Africa and beyond. The opinion of one of the beneficiaries of Hastings's publication attests to its significant impact: "If there has been one factor that made Vatican II known, then that is it!"[31] Regrettably, Hastings's initiative was short-lived.

29. De Jong, *Challenge of Vatican II in East Africa*, 83–89.
30. Gribble, *Implementation of Vatican II in Eastern Africa*, 77; see also 155.
31. Quoted in De Jong, *Challenge of Vatican II in East Africa*, 35.

African Ecclesial Review *(AFER)*

Hastings himself noted two other major factors that created "a real wave of pastoral renewal" in Africa following the conclusion of Vatican II, namely, the founding of the *African Ecclesial Review* (AFER) and the Pastoral Institute at Gaba.[32] Regarding the former, "in addition to the Council documents and the authorized commentary by Hastings, the pastoral theological periodical, *African Ecclesial Review* (AFER), was an important factor in the process of assimilating Vatican II."[33] In the wake of Vatican II, AFER gained prominence as the leading journal of theology in English-speaking Africa.

Prior to and during the council, AFER published columns on happenings at Vatican II. In the first two decades following the council, some of the most critical and incisive analyses of conciliar documents, themes, and innovations appeared in AFER. Its publications would later include full texts of the conciliar documents and critical commentaries. Articles in AFER treated topics as varied as catechetics, sacraments, liturgy, interreligious dialogue, inculturation, ecumenism, and seminary formation in the context of the church in Africa.

Regrettably, the publications would fizzle out as the years went by, giving credence to Hastings's poignant observation about the fleeting lifespan of Vatican II's reception and implementation in Africa: "By the late 1970s the period of postconciliar innovation was well-nigh over. . . . Clericalism at the top but congregationalism at the bottom proved the *de facto* compromise of the postconciliar African Church."[34]

AMECEA Pastoral Institute

One institution that bears lasting testimony to the legacy of Vatican II for Africa is the AMECEA Pastoral Institute. The launch of this initiative responded to the need to communicate the vision, promote the teaching, and implement the guidelines of Vatican II in all parts of the nascent African church. In the words of eyewitness Jean-Claude Lemay:

> The decision of the AMECEA Bishops to launch a pastoral and catechetical institute was a deliberate attempt to meet the needs made more urgent by the context described above: the need to bring to grass-root level the doctrinal and pastoral renewal of Vatican II; the need to help

32. Hastings, "The Council Came to Africa," 319.
33. De Jong, *Challenge of Vatican II in East Africa*, 35.
34. Hastings, "The Council Came to Africa," 322.

pastoral workers to update themselves in the field of catechetical and pastoral work; the need for personal renewal.[35]

Lemay continues: "The academic input (of Gaba) would be geared towards updating and deepening the existing wealth of knowledge, in the light of the teaching of Vatican II."[36]

Concretely, this program included "a two-week period set aside for the study of the Vatican II documents."[37] In time it expanded into a three-week course on the documents of Vatican II. The profile of the initial participants in this program reflected "the mixity [*sic*] of the local church . . . priests, religious, women and men, and laity, African and non-African."[38] In addition to pastoral and catechetical training, for a few short years, the Pastoral Institute conducted experimentation in appropriately adapted and creative African liturgies in response to the inspiration and directives of *Sacrosanctum concilium*, the Constitution on the Sacred Liturgy.

As with the previous efforts considered in this essay, with the passing of years, the impact of this institute as a prime facilitator and effective vehicle for the implementation of the directives and teaching of Vatican II would gradually diminish. Interestingly, this decline is attributable to the manifest conservatism within the church in Africa that resisted the orientation of Vatican II. Considering its status as a tool for implementing Vatican II, the Pastoral Institute owed its establishment and existence to the bishops of AMECEA. Curiously, however, the bishops took exception to the "liberal" and "progressive" direction of the Institute and adopted measures that not only curtailed the effectiveness of its programs, but would essentially engineer its gradual and eventual demise.[39]

Fifty Years On: The Council's African Legacy

The legacy of Vatican II is a matter of contention and debate among theologians in the world church. The same situation holds in Africa. Quite clearly, the perspectives of historians on Vatican II and Africa differ. These perspectives are not straightforwardly descriptive, but thematic and frag-

35. Jean-Claude Lemay, "Gaba: A Story of Renewal" AFER 26 (1984): 22–31, at 23.

36. Ibid., 24.

37. Ibid., 24, 25, 26; see also De Jong, *Challenge of Vatican II in East Africa*, 41.

38. Lemay, "Gaba: A Story of Renewal," 24.

39. De Jong, *The Challenge of Vatican II in East Africa*, 189; Gribble, *The Implementation of Vatican II in Eastern Africa*, 159.

mentary, and they contain multiple points of convergence and divergence. One major factor of interpretation lies in the fact that so far most of the accounts and interpretations are written by expatriates, reflecting interests, adopting methodology, and applying criteria that, far from being false, are radically partial. Unsurprisingly, favorable and flattering portrayals of the contributions of expatriate bishops and clergy dominate existing historical accounts.[40] A comprehensive, critical, and scholarly account of Vatican II and Africa awaits realization—such an undertaking would avoid the pitfall of simply narrating Africa's presence and encounter with Vatican II in broad strokes. Conflicting perspectives aside, the positive impulses released by Vatican II for the church in Africa are beyond dispute:

> For Bishops of the Catholic Church in East Africa, as for Bishops everywhere, the Council was not only an impressive assembly of the Universal Apostolic College; it was also a deep experience of learning, at times challenging and even disturbing, but also liberating and rewarding. . . . For the leaders of the Church in East Africa, the sharing of the Council's experience became a priority. How could such renewal as they lived at Vatican II be brought to their people and in particular to their close collaborators in the ministry?[41]

Still, there are those, like Vincent Donovan, who contended that Vatican II's program for "young churches" produced a carbon copy of Eurocentric ecclesiology laden with all the trappings and flaws of the Western church.[42] Donovan's unflattering characterization should not surprise us. As mentioned above, an "African" church could hardly be said to exist at the time of Vatican II.

Nevertheless, there are several useful areas for positively assessing the impact of Vatican II on the church in Africa in the past, at present, and for the future. Three such areas may be found distributed in the analyses of African theologians since Vatican II.

40. Notably, De Jong, *Challenge of Vatican II in East Africa*; Gribble, *Implementation of Vatican II in Eastern Africa.* De Jong's bias is unmistakable in his claim that "Dutch missionaries and their colleagues from other countries were the reformers and renewers of the Church, while the African clergy in general remained dismissive of the renewals because of their clinging to conservative ecclesiological positions" (187).

41. Lemay, "Gaba: A Story of Renewal," 23.

42. Vincent J. Donovan, *Christianity Rediscovered*, 25th Anniversary Edition (1978; Maryknoll, NY: Orbis, 2003), 97, 131.

Dining with the Devil

In the missionary church, a key challenge of Christianity is how to fashion a constructive relationship with indigenous African religion. Despite deliberate attempts of Eurocentric missionaries and evangelists, Christianity could neither circumvent nor suppress the claims of indigenous religion in Africa. In general, "the encounter between Christianity and indigenous beliefs, rituals, and customs involved a massive and continuous process of interpretation and reassessment."[43] In many instances, ignorance and antagonism dominated the relationship and skewed the process, judging by the approach of missionaries obstinately committed to their avowed mission to demonize, oppose, and eliminate all manifestations of indigenous religion and worship. Vatican II inaugurated a new approach that acknowledged the claims of "other religions" and attempted fresh interpretation and reassessment of interreligious encounter, while at the same time tenaciously asserting the superiority of Christianity and the preeminence of the Roman Catholic Church as the sacrament of salvation.

Nostra aetate, the Declaration on the Relation of the Church to Non-Christian Religions, and *Ad gentes*, the Decree on the Church's Missionary Activity, provided the basis for adopting a fresh approach to non-Christian religions in the missionary context of Africa. In particular, *Nostra aetate*, as Emmanuel Ifesieh noted, "is in some ways one of the Council's most radical and far-reaching products, and it has many implications for the Church in Africa."[44]

Although African religion—perhaps glibly subsumed under the category of people who seek God "in shadows and images" (*Lumen gentium* no. 16)—did not get a mention in these seminal documents, it is reasonable to argue that if one reads between the lines, Vatican II led to a shift in attitude vis-à-vis indigenous religion in Africa.[45] The fundamental attitude of considering the latter solely and merely as *preparatio evangelii* remained dominant; but the council opened the way for the emergence of a marginally more sensitive approach that acknowledges goodness, truth, and holiness in other religions (*Ad gentes* nos. 3, 9, 11, 22; *Nostra aetate* no. 2; *Sacrosanctum concilium* nos. 37–40).[46] Furthermore, the openness toward dialogue

43. Richard Gray, *Christianity, the Papacy, and Mission in Africa* (Maryknoll, NY: Orbis, 2012), 155.

44. Emmanuel I. Ifesieh, "Vatican II and Traditional Religion," AFER 25 (1983): 230–36, at 230.

45. Ibid., 231.

46. Eugene Hillman, *Toward an African Christianity: Inculturation Applied* (New York: Paulist, 1993), 38–40.

with, and respect for, indigenous African religion as contained in the analysis that exists in the corpus of African theology owes its origins to Vatican II.[47]

Inculturation—To Drum or Not to Drum

In light of the preceding point, within the wider field of theological scholarship, a central topic that claims the attention of the postconciliar generation of African theologians concerns defining the meaning, delineating the scope, and regulating the application of the principle of inculturation. The primary aim of this process, as Eugene Hillman put it, is to determine "whether and to what extent Christian faith is supposed to bypass, negate or affirm the claims any culture has on the loyalty of its people."[48] As a theological initiative or project, we can rightly trace the origins of inculturation of the church to the teaching, guidelines, and direction of Vatican II. De Jong emphatically argues that "the foremost driving force for inculturation of the Church in this region [East Africa] consists in the new theological perceptions of Vatican II."[49] The scope is continental. Yet, ironically, the direction of this project, at least in the initial phase of the implementation of the council, was not only attenuated but also strongly contested by a constellation of local factors and personalities.

De Jong also argues that the inculturation issuing from Vatican II was superficial. Not only does he regret this superficiality, but, as already mentioned, he also lays the blame squarely at the feet of conservative African episcopate and clergy. Credit for whatever simulacrum of postconciliar adaptation, Africanization, or inculturation that existed belonged to European bishops and clergy, not to—if I might paraphrase—their inferior, illiterate, and retrograde African counterparts bereft of theological imagination.[50] This statement oversimplifies attitudes, facts, and processes in the church in Africa vis-à-vis Vatican II. It is largely biased, even though it identifies some exceptional cases of outright resistance. It is possible and necessary to perceive things in a different optic.

Hastings, who wields incontestable authority on this matter, contradicts De Jong's claims and provides a list of outstanding African ecclesial leaders,

47. Laurenti Magesa, "On Speaking Terms: African Religion and Christianity in Dialogue," in *Reconciliation, Justice, and Peace: The Second African Synod*, ed. Agbonkhianmeghe E. Orobator (Maryknoll, NY: Orbis, 2011), 25–36, at 26.

48. Hillman, *Toward an African Christianity*, 29.

49. De Jong, *Challenge of Vatican II in East Africa*, 187; see Gribble, *Implementation of Vatican II in Eastern Africa*, 78–82.

50. De Jong, *Challenge of Vatican II in East Africa*, 186–90; Gribble, *Implementation of Vatican II in Eastern Africa*, 80–81.

pioneers, and reformers inspired by the spirit of Vatican II, which De Jong's partial and biased account does not consider. The postconciliar movement of inculturation, reform, and renewal benefitted immensely from the activities of African ecclesial leaders who "were men of imaginative commitment, exuberance and charism."[51] The cast of postconciliar reformers included: Bishops Joseph Malula (Kinshasa, DRC), Christopher Mwoleka (Rulenge, Tanzania), Peter Sarpong (Kumasi, Ghana), Dennis Hurley (Durban, South Africa), Patrick Kalilombe (Lilongwe, Malawi), Peter Dery (Wa, Ghana), and Emmanuel Milingo (Lusaka, Zambia). These ecclesial leaders understood postconciliar liturgical, sacramental, and theological inculturation as constitutive of the mission of the church in Africa.

Naturally, inculturation has created a rich terrain for evaluating the depth and extent of renewal generated by Vatican II in Africa. A much-debated and celebrated quintessence of this renewal was the introduction of African music and instrumentation into Catholic liturgy, the focal point of which was the African drum. While some would dismiss this as superficiality,[52] others would perceive it as an initiative of immense symbolic value for the identity of the African church. "The drum was the great symbol of post–Vatican II liturgy—a symbol at once of cultural pluralism and popular participation, the arrival of an active laity, but still more the arrival of Africa in all its vibrant, populist, rhythmic vitality as a major reality within Catholicism."[53]

Taking account of the liturgical innovation inspired by Vatican II, especially via *Sacrosanctum concilium*, opinion on the progress in liturgical adaptation and inculturation in Africa has been consistently divided. Twenty years after Vatican II, Alex Chima made the following assessment: "Our liturgy is still far from having African 'flesh and blood,' as Vatican II, indirectly, says it should."[54] He concluded: "It seems we have not gone much further than the stage of relatively insignificant adaptations."[55] To recall De Jong's position, if Chima's analysis is correct, African bishops and priests are to blame for resisting postconciliar liturgical adaptation, whereas Dutch missionaries led the process of creative liturgical adaptation. Through De Jong's lens, one sees that it was only European ecclesiastics who presided over the presence of Africa at Vatican II and controlled the implementation of the teaching and directives of the council in some parts of Africa.

51. Hastings, "The Council Came to Africa," 321.
52. De Jong, *Challenge of Vatican II in East Africa*, 181–85, 189.
53. Hastings, "The Council Came to Africa," 320.
54. Chima, "Africanising the Liturgy," 283.
55. Ibid., 290.

As shown above, however, it may be questioned whether De Jong's perspective does justice to the wider continental context. The situation in West and Central Africa could hardly be described as superficial, uninspiring, and lacking creativity or imagination. In these regions, it can be plausibly argued that Vatican II created a liturgical revolution in Africa of immense practical and pastoral significance.[56] In Central Africa, for example, in the aftermath of Vatican II, legendary African ecclesiastic Cardinal Malula of Kinshasa initiated and led liturgical reforms that have lasted well into the 21st century. Undoubtedly, the impetus for this reform emanated from the inculturation movement triggered by Vatican II. A firsthand account from Nigeria in West Africa corroborates this claim: "Led by the themes of Vatican II, sensitivity to popular religion and culture and a commitment to inculturation made it possible to refashion liturgy, celebrating rites to be relevant and familiar, intelligible, and also emotionally stimulating. . . . Now there was permission for Africans to be Africans."[57]

In contemporary African theology and ecclesiology, inculturation represents an effective methodology of reflection, analysis, and praxis.[58]

Ecclesial Pan-Africanism and Result-Oriented Particular Churches

Another significant development that owes its origins to Vatican II is the awareness of African ecclesial leaders "that they belonged together, and should work in collaboration."[59] The immediate outcome of this realization was the creation of continental and regional forums. "The collegiality experienced by the African bishops at Vatican II generated action for some form of permanent episcopal association, linking all African countries."[60] One example of this episcopal association is the Symposium of Episcopal Conferences of Africa and Madagascar (SECAM), founded in 1969. For several decades SECAM has served as the umbrella body for episcopal conferences on the continent in areas of evangelization, theological formation, social action, leadership development, and pastoral initiative.

56. Hastings, "The Council Came to Africa," 320; for examples from West, Central, and East Africa, see Elochukwu E. Uzukwu, *Worship as Body Language: Introduction to Christian Worship: An Orientation* (Collegeville, MN: Liturgical Press, 1997), 270–317.

57. Jagoe, "Vatican II Comes to Africa," 550; see also Brian Hearne, "Conciliar Fellowship and the Local Church: A Catholic View from Africa," *Ecumenical Review* 29 (1977): 129–40, at 129.

58. See Laurenti Magesa, *Anatomy of Inculturation: Transforming the Church in Africa* (Maryknoll, NY: Orbis, 2004).

59. Kalilombe, "Effect of the Council on World Catholicism: Africa," 311.

60. Gribble, *Implementation of Vatican II in Eastern Africa*, 164.

The momentum for creating and sustaining pan-African movements inspired the establishment and development of fledgling regional and national bodies. An example of a highly effective regional body is Association of Member Episcopal Conferences in East Africa (AMECEA). This organization has developed an admirable profile in the African church in the area of regional ecclesiastical collaboration. Arguably, the most concrete and best achievement of AMECEA is its pioneering role in developing Small Christian Communities (SCCs) as a new way of being church[61] and establishing a flagship higher education institution, the Catholic University of Eastern Africa (CUEA) in Nairobi, Kenya.

Taken as a whole, these organs, forums, or platforms of ecclesiastical collaboration stand as structural, contextual, and appropriate expressions of the conciliar idea of "particular churches" (*Ad gentes* no. 22).[62] Yet, reflecting on the five decades of ecclesial growth and development in Africa since Vatican II, I would see such optimistic characterization as contradicted by the intense centralization and concentration of the understanding of church in hierarchical structures of governance and control. At least in Africa, the promise or optimism of national and regional ecclesial structures as credible and vibrant loci of church and embodiment of catholicity has been fulfilled only partially. This, however, is in contrast to the growing prominence of national episcopal conferences in dealing with domestic socioeconomic and political issues since the 1980s. National conferences continue to be active in the public sphere. Examples of their zones of influence include facilitating political transitions, resolving social conflict, and negotiating peace and reconciliation in situations of armed violence. Such focus *ad extra* remains imbalanced in the absence of a commensurate focus *ad intra* on organizational and ecclesial matters affecting the Roman Catholic Church.

Conclusion

"The Church in Africa is greatly indebted to Pope John XXIII and to the Council that he convoked: the Second Vatican Council."[63] Thus began

61. See Joseph G. Healey and Jeanne Hinton, eds., *Small Christian Communities Today: Capturing the New Moment* (Maryknoll, NY: Orbis, 2005); Joseph Healey, "Timeline in the History and Development of Small Christian Communities (SCCs) in Africa, Especially Eastern Africa," http://www.smallchristiancommunities.org/africa/africa-continent/107-timeline-in-the-history-and-development-of-small-christian-communities-sccs-in-africa-especially-eastern-africa.html (accessed February 21, 2013).

62. Hearne, "Conciliar Fellowship and the Local Church," 133.

63. Ifesieh, "Vatican II and Traditional Religion," 230.

Ifesieh's article assessing two decades of Vatican II and its impact on traditional religion in Africa. His conclusion pays glowing tribute to the legacy of the council for Christianity and the church in Africa: "Vatican II, by its openness to the God-given values in African traditional religion and culture, has initiated a new era for the Church in Africa, when Christianity will no longer appear as a foreign religion but as one that brings to fulfillment the deepest longings of African religiosity."[64] Fifty years after the council, this positive and optimistic assessment bears the endorsement of several theologians and historians in Africa. Although numerically and theologically insignificant, Africa's dignified presence and participation at the council contributed to what historian of Vatican II Alberto Melloni designates as "multi-coloured universality" of the church.[65]

The currents of renewal and reform unleashed by the central affirmations of Vatican II continue to wax and wane against the retaining wall of legalism, clericalism, and conservatism.[66] It goes without saying that all the accounts of the experience and reception of Vatican II in Africa focus on bishops as key players, primary implementers, authoritative interpreters, and incontestable guardians of the legacy of the council. There is nothing surprising about this approach in a church that continues to labor under clericalist and hierarchical tutelage and where the vast majority of the people of God minister, serve, and worship at the behest of the clergy. Clearly, certain features of the church in Africa continue to resist and hold out against the renewal and reforms inaugurated by Vatican II. Forms of this resurgent clericalism and conservatism exist in matters of sexual morality, control of liturgical development, gender discrimination, and the exercise of ecclesial authority.

As it should be clear to a keen observer of the history of Christianity in Africa, notwithstanding the multiple negative factors that have conditioned the reception and limited the implementation of Vatican II in the African church, the impact of this ecclesial watershed limns more than just a trajectory of decline. Since the council, studies in African Christianity provide incontrovertible evidence of demographic progress, theological creativity, and religious effervescence.[67] In this sense, the Second Vatican

64. Ibid., 236.

65. Alberto Melloni, "The Second Vatican Council," *Asian Horizons* 6 (2012): 423–55, at 431.

66. See Adrian Hastings, "Opting for Vatican II Plus," *Journal of Theology for Southern Africa* 41 (1982): 25–28, at 26.

67. See Philip Jenkins, *The Next Christendom: The Coming of Global Christianity* (New York: Oxford University, 2002); John L. Allen Jr., *The Future Church: How Ten*

Council is best understood in the currents of change and growth in African Christianity. While the council cannot be facilely credited for this growth, nevertheless it laid the foundation for the emergence and existence of a truly local African church and continues to inspire contextualized theological production.

Although the "letter" of the Second Vatican Council proved somewhat esoteric, indecipherable, and incomprehensible to the majority of Catholics on a largely nonliterate continent, the spirit of the council continues to animate, motivate, and support the demographic and theological flourishing of the African church. Adopting Adrian Hastings's words, we can sum up the theological and ecclesiological achievement of Vatican II in Africa as follows: "The Catholic Church of Africa of the 1980s is unthinkable without Vatican II and the many great endeavours which followed close upon it."[68] Hastings's claim holds true not only for the 1980s but also for present times.

Trends Are Revolutionizing the Catholic Church (New York: Doubleday, 2009); Kwame Bediako, *Christianity in Africa: The Renewal of a Non-Western Religion* (Maryknoll, NY: Orbis, 1995).

68. Hastings, "The Council Came to Africa," 322.

13 Reception of and Trajectories for Vatican II in Asia

PETER C. PHAN

The article offers a historical analysis of the impact of Vatican II on the Asian Catholic churches. It places this reception of the council within the various contexts of Asia and Asian Christianity and argues that this reception includes an expansion of the council's trajectories insofar as Asian Catholicism, led by the Federation of Asian Bishops' Conferences, carries out the council's renewal agenda to respond to the internal and external challenges facing the Asian Catholic churches in the last five decades.

The focus of this article is quite precise and narrow: the impact of the Second Vatican Council on the Asian churches or, stated positively from the perspective of the Asian churches, their "reception" of Vatican II since its convocation five decades ago. It is not a historical study of the contributions of the Asian churches to the council as such.[1] Nor does it

1. A comprehensive and critical historical study of the contributions of the bishops of Asia to Vatican II during the antepreparatory, preparatory, and conciliar periods is still to be written. The celebrated 5-volume *Storia del concilio Vaticano II*, ed. Giuseppe Alberigo (Bologna: Il Mulino, 1995–2001), ET, *History of Vatican II*, ed. Joseph Komonchak (Maryknoll, NY: Orbis, 1996–2006), provides only sketchy information on this subject. This study is now made easier by the publication of all the official documents of the council: *Acta et documenta Concilio Oecumenico Vatican II apparando: Series I—Antepraeparatoria* (Vatican City: Typis Polyglottis Vaticanis, 1960–1961); *Series II—Praeparatoria* (Vatican City: Typis Polyglottis Vaticanis, 1964–1994); *Acta Synodalia Sacrosancti Concilii Oecumenici Vatican II* (Vatican City: Typis Polyglottis Vaticanis, 1970–1999). For a brief survey of the presence and contributions of the

treat of the theoretical issues such as the principles that should guide the interpretation of Vatican II as an "event" and of its 16 documents,[2] the various "narratives" of the council,[3] and the "rupture/discontinuity" and/or "reform/continuity" between the council and the alleged "pre-Vatican II church."[4] Rather, it is intended as a companion piece to the surveys of the reception of Vatican II in Latin America and Africa.[5]

A few preliminary remarks are in order before undertaking the proposed assessment. First, by "Vatican II" is meant the council itself and its 16 documents. However, since Vatican II could not, of course, implement its own reform programs and even called for the establishment of postconciliar commissions to carry out its reform policies, it is reasonable that, in assessing the impact of Vatican II, attention should be paid to the major postconciliar documents, institutions, and, indeed, to the pontificates of Paul VI, John Paul II, and Benedict XVI.[6]

---

bishops of Asia at Vatican II, see Peter C. Phan, "'Reception' or 'Subversion' of Vatican II by the Asian Churches? A New Way of Being Church in Asia," in *Vatican II: Forty Years Later*, ed. William Madges (Maryknoll, NY: Orbis, 2005), 26–32.

2. On the hermeneutics of Vatican II, see the magnificent articles celebrating the 50th anniversary of the council in the pages of this journal: John O'Malley, SJ, "'The Hermeneutics of Reform': A Historical Analysis," *Theological Studies* 73 (2012): 517–46; and Ormond Rush, "Toward a Comprehensive Interpretation of the Council and Its Documents," *Theological Studies* 73 (2012): 547–69.

3. On the three "narratives"—ultratraditionalist, ultraliberal, and neoconservative—of the council, see Massimo Faggioli, "Vatican II: The History and the Narratives," *Theological Studies* 73 (2012): 749–67.

4. On the debate over the "continuity" and "discontinuity" of Vatican II, see Gerald O'Collins, SJ, "Does Vatican II Represent Continuity or Discontinuity?" *Theological Studies* 73 (2012): 768–94.

5. See O. Ernesto Valiente, "The Reception of Vatican II in Latin America," *Theological Studies* 73 (2012): 795–823; and Agbonkhianmeghe E. Orobator, SJ, "'After All, Africa Is Largely a Nonliterate Continent': The Reception of Vatican II in Africa," *Theological Studies* 74 (2013): 284–301. A decade ago I published an essay titled "Reception of Vatican II in Asia: Historical and Theological Analysis," *Gregorianum* 83 (2002): 269–85. This article assumes and extends the research presented in that essay by focusing on the reception of Vatican II by the Asian churches in the last ten years.

6. Note that the issue here is not a distinction between the "letter" and the "spirit" of Vatican II, which figures prominently in the recent debate on the hermeneutics of the council. Rather it is a recognition that the impact of Vatican II cannot fairly and fully be assessed apart from what has been officially promulgated as council-mandated reforms (e.g., new liturgical books and rites, the 1983 Code of Canon Law, the *Catechism of the Catholic Church*, the reform of the Roman Curia, and so on) and is thus a measure of its impact itself.

Second, "reception" refers to the ongoing process by which the community of faith, with its *sensus fidei/fidelium*, makes a teaching or a practice of the faith its own, acknowledging thereby that it is a true and authentic expression of the church's faith. Reception is not to be understood as a juridical ratification by the community of such a teaching or practice whose truth and validity would derive from such ratification. Rather, it is an act whereby the community affirms and attests that such teaching or practice really contributes to the building up of the community's understanding and life of faith.[7] Such a process of reception, however, is not a simple act of obedience and passive absorption. It is not always and necessarily a full acceptance of what is enjoined by ecclesiastical authorities. It may at times involve a partial and even total rejection of what has been taught or commanded. Thus, reception is necessarily a remaking or "inventing" of a creative fidelity to the tradition in the light of the contemporary situation; the reception of Vatican II is no exception.[8]

7. On reception, see Yves Congar, *Tradition and Traditions: An Historical and a Theological Essay*, trans. Michael Naseby and Thomas Rainborough (New York: Macmillan, 1967). See also Robert Dionne, *The Papacy and the Church: A Study of Praxis and Reception in Ecumenical Perspective* (New York: Philosophical Library, 1987); Hans Robert Jauss, *Toward an Aesthetic of Reception* (Minneapolis: University of Minnesota, 1982); Edward J. Kilmartin, "Reception in History: An Ecclesiological Phenomenon and Its Significance," *Journal of Ecumenical Studies* 21 (1984): 34–54; and Dale T. Irwin, *Christian Histories, Christian Traditioning: Rendering Accounts* (Maryknoll, NY: Orbis, 1998).

8. Among the immense bibliography on the reception of Vatican II, see Giuseppe Alberigo, Jean-Pierre Jossua, and Joseph Komonchak, eds., *The Reception of Vatican II*, trans. Matthew J. O'Connell (Washington, DC: Catholic University of America, 1987); Rene Latourelle, ed., *Vatican II: Assessment and Prospectives; Twenty-Five Years after (1962–1987)*, 3 vols. (New York: Paulist, 1988–1989); Pierre-Marie Gy, *The Reception of Vatican II: Liturgical Reforms in the Life of the Church* (Milwaukee: Marquette University, 2003); Austin Ivereigh, ed., *Unfinished Journey: The Church 40 Years After Vatican II* (New York: Continuum, 2003); Günther Wassilowsky, ed., *Zweites Vaticanum: Vergessene Anstösse, gegenwärtige Fortschreibungen* (Freiburg: Herder, 2004); Ladislas Orsy, *Receiving the Council: Theological and Canonical Insights and Debates* (Collegeville, MN: Liturgical Press, 2009); Christoph Theobald, *La réception du concile Vatican II, I: Accéder à la source* (Paris: Cerf, 2009); Theobald, *"Dans les traces . . ." de la constitution "Dei Verbum" du concile Vatican II: Bible, théologie et pratiques de la lecture* (Paris: Cerf, 2009); Gilles Routhier, *Vatican II: Herméneutique et réception* (Montreal: Fides, 2006); Routhier, ed., *Réceptions du Vatican II: Le concile au risque de l'histoire et des espaces humaines* (Louvain: Peeters, 2004); Gilles Routhier and Guy Robin, eds., *L'Autorité et les autorités: L'Herméneutique théologique du Vatican II* (Paris: Cerf, 2010); James L. Heft and John O'Malley, eds., *After Vatican II: Trajectories*

Since the reception of Vatican II in Asia consisted in a conscious attempt at applying the council documents to the specific contexts of Asia and the Asian churches, I begin with a brief overview of these manifold contexts. Next, since Vatican II's achievements, as many commentators on the council have suggested, can be categorized *ad intra* and *ad extra*, I consider how they have impacted Asian Catholicism under both of these aspects. I end with reflections on the prospects of the Asian Catholic Church in the light of Vatican II.

A Church in the "Asian" Context

Many Asian theologians have argued that the church in Asia must be not simply *in* but *of* Asia, that is, a fully and wholly inculturated church.[9] The context is not merely the location in which the church exists; rather it determines the church's self-understanding and its mode of being. Consequently, to understand how Vatican II has shaped the church of Asia requires knowledge of the contexts in which the church exists and to whose challenges the church seeks to respond theologically and pastorally.

With regard to Asia, several features should be kept in mind, and it will be clear that its extreme diversities make it a near impossibility to refer to anything—Christianity included—as "Asian." First, immense geography and population. Conventionally divided into five regions: Central Asia (mainly the Republics of Kazakhstan, Kyrgyzstan, Tajikistan, Turkmenistan, and Uzbekistan), East Asia (mainly China, Japan, Korea, and Taiwan), South Asia (mainly Bangladesh, India, Myanmar, Nepal, Pakistan, and Sri Lanka), South-East Asia (mainly Cambodia, Indonesia, Laos, the Philippines, Singapore, Thailand, and Vietnam), and South-West Asia (the countries of the Middle East, Near East, or West Asia). Asia is the largest

---

and Hermeneutics (Grand Rapids, MI: Eerdmans, 2012); and Massimo Faggioli, *Vatican II: The Battle for Meaning* (New York: Paulist, 2012).

9. The Jesuit Filipino Bishop Francisco Claver (1929–2010) reports that during the 1998 Asian Synod in Rome, a curial cardinal told the assembled Asian bishops that they should not use the expression "Church *of* Asia" but "Church *in* Asia" (Francisco Claver, *The Making of a Local Church* [Maryknoll, NY: Orbis, 2008], 2). Indeed, Pope John Paul II's postsynodal exhortation (1999) is entitled Ecclesia in Asia, http://www.vatican.va/holy_father/john_paul_ii/apost_exhortations/documents/hf_jp-ii_exh_06111999_ecclesia-in-asia_en.html. All URLs referenced herein were accessed on March 5, 2013. Among Asian theologians who have strongly argued for a church *of* Asia is the Sri Lankan Jesuit Aloysius Pieris.

and most populous continent, with nearly two-thirds of the world's seven billion population.

Second, overwhelming poverty. Despite the presence of some economically developed countries such as Japan and the so-called Four Asian Tigers (Hong Kong, Singapore, Republic of Korea/South Korea, and Taiwan) and despite the dramatic rise of China and India as global economic powers, Asia still remains mired in widespread poverty, with some of the poorest countries on Earth (e.g., North Korea, Cambodia, Laos, Myanmar/Burma, and Bangladesh).

Third, political heterogeneity. In addition to having the largest democratic country, namely, India, Asia also features three remaining Communist countries of the world, namely, China, Vietnam, and the Democratic People's Republic of Korea (North Korea), and several countries struggling to transition from military dictatorship or single-party states to democratic forms of government and from socialist economy to market economy.

Fourth, cultural diversity. Though East, South, and Southeast Asia are dominated by the Indic and the Sinic cultures, and West and Central Asia by the Arabic-Islamic culture, Asia is a tapestry of extremely diverse cultures and civilizations, often within the same country. For instance, ethnically and culturally, India and China are teeming with astonishing diversity—more than 100 and 700 languages spoken in the Philippines and Indonesia respectively.

Fifth, religious pluralism. Asia is the cradle of all world religions. Besides Christianity, other Asian religions include Bahá'í, Bön, Buddhism, Confucianism, Daoism, Hinduism, Islam, Jainism, Shinto, Sikhism, and Zoroastrianism, as well as innumerable tribal and primal religions.

It is within the context of these mind-boggling diversities—geographic, linguistic, ethnic, economic, political, cultural, and religious—that Christianity and, more narrowly, the Catholic Church in Asia should be broached, especially when assessing the impact of Vatican II. With regard to Asian Christianity, several features should be kept in mind.[10] First, ancient historical roots. Christianity may be said to be an Asian religion since it was born in Palestine, part of West Asia or the Middle East. Furthermore, though West Asia is now dominated by Islam, it was the main home of

10. For an introduction to contemporary Asian Christianity, see Peter C. Phan, ed., *Christianities in Asia* (Oxford: Wiley-Blackwell, 2011). For a history of Asian Christianity, see Samuel H. Moffett, *A History of Christianity in Asia*, vol. 1, *Beginnings to 1500* (Maryknoll, NY: Orbis, 1992); and *A History of Christianity in Asia*, vol. 2, *1500–1900* (Maryknoll, NY: Orbis, 2005).

Christianity until the Arab conquest in the seventh century. The conventional narrative of Christianity as a Western religion, that is, one that originated in Palestine but soon moved westward, with Rome as its final destination, and from Rome as its epicenter, spread worldwide, belies the fact that in the first four centuries of Christianity, the most active and successful centers of mission were not Europe but Asia and Africa, with Syria as the center of gravity. But even Asian Christians outside West Asia can rightly boast an ancient and glorious heritage, one that is likely as old as the apostolic age. For instance, Indian Christianity, with the Saint Thomas Christians, can claim apostolic origins, with St. Thomas and/or St. Bartholomew as its founder(s). Chinese Christianity was born in the seventh century, with the arrival of the East Syrian (misnamed "Nestorian") monk Aloben during the T'ang dynasty. Christianity arrived in other countries such as the Philippines, Japan, Vietnam, Thailand, Cambodia, and Laos as early as the 16th century.

Second, colonial heritage. One of the bitter ironies of Asian Christianity is that though born in Asia, it returned to its birthplace, and is still being regarded by many Asians as a Western religion imported to Asia by Portuguese and Spanish colonialists in the 16th century, and later by other European countries such as Britain, France, Germany, Denmark, and the Netherlands, and lastly by the United States.

Third, numerical minority. In 2010, in Asia, Christians predominate in only two countries, namely, the Philippines and the Democratic Republic of Timor-Leste (East Timor)—over 85% of their populations are Christian (mainly Catholic)—but their total Christian population remains relatively small.[11] In South Korea and Vietnam, Christians constitute an important but by no means numerically overwhelming presence.[12] In other countries, especially China, India, and Japan, to name the most populous ones, and in countries with a Muslim majority such as Bangladesh, Indonesia, Malaysia, and Pakistan, and in those countries where Buddhism predominates such as Cambodia, Hong Kong, Laos, Mongolia, Myanmar, Nepal, Singapore, Sri Lanka, Taiwan, and Thailand, Christians form but a minuscule por-

11. The total Christian population of these two countries is approximately 84 million (83 million in the Philippines and slightly over one million in Timor-Leste). These and the following statistics are taken from Todd M. Johnson and Kenneth R. Ross, eds., *Atlas of Global Christianity 1910–2010* (Edinburgh: Edinburgh University, 2009).

12. South Korea's Christianity (overwhelmingly Protestant) accounts for about 41.1% of the population of 50 million; Vietnamese Christianity (overwhelmingly Roman Catholic) represents 8.6% of the population of 85 million.

tion of the population.[13] Without counting the Middle East, Christians constitute only slightly over 9% of the Asian population.[14]

Fourth, ecclesial diversity. Asia is the home of many different Christian ecclesiastical traditions, rites, and denominations, so that it is more accurate to use "Christianities" (in the plural) to denominate them. Due to its past extensive missions in Asia, Roman Catholicism is the largest church. Older than the Roman Catholic Church is the Malabar Church of India ("Saint Thomas Christians"). The Orthodox Church also has a notable presence in China, Korea, and Japan. The Anglican Church (including the Anglican Church of Canada) is well represented, especially in Hong Kong, India, Malaysia, and Pakistan. Various Protestant Churches have also flourished in almost all Asian countries, e.g., the Baptists (especially in North India), the Lutherans, the Mennonites, the Methodists, the Presbyterians (especially in Korea), and the Seventh-Day Adventists.[15]

Fifth, extensive migration. One of the best-kept secrets about Asian Christianity is that migration, national and international in scope, forced

13. The following numbers represent the percentages of Christians vis-à-vis the population of each country in 2010 (though it must be remembered that the statistics are notoriously unreliable, especially in Communist countries): China (8.6), Taiwan (6.0), Japan (2.3), North Korea (2.0), Mongolia (1.7), Sri Lanka (8.8), India (4.8), Nepal (3.1), Pakistan (2.3), Bangladesh (0.59), Brunei (15.3), Singapore (16.1), Myanmar (8.0), Malaysia (9.1), Cambodia (2.0), Indonesia (12.1), Thailand (0.6), Laos (3.1), Kazakhstan (13.4), Kyrgyzstan (5.9), Tajikistan (1.4), Turkmenistan (1.5), and Uzbekistan (1.3). Dyron Daughrity provides helpful statistics of Asian Christianity in his *Church History: Five Approaches to a Global Discipline* (New York: Peter Lang, 2012), 234–38.

14. There are 350 million Christians in Asia out of the population of almost four billion. In absolute numbers Asia has more Christians than Western Europe, Eastern Europe, or North America. However, in relation to the total population of Asia, Christians constitute a minority and will likely remain so in the foreseeable future. On the place of Asian Christianity in world Christianity, see Dale T. Irwin and Scott W. Sunquist, *History of the World Christian Movement*, vol. 1, *Earliest Christianity to 1493* (Maryknoll, NY: Orbis, 2001); Irwin and Sunquist, *History of the World Christian Movement*, vol. 2, *Modern Christianity from 1454–1800* (Maryknoll, NY: Orbis, 2012); Dyron B. Daughrity, *The Changing World of Christianity: The Global History of a Borderless Religion* (New York: Peter Lang, 2010); Daughrity, *Church History: Five Approaches to a Global Discipline* (New York: Peter Lang, 2012); Douglas Jacobsen, *The World's Christians: Who They Are, Where They Are, and How They Got There* (Oxford: Wiley-Blackwell, 2011); Noel Davies and Martin Conway, *World Christianity in the 20th Century* (London: SCM, 2008); and Charles E. Farhadian, ed., *Introducing World Christianity* (Oxford: Wiley-Blackwell, 2012).

15. A helpful guide to Asian Christianity is Scott W. Sunquist, ed., *A Dictionary of Asian Christianity* (Grand Rapids, MI: Eerdmans, 2001).

and voluntary in nature, economic and political in intent, has changed the faces of many Asian churches. Thanks to the groundbreaking research of scholars such as Kanan Kitani and Gemma Cruz, a fuller picture of contemporary Asian Christianity has emerged in which migration has played a key role in reshaping the membership and organization of the local churches and producing difficult pastoral and spiritual challenges for the churches.[16]

Sixth, the rapidly growing presence of Pentecostals and Evangelicals. These recent comers to Asia, often part of the waves of migration, have grown by leaps and bounds, particularly among ethnic minorities and disenfranchized social classes; and their brands of Christianity, with their emphasis on the literalist interpretation of the Bible, glossalalia, prophecy, and healing, differ greatly from, and often are in severe conflict with, those of mainline Christian churches. The popularity of Pentecostals is well illustrated by the Yoido Full Gospel Church, located in Seoul, Korea, which is the largest Pentecostal church in the world, with nearly one million members. Furthermore, Pentecostal Christianity with its system of house churches is believed to be spreading like wildfire in China (such as the True Jesus Church and the Jesus Family) and to pose a serious threat to the government because it is unregistered and therefore beyond government control.[17]

16. Kitani has focused on the Pentecostals and Evangelicals, especially in Japan, and Cruz on Roman Catholics, especially in Hong Kong. See Kanan Kitani, "Invisible Christians: Brazilian Migrants in Japan," in *Latin America between Conflict and Reconciliation*, ed. Susan Flämig and Martin Leiner (Göttingen: Vandenhoeck & Ruprecht, 2012), 195–214; and Gemma Cruz, *An Intercultural Theology of Migration* (Leiden: Brill, 2010). As an illustration of how migration has radically changed the faces of the Asian churches, Kitani points out the astounding fact that of the 1.1 million Christians in Japan, more than half are Brazilians, Filipinos, Chinese, and Koreans. This makes the expression "Japanese Christianity" rather misleading, as it may suggest that the majority of Christians in Japan are Japanese-born. Perhaps it is more accurate to speak of "Christianities in Japan." See Kanan Kitani, "Emerging Migrant Churches in Japan: A Comparative Analysis of Brazilian and Filipino Migrants' Church Activities," in *Migration and Church in World Christianity: Contextual Perspectives*, ed. Elaine Padilla and Peter C. Phan (New York: Palgrave, forthcoming).

17. On Pentecostalism in general, see the works of Walter J. Hollenweger and Allan H. Anderson. On Pentecostalism in Asia, the most authoritative and informative book is Allan Anderson and Edmond Tang, eds., *Asian and Pentecostal: The Charismatic Face of Christianity in Asia* (Oxford: Regnum Books International, 2005). From the Roman Catholic perspective, John Mansford Prior, *Jesus Christ the Way to the Father: The Challenge of the Pentecostals*, FABC Papers 119 (Hong Kong: FABC, 2006) is groundbreaking.

Finally, indigenous and independent Christianity. Numerous indigenous and sectarian Christian churches and movements have been established, often inspired by nationalism, biblical fundamentalism, or charismatic leadership, and possessing little or no relationships among themselves and with mainline Christianity. Among the most famous are the Iglesia Filipina Independiente (founded by Gregorio Aglipay in 1902) and the Iglesia ni Cristo (founded by Felix Ysagun Manalo in 1914), both in the Philippines. In 1951 the Three-Self Patriotic Movement was formed to unite all Protestant churches in China and to promote a strategy of self-governance, self-support, and self-propagation. In 1957 the Chinese Catholic Patriotic Association was established to enable China's Religious Affairs Bureau to exercise control over Chinese Catholics. In 1980 the China Christian Council was founded as the umbrella organization for all Protestant churches in the People's Republic of China, allowing them to participate in the World Council of Churches.

This bird's-eye view of both Asia and Asian Christianity serves as the indispensable background and context for understanding the impact of Vatican II on the Asian Catholic Church. Indeed, it may be argued that the Asian Catholic Church's reception of Vatican II consisted mainly in appropriating the council's teachings and reform agenda to meet the challenges posed by this double context. Like the council, Asian Christianity has an essentially "pastoral" character. It "received" the council only to the extent that the teachings and the pastoral policies emanating from the council have proved helpful in meeting both the external challenges of Asia: geographical and demographic immensity, linguistic and ethnic diversity, economic poverty, Communist and military regimes, cultural richness, and religious pluralism; and the challenges internal to the church itself: ancient historical roots, colonial heritage, numerical minority, ecclesiastical diversity, widespread migration, Pentecostalism and Evangelicalism, and the emergence of independent and charismatic churches.

These two distinct sets of challenges correspond to Vatican II's *ad intra* and *ad extra* foci, and it is under these two aspects that an assessment of the Asian Catholic Church's reception of the council will be offered. Of course, these two aspects cannot be fully separated from each other. Indeed, they mutually influence each other: the better the church understands itself, the better it can relate to the world, and, vice versa, a better relation of the church with the world leads to the church's deeper self-understanding. Nevertheless, considering them separately serves as a useful heuristic device to put some order to what will otherwise prove a mass of unmanageable data about the Asian churches' recent past.

Before describing this process of reception it may be useful to take into account the helpful distinction suggested by church historian John O'Malley between "reception" and "trajectory":

> Whereas "reception" generally indicates a direct application (or nonapplication) of explicit norms or directives, such as the revised liturgical forms, "trajectory" suggests something less obviously based on the council's norms and directives. It is related to reception, and perhaps can be considered a species of it. Introduction of it as a category of interpretation expands what we usually mean by reception.[18]

In what follows I speak of "reception" in the expanded sense of "trajectory" as suggested by O'Malley.

Ad Intra Reception of Vatican II by the Church of Asia

Vatican II is the first council to reflect at great length on the church's own nature (*Lumen gentium*) and on the various aspects of its internal life such as worship (*Sacrosanctum concilium*), reception of divine revelation (*Dei verbum*), the role of the laity (*Apostolicam actuositatem*), episcopal and priestly ministry (*Christus Dominus* and *Presbyterorum ordinis*), religious life (*Perfectae caritatis*), and the Eastern Catholic Churches (*Orientalium ecclesiarum*). In addition to these *ad intra* issues, the council has also considered the *ad extra* relations and tasks of the Catholic Church vis-à-vis the outside world: other Christian churches and communities (*Unitatis redintegratio*), other believers (*Nostra aetate*), evangelization and mission (*Ad gentes*), education (*Gravissimum educationis*), the mass media (*Inter mirifica*), religious freedom (*Dignitas humanae*), and the modern world in general (*Gaudium et spes*).

Of course, Vatican II as a corpus of 16 official documents has had a decisive impact on the Asian Catholic Church. Asian Catholicism has received all these documents as authoritative guides for its *ad intra* and *ad extra* activities. However, as to be expected, it grants priority to some over others. From the frequency of citations, *Lumen gentium*, *Sacrosanctum concilium*, *Dei verbum*, *Gaudium et spes*, *Ad gentes*, and *Nostra aetate* have obtained pride of place. Important as Vatican II as a textual corpus has been for the Asian churches, it would be a mistake in assessing the council's impact on the Asian churches to limit one's attention to its 16

18. O'Malley, *After Vatican II*, xii.

documents, even if interpreted as a coherent and intertextually integral theological corpus. One must also attend to Vatican II as "event," that is, a happening in, to, and by the church brought about under the impulse of the Holy Spirit, in which the participants of the council as well as the church as a whole underwent a profound religious "conversion" that requires a new language and a new rhetoric to express itself adequately.[19] Among Asian theologians who have eloquently and insistently argued for a reception of Vatican II as an "event" is the Sri Lankan Jesuit Aloysius Pieris. Contrasting "reform" with "renewal," Pieris calls Vatican II a "crisigenic" council, a "council of renewal, not a council of reform,"[20] the latter starting from the center, often forced upon the periphery and designed to proceed smoothly and gradually; the former beginning from the periphery and moving to the center, from the bottom to the top, and often with a stormy process.

With regard to Asian Catholicism's *ad intra* reception of Vatican II, one helpful way to chart this appropriation is by examining the teachings and activities of what is without the slightest doubt the most important organizational innovation of the Asian Catholic Church as a whole, namely, the Federation of Asian Bishops' Conferences (FABC).[21] The Asian bishops at the Asian Bishops' Meeting in Manila in 1970 decided to establish a permanent structure, not unlike the Latin American Episcopal Conference

19. O'Malley has identified four issues that Vatican II had to deal with: "how to deal with change, how to deal with the implications of a truly world church, with the relationship between center and periphery, and with the style in which the church conducts its mission" (ibid., xiv).

20. See Aloysius Pieris, *Give Vatican II a Chance: Yes to Incessant Renewal, No to Reforms of the Reforms* (Gonawala-Kelaniya: Tulana Research Centre, 2010). Pieris recounts the astonishing advice that Karl Rahner gave his young audience during his *lectio brevis* at the Facoltà Teologica San Luigi in Naples: "Don't waste time on Vatican II." By this Rahner means that the task of expounding Vatican II should be left to him and the cohort of his age (the younger theologians have other tasks to do), because in Rahner's view, "*his* own contemporaries (the older generation to which he belonged, including some of the bishops who signed the documents) would find it well nigh impossible to grasp the totally *new perspective* within which the Council was formulating its message. If this new orientation was not recognized, the teachings of Vatican II could be misinterpreted along the beaten track of a theology which it was trying to leave behind as inadequate" (ibid., 70). This "new perspective" is what O'Malley and others refer to as "event."

21. For information on the FABC, see its website: http://www.fabc.org. For a history of the FABC's first three decades, see Edmund Chia, *Thirty Years of FABC: History, Foundation, Context, and Theology*, FABC Papers no. 106 (Hong Kong: FABC, 2003).

(CELAM), to help implement their resolutions. Approved by the Holy See in 1972, the FABC is a voluntary association of episcopal conferences in Asia. Its decisions do not juridically bind its members; acceptance of them is more an expression of collegial responsibility and ecclesial solidarity than canonical compliance. Its goals and objectives, to quote from its mission statement, include:

- To study ways and means of promoting the apostolate, especially in the light of Vatican II and post-conciliar official documents, and according to the needs of Asia
- To work for and to intensify the dynamic presence of the Church in the total development of the peoples of Asia
- To help in the study of problems of common interest to the Church in Asia, and to investigate possibilities of solutions and coordinated action
- To promote inter-communication and cooperation among local Churches and bishops of Asia
- To render service to episcopal conferences of Asia in order to help them to meet the needs of the People of God
- To foster a more ordered development of organizations and movements in the Church at the international level
- To foster ecumenical and interreligious communication and collaboration[22]

It is clear from these goals and objectives, especially the first, with its explicit insistence on following Vatican II and the postconciliar documents, that the FABC intends to be an official organ for the reception of Vatican II in Asia, as it seeks to implement the three ecclesiological principles advocated by the council: episcopal collegiality, ecclesial communion, and dialogue as the mode of being church. On the other hand, it is equally clear that the FABC could not have come into being without the impetus of Vatican II. Thus, it is as much the most mature fruit of the process of reception of the council as the most effective instrument for the implementation of the council's teaching and reform agenda.

In constituting its membership, the FABC has also sought to meet most, if not all, of the above-mentioned challenges facing Asian Christianity. Geographically, the 18 episcopal conferences that are the FABC's full members and the nine that are its associate members hail from all the five regions of Asia, including Central Asia.[23] Linguistically, ethnically, eco-

22. At http://www.fabc.org/about.html.

23. The episcopal conferences that are the FABC's full members come from Bangladesh, East Timor, India (comprising three episcopal conferences based on their distinc-

nomically, politically, and culturally, the FABC is marked by the same kind of diversity and multiplicity prevalent in Asia. (English is by default the common language.) Also represented are churches of ancient origins, with their different rites and ecclesiastical disciplines; their presence provides unique opportunities for the implementation of the council's decree on the Catholic Eastern Churches (*Orientalium ecclesiarum*). In this way, more than any other continental episcopal conferences, the FABC embodies the ideals and reality of the "world church" that Vatican II ushered in.

The structure of the FABC also promotes and facilitates collaboration among the churches and among the laity and the clergy. Besides the General Assembly, which is its supreme body and meets in regular session every four years,[24] the FABC has the Central Committee (composed of the presidents of the member episcopal conferences or their officially designated bishop-alternates), the Standing Committee (composed of five bishops elected from the five regions of Asia), and the Central Secretariat.

---

tive "Rites," namely, the Conference of Catholic Bishops of India [the Latin Rite], the Syro-Malabar Bishops' Synod, and the Syro-Malankara Bishops' Conference), Indonesia, Japan, Kazakhstan, Korea, Laos-Cambodia, Malaysia-Singapore-Brunei, Myanmar, Pakistan, Philippines, Sri Lanka, Taiwan, Thailand, and Vietnam. The FABC's associate members come from Hong Kong, Macau, Nepal, Novosibirsk (Russia), Kyrgyzstan, Tajikistan, Turkmenistan, and Uzbekistan. To be a full member, an episcopal conference must have a minimum of three dioceses. The absence of an official organization representing the bishops of mainland China is conspicuous.

24. The General Assembly is composed of (1) all the presidents of the episcopal conferences that are members of the FABC, or their officially designated bishop-designates; (2) bishop-delegates elected by the episcopal conferences that are full or associate members; and (3) members of the Standing Committees. Up to 2013 there have been ten General Assemblies, each with a distinct theme. The last assembly met in Vietnam, December 10–16, 2013, with 111 official participants. That the Communist government allowed the FABC's tenth General Assembly to be held in Vietnam was in itself an extraordinary diplomatic success for the Vietnamese church leaders. At the conclusion of each assembly the FABC issues a "Final Statement." For the Final Statements of the first seven General Assemblies, see FABC and its various institutes; and see *For All The Peoples of Asia: Federation of Asian Bishops' Conferences*, vol. 1, *Documents from 1970 to 1991*, ed. Gaudencio Rosales and Catalino G. Arévalo (New York/Quezon City: Orbis/Claretian, 1992); vol. 2, *Documents from 1992 to 1996*, ed. Franz-Josef Eilers (Quezon City: Claretian, 1997); vol. 3, *Documents from 1997 to 2002*, ed. Eilers (Quezon City: Claretian, 2002); vol. 4, *Documents from 2002 to 2006*, ed. Eilers (Quezon City: Claretian, 2007). These four volumes also contain the documents of the various "offices" of the FABC. Most of the documents related to the FABC are available online and at the FABC Documentation Centre located in Bangkok, Thailand, which is part of the General Secretariat of the FABC located in Hong Kong.

Though the members of the Central and Standing Committees are all bishops, the members of the General Secretariat, which is the principal service agency and an instrument of coordination of activities within and outside the FABC, is composed of nine "offices" whose members are mostly priests, religious, and lay persons, whose expertise and work are vital to the FABC.[25] These offices regularly organize workshops and seminars for all kinds and levels of church ministers, thus enabling an effective collaboration among the bishops and their collaborators, and among the local and national churches. The written statements and summaries of these meetings, readily accessible online, serve as a convenient and reliable means for church leaders and rank-and-file Asian Catholics to update themselves on the current issues and problems confronting the Asian churches and their possible solutions. From the names of these nine offices it is clear that no area of Christian life, including the teachings and reforms of Vatican II itself, is left untouched by the FABC.

In addition to the FABC, perhaps the major landmark in the history of Asian Catholicism's reception of Vatican II is the Special Assembly of the Synod of Bishops. Convoked by John Paul II to celebrate the second millennium of Christianity, the Asian Synod met in Rome, April 18 to May 14, 1998. It has been rightly hailed as the coming of age of the Asian Catholic Church. A careful reading of the responses of the Asian episcopal conferences to the *Lineamenta*, the individual bishops' speeches during the synod, and John Paul II's postsynodal apostolic exhortation, Ecclesia in Asia, readily shows how far the Asian Catholic Church has moved forward from its barely noticeable contributions to Vatican II to the Asian Synod, and all that thanks to its wholehearted reception of Vatican II, or more precisely, the council's trajectories.[26]

Reception of Vatican II for the Church's Relations *Ad Extra*

The reception of Vatican II by the Asian Catholic Church *ad intra* has been extensive and enduring, especially through the agency of the FABC and as demonstrated by the Asian Synod. Ironically, however, if one were to survey the abundant official documents of the FABC and the writings

25. The nine offices are: Human Development, Social Communication, Laity, Theological Concerns, Education and Student Chaplaincy, Ecumenical and Inter-religious Affairs, Evangelization, Clergy, and Consecrated Life.

26. On the Asian Synod, see Peter C. Phan, ed., *The Asian Synod: Texts and Commentaries* (Maryknoll, NY: Orbis, 2002).

of Asian theologians, one would be struck by the dearth of explicit treatments of ecclesiology. If anything, there is a conscious shying away from "churchy" themes such as papal primacy and infallibility, apostolic succession, magisterium, episcopal power, the hierarchical structure, canon law, the Roman Curia, ordination of women, and the like. Not that these issues are of no importance for the Asian churches. They are. But they do not occupy the central position on the theological radar of the Asian churches.

Instead of developing an ecclesiocentric or church-centered ecclesiology, Asian bishops and theologians have fostered what may be called a regnocentric or kingdom-of-God-centered way of being church. Their emphasis is not on establishing new church organizations or on instituting structural reforms, much less elaborating a theoretical ecclesiology. Rather, their main, if not exclusive, concern has been to implement, pastorally and spiritually, ways of being church that are appropriate to the sociopolitical, economic, cultural, and religious contexts of Asia, as these have been sketched out above. In other words, in appropriating Vatican II, the Asian Catholic Church has been more interested in those conciliar and postconciliar documents that deal with the church's *ad extra* relations. Among these *Gaudium et spes*, *Ad gentes*, and *Nostra aetate* have been most frequently invoked.

A quick glance at the themes of the ten past General Assemblies as well as those of the innumerable seminars and workshops organized by the FABC's nine offices will confirm this assessment.[27] In addition to these official and semiofficial documents, the FABC also publishes what it calls "FABC Papers." These booklet-size publications are theological writings, mainly by native Asian theologians, addressing particular issues affecting Asian churches.[28] By and large all these writings focus on what has become a mantra among Asian Catholic churches, namely, the "triple dialogue": dialogue with the poor (liberation), with cultures (inculturation), and with other Asian religions (interreligious dialogue). By dialogue is meant not theoretical discussions among religious experts but the fundamental mode-of-being-church toward outsiders, be they other Christians (ecumenical

27. The themes of the FABC's ten General Assemblies are, in chronological order: evangelization (1974), life of the church (1978), church as community of faith (1982), the laity (fourth, 1986), a new way of being church (1990), discipleship (1995), church as love and service (2000), family (2004), the Eucharist (2008), and new evangelization (2012). The tenth General Assembly celebrated inter alia the 40th anniversary of the approval of the statutes of the FABC by the Holy See and the 50th anniversary of the convocation of Vatican II. Underlying these diverse themes is the leitmotif of the new way of being church in Asia.

28. These booklets, numbering nearly 150, are available on the FABC website.

dialogue), non-Christian believers (interreligious dialogue), or nonbelievers (humanistic dialogue). This dialogue takes a fourfold form: common life, working together for the common good, theological discussion, and sharing religious experiences.

Continuing further the assessment of the impact of Vatican II on Asian Catholic Christianity, I will examine how this triple dialogue has been understood by the FABC and some influential Asian Catholic theologians. Here, O'Malley's distinction between "reception" and "trajectory" is highly relevant. In fact, this triple dialogue belongs more to extending the council's trajectories than to its reception. Needless to say, all three dialogues have been recommended by the council, as the three conciliar documents mentioned above, repeatedly invoked by the FABC, testify. It is true as well that liberation theology is the original contribution of the Latin American church (with an emphasis on liberation from economic poverty), and that inculturation has been a deep concern of African Christianity (with a stress on liberation from cultural and anthropological domination). Nevertheless, it is the Asian Catholic churches that have consistently, insistently, and officially adopted the three dialogues in all their reciprocal and intrinsic connections as the overall agenda for pastoral ministry, church life, and spirituality, so much so that "dialogue" has become synonymous with the new way of being church in Asia.[29]

Perhaps the most comprehensive summary of this new way of being church is found in the Final Statement of the FABC's Seventh General Assembly (2000), with its theme "A Renewed Church in Asia: a Mission of Love and Service." The General Assembly sees the 30-year history of the FABC as woven by eight movements: toward a church of the poor and the church of the young, toward a truly local and inculturated church, toward an authentic community of faith, toward active integral evangelization and a new sense of mission, toward empowerment of lay men and women, toward active involvement in generating and serving life, and toward the triple dialogue with other faiths, with the poor, and with the cultures.[30]

29. See Peter C. Phan, *Christianity with an Asian Face: Asian American Theology in the Making* (Maryknoll, NY: Orbis, 2003); Phan, *In Our Own Tongues: Perspectives from Asia on Mission and Inculturation* (Maryknoll, NY: Orbis, 2003); and Phan, *Being Religious Interreligiously: Asian Perspectives on Interfaith Dialogue* (Maryknoll, NY: Orbis, 2004).

30. See the full text of the Final Statement in *For All the Peoples of Asia*, 3:1–16. See also Peter C. Phan, "A New Way of Being Church in Asia: Lessons for the American Catholic Church," in *Inculturation and the Church in North America*, ed. T. Frank Kennedy (New York: Crossroad, 2006), 145–62.

This new way of being church had been elaborated at length by the Fifth General Assembly (1990), with its theme "Journeying Together toward the Third Millennium." Its Final Statement envisions "alternative ways of being church in the Asia of the 1990s" and describes them as constituting the church in Asia as a "communion of communities," a "participatory church," a "church that faithfully and lovingly witnesses to the Risen Lord Jesus and reaches out to people of other faiths and persuasions in the dialogue of life towards the integral liberation of all," and as "a prophetic sign daring to point beyond this world to the ineffable Kingdom that is yet to come."[31]

This new way of being church is the consistent and pervasive perspective in which Vatican II has been received and its trajectories carried forward in Asian Catholic Christianity. This is supremely true not only of the FABC and its offices in general but also of most Asian Catholic theologians of both the older and younger generations. Among the former group mention has already been made of Aloysius Pieris, who may rightly be regarded as one of the most innovative theologians of Asia. Together with him are to be named, among many others, Cardinal Luis Antonio Tagle, Carlos H. Abesamis, Georg Evers, Felix Wilfred, Michael Amaladoss, Virginia Fabella, Kathleen Coyle, José M. De Mesa, Jacob Kavunkal, Jacob Parappally, Soosai Arokiasamy, Antoinette Gutzler, Mark Fang, James Kroeger, John Mansford Prior, and Vu Kim Chinh.[32] Among the younger generation, mention should be made of Jonathan Tan, Edmund Chia, Gemma Cruz, Vimal Tirimanna, and the theologians associated with the FABC's Office of Theological Concerns.[33] A growing number of doctoral dissertations and master's theses have been written on the FABC and Asian theology.[34]

31. For the full text of the Final Statement, see *For All the Peoples of Asia*, 1:273–89.

32. See M. Amaladoss and R. Gibellini, eds., *Teologia in Asia* (Brescia, Italy: Queriniana, 2006), which also contains essays by non-Catholic theologians. Deserving special mention is James H. Kroeger, an American Maryknoller and long-time professor of missiology at the Loyola School of Theology, Manila. With his prolific writings he is a tireless and ardent advocate of the FABC and Asian Catholic theology.

33. See Vimal Tirimanna, ed., *Harvesting from the Asian Soil: Towards an Asian Theology* (Bangalore: Asian Trading Corporation, 2011); and Kathleen Coyle, ed., *40 Years of Vatican II and the Churches of Asia and the Pacific: Looking Back and Moving Forward*, *East Asian Pastoral Review* 42, nos. 1/2 (2005).

34. See James H. Kroeger, *Theology from the Heart of Asia: FABC Doctoral Dissertations I (1985–1998)*; and *Theology from the Heart of Asia: FABC Doctoral Dissertations II (1998–2008)* (Quezon City: Claretian, 2008).

Trajectories of Vatican II in Asia

As we celebrate the 50th anniversary of the convocation of the Second Vatican Council and as we take stock of the council and its reception throughout the world, it is clear that the Catholic Church as a whole is at a crossroads. There is a widespread sense of an urgent need for renewal and even moral and spiritual purification in the whole church *a capite ad calcem*. This realization is made more insistent by the discouraging perception that the "reforms" of Vatican II have been "reformed" in the last few decades and by the numerous scandals of various sorts (not only of a sexual nature) that have wrecked the credibility of the church as a sign of God's presence in history. By happenstance, as this essay is being composed, the cardinals are meeting in Rome to elect a new pope after the unexpected resignation of Pope Benedict XVI, who felt no longer up to the task of shepherding the church because of advanced age and ill health.

The question naturally arises: Can the Asian Catholic Church, with its manifold attempts at receiving Vatican II *ad intra* and *ad extra*, provide some useful hints for the "renewal" (and not simply "reform," to reprise Pieris's expressions) of the church? In other words, are there "trajectories" and unfinished business from Vatican II that need to be carried forward to achieve or restore the true renewal of the church at this critical juncture? Like any genuine church renewal, this renewal must be both *ressourcement* and *aggiornamento*, the two movements working in tandem and in support of each other.

An answer may be derived from the Final Statement of the FABC's Tenth General Assembly with the theme "Renewed Evangelizers for New Evangelization in Asia," which met December 10–16, 2012, in Xuan Loc, Vietnam, an event that has been hailed as a "miracle" because of the location of the meeting. As the General Assembly sees it, the fundamental task of the church is to respond to the specific challenges of our time, and like Vatican II, it sets out to "read the signs of the times." Its *instrumentum laboris*, titled "FABC at Forty Years: Responding to the Challenges of Asia: A New Evangelization," analyzes 15 megatrends currently affecting Asia and Asian Christianity:

- globalization as an economic process and a cultural phenomenon
- a secular, materialist, consumerist, and relativist culture
- widespread and systemic poverty
- the phenomenon of migrant workers and refugees
- the oppression of the indigenous peoples
- immense population

- threat to religious freedom
- threats to life
- the increasing role of social communications
- the endangerment to ecology
- the lack of empowerment of the laity
- discrimination against women
- the majority of youth
- the presence of Pentecostalism
- and the rise of Asian missionary societies

An essential part of the effort to meet these challenges, according to the FABC's Tenth General Assembly, is to continue the process of reception of Vatican II and expansion of its trajectories, as the following statement of the General Assembly makes clear: "The same Spirit who animated Vatican II now summons us to become *renewed evangelizers for a new Evangelization*" (emphasis original). This reception and expansion of Vatican II requires a new spirituality: "To be renewed as evangelizers we have to respond to the Spirit active in the world, in the depths of our being, in the signs of the times and in all that is authentically human. *We need to live a spirituality of New Evangelization*" (emphasis original).

In elaborating this spirituality of New Evangelization, the General Assembly lists the following ten recommendations:

- personal encounter with Jesus Christ
- passion for mission
- focus on the kingdom of God
- commitment to communion
- dialogue as a mode of life and mission
- humble presence
- prophetic evangelization
- solidarity with victims
- care for creation
- and boldness of faith and martyrdom[35]

It is interesting to note that all ten recommendations, though deeply rooted in Christian spirituality (especially the first), are oriented *ad extra*,

35. For the full text of the Final Statement of the Tenth General Assembly, see http://www.fabc.org/10th%20plenary%20assembly/Documents/FABC%20-%20X%20PA%20Final%20Message%20-%202012.pdf.

as ways of being church toward others in contemporary Asia. The FABC's dominant concern is centered on the kingdom of God (not on the institutional church); mission (not inward self-absorption); communion (not splendid isolation); dialogue (not imperialistic monologue); solidarity with victims (not victim-blaming and withdrawal into an otherworldly "spirituality"); care of creation (not exploitation of natural resources); and witness/martyrdom (not cowardly compromise).

Perhaps it is not too far-fetched to see in these extensions of Vatican II's trajectories by the Asian Catholic Church a way forward for the Catholic Church in these dark times. If so, we will come full circle: the gift that Rome gave to Asia 50 years ago is now brought back to Rome enlarged, enhanced, enriched.

14 The Reception of Vatican II in Latin America

O. ERNESTO VALIENTE

Since Vatican II the Latin American church has come of age becoming an autochthonous and distinctive expression of the universal church. The article enlists the postconciliar general conferences of Latin American bishops to explore the creative reception of the council and how it has shaped the identity and mission of this church. Three theological elements reflect the renewal that Vatican II made possible in the Latin American church: reading the signs of the times, the preferential option for the poor, and the communion ecclesiology expressed in the Christian base communities.

In the early 1960s, the Latin American church, due to demographic, social, economic, and political changes, was ripe for change and renewal. But the Second Vatican Council provided the catalyst for the development of a truly autochthonous church. While the council did not directly address the concerns of the Latin American continent, it did chart a new course for its church. The Second General Conference of Latin American Bishops, which gathered at Medellín, Colombia, in 1968, formally began the process of reception, whereby the Latin American church began to appropriate the resolutions arrived at by Vatican II a few years earlier.[1]

1. Differences among Latin American countries must be acknowledged, as generalizations about the whole continent are always vulnerable to inaccuracies. Yet, I believe that some generalizations are legitimate, given the fact that most countries of Latin America share a similar faith, history, culture, and language.

I am grateful to Richard Lennan, Gene McGarry, and the anonymous referees of this article for their help on earlier versions.

This article does not focus on liturgy, religious life, or other topics directly addressed by the council, but rather on how the council helped shape the identity and mission of the Latin American church. It is possible to summarize the council's contribution to the Latin American church by using three theological principles that have come to characterize it: (1) attention to the signs of the times as the point of departure for pastoral directives and theological reflection; (2) the adoption of the preferential option for the poor as the stance that ought to inform all aspects of the church; and (3) an ecclesiological vision rooted in the idea of communion and expressed in the formation of Christian base communities. These three elements have been consistently engaged across the general conferences of Latin American bishops since Vatican II. Thus, following a discussion of the council from the Latin American perspective, this article focuses on the development of these principles at the episcopal gatherings held at Medellín (1968), Puebla (1979), Santo Domingo (1992), and Aparecida (2007).

This focus on the general conferences of bishops as key agents and indicators of reception is justified by three considerations: (1) the participating bishops represented all the national episcopal conferences in Latin America and the Caribbean; (2) the general conferences explicitly placed themselves in the trajectory of Vatican II; and (3) the general conferences, which usually take place every ten years, set the pastoral directives for the whole continent in light of the challenges experienced by the church. I engage each general conference as an event constituted by many elements in order to illustrate the different forces that converged in the formulation of its final documents.[2]

Vatican II from a Latin American Perspective

Although Vatican II was, as Karl Rahner famously argued, a gathering of the "world church," including 600 bishops from Latin America, it is important to keep in mind that the council was an event driven primarily

2. It is important to distinguish a "National Conference of Bishops," which refers to a permanent episcopal structure of a particular nation (e.g., The National Conference of Bishops of Brazil), from a "Regional Conference of Bishops," which clusters the bishops of nations in close proximity to one another (e.g., the Episcopal Secretariat of Central America and Panama), and the "General Conferences of Latin American Bishops" (e.g., The Second General Conference of Latin American Bishops at Medellín), which are events that include representative bishops from Latin America and the Caribbean.

by the concerns of the European church.[3] European bishops led the theological and pastoral discussions during the assemblies, and "very little if anything referring directly to Latin America found its way into the final document of the Council."[4]

This subordination of the needs of the Latin American church to the concerns of the European church has historical roots. The Latin American church of the mid-20th century was in many ways still a European transplant, its identity shaped by its historic and institutional ties to the Spanish and Portuguese colonial powers. These connections contributed to the church's later tendency to oppose independence movements during the 19th century, even as it was strengthening its ties to groups representing the traditional alliance of "conservative parties, landowners, and the old aristocracy."[5] Indeed, until the mid-20th century the church honored this alliance and tacitly endorsed the socioeconomic structures that relegated the majority of the population to substandard living conditions.[6]

After World War II, however, the continent experienced a demographic explosion that accelerated internal migration among the rural poor, who sought better living conditions in urban areas. The rapid shift of population from the countryside to the slums surrounding the cities made it hard to overlook the acute economic inequality and poverty of much of the population. Alarmed by these injustices, many Catholics and non-Catholics struggled to respond to the situation of the whole continent.[7] Their efforts took the form of movements that sought to change not only the broader society but also the church's priorities and alliances. These renewal movements would give direction to the Latin American church's reception of Vatican II.

3. See Karl Rahner, "Towards a Fundamental Theological Interpretation of Vatican Council II," *Theological Studies* 40 (1979): 716–27, at 718; Massimo Faggioli, *Vatican II: The Battle for Meaning* (New York: Paulist, 2012), 3; and José Comblin, "Vaticano II: Cincuenta años después," *Revista latinoamericana de teología* 84 (2011): 271–72.

4. Enrique Dussel, "Latin America," in *Modern Catholicism: Vatican II and After*, ed. Adrian Hastings (New York: Oxford University, 1991), 319 –25, at 319.

5. Christian Smith, *The Emergence of Liberation Theology: Radical Religion and Social Movement Theory* (Chicago: University of Chicago, 1991), 13.

6. This is not to deny that the church was in some ways an advocate for the poor, but the church did not identify herself with the great majority of the Christian faithful or recognize their concerns as her own.

7. See Enrique Dussel, *A History of the Church in Latin America: Colonialism to Liberation (1492–1979)* (Grand Rapids, MI: Eerdmans, 1981), 101–24; Smith, *Emergence of Liberation Theology*, 71–121.

Lay movements such as Catholic Action, *Cursillos de Cristiandad*, and the Legionaries of Mary, which had come from Europe earlier in the century, stressed the active role of lay people in the world and expanded at an exponential rate.[8] Catholic Action, arguably the largest and most influential among these groups, stimulated the formation of labor unions as well as professional and student organizations, and eventually inspired the formation of Christian Democratic parties. Although these movements did not call for the structural transformation of society per se, by inculcating Christian social values in their members they encouraged sectors of the church to make a more radical commitment to alleviate poverty.

Another important lay movement was the formation of *comunidades eclesiales de base*, the base ecclesial communities (CEBs). These grew from a successful catechetical experiment initiated in 1956 at Barra do Pirai, Brazil. In an effort to overcome the shortage of priests in rural areas, lay members were trained to serve as catechists, animators, and leaders of small communities. These lay-led Christian communities anticipated the important responsibilities that Vatican II and Medellín would later ascribe to the laity, and the CEBs would eventually play a crucial role in the development of an indigenous Latin American church.[9]

The shortage of priests in rural areas also led to an influx of North American and European clergy during the 1950s and 1960s.[10] These missionaries introduced new European currents of theological thought, such as the *nouvelle théologie*, thus bridging the distance between Latin American communities and those of the First World. At the same time, other intellectual and historical developments sharpened the Latin American church's awareness of the distinctive challenges it faced: local scholars achieved an understanding of the causes of poverty in the region that challenged explanations put forward by scholars from industrialized nations, and this new understanding would later inform the discussions at the general con-

8. See Dussel, *History of the Church in Latin America*, 101–24.

9. The terms "base ecclesial community," "Christian base community," and *comunidad ecclesial de base* (CEB) are used interchangeably. On the origins of these communities, see Marcello de C. Azevedo, *Basic Ecclesial Communities in Brazil: The Challenge of a New Way of Being Church*, trans. John Drury (Washington, DC: Georgetown University, 1987); and Andrew Dawson, "The Origins and Character of the Base Ecclesial Community: A Brazilian Perspective," in *The Cambridge Companion to Liberation Theology*, ed. Christopher Rowland (New York: Cambridge University, 2007), 139–58.

10. See Renato Poblete, "The Church in Latin America: A Historical Survey," in *The Church and Social Change in Latin America*, ed. Henry A. Landsberger (Notre Dame, IN: University of Notre Dame, 1970), 39–52.

ferences held after Vatican II. The Cuban Revolution, however ambivalent its legacy, at the time inspired many emancipatory movements elsewhere on the continent, while the liberation of many African nations from their colonial ties made the Western world more aware of the ubiquity of oppression and raised, in the developing nations, the hope for liberation.

The Latin American church's increasing awareness of itself as a distinct branch of the global church was fostered by the establishment in 1955 of the Latin American Episcopal Council (CELAM) in Rio de Janeiro.[11] This first general conference of bishops did not publish any significant documents and is scarcely mentioned in the history of the Latin American church.[12] Yet, within a relatively brief time, CELAM broke down the isolation that had hampered relationships among bishops and would eventually lead the effort to appropriate Vatican II faithfully and creatively. The episcopal council would become, in Enrique Dussel's words, "the only effective entity operating as a united force in Latin America, promoting integration in the programs of the political parties and diverse lay movements in general."[13]

Thus, when the 600 Latin American bishops arrived in Rome, they saw themselves as representing the distinctive political and economic concerns of the continent. Although their overall participation is often described as limited, these bishops sought to convey the reality of global poverty to their colleagues both in formal discussions and in the corridors outside the *aula* of the council.[14] Their concerns resonated with European bishops, but there were notable differences between the Latin American and European views of the role the church should play in responding to such needs. Panamanian bishop Marcos McGrath recounts that during the discussions around *Gaudium et spes*, some European bishops were very anxious to note that the church was not directly responsible for building the temporal order. While agreeing with this basic principle, McGrath and other Latin American bishops objected to the way it was phrased and sought to make room for the church's participation in society. McGrath writes:

11. The first conference of Latin American bishops, the Plenary Council of Latin America, was convoked by Pope Leo XIII in Rome in 1889, but it did not constitute a regional body.

12. Segundo Galilea notes that this first conference had a minimal impact because "as yet there were few established channels in the continent to spread its message" ("Between Medellin and Puebla," *Cross Currents* 28 [1978]: 71–78, at 71).

13. Dussel, *History of the Church in Latin America*, 134.

14. Smith, *Emergence of Liberation Theology*, 97– 98.

> We did not want to give the impression in a Council statement that the church, as an institution, could not and must not in any instance inaugurate programs and instill in the people the spirit of working together for justice, a spirit which is required if they are going to raise themselves up by their own bootstraps and develop organic communities.[15]

Prior to the opening of the council, Pope John XXIII asked the assembled bishops to engage three key issues: (1) updating the church in relation to the modern world; (2) overcoming division among Christians; and (3) addressing the challenge that the poverty of underdeveloped countries posed for the church.[16] The question of the church's response to modernity received the broadest attention, and the council went to great lengths to foster ecumenical dialogue. But with the exception of a few texts, including the fine christological passages in *Lumen gentium* no. 8 and *Ad gentes* no. 5, the relationship between the church and the poor was given little prominence in the council's documents. This modest response to the problem of poverty is not difficult to explain. The majority of the council's participants represented European and North American sees and had little knowledge of the problems of the underdeveloped nations. They focused instead on the challenges of modernity and ecumenism they themselves faced.[17]

If Vatican II sidestepped the economic challenges facing the Latin American church, the council nevertheless equipped that church with the tools required to confront them. The council's renewed attention to the historical dimension of the church, along with a corresponding change in attitude toward the modern world, would provide a crucial methodological framework for the church in Latin America. The opening lines of *Gaudium et spes* state that the church "realizes that it is truly linked with mankind and its history by the deepest of bonds" (no. 2).[18] This attention to history was expressed in a scriptural image that would become a guiding principle in the Latin American reception of the council: discerning the signs of the times. The call to heed the signs of the times was already present in John XXIII's convocation of the council, and it was further articulated in the

15. McGrath, "Church Doctrine in Latin America after the Council," 111.

16. Gustavo Gutiérrez, "The Church and the Poor: A Latin American Perspective," in *The Reception of Vatican II*, ed. Giuseppe Alberigo, Jean-Pierre Jossua, and Joseph A. Komonchak (Washington, DC: Catholic University of America, 1987), 175.

17. Gutiérrez, "The Church and the Poor," 183–88.

18. All references to the documents of Vatican II come from *Vatican Council II: The Conciliar and Post Conciliar Documents*, ed. Austin Flannery, OP (Northport, NY: Costello, 1996). I use gender-inclusive language except for when directly quoting church documents.

council's documents (nos. 4, 11).[19] In these texts the church embraces her place within history and acknowledges her dialogical relationship with a historical world. In attending to the signs of the times, the church inductively determines from everyday facts the signs of consistency between the Christian tradition and the desires of human beings. The signs, then, "call for the positive acknowledgement of history as an authentic 'place' wherein the imminent presence of the kingdom may be perceived."[20]

The Latin American church quickly discerned that there was one historical sign of the presence of God that overshadowed all others and required her immediate attention. A few years after the council, Gustavo Gutiérrez referred to this sign as the "irruption of the poor," which gave rise to his central theological question: "How is it possible to tell the poor, who are forced to live in conditions that embody a denial of love, that God loves them?"[21] Leonardo Boff approached the issue from a different direction, asking, "What does it mean to be Christian in a world of the oppressed?"[22] And Jon Sobrino, following Ignacio Ellacuría, explicitly asserts "that the sign of the times . . . par excellence, is the 'existence of a crucified people' . . . and that the prime demand on us is that we 'take them from the cross.' "[23] In heeding Vatican II's call to discern the signs of the times, the Latin American church encounters the poor—the crucified—and in solidarity with them recognizes the stance that still guides its liberating mission: the church's preferential option for the poor.

From Vatican II to Medellín (1968)

Even before Pope Paul VI delivered the concluding address of Vatican II on December 8, 1965, preparations had already begun for the Second Episcopal Conference of Latin American Bishops, who would assemble in Medellín, Colombia. Brazilian church historian José Oscar Beozzo

19. John XXIII, *Humanae salutis*, Apostolic Constitution, December 25, 1961, http://www.vatican.va/holy_father/john_xxiii/apost_constitutions/1961/documents/hf_j-xxiii_apc_19611225_humanae-salutis_sp.html (all URLs cited herein were accessed on September 5, 2012).

20. Giuseppe Ruggiere, "Faith and History," in *Reception of Vatican II*, 91–114, at 98.

21. Gustavo Gutiérrez, *A Theology of Liberation: History, Politics, and Salvation* (Maryknoll, NY: Orbis, 1988), xxxiv.

22. Leonardo Boff, *When Theology Listens to the Poor*, trans. Robert R. Barr (San Francisco: Harper & Row, 1988), 10.

23. Jon Sobrino, *The Principle of Mercy: Taking the Crucified People from the Cross* (Maryknoll, NY: Orbis, 1994), vii.

convincingly argued that the initial incentive for the conference at Medellín was the bishops' realization that many of their concerns would not be addressed by the council.[24] Hence, during the last session of the council in 1965, Chilean bishop Manuel Larraín, president of CELAM at the time, and his vice-president, Brazilian bishop Hélder Câmara, decided that an assembly of Latin American bishops was needed to examine the continent's situation in light of Vatican II. Taking advantage of a CELAM meeting in Rome later that year, the contingent of Latin American bishops officially proposed such a gathering to Paul VI, who approvingly suggested a wider consultation among the bishops on the continent. Three years later, in January 1968, the pope officially convoked the conference at Medellín.[25]

Since the late 1950s, converging historical and ideological forces had inspired in many Latin Americans the desire to transform the dismal reality in which they lived. The popular movements that began to develop in the early 1960s confronted new military dictatorships that began to take power in the middle of the same decade. Military repression only aggravated a restless population and stirred their hope for change. Paul VI's encyclical *Populorum progressio*, published in 1967, a year before Medellín, also helped foster a climate of high expectations for the conference.[26] The pope's analysis of the inequalities resulting from the international economic order anticipated many of the themes articulated at Medellín.[27] Gutiérrez notes that the encyclical also had a significant influence on the overall soteriological vision of Latin American theologians because it stressed salvation as a holistic event that incorporates the personal, social, and spiritual dimensions of the human person.[28] On a continent where the majority of the population was culturally and sociologically Catholic, the urgent desire for social change went hand in hand with the need for a renewed understanding of how the church should relate to the social sphere.[29]

24. José Oscar Beozzo, "Medellín: Inspiração e raízes," August 31, 1998, http://www.servicioskoinonia.org/relat/202.htm.

25. Fernando Torres Londoño, "Medellín 1968," *Revista anuario de historia de la iglesia* 5 (1996): 416–17.

26. Smith, *Emergence of Liberation Theology*, 126. See also Edward L. Cleary, *Crisis and Change: The Church in Latin America Today* (Maryknoll, NY: Orbis, 1985), 40.

27. *Populorum progressio* became an important source for the final Medellín documents; it was quoted more than 30 times.

28. Gustavo Gutiérrez, "The Meaning and Scope of Medellín," in *The Density of the Present: Selected Writings* (Maryknoll, NY: Orbis, 1999), 59–101, at 74.

29. Segundo Galilea, "Latin America in the Medellín and Puebla Conferences: An Example of Selective and Creative Reception of Vatican II," in *Reception of Vatican II*, 59–73, at 60.

In the years between Vatican II and Medellín, CELAM organized a number of regional meetings to examine and discuss "the signs of the times in Latin America and their interpretation for the theological and pastoral mission of [the] Church."[30] In these preparatory consultations, the participating bishops were joined by experts, including economists, anthropologists, sociologists, and theologians, who presented papers (*ponencias*) on their areas of specialization. These presentations widened the bishops' horizons and equipped them to better articulate the church's evangelizing mission in Latin America.[31] Among the meetings, those held in Melgar, Colombia, and Itapoán, Brazil, in 1968 are particularly noteworthy.[32] Melgar's recognition of Christ's active presence in history would become a key feature of Medellín's theology of revelation. It explicitly rejected the existence of two different histories—one sacred and the other profane. To the contrary, Melgar insisted on the fundamental unity of history in which God and humans participate. Christ's salvific work encompasses all the dimensions of human history and sets the mission for a church squarely planted in this same history. The document from the meeting states:

> All the dynamism of the cosmos and of human history; the movement for the creation of a more just and fraternal world, for the overcoming of social inequalities among people from all that depersonalizes them . . . have their origin, are transformed, and are perfected in the salvific work of Christ. In him and through him salvation is present in the heart of human history, and in the final analysis, every human act is defined by that salvation.[33]

At Itapoán, meanwhile, the Latin American bishops began to distance themselves from the social reformism of Vatican II and the models of economic development proposed by the industrialized nations. They

30. Marcos McGrath, "The Impact of *Gaudium et Spes*: Medellín, Puebla, and Pastoral Creativity," in *The Church and Culture since Vatican II: The Experience of North and Latin America*, ed. Joseph Gremillion (Notre Dame, IN: University of Notre Dame, 1985), 61–73, at 67.

31. Ibid., 66. See also Cleary, *Crisis and Change*, 34–35.

32. In addition to these meetings at Melgar and Itapoán, in 1966 the bishops gathered in Baños, Ecuador, to discuss pastoral ministry, social action, and the laity. In Mar del Plata that same year, the gathering focused on development and integration in Latin America; the 1968 meeting in Buga, Colombia, addressed the mission of Catholic universities in Latin America. See Agenor Brighenti, "América Latina—Medellín: 40 Años," *Adital*, http://www.adital.com.br/site/noticia.asp?lang=ES&cod=34474.

33. CELAM Department of Mission, Melgar meeting, quoted in Gutiérrez, "The Meaning and Scope of Medellín," 81.

instead invoked the dependency theory that had been formulated by Latin American social scientists in the mid-1960s. This theory essentially argues that the wealth enjoyed by developed countries is made possible by the poverty of the underdeveloped ones. As the Brazilian economist Theotonio Dos Santos summarizes, "Dependency is a situation in which certain groups of countries have their economies conditioned by the development and expansion of another country's economy."[34] Although this socioeconomic theory is rightly criticized for not sufficiently accounting for the internal factors that foster dependency within the underdeveloped nations, it made clear the need for a global and historical approach that would incorporate structural analysis into its examination of Latin America's underdevelopment.[35]

The period just prior to the Medellín conference saw an intensification of the fundamental concern that had informed the two-year-long process of preparation: how best to proclaim the gospel on the continent. The preparatory document for the conference stated the problem concisely: "Free of temporal partnerships, which she rejects; free from the burden of ambiguous prestige, which does not serve her interests, the Church seeks to understand a new evangelization of the continent."[36] The document called the Latin American church to a deeper conversion in order to more credibly proclaim the word. She was to place herself at the service of all and break with the ambiguous legacy of her legitimization of the political and economic domination exercised by both colonial rulers and local oligarchies.

On August 24, 1968, Paul VI—the first pope to visit the Americas—delivered the opening address of the general conference.[37] The 249 participants aimed to articulate an interpretation of the church's mission that would reshape the identity of the Latin American church. The introduction to the final documents shows that the bishops were mindful of the historical significance of the occasion: "We are on the threshold of a new epoch in the history of our continent. It appears to be a time full of zeal for full emancipation, of liberation from every form of servitude, of personal

34. Theotonio Dos Santos, "La crisis de la teoría del desarrollo y la relaciones de dependencía en America Latina," quoted in Smith, *Emergence of Liberation Theology*, 145.

35. Gutiérrez, "Meaning and Scope of Medellín," 77.

36. *Signos de renovación*, 215 (my translation); quoted in Gutiérrez, "Meaning and Scope of Medellín," 78.

37. In *Aparecida renacer de una esperanza* (San José: Fundación Amerindia/Indo-American, 2007), 35–52, at 40. See also http://www.scribd.com/doc/40528082/Amerindia-2007-Aparecida-Renacer-de-Una-Esperanza.

maturity and collective integration. In these signs we perceive the first indications of the painful birth of a new civilization."[38]

The direction of the conference was set early on with a sociological overview and the presentation of seven papers (*ponencias*) that addressed the social and religious situation of the continent.[39] Speaking on "Signs of the Times in Latin America Today," Bishop Marcos McGrath of Panama called the assembly to interpret these signs for the mission of the local church.[40] The "see, judge, act" approach to reading the signs, popularized by the Belgian priest Joseph Cardijn, called for looking at reality through the appropriate scientific disciplines; judging the results in the light of Christian revelation—that is, through theological reflection; and acting or responding through the implementation of pastoral recommendations. This inductive process guided the final drafting of the conference's final document.

Latin American theologians often assert that the strength of the Medellín conference resides in its "creative and selective reception" of Vatican II.[41] What they mean by "selective" and "creative" can be inferred from the official formulation that articulates the theme of the conference in its final document, "The Church in the Transformation of Latin America in the Light of the Council." This church "reflected on itself both 'in the light of the council' and in the context of 'the present day transformation of Latin America.' "[42] It is this contextualization of Vatican II in contemporary Latin America that characterizes its creative reception by the Medellín conference. The bishops "incarnated" the insights of the council in a way that would empower the local Latin American church to become an evangelizing force in the dynamic transformation of its own culture and society. Their indebtedness to Vatican II is always palpable: "Of 340 references which Medellín makes, 219 are from the Council."[43] At the

38. Second General Conference of Latin American Bishops, "Introduction to Final Documents," in *The Church in the Present-Day Transformation of Latin America in the Light of the Council*, 2 vols. (Bogota: General Secretariat of CELAM, 1970), 2: no. 4.

39. See Cleary, *Crisis and Change*, 41.

40. Marcos McGrath, "The Signs of the Times in Latin America Today," in *Church in the Present-Day Transformation*, 1:81–106.

41. See Brighenti, "America Latina—Medellín: 40 Años"; see also Segundo Galilea, "Latin America in the Medellín and Puebla Conferences: An Example of Selective and Creative Reception of Vatican II," in *Reception of Vatican II*, 59–73, at 61.

42. Joseph A. Komonchak, "The Local Realization of the Church," in *Reception of Vatican II*, 77–90, at 82.

43. McGrath, "Impact of *Gaudium et Spes*," 67; 47 references come from *Gaudium et spes*, 28 from *Lumen gentium*.

same time, Medellín's reception of the council was selective: the bishops had to analyze and interpret the continent's current economic, political, and cultural developments in order to discern the issues that demanded their immediate attention. They determined that the most important and pressing historical signs were overwhelming poverty and injustice.[44] Other issues of import to the council, such as secularism and religious pluralism, would be addressed more fully in later conferences. In this sense, Medellín was a hermeneutical accomplishment that brought together text and context—the good news and a particular situation—in such a way that each interprets and illuminates the other.[45]

The bishops' analysis of the signs of the times—Latin American realities and the experience of the poor—marked Medellín's point of departure in formulating the church's vision and mission. The conference took an honest view of the people's situation, describing it as "dismal poverty, which in many cases becomes inhuman wretchedness" that is accompanied by a "deafening cry from the throats of millions of men asking their pastors for liberation" (Medellín, "Poverty," nos.1, 2).[46] This description of the situation was complemented by a vigorous attempt to identify its underlying causes. Medellín's inductive approach to the continent's social reality incorporated the expertise of different social scientists and appealed to the theory of dependency and other structural analyses (Medellín, "Peace," nos. 3, 5, and 9). This careful attention to the situation of the human person was also present in the conference's treatment of other areas, such as education, preaching, catechesis, liturgy, and other ministries.[47] In the reception of Vatican II's *Sacrosanctum concilium*, for instance, Medellín insists that "In Latin America . . . the liturgical celebration crowns and implies a commitment to the human situation, to development and human promotion" (Medellín, "Liturgy" no. 4).

The bishops fiercely denounced the extreme inequality among social classes, the forms of oppression exercised by the dominant groups, and the unjust actions of world powers. Indeed, their pronouncements against

44. The bishops explicitly acknowledge that "'the signs of the time,' . . . on our continent are expressed *above all else* in the social order'" (Second General Conference of Latin American Bishops, "Pastoral Concern for the Elites," in *The Church in the Present-Day Transformation of Latin America*, 2, no. 7, 98–105, at 101, emphasis added.

45. Komonchak, "Local Realization of the Church," 83.

46. These and all direct references to the text of the Medellín Conference are taken from *Church in the Present-Day Transformation of Latin America*, vol. 2.

47. Galilea makes a similar point; see "Latin America in the Medellín and Puebla Conferences," 63.

injustice go beyond ethical condemnation: they raise this historical reality to the status of a theological concept by declaring it to be a situation of sin, contrary to God's will (Medellín, "Peace" no. 1). As one author notes, the bishops put forward "the first magisterial articulation of structural and institutional sin."[48]

The church's faithful observance of the signs of the times led her directly to the concept of the preferential option for the poor,[49] itself a development of the position of John XXIII, who envisioned the church of Christ to be a "church of the poor."[50] The bishops at Medellín asserted that "the Church in Latin America should be manifested, in an increasingly clear manner, as truly poor, missionary, and paschal, separate from all temporal power and courageously committed to the liberation of each and every man" (Medellín, "Youth" no. 15). Their application of the pope's insight to the context of Latin America is rooted in faith in a God who incarnates in history—who himself becomes poor in order to extend his friendship to us. In a similar vein, for Medellín, the church's solidarity with the poor "is directed to the fulfillment of the redeeming mission to which it is committed by Christ" (Medellín, "Poverty" no. 7). Hence, the conference clearly understood that the church's solidarity with the poor is at the center of her vocation to follow Christ and serve as he did (Medellín, "Poverty" nos. 4, 6, and 7). Speaking of this solidarity with the poor, Clodovis Boff somewhat dramatically notes, "Everything happened as if Providence had reserved for the Latin American Church the task of developing, on behalf of the universal Church, what Vatican II had only intuited. And this is perhaps the most creative element of reception of the Council by the Church of the Continent."[51]

Closely related to the church's preferential option for the poor is her message of integral liberation. Building on *Gaudium et spes* and *Populorum progressio*, but speaking with more precision of the fundamental unity of history and an understanding of salvation that encompasses all aspects of the human person, the Latin American bishops affirmed that

48. Daniel J. Daly, "Structures of Virtue and Vice," *New Blackfriars* (2010), http://catholicethics.com/sites/default/files/u3/Daly%20article.pdf.

49. Although the formula is not explicitly stated in Medellín, we already find here the foundations of the church's "preferential option for the poor." The formula would be articulated explicitly later in the conference at Puebla and in liberation theology.

50. John XXIII, message of September 11, 1962, in Angelina and Giuseppe Alberigo, *Giovanni XXIII: Profezia nella fedeltá* (Brescia: Queriniana), 365, quoted in Gutiérrez, "Meaning and Scope of Medellín," 67.

51. Clodovis Boff, "La originalidad histórica de Medellín," *Revista electrónica latinoamericana de teología*, http://servicioskoinonia.org/relat/203.htm (my translation).

"while avoiding confusion or simplistic identification, [catechetical teaching] must always make clear the profound unity that exists between God's plan of salvation realized in Christ and the aspirations of man; between the history of salvation and human history" (Medellín, "Catechesis" no. 4). Upholding a holistic soteriology, the bishops noted that "Christians cannot but acknowledge the presence of God, who desires to save the whole man, body and soul" (Medellín, "Introduction" no. 5).[52]

Consideration of the church as a mystery in which all the people of God are invited to participate enabled Vatican II to conceive of the church as a communion whose charisms and ministries are oriented toward the edification of the community.[53] The council proclaimed that "[the] Church of Christ is truly present in all legitimate local congregations of the faithful which, united with their pastors, are themselves called churches in the New Testament" (*Lumen gentium* no. 26). Medellín echoed this insight:

> The Church is, above all, a mystery of catholic communion, because in the heart of its visible community, by the call of the Word of God and through the grace of its sacraments, particularly in the Eucharist, all men can participate in the common dignity of the sons of God, and also share in the responsibility and the work to carry out the common mission of bearing witness to the God Who saved them and made them brothers in Christ (Medellín, "Joint Pastoral Planning" no. 6).

As José Comblin has noted, "the concept 'people of God' offered the gateway to a church of the poor."[54] Indeed, Vatican II's communion model of church was creatively expressed in Latin America's CEBs. Before Medellín these communities, usually constituted by poor people, existed largely as scattered groups, but the conference outlined their central identifying features and treated them as an official expression of the renewed Latin American church.[55] Medellín recognized the CEBs' role as protagonists

52. Here, the words of *Gaudium et spes* no. 39 are a helpful reminder: "While earthly progress must be carefully distinguished from the growth of Christ's kingdom, to the extent that the former can contribute to the better ordering of human society, it is of vital concern to the Kingdom of God."

53. Consuelo Velez, "Verdaderas luces y urgentes desafíos," *Voices* 4 (2011): 273–83, at 276; http://internationaltheologicalcommission.org/VOICES/VOICES-2011-4.pdf.

54. José Comblin, *People of God*, ed. and trans. Phillip Berryman (Maryknoll, NY: Orbis, 2004), 41.

55. William T. Cavanaugh, "The Ecclesiologies of Medellín and the Lessons of the Base Communities," *Cross Currents* 44 (1994): 67–84, at 74.

in the renewal of the Latin American church and thus considered them to be the "initial cell of the ecclesiastical structures" as well as "the focus of evangelization . . . and the most important source of human advancement and development" (Medellín, "Joint Pastoral Planning" no. 10).

While the conference ascribed responsibility for the selection and formation of community leaders to the parish priests and bishops, it also noted that the leaders of CEBs could be ordained, religious, or lay ministers (Medellín, "Joint Pastoral Planning" no. 11). Thus, the Christian communities introduced a new church structure in which the laity could participate while exercising a measure of authority. After Medellín the CEBs spread throughout Latin America, spearheading the Bible-reading movement and nurturing reflections that would strengthen the development of Latin American liberation theology. Ten years after Medellín, Galilea noted that Latin America's evangelization could not be understood in the context of justice and liberation alone; it had to be understood in the context of the CEBs. "These communities embody the originality of the Latin American Church," he wrote. "They represent one typical way in which Latin American Christians are trying to preach the gospel and assemble as church. Indeed, they offer a new 'model of the church.' "[56]

The reception of Vatican II by the Second Episcopal Conference at Medellín set the course the Latin American church has followed to this day. In spite of the struggles and conflicts that Medellín would generate, many Latin Americans continue to see Medellín as a true rebirth and a new Pentecost for the Latin American church. In the words of Chilean theologian Víctor Codina, "Medellín became the point of departure in [Latin Americans'] march as a people of God . . . [and] has become the necessary test and point of reference to discern the path of the Latin American church for years to come."[57]

From Medellín to Puebla (1979)

Medellín provided Latin Americans with the foundation to develop as an autochthonous and renewed church. Ten years later, the general conference held in Puebla, Mexico, "shows decisively that the spirit of both Medellín and Vatican II is still very much alive within the Roman Catholic

56. Segundo Galilea, "Between Medellín and Puebla," *Cross Currents* 28 (1978): 71–78, at 75.

57. Víctor Codina, "Eclesiología de Aparecida," in *Aparecida: Renacer de una esperanza*, 105–25, at 109 (my translation).

Church."[58] At Puebla the three central theological elements of Medellín that came to define the post–Vatican II Latin American church—attention to the signs of the times, the preferential option for the poor, and a communion ecclesiology expressed in the Christian base communities—would be confirmed, clarified, and further developed. In a different historical and ecclesial context than Medellín, Puebla represents a new stage in the selective and creative reception of the council.

The decade between the Medellín and Puebla conferences saw vast political and social deterioration throughout the continent. In 1978, the Theological Commission of Northeast Brazil observed, "If the Church were to summarize the past decade of 'development' in Latin America, it would have to state that the result is more hunger."[59] Medellín had spurred the development of well-considered pastoral programs and training institutes and the unprecedented growth of CEBs and groups actively engaged in civil society, fostering the urgent sense that society had to be transformed. As theologian Pablo Richard observed, "The Church now has a full-blown popular movement with its own theological thought commonly known as liberation theology."[60] On the other hand, the increased social deterioration in many Latin American nations gave rise to widespread political unrest. At a time when most of the continent was still under military dictatorship, unrest led to human rights abuses and the targeting of those who opposed the current regimes. In the persecution of some of her lay and ordained members, the church began to experience the cost of the option for the poor exercised at Medellín.

Puebla also needs to be understood within its particular ecclesial context. In the years prior to the conference, a growing division had emerged among the Latin American bishops. While the final documents of the Medellín conference had been approved overwhelmingly (only five negative votes out of 130), a number of bishops were now questioning what the future direction of the church should be in her relationship to society.[61] Two distinct pastoral tendencies became clear. In line with Medellín, some

58. Jon Sobrino, "The Significance of Puebla for the Catholic Church in Latin America," in *Puebla and Beyond*, ed. John Eagleson and Philip Scharper (Maryknoll, NY: Orbis, 1980), 289–309, at 302.

59. Quoted in Penny Lernoux, "The Long Path to Puebla," in *Puebla and Beyond*, 3–25, at 25.

60. Pablo Richard, "Puebla: Hope of the Poor," *Missiology* 7, no. 3 (1979): 287–93, at 288.

61. Cleary, *Crisis and Change*, 44.

bishops insisted that the main challenges before the church remained the realities of poverty and injustice. An influential minority, however, argued that the main challenge now was the continent's increasing secularism and a corresponding weakening of the faith.[62] This camp argued that "liberation without evangelization [is] the breech through which secularism penetrates," and thus Puebla should make evangelization its main concern.[63]

Meanwhile, in the public square, Catholics were embroiled in disagreements over the church's proper role vis-à-vis the political sphere. While the Medellín conference had insisted on the need to humanize and transform society through peaceful means and did not endorse any particular social or political agenda, the acute deterioration of the social and political situation influenced Catholic groups to take more radical and revolutionary positions.[64] Moreover, liberation theology, which had gained strength during Medellín and flourished thereafter, became both a source and symbol of conflict on the continent.

The mistrust of liberation theology among some members of the church—clergy and laity alike—arose in part because of a lack of clarity in the early writings of some theologians who enlisted Marxist elements in their theological approach.[65] But it was also fueled by what appears to have been a smear campaign organized against this theology by some influential members of the church.[66] At a more fundamental level, this mistrust also reflected the authoritarian and repressive context in which

62. This prompted Sobrino just a few months after the conference to assert that "Puebla was a struggle between the people who were more interested in watering down the novel and conflict-ridden aspect of [Latin American] reality and that reality itself as brought out by other spokes-persons" ("The Significance of Puebla for the Catholic Church in Latin America," in *Puebla and Beyond*, 289–309, at 295–96).

63. Albertho Methol Ferre, "Puebla procesoy tensiones," quoted in Smith, *Emergence of Liberation Theology*, 210.

64. Unfortunately, some Christians saw no other political alternative but armed struggle. Others, such as the Chilean movement of Christians for Socialism, seized on the Medellín document to justify their support for specific political programs and took sides in party politics. See Smith, *Emergence of Liberation Theology*, 180–88; Lernoux, "Long Path to Puebla," 12–14; and Paul E. Sigmund, *Liberation Theology at the Crossroads: Democracy or Revolution* (New York: Oxford University, 1990), 46–47.

65. See, for instance, Nicolas Lash's assessment of Porfirio Miranda's early work in Lash, *A Matter of Hope: A Theologian's Reflection on the Thought of Karl Marx* (Notre Dame, IN: University of Notre Dame, 1981), 4.

66. See Lernoux, "Long Path to Puebla," 20–23; Smith, *Emergence of Liberation Theology*, 185–86; and Gregory Baum, "German Theologians and Liberation Theology," in *Puebla and Beyond*, 220–24.

the church was trying to renew itself. During the Cold War, particularly on a continent governed by the "national security" ideology of the then-ubiquitous military dictatorships, the term "Marxist" inspired fear and was even seen as a just cause for persecution in some Latin American circles. Thus some church members were apprehensive of a theology that enlisted Marxist analysis as a tool to better understand the church's social world. Liberation theologians themselves were critical of many aspects of Marxism, but some Catholics, within and beyond the continent, questioned whether these theologians could appropriate Marxist elements without also endorsing Marxism's atheistic philosophical framework.[67]

Disagreements between some bishops over the direction of the Latin American church and reservations about liberation theology on the part of some influential members of the hierarchy contributed to a change of leadership in CELAM. In November 1972, Colombian Archbishop Alfonso López Trujillo, an outspoken critic of liberation theology, was elected CELAM's general secretary and was charged with organizing the Third General Conference of Latin American Bishops to be held in Puebla, Mexico. The theme of the conference, "The Present and the Future Evangelization of America," was inspired by the 1974 Synod on Evangelization and Paul VI's postsynodal apostolic exhortation *Evangelii nuntiandi* (1975).[68] Given the theme, the apostolic exhortation became an important point of reference for Puebla, just as *Populorum progressio* had been for Medellín.[69]

In 1977, the new general secretary of CELAM circulated the preliminary consultative document for the upcoming conference. Abjuring Medellín's inductive approach to the signs of the times, this document enlisted a

67. This helps explain why the letter of Pedro Arrupe, former superior general of the Society of Jesus, on the use of Marxist analysis was so timely and significant. See "Marxist Analysis by Christians," in *Liberation Theology: A Documentary History*, ed. Alfred T. Hennelly (Maryknoll, NY: Orbis, 1997), 307–13. See also Paul VI's apostolic letter *Octogesima adveniens* (1971). This issue came to a climax in 1984 when the Vatican's Congregation for the Doctrine of the Faith published its Instruction on Certain Aspects of the "Theology of Liberation," which argued that Marxism was a "totalizing ideology that could not be selectively endorsed." See Denys Turner, "Marxism, Liberation Theology and the Way of Negation," in *The Cambridge Companion to Liberation Theology*, ed. Christopher Rowland (New York: Cambridge University, 2007), 229–47, esp. 231–33.

68. Alfonso López Trujillo, "On the 25th Anniversary of the Puebla Conference," http://www.vatican.va/roman_curia/pontifical_councils/family/documents/rc_pc_family_doc_20040212_trujillo-puebla_en.html.

69. Galilea, "Latin America in the Medellín and Puebla Conferences," 70.

deductive theological approach to argue that secularism, and not social injustice, was at that time the main challenge facing the Latin American church. The preliminary document was widely discussed by the national episcopates and ultimately rejected because it did not reflect the questions and concerns of their CEBs and grassroots groups.[70] A second round of consultations, now including delegates representing a wider constituency—priests, religious, parishes, and the CEBs—was held in 1978, after which a more comprehensive working document was drafted under the direction of CELAM's president, Brazilian Cardinal Aloísio Lorscheider.

John Paul II, who had been elected pope just three months earlier, opened the general conference on January 28, 1979. Both pastoral preoccupations noted above—economic injustice and secularism—were represented in the discussions and are evident in the final document.[71] However, as at Medellín the situation of poverty and oppression endured by most Latin Americans came to the fore in the document as the sign of the times that most urgently required the church's attention.[72] Early in the final document, the bishops state, "We place ourselves within the dynamic thrust of the Medellín Conference . . . , adopting its vision of reality that served as the inspiration for so many pastoral documents of ours in the past decade" (Puebla no. 25).[73] Puebla also endorsed the "see, judge, act" methodology of *Gaudium et spes* and Medellín, and again took the experience of the human person as the point of departure for theological reflection.

In a style reminiscent of *Gaudium et spes*, the final document begins with a pastoral description of the human situation on the continent.[74] The bishops note the increased deterioration of economic, social, and political conditions since Medellín (Puebla nos. 27–50). To a greater extent than Medellín, the bishops' treatment identifies the structural causes, both domestic and international, that undergird the ongoing violations against human dignity. These causes include an economic system that disregards

70. See Gustavo Gutierrez, "Liberation and the Poor: The Puebla Perspective," in *The Power of the Poor in History* (Maryknoll, NY: Orbis, 1993), 125–65, at 130. See also Sobrino, "Significance of Puebla," 291; and Laura Nuzzi O'Shaughnessy and Luis H. Serra, *The Church and Revolution in Nicaragua* (Athens: Ohio University, Center for International Studies, 1986), 3.

71. Moíses Sandoval, "Report from the Conference," in *Puebla and Beyond*, 28– 43, at 41.

72. Sobrino, "Significance of Puebla," 296.

73. This and all direct references to the final document of the Puebla Conference are taken from "The Final Document," in *Puebla and Beyond*, 123–285.

74. McGrath, "Impact of *Gaudium et Spes*," 70.

the human person; a prevailing social order that generates structural conflict; economic, political, and cultural dependence on industrialized nations; political oppression; and the arms race. Thus, the bishops repeatedly declare that the continent is caught in a situation of "institutionalized injustice" and that "the contradictions existing between unjust social structures and the demands of the Gospel are quite evident" (Puebla no. 1257).

At Puebla the bishops also addressed an issue that was very much on the agenda of Vatican II but had barely been considered by Medellín: the relationship between culture and the church. Drawing heavily from *Ad gentes* (Puebla nos. 366, 375) and *Gaudium et spes* (Puebla nos. 386, 391–93, 401, 404),[75] the bishops encouraged the integration of the continent's three main cultural groups, Mestizos, African-Americans, and Amerindians; following *Evangelii nuntiandi,* the conference called for the evangelization of their cultures (Puebla nos. 385–87, 394, 395, 404). In spite of the church's relative lack of human resources, the bishops for the first time called Latin Americans to participate in the universal evangelizing mission of the church (Puebla no. 368).

Puebla further developed Medellín's initial insights into the church's option for the poor. The bishops were mindful that poverty is the result of a dialectical relationship between the haves and the have-nots. Thus the bishops often observed that the poor are not simply "poor," but rather are *impoverished* by mechanisms of oppression. Puebla drew from Matthew 25 to stress Christ's identification with the poor and his presence *in* those who suffer:[76] "[The] situation of pervasive extreme poverty takes on very concrete faces in real life. In these faces we ought to recognize the suffering features of Christ the Lord who questions and challenges us" (Puebla no. 31). This deepening understanding of the poor as subjects includes the conference's recognition of their evangelizing potential (Puebla no. 950). This constitutes an important advancement over Medellín, which spoke of the plight of the poor and their role as protagonists but did not formally identify the poor as agents of the gospel able to lead others to conversion.

Memorably, Puebla introduced the explicit use of the formula "preferential option for the poor." Indeed, a chapter is dedicated solely to this topic.[77] While both Medellín and Puebla ground the church's preferential option for the poor in our vocation to follow Christ, Puebla also stresses

75. Galilea, "Latin America in the Medellín and Puebla Conferences," 71.

76. Gutiérrez, "Liberation and the Poor," 142.

77. The Third General Conference of Latin American Bishops, "Final Document," in *Puebla and Beyond*, 264– 67.

that this preference is grounded in Christ's gratuitous love. The bishops explain that "[Christ] established solidarity with [the poor] and took up the situation in which they find themselves. . . . For this reason, the poor merit preferential attention, whatever may be the moral or personal situation in which they find themselves" (Puebla nos. 1141–42).

In this third general conference, the ecclesiology articulated in *Lumen gentium* and appropriated by Medellín as "the communion of the poor people of God" continued to shape the Latin American church. Puebla's final document describes a church that is both missionary and a sacrament of communion, characteristics that arise from God's trinitarian fellowship. The church's mission is that of the Son, and it is by proclaiming the good news that the church calls others to participate in the trinitarian communion. Thus the bishops summon the church "to preach conversion, to liberate human beings, and to direct them toward the mystery of communion with the Trinity and with all their brothers and sisters, transforming them into agents and cooperators in God's plan" (Puebla no. 563). As a polyvalent category, *communion* expresses different meanings throughout the document: presence, participation, sharing, and community. It is "because *communion* has this many-leveled meaning, [that] it could express sharing in a common good and mean participating at the same time in trinitarian life, in eucharistic community, and in human and material goods (property, wealth, the economic consultative process, political action)."[78]

In fact, one reason for the growth of CEBs lies in their capacity to foster a Christian life that integrates participants' religious experience with their commitment to communal and social transformation. At Puebla the bishops reaffirmed the importance of the CEBs and asserted that they "are determined to promote, guide, and accompany the CEBs in the spirit of the Medellín Conference . . . and the guidelines set forth by *Evangelii Nuntiandi* (no. 58)" (Puebla no. 648). As embodiments of the church's preferential option for the poor (Puebla no. 644), these communities were praised for their capacity to foster a close following of Christ while helping Christians strive for an evangelical life that challenges the egotistical and consumerist roots of today's society and to "make explicit their vocation to communion with God and their fellow humans." Thus "they offer a valid and worthwhile point of departure for building up a new society, 'the civilization of love' " (Puebla no. 643).

78. Kilian McDonnell, "Vatican II (1962–1964), Puebla (1979), Synod (1985): Koinonia/Communion as Integral Ecclesiology," *Journal of Ecumenical Studies* 25 (1988): 399–427, at 414.

In the final analysis, Puebla was not an innovative assembly, in that its primary accomplishment was to deepen and sharpen the themes and insights first developed at Medellín. At Puebla the Latin American church renewed the hope of the poor, continued the renewal brought forth by the council, and confirmed the features that have shaped her into a distinctive church.

From Puebla to Santo Domingo (1992)

In the decade following the Puebla conference, the Latin American military regimes that controlled the continent began to give way to democracies. This political liberalization did little to alleviate the perennial economic and social inequality between small, affluent groups and the great majorities. Slow growth, increased inflation, and the international debt crisis led the United Nations to call the 1980s Latin America's "lost decade."[79] At the same time, the emergence and consolidation of new Protestant churches and other religiously identified social movements that had been growing since the 1960s presented a challenge to the Catholic Church's traditional role as the *only* church on the continent.[80]

In commemoration of the quincentennial celebration of the first evangelization of the Americas, the Fourth General Conference, convened in October 1992 in Santo Domingo, Dominican Republic, on the theme of the "New Evangelization." The theme had been announced to the Latin America bishops by John Paul II in a 1983 address delivered in Haiti; it was a recurring motif in John Paul's papacy and can be traced to his Christocentric reading of *Gaudium et spes*.[81] In his address, the pope asked

79. United Nations Conference on Trade and Development (UNCTAD), "A Brief History of UNCTAD," http://unctad.org/en/Pages/About%20UNCTAD/A-Brief-History-of-UNCTAD.aspx.

80. Daniel Levine, "Pluralism as Challenge and Opportunity," in *Religious Pluralism, Democracy, and the Catholic Church in Latin America*, ed. Frances Hagopian (Notre Dame, IN: University of Notre Dame, 2009), 405–28, at 408. See also Edward Cleary, "The Journey to Santo Domingo," in *Santo Domingo and Beyond: Documents and Commentaries from the Historic Meetings of the Latin American Bishops' Conference*, ed. Alfred Hennelly (Maryknoll, NY: Orbis, 1993), 3–23, at 9.

81. Uruguayan theologian Fernando Verdugo asserts that while the conference was carried out in the context of the Americas' conquest and first evangelization, the "New Evangelization" was John Paul II's large personal project. It is not a coincidence, Verdugo notes, that in practice this conference was not led by CELAM but by the Latin American Pontifical Commission ("Aparecida: Perspective teológico-cultural," *Teología y vida* 49 [2008]: 673–84, at 677).

the bishops for a "commitment not to re-evangelization but to a new evangelization, new in ardor, methods, and expression."[82]

More so than its predecessors, this episcopal gathering was complex and at times conflicted, reflecting the ambiguities inherent in the process of interpreting and receiving an event such as Vatican II. The conference was preceded by a long preparation filled with tensions, reservations, misgivings, and at least two distinct visions of how the Latin American church should carry out this "New Evangelization."[83] Santo Domingo's process involved the same tensions over pastoral priorities that had been operative at Puebla. Here again some bishops maintained that the greatest need was to confront the challenges presented by contemporary culture, such as secularization and the increased presence of Protestant churches; for others, the most important matter was the prevalence of poverty in Latin America and the lack of an inculturated proclamation of the gospel among the indigenous population and the great majorities. Where Santo Domingo differed was in the increased number and influence of bishops representing the former stance, largely because of John Paul II's appointments in the preceding decade.[84]

Under the supervision of the Latin American Pontifical Commission, CELAM drafted three preparatory documents. The Consultative Document published in 1991 proposed that the main challenge faced by the church came from modern culture, as noted above. This was subsequently rejected by the bishops because it did not incorporate the contributions of the recent national bishops' conferences. A second document, aptly named *Segunda relation*, did gather ideas from the national bishops' conferences and other ecclesial organizations. This document proposed that the problems of modern culture and poverty facing the church should be addressed in a unified manner, beginning with the problems of poverty and marginalization.[85] This second document was rejected by Vatican officials,

82. "The Task of Latin America's Bishops, Address of Pope John Paul II to the Latin American Bishops' Council," *Origins* 12 (1983): 659–62, at 661.

83. Many conference observers were unsettled by the excessive intervention of Vatican officials in the preparation, discussion, and drafting of the final document in the Santo Domingo conference. See Jon Sobrino, "The Winds in Santo Domingo and the Evangelization of Culture," in *Santo Domingo and Beyond*, 167–83, at 170. See also Codina, "Eclesiología de Aparecida," 107–8.

84. Víctor Codina, "IV Conferencia del Episcopado Latinoamericano: Santo Domingo; Dos visiones differentes," *Revista electronica de teología*, no. 14, http://www.servicioskoinonia.org/relat/014.htm. See also Gustavo Gutiérrez, "An Agenda: The Conference at Santo Domingo," in *Density of the Present*, 113–23, at 114.

85. Gutiérrez, "An Agenda: The Conference at Santo Domingo," 114.

as well as by some of the Latin American bishops.[86] A final Working Document that incorporated the previous two documents was then drafted by the secretary general of CELAM and sent to Rome for approval. Rome initially approved this final Working Document, but at the beginning of the conference reclassified it as one of the consultative documents to be used in the discussions.[87]

The three distinct theological elements I have been tracing—reading the signs of the times, the preferential option for the poor, and the CEBs—are treated in the final document within the framework set by the main themes of the conference: New evangelization, human development, and Christian culture. Yet, the document to emerge from this conference differs notably from those produced by previous conferences in that it does not begin with an analysis of reality, a discernment of the signs of the times. Instead of adopting as its method the inductive approach of "see, judge, act," Santo Domingo took as its point of departure the bishops' rather ahistorical christological reflections.[88] While the document does not mention liberation theology, it reaffirmed its continuity with Medellín and Puebla as the bishops committed themselves to "renew [their] intention to further the pastoral guidelines, set by Vatican II, which were applied at the General Conferences of Latin American Bishops at Medellín and Puebla, and bring them up to date by means of the pastoral guidelines laid down at this conference" (Santo Domingo no. 298).[89]

Consequently, Santo Domingo upholds the church's preferential option for the poor (Santo Domingo nos. 50, 179, 180, 275, 296, 302), which informs the pastoral priorities for the church's evangelizing mission. Theologically, the conference grounds this in the church's vocation to follow Jesus Christ, who "[came] to bring 'glad tidings' to the poor" (Santo Domingo no. 179). Nonetheless, the issue of economic poverty and injustice is not treated with the same depth and vigor of previous conferences, as

86. Alfred Hennelly, "A Report from the Conference," in *Santo Domingo and Beyond*, 24–36, at 26.

87. Alfred Hennelly (ibid., 26–27) notes that on the first day of the conference the bishops were instructed to discard the Working Document, sabotaging years of work by the Latin American bishops.

88. Some chapters, such as the one on human development and Christian culture, do pay relatively more attention to the Latin American context. See Sobrino, "The Winds in Santo Domingo and the Evangelization of Culture," 177.

89. This and all direct references to the final document of the Santo Domingo Conference are taken from "Santo Domingo Documents," in *Santo Domingo and Beyond*, 39–150.

the bishops dedicated significant attention to the need for a new evangelization and to the relationship between religion and culture.[90]

The relation between culture and the church had already been noted at Medellín and initially developed at Puebla, but the bishops now turned to the task of inculturating the gospel.[91] Here again they grounded this pastoral task in the Incarnation, noting that "Jesus Christ is the measure of all things human, including culture" (Santo Domingo no. 228). Drawing from John Paul II's encyclical *Redemptoris missio* (1990), the bishops noted that "through inculturation, the Church makes the gospel incarnate in different cultures and at the same time introduces peoples, together with their cultures, into her community" (Santo Domingo no. 230). In this, Santo Domingo marks the first time in Latin America that a synod or episcopal conference developed a pastoral plan directed to the evangelization of the indigenous, African-American, and Mestizo cultures.

The conference also endorsed Medellín and Puebla's communion ecclesiology, but this theme was not furthered. The final document refers to the church as a "sacrament of evangelizing communion" (Santo Domingo no. 123), but although the bishops summon the church to "embody the driving forces of communion and mission" (Santo Domingo no. 55), they do not offer a systematic treatment of ecclesiology. In the same vein, Santo Domingo "reaffirm[s] the validity of basic Christian communities" (Santo Domingo no. 62), but its reflections on them are limited. Some Latin American theologians and bishops lamented that the themes of Medellín and Puebla were not advanced at Santo Domingo, and that the conference's final document does not have the "prophetic energy" of Medellín or the "theological density" of Puebla.[92]

From Santo Domingo to Aparecida (2007)

For many Latin Americans the conference at Aparecida, Brazil, was a welcome surprise. John Paul II's 1997 call for continental synods had

90. Roberto Goizueta argues that Santo Domingo, departing from Medellín and Puebla, reduces the preferential option for the poor to an "ethical injunction" and "no longer primarily a privileged epistemological criterion of faith." See "The Preferential Option for the Poor: The CELAM Documents and the NCCB Pastoral Letter on U.S. Hispanics as Sources for U.S. Hispanic Theology," *Journal of Hispanic/Latino Theology* 3, no. 2 (1995): 65–77, at 72.

91. One can trace the beginnings of a theology of inculturation to *Ad gentes* no. 11, which speaks of the "seed of the Word" said to be contained in various cultures.

92. Gutiérrez, "An Agenda: The Conference at Santo Domingo," 123.

given rise to speculation that they would henceforth replace the general conferences of Latin American bishops.[93] The Synod for the Americas would have included the bishops from Latin America, Canada, and the United States assembled in Rome, and it would have submitted its work to the pope, who would later publish a document under his authority.[94] Many Latin American church leaders and observers were concerned that this change would erode the identity that the Latin American church had forged, beginning with Medellín. Yet by 2003, after a number of unsuccessful attempts, the office of the new CELAM president, Cardinal Francisco Javier Errázuriz, was able to convince John Paul II to convene a general conference instead of a synod.[95] There was much relief two years later when Benedict XVI endorsed CELAM's proposal to celebrate its 50th anniversary with a general conference that he himself would convene at Aparecida in Brazil.

The assembly was held, once again, against the backdrop of a deeply troubled region. Though military dictatorships were almost entirely a thing of the past, the new century was marked by increasing dissatisfaction with the young democracies' apparent incapacity to overcome the structural problems that undergirded the acute social and economic inequalities of much of the continent.[96] The promises made by proponents of globalization in the early 1990s had not materialized. Rather, globalization and 15 years of "neo-liberal" policies of structural adjustments had increased the gap between the rich and poor nations, generated poverty and marginalization for the great majority, undermined local cultures, and further devastated natural resources.[97] The same 15 years had witnessed the departure of an unprecedented number of Catholics from the church, and the progressive

93. João Batista Libanio, "Conferencia de Aparecida: Documento final," *Revista iberoamericana de teología* (2008): 23–46, at 24.

94. Sergio Torres, "Amerindia: Return from Internal Exile," in *Aparecida: Quo Vadis?*, ed. Robert Pelton (Scranton, PA: University of Scranton, 2008), 137–58, at 149.

95. Aparecida marks the first time that bishops representing Canada and the United States were invited to a general conference [assembly?] not just as observers but also as voting members.

96. See "The Results of Aparecida: Monographic Issue," *Revista proceso* 1247 (June 27, 2007), http://www.uca.edu.sv/publica/cidai/proceso.1247i.pdf.

97. See United Nations Economic Commission for Latin America and the Caribbean, "Inequalities and Asymmetries in the Global Order," chap. 4 in *Globalization and Development: A Latin American and Caribbean Perspective*, ed. José Antonio Ocampo and Juan Martin (Washington, DC: World Bank, 2003), 99–128; available at http://www.eclac.cl/publicaciones/xm/0/10030/Globalization-Chap3.pdf.

transformation of the continent into an increasingly secular and religiously pluralized region.[98]

Preparation for the fifth general conference, which was given the title "Missionary Disciples of Jesus Christ: That Our Peoples May Have Life in Him," began in 2006 with the Document of Participation (past conferences referred to this as a Document of Consultation). As in the previous two conferences, this preliminary document was roundly criticized by most local churches.[99] Many veterans of Puebla and Medellín note that the Document of Participation again ignored the "see, judge, act" method and proposed an abstract and deductive Christology; it also put forth an ecclesiology that was centered in the institutional church and barely mentioned God's kingdom.[100] Others noted that the document paid no attention to the CEBs or to the witness of the recent Latin American martyrs.[101] In all, 22 national episcopal conferences submitted formal responses to the Document of Participation. Based on these contributions, a task force from CELAM prepared a Synthesis Document (in past conferences referred to as a Working Document) that heeded the request made by most of the national conferences to reinstate the "see, judge, act" method and to stress the centrality of God's kingdom.[102]

Aparecida's final document describes the conference as "a new step in the church's journey, especially since the ecumenical council Vatican II" (Aparecida no. 9).[103] In accord with the bishops' insistence on retaining the "see, judge, act" method, the document begins with a detailed evaluation of the social, economic, political, ecclesial, and cultural signs of the times. For the bishops, globalization is the complex phenomenon that best explains the challenges currently faced by the church (Aparecida no.

98. In the last ten years, approximately 30 million Catholics have left the church in Latin America and the Caribbean. See Pablo Richard, "Será possible ahora construir un nuevo modelo de iglesia?," in *Aparecida: Renacer de una esperanza*, 93–98, at 94; and Edward Cleary, "Aparecida and Pentecostalism in Latin America," in *Aparecida: Quo vadis?*, 159–72.

99. See Agenor Brighenti, "Crónica del desarrollo de la V Conferencia," in *Aparecida: Renacer de una esperanza*, 25–34, esp. 27.

100. Codina,"Eclesiología de Aparecida," 109.

101. See Brighenti, "Crónica del desarrollo de la V Conferencia," 25–34, esp. 26 –27.

102. Codina, "Eclesiología de Aparecida," 110.

103. This and all direct references to the final document of the Aparecida Conference are taken from V General Conference of the Bishops of Latin American and the Caribbean, Concluding Document (Washington, DC: United States Conference of Catholic Bishops, 2008), http://old.usccb.org/latinamerica/english/continentalmission.shtml/.

43): in Latin America, globalization has become the cause of new types of poverty. Focusing on the core economic values that fuel this new process of internationalization, the bishops warn that "in globalization, market forces easily absolutize efficacy and productivity as values regulating all human relations" (Aparecida no. 61). This instrumental way of thinking excludes transcendent values such as justice, truth, and human dignity, particularly the dignity of those not included in the market. The bishops thus conclude that a new type of globalization is necessary: "one characterized by solidarity, justice, and respect for human rights" (Aparecida no. 64).

In his inaugural address on the morning of May 13, 2007, Benedict XVI firmly embraced the preferential option for the poor that had distinguished the Latin American church since Medellín. He reminded the bishops that "the preferential option for the poor is implicit in the Christological faith in the God who became poor for us, so as to enrich us with his poverty (cf. 2 Cor 8:9)."[104] Aparecida quotes the pope directly and builds on *Lumen gentium* no. 8 to insist that "We Christians . . . are called to contemplate, in the suffering faces of our brothers and sisters, the face of Christ who calls us to serve Him in them" (Aparecida no. 393). The bishops offer a complex understanding of poverty that is not limited to economic factors but includes "the silenced cry of women who are subjected to many forms of exclusion and violence" (Aparecida no. 454) and the marginalization of indigenous and African populations (Aparecida no. 89). They are subjects that "need to shape their own destiny" (Aparecida no. 53) and through the recuperation of their identities "participate actively and creatively in building this continent" (Aparecida no. 97).[105] Rounding out the teaching on the option for the poor, the bishops, for the first time in a general conference, elaborate on the personal dimension of this option rooted in what can be described as a christological friendship: "Only the closeness that makes us friends enables us to appreciate deeply the values of the poor today, their legitimate desires, and their own manner of living the faith" (Aparecida no. 398). Moreover, the bishops affirm that the preferential option for the poor is not just a matter of ethics, but rather is also a holistic stance inherent in the Catholic faith: "That it is preferential means that it should

104. Benedict XVI, Inaugural Session of the Fifth General Conference of the Bishops of Latin American and the Caribbean, May 13, 2007, http://www.vatican.va/holy_father/benedict_xvi/speeches/2007/may/documents/hf_ben-xvi_spe_20070513_conference-aparecida_en.html.

105. See Gustavo Gutiérrez, "Aparecida: La opción preferencial por el pobre," in *Aparecida: Renacer de una esperanza*, 127–38, at 133.

permeate all our pastoral structures and priorities. The Latin American church is called to be [a] sacrament of love, solidarity, and justice within our peoples" (Aparecida no. 396).[106]

Aparecida's *communio* ecclesiology (Aparecida nos. 304, 305) stands in close continuity with the ecclesiology developed by Vatican II and appropriated by Medellín, Puebla, and Santo Domingo.[107] The bishops articulated this ecclesiology according to their appreciation of the Latin American church's most pressing task in the 21st century: "to show the church's capacity to promote and form disciples and missionaries who respond to the calling received and to communicate everywhere . . . the gift of the encounter with Jesus Christ" (Aparecida no. 14). Within this pastoral directive, the bishops note that the CEBs "have been schools that have helped form Christians committed to their faith, disciples and missionaries of the Lord" (Aparecida no. 178). Indeed, "they deploy their evangelizing and missionary commitment among the humblest and most distant, and they visibly express the preferential option for the poor" (Aparecida no. 179). These communities then continue to be a significant structure of the Latin American church even though the support of the hierarchical church has not always been consistent, and unfounded rumors of their suppression are sometimes spread.[108]

At Aparecida, the bishops unequivocally endorsed, and in some cases expanded, their teaching on the three central theological principles I have been tracing in the reception of Vatican II since Medellín: the signs of the times, the preferential option for the poor, and an ecclesiology of communion expressed in the CEBs. The dynamism in this process of reception is evinced in some of the new themes engaged by Aparecida, including

106. On the impact of the preferential option for the poor on the following of Jesus, the task of theology, and the proclamation of the gospel, see Gustavo Gutiérrez, "The Option for the Poor Arises from Faith in Christ," *Theological Studies* 70 (2009): 317–26.

107. While some theologians contend that Aparecida has a balanced view of the collaboration between grassroots and hierarchical leaders, others argue that it favors an ecclesiology from above, in which "the Church understands itself as the one who possesses, keeps, and guards the transmitted doctrine and creates the necessary space for living such doctrine" (João Batista Libanio, "Conferencia de Aparecida: Documento final," *Revista iberoamericana de teología* 6 [2008]: 23– 46, at 37 [my translation]).

108. Robert Pelton, "Medellin and Puebla: Dead or Alive in the 21st Century Catholic Church?," in *Aparecida: Quo vadis?*, 25–48, at 33. It should be noted that the sections on the CEBs were those most altered by the Vatican before Aparecida's final document was approved. For a detailed study of these changes, see Rolando Muñoz, "Los cambios al documento de Aparecida," in *Aparecida: Renacer de una esperanza*, 298–308.

the continent's ecological devastation, popular religion, and martyrdom. There is a clear consensus among many Latin American theologians that Aparecida was a reaffirmation of the distinct features of the post–Vatican II Latin American church and a ratification of the theological-pastoral direction first assumed at Medellín in the wake of the council.[109] Indeed, some see in Aparecida the rebirth of a hope ushered in 50 years ago by Vatican II and first appropriated by Medellín.[110]

Conclusion

The transformation of the Latin American church in the wake of Vatican II can be characterized as a process through which the church came into its own. While Latin America was poised for change on the eve of the 1960s, the council provided the theological catalyst for the regional church to deepen its authentic identity and mission, and to refashion the relationships that had historically tied her to the continent's structures of economic and political power. Far from a mere repetition of the theological insights, teachings, and practices formulated during the four productive years of the council, the reception of Vatican II has been a decades-long creative interpretation and selective appropriation of the council's message according to the circumstances and needs of the Latin American people. Through this process, the church began to draw closer to the great majorities of the continent and to incorporate their concerns and aspirations into her life and mission.

Amid the diversity and complexity of the Latin American Catholic Church, the theological development that has taken place there since Vatican II reflects an overall theological and pastoral continuity that has helped it emerge as a distinctive expression of the universal church. Across the ecclesial gatherings rehearsed above, three theological elements have been consistently engaged: attentive discernment of the signs of the times

109. Gutierrez, "Aparecida: La opción preferencial por el pobre," 127. Clodovis Boff, for example, claims that Aparecida is the highest achievement of the Latin American magisterium, and that it best recapitulates the previous CELAM conferences. See *Revista do Instituto Humanitas Unisinos*, quoted by Jose Carlos Caamaño in his "Cristo y la vida plena: Aportes a la recepcion de Aparecida," *Revista teologica* 94 (2007): 445–56, at 447.

110. The title of the anthology and commentary published on Aparecida by the Amerindia group of Latin American theologians, which includes authors such as José Comblin, Víctor Codina, Gustavo Gutiérrez, Pablo Richard, Sergio Torres, is telling: *Aparecida el renacer de una esperanza* (Aparecida, the Rebirth of a Hope).

in light of the gospel; the preferential option for the poor, which is rooted in a christological faith; and the development of a *communio* ecclesiology as expressed in the CEBs. Though these principles continue to be contested by certain sectors of the church, they represent the most distinctive components of a region-wide effort to live out Vatican II in Latin America.

These three elements are deeply interrelated. It is the turn to history and the discernment of the signs of the times that leads the church to take a preferential stance on behalf of the poor; and in Latin America this option has been clearly expressed in the life and structure of the CEBs. Among these three theological principles, the preferential option for the poor is the most defining and prophetic. It provides a hermeneutical perspective that guides the church's pastoral directives and priorities, orients Christian praxis toward a more authentic following of Jesus Christ, and should be incorporated into the church's theological reflection. Thus understood, the preferential option for the poor is the most important contribution of the Latin American church to the universal church and is a necessary step in fulfilling John XXIII's wish for the Second Vatican Council: that it would lead us to become "a church of the poor."

Part 5

Specific Documents

15 The Divine Dignity of Human Persons in *Dignitatis Humanae*

LADISLAS ORSY, SJ

The author inquires about the idea of human dignity that inspired Dignitatis humanae, *the Declaration on Religious Freedom. The idea is grounded in the fact that human beings are created in the image of God; they are intelligent and free, replicas of divine nature. They are called to meet God in their consciences, and serve God in obedience and love. Such a response must take place in an environment of freedom, internal and external. Five decades later the question is still alive: How ought the Church respect consciences? Further, the implementation of the Declaration in our contemporary world may demand that the "new evangelization" should begin with awakening human persons to their own dignity.*

One of the most insightful of the commentators on the Second Vatican Council, French Benedictine Ghislain Lafont, writes in his book *L'Église en travail de réforme*, "The history of the Christian churches is perhaps the history of their struggle to believe finally in man."[1] The sentence is not

1. "L'histoire des Églises est peut-être celle d'un combat pour finalement croire en homme," in *L'Église en travail de reform*, Imaginer l'Église catholique 2 (Paris: Cerf, 2011), 23. Lafont also poses the question, Why has Christ not yet returned, why so long a wait for the end of times? His response is, "Pour nous donner le temps de croire en l'homme" (to give us time to believe in the human person (ibid). This is not a silly play with eschatology: Christ died because he "believed" in the human person. The last chapter of *L'Église en travail*, entitled "L'Espérence de l'Église est dans l'Amour" ("The Hope of the Church Is in Love") (319–35), offers the ultimate hermeneutical clue for the interpretation of the Council and for its implementation.

so much a quiet affirmation as it is a loud cry. It conveys relief after past exasperation: "finally!"—as if the church had failed to have such belief in the past. Then Lafont expresses hope: "perhaps!"—the struggle is over and we are ready to sing a new creed: We believe in God, we believe in human persons. That is, we believe in both with one act of divine faith.

This "belief in man," that is, the Catholic doctrine of the dignity of individual human beings as Vatican II states it explicitly and asserts it implicitly in *Dignitatis humanae*, the Declaration on Religious Freedom, is the principal focus of my inquiry. The Council Fathers were mainly concerned with the political and social aspects of religious freedom, but to find their conclusions they had to ground their reflections in the Christian idea of the human person that is latent yet dominating throughout the document. My intent is to gather what is explicit and to bring to light what is implicit in the Declaration. I do so in four steps.[2]

First, as a somewhat prolonged introduction, I lay out the context of the Declaration, since the full meaning of a part cannot be found unless it is seen as a component of the whole. The context here is nothing other than an ecumenical council—a holistic approach, one might say. Second, I draw attention to the document's inspirational sources, its internal complexities, and its painfully achieved clarities. Third, I bring human persons into full focus and explain their dignity though the "sovereignty" of their conscience. Fourth, I write briefly on the present state of the Catholic Church and inquire about its task in the foreseeable future.

Of course, I am aware of the social dimension of *Dignitatis humanae* that concerns religious freedom in the political community.[3] I hold, how-

2. This article is the development of a talk I gave at the Centro Pro Unione in Rome, January 25, 2013, celebrating the 50th anniversary of Vatican II.

3. The social and political significance of *Dignitatis humanae* should be the subject of a separate inquiry. Although the Declaration is commonly referred to as the document on "the separation of church and state," it could just as well be called a guide for creating organic unity between the secular and the sacred authorities in the state. To date, the nature and the demands of such unity received but limited attention from commentators. For the council the ideal is not a confessional state but a political society in which each authority preserves its own identity and operations but respects and supports the other's. The authorities have a common purpose, namely, the overall well-being of the citizenry (human persons) to which each authority must contribute according to its own specific character. Excesses in separation of authorities can produce a split mentality and divided loyalties in individual citizens; attempts to create a unity by giving undue advantages either to religion or to secularity may lead to tensions and violent reactions in the community.

ever, that without first understanding the Council's[4] teaching on human dignity, a comprehensive vision of the ideal relationship between the sacred and the secular authority is not possible; or, at most, it remains imperfect.

The Context: An Ecumenical Council

Fifty years after Vatican II, as we survey the literature on and around the Council, we are bound to find—not without surprise—that many scholars have put admirable acumen and effort into reporting on and recreating the conciliar event, or labored intensely on interpreting the documents, but few of them paused and asked the foundational question, What is an ecumenical council?[5] Yet, raising this question should be the starting point for all research concerning an ecumenical council, because only a proper response to it can provide the needed horizon for understanding it and its achievement. But to construe a well-rounded theology of ecumenical councils built on old tradition and refreshed with new insights is a daunting enterprise—certainly beyond the purpose of this article. Much research and reflection should go into it, and it ought to be a labor of love. Such studying, however, is necessary because as long as we have only partial conclusions, we have precisely that—parts to be inserted into the whole. The danger exists that we may follow the proverbial wanderer in the woods who sees the trees but not the forest.[6]

I am not suggesting that the study of Vatican II should come to a halt until we have a definitive treatise on councils in general. We know enough

4. In this article the word "Council" spelled with an uppercase "C" refers specifically to Vatican Council II; spelled with a lowercase "c" it signifies an ecumenical council unless the context indicates otherwise. I am not dealing specifically with particular councils (regional, provincial, etc.).

5. See Massimo Faggioli, "Council Vatican II: Bibliographical Overview 2007–2010," *Christianesimo nella storia* 32 (2011): 755–91. A recent installment of the running series on publications about Vatican Council II, Faggioli's reports are comprehensive, informative, and balanced.

6. An ecumenical council can be approached at different levels, and our understanding of it will correspond to the level of our questions. On the level of reason and human sciences, historians may ask, What happened at the council? Their response will contain what their standard historical-critical method can discover. Literary critics may inquire, What literary forms do the texts represent? What hermeneutical principles are applicable? Their answers will consist of explanations that are acceptable within their horizon. Every council, however, happens and speaks on both a human and divine level (within the realm of reason *and* faith), hence a holistic approach cannot exist without "faith seeking understanding." For a comprehensive inquiry, reason and faith must blend.

right now to engage with it—no less than did the Fathers who produced the documents. We have a fair notion of what a council is about—a "working knowledge" that can be accounted for and described in various ways while we await the consummate synthesis.

An ecumenical council is both *a human reality and a divine mystery*. It is the product of human effort and the gift of our saving God. It is human through and through, and it is sustained by divine assistance.

Or, an ecumenical council is *a vital act of an earthly community that has the Risen One for its head and draws energy from the Spirit* dwelling within it. "I am with you always, to the end of the age" (Mt 28:20), and "when the Spirit of truth comes, he will guide you into all truth" (Jn 16:13).

Or, an ecumenical council is an *immense wave of divine energy moving a human community* that was gathering strength for a long time before the bishops assembled, and after the event, it remains fresh and forceful to the end of the times. It is not an isolated occurrence in our salvation history. The same Spirit who prompted and supported the council assists the people in appropriating and implementing it. An ecumenical council has a staying force in the community of believers because the Spirit is permanently with them. As the kingdom of God unfolds in time and space, the people reach new depths in understanding a council.

Or, an ecumenical council is *a sacramental event*: the community of bishops—sacramentally mandated to guide the people—speaks and interprets the word of God. Then, the believers at large—sacramentally enabled and moved by the Spirit—respond with an *Amen*. For this immense dialogue between the shepherds and the flock, the examples are at hand. The bishops of the Councils of Nicaea (325) and Constantinople (381) called out to the church with a profession of faith, and people from generation to generation are responding to them whenever they sing the councils' creed. The Council of Ephesus (331) honored Mary of Nazareth as *theotokos*, "God-bearer," and ever since the faithful greet her in every "Hail Mary" as "holy Mary, Mother of God." When we do our Easter duty, we respond to Lateran IV (1215). Whether we are aware of it or not, we are, in our present moment, participating in an ongoing vital response to every one of the past ecumenical councils.

The Content of the Declaration

On the last of its working days, December 7, 1965, the Council approved a document that was long in the making, brief in its composition, and powerful in its content: *Dignitatis humanae*, the Declaration on Religious Freedom. Its text moves from the conceptual realm of philosophical reflections into the luminous world of faith. It culminates with a proclamation that amounts to a profession of faith in the dignity of human persons.[7]

Dignitatis humanae is one of the most mature products of the Council.[8] It contains more than what a first reading may reveal. A document of contrasts and paradoxes, it regularly refers to tradition but opens new vistas by expanding the tradition. It invokes Scholastic philosophy but soon transcends it by arguing from the Scriptures and patristic writings. It presents an uncompromising ideal from the viewpoint of Catholic philosophical and theological tradition, but it leaves ample space for practical accommodations. It demands faith in absolute principles yet appears as if it left truth unprotected. Its greatest paradox, however, is that, while it vindicates the unique God-given mandate of the church as the carrier of the word of God, it claims no privileged political position for the church either among the nations or within any nation.

Admittedly, the Council Fathers struggled to find adequate and defensible responses to highly complex demands and puzzles that had accumulated over the centuries.[9] They debated endlessly—mainly outside the conciliar hall. They went through confounding obscurities and promising

7. There is a striking contrast between the subject matter of the great councils of antiquity and Vatican II. The early Fathers focused mostly on God's mighty deeds in our salvation history: on the Word who became flesh, died, and was raised; on the inner nature of God who is one and three; on the two natures of Christ, and so forth. The attention of the bishops of Vatican II centered on the church, its internal structures, and its place and role in the larger human society.

8. For a comprehensive history of the text and its exegesis, see Pietro Pavan (one of the chief architects of the Declaration), "Declaration on Religious Freedom," in *Commentary on the Documents of Vatican II*, 5 vols., ed. Herbert Vorgrimler (New York: Herder & Herder, 1967–69), 4:49–86; also Louis Tagle, "The Declaration on Religious Liberty," in *History of Vatican II*, 5 vols., ed. Giuseppe Alberigo and Joseph A. Komonchak (Maryknoll, NY: Orbis, 1995–2006), 4:395–406; and Peter Hünermann's brief but excellent reflections in "*Dignitatis humanae*: A Creative Solution," in ibid., 5:395–406, at 451–57. For a summary of the genesis and maturation of the document through the conciliar process, see John T. Noonan Jr., *The Lustre of Our Country: The American Experience of Religious Freedom* (Berkeley: University of California, 1998), 323–53.

9. The celebration of the Council was an evolving event. For example, in matters of collegiality the participants first practiced it without articulating it; the majority then insisted on articulating their intuitive vision and making it normative. They succeeded in inserting their idea of collegiality into the final version of *Lumen gentium* but not in having it formally accepted as a universally binding norm. In spite of such failure, they left to the church a far more developed doctrine of collegiality than was present at the beginning of the Council.

enlightenments, but at the end they succeeded "like a householder who brings out of his treasure what is new and what is old" (Mt 13:52), all in a happy blend. They reached a resolution remarkable for its clarity in simplicity. They discovered—conceivably once and for all—that in the hierarchy of human and Christian values living human persons (imperfect as they are) have priority over abstract propositions (true as they may be). Humans have rights; propositions have meanings but no rights.

The central point of the Declaration is the sacred event where human persons meet God—an event that occurs in human consciences. Toward this central event everything in the Declaration converges; from the recognition of its importance, its conclusions follow. The meeting between creature and Creator is an intimate episode, but it has a cosmic significance because it concerns not only the salvation of an individual but also the composition (building) of God's eternal kingdom.

Peter Hünermann calls the resolution of the problem of religious freedom "a creative solution":

> What, then, was at the heart of the solution and at the same time the innovative element in this document? The document does not take as its starting point either the freedom of conscience of the individual or the necessity that the state should issue legal regulations touching on questions of morality or religion. Nor does it start from the claim of the religions or the Church to proclaim the truth and the will of God. Instead, the fathers chose as the point of departure of their arguments the dignity of the human person as something that must be respected in principle by all institutions. But *part of the very core of the dignity of the person is the religious relationship with God.*[10]

Sources of Inspiration

The ecclesiological significance of the introductory paragraph of the Declaration goes well beyond the theme of freedom of religion: it is about the Council's source of inspiration. A seemingly secular movement—the demand for human rights—in the human family at large caught the Fathers' attention. They present themselves as learners, honoring the nations as their teachers. In so doing they acknowledge the common sense of humanity as a *locus theologicus*, a legitimate source for theological information:

> The dignity of the human person is a concern of which people of our time are becoming increasingly more aware. In growing numbers they

10. Peter Hünermann, "The Final Weeks of the Council," in *History of Vatican II*, 5:363–483, at 453, emphasis added.

> demand that they should enjoy the use of their own responsible judgment and freedom, and decide on their actions on grounds of duty and conscience, without external pressure and coercion. . . . Keenly aware of these aspirations, and wishing to assert their consonance with truth and justice, this Vatican synod examines the sacred tradition and teaching of the church from which it continually draws new insights in harmony with the old. (DH no. 1)[11]

The bishops in council sensed the presence of the Spirit in the human community at large. They responded positively; hence the unheard of opening in a conciliar document.[12] Then they turned to the "sacred traditions."

Traditional Philosophy

Officially the Council shied away from doing any philosophy. It had no intention of canonizing any system. But to understand their deliberations and determinations, we need to keep in mind that virtually all the participants were educated in a variety of Aristotelian-Thomistic interpretations of the universe. The elements of what used to be called *philosophia perennis* may be detected and even seen to dominate—especially in the Declaration's chapter 1, in some translations entitled "The General Principle of Religious Freedom" (*DH* nos. 2–8).

Theological Tradition

In *Dignitatis humanae* nos. 9–12, the Council recalls the ministry of Christ and his respect for human freedom, the practice of the apostles, and the opinions of early Christian writers.

A theologically significant statement in the Declaration is a reference to previous papal teaching: "in treating of this religious freedom the synod intends to develop the teaching of more recent popes" (*DH* no 1). The Fathers indeed developed previous papal teaching, but they went beyond it: they corrected it. Pope Pius IX in his Syllabus of Errors condemned as

11. All translations of *Dignitatis humanae* are taken from *Decrees of the Ecumenical Councils*, vol. 2, ed. Norman T. Tanner, trans. John Coventry (Washington, DC: Georgetown University, 1990).

12. Pope Francis writes in his Apostolic Exhortation, *Evangelii gaudium* no. 68, "The Christian substratum of certain peoples—most of all in the West—is a living reality. Here we find, especially among the most needy, a moral resource which preserves the values of an authentic Christian humanism. *Seeing reality with the eyes of faith, we cannot fail to acknowledge what the Holy Spirit is sowing*" (emphasis added), http://www.vatican.va/holy_father/francesco/apost_exhortations/documents/papa-francesco_esortazione-ap_20131124_evangelii-gaudium_en.html (accessed December 3, 2013).

erroneous the proposition "The Church is to be separated from the State, and the State from the Church."[13] This is a delicate matter: an ecumenical council correcting a previous pope. Of course, what he decreed must be understood within his historical, ecclesial, and cultural context. The pope responded to a specific historical situation with the help of a doctrine that was in the process of development and had not reached full maturity. At any rate, this correction stands as a warning to interpreters of papal pronouncements; caution is needed in assessing their authority.

The Intended Recipients of the Message

The Declaration has a universal scope: the entire human family. Within that broad range we can discern messages to particular groups: states—secular or otherwise; "religions" in their great variety; Christian churches and communities not in union with Rome; and, of course, the Roman Catholic faithful.

The transparent purpose of the Declaration is to describe and promote a measured equilibrium in human society; in particular, a prudent balance between the roles of the secular and the sacred authorities. Both are entitled to proportionate freedom of action; each has a duty to abstain from intruding into the other's field of operation.

For the whole world, the Fathers profess their faith not only in the one Creator but also in Jesus Christ as the universal savior. They state in a matter-of-fact way that Christ entrusted his church, their church, with the task of spreading the Good News of salvation far and wide and offering the means of justification to all who are willing to receive it.

After the affirmation of being in possession of such privileged gifts, the Fathers—speaking in the name of the church—want it to be known that they do not wish for and do not claim any privileged political position for the church within the international or national communities. They want only freedom for their church to speak the word of God, and they want freedom for anyone who wants to follow that word on the testimony of the Holy Spirit. Further, they are not self-centered: the freedom they claim for their own religion they wish to be granted to all others. This is an immense project for all to see—for all to take up.

Accordingly, the Council is mandating the Roman Catholic community to "have the mind which is theirs in Christ." That is, while they have the

13. Proposition 55, in *Enchiridion symbolorum . . .*, 43rd ed., English and Latin, ed. Heinrich Denzinger and Peter Hünermann (San Francisco: Ignatius, 2012) (hereafter Denzinger-Hünermann).

word of God and the energy of the Spirit, they should not boast vainly about their rich gifts but empty themselves, "taking the form of a servant" (Phil 2:5–11).

Conscience: Creature Meets Creator

Dignitatis humanae is grounded in the Christian idea of a human person: in it faith seeks understanding. But who is a human person in the light of faith, that is, in the sight of God?

The Scriptures are eloquent about the dignity of human persons. The Psalmist sings that humans persons are little less than God and that God crowns them with glory and honor (Ps 8:5). In what does this honor and glory consist? The standard reply comes from Genesis's story of creation: a person is the image of God—"Let us make humankind in our image, after our likeness" (Gen 1:26, RSV). But the meaning of the original Hebrew term for "image" used by the author of Genesis is stronger than what our English word "image" can convey. A human person is not a mere semblance—like a mirror image—but a reproduction, a "replica," of God, as a child is a replica of his or her parents—"flesh from their flesh"—to use the biblical expression (Gen 2:3).[14]

Human persons are therefore endowed with dominion over the works of God's hands (see Ps 8:6), but that is not the noblest and the highest mark of their dignity. They have a divine quality: they are sovereign; they have dominion over their eternal destiny. They are free to say yes or no to God, to serve him or to reject him. Whatever they decide, God will accept and respect—a dignity that has no parallel in our visible universe.[15]

The Council also remarks that human persons have the capacity to recognize

> divine law itself, the eternal, objective and universal law by which God out of his wisdom and love arranges, directs, and governs the whole world and the paths of the human community. God has enabled people to share in this divine law, and hence they are able under the gentle

14. Adam "became the father of a son in his own likeness, after his image" (Gen 5:3). See explanatory note in *La Bible: Traduction oecuménique* (Paris: Cerf, 2010), 62.

15. The teaching of Vatican II on the "divine dignity of human persons" is in continuity with the patristic (especially Greek) tradition of "divinization." The Council's practical provisions receive their full and rich meaning in a historical-theological context; for such an "introductory framework" see Myrrha Lot-Borodin, *La déification de l'homme selon la doctrine des pères grecs* (Paris: Cerf, 2011).

> guidance of God's providence increasingly to recognize the unchanging truth (*DH* no. 3).

Integrity

While human dignity flows from the God-like nature of a human person (hence, it is universal), the authenticity of a human person is grounded in her or his integrity (hence, it is personal).[16] Admittedly, the Council did not use the term "integrity" in *Dignitatis humanae*. Yet it must have been in the minds of the Fathers because what integrity signifies played a consistently directive role in the composition of the document.

Persons have integrity when their inner being is transfused by harmony; when their decisions and actions flow from their honest judgment; when they faithfully pursue the values that they comprehend as means to their perfection. In contrast, they lose their integrity when their volitions and operations are divorced from their vision. Should such a disaster happen, the persons in question become traitors to themselves. Their inner world shatters; it becomes fragmented.

Integrity, however, does not mean that the individual judgments held by persons of integrity are by that fact alone correct and critically unassailable. Quite the opposite: their convictions must be open to critical examination and verification. Integrity speaks of honesty; it is not the final guarantee of the truth of any proposition or of the prudence of any intended action.

It follows that persons holding a mistaken opinion in good faith are not diminished in their dignity. They should be aware, however, that they have the duty to submit their position to detached probing: integrity does not include the gift of infallibility or the highest degree of prudence. To pursue honest self-examination and to be open to an external critical process always remains a duty.

Conscience: The Guardian of Integrity

In *Gaudium et spes* we find a working description of conscience, rich in its intuitive simplicity:

> In the depth of his conscience, man detects a law that he does not impose upon himself but that holds him to obedience. Always summoning him to love good and avoid evil, the voice of conscience when necessary speaks to his heart: Do this, shun that. For man has in his heart a law written by God; to obey it is the very dignity of man; according to it he will be

16. Cf. Jesus' saying about Nathanael "in whom there is no guile" (Jn 1:47).

> judged. Conscience is the most secret core and sanctuary of a man. There he is alone with God, whose voice echoes in his depths. (*GS* no. 16)[17]

Briefly, integrity does not guarantee the truth of a judgment or the prudence of an intended action. For that it *must* rely on critical intelligence. The task of conscience is not to create infallible knowledge or unfailing wisdom but to keep a person faithful to his or her honestly acquired conviction.

Such an understanding of integrity has far-reaching consequences for sound policy toward persons who advocate the truth of a proposition (theoretical or practical) by invoking their "dictate of conscience." The community must honor their honesty and in no way invade or destroy it. At the same time, the community has the right—and may have the duty—to examine critically by ordinary and universal criteria the soundness of a position. Further, the community has the right to defend and support the value of unity.

The Inner Drama: Struggle with God

God shared his nature with human persons by creating them intelligent and free. But, I venture to say, it would hardly make sense for God to create such beings without wanting to meet them. In fact, we read in the Scriptures that from the first moment of human beings' consciousness God was conversing with them. Such conversation, symbolically described in Genesis, has never ceased. It continues not only through the external acts of revelation but also in the conscience of every single person.

According to Genesis, there was drama in the Garden of Eden between God who demanded obedience and the humans who wanted to be sovereign like God. This same drama has resided ever since in the inner depths of every human person. God talks to each of his creatures; each is invited to surrender to God's love. Still, anyone—to his or her ruin—may refuse it; the sanctuary of conscience is the scenery of this divine play. God recognizes the freedom of each person and respects it. The outcome of the drama depends on the created human person. The dignity of the human person is ultimately grounded in the freedom of each one to surrender to God.

Freedom: A Divine Attribute

Freedom is self-revealing; it is a prime experience for every human person. Even little children, long before they are capable of understanding

17. Translation from Denzinger-Hünermann, 4316.

the word, can and do vindicate their freedom with resounding "noes" to their parents' demands.

Only God is perfectly free: God freely communicates himself in creation, and freely receives the surrender of his creatures. God gives and takes: God gives himself, the Supreme Good, and takes the homage of the person intent on serving him. Ultimately freedom is the autonomous capacity to opt for what is truly good.

Persons are free internally when their spirit in its deliberations, decisions, and actions is independent, when it is not imposed or hampered by an outside agent or by their own unruly passions. They are free externally when no outside power coerces them physically or sets up obstacles for their intended actions.

Dignitatis humanae is primarily concerned with the latter, external freedom in religious matters within human society—with a view toward securing internal freedom for the demands of faith. The document demands external "space" for the profession of religious beliefs and for worship, individually or in community. At the same time, it recognizes a limit to this demand: freedom for religion must not interfere or diminish secular authority within its own domain, that of caring for the temporal well-being of the citizens.[18]

Dissent

While *Dignitatis humanae* advocates religious freedom in human society, how is the doctrine of the primacy of conscience applicable within the Catholic Church? In other words, what can our postconciliar church do? What ought it do to respect the "claim of conscience" within its own boundaries?

Good-faith conflict situations in the church are arising with some frequency, and often with urgency.[19] The cases are of similar pattern: recog-

18. For example, when parents, following their religious belief, refuse medical care for their child, the secular authority has the right to intervene; it has a duty to care for the temporal welfare of the child. An essential human value is at stake.

19. I am not referring here to crimes of heresy, apostasy, and schism as defined in canon law: obstinate denial or obstinate doubt of Catholic truth, the total rejection of Christian faith, the refusal of submission to the pope, or the denial of communion with the members. Please note the adjective "obstinate": it signals that the person is aware of his or her wrongdoing but does it anyway (see canon 751). Persons of good faith who are holding an erroneous doctrine keep their integrity. They have no criminal intent; hence they are not criminals. Canon law has no particular provisions (procedure, court, sentencing) for such cases and admits only two possibilities in their resolutions. One is excommunication; another is submission with little or no regard to conscience (mistaken

nized values are in conflict. On the one hand there is the value of unity in belief and action as Luke describes it in the Acts of the Apostles: "the company of those who believed were of one heart and soul" (Acts 4:32). On the other hand there is the value of the integrity of a person—member of the community—who finds him- or herself in conscience opposed to official doctrine or practice. That is the well-known issue of dissent.

When such a conflict happens, there is a crisis. For the resolution of such a conflict we may begin by referring to some venerable principles, old and new:

- "Unity in all that is necessary; freedom in all that is doubtful; charity in all"—a maxim often quoted at the Council;
- the dignity of the persons must be upheld by respecting their integrity;
- the objective correctness of all judgments held "in conscience" must remain subject to critical examination, using the criteria that faith and reason can provide;
- the identity of the community in its essential beliefs and practices must be preserved.

So much for principles: they have their role, but they remain abstract, general, and impersonal. They offer universal guidance but no solution for individual cases, because each case is concrete, particular, and personal. It can hardly be otherwise: consciences differ.

The solution consists in admitting that such cases do not, cannot, fall under the law. Since they are concrete, particular, and personal, so must be their resolutions. Peter Hünermann, however, thinks that the Council should have taken care of this problem, possibly by universal legislation:

> There is one consequence that the Council fathers did not have in mind. The strict distinction between, on the one hand, the legal level with its element of compulsion, and, on the other, the religious level, the freedom of faith, also has consequences for defining the relationship and distinction between institutional and juridical regulations within the Church . . . and the questions of faith and the duty of believing. . . . The history of the postconciliar period bears painful witness to the continued existence of this blind spot.[20]

as it may be). In either case, the result is bound to be the violation of human dignity that should be respected in all persons of integrity. Excommunication is humiliating; it implies guilt. Pressure to conform may destroy the integrity of the person. There should be a third alternative: "Let us part in peace and in mutual respect."

20. See Hünermann, "A Creative Solution," 457.

Hünermann is right. The Council did not give any indication as to how church authorities should handle cases where a person asserts that, in conscience, he or she cannot accept some official teaching or practical order. He is also right that in the postconciliar decades we have had plenty of experience with painful situations—at times unresolved, at times terminated in a manner that left the impression that justice was not done.

I doubt whether the Council Fathers could have given any clear and workable rules (to be placed into the Code of Canon Law) even if they had wanted to. The reason is that in such cases the concrete variables are so numerous and subtle, so singular and personal, that laws—by nature always abstract, general, and impersonal—cannot do justice to them. They belong to the realm of equity.[21]

I do not see any other way of resolving cases than by handing each case over to a wise and learned person (or persons) who can search for a fair resolution and advise the interested parties accordingly. Such an approach in a spirit of reconciliation could be supported by some institutional structure. Is it too far-fetched to think of an Office of Reconciliation (Conflict Resolution? Arbitration?) in the territory of an episcopal conference or, for that matter, in the Roman Curia? When good faith is ascertained, there is no need for a criminal process.[22]

Admittedly, there will be cases (as there have been from apostolic times) where no reconciliation is possible. Then the two sides may have no other option than to agree to separate, with respect for each other's integrity. It may be a far better solution than the fulmination of an excommunication.

21. Whenever the conscience of a person is involved in a case, the issue becomes so personal that the law conceived for general occurrences may not be able to handle it. Yet justice ought to be done. For such circumstances, Aristotle invoked equity as a balancing factor and an instrument of justice (not of mercy). Equitable consideration takes into account the concrete, particular, and personal circumstances of the individual involved. See Aristotle, *Nicomachean Ethics*, Book 5. Further, to the point: "Thus, there is no magic in equity. There is no fuzziness either. The life of human communities is regulated by various norms, legal, philosophical, religious. Each group of norms has its own built-in limits. When in concrete life a case arises which cannot be justly resolved by law, it is right that the community should turn to philosophy or to religion and let them prevail over the positive law. When this happens, there is authentic equity" (Ladislas Orsy, *Theology and Canon Law* [Collegeville, MN: Liturgical Press, 1992], 63).

22. At the present we have only the "tribunal" of the Congregation for the Doctrine of Faith with its procedure conceived principally to take care of criminal situations, such as heresy or schism. We have no institutional structure and procedure to deal with good-faith cases of disagreement or error.

Five Decades Later

History, including church history, has its own rhythm. Once an ecumenical council is concluded the church at large needs to receive it by making its teachings and practical directions vital forces in the lives of the faithful. The essential pronouncements must become existential events. This transition can be described also from a different (opposite) point of view: once a council is concluded, the Holy Spirit wants to bring the people of God into the movement that the Spirit has initiated. Bishops debate, make decisions, and produce documents, but the purpose of the council is fulfilled only when the universal faithful make it their own and live by it.

Reception

The reception of an ecumenical council is a long, dynamic, and variegated process. On the one side the Council Fathers communicate their inspiration, vision, insights, and determinations. They do it with authority: *Placuit Spiritui sancto et nobis* (it pleased the Holy Spirit and us). On the other side the communities (local churches, parishes, religious communities, etc.) respond first by accepting the information on a human level, and then by progressively *believing* in the council on the testimony of the one Spirit who moves in both the Fathers and the faithful. They achieve this grace-filled act with the gift of the theological virtues (as a sacramental community): faith brings them light to see, hope gives them courage to surrender, and love moves them to be disciples. Although every community receiving the council participates in the same gift, each one absorbs it according to its capacity; one does it slowly, another tries to do it rapidly; none can do it instantaneously.

The process of reception, therefore, displays innumerable degrees and modalities that cannot be described with precision. Four stages, however, are always recognizable in these movements. Initially the communities learn in a human way about *what happened at the council*; then they want to know in a historical-critical context *what meanings can be found in the texts*; then, in the light of their faith they wonder *how the word of God is unfolding in the council's message*; and finally, on the strength of their hope and love, they reshape and reorder their lives according to the Council.[23]

23. The 50th anniversary of Vatican II offers a good opportunity for each person and community to make a detached assessment of their progress in assimilating the Council—or of letting themselves be absorbed into the conciliar movement initiated by the Spirit. Here one question, among others, suggests itself: Have we not spent effort

The reception of the Council demands the transformation of minds; it requires the appropriation of a vision of faith that touches every aspect of the lives of individual Christians and of their communities. This is especially true of Vatican II, as it was a seminal council that aimed to bring about a fresh way of thinking and acting concerning issues human and divine. The evangelical parables about the kingdom of God can help us understand what is happening. The Council has thrown leaven into the dough; it has sown seeds bursting with energy; it has put a lamp on a stand. Now we are watching fermentation; we see growing plants splitting rocks; and we find light in the dark corners of our house (see Lk 18–20; Mt 5:15). But we need patience: the tasty bread, the mature tree laden with fruit, the light that radiates afar will come only in God's own time.

The energies of the Spirit are explosive by nature; impeded in one direction, they find another. After the Council of Trent theological reflection went into a recession due mainly to Pius IV's bulla *Benedictus Deus* of 1564 forbidding any insightful commentaries on the decrees of Trent.[24] It did not recover until the 19th century when Newman's genius broke into the field. Yet, after the Council of Trent there was an explosion of other fields. Fresh initiatives abounded in religious life (Carmelites, Jesuits), in schools of arts (baroque), in education (seminaries, colleges), in propagating the faith (Far East, South America, Canada), and so forth. Meanwhile reflections on the tradition displayed little originality and liturgy stagnated. But the Spirit cannot be extinguished.

The mandate of Vatican II for the hierarchy is not so much to preserve discipline in the Church as to support and manage creative communities by providing space for their immense energies—they have the Spirit. The primary guidebook for such a task cannot be anything other than the book of the Gospels. *Mutatis mutandis*, the words of the Lord for the times of persecution are valid for peaceful times too: "Do not be anxious . . . [about] what you are to say"—"for the Holy Spirit will teach you in that

---

and energy beyond measure in discussing hermeneutical principles and less than what would have been necessary to introduce collegiality?

24. "Furthermore, in order to avoid the distortion and confusion that could arise if it were permitted to every individual, as he pleased, to publish his own interpretations and commentaries on the decrees of the council: by apostolic authority We order all . . . that none, without Our authorization, should dare to publish any commentaries, glosses, notes, explanations, or any kind of interpretation at all concerning the decrees of the said council" (Denzinger-Hünermann, 1849). The same pope, also in 1564, reinforced this order by the Rules for the Prohibition of Books in the constitution *Dominici Gregis* (Denzinger-Hünermann, 1851–61).

very hour what you ought to say"—and, we may add, what you ought to do (Lk 12:11–12). The task of ecclesiastical laws is to create freedom for the subjects to follow the Spirit, and, more importantly, to create freedom for the Spirit to lead the community.

New Evangelization

It is the great tragedy of Western society that so many persons have lost their faith in God. It may be an even greater tragedy that just as many, if not more, lost their faith in human persons. Those who have lost faith hold and proclaim that we humans have no capacity to know the truth and are not free to love. Such persons place themselves in a tragic situation indeed. A false state of mind prevents them from listening to the One who is the Truth. A wrong disposition hinders them from freely responding to the One who is Love. When we meet such people, their evangelization ought to begin with the proclamation that human beings have the capacity to know the truth, and that they have the gift of freedom to love. It follows that the God-given task of the church is never confined to preaching the gospel in a restricted sense only (that is, the Christ event) or to dispensing the sacraments in an internally purified church only, but in proclaiming openly—opportunely or not—the innate divine dignity of human persons.

Concluding Remarks

The reception of *Dignitatis humanae* is far from coming to a close; its meaning continues to unfold. The Council's vision is supported among the nations by an immense movement in favor of human rights. Interestingly, even governments who deny it in practice honor it in their "official" statements; they do not want to lose credibility in the worldwide forum of nations. A secular movement is supporting the Council's religious vision.

The Spirit of God was poured out in Jerusalem on the first believers. Soon after the first Pentecost, however, the community understood that the Spirit was sent to renew the face of the earth—the whole earth, that is, the whole human family. Is it too much, therefore, to see in the promptings of the same Spirit the ultimate origin of the movement for human rights? Granted, the movement is often marked by human sinfulness and provokes misery and bloodshed, but is it not conceivable that at its core is the Holy Spirit, present and active? In truth, how could it be otherwise? God has not abandoned his people; all nations belong to him.

Pope John XXIII liked to invoke the signs of the times. Surely, the Council's Declaration on Human Dignity and the people's demand for human rights are overt signs that the greatest value in this creation is, must be, the human person. The noble aspiration of the peoples and the holy inspiration of the Council converge to recognize and honor human persons for what they are: authentic "replicas" of God.

It is fitting to close these reflections with a quote from John XXIII (recently to be proclaimed holy; blessed be his memory) from his Allocution for the Opening of Vatican Council II, October 11, 1962:

> In our times Divine Providence is leading us to a new order of human relations which, by human effort and even beyond all expectations, are directed to the fulfillment of God's superior and inscrutable designs, in which everything, even human setbacks, leads to the greater good of the Church.[25]

Credo in Deum: credo in hominem. We believe in God; we believe in human persons;[26] we believe that by honoring them, we honor God.

25. Quoted and reaffirmed by Pope Francis in *Evangelii gaudium* no. 84.

26. It would be difficult to think of persons in a more tragic situation than those who lost faith in the capacity of their own intelligence to know the truth and in their ability to reach freely for what is good. Such persons have no home; they are strangers in the universe. They cannot enter freely into any human relationships; they can only experience interactions imposed by irrational forces. Whenever an evangelizer meets such persons, his or her first task is to lead them to believe in themselves, to accept their innate dignity—with their own divine gifts of intelligence and freedom. Sages of old called such an operation preevangelization. In the Western world, where today such an attitude is widely spread and shared by many, it should be seen as the beginning of new evangelization. No one can believe in the gospel if he or she does not believe in his or her own dignity.

16 Scripture Reading Urged *Vehementer* (*Dei Verbum* No. 25)

Background and Development

JARED WICKS, SJ

This article relates the itinerary of Vatican II's exhortation to Catholics to practice prayerful Scripture reading. In 1961 the Preparatory Theological Commission treated Bible reading in a cautionary and admonitory mode that highlighted guidance by the Magisterium. But the Secretariat for Promoting Christian Unity insisted that pastoral ministers should introduce the faithful to devout reading of Scripture leading to personal encounters with God. The conciliar encouragement of lectio divina *deserves appreciation and further application as a pastoral consequence of Vatican II's* Dei verbum.

This contribution presents the main stages in the genesis of *Dei verbum* (*DV*), the Dogmatic Constitution on Divine Revelation, no. 25, in which Vatican Council II states a central pastoral consequence of biblical inspiration by issuing a forceful and specific exhortation directed to all the faithful to engage in frequent and prayerful Scripture reading. Added to this presentation are five appendixes giving draft texts formulated along the itinerary to *DV* no. 25, which include *De verbo Dei: Schema decreti pastoralis* prepared by the Secretariat for the Promotion of the Unity of Christians. At the end, I offer my initial reflections on this Vatican II word to Christians. But I begin well before the council, with the promotion of Bible reading in Venice in 1956 by the future Pope John XXIII.[1]

1. Capitalization of words in this article follows, for the most part, the practice found in the conciliar texts quoted or referred to. Translations throughout are mine unless otherwise indicated.

Prelude: Cardinal Patriarch Roncalli's Pastoral on Scripture Reading, 1956

In 1956, the Archdiocese of Venice celebrated the fifth centenary of the death of its proto-patriarch, St. Lorenzo Giustiniani (1381–1456). In his Lenten pastoral letter of 1956, Cardinal Patriarch Angelo G. Roncalli called attention to St. Lorenzo's deep immersion in Scripture and urged the Venetian faithful to turn to Bible reading as a way to follow the counsels and example of their first patriarch. Roncalli made the centenary into a pastoral call to take up Scripture.[2]

Roncalli's pastoral opens by celebrating the biblical books as grand monuments to divine relations with humanity, being God's testimony that, in the Scriptures of Israel, prepares for the union of divinity with humanity in the incarnation. The further biblical narratives, especially the Gospels, manifest sublimity and the fullness of holiness, as they teach humans to worship God in spirit and truth. His episcopal consecration had impressed on Roncalli his duty to teach Scripture and to inculcate in people a familiarity with the sacred book. While church measures that restricted biblical reading during the Reformation era were conditioned by particular circumstances, under recent popes the promotion of Bible reading has become a characteristic mark of the Catholic apostolate.

Roncalli's letter then offers a brief anthology of citations from St. Lorenzo Giustiniani to impress on readers the beauties of Scripture and to stir their desire to taste and see the solid and life-giving spiritual nourishment that the biblical books offer. The letter closes with a concise appeal to turn to the biblical wellsprings of the Christian life so as to further the spread of evangelical truth, which is the living substance of the two Testaments of the Bible.

This action of 1956 gives us a good example of what Pope John XXIII had in mind later, when he named the spiritual reinvigoration of the faithful as a primary aim of Vatican II, which came to expression in the initial paragraph of the council's first promulgated document, *Sacrosanctum concilium*.

2. "La Sacra Scrittura e S. Lorenzo Giustiniani: Lettera pastorale per la Quaresima," in Angelo Giuseppe Card. Roncalli, *Scritti e discorsi,* 3 vols. (Rome: Edizioni Paoline, 1959), 2:329–51. On February 22, 1956, when he finished writing the pastoral, Roncalli wrote in his diary that his letter should give rise to "un buon movimento per lo studio della Bibbia" (a good movement of Bible study) (*Pace e Vangelo: Agende del patriarca*, ed. Enrico Galavotti, Edizione nazionale dei diari di Angelo Giuseppe Roncalli – Giovanni XXIII 6/2, 1956–58 [Bologna: Istituto per le scienze religiose, 2008], 48).

Bible Reading in the Preparatory Theological Commission's Schema *De Fontibus Revelationis*, 1960–1961

To begin work on the schema *De fontibus revelationis*, Sebastian Tromp, secretary of the Preparatory Theological Commission, composed on July 18, 1960, a *primum tentamen* of theses treating Scripture and tradition (the sources of revelation), biblical inerrancy, literary genres, Gospel historicity, and the Protestantizing danger of a theology based solely on Scripture to the neglect of tradition and the Magisterium.[3] Tromp's Thesis 2 stated that Scripture, being in many passages obscure, has not been given by God to individual believers, but to the Church's Magisterium for explaining the text. After a meeting of a small group of Rome-based consultors on July 20, the text had a new thesis, no. 3, on biblical reading, which stated that while Scripture reading should be highly commended, it is not appropriate for every believer, because of the obscurity of many passages and because the religion and morality of the Old Testament has been raised by Christ to a higher perfection.[4] The text underwent slight modifications in the coming weeks, and on September 24 it went out as a *schema compendiosum* of 13 theses to the Commission's members in view of a late October 1960 meeting to discuss them.[5] The importance of this schema *De fontibus* for Tromp appears in its thesis form, by which it gives positions to be maintained, and not just topics to be developed, as was the case in the other three "compendious schemas" prepared at the same time.[6]

3. The text is in *Konzilstagebuch Sebastian Tromp SJ*, edited by Alexandra von Teuffenbach, vol. 1/2 (Rome: Gregorian University, 2006), 834–35. Tromp discussed his theses with Salvatore Garofalo, professor of Scripture at the Pontifical Urban University. Later in the work of the Commission, Garofalo chaired the consultors' subcommission that drafted *De fontibus*, which the Commission members approved on September 21, 1961.

4. These early developments are narrated by Karim Schelkens, *Catholic Theology of Revelation on the Eve of Vatican II: A Redaction History of the Schema* De fontibus revelationis *(1960–1962)* (Leiden: Brill, 2010), 76–85.

5. In the distributed text the order was changed, with the former nos. 2–3 now being: "9. Sacra Scriptura non est a Deo immediate data singulis fidelibus, sed Ecclesiae. 10. Licet sacrae Scripturae lectio summopere sit commendanda, tamen non omnibus et singulis indiscriminatim convenit, tum prae obscuritate aliquarum partium, tum quia religiositas et moralitas Veteris Testamenti a Christo Domino ad altiorem perfectionem sunt elevatae" (given by Riccardo Burigana, *La Bibbia nel concilio: La redazione della costituzione "Dei verbum" del Vaticano II* [Bologna: Il Mulino, 1998], 468).

6. Along with the theses of *De fontibus*, Tromp also composed in early July 1960 topical outlines for three more theological schemas: *De ecclesia*, *De deposito fidei pure custodienda,* and *De rebus moralibus et socialibus*.

In early 1961 a subcommission expanded the original theses into a complete schema *De fontibus revelationis* in five chapters. The prioritized issues were (1) the insufficiency of Scripture, because important revealed truths come to the Church through tradition (vs. J. R. Geiselmann); (2) the proper methods of literary interpretation, which were central in the Roman controversy ignited by the early 1961 attack of Msgr. Antonino Romeo on the Biblical Institute; and (3) the historicity of Gospel narratives, on which the schema formulated condemnations of mythical and reductive interpretations.

The schema's chapter 5 on Scripture in the Church had come onto the *De fontibus* subcommission's agenda in June 1961, leading to the text approved as chapter 5 on June 23.[7] This text was modified in only small ways at the plenary meeting of the Theological Commission on September 20–21,[8] and in early October the whole schema went to the Central Preparatory Commission where it became the object of some severe critical objections on November 9–10, 1961.

The draft text that the Theological Commission gave to the Central Commission in *De fontibus* began its chapter 5 with no. 24, on the Church's perennial protective care and diffusion of Scripture through homilies and liturgical readings.[9] No. 25 set forth the special standing of the Vulgate Latin version, which "is immune from any error in matters of faith and practice" and is "so closely connected with the Church's Magisterium that it should be acknowledged to share in the authority of tradition."

Chapter 5 then devoted paragraphs 26–27 to Scripture reading.[10] These expand considerably the earlier theses of Tromp, by working in biblical and patristic citations, but no. 26, directed to priests as preachers, includes as well Tromp's original point that one receives Scripture from the Church, its first depository, in view of spiritual growth, which requires docility. No. 27, on Scripture reading by the faithful, noted positively the spread of modern-language translations for reading that fosters spiritual enlightenment and motivation. But over half of no. 27 was admonitory, on the lines

7. See Schelkens, *Catholic Theology of Revelation*, 213–17. Garofalo composed the first draft of chapter 5.

8. Ibid., 232.

9. This overture to the chapter states succinctly what the major biblical encyclicals of the popes had treated at greater length on the Church's protection and promotion of Scripture. See Dean Béchard, ed., *The Scripture Documents: An Anthology of Catholic Teaching* (Collegeville, MN: Liturgical Press, 2002), 42–44 (Leo XIII, *Providentissimus Deus* [1893]) and 116–21 (Pius XII, *Divino afflante Spiritu* [1943]).

10. Below, the Appendix (pp. 382–83) gives these paragraphs in English translation.

of Tromp's thesis no. 3 (later no. 10). Biblical reading must be done in the light of church teaching and "with a secure and appropriate formation," because both Testaments contain obscure and difficult texts, which 2 Peter 3:16 states regarding the Pauline letters. Translations need episcopal approval and must include explanatory passages "which agree with the mind of the Church, whose living Magisterium is for the faithful the proximate norm of belief."[11] The "authentic meaning" of biblical passages is ascertained by the Magisterium, to which Scripture has been entrusted for its interpretation. In fact, every initiative for spreading Scripture among the faithful must be under episcopal oversight, since, as mentioned a few lines earlier, the bishops are the bearers of apostolic teaching.

The concluding paragraphs of the schema that the Preparatory Theological Commission sent to the Central Preparatory Commission reminded Catholic exegetes, in no. 28, that they need the Holy Spirit's aid in their interpretive work and that this work should above all bring out Scripture's theological and spiritual doctrine. Catholic exegesis has its criteria, and so must be "always attentive to the analogy of faith, to the church's tradition, and to the norms given by the Apostolic See in this regard." No. 29, on theology and the Bible, stated that Holy Scripture, along with tradition, is like the soul of theological work. But while biblical interpretation contributes to good theology, one must be mindful that right interpretations of Scripture cannot be in dissonance with church teaching, because the same God is author of both the Bible and the church's doctrine. The schema concludes with the directive that the work of theologians should aim to show the *concordia* of perennial and current Catholic doctrine with the foundational and inspired texts of Scripture.[12]

Before following the *iter* of *De fontibus*, with special attention to its chapter 5, I turn to another text of Vatican II's preparation, which addressed the topic of Scripture reading in the Church.

11. The schema gives no reference to a source of this statement, but it comes from Pius XII's *Humani generis* of 1950, in a passage regarding theologians, for whom "the proximate and universal norm of truth" is the Church's magisterium, "because Christ entrusted the scriptures and apostolic traditions to this authoritative office for their defense and interpretation" (Claudia Carlen, IHM, ed., *The Papal Encyclicals* 5 vols. [Ann Arbor, MI: Pierian, 1970], 4:177).

12. This directive also comes from Pius XII's *Humani generis*, which the schema again does not reference. Theology can pursue confidently its demonstration of agreement between the Bible and later doctrine, for "together with the sources . . . God has given to his church a living magisterium to elucidate and explain what is contained in the deposit of faith obscurely and implicitly" (Carlen, ed., *Papal Encyclicals*, 4:178).

The Unity Secretariat on Scripture Reading: The 1962 Schema *De Verbo Dei*

From the start of its work in late 1960, Cardinal Augustin Bea's Secretariat for Promoting the Unity of Christians (SPCU) had a subcommission no. 4 on the word of God, whose task was to give the council an account of the importance of God's word in Catholic teaching and life.[13] The subcommission's chair was Professor Hermann Volk, who then held the Dogmatic Theology Chair in the Faculty of Catholic Theology in the University of Münster. Volk had been for some time pondering Protestant criticisms of a perceived contrast between Catholic emphasis on the sacraments and the relatively small Catholic concern for biblical preaching and personal Bible reading.[14]

A first result of the Word of God subcommission's work came before the SPCU plenary meeting of April 1961 in a seven-page draft, in French; it had four sections: (1) the word as both a gift to and task of the Church, (2) the word and the sacraments, (3) the word in pastoral ministry, and (4) possible consequences in the council's treatment of the word of God.[15]

Section 1 of the draft distributed by Volk's subcommission recalls how recent popes have spoken emphatically about the importance of the word of God and have urged Bible reading on priests and laypeople, with Bene-

13. At the SPCU's first plenary of November 1960, the list of subcommissions included "4. 'Verbum Dei' in Ecclesia; eius momentum in doctrina et vita; eius praedicatio: in Missa (Epist. et Evang. in lingua vulgari) et catechesis." The creation of new subcommissions led in August 1961 to this one becoming no. 6, with its topic reformulated as "De Dei Verbi virtute et principalitate," which implied that its schema would develop a theological basis for the spiritual power of the proclaimed word and for showing the high ranking of God's word among the constitutive elements of the Church. My source for these SPCU working documents is Mauro Velati, ed., *Dialogo e rinnovamento: Verbali e testi del segretariato per l'unità dei cristiani nella preparazione del concilio Vaticano II (1960–1962)*, Testi e ricerche di scienze religiose, Serie Fonti e strumenti di lavoro 5 (Bologna: Il Mulino, 2011), 97–98.

14. Also on Volk's "word of God" subcommission were Johannis Feiner (Chur, Switzerland), Frans Thijssen (diocese of Utrecht), Charles Boyer (Gregorian University), and George Tavard (then at Mount Mercy College, Pittsburgh).

15. Velati, ed., *Dialogo e rinnovamento*, 395–403, followed on 403–9 by the minutes of the discussion, in which Bea underscored the ecumenical importance of the topic, adding that while Volk's text was that of a dogmatic theologian, the Secretariat should especially develop the pastoral consequences mentioned at the end, to avoid having a document that would encroach on the proper area of the Theological Commission. Volk insisted on treating God's word not just on its instructional content, but as well on the word as a mode of God's saving gift of life to believers.

dict XV cited in this sense.[16] The council should underscore the importance of the word in the Church, which must show by its proclamation and interpretation that "the Church is not above, but under the Word, and by this is under God's sovereignty."[17] Also the council could well, as a possible consequence, urge the faithful to pray more frequently with Scripture texts, especially the Psalms.[18]

During 1961, Volk developed his text into a longer systematic treatment, especially by adding many biblical passages, and this was on the agenda of the November 1961 plenary of the Secretariat.[19] The concluding section spoke of Holy Scripture as "the source and constant nourishment of the spiritual life, by which the pastoral ministry should orient itself in order to be fruitful in all its forms."[20] Applications are then made to homiletic preaching, to vernacular recitation of the Breviary, to the centrality of Scripture for novice religious, and to the need of easily usable editions. The last point gives rise to this statement:

> An important duty in pastoral ministry is to carefully introduce the faithful to the spiritual reading of Scripture. . . . For Holy Scripture brings a person in a unique way into the mysteries of the Kingdom of God, helping one to recognize its hidden reality and fortifying one's confidence in

16. Benedict XV had written, "Who can fail to see what profit and sweet tranquility will result in well-disposed souls from such devout reading of the Bible? Whosoever comes to it in piety, faith, and humility, and with determination to make progress, will assuredly find therein and will eat the 'bread . . . that comes down from heaven' (Jn 6:33) and will personally experience what David speaks of, 'What is unknown and hidden in your wisdom you manifested to me' (Ps 50:8 Vulg.). . . . As far as in us lies, Venerable Brethren, we shall, with St. Jerome as our guide, never cease urging all the faithful to peruse daily the Gospels, Acts, and Epistles, with the intent to absorb these into their own flesh and blood" (Encyclical *Spiritus Paraclitus*, September 15, 1920, on the 15th centenary of the death of St. Jerome, which Volk's draft cited from *Acta apostolicae sedis* [AAS] 12 [1920]: 405. My translation corrects that given in Béchard, ed., *Scripture Documents*, 97).

17. Velati, ed., *Dialogo e rinnovamento*, 402. Secretariat member Archbishop John C. Heenan (Liverpool) asked for a further explanation of this, to which consultor Gregory Baum responded with a line from St. Francis de Sales to the effect that the Church does not issue judgments on God's word itself, but on interpretations of it (404–5).

18. Velati, ed., *Dialogo e rinnovamento*, 403.

19. The text is found in ibid. 676–87, with added paragraph numbers 1–41. Sections remained on the word as gift to the Church, that is, on it as a means of God's saving presence (especially revered in the liturgy) and as the Church's task in theology and in the pastoral ministry, where the word shows its spiritual fruitfulness.

20. Ibid., 685.

> Christ who works efficaciously in us, in virtue of the power by which he triumphed over all the powers of the world.[21]

But the SPCU discussion of Volk's developed text on the word of God was cut short, because on November 9–10, 1961, Cardinal Bea had taken an active part in the Central Preparatory Commission's critical treatment of the Theological Commission's schema *De fontibus revelationis*. This draft contained its chapter 5 on the Bible in the Church, which would be revised. But for the SPCU Bea saw an opening because the theological schema gives no recognition to the high value of God's word in the liturgy and for the spiritual life. Also, the Theological Commission was reserved about commending biblical reading and preaching, both of which are ecumenically important. The outcome was a mandate given to Volk to compose—for the council itself—a succinct *pastoral* decree on the word of God.[22]

In early 1962 Volk prepared a concise theological gem, of 1300 words in 13 paragraphs.[23] This came to the Central Preparatory Commission, which approved the text for the council on the Commission's last working day, June 20, 1962. The SPCU text eventually supplied formulations to *Dei verbum*'s chapter 6 on the place and role of the biblical word and Scripture reading in Catholic life.

This pastoral schema commends insistently the "living and life-giving word of God, in which God's saving power is most certainly present in an efficacious manner" (no. 1). This is the word proclaimed in the Spirit and through the Church, . . . primarily by Scripture . . . , which not only contains God's word but in an eminent sense is God's word" (no. 2). Nos. 3–7 expand on the spiritual power of the word, on Christ's words mak-

21. Ibid., 686.

22. Ibid., 687–91, giving the minutes of the November 30 and December 1, 1961, discussion. But Volk also reworked his longer text, giving it out in French at the SPCU plenary of March 6–10 (872–83) and publishing it in the original German as "Wort Gottes: Gabe und Aufgabe," *Catholica* (Münster) 4 (1962): 241–51.

23. Velati, *Dialogo e rinnovamento*, 883–89, giving the March draft in Latin and the changes introduced during the plenary meeting of March 1962 to fill out and polish the text for submission to the Central Preparatory Commission with a view to its coming before the council. The text received by the Central Commission, "De verbo Dei—Schema decreti pastoralis," is given in *Acta et documenta Concilio Oecumenico Vaticano II apparando*: *Series II*, *Praeparatoria*, 3 vols. in 7, ed. Commissio Centralis Praeparatoria Concilii Vaticani II (Vatican City: Typis Vaticanis, 1969), 2/4:816–19; and in a revised form that went to the Council members, in *Acta commissionum et secretariatum*, 3/2:454–57. In the Appendix below (pp. 383–87), I give the latter version in my English translation from the Latin.

ing known divine mysteries, on God's personal and paternal conversation with believers, and on the apostolic word concerning Christ, by which the content and saving power of God's revelation enters into well-disposed minds and hearts. By its power, it truly becomes for believers in Christ a vital source of sturdiness in faith and of a characteristic spirituality, so as to give the Church support and strength (no. 3). What began in Jesus' words of spirit and life to convert hearts and draw disciples to follow him, resounded then in apostolic preaching and continues to echo in the Church as the principal means of the unfolding Christian economy.

Nos. 8–13 present Scripture in its nourishing and formative effectiveness. "Believers must be marked and interiorly formed by reverence for this word and by a piety drawn from the wisdom of the Scriptures, 'for ignorance of the Scriptures is ignorance of Christ (Jerome)' " (no. 8). The word informs liturgical worship, where readings and preaching lead into the narrative of thanksgiving proclaiming the Lord's death until he comes (no. 9). Biblical vocabulary is central in the sacraments; thus, word and sacrament should never be sundered but be ever coalescing (no. 10). The care of souls centers on communicating the word that nourishes unto eternal life (no. 11). Therefore Bible reading, study, and meditation must be habitual for priests and seminarians. Theological work should develop in the greatest possible proximity to Scripture, for along with tradition, Scripture study keeps theology ever fresh, as Pius XII had pointed out (no. 12).[24]

In no. 13 the schema makes devout Scripture reading by the faithful a main concluding point, connected with what went before in the text's recommendations to priests. In their practice of pastoral care, a key component is to guide their people "to practice frequent and devout Scripture reading." This will lead believers to contemplate God in his nearness and will engender firmness against temptation. The main aim of Scripture reading is personal encounter with God, through individual hearing and appropriation of his word. A brief reference to magisterial guidance introduces

24. In *Humani generis* Pius XII had written: "Theologians must always return to the sources of divine revelation. . . . Each source of divinely revealed doctrine contains so many rich treasures of truth, that they can really never be exhausted. Hence it is that theology through the study of its sacred sources remains ever fresh; on the other hand, speculation which neglects a deeper search into the deposit of faith proves sterile, as we know from experience" (Carlen, ed., *Papal Encyclicals*, 4:178). I cite this because the main point about theology has fallen victim to a printing error in Joseph A. Komonchak's reference to the passage in his "*Humani Generis* and *Nouvelle Théologie*," in *Ressourcement: A Movement for Renewal in Twentieth-Century Catholic Theology*, ed. Gabriel Flynn and Paul D. Murray (New York: Oxford University, 2012), 138–56, at 151.

a protective factor against spiritual subjectivism, before the final sentences point to the support of devout reading that is expected from liturgical renewal. The general conclusion is that esteem and reverence for God's word will bring to the whole church new spiritual impulses.[25]

The Further *Iter* of Vatican II's Recommendation of Scripture Reading, 1961–1965

De Fontibus Revelationis *in the Central Preparatory Commission, November 1961*

An anticipation of the famous Vatican II clash of November 1962 over *De fontibus revelationis* occurred a year earlier when the Central Preparatory Commission took up the Preparatory Theological Commission's text on November 10, 1961.[26] On that day several cardinals spoke to the passages on Scripture in the Church. Cardinal Julius August Döpfner (Munich/Freising) found no. 27 exaggerating on the Magisterium in connection with Bible reading, since the teaching office focuses its attention elsewhere, namely, on formally taught church doctrine. Bea delivered a sweeping critique of the schema, especially of its account of biblical inspiration and generally on its minimal use of the recent biblical encyclicals. Bea's intervention included (1) precisions on the "juridical authenticity" of the Vulgate (clarified in *Divino afflante Spiritu*), (2) a call for more charity toward exegetes, and (3) the bad impression given by the multiplied references to the Magisterium. Also (4) in drawing on *Humani generis*, the Theological Commission had omitted the encyclical's celebration of

25. In a preliminary evaluation of September 1962 of the first seven Vatican II schemas, Cardinal Joseph Frings (Cologne) used a text composed by Professor Joseph Ratzinger; it contained the suggestion about *De fontibus revelationis* that "in place of Chapter V, much of the draft text presented by Cardinal Bea, *On the Word of God*, could well be substituted, since it treats the same topic and does this better" (citing my translation from "Six Texts by Prof. Joseph Ratzinger as *Peritus* before and during Vatican Council II," *Gregorianum* 89 [2008]: 233–311, at 277). Later, during the 1962 Vatican II debate on the Theological Commission's *De fontibus revelationis*, Archbishop Denis Hurley (Durban, South Africa) mentioned, on November 19, the SPCU schema *De verbo Dei* as exemplifying a pastorally enriching schema, whose language shows the expansive power of God's word, which was notably lacking in *De fontibus*. See *Acta synodalia Sacrosancti Concilii Oecumenici Vaticani II* (hereafter AS) 6 vols. in 31 (Vatican City: Typis Vaticanis, 1970–), 1/3:198.

26. Schelkens (*Catholic Theology of Revelation*, 234–44) introduces the procedures of the Central Commission and reviews the November 10, 1961, debate on *De fontibus*.

the inexhaustible power of the biblical source for "rejuvenating" theology and life.[27] Bea's intervention had a notable impact on the members of the Central Commission, and when they voted on *De fontibus*, 55 of 70 members voted *placet iuxta modum* and indicated that Bea's intervention expressed the content of their reservations.

However the Theological Commission held its ground against criticisms of *De fontibus* in the Central Commission, because votes *placet iuxta modum* counted as votes of approval of the text. As a result only minor changes appeared in the paragraphs on Scripture reading in the published *De fontibus* sent out with six other texts to all the Council Fathers in late summer 1962.[28] Although *De fontibus* stood first in the booklet, it gave way to liturgy as the topic treated during Vatican II's first three weeks of debate. But the turn of *De fontibus* came on November 14, 1962.

It is well known that the council's conflicted discussion of *De fontibus,* November 14–20, 1962, led to an impasse when the Fathers were asked to vote on taking the schema off the immediate agenda. The 62% who voted *placet* to this motion fell short of the two-thirds majority needed to carry it and so the council seemed destined to evaluate each chapter of a schema rejected by a majority. But on November 21 Pope John XXIII exercised his authority by informing the Fathers that he was remanding the schema *De fontibus* for revision by a newly created Mixed Commission, composed of the council's Doctrinal Commission and the Unity Secretariat, to which the pope added some cardinals.

The Textus Prior *of the Mixed Commission on Scripture in the Church, 1962–1963*

The Mixed Commission went to work in November 1962 and made an early decision to give the schema the new title, *De divina revelatione*, and to have it open with a *prooemium* on revelation in itself (eventually, nos. 1–6). For revising chapter 5 on Scripture in the Church, a subcommission of six members was named, including Cardinal Paul-Émile Léger (Montréal) and Hermann Volk (recently made bishop of Mainz). The group

27. *Acta et documenta: Series II*, 2.1:540 (Döpfner) and 546 (Bea).

28. When the future Council Fathers got the booklet of seven texts, they were asked to respond in letters giving their initial evaluation of the schemas. In his response, Frings called for a major revision of the schema *De fontibus*, including the recommendation that the whole chapter 5 be replaced by the SPCU schema *De verbo Dei*, which "treats the same topic and does this better." Frings's evaluation was the work of his *peritus*, Ratzinger. I give this response in "Six Texts by Prof. Joseph Ratzinger," 233–311, at 264–68.

had a new text ready by December 3, which the whole Mixed Commission discussed, emended, and approved two days later. This revised chapter 5, now entitled *De Sacrae Scripturae usu in Ecclesia*, entered the version of the schema that went out to the Fathers along with several other revised schemas on April 22, 1963. Because other intermediate revisions followed, this draft is known as the *Textus prior*.[29]

In the draft, the paragraphs recommending Scripture reading gained importance by becoming the concluding two numbers, with the paragraphs on exegesis and theology moving ahead to the middle of the chapter. This change, together with others, gave a decidedly pastoral orientation to the treatment of Scripture in the Church. This treatment begins in the first paragraph (now no. 21, because of omissions in earlier chapters), where the SPCU's *De verbo Dei* (no. 8) contributes the notion of a personal encounter between the divine Father and his children through the sacred books. Also, no. 3 of *De verbo Dei* adds the affirmation of the saving efficacy of God's word in giving vigor to the Church and spiritual nourishment to the faithful. No. 22 now makes no reference to the Vulgate, but speaks only of translations from the original texts, in biblical versions to spread a more profound and widespread knowledge of Scripture. No. 23, on exegetes, simplifies notably *De fontibus* no. 28 to urge that biblical experts collaborate with theologians to aid the Church in pastoral care that nourishes the faithful. No. 24 asserts that theology has from Scripture its "primary and inalienable foundation and content," with Scripture conveying constant theological rejuvenation, as *De verbo Dei* had cited from Pius XII. The same *De verbo Dei* no. 2, also gave no. 24 the affirmation that Scripture both contains God's word and *is* God's word. Theology is to serve ministry, especially by its contribution to homilies on the Scripture readings.

No. 25, on priests, no longer cites 2 Timothy 3, as in *De fontibus* no. 26, since this text on the effects of inspiration had moved forward to chapter 2, no. 11, on inspiration itself. No. 24 cites only one of the previous three patristic texts and moves quickly to communicating the word during the liturgy.

No. 26, on Scripture reading by the faithful, condenses notably no. 27 of *De fontibus* by, for example, dropping the earlier references to obscurities in the Bible. The people are to "freely" approach Scripture as it is available in the liturgy and other means now widespread. Church authority appears in a positive light as approving these means of formation. Bishops are guides

29. I give the whole text of the *Textus prior*, chapter 5, in the Appendix, pp. 387–89 below.

in the use of Scripture by promoting well-annotated translations. A final passage adopts the last two sentences of *De verbo Dei* no. 13 on the hope for spiritual renewal in the Church from the greater esteem and reverence for the word promoted by this text. "For, the word of the Lord remains forever."

The *Textus prior* thus concludes by featuring elements of a biblically based spirituality as the pastoral goal of the combined work of exegetes, theologians, pastors and homilists, and the bishops who promote programs of biblical formation.

The Doctrinal Commission's Revision on Scripture in the Life of the Church, 1964

In response to the May 1963 distribution of the *Textus prior*, numerous written comments came in from the council members, with chapter 5 on the use of Scripture in the Church being treated in 44 interventions by individual council members and in ten responses by episcopal conferences. But when the announced agenda of the 1963 period of the council did not include *De revelatione*, the Doctrinal Commission suspended work on further revising this text on the basis of the written comments. But Pope Paul VI, in his closing discourse of period 2 on December 4, 1963, gave notice that the revelation schema would be taken up again in period 3 in 1964. Time was given for further written interventions, and in March 1964 a doctrinal subcommission on the revelation schema, with Bishop André-Marie Charue (Namur, Belgium) as president, began work on revising the *Textus prior* on the basis of the council members' many recommendations.

The assignment of *periti* to review the Fathers' comments and initially propose revisions of chapter 5 brought together two Jesuits, Alois Grillmeier and Otto Semmelroth, professors at Sankt Georgen, Frankfurt/ Main, with Professor Ratzinger of Münster. At meetings of April 20–24, the Charue subcommission reviewed proposals by the *periti* for revising the biblical chapters, 2–5, with Grillmeier presenting the revision on Scripture in the Church.

One of the most frequent critical reactions by the Council Fathers to the *Textus prior* had been that it said far too little in no. 26 by way of exhorting the faithful to read Scripture frequently for strengthening their faith and personal spirituality.[30]

30. Calls for this exhortation came in the comments of Bishop Dammert Bellido of Cajamarca, Peru (AS 3/3:827); of Bishop Henriques Jimenez, Auxiliary of Caracas, Venezuela (AS 3/3:840, citing *De imitatione Christi* 1.5); Bishop Jaeger of Paderborn, Germany (AS 3/3:844); Bishop Przyklenk of Januária, Brazil (AS 3/3:869); Bishop Schoemaker of Purwokerto, Indonesia (AS 3/3:876); the Southern African bishops' conference (AS 3/3:894); the Belgian episcopal conference (AS 3/3:897); the bishops of

The revision, called *Textus emendatus*, consolidated no. 25 and the first part of no. 26 into a single no. 25 that recommended Scripture reading to various persons. The last part of the previous no. 26 became the epilogue to the chapter on Scripture in the Church.

The emended no. 25 first extended the exhortation to practice constant biblical study for the enrichment of the ministry of the word from priests (as in *Textus prior* no. 25) to deacons and catechists as well. A second major change transformed the colorless statement of the previous no. 26 about the faithful freely approaching Scripture into an energetic exhortation directed *vehementer particulariterque* to all the faithful, with special mention of those in religious life, calling them to read and study Scripture in order to grow in the knowledge of Christ.[31] A third change responded to the requests of a number of Council Fathers that the text should go beyond the liturgical readings and programs of formation, which were already mentioned in the *Textus prior*, by adding a reference to the practice of personal devout reading (*sive per piam lectionem*) of the Bible.[32] The fourth change added a long sentence urging the preparation of well-adapted editions of Scripture for non-Christians, to give the exhortation its missionary outreach.

The *Textus emendatus* of the whole schema on revelation gained the approval of the Doctrinal Commission in early June 1964, to which was added a satisfied word from Bea that members of the Unity Secretariat need not be called together for a further meeting of the Mixed Commission. The revision went out to the Council Fathers in mid-July and was treated in the council aula from September 30 to October 6, 1964. This week

---

southern France (AS 3/3:900–01, with explicit mention of *lectio divina*); the German and Scandinavian bishops (AS 3/3:905, 913); and the Indonesian bishops' conference (AS 3/3:917).

31. The first two changes depended on the written comments of Bishop João Batista Przyklenk of Januária in the state of Minas Gerais, Brazil (see the previous note). He was a German-born member of the Missionary Congregation of the Holy Family, who included in his written intervention a text offered to express his main desires, namely, to include deacons and to speak an insistent word on Bible reading by religious. The Grillmeier-Semmelroth-Ratzinger team found Bishop Przyklenk's formulation so good that they adopted much of it, while incorporating the word to religious into the insistent exhortation of all the faithful. The phrase "*vehementer particulariterque*" came from Bishop Przyklenk's suggestion that the council address religious on this "*vehementer peculiarique amore*" (AS 3/3:869).

32. Those wanting this insertion included the episcopal conferences of Indonesia, Germany and Scandinavia, and southern France (as in n. 30 above). The emended text of no. 25 is given in the Appendix, pp. 389–90, below.

was a decisive step toward *Dei verbum*, because many Fathers, including leading Cardinals like Döpfner, Meyer (Chicago), Léger, König, and Bea announced their judgment on the revision as *placet* or even *valde placet*.

Final Emendations of De Revelatione *on Scripture Reading, 1964 and 1965*

After the aula discussion, the Charue subcommission reviewed the further recommendations that had been offered for improving the text. From this review, a further revision, the *Textus denuo emendatus*, went to the full Doctrinal Commission, which gave its approval in meetings of November 10–11, 1964. On November 20, all the Council Fathers received the new version in a booklet giving it side-by-side with its predecessor text and accompanying it with explanations of the further emendations.

In no. 25, two changes occurred in the second text of 1964. First, the maxim from Jerome on ignorance of Scripture being tantamount to ignorance of Christ was moved ahead so as not to imply that this pertained especially to those in religious life. Second, at the behest of some Council Fathers, an elegant sentence was added to the exhortation to read the Bible, with its commendation of biblical programs. The addition brought out the need for prayerful interiorization of the content that a person takes from Bible reading: "Let them remember, however, that prayer should accompany the reading of Sacred Scripture, so that it becomes a dialogue between God and the human reader. For 'we speak to him when we pray; we listen to him when we read the divine oracles' (Ambrose, *De officiis*)."[33]

Voting on the schema of *Dei verbum*, the Dogmatic Constitution on Divine Revelation, took place in period 4 of Vatican II, beginning on September 20, 1965. In this vote, the Council Fathers accepted the chapter on Scripture in the Life of the Church by 1,915 votes of *placet*, 212 votes of *placet iuxta modum*, and only one *non placet*. The Doctrinal Commission, in meetings from September 29 to October 11, reviewed the amendments proposed by those voting *placet iuxta modum*, including seven on no. 25. But the outcome was that none of the amendments offered to no. 25 were found necessary or even compatible with the text that had been overwhelmingly approved.

In this amendment process, some Council Fathers had asked for a restrictive modification of the recommendation of biblical reading. In the

33. This came from recommendations submitted by Archbishop Modrego y Casáus of Barcelona (AS 3/3:483) and Volk of Mainz (AS 3/3:345). The further emended text is given in the Appendix, p. 390, below.

amendment proposed by 51 members, the early reserved outlook of Tromp and Garofalo came back in the request that the insistent recommendation of Scripture reading be accompanied by a reference to the Church's past and present teaching that reading all of Scripture is not necessary for each and every member of the faithful.[34]

But the Doctrinal Commission dismissed this restrictive clause, first, as not cohering with the citation from Jerome about ignorance of Scripture being tantamount to ignorance of Christ; second, because a following passage is equivalently protective against erroneous reading, by noting the duties of bishops regarding translations and regarding the explanations that must come with published Bible texts; third, because for some time the popes have been urging Scripture reading upon all Catholics, and, to show this, references to such passages in the biblical encyclicals of Benedict XV and Pius XII were to be added to note 5, which gave the source of the citation from Jerome.

On November 18, 1965, the final voting on *De revelatione* resulted in 2344 votes of *placet* and only six of *non placet*, after which Pope Paul VI promulgated the constitution *Dei verbum* on divine revelation itself, the transmission of revelation by tradition and Scripture, and how the inspired Scriptures should be central in the life of Catholic Christians.

Concluding Reflections

The Second Vatican Council's vigorous exhortation of the faithful to engage in devout Scripture reading (*Dei verbum* no. 25) could not have been foreseen on the basis of the work in 1961 of the Preparatory Theological Commission. What prevailed at that time was instead the Commission's concern over potential dangers to faith and Catholic doctrine that could arise from reading the Scriptures, which in places are quite obscure in their meaning for believers. This was an echo in the mid-20th-century preparation of Vatican II of a staple of traditional anti-Protestant controversial arguments that aimed to refute the position that the Scriptures were clear to everyone regarding the gospel, and, even more, to exclude attributing

34. The proposed modification: "Licet autem Ecclesia docuerit et doceat lectionem totius S. Scripturae non omnibus et singulis necessarium esse, nihilominus *Sancta Synodus* christifideles cunctos, *praesertim sodales religiosos* . . ." (italicizing the proposed additions; citing from Francisco Gil Hellin, ed., *Concilii Vaticani II Synopsis: Constitutio dogmatica de divina revelationis Dei verbum* [Vatican City: Typis Vaticanis, 1993], 167).

to the Holy Spirit an assuring guidance of the devout reader and his or her private judgment on the biblical message for one's salvation.

The schema *De fontibus revelationis*, which the Vatican II membership received before the council opened, bore several traces of passages in Pius XII's *Humani generis*. This appeared in words about the Magisterium being the proximate norm of biblical interpretation and on the task of Catholic theologians to show the agreement between present-day Catholic doctrine and the message and doctrine of the Bible. In time, these lines from Pius XII all but disappeared as the schema *De revelatione* was several times revised. Instead, another text of *Humani generis* came to the fore, namely, Pius XII's charter for *ressourcement*, when he affirmed the inexhaustible potential of the Bible to contribute ongoing rejuvenation to faith and theological instruction.

This study has shown the influence exercised on *Dei verbum*, in chapter 6 on the Bible in the life of the Church, by the Secretariat for Promoting Christian Unity, especially through the introduction into the constitution of passages from the Secretariat's pastoral schema *De verbo Dei*. While it remains true that *Dei verbum* benefitted greatly from the preconciliar biblical movement, one has to note that the ecumenical pioneers brought together in Bea's Unity Secretariat also made a valuable contribution. However, it was fateful that one point of the Secretariat's text did not enter *Dei verbum*, namely, the affirmation in *De verbo Dei*'s final paragraph, no. 13, that pastors have the duty to instruct and guide their people in devout reading of Scripture. This, one has to say, is an element sadly missing from much of the pastoral practice that followed Vatican II.

In revising the schema *De fontibus revelationis*, a crucial change came when the paragraphs of the final chapter were given a new order. Directives on the work of exegetes and theologians moved from the end of the chapter into its center, which allowed the exhortation on Bible reading to have a more emphatic final place in the text. This was a textual realization of the desire of John XXIII and of many Council Fathers that Vatican II should have a primarily pastoral aim and character. Then the little-known German-Brazilian missionary bishop, João Batista Przyklenk, recommended greater insistence on personal Scripture reading than was present in the 1963 text. From his suggestion came the forceful *vehementer* that qualifies the council's recommendation in *Dei verbum* no. 25. A profound "final touch" to no. 25 insisted on prayer before and during one's encounter with God while reading the inspired and inspiring biblical text.

Thus, Vatican II's dogmatic constitution *Dei verbum* has a significant pastoral conclusion concerning what is today known as *lectio divina*. In the reception of the Constitution, commentators have given much attention to its Christocentrism of revelation (chap. 1), to its elegant account of tradition as vital and dynamic (chap. 2), to the great care evident in its expression of the truth of the inspired Scripture (chap. 3), and to its illuminating statement on the genesis of the Gospels (chap. 5). But *Dei verbum* also deserves appreciation and a ready application of its chapter 6 on all that Scripture can give to rejuvenate church members, especially by the practice of devout Bible reading, which is forcefully (*vehementer*) urged on them in no. 25 of the constitution.

Appendix

Preparatory Theological Commission

SCHEMA *DE FONTIBUS REVELATIONIS*[35]

CHAPTER 5, SACRED SCRIPTURE IN THE CHURCH (SELECTIONS)

26. [*Reading of Scripture by Priests*] Every minister of the Church should recall the admonition of St. Paul the Apostle, "all Scripture is divinely inspired and useful for teaching, convincing, correcting, and instructing in justice, so that the man of God may be complete and fully taught for every good work" (2 Tim 3:16-17). As with the Church Fathers who have gone before us, "those who carry out the duty of preaching must not neglect the study of sacred letters,"[36] for the word of the priest should "be grounded in reading of the Scriptures"[37] to prevent a preacher from becoming externally empty "by not being interiorly a listener."[38] The sacred books "can prepare one for salvation through faith in Christ Jesus" (2 Tim 3:15), when they are received from the hands of the Church and a devout reader is moved by docility of spirit and a desire of learning, which promotes spiritual growth.

27. [*Reading of Scripture by the Faithful*] In our times, by the blessing of divine providence, not a few of the faithful have taken up the praiseworthy practice of reading Sacred Scripture in the original texts. Above

35. The Theological Commission approved this schema on September 21, 1961, for forwarding to the Central Preparatory Commission, which would evaluate it regarding its adequacy for distribution to the council members and eventual deliberation on it in the council aula. The Latin original of nos. 26–27 is in *Acta et documenta: Series II*, Praeparatoria 2/1 (1965): 530–31.

36. Gregory the Great, *Pastoral Rule* 2.11; PL 77.50.

37. Jerome, Letter to Nepotianus 8; PL 22.534.

38. Augustine, Sermon 179; PL 38.966.

all, many translations of the sacred books in current languages, made from the original languages, have come out for the use and benefit of many. One has to especially rejoice over the active love that is promoting the publication and diffusion of the Gospels of Christ and writings of the Apostles. This holy reading, as the Fathers and Doctors of the Church give witness and as holy individuals know by experience, enlightens the mind, makes firm the will, and inflames the heart with love of God. But this most holy Vatican council adds its warning that the faithful of Christ should approach the sacred text in awareness of the Church's teaching and with a secure and appropriate formation. This holds especially for the reading of the Old Testament, but also for the New Testament, in which "some things are hard to understand, which ignorant and unstable individuals twist to their own perdition, as they do with the other parts of Scripture" (2 Pt 3:16). Therefore translations used by the faithful must be examined and approved by the bishops "with whom is the apostolic teaching."[39] Also, translations should offer necessary and sufficient explanations that agree with the mind of the Church, whose living Magisterium is for the faithful the proximate norm of belief. In fact the authentic meaning of the divine words cannot be determined by any individual, even if he or she be learned, but by the Magisterium of the Church, to which is entrusted the deposit of Holy Scripture for its interpretation. Every initiative for the diffusion and explanation of Holy Scripture among the Christian people must take place under the authority of the bishops.

Secretariat for Promoting the Unity of Christians

THE WORD OF GOD: SCHEMA OF A PASTORAL DECREE[40]

1. The Church commends to all believers in Christ God's living and life-giving word, which is God's gift from on high and the shield of faith, a reality that the Church never ceases to revere with highest honor and devout affection. This commendation is of greater importance today, when the sower of tares does not oppose single doctrines but the very fact of

39. Irenaeus, *Adv. haer.* 4.32; PG 7.1071.

40. This schema was approved by the council's Central Preparatory Commission on June 20, 1962. The Council Fathers received the text, revised in nos. 2, 7, 9, and 13 (noted by underlining), in *Schemata constitutionum et decretorum de quibus disceptabitur in Concilii sessionibus: Series IV* (1963): 378–82, from which this translation has been made. The schema itself was not debated, but it did contribute several passages to chapter 5 [later, 6], on Scripture in the Church, of the *Textus prior* on divine revelation produced by the Mixed Commission (Doctrinal and SPCU) of 1962–1963.

revelation and the whole deposit of revelation by seeking to weaken the assent of believers to God's word. Against these growing dangers for faith, the Church sets in opposition, from among the other gifts of grace, the living and life-giving word of God, in which God's saving power is most certainly present in an efficacious manner.

2. This word embraces all of what God says to us in revelation, as it echoes through Scripture and tradition in the Church's worship and life. This is the word proclaimed in the Spirit in and through the Church, where it becomes present and operative as an "efficacious word" (Heb 4:12). This occurs primarily by the Holy Scriptures of the Old and New Testaments, which not only contain God's word but in an eminent sense are God's word, and which moreover give witness through the Church to "God's mighty deeds" (Acts 2:11) and to all his saving activity.

3. The Church knows that God's word is wholly unlike human words, since it transcends them by far. God's word is filled with spiritual strength and force, with heavenly vigor and supernatural power, being "the power of God" (1 Cor 1:18), the word of salvation (Acts 13:26) and of life (Acts 5:20), so as to be for all Christians the wellspring of the spiritual life, food for the soul, the strength of faith, the support and vigor of the Church. When lived out faithfully each day it can instill authentic faith and unshakeable hope in opposition to the attractions of pseudo-science and to the anxieties of this life, which today oppress a vast number of souls.

4. "God spoke in many and various ways to the fathers by the prophets, but in our days he has spoken in his Son" (Heb 1:1-2). The words of the Word Incarnate make known the mysteries of God, so that in faith one becomes truly united with God. The God who addresses man in his word approaches us personally, coming near in spirit and grace as a Father embracing all his children. For believers, God's word is life, grace, and spiritual food. "Man does not live by bread alone, but by every word coming forth from the mouth of God" (Mt 4:4). "The words I have spoken to you are spirit and life" (Jn 6:63). God's word works chastely in souls, inviting them to the highest realities, while disposing them to choose a life of conversion to God and of following him by their deliberate decision. One who receives God's word in himself in faith "has eternal life and . . . passes from death to life" (Jn 5:24).

5. God's word is above all a divine gift to the Church, in which many ecclesial duties and tasks concern this divine word. It was given in this way that Jesus the Redeemer mandated the Apostles, and in them the Church,

to preach by the Holy Spirit's empowerment the Gospel of Christ to all nations. For this he gave them full power. This is the fullness of revelation, brought to completion in the Apostles, for "whoever hears you hears me" (Lk 10:16). Therefore the Apostles' discourse was never a merely human word telling about Christ and his saving work, but instead a ministry of the word of Christ himself. First from the mouths of the Apostles and then by the voice of the Church this was passed on and has come to us, to work effectively and salvifically in us, "because in accepting the word of God by hearing us, you received not a human word but, as it truly is, the word of God, which is now at work in you who believe" (1 Thes 2:13).

6. This same apostolic word, "the word of truth, the gospel of salvation" (Eph 1:13), contains in itself force and power to transform everyone and bring them to rebirth, so they may live no longer "from a perishable but from an imperishable seed, the living word of God" (1 Pt 1:23). This same apostolic word echoes through the successive centuries, never dying out or fading away, but instead always living and operating in the catholic and apostolic Church built "on the rock" (Mt 16:18). Therefore God's word not only lays the foundation of Catholic doctrine, but at the same time, when it becomes present among us by the Church's preaching, it has to be taken as a mode and means of the economy of salvation, by which God himself touches the souls of believers by his word and saving grace to lead them to share in divine life. But no one is able to listen to God's word who is not prepared to accept it by having the interior disposition and docility given effectively by grace. But the word received in souls becomes fruitful by the grace of the Holy Spirit.

7. The Church can never be nor even thought of without God's word. The Apostles . . . wanted to be "ministers of the word" (Lk 1:2) who proclaimed not themselves but Christ. In just this way the apostolic Church is truly the minister of the word under the supreme authority of God who speaks. Thus, nothing new may ever be added to and nothing handed on may ever be removed from the divine revelation that is complete in the Apostles.

8. The word of the revealing God comes to expression not only in dogmatic truths defined by the Church, but it also continually offers believers nourishment of their spiritual lives especially by the inspired passages of the Holy Scripture of both Testaments. For this reason believers must be marked and interiorly formed by reverence for this word and by a piety drawn from the wisdom of the Scriptures, "for ignorance of the Scriptures is ignorance of Christ," as St. Jerome pointedly affirmed. Hearing this

sacred discourse is not like reading any other book, for in Scripture the heavenly Father carries on a living and vital conversation with his children. In the Church no other reality but the Gospel receives the recognition given by saying, *Per evangelica dicta deleantur nostra delicta* ("Through the words of the Gospel may our sins be wiped away").[41]

9. The Church celebrates God's word with special solemnity in its liturgical action of praise, in which a necessary part has been from the beginning the reading of Scripture to the faithful for their formation in the mysteries of faith. But God's word is present beyond the reading of Scripture, for this word is undoubtedly present to us in other and varied ways. This occurs above all in preaching and when the faithful assemble to celebrate in thanksgiving "God's great deeds" (Acts 2:11). Then they announce and commemorate the death of the Lord "until he comes" (1 Cor 11:26). Also every testimony to Christ in the Spirit (1 Cor 12:3), every conferring of a sacrament (see Rom 6:3ff, on baptism), and every teaching of "sound doctrine" (1 Tim 1:10) entails the saving proclamation of the power of Christ and by this shares to some extent in the power of the word of God.

10. In the ministry of the Church, God's word acquires its supreme saving efficacy when it enters into the constitution of the sacraments, which are often performed by using words taken directly from Scripture. Consequently, word and sacrament should never be dissociated or separated from each other, but instead should be understood as coalescing in one reality when Christ makes operative our salvation by their coming together at the same time.

11. In its ministry the Church protects and honors the word that it receives from the Lord by preaching it to the faithful in such a way as to offer them the spiritual food that by God's word nourishes them for eternal life, which is a notable spiritual function of the care of souls. For this reason the homily should be practiced as the supreme form of preaching, as the example of the Church Fathers shows us. Because God's word has an exalted place in the economy of salvation, its clear doctrine is most profitable, not only by serving to ground doctrine and truth, but also to the extent that God's word in the Church and through her becomes actualized as "God's living and effective word" (Heb 4:12).

12. Priests should from their time as seminarians be accustomed to reading Scripture and never cease meditating on it. By this they will become

41. A prayer prescribed in the Roman Missal to be said quietly by the priest after he proclaims the Gospel as he kisses the opening words of the text in the Missal or Lectionary.

assiduous hearers of God's word and develop into excellent preachers. The theological disciplines, in debates and in giving their account of profound truth, should follow as close as possible the words of Scripture and take it as normative. For Scripture and tradition "contain so many rich treasures of truth, that they in fact can never be exhausted. Hence it is through the study of the sacred sources that theology remains ever youthful, while, on the other hand, speculation that neglects to search more deeply into the sacred deposit proves sterile, which we know from experience."[42]

13. A duty of pastors is to gently lead all the faithful as early as possible to practice frequent and devout Scripture reading. Thereby the people will become accustomed to contemplate in themselves the mysteries of God and from this to draw spiritual strength against all the attacks of impiety. Let everyone be fully convinced that the primary purpose of Scripture reading is that one hears God speaking to oneself and accepts His word into oneself with an open and docile spirit—under the guidance of the Magisterium to which God has entrusted his word. An aim of preaching and of a worthy and competent renewal of all liturgical worship should be that the continual proclamation of God's word will have an eminent place as well in the solemnities of sacraments. Just as increased devotion to the Eucharist has enriched the Church's life, so one may hope that in the same way the Church will receive new impulses of spiritual life from the proper esteem and reverence for the word. For the word of the Lord remains forever.

Mixed Commission (Doctrine and SPCU) for Revising De fontibus revelationis

TEXTUS PRIOR APPROVED AND SENT TO THE COUNCIL FATHERS (APRIL 22, 1963)[43]

CHAPTER 5, THE USE OF HOLY SCRIPTURE IN THE CHURCH (COMPLETE TEXT)

21. [*The Church Venerates Holy Scripture*] The Church has from the beginning shown the heavenly treasure of the sacred books of the Old and

42. Pope Pius XII, *Humani generis*, August 12, 1950; AAS 42 (1950): 569.

43. Although the supervisory Coordinating Commission approved this draft text for distribution, the initial written comments sent in by the Fathers in summer 1963 made clear that it was not yet a satisfactory basis for treatment in the council aula. Therefore, in spring 1964, it underwent another revision, based mainly on the Fathers' written observations. The translation offered here is from the Latin text given in *Acta synodalia* 3/3:101–5, left-hand column, which was given so that readers could appreciate the subsequent *Textus recognitus* of 1964, given in the right-hand column.

New Testaments great veneration and has never ceased to distribute this singular gift of God to the faithful, especially in its sacred liturgy, commending them for devout reception as a precious gift from God. In the sacred books, the Father who is in heaven meets his children lovingly and in a way converses with them. God's word has in itself so much strength and force that it is in reality the support and vigor of the Church and for her children, the strength of faith, food for the soul, and wellspring of the spiritual life.

22. [*Recommendation of Accurate Translations*] To open the access to Holy Scripture widely for believers in Christ, the Church by her authority and maternal solicitude recommends and takes care that accurate translations be prepared from the most excellent original texts, so that God's word may be known more deeply and declared more abundantly.

23. [*The Apostolic Office of Catholic Teachers*] The Spouse of the Word incarnate, the Church taught by the Holy Spirit of God and Christ, is always seeking to gain a deeper understanding of the Scriptures (see Jn 16:13), so that she may pasture her children with divine discourses. Catholic exegetes, along with theologians, must dedicate their efforts so that, under the lead of the Church's Magisterium, they study more deeply the divine texts, and thereby many ministers of the divine word may be able to offer to God's people nourishment from Scripture, so as to illumine minds, make wills firm, and inflame human hearts with love of God.

24. [*Theology Is Based on God's Word*] Theological science has from the word of God its primary and inalienable foundation and draws from Scripture the contents that give it great solidity and constant rejuvenation. Scripture not only contains God's word, but is truly God's word. From this, the ministry of the word of God, namely, pastoral preaching in which the homily has pride of place, is nourished to good health and flourishes with holiness.

25. [*Scripture Reading Recommended for Priests*] Therefore priests of Christ must give themselves to assiduous reading and diligent study of the Holy Scriptures, both to prevent a preacher from becoming "an externally empty preacher by not being interiorly a listener" (Augustine, Sermon 179) and so they may be able to communicate to their flock all the many riches of the divine word, especially during liturgical worship.

26. [*Scripture Reading Also Recommended for the Faithful*] The faithful as well should freely approach the sacred text itself, whether through the

liturgy so filled with divine discourse or through other programs for this purpose, which with the approval of church authority are happily spreading everywhere in our times.

It is for the bishops, "with whom apostolic doctrine resides" (Irenaeus, *Adv. haer.* 4.32), to guide the faithful entrusted to them in the right use of the divine books and to see to it that they have translations of the sacred texts accompanied with necessary and truly sufficient explanations, so that their converse with Holy Scripture may be safe and fruitful.

Just as increased devotion to the Eucharist has enriched the Church's life, so one may hope that in the same way the Church will receive new impulses for the spiritual life from the rightful esteem and reverence for God's word, which "remains forever."

Doctrinal Commission

TEXTUS EMENDATUS, APPROVED IN JUNE 1964 AND SENT TO THE COUNCIL FATHERS JULY 14, 1964 (SELECTION)
(MODIFICATIONS OF THE *TEXTUS PRIOR* INDICATED BY UNDERLINING)

25. [*Reading of Sacred Scripture Recommended*] Therefore, all clerics, especially priests of Christ and others, who as deacons or catechists, are officially engaged in the ministry of the word, should give themselves to assiduous reading and diligent study of the Holy Scriptures, both to prevent any of them from becoming "an externally empty preacher by not being interiorly a listener" (Augustine, Sermon 179) and to make them able to communicate to the faithful entrusted to them the abundant riches of the divine word, especially during divine worship.

Likewise, the Holy Synod exhorts forcefully and specifically (*vehementer particulariterque exhortatur*) all the Christian faithful, especially those in religious life, lest "by ignorance of the Scriptures they may be ignorant of Christ" (Jerome, *Comm. in Is.*), to learn instead by frequent study of the Scriptures "the surpassing worth of knowing Jesus Christ" (Phil 3:8). Let them therefore turn gladly to the sacred text itself, when it is offered by the sacred liturgy or approached by devout reading or through programs and other aids for this purpose, which with the approval and guidance of the Church are happily spreading everywhere in our times.

It is for the bishops "with whom apostolic doctrine resides" (Irenaeus, *Adv. haer.* 4.32), to guide the faithful entrusted to them in the right use of the divine books, especially of the New Testament and above all of the Gospels. This is done by translations of the sacred texts that are equipped with necessary and truly adequate explanations. Thus members of the

Church may become familiar with the Holy Scriptures safely and to their profit, so as to be steeped in their spirit.

Moreover, editions of Sacred Scripture, provided with suitable notes, should be prepared for the use of non-Christians as well and adapted to their circumstances. Let these be prudently circulated, either by pastors of souls or by Christians of any walk of life.

Doctrinal Commission

TEXTUS DENUO EMENDATUS, APPROVED NOVEMBER 10–11, 1964, AND GIVEN TO THE COUNCIL FATHERS NOVEMBER 20 (SELECTION) (MODIFICATIONS OF THE *TEXTUS EMENDATUS*, NO. 25, PARA. 2, INDICATED BY UNDERLINING)

Likewise, the Holy Synod exhorts forcefully and specifically (*vehementer particulariterque exhortatur*) all the Christian faithful, especially those in religious life, to learn by frequent study of the Scriptures "the surpassing worth of knowing Jesus Christ" (Phil 3:8). "For ignorance of the Scriptures means ignorance of Christ" (Jerome, *Comm. in Is.*).[44] Let them therefore turn gladly to the sacred text itself, when it is offered by the sacred liturgy or approached by devout reading or through programs and other aids for this purpose, which with the approval and guidance of the Church are happily spreading everywhere in our times.

Let them remember, however, that prayer should accompany the reading of Sacred Scripture, so that it becomes a dialogue between God and the human reader. For "we speak to him when we pray; we listen to him when we read the divine oracles" (Ambrose, *De officiis*).

44. The Jerome citation now comes after the passage on learning Christ, so as to clearly apply to all, not just religious.

17 Religious Life in the Vatican II Era
"State of Perfection" or Living Charism?

MARYANNE CONFOY, RSC

Religious life has consistently played a prophetic role in the church; its post–Vatican II era is no exception. The failure of dialogue between those leaders whose ecclesiology is described as traditionalist and those labeled progressive continues to wound the Body of Christ. This article argues that it is in and through the dialogical living of their charism in service of the global church and society of the 21st century that religious offer healing and hope in and through their prophetic, ecclesial witness.

Religious Life: Pre–Vatican II

Throughout the life of the Christian church, religious life has been in dialectical tension with both its ecclesial and cultural contexts. The various histories of religious life attest to the presence in the church almost from the beginning of lifestyles different from that of the baptismal norm.[1] The early eremitical and monastic forms were ways of commitment to God different from those of the typical "faithful." The monastic, ministerial, or secular institute forms of religious life[2] have usually been generated by the inspired

1. Elizabeth Rapley, *The Lord as Their Portion: The Story of the Religious Orders and How They Shaped Our World* (Grand Rapids: Eerdmans, 2011). This study focuses on the missionary initiatives of religious through history.

2. There are various forms of naming active religious life in contrast to the monastic. I use the term "ministerial lifestyle," following Sandra M. Schneiders, *Prophets in Their Own Country: Women Religious Bearing Witness to the Gospel in a Troubled Church* (Maryknoll, NY: Orbis, 2011).

response of a significant leader who saw a situation of need, of people suffering on life's margins for one reason or another, and who reached out to them in compassionate response. In most cases the charismatic leader was joined by a group of other dedicated Christians inspired to serve Christ and to live the Christian life in and through a community of discipleship.[3]

The pre–Vatican II church was predominantly European in terms of identity, discipline, and the exercise of power. It was a church in a problematic state as a consequence of the two world wars, global depression, and rebuilding that followed. In face of local or global upheaval or radical change, the tendency to solidify roots and identity in a familiar form is a common occurrence. The strong resistance of the institutional church to the uncertainties of the post-Enlightenment world along with the maintenance of a 19th-century fortress identity at its institutional center had set up tensions within the various European Catholic communities.

Religious life in the early 20th century was a largely northern hemispheric reality. While there were significant differences between the experience of ministerial religious life and its demands in Europe and that of North America, the demands of the 1917 Code of Canon Law had engendered a control and structuring of religious life that was not characteristic of previous eras.[4] The repression of European religious congregations and communities during the two wars had its own impact. In postwar years, religious were active in ministry but their numbers were decreasing. There were more calls to open new institutions even though there were no religious to minister in them. Awareness of the dire situations faced by many European congregations led some bishops to envisage

3. While religious life in the present era has been characterized by women and men who experienced a call to the contemplative or ministerial life of prayer and service, this was not always the case. Both Jo Ann McNamara and Elizabeth Rapley point out that in earlier centuries, women joined religious life as an alternative to marriage, and it was quite usual for affluent women to take up this lifestyle. See McNamara, *Sisters in Arms: Catholic Nuns through Two Millennia* (Cambridge, MA: Harvard University, 1996); and Rapley, *Lord as Their Portion*.

4. The Code of Canon Law, based on the previous *Codex juris canonici*, was promulgated under Pope Benedict XV in 1917 and published in English in 1918. For the implications of the new code and the transition of religious life from "extralegal if not illegal" aspects of lifestyle and ministry see Margaret S. Thompson, *The History of Women Religious in the United States* (Now You Know Media, https://www.nowyouknowmedia.com/the-history-of-women-religious-in-the-united-states.html, 2010, Topic 7. Thompson's work is available only on audio CD; a second CD allows one to print the text; I refer to the latter as "Written Guide"; topic and page numbers refer to it). All URLs cited herein were accessed on March 10, 2013.

and argue for alternative religious lifestyles to meet the changing needs of the time. During Pius XII's papacy and into the 1960s, the Vatican Congregation for Religious Affairs commented on the situation of many religious communities:

> It is unfortunately true that there are convent communities which are nearly dying of hunger, neglect and privation; and others which, because of material difficulty, lead a very painful life. There are other communities which, without living in need, often decline, because they are separated and isolated from all the others. Moreover, laws of the cloister, often too strict, frequently provoke great difficulties.[5]

Concerns about declining numbers of vocations, aging and overworked religious, ministerial burnout, and loss of an authentic religious spiritual life were major issues for the church hierarchy in the first half of the 20th century; they were not simply a post–Vatican II phenomenon.

Although their history was different from that of European religious, North American women religious were experiencing similar struggles. Along with the ever-expanding demands of their ministries as women, they faced the problem of antiquated but romanticized religious habits that not only set them apart from those they ministered to, but required hours of time in their laundering and maintenance.[6] The significance of this did not receive much attention at the time.[7] Aware of the pressures on religious and the difficulties they faced mainly as a result of the tensions between the required monastic practices and the competing ministerial demands, Pope Pius XII called religious leaders to Rome to address the problems they were facing, including the need to adapt to the present.[8]

5. Quoted in Gérard Huyghe, *Tensions and Change: The Problems of Religious Orders Today*, trans. Sister Marie Florette (London: Geoffrey Chapman, 1965) 7.

6. The romantic attitude of many older Catholics toward the habit in both the pre–Vatican II period and at present fails to take into account the elitism of the habit and its privilege rather than its witness to service. The situation of congregations that were refused the right to wear their religious habit during the war and were oppressed is quite different.

7. While issues of numbers, problematic lifestyles, and religious habits were important, far greater problems were being faced by both male and female religious in their dealings with bishops, whose sometimes autocratic demands created significant pressures on communities and their leaders. For a comprehensive examination of the history of women religious in the United States, see Thompson, *History of Women Religious in the United States*.

8. See Pius XII, *Menti nostrae* (September 23, 1950), *Acta apostolicae sedis* 42 (1950): 657–702. Friedrich Wulf, "Decree on the Appropriate Renewal of the Religious Life," trans. Ronald Walls, in *Commentary on the Documents of Vatican II*, 5 vols., ed.

This was the pre–Vatican II period that is remembered nostalgically by many as a time of flourishing religious life. In the mid-20th century, religious congregations were exercising significant ministerial leadership in education, health care, and community service. But this was also a period when few options other than religious life were available, particularly for women, to exercise a life of dedicated service to the church. With the rise of feminism leading to the awakening of women to issues of long-standing oppression, new questions and concerns began to surface especially for women.[9] This was the heritage and the reality of the diverse forms of religious life that were to be the object of concern for the bishops of Vatican II.

Vatican II: Static versus Dynamic Worldviews

A more expansive understanding and appreciation of the contribution that Pope John XXIII believed the church could make to the 20th-century world inspired him to call the Second Vatican Council. It was to be a pastoral council, not an easy concept to grasp for those in curial power at the time. The first documents produced by the curial committees on church, liturgy, Scripture, priesthood, and religious life were juridical and disciplinary in character. The council members rejected these documents almost immediately. From that early period onward the council was characterized by polarization.[10] The vision of church that was integral to Vatican II as it progressed through the five sessions was one that moved from a static worldview to a more dynamic approach of connectedness to and service of the world.[11] As Yves Congar noted:

> The church of Vatican II relates to the world and wants to serve. Of course, the first article of the Christian mission in the world talks about

---

Herbert Vorgrimler (New York: Herder & Herder, 1967–1969), 2:301–70, at 301, points out that an account of Pius XII's efforts at renewal of religious life can be found in P. Lombardi, SJ, "Il rinnovamento dei religiosi," *Civiltà Cattolica* 100, no. 1 (March 12, 1949): 615–29.

9. See Rapley, *Lord as Their Portion*, 321–25.

10. Massimo Faggioli comments that the death of Pope John Paul II and the election of Pope Benedict XVI were two important elements in the "broad theological and ecclesiastical landscape of the debate on Vatican II in the last few years" (*Vatican II: The Battle for Meaning* [New York: Paulist, 2012], 17).

11. While the debates and divisions between factions continued throughout the council, voting on the documents showed the movement toward aggiornamento and the pastoral intent of John XXIII.

> conversion to the Gospel but the mission of the church entails a second article, service to the world as it is, until, in the eschatological kingdom, church and world will be one.[12]

This commitment to presence in and service of the world has played a major part in the strategies for renewal and adaptation of religious life in the post–Vatican II era.

While the aim of John XXIII was intrinsically pastoral, the vision and mind-set of many of the bishops who attended the council was less so. Caught within the textbook certainties of their own juridical training for sacramental ministry and the questions and ambiguities raised by their pastoral roles and experience over the decades of their ministerial lives, many of the Council Fathers struggled between the two extremes of openness and closure to the world as exemplified by various conciliar leaders during the debates. From the council's opening to its close, the polarized positions were clearly evidenced in the membership of the various committees appointed to write the document on religious life.

Among the significant bishops calling for openness to a less juridical approach to religious life were Cardinals Julius Döpfner, Léon Joseph Suenens, and Bishop Gérard-Maurice-Eugène Huyghe. Döpfner played a significant role in shaping the documents on the church and on religious life. He argued for the importance of recognizing the foundations of religious vocation in Christ and in the life of the church and the importance of moving beyond the perspective focused simply on personal salvation.[13] Commentators point out that those involved in writing *Perfectae caritatis* (*PC*), the Decree on the Adaptation and Renewal of Religious Life, had not grasped key issues that would have to be faced by religious in their efforts at renewal and adaptation due to the long history of accretions of stylized and ritualized ways of living, dressing, and apostolic service that had virtually become the essence of religious life.[14]

12. Quoted in Massimo Faggioli, "The Battle over *Gaudium et Spes* Then and Now: Dialogue with the Modern World," *Origins* 42 (2013): 545–51, at 551 n. 16.

13. I do not intend to address the history of the development of *PC*; for that see Friedrich Wulf, "Decree on the Appropriate Renewal of the Religious Life"; and Maryanne Confoy, *Religious Life and Priesthood:* Perfectae caritatis, Optatam totius, Presbyterorum ordinis (New York: Paulist, 2008), 177–206.

14. Ian Linden describes the degree of control over horarium and clothing exerted within religious life by authoritarian religious superiors in the pre–Vatican II era: *Global Catholicism: Diversity and Change since Vatican II* (New York: Columbia University, 2009), esp. chap. 10. See also Wulf, "Decree on the Appropriate Renewal," 306. The

Perhaps the greatest and most practical challenges to the document on religious life and to the mentality of the bishops present especially in regard to religious, particularly women religious, were offered by Suenens, whose writings and exhortations on religious life were inviting religious into more contemporary and much-needed ministries. He lamented the fact that particularly women religious were limited in how they could serve the church and world of the time because of outmoded customs and habits, and by their apparent institutional confinement to roles of education of children. Suenens also commented that religious women were treated as less than adults themselves because of the oppressive lifestyles and relational structures in their communities. Although the traditional ministries of health care, community care, and education of children were seen to make a valuable contribution to the church, Suenens believed that religious could play a significant role in evangelizing and by working with laity through other ministerial outlets.[15] He recognized that with the numbers of religious in that period—300,000 men and 1,200,000 women—new ways of serving church and world that addressed the cultural needs of the time could be generated. He argued that the council must elaborate a spirituality of the active life for religious, so that they can get away from "the traditions and mentality of the cloister."[16] Huyghe criticized the various early drafts and the static approach they presented for being preconciliar, Occidental, and juridical. His hope was for religious whose role would be a source of unity among Christians and contribute to dialogue with non-Christians: "Within the church, religious should exercise a unifying role both by example and by action. They should not separate themselves from other members of the church; on the contrary, they should forge bonds with them, cooperate with all and fulfill an ecumenical role."[17]

---

surrendering of both autocratic control and these accretions was a costly experience. It is ironic, and perhaps an example of the depth of the traditionalist mind-set of some religious that, at a postconciliar meeting of leaders of religious congregations called by Paul VI shortly after the conclusion of Vatican II to express his gratitude to religious for their service of the church, one angry superior general, apparently unwilling to implement any form of renewal asked, "Could I have Cardinal Suenens's head on a plate?" Neither the superior's facial expression nor her tone of voice gave the appearance of a comment made in jest! See "Author of Reform: The Cardinal Suenens Story" (Alexandria, VA: Journey Films, 1999) VHS tape.

15. Léon Joseph Suenens, *The Nun in the World: New Dimensions in the Modern Apostolate*, trans. Geoffrey Stevens (Westminster, MD: Newman, 1962), 209.

16. Ibid.

17. Ibid., 210.

In contrast to the understanding of Döpfner, Suenens, and Huyghe, which highlighted the dynamic dimensions of religious life, was the static mind-set of, for example, Cardinals Francis Spellman and Ernesto Ruffini. Spellman disagreed with Suenens's interventions that promoted adaptation and renewal of religious life and ministry. Spellman wanted to maintain the ministries of religious in his archdiocese as they were. The need to reinforce the regulatory practices of both convent and cloister along with the fear of losing the religious workforce in their dioceses informed the interventions of those bishops who resisted what was seen as a more liberal approach.[18] Opposition to any idea of renewal and adaptation was led by Ruffini, who worried about "imprudent demands for reform" and the danger that this might mean for the call to the life of perfection.[19]

The dissension between the two groups continued in debates in both the committee meetings and the council hall on the document's sections relating to the baptismal and religious consecration and on the vowed life. The baptismal call to participate in the saving mission of the world is present to all people in Christ, and the love of God and neighbor cannot be separated. Monastic or ministerial religious life is not an individualistic way of living "for God alone" (nos. 5, 6). This expresses the foundational ecclesiology of both *Lumen gentium* and *Gaudium et spes* that is integral to the call and response of all Christians in general and of religious in particular through their public profession of following Christ in a communal life. As Gregory Baum notes, "Essential to religious life . . . is the commitment to a community as a way of intensifying obedience to the Gospel."[20]

Wulf comments that in the post–Vatican II era, it is not so much the contemplative life that nourishes the love of God and of neighbor within the individual and thus gives "life and direction" to the practice of the counsels; rather, it is ordinarily "the distress of the neighbor who needs our help, the worldwide concerns of the church, the helplessness of so many nations facing catastrophe . . . that bring evangelical counsels to

18. For the concern expressed by those bishops who wanted to maintain the status quo of religious in terms of both lifestyle and ministry, see Hanjo Sauer, "The Doctrinal and the Pastoral: The Text on Divine Revelation," in *History of Vatican II*, 5 vols., ed. Giuseppe Alberigo and Joseph A. Komonchak, vol. 4, *Church as Communion: Third Period and Intersession, September 1964–September 1965* (Maryknoll, NY: Orbis, 2004), 196–233, at 211.

19. Ibid.

20. Gregory Baum, "Commentary," in *The Decree on the Renewal of Religious Life of Vatican Council II*, trans. Austin Flannery (New York: Paulist, 1966), 9–55, at 41.

mind and reveal afresh their urgent necessity."[21] This is ordinarily the basic dynamism of ministerial religious life. This is certainly the basis of many of the diverse forms of ministry that have characterized religious life in subsequent decades, and that have been judged by traditionalists as deviations from the state of perfection.[22] The dynamic dimension of the vowed life and its broader foundations are described in *SC* no. 12, par. 1. The meaning of celibacy has its foundations in the christological, ecclesiological, and eschatological dimensions:

> It not only symbolizes in a singular way the heavenly goods but also the most suitable means by which religious dedicate themselves with undivided heart to the service of God and the works of the apostolate. In this way they recall to the minds of all the faithful that wondrous marriage decreed by God and which is to be fully revealed in the future age in which the Church takes Christ as its only spouse. (Translation from the Vatican website.)

This relational understanding is in contrast to the more static articulation of pre–Vatican II treatments of celibacy, which were, in terms of an unqualified and unexplained exhortation to religious to embrace "the chastity of angels," an approach that failed to take human reality into account.[23] Rather, religious are encouraged not to "overestimate their own strength but practice mortification and custody of the senses. Neither should they neglect the natural means which promote health of mind and body" (*PC* no. 12). A more holistic and human approach is recommended, along with some form of personal discipline that will support a lifelong commitment.[24] Attention to the relational aspect of celibacy came as a result of the endeavors of those bishops who promoted the living charism of religious life in the mandate that all, "especially superiors, remember that chastity is guarded more securely when true brotherly [or sisterly] love flourishes in the common life of the community" (*PC* no. 12). The

21. Wulf, "Decree on the Appropriate Renewal," 348.

22. In his "Extending the Dialogue about Religious Life," a 1983 address to the Leadership Conference of Women Religious Assembly, Archbishop John Quinn of San Francisco observed that during the past 20 years of renewal, American nuns have been "exposed to an unprecedented level of misrepresentation and attack from both the right and the left" (*Origins* 13 [1983]: 213–21, at 216).

23. The implications of the formation of religious in the pre–Vatican II period when the "chastity of angels" is the model are surely evident in the exposure of abuse at both administrative and ministerial levels in the post–Vatican II decades.

24. For a more detailed development of the vows according to *Perfectae caritatis*, see Confoy, *Religious Life and Priesthood*, 216–23.

emphasis on the mutuality of responsibility for authentic communal relationships and the special emphasis on the leadership of the superior in this matter is a fruit of the greater awareness of the coresponsibility of all for the common life, and a breaking down of autocratic approaches and the subordination of subjects.

The closing section of *Perfectae caritatis* (no. 25) offered a vision for the future of religious life that was in sharp contrast to the carefully separated identities and ministries of the past, reinforced by the narrow canonical interpretation of the period. It affirms the importance of encouraging vocations, recognizes the generosity of religious, and recommends more initiatives in collaboration and communication.

While the new understanding of religious life and the recognition of its importance for the church of the future energized many of the council members with the possibility of renewal and adaptation that opened up ways of collaboration and cooperation within parishes, dioceses, and between institutions, many Council Fathers were fearful of what might be let loose as the well educated and committed religious envisaged alternative ways of living their charism in different ministerial contexts.[25] The Tridentine understanding that had remained active, or that simply stayed below the surface throughout the council sessions, kept numbers of bishops insulated in their traditional mind-set and unable to hear the significance of the pastoral and dogmatic constitutions on the church or of the call for a new approach to ecclesial ministry in relation to religious life.[26] Commentators on the outcomes of Vatican II point out that *Perfectae caritatis* ranked among the weakest and most limited of all the documents produced.[27] The polarization that characterized the committees that produced the document has continued throughout subsequent decades and extended its influence in the Catholic community at large.[28]

25. For a long time frustration has characterized the relationship between bishops and members of religious orders, particularly clerical orders. This seems to be primarily due to the fact that many council members were against the rights and privileges of exempt religious. Some bishops felt religious should be more accountable to the local bishop than to the works of the congregation.

26. For an alternative reading of the Council of Trent, see John O'Malley, *Trent: What Happened at the Council?* (Cambridge, MA: Harvard University, 2013).

27. Wulf commented that there was little unity in the document, or in the commission that produced it. Evident throughout the deliberations were the different approaches to, and understandings of, religious life in the authors of not only *Perfectae caritatis* but also *Lumen gentium* chaps. 5 and 6. See "Decree on the Appropriate Renewal," 301.

28. It was questioned consistently within various meetings and debates whether the traditional doctrine of the counsels, which so decisively characterized the

Renewal and Adaptation Versus Resistance in the Post–Vatican II Decades

Commentators on the post–Vatican II period describe the wide-ranging polarities of interpretation of the 16 documents in various ways. Faggioli expands and deepens the understanding of these divergent viewpoints.[29] In addressing the question of the impact of Vatican II over the past 50 years, Joseph Komonchak describes three interpretations of Vatican II that have taken shape that are most apt for this analysis. He describes a progressive interpretation that dichotomizes "the pre- and postconciliar Church." This stance is more negative on the preconciliar church and more positive on the council itself and on the postconciliar church and its reforms. The second group, described as taking a traditionalist approach, also dichotomizes but with reversed polarities. The preconciliar church had responded appropriately to the challenges it had faced, while the postconciliar church had generated chaos, a chaos for which the council was responsible. The third interpretation, between the other two, is described as reformist. This stance rejects the dichotomizing approach and stresses "elements of continuity in the conciliar teachings and reforms. . . . It argues that the popes and bishops of Vatican II never intended revolution but rather reform and especially spiritual renewal."[30] It is surely the understanding of a reformist response to Vatican II that has characterized religious in the past 50 years. While "reformist" carries its own accretions of meaning and interpretation, the meaning I intend here is that of religious re-forming and renewing religious life spiritually in dynamic response to the call of Vatican II.

The resistance to the renewal and adaptation endorsed by *Perfectae caritatis* by those described as traditionalist during the council debates was to any understanding of religious life other than that of the call to a state of perfection; and in subsequent years, they carried this understanding back to their dioceses. The polarized perspectives and the tensions that had been present in the debates in the aula were echoed in most congregational meeting rooms as the concrete issues and implications of the meaning of renewal and adaptation came into action. While the authors of *Perfectae caritatis* had worked on the renewal of religious life with both intensive

---

self-understanding of the religious orders of the past could still be maintained in the postconciliar years. See Wulf, "Decree on the Appropriate Renewal," 306.

29. Faggioli, *Vatican II: The Battle for Meaning.*

30. Joseph A. Komonchak, "Interpreting the Council and Its Consequences: Concluding Reflections," in *After Vatican II: Trajectories and Hermeneutics*, ed. James L. Heft, with John O'Malley (Grand Rapids, MI: Eerdmans, 2012), 164–72, at 164–65.

and expansive theological and canonical understandings of "constant return to the sources" and "to the original spirit of the institute" (*PC* no. 2), religious in their own contexts worked to understand what this might mean in their own concrete situations, in their own local efforts to adapt to the changed conditions of our time.

One of the difficulties for ministerial religious was that they were facing the immediacy of the task in their communal lives at the same time as they were trying to promote and implement Vatican II in their ministries. As they endeavored to reconnect with their "founding identity" as the council had mandated, some religious realized that they did not have a founder in the way the document assumed. They had come into being not because of any charism handed on by a founder, but rather as a consequence of a ministerial need at a particular time, and at the invitation or mandate of a bishop or other founding cleric.[31] Thompson describes the origin of the Sisters of the Assumption of the Blessed Virgin, where the parish had a school but no teachers, and where no religious were forthcoming from any of the local religious congregations. The comment of the parish priest at the time was, "We cannot obtain nuns? Then let us make some."[32] The fact that the congregation of the Assumption of the Blessed Virgin came into existence and that young women generously gave their lives for this ministry indicates something of the ethos of the period and its understanding of the religious vocation. The contrast between the experiences of those congregations that were intentionally founded and those that seemed to arise "accidentally" was emphasized in the early decades after Vatican II as the decisions by the religious leaders of the period came into conflict with the will of the bishops in the diocese where they were located, or who saw themselves as the founders of the communities.[33]

31. Schneiders comments that congregations typically begin "in the charismatic experience of one or more founders who feel impelled to give themselves to God and God's work, almost always in response to some historically pressing need. Subsequent members respond to a personal call to join the founders in this divinely originated enterprise" (*Prophets in Their Own Country*, 100).

32. Thompson, *History of Women Religious of the USA*, "Written Guide," 42. See especially Topic 10, "Charism and Personality: Individuals as Shapers of Communities" (42). In describing the diverse origins of religious communities Thompson comments that not all congregations have a founding charism; rather, their origin is in an "instrumental" need for religious to minister, rather than in a founder's charismatic response to a perceived need. She describes the ensuing experience and history of such religious congregations as a "deep story."

33. Ibid., Topics 11 and 12, in "Father Didn't Always Know Best: Relations and Tensions with the Clergy," Parts I and II.

The polarization between those religious who were locked into the status quo of religious life as a state of perfection and those who responded to the dynamic of renewal that was a constant issue during the council had destructive consequences both within some religious congregations and between the congregation and the local bishops.[34] This was particularly the case for some women's congregations in the United States. Los Angeles Cardinal James McIntyre's 1968 rejection of the Immaculate Heart of Mary Sisters' renewal and adaptation decisions created division within the community.[35] The IHM chapter had mandated adaptation in five areas: more autonomy in choice of ministry, choice of dress, and issues related to prayer, leadership, and formation. This was anathema to the cardinal, and the appeals of both the cardinal and the congregational leader, Sister Anita Caspary, to Rome resulted at first in an uneasy stalemate. The cardinal was forced to back down to a certain extent and to recognize the authority of the chapter. But there was uneasiness among some members of the community in this unusual resistance to episcopal authority. When the sisters proceeded with their adaptation decisions along the track of renewal, the cardinal saw this as defiance and issued the ultimatum that if their decrees were not retracted, he would expel them from the archdiocesan schools.[36]

McIntyre referred the case to the Vatican, which censured the IHM leadership and congregation, classifying the changes they had made as

34. Thompson also records some horrendous examples of the suffering of some women religious leaders and their congregations at the hands of their local bishops (Topics 11 and 12, on audio CD only).

35. Although this conflict between the cardinal and the IHM leadership took place shortly after the council, I believe it is important to see the continuity of resistance and of the abuse of power exercised by some bishops in reaction to the ministerial leadership of religious in their diocese. There are multiple examples of the suffering caused by autocratic and sometimes inadequately informed bishops in reaction to leadership exercised by individual religious as well as in congregational initiatives. The public censuring of religious has been occasionally scandalous and tragic in their consequences—e.g., the 2009 excommunication of Sister Margaret McBride, RSM, without full knowledge of the facts surrounding an induced abortion case at St. Joseph's Hospital and Medical Center, Phoenix, Arizona. This action and the inadequacy of the follow-through of the situation at the level of leadership has been a cause of unnecessary suffering and misunderstanding at many levels of Catholic church life. Such occurrences have been repeated in contemporary civic cases of administrative failures of Catholic church leaders in relation to situations of sexual abuse globally.

36. Helen Rose Fuchs Ebaugh, *Women in the Vanishing Cloister: Organizational Decline in Catholic Religious Orders in the United States* (New Brunswick, NJ: Rutgers University, 1993), 139–40.

deviations rather than adaptations. The Vatican required compliance with the cardinal's demands and ordered the dissemination of its findings to other religious women's communities. The public conflict that followed resulted in a division in the IHM community and their eventual decision to move to a noncanonical status.[37] The division was highly publicized and caused concern and even dissension within some religious communities and in other dioceses and parishes. As a consequence, hundreds of letters of support were sent to the dissenting IHMs, and Catholic newspapers published editorials and articles on the scandal.

The issue of "appropriate" adaptation, however, was not confined to Los Angeles. The Major Superiors of Religious Women at the time took varying stances on this issue. Some wanted the relatively newly established Leadership Conference of Women Religious (LCWR) to speak out against McIntyre's action and in support of their fellow religious leader.[38] Others were concerned that this could be seen as disobedience and a lack of loyalty. The resultant establishment of an alternative leadership group in the United States, the only country with two such leadership groups for religious women, has had its own deleterious consequences over the decades, with the Stonehill "Symposium on Apostolic Religious Life since Vatican II" being an example of the divisiveness in action.[39]

37. While 50 sisters opted to comply and stay within the Los Angeles schools system, 400 others were dispensed from their vows and reconstituted themselves as a lay community in the church. A contemporary perspective on this from outside religious orders is found in Kenneth Briggs, *Double Crossed: Uncovering the Catholic Church's Betrayal of American Nuns* (New York: Doubleday, 2006), 154–55.

38. The opponents of the California IHM sisters decided to rename their organization Consortium Perfectae Caritatis after the title of Paul VI's Decree on the Adaptation and Renewal of Religious Life, October 28, 1965 (http://www.vatican.va/archive/hist_councils/ii_vatican_council/documents/vat-ii_decree_19651028_perfectae-caritatis_en.html); they were concerned for the status quo of religious life and the current direction of leadership. In this decision they had the support of conservative bishops. When Cardinal James Hickey of Washington, DC, obtained Vatican recognition for the organization's dissenting position, the Consortium was renamed Council of Major Superiors of Women Religious. See Thompson, *History of Women Religious in the United States*, Topic 17: "Reaction and Response: Adjusting to New Circumstances."

39. For an analysis of the contemporary equivalent of the IHM conflict that was provoked by a meeting of traditionalist religious and bishops at a 2008 symposium entitled "Apostolic Religious Life since Vatican II . . . Reclaiming the Treasure: Bishops, Theologians, and Religious in Conversation," see Schneiders, *Prophets in Their Own Country*, esp. 4–7. It was on this occasion and in her symposium address that Sara Butler, SMBT, called on Cardinal Franc Rode, prefect of the Vatican Congregation for Institutes of Consecrated Life and Society of Apostolic Life, to initiate an apostolic

The different and inconsistent interpretations of the meaning of renewal and adaptation, along with the formalized expectations of what postconciliar religious lifestyle and ministry might be, generated a range of publications both from the Vatican and from conciliar participants. Within twelve months of the conclusion of the council, the apostolic letter *Ecclesiae sanctae* (*ES*) (August 6, 1966) was published with the essential norms for religious congregations that had been promised in *Perfectae caritatis* no. 1.

This document spelled out the implementation of the spirit and practice of religious life. The approach taken was an enabling one; for example, where *PC* no. 4 required the "cooperation of all the members of the institute," *ES* reads: "The cooperation of all superiors and members is necessary to renew Religious life in themselves, to prepare the spirit of the chapters, to carry out the works of the chapters, to observe faithfully the law and norms enacted by the chapters" (Part I, I., no. 2). The choice of the word "members" rather than "subjects" is important in the new movement toward mutuality of responsibility within orders.[40]

It took time and much work for religious to deal with the diversity of interpretations generated in those early post–Vatican II years. While many congregations were characterized by either one or the other polarized response to the implementation of renewal and adaptation in terms of identity, lifestyle, and mission, some congregations suffered division within their ranks. Some split into two groups, one clinging to the traditional lifestyle and the other opening up to new possibilities of lifestyle and ministry. Conferences and congregational gatherings were held, and numbers of books were published to help religious discover their founding charism or originating story.

The gospel and ecclesial foundations for religious life were the basis of much of the ongoing post–Vatican II research and implementation of the living charism in religious life. Founding stories, rules, and constitutions

---

visitation of American women religious. Such an investigation followed this small but powerful symposium. In February 2009 the Congregation for the Doctrine of the Faith (CDF) announced that it would conduct a Doctrinal Assessment of the LCWR; the findings were released in April 2012. The responses to it both nationally and internationally were largely in support of the LCWR and US religious women. The consequences for the 80% of US women religious represented by the leadership of LCWR are yet to play out.

40. For a more extensive analysis of the implementation of *PC* over the decades following *ES*, see Confoy, *Religious Life and Priesthood*, 224–54. *ES* can be found at http://www.vatican.va/holy_father/paul_vi/motu_proprio/documents/hf_p-vi_motu-proprio_19660806_ecclesiae-sanctae_en.html.

were reviewed and reformulated using a scriptural rather than a juridical lens; the intent was a renewal that would enable religious to minister more effectively in the church and society of their cultural contexts.

Huyghe describes some of the responses that were taking place among European religious orders. They seemed to be following the patterns that prevailed in the council itself. The conciliar tensions were echoed in the receptivity or resistance to the vision of Vatican II:

> Some have completely accepted this new world along with its dangers and hopes. Resolutely detached from the sociological milieu in which former generations lived, they are alert to the needs of the people who now expect a new type of evangelization. Others cling desperately to the earlier forms of religious and apostolic life which, they declare, have stood the test of years; and in the shelter of their institutions which have become for them a sort of artificial Christianity, they do not see that the world is being formed without them and, unfortunately, without the message of Christ which they should be bringing to it.[41]

New ministries, new ways of being present and of service to those in need in the world continued to challenge the entrenched understanding of those traditionalists who saw loyalty and orthodoxy expressed in maintaining established institutions and lifestyles of the early 20th century. The religious habit was and continued to be a key source of conflict for traditionalists and for bishops who used the criterion of a religious habit as a basis of invitation into their diocese.[42]

> Wearing a habit as a symbol of consecration (and, therefore, separation from the world) and maintaining institutional works in preference to newer services in the public sphere (again, a curtailment of involvement in the world) were particularly controverted points. Since many American communities besides the IHM sisters had adopted similar provisions, discussions focused specifically on whether religious life was what church law stipulated it to be or what was developing through the experience of communities.[43]

41. Huyghe, *Tensions and Change*, 4.

42. Sometimes traditionalist religious were brought into a diocese to administer parish elementary schools even though they had neither the educational competence nor the language skills to accomplish the tasks given them.

43. See Lora Quiñonez and Mary Daniel Turner, *The Transformation of American Catholic Sisters* (Philadelphia: Temple University, 1992), 42.

The confusion and turmoil within religious life that characterized the early response to Vatican II continued into the next decades. Review and revision of their founding charism and the examination of the trajectories of their congregations had led to the redirection of ministries and the consequent adaptation of lifestyle to engage in such ministries. The mandate for a "preferential option for the poor"[44] rather than for a maintenance of established ministries was taking shape in the context of new levels of collaboration of religious and laity in education, health care, and welfare initiatives. Laity who had been looking for ways to exercise their baptismal vocation more ministerially began to take on leadership roles that previously had not been open to them. It cannot be ignored that this was disturbing both within the ranks of religious themselves, who felt that they were being passed over, and among the laity who looked for carefully differentiated levels of leadership.

Attitudes of authority and subordination instilled in both the civic and Catholic cultures of the 20th century saw women's roles as in the home or in the church and exercised in traditionalist modes. The rise of feminism, the awakening by women and men to the mutually enriching possibilities of collaboration in ministry, home, and workplace were shaping relationships in the community at large as well as in home and church. This unsettled the very settled world of the Catholic community, particularly that of the Western world.

Sociologists began to analyze the consequences of the council. In religious life, Maria Augusta Neal was a leading figure of this analysis.[45] Her research showed the courage alongside the suffering that characterized religious women of the post–Vatican II decades, as they worked to transform the monastic asceticism of the vowed life for their contemporary ministry and communal lifestyles. For example, the radical change from the conventional understanding of the vow of obedience as one of unquestioning submission to one of mutuality and careful attentiveness to one's own conscience as well as to the voice of the superior or "community leader"

44. This phrase seems to have been first used by Jesuit Superior General Pedro Arrupe (1907–1991) in "The Jesuits of Latin America," a 1968 letter republished in *Liberation Theology: A Documentary History*, ed., intro., comm., and trans. Alfred T. Hennelly (Maryknoll, NY: Orbis, 1990), 77–83.

45. From 1950 to 1984 Neal surveyed over 139,000 sisters to "determine the readiness of American sisters to implement the directives of the Vatican Council" (Maria Augusta Neal, *Catholic Sisters in Transition: From the 1960s to the 1980s* [Wilmington, DE: Michael Glazier, 1984], 16).

required new acceptance of personal and communal responsibility and depth of spirituality.[46] The publication of Neal's research confirmed the dynamic response of religious to the call to exercise their commitment to God and their ministry in the church in the modern world. The ecclesial consequences of returning to the sources of religious life and of reclaiming their charism or "deep story"[47] were transforming for religious and those with whom they ministered in church and society. This was not an easy transition; misunderstandings ensued between religious and laity, and between religious and their ecclesiastical leaders, and a heavy price was paid in many cases. But Neal argues that regardless of issues of declining membership and the high costs of living that followed from the new movements of vowed religious toward the poor and away from the financial support and recognition that came with ministering in traditional institutions, there was a revitalization of the experience of the call and the mystery of religious life:

> It might seem that as we have moved with the church to this new mission embodying a special option for the poor, we have lost the security that others envied in our lives: the contemplative serenity, a dependable community, care in retirement and something important and significant to do, i.e. relevant work. Yet in reality, all these advantages have been heightened, not lost as we have responded in new ways to the mission of Jesus.[48]

Neal sustained her analysis of post–Vatican II religious life into the 1990s. The consistent commitment of religious to serve the marginalized was not unequivocally approved or understood by the Catholic communities in which they ministered. Neal used the metaphor of a tortoise shedding its shell, accepting vulnerability for the possibility of new life.

46. The range of interpretation of the vows in those decades was extraordinary. Diarmuid O'Murchu wrote of obedience as the "vow of mutual collaboration" (*Consecrated Religious Life: The Changing Paradigms* [Maryknoll, NY: Orbis, 2005], 209). His renaming of vows in relation to the evangelical counsels was a creative and provocative initiative. In this study his research on quantum theory and evolutionary science was foundational to his approach to the vowed religious life. Vadakethala Vineeth, in an alternative approach to religious life and the vows, takes into account the cosmos and a transformation of consciousness informed by "Indian genius and modern psychology" (*Call to Integration: A New Theology of Religious Life* [New York: Crossroad, 1981]); he also renamed the vows against an alternative horizon of meaning (33–70).

47. As the initial story takes shape in the living memory of the congregation, Thompson describes it as a "deep story"; see her "Written Guide," Note III B, p. 42.

48. Neal, *Catholic Sisters in Transition*, 78.

"The composite carapace of an outmoded institutional framework and accumulated customs finally shed, these congregations now allow their members an environment for a more faithful response to their apostolic ministry in the church."[49] This metaphor for religious life was appropriate for the renewed claiming of the prophetic role of religious women and men that was taking shape in these decades.

A different approach to postconciliar religious life was taken by Patricia Wittberg, who called the decline in religious orders an "ideological limbo."[50] The various changes taking place, along with the reactions within the Catholic community in the United States led to an unprecedented intervention by Pope John Paul II. A gathering of bishops and leaders of religious congregations was asked "to enter into the process in order to support and to second the efforts of the religious to strengthen and renew their communities."[51] During this period traditionalist documents continued to be promulgated, such as the Congregation for Religious and Secular Institute's Essential Elements of Religious Life.[52]

The work of the joint commission of bishops and religious that resulted from the papal intervention acted as a discernment process contributing to a deeper understanding of the mission and ministry of religious women and men.[53] After his experience of listening to the religious of the time,

49. Mary Augusta Neal, *From Nuns to Sisters: An Expanding Vocation* (Mystic, CT: Twenty-Third, 1990), 114.

50. Patricia Wittberg, *The Rise and Fall of Catholic Religious Orders: A Social Movement Perspective* (Albany: State University of New York, 1994), 265. Wittberg analyzes the cultural context and illustrates the historic and systemic problems that were operating during these decades of renewal and adaptation.

51. John R. Quinn, "Addresses of the Pontifical Delegate, John R. Quinn D.D., Archbishop of San Francisco," in *Religious Life in the U.S. Church: The New Dialogue*, ed. Robert J. Daly et al. (New York: Paulist, 1984), 11–53, at 11.

52. This document, while appearing to draw on John Paul II's letter to the American bishops (April 3, 1983), in fact misrepresented aspects of it. See http://www.vatican.va/roman_curia/congregations/ccscrlife/documents/rc_con_ccscrlife_doc_31051983_magisterium-on-religious-life_en.html. For an analysis see Confoy, *Religious Life and Priesthood*, 240–43.

53. At one of these meetings the term "charism" came under discussion. A panel contributor to the discussion, Howard Gray, SJ, described his understanding of the term: "By charism I mean the gift given to individuals within the church for the good of the church and for the good of humankind. Founders of religious communities were gifted both to do good and to establish a way of life in which others could sustain that good work" ("Religious Life: Continuing Summons to Renewal and Reorientation," *Origins* 23 [1993]: 115–20, at 117).

Quinn commented that "American nuns have been exposed to an unprecedented level of misrepresentation and attack, from both the right and the left."[54] His endorsement of the state of religious life was wholehearted and validating for religious life. He recognized the new directions that were taking shape in religious life in general and the fruit of these directions particularly for religious women:

> In these United States toward the close of the twentieth century, for the first time in history there is appearing a radically apostolic form of religious life for women, which heretofore had been possible for men only—a life characterized by professional personal ministries, and by small and flexible communities.[55]

While the primary tension between those whose focus was on the religious life as a state of perfection and those who maintained the commitment to the living charism of the founder or to the sustained commitment to the deep story of their congregation seemed to be focused primarily on the northern hemisphere. The Catholic Church, however, was expanding globally, and religious life has been taking its own shape in the diverse cultural contexts in which it was being lived.[56]

What has been described as a seismic shift that has taken place both locally and globally in the experience of Catholic communities cannot be ignored or trivialized. Theological debates about whether Vatican II was an "event" or an "occurrence," whether it represented "continuity" or "discontinuity" in the life of the church, are important for both Catholics and other Christians in terms of the sustained openness to dialogue that was integral to the spirit of Vatican II, if not always lived out in the debates in the aula.[57] However, of equal importance at every level of church life and integral to ecumenical engagement is the reality of accountability to ministry in the changing world in which the call to evangelization must be lived out. As Gray put it:

54. Quinn, "Addresses of the Pontifical Delegate," 26.

55. John Manuel Lozano, CMF, "The Theology of 'The Essential Elements' in the Teaching of the Church," in *Religious Life in the U.S. Church*, 98–133, at 102.

56. Space restrictions require the omission of a detailed description of the impact of Vatican II on religious life in Latin America, but on this topic and Medellín's impact on religious life in Latin America see Confoy, *Religious Life and Priesthood*, 242–52.

57. See especially Faggioli, *Battle for Meaning*; Komonchak, "Interpreting the Council and Its Consequences," in *After Vatican II*, 164–172; and Gerald O'Collins, SJ, "Does Vatican II Represent Continuity or Discontinuity?" *Theological Studies* 73 (2012): 768–93.

> When our renewal followed the leadership of Jesus best, it did so in our obedient listening, like Christ, to God's voice in the community of faith, in the needs of God's people everywhere, in the wisdom of our tradition, in the struggles within our cultures for justice and human dignity—in brief, in all that constitutes God's action and invitation in our Catholic and human lives. Renewal was for us closely allied to our membership in the church's communion, but it was also allied to our graced solidarity with human history and experiences.[58]

Obedient listening in the multiple levels described above is the energizing force for enabling the founding charism to take authentic shape in religious life in today's world. Such listening is an integral element in the contemporary initiatives and in ministerial outreach exercised by significant numbers of religious in church and society.

Transition and Transformation: Religious Life in the Global Context of the 21st Century

The tension between those who have wanted to hold the Catholic church in a nucleated European identity that no longer exists except in closed, monological mind-sets and those whose response to the call of Vatican II has been one of prophetic discernment of and dialogical response to the needs of the time, both locally and globally, is still operative. But the demography of the 21st-century Catholic Church has changed radically. The importance of attending to this is described by Phan, who recognizes that despite the openness of its ecclesiology, Vatican II could not have foreseen the impact of cultural and religious pluralism and interreligious dialogue on the church of the 21st century:

> In the post-Conciliar period, battles were waged not only within the Catholic church on intra-ecclesial issues (e.g. collegiality, liberation theology, liturgical reforms etc.), but the church itself had to confront a new situation caused by the massive demographic shift of Christians and Catholics (from) the global North (Europe and North America) to the global South (Africa, Asia and Latin America). In this new predicament the church has become truly multicultural—again one might say—and can no longer pretend to possess cultural and religious homogeneity, of course, not for lack of effort.[59]

58. Gray, "Religious Life: Continuing Summons," 117.

59. Peter C. Phan, "World Christianity: Its Implications for History, Religious Studies, and Theology," *Horizons* 39 (2012): 171–88, at 186.

The transition from a Western church to an authentically global church, Phan reminds his readers, requires a radically new approach, and he sees that intercultural and interreligious dialogues are not simply essential for the survival of Christianity, but that they are issues of justice and peace. To understand the present reality, he suggests that instead of the traditionalist approach to an understanding of church and of leadership, "attention should be turned to the contributions of the people who have been marginalized in church history, such as lay men and women, religious sisters, the poor, the tribals, and those accused of heresy, schism, and syncretism."[60] This level of attention has certainly been the subject, as well as the prophetic engagement, of religious, particularly of religious women in this period.

It is the awareness of the changing demands of a changing church and society that has shaped much of the contemporary transformation in religious life. *Lumen gentium*, the Constitution on the Church, with its emphasis on religious and its call to new collaborative relationships with laity, and *Gaudium et spes*, with its call to service in and for the modern world, have generated the breakthrough and breaking down of the exclusivist barriers of the pre–Vatican II church for ministry in general and for religious in particular. Openness to the dynamism of renewal and engagement with both the constant and changing issues being faced in the context in which they live has characterized the adaptations of religious in the 21st century. Gray sums up the responses of religious in the United States as having two directions:

> that of renewal and that of apostolic reorientation. The movement of renewal was inspired by a return both to the Gospel and to the founding charism of each institute as well as a discerning sensitivity to the needs of the times. The movement of apostolic reorientation of ministries was inspired by a faith that testified to its authenticity by works of justice. These two movements summarize how religious men and women integrated their communal and apostolic lives into a single mission.[61]

A major transition of apostolic life of religious women in the present time has been in relation to governance of major institutions. The call for ministerial collaboration between all the baptized has taken shape

60. Ibid., 178. He also gives a timely reminder of the importance of reading the works of Dana L. Robert on the role of women, e.g., *Christian Mission: How Christianity Became a World Religion* (Malden, MA: Wiley-Blackwell, 2009).

61. Gray, "Religious Life: Continuing Summons," 119.

in the movement away from previous governance models of the major institutions of many congregations of men and women religious. The transition of governance of many of the health care, community care, and educational institutions from congregational ownership to lay governance through the establishment of public juridic persons[62] is an expression of the everexpanding and deepening understanding of the collaborative call to holiness of *Gaudium et spes*. Such transitions may be seen by observers simply to be a consequence of diminishing numbers of religious, but the reality is that religious and laity are collaborating in ministry, so that religious may focus on more evangelical and communal ways of living their founding charism. Those in lay governance in the not-for-profit corporate context enable the charism to continue to both deepen and expand in new ways of meeting the needs of the present and future world.

In addressing the issue of a dynamic or "ever-re-forming" understanding of charism versus a traditionalist understanding of religious life as "state of perfection," it is essential to acknowledge the reality of suffering that is a consequence for contemporary women and men in relation to the gender oppression that continues to impact church and societal relationships. This is something that religious women in particular have suffered from, protested against, and are working to eradicate.[63] The present situation in which the 21st-century Catholic Church finds itself—the public disclosure of both administrative and sexual abuse—is an issue for all Catholics, women as well as men. That it is a global situation can be seen in the issues being addressed in the Asian church and that women religious have brought to light.

> The phenomenon of women's movements is yet another positive development. They are increasing in Asia, making women aware of their potentialities and resources, challenging centuries of subordination to men, enabling them to claim their rights and participation in public life. The Spirit of God is present in these developments.[64]

62. A public juridic person is a legal entity under canon law that allows the church's ministries to function in the name of the Catholic Church. See John P. Beal, James A. Coriden, and Thomas Joseph Green, *New Commentary on the Code of Canon Law* (New York: Paulist, 2002), 171.

63. That this is a global and urgent issue is apparent in the recent outcry in the world media against the vicious rape of a woman in India and shooting of a teenage girl in Pakistan as punishment for her outspoken stance on behalf of the education of girls. These occurrences in relation to the endemic issue of violence against women cannot be reduced to the issue of women's ordination.

64. FABC Theologians, "The Church in Contemporary Asia" I, 5, *Origins* 24 (1994): 85–90, at 86.

In a July 2005 symposium on "The Role of Religious in the Building Up of the Local Church in Asia" organized by the Federation of Asian Bishops' Office of Consecrated Life, the gathered bishops, women religious, and laity from 20 Asian countries passed the resolution to "enhance and strengthen greater knowledge, esteem and promotion of all forms of Consecrated Life and Societies of Apostolic Life, particularly that of Religious Sisters and Brothers."[65] Integral to their deliberations was the expressed importance of mutuality between the various ecclesial vocations in accord with *Lumen gentium* and the recognition that "charisms are cultural in that their externalization is always mediated by culture; they are transcultural in that they transcend cultures; they are countercultural in as much as they provide criteria against which cultures can be judged."[66] If these affirmations take hold, they will impact the ways religious life is lived in Asia surely, but globally as well.

Asian, African, and Latin American religious have been meeting together, both in the Ecumenical Association of Third World Theologians (EATWOT) and in other groupings, to share their understanding of church in other than a Western environment.[67] Many of the women religious present have a more comprehensive picture of the needs of their church, their society, and of religious life than do their local leaders. Indications of the impact of these new voices on the postconciliar discussion are now being heard in a variety of meetings and publications. One expression of the Asian voice can be heard in a comment by a Korean religious woman at a 2002 Bangkok meeting of the Ecclesia of Women in Asia:[68]

> The Second Vatican council proclaimed the mystery of the church to all wo/mankind. The mystery of the church is a symbol of the deep unity of all the people with God, and it is the sacramental sign and instrument of Christ (GS 2, LG 1). However, in 1976 the Vatican Sacred Congregation of Faith and Doctrine [sic] reaffirmed that women could not be ordained

65. Federation of Asian Bishops Office of Consecrated Life, http://www.fabc.net/offices/ocl/ocl.html.

66. Ibid.

67. For a more detailed analysis of the Latin American and Asian churches and religious life, see Richard R. Gaillardetz, *Ecclesiology for a Global Church: A People Called and Sent* (Maryknoll, NY: Orbis, 2008), esp. 190–202.

68. See Evelyn Monteiro and Antoinette Gutzler, *Ecclesia of Women in Asia: Gathering the Voices of the Silenced* (Delhi, India: ISPCK, 2005.) The six areas addressed in the conference were: women and violence, women and the Bible, women and church structures, women and spirituality, eco-feminism and theological method, and women and world religions.

> priests. The reason why I am discussing the issue of women's ordination here is the following. Today, thirty-eight years after the close of the Second Vatican Council, the issue of ordination negates the call of Vatican II for the deep unity of all humankind with God. . . . The church, through a dynamic relationship with human persons in each age, always establishes and transmits new traditions. Just as Jesus broke down prejudices of his time, now we must break down the prejudices of our time.[69]

A serious issue for Asian women religious stems from the fact that although women comprise over 60% of church congregations, and that over 70% of those who are active in the churches are women, they occupy only around 5% of appointed leadership roles. It is particularly important in the new millennium, which has been dubbed "the age of women," and in a culture where "at least one family in ten experiences serious violence" and "nearly all married women experience some kind of violence from their husbands."[70] This is a necessary concern for religious women and men in their ministries on behalf of the church, which is struggling with its own failures. The question of women in ecclesial leadership is much larger and more urgent than simply the question of who can or cannot be ordained.

Members of religious congregations are not free from accusations regarding both aspects of the abuse that has taken place. Whatever form it takes, abuse is sinful, and the whole Body of Christ is suffering in the necessary cauterization that is taking place in our civic as well as our ecclesial context. The prevailing resistance to an open and just dealing with this evil and the awareness of the failures of church leaders at key levels is confronting all the baptized. The Catholic Church has been brought to its knees publicly for what it failed to do within the institution for longer than we may realize. This is tragic, but in and beyond the despair felt by all, and in the reality of the breaking down of the barriers of ecclesiastical elitism, Catholics are being invited to a new level of active hope and to move beyond the culture of unquestioning submission of conscience by laity to their ecclesiastical leaders. Religious can play an important role here. Where they have also been complicit in administrative and sexual abuse, they can continue to acknowledge their sinfulness and ask for forgiveness. The choice of many religious today to side with those on the margins who suffer from injustice and rejection is one that redounds on

69. Jeong Ja Leo Kim, LSHF, "God our Ma/Father's Korean Women's Church," in *Ecclesia of Women in Asia*, 170–71.

70. Kim, "God our Ma/Father's Korean Women's Church," 172.

the religious themselves in their local communities. They have experienced and continue to experience insecurity and social disfavor because of their radical commitment to justice and peace.[71] Their outreach and commitment has been recognized in Ian Linden's research on the changes in global Catholicism that have taken place since Vatican II:

> The response of Women Religious to sexual trafficking in the last decade is an unsung story of globalization, building on earlier changes in the Religious Orders. By the 1990s in North America and Europe the crisis in religious life that struck after the Council had abated. Changes since preconciliar days were dramatic as a result of a wider interpretation of the "charism" of each Society's founder: from a pervasive subordination to authority in the convent and work circumscribed by bishops, to a spiritual life in small communities employed in innovative forms of catechetical, social or medical work.[72]

The work of religious on behalf of those people who are the subject of human trafficking has increased and become a collaborative initiative between laity and religious.[73] This stance has not found favor or support with those conservative members of the hierarchy or members of the Catholic community for whom the maintenance of the status quo is of the highest importance. The consequence of disfavor is a risk that many religious are already taking, in the various ways in which religious have collaborated with diverse groups to advance the common good. "The charism of religious life is about the transformation of life."[74]

71. In his commentary on *PC*, Baum pointed out that the two marks of poverty in ordinary society are "insecurity and social disfavor" ("Commentary," 45).

72. Ian Linden, *Global Catholicism: Diversity and Change Since Vatican II* (New York: Columbia University, 2009), 271.

73. These organizations are working internationally and nationally. For example, "UNANIMA International is a non-governmental organization (NGO) advocating on behalf of women and children (particularly those living in poverty, immigrants and refugees, and the environment. Our work takes place primarily at the United Nations headquarters in New York, where we and other members of civil society aim to educate and influence policymakers at the global level. In solidarity, we work for systemic change to achieve a more just world" (http://www.unanima-international.org/eng). National groups, such as Australian Catholic Religious against Trafficking in Humans, are endorsed by Catholic Religious Australia, the peak body for 190 religious orders in Australia, representing 8,000 religious sisters, brothers, and priests; see http://acrath.org.au/.

74. Margaret R. Brennan, IHM, "Religious Life's Charism: Transforming Life," *Origins* 23 (1993): 207–11, at 211.

This comment of Margaret Brennan calls readers to attend not simply to human life but to all aspects of living together in the cosmos in which we find ourselves. This is another area in which religious have made their presence felt in the 21st century. The global crisis of human trafficking is connected to the global crisis of "unprecedented poverty, environmental destruction and social disintegration that have disrupted whole communities" and threatened the possibilities for healthy communities and environments for future generations.[75] The work that religious are doing with NGOs and other organizations whose concern is for the well-being of the cosmos, is deeply connected to the living charism that enables transformation that crosses the boundaries of religious and philosophical belief systems and enables religious to work with people from all walks of life for the benefit of the human community as well as the planet in which it lives, so that there will be a future for all.[76]

In discussing the future of religious life, Schneiders emphasizes the importance of the prophetic vocation in responding to the changing social and cultural contexts, and the revisioning of those on life's margins. She points out that religious are on the front lines in what Gray refers to as their "obedient listening, like Christ, to God's voice in the community of faith, in the needs of God's people everywhere"[77] and in their response to issues of oppression and discrimination in their world, especially in regard to sexual issues. Religious are active in, for example, addressing "the realities of marriage and procreation within the framework of a patriarchal moral theology, mandatory singleness and sexual apartheid in ordained ministry that is causing eucharistic famine throughout the Church." The ecumenical and interreligious commitment of religious in addressing the dominant "ecclesiastical elitism and exclusivism in relation to other Christian traditions" places them in the forefront of prophetic challenge to the status quo. Their concern for "intellectual freedom in theology and freedom of conscience in religion, and numerous other issues that the Vatican would like to declare 'settled,' or 'closed,' or 'forbidden' has led them to be the subject of attack from within traditionalist and ghettoist fortresses."[78]

75. Ibid.

76. The impact of Vatican II on religious life can be seen in the ways documents such as *Unitatis redintegratio* (On Ecumenism), *Nostra aetate* (On the Relations of the Church to Non-Christian Religions), and *Dignitatis humanae* (On Religious Liberty) have taken a human shape in and through the collaborative ministries of both religious and laity.

77. Gray, "Religious Life: Continuing Summons," 117.

78. The quotations and substance of this paragraph are from Schneiders, *Prophets in Their Own Country*, 25.

The basis of Schneiders's position is her understanding of religious life today as a prophetic life-form:

> Intrinsic to the prophetic vocation within the Judaeo-Christian biblical tradition is the tension between prophecy and institution. Jesus was executed not because he did good works but because his doing of good works, like his preaching and teaching, was in the service of the liberation of the oppressed—those oppressed by secular power but especially those oppressed by religious power. Jesus was a quintessential prophet, a deeply committed Jew who was profoundly loyal to his religious tradition and, for that very reason, an implacable opponent of its perversion by the institutional power structure and its enforcers.[79]

New depths and breadths of living the paschal mystery in our present era continue to challenge all the baptized, but surely this is particularly true of religious called to take the living of their charism or deep story seriously, as they respond to the universal call to holiness that was the hallmark of Vatican II.

Conclusion

While so much of the present Western discussions about religious life focuses predominantly on diminishing numbers, aging religious, loss of ministries, and other statistical or ecclesiastical preoccupations regarding property, this is not an accurate picture of religious life in its global reality. Arguments made about whether the numbers of religious in traditionalist congregations are growing more than those in ministerial religious life have missed the point of Vatican II and indeed of Christianity itself. Christianity has never been a numbers game. Actuarial studies will never do justice to the past, present, or future of religious life. It has always operated through the dynamic of the Holy Spirit and the graced response of individuals and the communities they generate in and through their depth of commitment to their call. Those who attempt to project the future through numbers alone have missed the story. The history of religious life defeats demographic projections. The impact of religious today transcends the limits of their physical presence. The witness to the vision engendered by Vatican II is alive and well globally in and through the range and diversity of ministries and in terms of prophetic witness of contemporary religious.

79. Ibid., 23.

M. Shawn Copeland, in her keynote address to the LCWR in 2010, reminded the religious present of their contribution to church and society:

> The fact and hard-won achievement of your openness incarnates creative, faithful Christian responses to situations that many of us have chosen to disregard or belittle. In your lived passion for the mission and vision of Jesus of Nazareth, you women religious have become a symbol of contradiction and scandal among the people of your time and place. You have become a living protest of a perhaps unintentional but nonetheless real reduction of ourselves as church to the law-abiding but lukewarm; the unthinking but self-righteous; the domineering but fearful. We "good Catholics" would like to make you—and you must resist—into the talisman, the good luck charm, of our call to holiness. You must not, indeed, you cannot allow or submit to this. The very nature of prophetic ministry opposes patronage, and true prophets are never on sale.[80]

This public recognition of the prophetic, ecclesial life-form of religious life in the 21st century is surely yet another indication among many that religious life is more significant in its dynamic service of the global church and society in the 21st century than in any other era, and perhaps never more needed.

80. M. Shawn Copeland, "Radical Openness, Suffering, and Hope," keynote address to the Annual Assembly of the LCWR, Dallas, TX, August 2010, https://lcwr.org/calendar/lcwr-assembly-2010.

Afterword

Vatican II

Relevance and Future

GILLES ROUTHIER

TRANSLATED BY JOHN J. CONLEY, SJ, AND
CHARLES T. KESTERMEIER, SJ

Vatican II has more than a simple historical interest. What truly counts is comprehending its contemporary relevance and bearing its heritage within ourselves today. If we focus on the council's governing ideas and adopt the Council Fathers' method of posing problems rather than limiting ourselves to commenting on the texts' conclusions, we can apply this heritage beyond what the council says to the questions that are ours 50 years on.

Following repeated requests by opponents of Schema XIII who wanted to reduce its scope and authority,[1] *Gaudium et spes* (*GS*), the Constitution on the Church in the Modern World, bears the following interpretive note:

1. Some wanted the schema to be titled simply *Nuntius* or *Epistola pastoralis a concilio ad homines huius temporis* or even *Litterae synodales a concilio ad mundum* or *Declaratio ecclesiae ad dialogum instituendum cum mundo huius temporis* or *Declaratio ecclesiae ad mundum hodierum* instead of being called a pastoral constitution. On this issue, see my article "Mener à terme l'oeuvre amorcée: L'éprouvante expérience de la quatriè me période," in *Concile de transition*, vol. 5 of *Histoire de Vatican II 1959–1965*, ed. Giuseppe Alberigo (Paris: Cerf, 2005), 177, 181–82, 222.

> In the first part, the Church develops her teaching on man, on the world which is the enveloping context of man's existence, and on man's relations to his fellow men. In part two, the Church gives closer consideration to various aspects of modern life and human society; special consideration is given to those questions and problems which, in this general area, seem to have a greater urgency in our day. As a result in part two the subject matter which is viewed in the light of doctrinal principles is made up of diverse elements. Some elements have a permanent value; others, only a transitory one. Consequently, the constitution must be interpreted according to the general norms of theological interpretation. Interpreters must bear in mind—especially in part two—the changeable circumstances which the subject matter, by its very nature, involves.[2]

Since the closing of the council, the opposition has not let down its guard. They have consistently promoted the theory that the teaching of Vatican II, in particular that of *Gaudium et spes*, does not have a permanent value due to its pastoral character. According to those who uphold this theory, Vatican II is a council marked by the situation and spirit of the 1960s. Because of this, it might speak to the baby-boomer generation, but it would no longer have anything to say to the new generation and to our current situation. In other words, it would not have any contemporary relevance. Since this teaching does not have any permanent value—so the argument goes—the change in social context renders the opinions of the council outmoded on the cardinal question of the relationship of the church to the world, to cultures, and to non-Catholics and non-Christians. As a circumstantial teaching, it concerns only one era. As a pastoral council, its teaching's value would be so limited to a particular social context that, given the evolution of this context,[3] its choices would be of little help for reflection on the future of Catholicism in the 21st century. In short, describing the council as "pastoral" becomes a pretext for denying it any significance today.

The current efforts to trivialize the teachings of Vatican II and to deny their contemporary relevance because of its alleged outdated character fail to notice that the theological qualification mentioned in note no. 1 of the preface to *Gaudium et spes* affirms that this teaching includes doctrinal

2. *Gaudium et spes (GS), preface*, note 1, http://www.vatican.va/archive/hist_councils/ii_vatican_council/documents/vat-ii_cons_19651207_gaudium-et-spes_en.html. All URLs cited herein were accessed on June 10, 2013.

3. See Antonio Acerbi, "La réception de Vatican II dans un contexte historique changé," *Concilium* 166 (1981): 123–33.

and permanent principles. They also fail to recognize the historical character of *all* magisterial teaching and, in consequence, that such teaching is always affected by the era of its composition.[4]

This being said, the objection merits consideration, and we should ask what the contemporary relevance of Vatican II is. In other words, what is the permanent value of the teaching of this council, and how might it still contribute to guiding the church's journey 50 years after its close, at a time when the cultural, social, political, economic, and ecclesial context has changed profoundly? The clear position of Pope John Paul II on the question of the relevance of Vatican II is well known:

> What a treasure there is . . . in the guidelines offered to us by the Second Vatican Council! . . . With the passing of the years, *the Council documents have lost nothing of their value or brilliance*. They need to be read correctly, to be widely known and taken to heart as important and normative texts of the Magisterium, within the Church's Tradition. Now that the Jubilee has ended, I feel more than ever in duty bound to point to the Council as *the great grace bestowed on the Church in the twentieth century*: there we find a sure compass by which to take our bearings in the century now beginning.[5]

The position taken by Benedict XVI during the celebration of the 50th anniversary of the council is no less clear concerning its contemporary relevance: "The Council documents contain an enormous wealth for the

4. On this subject, see the astute lesson in hermeneutics given by Pope Benedict XVI in his allocution to the Roman Curia on December 22, 2005. Discussing the 19th-century pontifical teaching on religious freedom and on church-state relations, he observed: "In this process of novelty in continuity, we must understand more clearly than we did before that the judgments of the Church concerning contingent facts—for example, certain particular forms of liberalism or the literal interpretation of the Bible—necessarily had to be themselves contingent, precisely because they referred to a particular reality that is by its nature mutable. It was necessary to learn to recognize that in such judgments only the principles express a durable aspect, often remaining in the background and motivating the judgment from the interior. The concrete forms of expression, on the other hand, are not as permanent. They are dependent on the historical situation and thus may be subject to change. Therefore, the fundamental judgments can remain valid, while the forms of their application in new contexts may vary" (*Acta apostolicae sedis: Commentarium officiale* 98 [2006]: 40–53, at 49–50 [my translation]). In this way Benedict shows the historicity of all magisterial teaching.

5. John Paul II, *Novo millenio ineunte* (January 6, 2001) no. 57, http://www.vatican.va/holy_father/john_paul_ii/apost_letters/documents/hf_jp-ii_apl_20010106_novo-millennio-ineunte_en.html (emphases original).

formation of the new Christian generations, for the formation of our consciences. Consequently, read it."[6]

Returning to the Council's Texts: Challenges, Difficulties, Promises

The two papal statements quoted above send us back to the texts of Vatican II, that is, to the richness of the council's documents. From that perspective, we might be tempted to think that the texts and the documents concern only a certain teaching or "content." This risks reducing the council to its pronouncements or to a certain content that we would appropriate for ourselves. Thus we would be tempted to search out the conciliar teachings that are still pertinent today and the ideas that we could take up to guide the church, to give it some vitality, and to give the church direction.

This approach to the documents, however, reduces them to their content and their teaching and treats them as mere vehicles for the diffusion of ideas. Undoubtedly, this approach, which consists in searching the texts and documents for propositional content or teachings, is familiar to theologians. This method leads to establishing a list of conciliar teachings on such topics as religious freedom, the participation of everyone in the life of the church, the bishops, ecumenism, culture, family, Communism, the laity, the word of God, the catechism, war and peace, exegesis, the renewal of religious life, the ministry of priests, non-Christian religions, etc. An approach to conciliar texts by this method of analysis of content leads us to establish a quasi-interminable list of specific topics.

Necessary and legitimate though this analytical method is, it tends, if it is not accompanied by a more synthetic method, to dismember the conciliar corpus by reducing it to so many instructions on specific questions. It tends to concentrate on particular, isolated pronouncements, thereby preventing a grasp of Vatican II as a coherent whole or a unified ensemble and reducing it to an aggregate of specific teachings.[7] In effect, it is possible to gloss and to comment *ad infinitum* on the teachings of the council—on *subsistit in*, for example, or on the hierarchy of truths—without ever arriving at a grasp of the council's central intuitions that should still be nourishing

6. Homily of Benedict XVI at Frascatti, July 15, 2012, http://www.vatican.va/holy_father/benedict_xvi/homilies/2012/documents/hf_ben-xvi_hom_20120715_frascati_en.html.

7. See Gilles Routhier, "L'herméneutique de Vatican II: De l'histoire de la rédaction des textes conciliaires à la structure d'un corpus," in *Vatican II: Herméneutique et réception* (Montréal: Fides, 2006), 389–99.

us today. Moreover, this method does not permit us to tie these teachings to the conciliar event in its varying dimensions; it detaches the texts and documents from the action of the Council Fathers themselves and from the conciliar milieu that produced them. They become disconnected from the experience that gave them birth and from the questions that constitute their origin. Although necessary, this analytic approach focuses on the content of the pronouncements and—if it is absolutized—risks being reductionist, in the sense that it cannot by itself truly give us access to the "teaching" of Vatican II. It risks fossilizing the living word addressed to the church for its growth and renewal. Reduced to the single dimension of a collection of pronouncements, Vatican II cannot represent the compass given to the church to guide it through the course of the 21st century, to use John Paul II's phrase, since it has been cut off from part of its vitality.

Fifty years after Vatican II, a narrow approach to the conciliar texts risks reducing the impact of the council and obscuring its innovative character, just as decadent Scholasticism and commentators—not to mention the neo-Scholasticism of the manuals—reduced the innovative power of the great, original Scholasticism and trivialized its intellectual élan and audacity to the point of making it sclerotic. If we limit ourselves to an analytical method developed within the framework and thought world of neo-Scholastics, we risk the same narrowing in our treatment of Vatican II, whose pronouncements we could endlessly comment on, and whose texts we could gloss to exhaustion. But this method arises from an intellectual framework foreign to the conciliar texts. To adopt it for reading these texts, which were not conceived and formulated within the framework of Scholastic categories, would therefore risk seriously distorting their teaching.

Attention to Foundational Ideas, Key Insights

From these considerations, I suggest that limiting ourselves to commentary on the texts and exegesis of their pronouncements is insufficient to bring into relief all the contemporary relevance, unity, and dynamic power of Vatican II. Another endeavor seems just as important: discerning the key insights of the council. I would like to recall here the example of Marie-Dominique Chenu, for whom Thomism must be considered not "as a defined system of inviolate propositions, but as a body of defining insights that are incarnate in conceptual ensembles only to the extent that they maintain their living light."[8] Without this perspective, we risk dulling

8. Marie-Dominique Chenu, *Une école de la théologie: Le Saulchoir*, 2nd ed. (Paris: Cerf, 1985), 123.

and fossilizing the thought of Aquinas or missing its essence altogether. It is the same with Vatican II. Detached from the broad perspectives of the ensemble and cut off from their foundational orientation, analyzing particular pronouncements commits the same error made by the Thomistic synthesis of the neo-Scholastic era. The central insights and fundamental orientations are naturally not detached from the conciliar texts themselves, but to access them, we must read them according to a method different from that of commentary on, or exegesis of, particular pronouncements.

A more adequate reading demands a grasp of the whole, a synthetic approach that highlights the central axes, the load-bearing structures, and the internal dynamic of each of the documents and of the global architecture governing the document's exposition. It would indicate the coherence and thrust, the movement of ideas, the cross-references of texts, the connections, the ideas that appear in several documents, the nodal questions, the categories that create structures, etc. The central insights, in my view, depend on the method that determined the composition of the texts and the styles used just as much as on the themes developed.

While we already have numerous textual commentaries, the council's central insights have not yet received sufficient attention. The commentaries, focused as they were on particular conciliar documents and pronouncements, were perhaps not capable of gaining the distance necessary to discern the fundamental posture of Vatican II. Recent works on the style of the council[9] or on its pastoral form[10] allow us to make some progress in this area, but much work remains to be done.

9. See Gilles Routhier, "El concilio Vaticano II como estilo," *Iglesia viva* 227 (2006): 3–44; "Il Vaticano II come stile," *La scuola cattolica* 136 (2008): 5–32; John W. O'Malley, "Erasmus and Vatican II: Interpreting the Council," in *Cristianesimo nella storia: Saggi in onore di Giuseppe Alberigo*, ed. Alberto Melloni et al. (Bologna: Il Mulino, 1996), 195–212, esp. 197–98; John W. O'Malley, SJ, "Vatican II: Historical Perspectives on Its Uniqueness and Interpretation," in *Vatican II: The Unfinished Agenda: A Look to the Future*, ed. Lucien Richard, OMI, Daniel Harrington, SJ, and John W. O'Malley, SJ (New York: Paulist, 1987), 22–32; John W. O'Malley, SJ, "Vatican II: Did Anything Happen?," *Theological Studies* 67 (2006): 3–33, esp. 23); and Joseph Famerée, ed., *Vatican II comme style: L'herméneutique théologique du concile* (Paris: Cerf, 2012).

10. See Giuseppe Ruggieri, "La lotta per la pastoralità della dottrina: La ricezione della '*Gaudet Mater Ecclesia*' nel primo periodo del concilio Vaticano II," in *Zeugnis und Dialog: Die Katholische Kirche in der neuzeitlichen Welt und das II. Vatikanische Konzil*, ed. Wolfgang Weiss (Würzburg: Echter, 1996), 118–37; and Christoph Theobald, "Le Concile et la 'forme pastorale' de la doctrine," in Bernard Sesboüé, *La parole du salut: La doctrine de la parole de Dieu, la justification et le discours de la foi, la révélation et l'acte de foi, la tradition, l'écriture et le magistére*, Histoire des dogmes 4, ed. Bernard Sesboüé and Christoph Theobald (Paris: Desclée, 1996), 471–510.

In short, I am pleading here for studies that, while remaining attached to the conciliar texts, which we must read and reread, gain sufficient distance to arrive at a holistic reading of the council's work rather than remaining at a microanalytic reading of pronouncements. That approach risks diminishing the amplitude of the council's teaching. I contend, to the contrary, that bathed in its leading insights Vatican II still reveals itself as a design for the church's future, in the sense that its major insights concerning attitudes, postures, practices, and institutions shape mentalities and engrave the *aggiornamento* desired by the council into the body of the church. These fundamental insights are still capable today of guiding the church on its path.

Return to the Method of Posing Problems

M.-D. Chenu, who deliberated over how to transport the Thomist heritage into the 20th century, warned his readers to pay as much attention to the questions Aquinas asked and to which he tried to reply as to his replies or conclusions. In sum, he invites the readers of the *Summa theologiae* to return again and again to his formulation of problems and to his manner of working on them, that is to say, to the intellectual procedure incorporated in his exposition. For the regent of Le Saulchoir, beyond the centuries of distance,

> connecting with Saint Thomas first involved finding again this state of inventiveness by which the mind returns, as to an ever-fertile source, to the *posing of problems* beyond the conclusions acquired since then. . . . It seems that the Thomist school, weighed down by its too-heavy heritage and concerned exclusively with its conservation, renounced at the beginning of the 16th century this innovative and creative power that was at the very root of Thomism.

Therefore, it was necessary to move beyond conclusions, "to go back to the beginning and to take the foundational givens, there where . . . the *problematic* continuously renews itself."[11]

This perspective is just as suggestive for the studies of Vatican II in proportion as the passage of time creates a gap between a situation prevailing at the time of the council and our own. It leads us not only to tease out the fundamental insights of the council but also to see how the Council Fathers posed problems and reflected on them. One must first identify the problems or the questions the Fathers had to confront; only then can one

11. Chenu, *Une école de la théologie*, 123.

reflect on the motives that led them to pose these particular questions. According to Benedict XVI, who, as Joseph Ratzinger, served as a peritus at the council,

> we can say that three circles of questions had formed that at the moment of the Second Vatican Council demanded a response. We had to find a new definition for the relationship between faith and modern science. This concerned not only the natural sciences; it equally concerned the historical sciences because, according to one school of thought, the historical-critical method claimed the last word in interpreting the Bible and claimed the total exclusivity of its interpretation of Sacred Scripture, being opposed on important points to the interpretation that the faith of the church had established. In the second place, we needed a new definition of the relationship between the church and the modern state that accorded a place to citizens of diverse religions and ideologies, comporting itself in an impartial way toward these religions and simply assuming the responsibility for an orderly and tolerant coexistence among citizens as well as for the freedom to exercise their religion. In the third place, this was tied in a more general way to the problem of religious tolerance—a question that demanded a new definition of the relationship between the Christian faith and the world's religions. In particular, in the face of the crimes committed by the National Socialist regime, and more generally within the framework of a retrospective view of a long and difficult history, we had to evaluate and develop a new definition of the relationship between the church and the faith of Israel.[12]

I might present these issues a bit differently, but I can also easily agree with this position. If I were to add something to the questions awaiting resolution at the time of the council, I would list those that had appeared as recurrent concerns during the century preceding Vatican II. First, there were questions concerning ecclesiology that were left hanging following the interruption of Vatican Council I. These questions had seen important developments as much in theology as in declarations by the magisterium in the first part of the 20th century: the exercise of authority and the magisterium, the theology of the episcopate and its corollary, collegiality.[13] There

12. Allocution to the Roman Curia 49 (my translation).

13. To the encyclical *Mystici Corporis* we must add all pontifical teachings concerning the laity, the holding of international congresses on the laity and the creation of COPECIAL (Permanent Committee for International Congresses of the Lay Apostolate of the Roman Catholic Church). Moreover, Pius XII had launched a renewal of religious life, beginning in 1951 with a series of Roman congresses for women religious educators and superiors general of papally approved religious congregations.

was also the Marian question raised not only by an impressive number of encyclicals and two dogmatic definitions but also by a vigorous Marian movement deeply rooted in the Catholic faithful and by a theological reflection that did not at all move in the same direction. The missionary question, which had not been the subject of a single encyclical prior to the 20th century, also occupied the ecclesiastical foreground since the developments of missiology and the increasingly numerous interventions of the magisterium.[14]

When we consider the questions advanced by the commission established by Pius XI in April 1923 concerning a possible reopening of Vatican Council I, we already find all these questions awaiting a reply. Among the 39 questions contained in the list drawn up by theologians Edward Hugon and Alexis Lépicier of the preparatory commission are notably those concerning the church, its nature, its powers, its relationship with secular states, Catholic Action and the social kingship of Christ, Communism and socialism, and the dogmatic definitions of the bodily assumption of Mary and her universal mediation. As for the commission established by Pius XII on March 15, 1948, it considered approximately 50 themes, including the origin of the jurisdiction of bishops, the relationship between the magisterium and tradition, the inerrancy of Sacred Scripture and literary genres, questions concerning sexuality, and once again Mary's assumption.[15]

It is in examining the new themes that spring up in the magisterium's discourse—themes representing a new development in the theological literature and those fostered by popular movements—that we can identify the list of questions awaiting answers. Several questions (on Catholic Action, the assumption of Mary, the church, and Scripture) had found answers, at least partial ones, in papal encyclicals or the dogmatic definition of 1950;

14. See the missionary encyclicals of Pius XI, *Rerum ecclesiae* (February 8, 1926); Pius XII, *Evangelii praecones* (June 2, 1951); and John XXIII, *Princeps pastorum* (November 28, 1959).

15. See Giovanni Caprile, "Pio XI e la ripresa del Concilio Vatican II," *La Civiltà Cattolica* 177, no. 3 (1966): 27–39, completed in "Pio XI, la curia romana e il concilio," *La Civiltà Cattolica* 120, no. 2 (1969): 121–33 and 563–75; Santiago Casas, "Nouvelles données concernant la reprise de Vatican I sous Pie XI," *Revue d'histoire ecclésiastique* 104, no. 3–4 (2009): 828–55; Giovanni Caprile, "Pio XII e uno nuovo progetto di concilio," *La Civiltà Cattolica* 117, no. 3 (1966): 209–27, reprinted and expanded as "Pius XII und das zweite vatikanische Konzil," in *Pius XII zum Gedächtnis*, ed. Herbert Schambeck (Berlin: Duncker & Humblot, 1977), 649–91; and François-Charles Uginet, "Les projets de concile général sous Pie XI et Pie XII," in *Le deuxième concile du Vatican (1959–1965), Acte du colloque de Rome (28–30 mai 1986), Mélanges de l'École Française de Rome* 113 (1989): 65–78.

but several questions remained to be answered, and new questions had emerged in the meantime. This is also true for the liturgy, which had been supported by a renewal movement that had developed since the beginning of the 20th century and that had been the theme of several pontifical documents from the time of Pius X,[16] the last one being Pius XII's encyclical *Mediator Dei*. Reform of the liturgy had been a primary concern—the liturgies of Holy Week and Holy Saturday and reform of the breviary, which is still getting started. Among the new questions were ecumenism and especially a group of questions rooted in the pastoral and theological renewal that had arisen after World War I.

It is not sufficient, however, to draw up the list of questions waiting for a response and, eventually, to see the solutions that would be given by the council. The principal task is to study how the Council Fathers approached these questions. How did they work on them, with what method, beginning with what references, using what categories? Congar, recalling in 1971 his approach to the theology of ministry, observes that "the door by which *one enters into* a question determines the chances for a happy or less happy solution. The concepts one uses largely determines all that follows."[17] As he remarks, his first approach to ministry considered it from the perspective of the concepts of Thomistic philosophy, in particular from the category of the efficient cause of the church. In retrospect, this approach seemed to him of limited value and required him to go beyond it.

Similarly in the case of Vatican II, it is not simply a matter of enumerating the questions it treats and the teaching it proposes on each of them; it is a matter of carefully examining in what perspective it situates the questions it considers, the method used to elaborate the conciliar teaching, the concepts that communicate this teaching, etc. In short, Vatican II takes up several questions from the second half of the 19th century and the first part of the 20th: on ecclesiology, Mariology, church-state relations, ecumenism, etc.; but it reframed the questions within a problematic that will permit them to be recast or situated in a new perspective. The

16. One often finds his motu proprio *Tra le sollicitudine* (1904) cited but not his motu proprio *Abhinc duos annos*, where he discusses the reform of the breviary: "It will take a good many years before this liturgical edifice, composed with intelligent care by the Spouse of Christ to express its piety and its faith, can appear with the incrustations of time cleansed away and newly resplendent in dignity and good order" (*Acta apostolicae sedis* 5 [1913]: 449–51, at 449–50; my translation).

17. Marie-Dominique Chenu, "Mon cheminement dans la théologie du laïcat et des ministres," in *Ministères et communion ecclésiale* (Paris: Cerf, 1971), 9–30, at 17–18.

conciliar texts themselves allow us to grasp this reframing (which concerns precisely the formulation of questions), because these texts contain much more than particular content or statement. Just as the reduction of Thomism to certain contents or conclusions, disconnected from the posing of problems that always arise in a given situation, had, as Chenu appreciated, fossilized and reduced Aquinas to a system, Vatican II today runs the same risk by a return to the texts and documents that is limited to a search for what was "said." Such an approach ignores *how* the texts "speak." The study of texts limited to an analysis of content leaves aside any recourse to more rhetorical approaches.

The Reading of Texts and the Appropriation of Their Method of Composition

We must take into account that Vatican II's teaching is also of a methodological order, and working with the texts today should lead us to appropriate and deepen this method. This is preeminently the case with *Gaudium et spes*; the disputes surrounding its composition are an outstanding witness to this. As Bishop Mark McGrath of Panama underscores in his presentation of the constitution, its "gestation was not easy":

> The traditionalists considered this project with a critical eye and an air of amused disdain. For them it was evident that such earthy issues were not worthy of a council's consideration. Even the so-called progressive theologians, who were already at work in brilliantly renewing the definition of the Church in the dogmatic constitution *Lumen gentium*, rebelled against anything that might resemble an empirical analysis of the world. They forcefully affirmed that a council must proceed according to the most certain theological method, that is to say, by starting from the principles of revelation, from which one draws norms of faith and morality. . . . During a tumultuous discussion between the members and experts of the mixed commission, held toward the end of November 1963, it became evident that the unusual character of the document still disoriented the commission. While a minority made clear its lack of interest in the document, the others were deeply divided over what method to follow. Some forcefully defended an exclusively doctrinal approach. Others referred to the two great social encyclicals of Pope John and claimed that it was only in starting with the problems of the world that one could interest the world, appreciate its problems, and enter into dialogue with it. . . . Confusing and painful at the time, this discussion was extremely fruitful. For the first time, the unique character of Schema XIII . . . appeared

> clearly to everyone. For this new type of document, it was necessary to invent a new method. It is this new method, slowly elaborated, imperfect even in the last version of the constitution, that the reader must grasp if he or she wants to interpret the constitution correctly and pursue with the world the dialogue it inaugurates.[18]

Throughout the redaction of this constitution, McGrath notes, there is a reflection on the method to be employed if the Fathers wanted to address their contemporaries without falling into the traps of "juridicism" and "moralism."[19] In this perspective, "certain Fathers and experts wanted the document—if it was to get a hearing from modern humanity—to follow the example of the encyclicals *Mater et magister* and *Pacem in terris* by using a style and arguments accessible to everyone and, consequently, flowing from natural morality."[20] The difficulties encountered in the course of the redaction of Schema XIII are "at the same time a question of tone and of substance,"[21] a question of method and of style as much as a question of doctrine or theology.

We should not think that methodological questions concern only *Gaudium et spes*; they concern all the other documents as well. To take another example, the originality of the teaching of Vatican II on the liturgy, compared to the teaching of the Council of Trent five centuries earlier, derives in large measure from the method used in each of the assemblies. The teaching of Trent on liturgy (but not only on liturgy) intended to reply to the Protestant reformers who were denouncing abuses, notably in the area of the celebration of the liturgy and the sacraments. As a result, the council essentially worked on the basis of catalogues of propositions extracted

18. Mark G. McGrath, CSC, "Présentation de la constitution: L'Église dans le monde du ce temps," in *Vatican II: L'Église dans le monde de ce temps*, 4 vols., ed. Yves Congar, OP, and M. Peuchmaurd, OP (Paris: Cerf, 1967), 2.1:17–30, at 18–19.

19. By which he means "that tendency to judge human and social situations in terms of abstract moral principles without sufficiently testing these principles by a constant return to the sources of revelation, a return that would prevent the principles and their formulations from hardening into outmoded schemas of thought and social situations; he is also referring to an insufficient investigation of moral conditions, that is to say, the real, current dimensions of human and social problems, studied by themselves before any application of moral judgments. This sort of a priori moralism lent itself easily to the formulation of unnuanced, inflexible, and unassailable moral positions" (ibid., 19).

20. Roberto Tucci, SJ, "Introduction historique et doctrinale à la constitution pastorale," in *L'Église dans le monde de ce temps*, 1.1:33–127, at 56.

21. Henri de Riedmatten, "Histoire de la Constitution pastorale sur 'L'Église dans le monde de ce temps,' " in Karl Rahner et al., *L'Église dans le monde de ce temps: Constitution 'Gaudium et spes'; Commentaires du schéma XIII* (Paris: Mame, 1967), 42–92, at 68.

from the writings of Luther and other reformers or from catalogues of abuses.[22] These catalogues contained propositions diverse in their origin and content. This explains the uneasy feeling one has when considering disparate measures of a varied nature that have not been integrated into a coherent ensemble. As Heinrich Holstein observes:

> One should also say that the way of proceeding imposed by Cervini beginning at the end of 1546, when [the Council Fathers] were preparing the decrees on the sacraments, conferred on the conciliar work a polemical vision and strongly restricted its field of vision. The sessions on the sacraments were prepared on the basis of catalogues of articles collected from the reformers, especially Luther. The regrettable consequence of such a procedure is threefold. It apparently gave the Council the negative task of refuting the Protestants instead of giving it the mission of illuminating and strengthening the faith of Catholics. It obliged the Council to let itself be guided by the reformers in a sort of endlessly pursued tit-for-tat debate instead of taking a broader perspective and discerning what the unacceptable "novelty" or betrayal of the tradition was in the reformers as well as recognizing the ways of proceeding based in their common faith; finally, it was going to make the Council narrowly focus on texts separated from their context, sometimes cited only approximately.[23]

As a result, we are not presented with an exposition on the nature of the liturgy or on the elaboration of the principles that might guide its renewal. Rather, the texts react either to abuses or to the words of reformers denouncing the abuses. The Council Fathers thus let themselves be guided in large measure by external events rather than proceeding to a holistic reflection on the liturgy.

22. As is well known, the decrees of Sessions 21 and 22 are the fruit of the examination of propositions contained in catalogues composed in 1547. They were first studied by theologians at Bologna in August 1547, then at Trent under Julius III in December 1551 and January 1552. Moreover, the Decree on What One Must Observe and Avoid in the Celebration of the Mass (Session 22, September 17, 1562) comes from a memorandum on Mass abuses drawn up at the end of July and dated August 8, 1562. "It is an interminable enumeration by chapters (celebration, vestments, time and place, conduct of the assembly) of everything it is possible to imagine—and to do—as a fault, a negligence, or carelessness" (Heinrich Holstein, "La 22e session: Doctrine et réforme," in *Histoire des conciles cecuméniques*, 12 vols., ed., Gervais Dumeige, vol. 11, *Le Concile de Trente 1551–1563*, 2nd ed. [Paris, Fayard, 2005], 296–326, at 309). This memorandum was discussed during the course of seven general assemblies held between September 10 and 15, 1562.

23. Heinrich Holstein, "Les décrets doctrinaux et réformateurs de la 13e session: L'Eucharistie," in *Le concile de Trente 1551–1563*, 39–73, at 57.

While Trent was being moved by a reforming and anti-Reformation current,[24] Vatican II also leaned on two movements: (1) on the one hand, a movement of liturgical restoration that developed in the West in the 19th century against the background of an antimodern reaction characteristic of the period before it saw a second founding with Dom Lambert Baudouin in the framework of a liturgical pastoral movement complemented by youth movements (scouting and Catholic Action), a movement accompanied by the reflection and the reforming measures of the Pius XI and Pius XII; (2) on the other hand, a considerable broadening of horizons with the emergence of the young churches in the 20th century.[25]

The waters of these two rivers were going to run together at Vatican II, which was going to benefit from the long period of maturation of the ideas of the century that prepared the council.[26] These different movements, moreover, are not simply tributaries of cultural and social evolutions; they are accompanied by serious developments in liturgiology because of important work on ancient liturgical sources. In effect, liturgiology at the

24. The call for church reform had become urgent especially after 1520. In 1537 a group of cardinals had collectively drawn up a document entitled *Consilium de emendanda ecclesia*, calling for deep reform of the church.

25. This emergence is too often neglected in studies of the liturgical renewal. On this question, see Johannes Hofinger, SJ, ed., *Liturgy and the Mission: The Nijmegen Papers* (New York: P. J. Kenedy, 1960). During the fifth study week session of the Central Preparatory Commission, Cardinal Valerian Gracias of Bombay, referring to this study week, said that it was a matter of the *Vox clamantis in deserto*. On the question of requests concerning liturgical adaptation in India, one could go further back to the study week on the relationship between Christianity and culture held in Madras in 1956. See the Madras Cultural Academy, *Indian Culture and the Fullness of Christ* (Madras: Madras Cultural Academy, the Catholic Centre, 1957). The report deals with art, architecture, music, etc. See Paul Pulikkan, *Indian Church at Vatican II: A Historico-Theological Study of the Indian Participation in the Second Vatican Council* (Trichur, Kerala: Marymatha, 2001), esp. 29–42, 98–107, and 210–20; Paul Pulikkan and Mathijs Lamberigts, "The Vota of the Indian Bishops and Their Participation in the Liturgy Debate during the Second Vatican Council," *Questions liturgiques* 78 (1997): 61–79; Mathijs Lamberigts and Anthony Njoku, "Vatican II: The Vota of the Anglophone West African Bishops concerning the Sacred Liturgy," *Questions liturgiques* 81 (2000): 89–121; and Gilles Routhier, "De nouvelles idées pour l'Église catholique: Contributions des jeunes Églises à Vatican II," in *L'espace missionnaire, lieu d'innovations et de rencontres interculturelles*, ed. Gilles Routhier and Frédéric Laugrand (Paris: Karthala, 2002), 247–70.

26. See Gilles Routhier, Philippe J. Roy, and Karim Schelkens, eds., *La théologie catholique entre intransigeance et renouveau: La réception des mouvements préconciliaires à Vatican II* (Leuven: Universiteitsbibliotheek, 2001).

time of Vatican II had gained appreciable depth and extension. It was not comparable to the state of liturgiology at the time of the Council of Trent.

Through this example, then, one can see concretely to what degree the posing of problems and the method used in their treatment is determinative. It is on this very point that Vatican II is innovative: if it arrives at a teaching that renews the questions, it is because it has proceeded from the beginning with a different methodology. This is not simply a question of Vatican II's originality; its contemporary relevance is equally in question. This appears in the guidelines given by John XXIII in his opening speech. The working method at Vatican II did not consist in refuting errors or repressing abuses grouped into catalogues but in positively exposing Christian doctrine or, in the pope's words, "by making the Church's doctrine stand out more advantageously."

As for *Sacrosanctum concilium*, the Constitution on the Sacred Liturgy, the council wanted to serenely present the fruit of conciliar discernment, which had been sorted out of what the various liturgical movements (reflections and experiences) prior to the council had to offer to the church. The discernment of the Council Fathers maintained, at the end of reading the long tradition and listening to the appeals of the church, what would best serve the welfare of the Western churches struggling with modernity and the young churches struggling with cultural diversity. The method of responses to errors and abuses adopted by Trent yielded to a method of discernment, the council being a moment of spiritual discernment par excellence. Because of this method Vatican II was able to offer a coherent and well-structured presentation of the liturgy; Trent could not arrive at this because of the method it had adopted. This methodological difference, resulting from a difference in context, is determinative if we want to understand what each of the councils ended up achieving.

Going even further, the awareness of the insertion of the Catholic Church into a great diversity of cultures led to posing the liturgical problem in other terms. At the time of Trent, Christendom was limited to a homogeneous part of the world—which can be seen in the very composition of the conciliar assembly: generally speaking it consisted of members from Spain and Italy and parts of France and Germany.[27] Consequently,

27. At Vatican II, the Council Fathers came from 116 nations, of which 849 came from Western Europe (32%), 601 from Latin America (23%), 332 from North America (13%), 250 from black Africa (8%), 174 from the Communist bloc (7%), 95 from the Arab world (4%), 256 from the Asian world (10%), and 70 from Oceania (3%). As far as the Council of Trent was concerned, although it was convoked to open on March

the preoccupation of the Fathers of Trent was the Reformation; it was sweeping the nations of Europe and manifested itself by adopting a vernacular liturgy, which had to be countered at all costs. By contrast, what preoccupied the Fathers at Vatican II was the encounter of the church with various cultures and the expression of Christianity in the diversity of cultures. This could not help but open a new chapter in the relationship between the church and the local traditions and customs of different peoples inhabiting territories unknown to the Fathers of Trent.[28]

In consequence, even if Trent and Vatican II wanted to foster a liturgical reform, the two councils developed disparate types of teaching, differentiated by their respective way of posing the problem. The method that directs the reflection thus ends by determining the content of the resulting presentation: the answer to give to a catalogue of abuses or of *dicta* of the reformers in the one case;[29] in the other case, the proposal of a future path for the church based on a long reflection that draws on traditions and liturgical precedents worldwide and is tested by prolonged experimentation and apprenticeship, all of which permits careful discernment. In one case, the horizon is limited to Latin and Mediterranean nations; in the other case, it includes the whole world and diversity of peoples and cultures.

This contrasting of Vatican II and Trent permits us to better grasp how the reading of texts and the recourse to documents enables us to understand not only the content or the teachings but also what Chenu calls "the posing of the problems"; thus the contrasting brings out the originality of Vatican II. The same exercise can be done with the other conciliar texts. In fact, when we examine the first debate on *De ecclesia* (December 4–7, 1962), it is clearly the "posing of the problems" that generates the entire

---

15, 1545, it could not commence before December 13 of that year because in March almost no one was present. When it finally opened, it counted 31 Council Fathers, the majority of whom came from Italy. In its first phase (1545–1547), the number of Fathers did not go above 70, practically all of whom were Spanish or Italian. In the last phase, the number of Fathers varied between 150 and 200.

28. See my article "La liturgie aux prises avec un monde et une Église en mutation," *La Maison Dieu* 260 (2009): 153–81, reprinted in *Il Concilio Vaticano II: Recezione e ermeneutica* (Milan: Vita e Pensiero, 2006), 85–104.

29. It seems to me that the instruction from the Vatican Congregation for Divine Worship *Redemptoris sacramentum* reconnects with the method set forth in the summer of 1562 without underestimating the influence that the use of such a method has on the results obtained. The term "abuse" appears 36 times in the text. Without denying that such abuses can exist, it is still important to reflect on the consequences that such a method of reflection, with its starting point in the question of abuse, might have.

discussion, without even taking into account that the debaters are clearly interested in the *modus loquendi*, in method, in basic structural concepts, and in the style of the presentation. Reading the conciliar texts thus comes down to interesting us in the elements that are too often neglected.

We can say that the problems taken up by Vatican II (church-state relations, religious freedom, Mariology, the relationship between the episcopacy and the papacy, the laity, liturgy, etc.) are not new. In fact, several were already the subject of teaching documents during the century preceding Vatican II. The novelty resides precisely in "the posing of the problems," the method used to treat them, the fundamental concepts on which the reflection is based, etc. In other words, learning from Vatican II consists not only in regularly studying its conclusions and commenting on its pronouncements; it also consists in relearning, with the Council Fathers, how to pose questions and work on them. That is where much of the contemporary relevance and fertility of Vatican II reveals itself.

If we are convinced, as Congar was, that it is "the door by which *we enter into* a question that determines the chances of a happy or less happy solution," we must take up today's questions by examining through which door the Council Fathers entered into a question, sometimes after months of debate during which they continually returned their work to the workshop—and then we must consider the method used in treating these questions. Finally, if it is true that "the concepts we use at that point are largely determinative for what follows,"[30] we must also pay attention to the dominant concepts they use. For example, the decision not to use *societas perfecta* to speak of the church, but to consider it rather in the light of *mysterium*, *populus Dei*, or *realitas complexa*, is determinative. Similarly, the designation of priests under the rubric *presbyteri* rather than *sacerdoti* in the decree *Presbyterorum ordinis* is critical for the conception of presbyteral ministry, even if it is recalled too infrequently today. We could multiply examples of this type.

Being prepared to learn from the Council Fathers by giving ourselves to a thorough reading of the council's texts permits us to enter into their way of proceeding, to assimilate it, and to make it ours today. That is where the contemporary relevance of Vatican II imposes itself. We could possibly approach the texts by beginning with our contemporary questions and ask ourselves how these had been posed at the time of the council and how they had been treated. If we did this, it seems to me that we could identify five

30. Congar, "Mon cheminement," 17–18.

broad groups of questions that belong as much to our current situation as they did to Vatican II. The Council Fathers handled these questions and so must the current generation. These questions are: (1) the encounter with others and the relationships we are called to maintain with non-Catholic Christians, non-Christians, and those who have rejected religion; (2) the insertion of Christian uniqueness into a pluralistic society or the proposing of the gospel to all people of good will; (3) the fraternal life of Christians, the relationship between Christians in the church, and the consecrated symbols and forms of their life together; (4) the perpetual reform of the church such that its witness to the gospel becomes more and more transparent; (5) the encounter with the living God through the liturgy, listening to God's word, diverse cultural expressions, diverse spiritual paths, etc. If we want to understand the teaching of Vatican II on each of these questions, we must not only know the content of this teaching, but we must also examine how the questions were asked at the time of the council: the choice of a perspective, the chosen point of entry, the concepts adopted, etc. We must also be attentive to the method adopted for the treatment of these questions. Reading these texts requires going to such a depth.

Conclusion

Claiming that Vatican II, its texts and documents, remain relevant 50 years after the council closed involves considering its documents as classics of Christian thought. Otherwise, they belong to one particular era, and they are outdated. In that case these texts would have nothing imperishable or permanent about them. They would only be texts of circumstance, limited to their world and too closely tied to the circumstances in which they were composed. They could not be contemporary for us. Only the classics have this power and capacity to speak to different eras, to transcend the contingencies of time and place. They can be made perennially current. It is only the classics that we reread, restage, reperform, and reinterpret.

So it is with the texts of Vatican II. These are documents that we must read and reread, following the lead of Benedict XVI because, as John Paul II wrote, "With the passing of the years, *the Council documents have lost nothing of their value or brilliance*." Certainly, we must reread them, but in order to let ourselves be surprised by them, in order to discover something always new in them. That is the real challenge, because calling a classic back into the spotlight involves making something new arise. It is not simply a matter of repeating what we know is found there or of endlessly glossing or commenting in a repetition of the first commentators. Otherwise, like the commentators on the *Summa theologiae*, we are going to sterilize the conciliar texts with our form of reductive neo-Scholasticism. The reading of a classic changes us; we do not simply find there what we were expecting to find.

At the time of the council, these texts "energized" the church, gave it vitality, because what they said did not simply correspond to what had been expected; rather, it represented a new language, a new way of speaking, a captivating style that drew and captured our attention. If today we merely read the conciliar texts to find in them what we expect and to confirm what we think, Vatican II is not a classic, and it immediately loses its relevance. As Hans Robert Jauss emphasizes, if the gap between the work and the measure of our hope narrows to the point "that the receptive consciousness is no longer forced to reorient itself toward the horizon of a still unknown experience, the work is similar to 'culinary' art, to a simple pastime," because the text no longer demands "any change of horizon, but on the contrary perfectly fulfills the aroused expectation" and "satisfies its desires."[31]

We do not read the conciliar texts simply to be comforted in our ideas, our ecclesiology, our own conception of ecumenism, etc. We read them in order to be changed, to be drawn forward, to be challenged to enter into the world of a text that draws us beyond our own world. This is as true for the defenders of Vatican II as for its detractors. We can refer to Vatican II in order to be comforted in our own positions by reducing the texts to a reservoir of *dicta* supporting our own theories. Conversely, we can oppose Vatican II because the content we find in it contradicts our own theories. These two positions are similar and merely represent two sides of the same coin. In neither case we do not want the reading of these texts to transform us, to take us somewhere else, to challenge us. Such reading becomes a dead letter, because we know in advance what the texts say and what they contain.

We must be prepared to find in these texts a power to transport us from our received ideas, locked away in glosses and commentaries, and we must agree to read these texts with new eyes, as if we were discovering them for the first time. This is what seems to me to be our most urgent task today. If we are not astonished by these texts, it is because they have become inert for us.

To bear within ourselves the heritage of Vatican II consists not in simply reviewing its history, nor in simply taking up the work of commentary

31. Hans Robert Jauss, *Pour une esthétique de la réception* (Paris: Gallimard, 1978), 53.

and restating what is already found in the earlier commentaries. In 1985 Hermann Joseph Pottmeyer called for a new generation of commentaries on the conciliar texts.[32] What should we understand by the term "a new generation of commentaries"? In my opinion, we can answer this only if we agree, starting with today's questions, to make a fresh interrogation of the conciliar documents, considered not as a collection of pronouncements and conclusions, but rather as the action of an assembly that grasped these questions in an original way, worked on them according to an appropriate method, and so managed to produce a discourse that astonished a generation and that can captivate a new generation today. At that moment we can grasp the "deed" of the Council Fathers and, with them, find again that state of effervescence that led them to think through in a fresh way the questions confronting the church during the second half of the 19th century and the first half of the 20th, by actually managing to speak a new language on the diverse questions that concern us today.

32. Hermann Josef Pottmeyer, "Vers une nouvelle phase de réception de Vatican II: Vingt ans d'herméneutique du Concile," in *La réception de Vatican II*, ed. Giuseppe Alberigo and J.-P. Jossua (Paris: Cerf, 1985), 42–64, at 61.

Contributors

STEPHEN B. BEVANS, SVD, received the PhD from the University of Notre Dame. He is the Louis J. Luzbetak Professor of Mission and Culture at Catholic Theological Union, Chicago, where he specializes in mission, ecclesiology, trinitarian theology, and contextual theology. He has recently published *Prophetic Dialogue: Reflections on Christian Mission Today* (2011), coauthored with Roger Schroeder; and two edited collections: *Mission and Culture: The Louis J. Luzbetak Lectures* (2012); and *A Century of Catholic Mission: 1910 to the Present* (2015). In preparation are an edited collection (with Cathy Ross) titled "Mission as Prophetic Dialogue"; "Practices of Mission: Trinitarian Practice" for an introductory text on practical theology; and essays on the New Evangelization.

MARY C. BOYS, SNJM, received her EdD from Teachers College, Columbia University, in cooperation with Union Theological Seminary in New York, where she is now the Skinner and McAlpin Professor of Practical Theology. Specializing in religious and theological education and theologies of Christian-Jewish relationship, she has recently published *Redeeming Our Sacred Story: The Death of Jesus and Relations between Jews and Christians* (2013); coedited *Christ Jesus and the Jewish People Today* (2011); and coauthored, with Sara S. Lee, *Christians and Jews in Dialogue: Learning in the Presence of the Other* (2006).

MARYANNE CONFOY, RSC, received her PhD from Boston College and is now professor of pastoral theology at MCD University of Divinity, Melbourne. Her areas of special competence are pastoral theology, psychology of religious development, and feminist theology in the two-thirds world. Her recent publications include *Religious Life and Priesthood*: Perfectae caritatis, Optatam totius, Presbyterorum ordinis (2008); and "Oceania, Women, and HIV/AIDS," in *Calling for Justice throughout the World: Catholic Women Theologians on the HIV/AIDS Pandemic*, ed. Mary Jo Iozzio with Mary M. Doyle Roche and Elsie M. Miranda (2008). In preparation is a work on effective leadership for ministry.

MASSIMO FAGGIOLI received his PhD from the University of Turin and is assistant professor at the University of St. Thomas, St. Paul, Minnesota. He has recently published, besides a number of books and articles, the following volumes: *Vatican*

II: The Battle for Meaning (2012) and *True Reform: Liturgy and Ecclesiology in* Sacrosanctum concilium (2012). He is now working on a book on the history of church government in the 20th century and after Vatican II.

ANNE HUNT received her DTheol from Melbourne College of Divinity and is currently Executive Dean of the Faculty of Theology and Philosophy at Australian Catholic University. Specializing in trinitarian theology, her most recently published book is *Trinity: Insights from the Mystics* (2010).

NATALIA IMPERATORI-LEE received her PhD from the University of Notre Dame and is currently associate professor of religious studies at Manhattan College, New York. Specializing in ecclesiology, feminist theology, and US Latina/o theologies, she has recently published "Hombres, Hembras, Hambres: Narration, Correction, and the Work of Ecclesiology," *Journal of Hispanic/Latino Theology* 17, no. 1 (November 2011); and "Mother Superior, Mother Inferior? Mary in the Thought of Hans Urs von Balthasar," *Listening Journal of Religion and Culture* 44 (Spring 2009). In progress is a book on the intersection of narrative theology and US Latino/a ecclesiology.

EDWARD KESSLER received his PhD from the University of Cambridge and is founder and director of the Woolf Institute in Cambridge, UK. Especially knowledgeable in Jewish-Christian relations, he has most recently published *An Introduction to Jewish-Christian Relations* (2010); *Jews, Christians, and Muslims in Encounter* (2013); and *What Do Jews Believe?* (2006). He edited *A Dictionary of Jewish-Christian Relations* (2005) and coedited with James Aitken, *Challenges in Jewish-Christian Relations* (2006).

GERALD O'COLLINS, SJ, received his PhD from Cambridge University and is currently professor emeritus of the Gregorian University, adjunct professor at the Australian Catholic University, Melbourne, and Honorary Research Fellow of MCD University of Divinity. Specializing in fundamental theology and Christology, he has most recently published *Rethinking Fundamental Theology* (2011); *Believing in the Resurrection: The Meaning and Promise of the Risen Jesus* (2012); *A Midlife Journey* (2012); and *The Second Vatican Council on Other Religions* (2013). In preparation are further studies on the teachings of Vatican II.

JOHN W. O'MALLEY, SJ, received his PhD from Harvard University and is currently University Professor at Georgetown University. Specializing in the history of religious culture, especially that of early modern Europe, he has recently published *A History of the Popes: From Peter to the Present* (2010); *What Happened at Vatican II* (2008); and *Trent: What Happened at the Council* (2012).

AGBONKHIANMEGHE E. OROBATOR, SJ, received his PhD from the University of Leeds and is now provincial superior of the Eastern Africa Province of the Society of Jesus and lecturer in theology at Hekima College Jesuit School of Theology. Concentrating on ecclesiology and ethics, he has recently coedited two volumes:

Feminist Catholic Theological Ethics: Conversations in the World Church (2014, with Linda Hogan); and *AIDS 30 Years Down the Line: Faith-Based Reflections about the Epidemic in Africa* (2012, with Paterne A. Mombé, SJ, and Danielle Vella). His recently published articles include: "The Struggle against Racism and the Global Horizon of Christian Hope," in *Ecclesiology and Exclusion: Boundaries of Being and Belonging in Postmodern Times*, ed. Dennis M. Doyle et al. (2012); and "Look Back to the Future: Transformative Impulses of Vatican II for African Catholicism," *Concilium International Journal of Theology* 3 (2012).

LADISLAS ORSY, SJ, is a graduate of the School of Law of Oxford University and received his Doctor's degree in Canon Law from the Gregorian University. He taught at Fordham University and The Catholic University of America; since 1993 he has been Professor of Law at Georgetown University where he lectures mostly on philosophy of law, Roman law and canon law. During Vatican II he served as *peritus* to the Archbishop of Salisbury (today Harare, Zimbabwe) and participated in numerous conciliar events and discussions. His most recent monograph is *Receiving the Council* (2009). In progress is his seminar at Georgetown on the Christian origins of modern international law.

PETER C. PHAN received the STD from the Salesian Pontifical University, Rome, and the PhD and DD from the University of London. He currently holds the Ignacio Ellacuría, SJ, Chair of Catholic Social Thought at Georgetown University. Specializing in systematic theology, inculturation, and religious pluralism, he has recently published *Christianities in Asia* (2011) and edited and introduced *The Cambridge Companion to the Trinity* (2012). Another monograph entitled "Catholic Christianities of Asia: History of Theology" is in progress.

GILLES ROUTHIER received his ThD from the Institut Catholique de Paris and his PhD in the history of religions and religious anthropology from the Université de Paris IV–Sorbonne. Now ordinary professor and dean of the Faculty of Theology and Religion at the University of Laval, Quebec, he specializes in ecclesiology, practical theology, and the history, reception, and hermeneutic of Vatican II. Among his recent publications are *Cinquante ans après Vatican II, que rest-t-il á mettre en oevre?* (2014); *Un concilio per il XXI secolo: Il Vaticano II cinquant'anni dopo* (2012); *La théologie catholique entre intransigeance et renouveau: La réception des mouvements préconciliaires* à *Vatican II* (2012), edited with Philippe Roy and Karim Schelkins; and "The Hermeneutic of Reform as a Task for Theology," *Irish Theological Quarterly* 77 (2012).

ORMOND RUSH received his STD from the Gregorian University, Rome, and is currently associate professor and reader in Australian Catholic University, Brisbane. His areas of special competence include fundamental theology, hermeneutics, theology of reception, and *sensus fidelium*. He has most recently published *The Eyes of Faith: The Sense of the Faithful and the Church's Reception of Revelation* (2009); and "Toward a Comprehensive Interpretation of the Council and Its

Documents," *Theological Studies* 73, no. 3 (2012). A monograph entitled "The Vision of Vatican II: A Framework for Assessing Its Reception" is under contract with Liturgical Press.

FRANCIS A. SULLIVAN, SJ, is professor emeritus of the Gregorian University, from which he earned his STD. Specializing in ecclesiology and ecumenism, he has recently published "The Development of Doctrine about Infants Who Die Unbaptized," *Theological Studies* (2011); and "Catholic Tradition and Traditions," in *The Crisis of Authority in Catholic Modernity*, ed. Michael J. Lacey and Francis Oakley (2011). Forthcoming is an article entitled "The Development of Doctrine on the Salvation of the Adherents of Other Religions, in Vatican II and the Postconciliar Magisterium." In preparation is an article entitled "The Challenge of Vatican II."

O. ERNESTO VALIENTE received his PhD in systematic theology from the University of Notre Dame and is currently assistant professor of systematic theology at the Boston College School of Theology and Ministry. Specializing in Christology, soteriology, political theology, and Latin American liberation theology, he has recently published: "Living as 'Risen Beings' in Pursuit of a Reconciled World: Resources from Jon Sobrino," *College Theological Society Annual Volume* (2007); and "From Utopia to Eu-topia: The Mediation of Christian Hope in History," in *Hope: Promise, Possibility, and Fulfillment*, ed. Richard Lennan and Nancy Pineda-Madrid (2013).

JARED WICKS, SJ, received his ThD from the University of Münster. After many years on the faculty of the Gregorian University, he is now writer-in-residence at the Pontifical College Josephinum, Columbus, Ohio. His interests include Martin Luther, Vatican II, and ecumenism. His most recent publications include "Vatican II on Revelation—From behind the Scenes," *Theological Studies* 71, no. 3 (2010); "Half a Lifetime with Luther in Theology and Life," *Pro ecclesia* 22, no. 3 (2013); and, since 2006, a series in the *Catholic Historical Review* on Vatican II studies appearing in European publications.